W9-AHA-723

COSBY

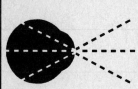

COSBY

HIS LIFE AND TIMES

MARK WHITAKER

THORNDIKE PRESS
A part of Gale, Cengage Learning

GALE
CENGAGE Learning·

Farmington Hills, Mich • San Francisco • New York • Waterville, Maine
Meriden, Conn • Mason, Ohio • Chicago

GALE
CENGAGE Learning®

OS
LT
Cosby,
Bill

LIBRARY OF CONGRESS CATALOGING-IN-PUBLICATION DATA

Whitaker, Mark.
    Cosby : his life and times / by Mark Whitaker. — Large print edition.
        pages cm — (Thorndike press large print nonfiction)
    Includes bibliographical references.
    ISBN-13: 978-1-4104-7295-3 (hardcover)
    ISBN-10: 1-4104-7295-7 (hardcover)
    1. Cosby, Bill, 1937- 2. Comedians—United States—Biography. 3.
    Actors—United States—Biography. 4. Large type books. I. Title.
    PN2287.C632W55 2014b
    792.7'6028092—dc23
    [B]   2014021178

Published in 2014 by arrangement with Simon & Schuster, Inc.

Printed in the United States of America
1 2 3 4 5 6 7 18 17 16 15 14

For my mother, Jeanne Theis Whitaker
And in memory of my grandmother,
Edith McColes Whitaker

CONTENTS

PART TWO

PART THREE

PROLOGUE:
ON THE ROAD AGAIN

"Thank you for my childhood!" a petite, thirty-something white woman calls out when she sees Bill Cosby in the Richmond International Airport. She does it from a distance and keeps walking, as though she doesn't want to intrude on his privacy, but she is an exception. Most of the travelers who recognize Cosby as he makes his way from New York City to Virginia for a concert date in Richmond want to come over and meet him, to shake his hand, to have a picture taken with him, to share details of their own lives as though he was a familiar visitor to their homes — which, of course, for much of four decades he was.

Like a walking tour of his career, the encounters recall its most treasured landmarks. In the airport lounge at LaGuardia Airport, a businessman wearing a blue blazer waxes nostalgic about listening to the comedy albums and watching *I Spy* as a kid. "Lifelong fan!" he says, pumping Cosby's hand. "What a treat for an old fucker like me!" As Cosby is driven to the gate in a motorized cart, devotees of the Saturday morning cartoon show chant "Hey, hey, hey!" On the plane, a flight attendant blurts out, "Oh my god, I *loved* Jell-O Pudding Pops!" And at the terminal in Richmond, a smartly dressed black man wants to declare his kinship with his most famous character.

"Mr. Cosby," he says. "My name is Cliff!"

"No, no, no, you can't be Cliff," Cosby responds in mock indignation. "I'm Cliff!"

Others want him to know about more personal connections. A curvaceous blonde woman wraps him in an embrace as he is about to duck into an airport restroom. "Thank you so much for what you've done for dyslexia!" she gushes. "I have a dyslexic son!"

As Cosby descends an escalator, a harried-looking mother who is standing below with a young boy in tow suddenly brightens up and breaks into song:

Let others sing of college days,
Their Alma Mater true,
But when we raise our voices,
'Tis only High for you!

Stepping off the escalator, Cosby puts his arm around the woman's shoulder and joins in:

10

We'll ne'er forget those days gone by,
Those glorious days of old,
When we sang the praises of,
The Crimson and the Gold!

The woman still hasn't announced her name, but she pushes her son forward to shake his hand as if he were an old family friend. "This is Mr. Cosby!" she says. "He went to Central High, just like Mommy!"

Near the door marked "Exit," three men in pressed green uniforms wait to greet him. Cosby's airport escort has alerted him in advance, so he calls out: "Where are the Marines? Come over and take a picture!"

"You know I was a marine, too, a merchant marine!" he jokes as the cameras snap.

"Really?" one of the servicemen asks.

"Navy!" he establishes for the record. "Hospital corpsman!"

Now everyone who passes by wants a picture, too, so he spends the next ten minutes posing with all of them, as the driver assigned to take him to the hotel hovers on the curb outside.

"We're such big fans!" says a woman in a sun hat who pulls her husband over to join the receiving line, and as soon as Cosby hears her bubbly voice, he senses an amusing exchange coming on.

"So I hope you bought a ticket to my concert tonight!" he says.

"You're giving a concert?" the woman says. "Well, we'd love to come, but we're just passing through."

"To where?" he asks.

"We're going on a cruise!" she says.

"So what three games do you like to play on the cruise?"

"Eating and drinking!"

"That's only two. What about shuffleboard or blackjack?"

"Eating and drinking and sunbathing!"

"How often do you go on cruises?"

"About three times a year!"

"Do you have children?"

"No."

"That's why you can afford the cruise, he-he-he!" Cosby jokes.

In an age of celebrity obsession and cell phone cameras, the sight of fans thronging a famous entertainer is not unusual, yet there is something different about this picture. To begin with, Bill Cosby is in his midseventies now. He is still fit for his age, with the erect posture of a former track star and only a slight paunch. But the balding head and the white stubble and the wrinkled jowls are very much the features of a grandfather, which he has been for a decade.

Still here he is, on the road performing at an age when most men are retired, if they're lucky enough to still be alive. And he isn't doing it occasionally, coming out of seclusion for a brief tour every decade or headlining a few charity events a year. The dates he is playing this weekend — an eight o'clock show on Friday night in Richmond and two back-to-back seven o'clock and nine thirty shows on Saturday in Greenville, South Carolina — are three of more than sixty concerts he will give in 2013, and he is already lining up just as busy a schedule for 2014 and 2015.

Despite his age and fame, Cosby is also traveling alone. He has no entourage: no bodyguard, no publicist, not even a baggage handler. He carries his luggage himself — a leather duffle bag and a matching knapsack — and wears the clothes he will perform in this evening: brown lounging pants, sandals and socks, and a white sweatshirt emblazoned with "Hello, Friend" in bright, multicolored letters. The housekeeper of his town house in Manhattan has accompanied him to the airport in New York and helped him get to the gate, and his concert promoter is there to greet him when he gets off the plane in Richmond. But otherwise he puts himself in the hands of employees of the commercial airline industry: the flight attendants (who fuss over or flirt with him), the pilots (who come out of the cockpit to get his autograph), and the security personnel (who ask him to pose for pictures while pleading with him not to tell their bosses).

Even more remarkable, Cosby can barely

see these people, or the scores of other facilitators and fans he will encounter on this trip, or the thousands of people in the audiences he will entertain. For two decades, he has battled a rare form of glaucoma that for a while clouded over one eye so badly that he took to wearing dark glasses in public. After multiple operations, the eye looks much better now, and he can go without the shades, which is a huge relief for a man who will tell you: "I perform with my face." But he still can't make out objects more than ten feet away. So as he travels across America, for more than thirty weeks out of the year, he has to navigate with other tools beside his vision: his acute senses of hearing, of smell, and of intuition about what lies in the fog beyond his sight.

Although Cosby's eyesight may be failing, he can already envision what historians will say about him. They will focus, rightly, on his iconic place in the annals of television. They will describe him as the first black man to star in a TV drama — *I Spy* — and talk about all the other roles for African Americans that the success of that show made possible. They will analyze his contributions to children's educational television with his early appearances on *Sesame Street* and *The Electric Company,* as well as his own creations *Fat Albert and the Cosby Kids* and *Little Bill.*

Most of all, cultural historians will measure the seismic impact of *The Cosby Show* on the entertainment industry and on American society. They will document how it revived the situation comedy format and laid the groundwork for other shows built around comedic personas, such as *Roseanne* and *Seinfeld.* And they will point out how, by implanting such a positive image of black family life in the national consciousness, it helped Americans envision sending a black president and his wife and daughters to live in the White House less than two decades later.

If you ask Cosby about them now, he will tell you how proud he is of his groundbreaking shows. But he will also say the same thing about many other TV and movie ventures that were deemed disappointments or flops. He is grateful for the extra measure of fame and wealth that television has afforded him, and he still likes to think that he has another show or two in him. As he waits to board the flight to Richmond, he imagines a prime-time drama about a Good Samaritan swat team that turns around the lives of troubled inner-city kids, and within months he will be pitching a new sitcom in which he would play grandfather in a multigenerational family to NBC and also developing a Fat Albert project with the Henson Muppet dynasty.

For all the attention TV success won him,

however, Cosby has always known that it is fleeting. What has lasted is what he is doing now, and has done consistently for more than fifty years: stand-up comedy. (Or more precisely, *sit-down* comedy, since he began his career perched on a chair at the end of a Philadelphia bar and still prefers to perform in a seated position.) Stand-up is what lifted Cosby's sights beyond becoming a junior high school gym teacher. It's what led to his biggest breaks in television and sustained him through his worst stumbles. And it's what first made him rich and still earns him millions of dollars a year, even though with a personal fortune in investments and real estate and artwork valued at close to a half billion dollars, he hardly needs to work.

Which raises an interesting question: why does Cosby continue to perform so much? (Beside the fact that it gets him out of the house and gives him the satisfaction of meeting and entertaining so many fans?) Is he is trying to retire the all-time record for stand-up, perhaps?

"No idea," he says with a dismissive shrug when asked if he knows how many comedy concerts he's given in his lifetime.

Then can he think of anyone else who has given more?

This question interests him, and he takes a minute to ponder the possibilities. (How many performers have lasted for a half century? And of that small number, how many have had the desire and the fortitude and the fan base to continue to tour success-fully?)

"Victor Borge?" he ventures finally. "He was out there for a long time! Don Rickles, maybe . . ."

He thinks a bit longer.

"Liberace!" he says. "Remember what they said about him? Liberace sold out wherever he went, but they said it wouldn't last. They said his audiences wouldn't be there next year. Then he'd come back, and he'd still be sold out. So I guess they kept making new old people!"

As Cosby nestles into an aisle seat on the flight to Richmond, he confesses that business over the last decade hasn't always been easy. Ever since the 1960s, he has worked a circuit of venues that seat 1,500 to 3,000 people, his preferred size. (Less than that, he says, and it's hard to make real money; more, and audiences in the back come away think-ing, *I might as well have had an 8-by-10 glossy.*) The venues include the casinos of Las Vegas and concert halls of New York and Washington, DC; but most are the college auditoriums, regional playhouses, and athletic arenas found in smaller cities and towns, and sometimes it's been hard to pack those houses.

Some in the concert business have whispered that Cosby's age was a factor in the falloff, or the intimidating sunglasses he wore for a while, or uneasiness with the outspoken stands he's taken on the failures of parenting and personal responsibility in parts of the black community. But he blames the impact of economic policies in Washington on his core audience of baby boomers. "After Clinton, the bottom fell out, and the weight was particularly heavy on the fifty-five-year-olds," he says. Things got even worse once the Great Recession of 2008 hit — "the last four years have not been pretty," he says — although lately the tide has turned, and ticket sales are up again. Still, he says, "The golden age is over."

If Cosby seems so sensitive to how well his concerts sell, it's not just a matter of pride. Like most star entertainers, he gets paid up front, so he makes a good living whether his promoters do or not. But he is famous — or notorious, among agents — for going into his own pocket to bail out the people who put up the money to stage his concerts if they stand to lose money. It's partly because he knows what a tough business it is. "I tell promoters, 'I didn't go into this so you could go broke,' " he says. But he also sees it as a way of winning their loyalty and protecting his own mystique.

He tells the story of a benefit concert he gave to help fund a new wing for a children's hospital in the 1980s. He was the biggest star in America at the time, with the top-rated show on television, a book at the top of the bestseller list, a ranking as the most highly paid celebrity in the country and his own private G4 jet that took him wherever he wanted. But the promoter of the concert was a "grunt," the son of a rich businessman who had fronted him the six figures to book Cosby. He didn't know what he was doing, and when Cosby arrived, he learned that a quarter of the house would be empty.

"Bring the kid in," he told his agent from William Morris. "I want to talk to him."

"Don't give money back!" the agent warned. "This is his fault."

Dressed in his tuxedo, the promoter appeared in the dressing room minutes later. Cosby could see his agent fuming, so he kicked him out.

"Sit down, son," he said to the promoter. "How are you doing?"

"We're a little short," the promoter confessed.

"Well, I want you to go the box office and find out exactly how short," he said.

The promoter did as he was told, and as he left the room, Cosby could see his agent hovering outside, his face flushed with anger.

"Fifty-five thousand dollars," the promoter reported when he got back.

"How much would it take to make you

whole, given your other expenses?" Cosby asked.

"Probably sixty thousand dollars," the promoter admitted.

"Okay," he said, "here's what I'm going to do. I'm going to let you cut sixty-five thousand dollars out of my fee, so you come out even and can tell Daddy you made a profit."

When the promoter left, Cosby's agent came back into the dressing room, still fit to be tied.

"You shouldn't have done that!" he said. "The kid needs to learn a lesson!"

"Listen!" Cosby snapped. "What is this benefit for?"

"A children's hospital?" the agent said.

"Well, think about this," Cosby said. "William Morris can't pay to get back the bad publicity I would get if I were to take the entire fee you negotiated, get on my private plane, and fly home while leaving this hospital more than fifty thousand dollars in debt. There's no way I can win here."

In the car from the airport to downtown Richmond, Cosby explains why he gravitated toward the kind of mass-appeal observational humor that is his specialty and didn't go in for the kind of clubby, cerebral comedy that was fashionable when he was starting out in Greenwich Village — the kind designed to show audiences how smart the comedian is. "People forget that the second word in show

20

business is *business,*" he says.

The fact that he never has — that he's a master of the show and the business — explains why Cosby has risen so far and lasted so long, but it's also a lesson he learned the hard way. In his early thirties, just when he had become a huge star, he almost went broke when his manager squandered millions of dollars of his money on a mismanaged production company. He had to pull out and turn over supervision of his financial affairs to his wife, Camille, and ever since, he's been prepared to do legal battle with anyone — business associates, would-be copyright infringers, even personal employees — whom he suspects of trying to take advantage of him.

Experiences with the media have only compounded his wariness. As far as Cosby is concerned, it's been annoying enough that for fifty years reporters and critics have persisted in dwelling on the presence — or lack — of racial themes in his work, when he's always viewed himself as searching for universal humor that can touch anyone. But in recent decades, he's endured invasive coverage of a devastating family tragedy and an embarrassing personal scandal. He's had to respond to what he sees as deliberately mean-spirited questioning of his lavish phi-lanthropy and his advanced academic de-grees. He makes no secret that he doesn't trust reporters, and in return some of them have spiked coverage of him with words like *angry* and *difficult* to insinuate that there's another side to his personality besides the soft and playful one so openly on display with fans and friends.

Yet to travel with Cosby is to be struck by several personal characteristics that provide clues to his complexity. One is how extraordinary his memory is. Even in his midseventies, he can summon up granular details from every phase of his life, from the trees on the street where he lived as a toddler to the sound of instruments in the jazz bands he played with in his teens to the home phone numbers of friends he hasn't seen in years. His prodigious powers of recall explain why he's been able to spin vivid threads of personal experience into so much comedy and why he can still improvise for two hours straight without losing his train of thought (unless it's part of the act). But they also suggest that he has equally vivid memories of every personal and professional slight he's absorbed along the way.

The second is how hard Cosby works. Not only does he perform somewhere almost every week; he shows up for every concert at least two hours early, so that he can inspect the hall, check production details, and spend ample time meeting with promoters, crew, and backstage well-wishers. Intimates will tell you that he is just following the example of his mother, who toiled twelve-hour days cleaning white people's homes, and his grandfather, who walked four miles back and forth to a factory job for forty years. But respect for hard work is also a key to Cosby's much-debated views on racial issues. It's not that he is oblivious to racism — far from it. It's just that he believes that playing its victim has never gotten blacks very far, and that ultimately his people always have and always will have to work for any meaningful advances they achieve.

Although Cosby won't be making one of his frequent appearances before black youth or black parents on this trip, his passionate and sometimes prickly opinions about race are never far from the surface. Recalling the deprivations of his youth, he uses the term *lower economic class* but refuses to utter the word *poor,* because of all the other negative characteristics it suggests ("lacking," "inferior," et cetera). Remembering the segregated world of strivers in which he grew up, he worries that black people today have "abandoned the old-time religion that got our grandparents from dirt floors to normal schools." When he travels to South Carolina tomorrow, he will explain to his promoter why he has returned to the state for the first time since 2005, after supporting an NAACP protest over its refusal to stop flying the

Confederate flag over the state capital. "I called the NAACP for an update on the boycott, but they never got back to me," he says with a shrug, "and I didn't see that it was doing any good."

The third characteristic is how keenly Cosby studies human behavior. It's been the wellspring of his observational humor, enough to fertilize years of successful sitcoms and decades of fresh stand-up material. But it also means that he can detect a potential con a mile away. In person, he doesn't appear to be angry or paranoid about it; in fact, there's an amused glint in his eye when he sees one coming. But he grew up in the projects and served in the navy and has been in show business for fifty years, so he's never surprised to see people trying to put one over on one another.

Cosby's antennae are up even as he lounges backstage before the show in Richmond. After catching a brief nap at the hotel, he's arrived at the Center Stage concert hall several hours early, as usual. In a spare room down the corridor from his official dressing room, a pizza box and a Starbucks cup sit on the coffee table as he holds a phone to his ear and listens to an agent update him on new concert offers.

"Take it! Take it! Take it!" he keeps repeating, in the tone of someone listening to an overlong argument for the obvious. Then he says, "Stop questioning, just tell them no! I just played Denver . . . We'll do it in 'fifteen." (Except for yearly appearances in Las Vegas and Washington, DC, which keep importing new tourists, he makes a point of waiting at least two years before he returns to most cities, so the locals don't get tired of him and he can come back with new material.)

Cosby's promoter looms in the doorway with last-minute personal requests. A man has dropped off a box from a place called Joey's Hot Dogs in Richmond, and the security men out back want to know if they should send it in.

"Is it just the hot dogs or Joey, too?" Cosby asks.

"I don't know," says the promoter.

"See!" Cosby says, rolling his eyes. "That's why they shoot the messenger. He comes with incomplete information!"

The promoter returns several minutes later with the box of hot dogs, but no Joey, and news of another request for a meet and greet. It's a war veteran in a wheelchair who is a huge fan of Cosby's and wants to get his autograph.

"Who's with him?" he asks.

"It's just him," the promoter says.

"That doesn't make sense," Cosby says. "How is he going to get back here by himself in a wheelchair?"

"He's with a group from a hospital for

wounded vets," the promoter says, "but they say only he wants to meet you."

"I bet!" Cosby says. "Better check that one out."

When the promoter reports back that four vets want to come backstage with four caretakers, Cosby says: "That's more like it, send them in." But after fifteen minutes, no one has arrived, and it's time for him to go the official dressing room to receive previously approved guests.

One is Stu Gardner, the longtime musical collaborator who helped write the famous theme for *The Cosby Show*. Gardner now lives in Richmond with his wife of forty years, whom Cosby greets as "the high school girl!" Gardner has brought along a white friend named Arthur Lisi, who composed the bridge for *The Cosby Show* tune, and Lisi's wife and daughter. But instead of the iconic theme, Cosby wants to reminisce about a mostly forgotten jazz-funk ensemble that Gardner helped him put together in the early seventies called Badfoot Brown and the Bunions Bradford Funeral and Marching Band. He prances around imitating the Bunions's bassist, Ron Johnson, and soon everyone in the room is weeping with laughter.

Next L. Douglas Wilder, the former governor of Virginia, arrives with his son. He explains that he first met Cosby after Bill and his wife, Camille, made a $100,000 donation to a state education fund. Then Wilder shares a story about an address that Cosby delivered at William & Mary College in 1993, when former Supreme Court chief justice Warren Burger was the chancellor.

"Burger was wearing his full regalia," Wilder says, "and Cos says to him: 'You've got on more jewelry than Amos 'n Andy!' Can you believe that? To Warren Burger? I almost fell out of my chair!"

Wilder also brings up about another, more controversial incident involving Cosby and the Supreme Court. "I was there!" he says about the tirade that Cosby unleashed at an event in Washington, DC, in 2004 to mark the fiftieth anniversary of the Court's *Brown v. Board of Education* decision. At the time, critics called him an elitist for blasting black Americans who didn't show respect for education, proper English, or responsible parenting, but Wilder points out that the speech was prescient. "Everything he was talking about is what's happening now," he says.

At five minutes to eight o'clock, a stagehand appears in the dressing room and encourages the guests to take their seats. Cosby begins to make his way to the backstage area, but just then the contingent of veterans in wheelchairs shows up. Introduced to the man who had requested to see him, he learns that the vet suffers from a brain injury. He was shot in the head and has no control over what he is saying, so he talks loudly and randomly even while others are speaking. But Cosby isn't fazed — he worked with stroke patients and brain damage victims as a physical therapist in the navy — and he patiently chats with the vet and poses for a photograph.

In the arena outside, a sold-out crowd of more than two thousand people is watching a reel of excerpts from an internet show called *OBKB* that Cosby produces at his home in Massachusetts and puts up on his website. The clips of him interviewing kids and family members hark back to his Jell-O commercials and guest host gigs on *The Tonight Show,* but they are also meant to demonstrate that he is up to speed with the digital era.

Then a black-and-white image of a pale, round-faced man appears on the screen. "Please join in a moment of silence for the memory of Jonathan Winters!" the stage announcer says. The mercurial comedian, who has just died, is one of Cosby's all-time favorites, a man he compares to the jazz saxophonist John Coltrane for his astonishing powers of improvisation. An interviewer once asked him if he had fifty dollars in his pocket, which comedian would he most want to buy a ticket to see, and Cosby answered without hesitation: "Jonathan Winters!"

Asked to expand on what the comedian means to him, Cosby cites Winter's professional words of wisdom. "You get tired of your material before your audience does," Winters told him when they first met in comedy clubs in the early sixties. Ever since, Cosby has taken that as a warning to keep retiring bits, no matter how famous, before they get stale. ("That's why 'Noah' and 'The Dentist' had to go!" he says.) "Some of us have to entertain ourselves while we're working," Winters also said. That too resonated with Cosby, who has never liked to rehearse or memorize, on stage or on television. He has always thought he works best when, like a jazz musician, he is riffing on well-developed themes rather than performing note-for-note.

Now the video intros are over and, without introduction, Cosby strolls onto the stage. The crowd rises, applauding and cheering. He motions for everyone to sit down, and then sits down himself in a chair draped with another of the "Hello, Friend" sweatshirts that he takes wherever he goes, as a greeting and a memorial.

In his mind, he has a rough outline of the stories he will unspool over the next two hours — where he will begin, how he will build, and how he will end — that still leaves plenty of room for his imagination to roam, depending on his mood and the vibe he feels from the audience. (The outline also ensures that each performance is unique; between the two-hour concert in Richmond tonight and the two in Greenville tomorrow, Cosby will repeat no more than twenty minutes of material.)

For Doug Wilder's benefit, he wants the climax of his performance to be a funny story that he has borrowed from the former governor: about a high school date that went awry when Wilder decided to pour a bottle of Canoe cologne in his bathwater before he went to the girl's house. Leading up to that story, Cosby plans to spend a good half hour charting his introduction to romance, from young boyhood to his late teens.

First, he will be nine years old, peeking through a stairway banister with his friend Poppy Whitehead to watch Poppy's older sister French-kiss a boy. Then he will be thirteen, playing spin the bottle at a birthday party and getting to brush lips with his junior high school sweetheart, Doris Mann. Finally, he will be sixteen, taking a stack of Miles Davis albums to the house of a girl named Bernadette Johnson but making the mistake of bathing in Canoe first. It will be a long, vivid reenactment that ends with Bernadette's father brandishing a gun to make Cosby go away. Then, in the punch line, the father sees him years later at Bernadette's wedding to another man. "I had nothing against you," the father explains, "but I didn't want to spend the rest of my life with that smell in the house!"

As Cosby eases into his routine, a voice can be heard at the rear of the concert hall. It's far up in the balcony, and it sounds like someone arguing with an usher or blurting out commentary about the show. Not everyone in the audience notices, but it's loud enough that more than a few heads turn to see what's going on.

Even though Cosby can't see more than a few of yards into the audience, his keen ears immediately recognize the source of the commotion in the balcony. It's the brain-damaged veteran in the wheelchair he has just met backstage. Now he understands why the encounter was arranged: the vet knew that he might talk uncontrollably during the show, and he wanted Cosby to be prepared. He also registers why no one is trying to silence the vet, because he can't help his outbursts. So even as Cosby continues to perform, offering no hint that anything is wrong, he is calculating how he will deal with that eternal bane of stand-up comics: the distractions from the audience or the room that can disrupt even the best of routines.

Cosby calls them "concentration thieves" — and it's not just the comic's focus but also the audience's attention that they can steal. He starts thinking about how he will vary his rhythm — how he will slow down in places and speed up in others — to keep the audience from being distracted. He also begins making snap alterations to the outline in his head.

When Cosby talks about his material, he divides it into two categories: "gourmet meals" and "fast food." The gourmet meals are the long stories he loves to tell, the ones that conjure a vivid setting and a world of characters that "put the audience *there.*" They don't always deliver a laugh a minute, but they leave the audience with a deep sense of satisfaction. The fast food is made up of the more obvious jokes and physical bits that are good for a quick laugh but don't linger in the memory.

Cosby's cologne story and his other tales of romantic misadventures are a classic gourmet meal. But to make sure that he keeps the audience laughing despite the distracting vet, he decides to add a few extra helpings of fast food. At one point, he veers off into a trusty Northerners versus Southerners joke about the difference between a "beating" and a "whooping." ("In a whooping, the parents give you a knife . . ." — he doesn't have to finish the sentence, and the crowd is laughing — "to cut the switch.") During his romantic reverie, he throws in a gag about asking his father what *platonic* means. "It means you won't get any!" his father says.

The stratagems work. As Cosby nears the end of the show, no one is paying attention to the noise in the back anymore, and he is able to serve up one last long story. He is in high school, and his Granddad Samuel, a religious man, tells him that he shouldn't play with a friend named Rookie Jackson because Jackson was "born out of wedlock." When Cosby asks his mother what that phrase means, she mistakenly assumes that her son has gotten a girl pregnant. He is sent to his room as his parents carry on an agitated conversation in the kitchen. Then his father comes to tell him that they've decided that "you'll bring the baby here." The conversation that ensues is funny and touching and, Cosby admits later, imagines the kind of rapport he might have had with his real father if the man hadn't been such an unreliable drunk.

The "out of wedlock" story goes over well, but Cosby wants to leave the crowd laughing a little harder. So as he slips on the sandals he took off at the start of the concert, he tells a slightly naughty story about a funny moment that he and his wife, Camille, shared at the very beginning of their fifty-year marriage. They had been wed for only four weeks and were still in the throes of young passion. Camille had taken a particularly long time preparing for bed one night, and when she emerged from the bathroom, she glanced at the sheets and witnessed the evidence of her husband's excitement.

Camille got down on her hands and knees and started looking under the bed.

"What's under there?" Cosby asked.

"I think there's a dog in this room!" Camille said, and they both roared with laughter.

And so does the audience in Richmond.

Missioned accomplished — having left his fans happy and shown again why younger comedians such as Jerry Seinfeld and Chris Rock and Louis C.K. worship Bill Cosby in the same way that he reveres Jonathan Winters — he rises to his feet. He scoops up the second "Hello, Friend" sweatshirt draped over the back of his chair and waves to the audience as they give him another standing ovation. Then he walks offstage as the house lights come up and satisfied reviews reverberate through the hall:

"He's so great!"

"I just love him!"

"I can't wait to tell my parents!"

As the crowd files toward the exits, the air fills with a jaunty whistle and a rhythmic clacking sound. It's "Sweet Georgia Brown," the tune that has ended Bill Cosby concerts for decades. There's a funny tale behind that, too, and it's as good a place as any to begin his story.

■ ■ ■ ■

PART ONE

■ ■ ■ ■

1
GRANDDAD SAMUEL'S BIBLE

The basketball game took place, as they always did in those days, on the black side of town. Sometimes it would be at a Negro high school. Sometimes it would be at a black boxing gym, or even between makeshift hoops erected in a Colored ballroom. On Saturday nights, there would be a dance afterward. Black folks would come from all over the host city and pay a quarter to watch their local men square off for four eight-minute quarters against a squad from out of town, and afterward they would stay to jitterbug until the wee hours. It was 1954, so there were never any white faces in the crowd.

The setting that night was Wilmington, Delaware, and the visiting team was called the Mount Airy Badgers. Or "The Philadelphia Mount Airy Badgers" as the poster outside billed them — "All the way from Philadelphia!" Their coach was a man named Berry, or Mr. Berry, as the players addressed him. He would pack all six men in his squad into his car and drive them to out-of-town games. He even paid them a few dollars, although sometimes he bought them hamburgers and milkshakes instead or made them bid for the chance to sit in the front seat, next to the heater.

The men who played for the Badgers were mostly college and former college players, some of them with wives and children already. But that day, there were two high school students in Mr. Berry's car, a fourteen-year-old named Herb Adderley and a sixteen-year-old named Bill Cosby. They went to school together, at Germantown High, but neither of them was allowed to play on the varsity basketball team. In Adderley's case, it was because he was only a sophomore, and the school coach, Mr. Webb, had a rule against sophomores playing on the varsity squad. In Cosby's case, it was because Mr. Webb also had a rule that you couldn't play varsity if your grades weren't good enough. And Cosby was a terrible student. In fact, he had transferred to Germantown that year after being held back in the tenth grade at Central High School — twice.

Instead of playing for Germantown, Cosby and Adderley would take the bus after school from East High Street to the corner of Pulaski and West Coulter, to play for the Wissahickon Boys Club. Wissahickon was a famous institution in black Philadelphia: the first all-

Negro boys club in America. It was a place where local Colored boys ranging in age from eight to eighteen could come in the afternoons and on the weekends to get extra instruction in math and reading and, most inviting of all, play basketball and swim in the club pool, nicknamed "the Bathtub." It was also a place where boys could learn and play alongside older black men from the neighborhood who volunteered their time to help keep the youngsters out of trouble.

That's how Cosby and Adderley came to play for the Mount Airy Badgers. Two older players from the Wissahickon Boys Club joined the traveling basketball squad and suggested to Mr. Berry that he bring along the teenage athletes. Cosby was gifted enough, they told him, six feet tall with the speed of a track and field man. But the real prize was Adderley. He was already a local legend for his prowess at any sport he tried: basketball, baseball, and particularly football. "Adderley's going to turn pro someday!" boys in the neighborhood were already predicting.

The Badgers arrived in Delaware dressed in their shorts and jerseys, as they always did, because they never knew if there would be a place to change. They made their way to the court and had begun their warm-up routine when they heard a musical whistle that they recognized instantly.

It was "Sweet Georgia Brown." Or, to be

precise, it was the version of the jazz classic recorded by Brother Bones, a bluesman known for accompanying himself with two sticks he slapped together called "the bones." And there was a reason the players knew this recording so much better than other versions by musicians such as Ethel Waters and Django Reinhardt. It was the whistled rendition by Brother Bones that had been adopted as a theme song by the most famous black basketball team in the world, the Harlem Globetrotters.

The Badgers worshiped the Globetrotters. All black people did. They were the Colored team that regularly beat the best white professional and college teams in exhibition matches. They were the Negro athletes who traveled the world to places such as Berlin and Rio de Janeiro — the 'Trotters were said to have been to more than thirty countries! — and made folks back home feel so proud when the newspapers reported that thousands of foreigners had packed stadiums to see their games.

Most of all, the Badgers loved the Globetrotters for the style of play that they had made famous. There was the fancy dribbling — behind the back, through the legs, lying on the ground — that delighted crowds and froze opponents in their tracks. There was the dazzlingly fast passing that made the other team look hapless. There were the lightning fast breaks that ended with the ball handler going up for a layup only to bounce the ball off the backboard so the player behind him could put it away. So beloved were the Globetrotters that every kid in every black neighborhood in America could tell you not only their names but also their nick-names: "Goose" Tatum, "Showboat" Hall, and the team's newest star, "Meadowlark" Lemon. And of course, there was the greatest of them all, the man who had all but invented the Globetrotters style, who didn't need a nickname. He was just Marques — Marques Haynes.

The coach from the Delaware team had brought a phonograph player and a 78 rpm recording of "Sweet Georgia Brown" that Brother Bones had made for Tempo Records. As soon as the record started playing, the Badgers forgot their warm-up drills and tried to play like their heroes. When the game began, they went on low dribbling and pass-ing behind their backs and leaping toward the rim. Their best player, Bozo Walker, forgot that there was anyone else at the court. He stood at the foul line, dribbling through his legs, back and forth, before hoisting lobs toward the basket.

Yet the Badgers weren't dazzling; they were dreadful. They lost control of their fancy dribbles and let the other team steal the ball. They tried to pass without looking and threw out of bounds. They heaved prayers from half court and missed the rim entirely. After two quarters, they were already losing badly.

As Mr. Berry huddled with his team on the sidelines during halftime, he gave them a tongue-lashing. "You are not the Harlem Globetrotters!" he scolded. "And they would be embarrassed to see you play this way!"

Then Mr. Berry tried to offer some positive encouragement. "This team can still be had if you play like you are supposed to," he said.

As the game resumed, "Sweet Georgia Brown" was playing again. Mr. Berry asked the referee to make the other coach turn it off, but it was too late. The music was back in his player's heads, and they fared as badly in the second half as they had in the first. At the end of thirty-two minutes, they had lost both the game and their pride.

It was a long, somber ride back to Philadelphia that night, except for one ray of comic relief. Young Bill Cosby started ribbing the rest of the team about how foolish they had looked. He hummed "Sweet Georgia Brown" and imitated their clumsy Globetrotter moves. His rubbery face and big brown eyes captured how smug they had looked while they were showboating and how confused they looked when they lost control of the ball. The way Cosby told it, it was already a funny story.

Cosby enjoyed making people laugh because, along with playing sports, it seemed like the only thing he could do well. At Germantown High, he was falling behind in his classes again. He was spending all of his free time hanging out with his friends and watching TV and trying to teach himself to be a jazz drummer, banging away on a $75 used kit that he kept in his bedroom. But he wasn't great at that either; he was never going to be the next Philly Joe Jones. Worst of all, he was starting to feel like a disappointment to the two people he looked up to most in the world: his mother Anna, the tireless maid who worked so hard to put food on the table and clothes on the backs of her three sons; and his Granddad Samuel, the proud factory worker who had tried to guide him with his Bible stories and words of wisdom.

Cosby didn't know it yet, but he was a year away from giving up. In his junior year, he would drop out of Germantown High and enlist in the navy like his father, Bill Cosby Sr., had done when Bill Jr. was in elementary school. It was ironic, because Cosby had always resented his father for leaving his mother and his little brothers alone to fend for themselves. In fact, *resented* was too gentle a word to describe how he felt about his namesake. But now Junior was about to run away from life's responsibilities and disappointments, too, just like his old man had done before him.

■ ■ ■ ■

One hundred and twenty-five years before that basketball game in Delaware, a white farmer named John Cosby died in a town in Nelson County, Virginia, deep in the Blue Ridge Mountains. He was hardly a big plantation baron, but he fit a more typical profile of white slave owners of the time, two-thirds of whom owned ten indentured servants or fewer. When an inventory of his property was prepared, it included four black slaves: a woman named Maria, valued at $230; two girls named Barbary and Anarchy, assessed at $120 and $100 respectively; and another child, a boy, named Sam, also valued at $100. But John Cosby didn't leave a will, so for the next thirteen years his six heirs fought over his estate.

In 1833, John Cosby's four slaves were sold at auction. The two girls went to two local white farmers for more than $750 each, reflecting the demand for young slave women who could do domestic chores. The mother and her boy were purchased together by Richard Cosby, one of John's sons, for only $350. But in the following decade, Richard mysteriously disappeared from Virginia, and when Maria died, she and Sam belonged to a man who was related by marriage to one of John Cosby's daughters.

How long Sam lived is unknown, but he was believed to have had three children. There was only family lore to attest to two daughters named Catherine and Louisa. But there were Nelson County records to confirm a son named Zachariah, known as Zack, born on January 17, 1841. When Zack died eighty-three years later, in 1924, his name was listed on his death certificate as Zachariah Cosby, son of Sam Thomas Cosby, the first official evidence that he and his black relatives had retained the family name of his father's original white owner.

After the Civil War ended and he became a free man, Zack Cosby married a local black girl named Louisa Johnson and stayed on in Nelson County as a sharecropper, farming a 133-acre plot of land. They didn't wait long after the passage of the Thirteenth Amendment abolishing slavery to start a family. A year later, in February 1866, Louisa gave birth to a girl named Mary, whom they nicknamed Molly. Seventeen more children followed, and when the thirteenth, a boy, was born in December 1881, he was given the name of his grandfather: Samuel Russell Cosby.

At the age of twenty, Samuel wed another local girl named Gertrude Thornhill and took to the life of farming like his parents. But by the time he turned thirty, more and more Southern blacks of his generation were chasing the promise of factory jobs in big Northern cities. The exodus called the Great Black Migration would see more than a million and a half African Americans relocate from the rural south to the industrial north in the two decades between 1910 and 1930. Blacks from deep southern states mostly traveled up the Mississippi and Ohio Rivers to cities in the Midwest like Chicago, Saint Louis, and Pittsburgh, but Virginia blacks also migrated up the Atlantic coast to the Northeast. In Samuel and Gertude's case, they set out toward Philadelphia, bringing with them an infant son who had been born in Virginia in 1913 named William Henry Cosby.

What the Cosby family found in Philadelphia, however, was far from the "promised land" that southern blacks imagined in the industrial north. Some one hundred and thirty thousand African American migrants arrived in the city in the 1910s and 1920s, and most of them met a chilly reception. Never mind Philadelphia's history as a cradle of abolitionism: the Irish, Italian, and Jewish immigrants who populated its leading industries — textiles, garment making, publishing, and shipbuilding — had no interest in competing for work with poor southern blacks and organized to keep those trades "Whites Only." Even low-skilled municipal jobs such as garbage collecting and street cleaning were reserved for Italian Americans. The black arrivals had to fight for scant skilled jobs with companies like the Pennsylvania Railroad and Midvale Steel that didn't hang out "No Negroes Need Apply" signs or otherwise had to settle for menial work as janitors in factories and maids in white people's homes.

The city's small population of established middle-class blacks was barely more welcoming. Known as "Old Philadelphians," they were descended from African Americans who had gained their freedom before the end of slavery, some as early as the Revolutionary War. Some had college degrees and professional training that allowed them to serve as doctors, lawyers, and teachers to other blacks within their segregated world, much of it centered downtown on a few blocks around South Street. They, too, were none too happy about the influx of the southern migrants, whom they looked down on as rural bumpkins and whose arrival they worried would inflame white racism.

For the new arrivals, finding housing was another of the ordeals that would lead historian W. E. B. Du Bois to write of Philadelphia that "there is more race prejudice here than in another city in the United States." In the Irish and Italian wards of South Philadelphia, riots broke out merely on the rumor that blacks might be moving into the area. The threat to white neighborhoods served as a powerful recruiting tool for the Ku Klux

47

Klan, which by the late 1920s had established twenty klaverns around the city, making Philadelphia the white supremacist group's largest outpost in the Northeast. Shunned elsewhere, virtually all the migrants settled in squalid slum housing in the "river wards" south of the city or in tiny, chock-a-block row houses in North Philadelphia.

When Samuel and Gertrude Cosby moved into the North Philadelphia district of Germantown, which had originally been founded by German Quaker abolitionists, it was still a racially and ethnically mixed neighborhood. But even there, a klavern of "the Klan" sprang up as the southern migrants began to stream in after World War I. At a local black church, a congregation of "Old Philadelphians" held a meeting to debate whether the migrants were "an asset or a liability" to the city's Colored community. Eventually, more white families would flee to the suburbs, an exodus that Samuel Cosby would watch gather force until, by the time his grandchildren had grown up, blacks outnumbered whites in Germantown by more than four to one.

For the next several decades, Samuel Cosby stoically endured the indignities that came with being black in the era before the end of legal segregation. He was lucky enough to be one of the southern migrants who found a manufacturing job — at the Ellwood Ivins

Tube Co. in Elkins Park, in the township of Cheltenham northeast of the city. Determined not to sit at the back of a bus or a trolley car, Samuel proudly walked the two-mile route to and from Germantown to the factory on Oak Lane, even through the snows of winter and damp heat of Philadelphia summers. He made the trek every day for three decades, until the day he retired.

At work Samuel stayed quiet, skipping lunch in the cafeteria so as to avoid any trouble with fellow workers. In the privacy of his own home, he shared his views on what he saw around him every day. "Racism is a waste of time," he told his children and grandchildren. But on the job, he kept his views to himself and his head down.

Samuel was a disciplined man who took pride in his work, which required great strength and mental focus. The Ellwood Ivins plant, known locally as "the Tube Works," was among the first in America to perfect the art of "cold drawing" steel to produce precision tubes for use in everything from airplanes and helicopters to refrigeration equipment. The process involved baking short, thick tubes in huge furnaces, covering them in acid, and then, once they were cool enough to handle, stretching them through a cylindrical cast to increase their length and narrow their width. The steps were then repeated several times to produce smooth, seamless metal tubes as long as twenty-five feet and as narrow as an inch or less in diameter.

In the days before fully automated assembly lines, factory hands had to carry the tubes from station to station. In Samuel's case, the years of porting long, heavy tubes of steel gradually stooped his tall frame and caused his muscle-bound, callused arms to hang permanently in front of him. A family friend who worked alongside him in the factory compared his posture to that of a powerful gorilla.

Yet for all his brute physical strength, Samuel was a gentle and deeply spiritual man. He kept only two books in his house: a copy of the Old Testament and one of the New Testament. After work, once he bathed the factory filth from his body and ate dinner with his family, he passed his evenings immersed in their pages. On the weekends, he spent so much time worshipping and singing in the choir at the Corinthian Baptist Church, a red brick sanctuary on North Twenty-First Street, that some of the parishioners mistook him for an assistant to the pastor, Reverend Hopkins.

After their oldest son William, Samuel and Gertrude had five more children, two boys and three daughters, including one girl who died shortly after they arrived in Philadelphia. The family moved into a row house on West Godfrey Avenue in an area within Germantown called Somerville. In his teens, William was sent to live with relatives in Virginia — he had "behavioral problems," family members recalled — but by his early twenties he returned to Philadelphia and began courting a petite, round-faced girl who lived around the corner.

Her name was Anna Pearl Hite, and they were an unlikely pair in several ways. She was spirited and bright, while William was moody and not as well educated. She was as tiny — less than five feet tall — as he was tall and strapping. She was also a year older, at a time when most men pursued younger women. Yet in other ways, their relationship had the trappings of an arranged marriage, since they lived so close to each other and both had Virginia roots and friends in common before they met. It seemed inevitable that they would wed, and finally, at ages of twenty-three and twenty-four, they did. The ceremony took place on the day before Labor Day 1936. Ten months later, on July 12, 1937, Anna gave birth to a baby boy at three o'clock in the afternoon at Germantown Hospital. He was named William Henry Cosby Jr. after his father. He was also given his father's nickname — Bill — although within the extended family they took to calling the baby "Junior."

The young family moved into a row house at 6058 Beechwood Street, around the corner

51

from Samuel and Gertrude and several blocks from Anna's parents. Although other nearby areas of Germantown had become ethnic strongholds — from "Irishtown" to predominantly black "Dogtown" — Beechwood was a diverse and relatively prosperous street. A Polish family named Jablonski and an Irish family named Gates lived down the block. Across the street, Italian men played bocce. Jews and Germans owned the stores on the corner, and at sunrise every morning, a "huckster man" arrived with a horse-drawn cart peddling regional delicacies of every kind, from porgies and whiting to rabbits and muskrats.

Two houses down, at 6062 Beechwood, there was another black couple named Gaines who had been childhood friends of Anna and Bill Cosby Sr. They also had a son, six months younger, and by the time they were toddlers, Johnny Baines and Bill Cosby Jr. were inseparable. "Johnny, come out and play!" Bill would call out from the street each morning, and they would set off on a new adventure.

Both boys had sweet natures and a knack for getting into mischief. They loved to climb trees and pick blackberries and search in the bushes for garden snakes, which they brought home in their pockets. Once they climbed over a neighbor's fence and let her dog out of the yard, then pretended to find the pet and return it to its distraught owner. Inside the Baines home, they stood on chairs to reach a candy dish hidden on top of a china cabinet and knocked the cabinet over.

"Uh-oh, we better run!" Bill cried, but it was too late.

"What happened here?" Mrs. Baines asked as she rushed into the room.

"We don't know!" the boys answered in unison, their mouths still stuffed with candy.

If Bill Cosby welcomed any opportunity to play on Beechwood Street or to visit the Gaines household, it was partly because of the tense atmosphere inside his own home. When he was just shy of two years old, his mother gave birth to another child, a second boy named James. The new baby battled one illness after another, and as the emotional and financial pressure grew, Bill's father began to drink heavily. On many nights, rather than come home from his factory job, Bill Sr. headed to a local tavern. Often it wasn't until Bill Jr. had gone to bed and was pretending to be asleep that he heard his father's heavy, stumbling footsteps in the hallway and listened as his parents argued about how much liquor he had consumed and how much money he had spent.

The confrontations were particularly heated on Friday, the day his father received his weekly wages.

"Well, you better take this, because that's

all I have!" Bill Sr. shouted.

"But you got paid today!" Anna pleaded.

"Well, this is all I have, so don't ask for more!" he snapped.

One week, Bill Sr. came home on Friday with no money at all in his wallet. He claimed that he had been robbed, but Anna finally forced him to admit that he had bought a round of drinks for everyone at the bar. After that, she tried to get to the tavern before he arrived on Fridays, to snatch the pay out of his hand before he could squander it. Yet even after he turned over the money, there would be more arguments on Saturday night when he wanted to go out again.

"Gimme ten dollars!" Bill Sr. demanded, as Anna cried that she needed the money to pay for groceries.

Decades later, Bill Jr. could still recall the precise number of nights that the fights between his parents turned violent. "I remember my father beating my mother up three times," he said. "I was too small to do anything about it."

For years, Bill Sr. had taken extra jobs as a handyman to help pay the bills, but the more he drank, the less he worked. By the time Bill Jr. was five years old, his parents didn't have money to afford the rent on Beechwood Street. So they moved the family to cheaper digs five miles away on Stewart Street, and Johnny Baines remembered the day his friend left the neighborhood as one of the saddest in his life. "When he moved," Johnny said, "I thought the world had ended."

The house on Stewart Street was a dilapidated hovel on a row of equally distressed buildings. There was no hot water and no tub in the bathroom. To bathe her sons, Anna had to heat water on the stove in the kitchen and sponge them down out of a large pot. Bill Jr. only had one change of clothes — two shirts and two pairs of pants — so his mother did a wash every day. She boiled the clothes he wasn't wearing and hung them on a line outside. If it was raining, she dried the clothes with an iron, leaving singe marks that he did his best to hide when he went out.

Frightened by his parents' fights and his brother's illnesses and heartsick over his separation from Johnny Baines, Bill Jr. had only one thing to look forward to: his visits with his grandparents. When his mother felt overwhelmed, she would send him to stay with her mother, Martha Hite, in Germantown. Anna's father had died when she was a child, and her mother had remarried a local minister named Robert Morgan. But the second husband never seemed to be in the house when Bill visited, so he had his Grandma Martha to himself.

He took special delight in one game they played together. Martha would lie on the sofa in her living room, pretending to be asleep.

When Bill approached, she sat up abruptly and spit the false teeth out of her mouth, and he ran away squealing in mock terror. He thought it was the funniest thing in the world, and later he would describe those rare moments of release as "the greatest laughs I ever had."

When Bill visited his father's parents, Granddad Samuel read stories aloud to him. They were always from the Bible: Adam and Eve, Noah and the flood, Joseph and his brothers. Samuel finished by drawing a lesson for his grandson — about the importance of not being wasteful or of telling the truth. Because of his thick Southern accent, Bill didn't always understand what his grandfather was saying, but he was mesmerized by the way Samuel told stories: how he gave each character a different voice, and wove words together into a long, spellbinding narrative.

At the end of each story, he got a reward. Samuel kept a sock filled with coins wrapped around his belt, and he would unspool the sock and pull out a quarter.

"Junior, take this quarter and put it in the bank," his grandfather said, trying to teach him a lesson in thrift. "Don't go wasting it on ice cream!"

Samuel liked to smoke cigars, but Gertrude didn't want the stench in her house. So he kept a stash of stogies in the basement, and when he wanted to smoke he would say that he needed to fix the furnace. Bill would tag after him — like "an open basket . . . trying to catch everything he had to say," he recalled. As he watched Samuel light his cigars and smelled the pungent fumes, he felt that they were sharing an exciting secret.

Gertrude had her own ways of making her grandson feel special. She was a talented seamstress, always sewing clothes when he visited. One day when Bill was five years old, she handed him her needle and asked him to thread it through a small hole in the garment she was mending.

"Will you please do this for Grandma?" she asked. "Her eyes are not as good as yours."

Bill didn't know exactly what that meant either — what was wrong with Grandma's eyes? — but being able to help her gave him a warm feeling.

Apart from the visits with his grandparents, Bill would remember the year he spent on Stewart Street as the worst time of his youth. But in the world beyond that dingy block, two historic events were unfolding that would reshape his family's life.

The first came on the morning of December 7, 1941, when the Imperial Army of Japan launched a surprise air and sea attack on the American naval base at Pearl Harbor, Hawaii. Aboard the USS *West Virginia,* a black Cook Third Class from Texas named Dorie Miller had just served breakfast and was gathering laundry when a torpedo struck the hull of the warship. Miller rushed to the deck and helped pull his wounded white captain out of the line of fire. Then he manned an antiaircraft gun and began firing on the swarming Japanese airplanes. Whether Miller shot down anything was never determined for certain, but his heroics earned him the only commendation for valor awarded after that historic battle to a Negro serviceman.

Once his identity became public, Dorie Miller became a folk hero in black America. The navy distributed recruiting posters across the country emblazoned with his portrait under the slogan "Above and Beyond the Call of Duty." Thousands of other Negro men were inspired to sign up for the global fight that Pearl Harbor forced the United States to join.

One of those men was Bill Cosby Sr. Suddenly he saw a way to flee the fights with his wife over money and drinking and the burdens of raising two demanding little boys. He decided to enlist in the navy and become a mess steward like Dorie Miller. Over the next decade and a half, he served three tours of duty at sea, never advancing in rank beyond a steward's mate. He returned only for brief leaves and short periods between tours, during which he sired two more sons but otherwise spent most of his nights drinking in local saloons.

The second development was the arrival of public housing in Philadelphia. In the US Housing Act of 1937, better known as the Wagner-Steagall Act, Congress had granted cities across the country the power of eminent domain to tear down slum areas and construct new residences for "families whose incomes are low enough that they cannot afford housing provided by private enterprise." In Philadelphia, $20 million were allocated to construct three so-called housing projects to accommodate the city's working poor. One, the Tasker Homes, would go up in a poor white area of southwest Philly, but the other two were planned for predominantly black areas of North Philadelphia: the James Weldon Johnson Homes, at Twenty-Fifth and Ridge Avenue, and the Richard Allen Homes, south of West Girard Avenue.

In 1940, the Philadelphia Housing Authority began razing scores of run-down row houses that lined nine square blocks running between Poplar Avenue to the north and Fairmount Avenue to the south, and between Twelfth Street to the west and Ninth Street to the east. In their places it erected more than four hundred squat, two-story brick structures modeled after British garden apartments. Each contained three units, two labeled "B" and "C" upstairs and one "A" apartment downstairs, with its own small yard. The sprawling complex also included a large playground, a recreational center, and a maintenance building where residents could buy seed for their gardens and borrow lawn mowers to cut their grass.

Named after the founder of the African Episcopal Methodist Church, the Richard Allen Homes were completed in 1941, and there was immediately a long waiting list of blacks from across North Philadelphia. One of them was Anna Cosby. When she visited a Hite relative who had moved into the homes, she was drawn to the clean, modern apartments and the prospect of living in a community of more than a thousand families who could keep an eye on one another's children. It seemed like a godsend for a hardworking maid raising two small boys largely on her own. So Anna filled out an application and was thrilled when a unit became available.

Apartment A at 919 Parrish Place was even smaller than the house on Stewart Street, with two tiny bedrooms separated by paper-thin walls, but at least there was hot water and a bathroom with a tub. There was no telephone because the Cosbys couldn't afford one. The railroad tracks running along Ninth Street were a half a block away, so the rattle of passing trains could be heard all day and night. But the apartment had new appliances and clean linoleum floors, and the rent was only forty-six dollars a month. So while

Bill Cosby Sr. was off to sea, Anna Cosby moved her sons into "the projects," and after the lonely year on Stewart Street her oldest son had a whole new world of playgrounds to explore and playmates to befriend.

2

A PLACE IN THE PROJECTS

One fall morning in the mid-1920s, when she was in her early teens, Anna Pearl Hite emerged from a small row house in Germantown and mounted a streetcar for the ride to her first day of high school. Two miles to the south, at the corner of Spring Garden and Seventeenth Street, she approached an imposing red brick building with tall Grecian columns and joined the hundreds of girls climbing its marble steps, her round brown face standing out in a sea of white.

Anna had arrived at the Philadelphia High School for Girls, better known as Girls' High. Opened in 1848, it was one of the first public secondary schools in America founded for the unique purpose of educating female students. For three quarters of a century, its graduates had grown up to become pioneers in the fields of law, medicine, politics, and the arts. Every year hundreds of applicants from around Philadelphia vied for a place in the freshman class, and only those with the most impressive records stood a chance of being chosen.

By the 1920s, Girls' High had begun to admit a small number of Negro students. Yet while they were welcomed into the classrooms, they were still excluded from many social activities. One year, the Colored girls banded together to petition for the right to attend the all-white senior prom; rather than allowing it to be integrated, the principal canceled the annual dance.

The previous spring, Anna had learned that she would be among that elite group of black girls. One of seven children, she was an avid reader and had done well enough in elementary school in Germantown that her teachers encouraged her to apply to the prestigious school. She was delighted by the opportunity and determined to make the most of it. Outgoing and talkative, she began to make friends from that very first day, with the other Colored students and with some of the white girls, too, and with one of them in particular.

The white friend's name was Mary Forchic, and she and Anna had a lot in common. They were both tiny: even as adults, neither would grow to be more than four feet, eleven inches tall. They were both quick-witted; in fact, Mary had leapt ahead several grades and would graduate from Girls' High when she was sixteen. And they both had their hearts set on becoming teachers. But each of them had families that stood in the way. Mary's parents were Russian Orthodox immigrants who considered teaching too ordinary a profession and wanted their precocious daughter to become something grander: a doctor, perhaps, or an engineer. In Anna's case, the hurdles were more mysterious and even more daunting.

Like Bill Cosby's father's ancestors, his mother's were slaves from Virginia. The Hites were more dark-skinned than the Cosbys and came from farther downstate — just over the border from North Carolina, in Brunswick County, the home of Brunswick stew, the famous dish first concocted with squirrel meat by a black slave cook. One of ten children, Anna's father, William Sidney Hite, married another Virginia girl named Martha Rice and came north to Philadelphia during the Great Black Migration. But he died in his midforties, when Anna was only ten years old, and her mother remarried Robert Morgan, the local preacher.

For some reason that her children would never fully understand, by the time Anna entered Girls' High she was living with one of her father's younger brothers. Robert Hite had married an imposing, six-foot-tall woman named Bell. When Anna completed the fall semester of ninth grade, known as 9A, her uncle Robert and aunt Bell signed her report card as her guardians. But she never returned for 9B.

There is no evidence that Anna flunked out of Girls' High, so the cause of her departure was likely some kind of family hardship. As a child, Bill Cosby remembered Robert Morgan as a prosperous-seeming man with a green Ford truck, but also with a meticulously clean home that bore no trace of children. When Bill went to the home of Uncle Robert and Aunt Bell, they were always kind to him but never offered him any food. So whether it was because her stepfather wouldn't support her or because her guardians needed financial help, Anna left high school after only one semester. At fourteen she began earning her living the way she would for the next forty years, cleaning and sewing and cooking for as little as eight dollars a day rather than fulfilling her dream of becoming a teacher.

Once Anna Hite married Bill Cosby Sr. and became a mother herself, she was determined to see that her children got the proper education that she did not complete. As soon as Bill Jr. was able to sit up in bed, she began reading aloud to him at night. She recited passages from the Bible, like her father-in-law Samuel had. She also read him stories by Mark Twain, her favorite writer, whom she admired for his wry humor and knack for creating funny characters, white and black.

By the time Bill Jr. started formal schooling, at Pennell Elementary School in Germantown, he was reading. He could even write a few words, although his spelling wasn't very good. His father had taught him to count money, so he had a sense of addition and subtraction. When the family moved to the Richard Allen Homes, he entered Mary Channing Wister Elementary School, a gray stone building two blocks east of Parrish Street, on the other side of the railroad tracks that ran above Ninth Street. His first-grade teacher was so impressed with what Bill already knew that she gave him extra work to do, until one day she told him that she didn't have anything more to teach him.

"Can I have some second-grade work?" Bill asked.

"No," the teacher said.

"Why?" he asked.

"Because I only know first-grade stuff," she confessed.

Yet Bill did learn something new and exciting in his first year at Mary Channing Wister: the art of making friends. Instead of living on a mixed city block with one black playmate down the street, he was now in a rambling housing project full of hundreds of children of similar age and background. In first grade, he met a group of boys from the Richard Allen Homes who quickly formed a loyal gang that for the next six years would spend all their free time outside of school together.

From the beginning, they had nicknames for each other. There was "Bootsie" Barnes and "Skeet" Matthews, "Buddy" Mason and "Sonny" Barnett. To his friends, Bill Cosby was known as "Shorty." Later, no one could remember exactly who started calling him that. Although he was still short at the time — he wouldn't have a growth spurt until his mid-teens — he was no smaller than the rest of them. His friends speculated that it might have been one of the "old heads," their name for the older kids in the neighborhood.

In the social hierarchy of the Homes, the old heads were a source of fascination for the younger boys. They were particularly envied for their long pants, since according to the dress code of the projects, boys under the age of ten were kept in knickers or "stove pipes": the embarrassing pants that hung down below the knees. Some of the younger boys were too intimidated to socialize with their older brothers and their friends, but Bill Cosby, because he was an eldest child himself and had grown up around adults, was at ease tagging along with the old heads. So it may have been one of them — Junior Barnes, Bootsie's older brother, or another older boy named Bobby Stevenson — who started calling him Shorty because he was shorter than they were.

In the Richard Allen Homes, there was always a group of boys gathered in the playground or hanging out on the stoop of one of the apartments, ready to play. Between them, they knew every game invented for city kids with little money, and when they ran out of those, they invented new ones. They played touch football in the alleyways and basketball using trashcans for hoops and handball against the red brick walls of the housing project. They played stickball, with the pink Spaldeen ball that sailed in the air forever when given a good whack with a broom handle. But they also had other variations called "wall ball" and "king ball" and "half ball," a contest that involved cutting a Spaldeen in half and trying to hit it with a wooden stick.

Imitating the sports calendar, Bill and his friends would declare the opening of "yo-yo season," with its walk-the-dog and rock-the-cradle contests, "tops season," and "deadbox season." The latter took place in the summer, when the boys commandeered the hopscotch grids that girls had drawn in the playground and shot bottle caps harvested from the garbage. For "jacks season," the girls were invited to play, too, since their fast hands made them worthy competitors at onesies, twosies, and threesies.

When the boys weren't inventing new games to win, they were creating ever more elaborate penalties for losing. The object of a game called "root the peg" was to throw a penknife so that it stuck in the ground. But doing that with their hands was easy, so they added increasing degrees of difficulty. They would flip the knife off their elbows or their knees. In a move called "spank the plank," a boy suspended the knife on his wrist and slapped the handle to make it somersault to the ground. At the start of the competition, a Popsicle stick was planted in the ground, and each time a player successfully stuck the knife he pushed it farther down with his thumb. At the end of the contest, the losing player had to get down on his hands and knees and extract the Popsicle stick from the dirt with his teeth.

The ultimate punishment, to which a boy could be sentenced for placing last in any competition, was called "bunkies up." The loser stood with his face to a wall and pulled down his pants, while the victors threw Spaldeens or snowballs at his naked rear end. When it came to bunkies up, however, the other kids accused Shorty Cosby of having an unfair advantage. "Your ass is too small!" a boy named Eddie Robinson complained one day after he missed the strike zone several times. Unfortunately for Bill, it happened to be the day that his mother looked out the window of their apartment and saw her oldest son exposing his nether regions to the entire neighborhood.

"Don't you ever take off your pants on the

street again, you hear!" Anna scolded him when he got home. "You ever see your father doin' that?"

"Well, he don't play too much bunkies up," Bill responded meekly.

Then there was the game that in Philadelphia they called "buck, buck." A version of "Johnny on the pony," its name in New York and other cities, it was a contest between two teams of five boys each. One team lined up in a horse formation, as a boy bent over with his hands against a wall and his four teammates arrayed themselves behind him, grabbing one another by the waist. Then, one by one, the members of the opposing team jumped on the backs of the first team, until the formation collapsed.

"Buck, buck number one!" cried the first player as he mounted the human steed.

"Buck, buck, number two!" the next player called out.

Surrounded by a familiar band of comrades every day, Bill began to discover a talent for making them laugh. He became a ringleader in the pranks they played on one another, and the verbal jousting that, though they had no way of knowing it, harked back to a long black cultural tradition known as "playing the dozens." He took particular delight in mocking his friends with "Your mother" jokes. "Your mother looks so scary, she gives Frankenstein nightmares!" he would call out, always at a safe distance from apartment A so Anna wouldn't hear.

Bill learned quickly that joking around was an effective way of avoiding the violence that broke out in the projects. Like all the boys in the Homes, he had to learn to use his fists, and he wasn't afraid to. What he dreaded was coming home with ripped clothes, because he knew that his mother couldn't afford to buy new ones. So he used humor to charm the group of toughs who loitered underneath the Ninth Street railroad tracks waiting to rough up younger kids. The "gangsters," as his friends called them, would order their victims to turn over all their pocket money; if the little ones refused or didn't have any, they got a beating. But Shorty made the gangsters laugh, so they allowed him and his friends to pass through unharmed.

Sometimes he used his comic imagination to delay a fight. One day Junior Barnes asked Bill for a sip of his soda and proceeded to spit in it. Rather than strike back, Bill plotted a delayed revenge: he made a snowball and put it in the refrigerator so he could launch a surprise attack in the summer months.

As Bill looked for ways to amuse his friends, he found that he had a special gift for mimicry. He could re-create the many noises that reverberated through the projects: the sound of cars driving by, of airplanes flying overhead, of guns and firecrackers going off. He could make the sound of a fist hitting a jaw as he pretended to throw a punch at another boy. He imitated the walks of his favorite athletes, like Jackie Robinson's pigeon-toed gate. And he did dead-on parodies of the B movies that the boys snuck into on the weekends.

On Saturday mornings, the gang would gather at the Booker Theater on Fairmount Avenue. One boy would buy a ticket at the box office booth for ten cents, and then go inside and open a side door a crack. Before the ushers could catch them, the rest of the boys would rush in and dive between the upward-turned seats until the show started. When the lights went down, they would sit transfixed through another cowboy serial or horror movie, and as they emerged from the theater Shorty would treat everyone to his impersonations of Red Ryder or the Mummy.

At home, Bill listened to a small Philco radio that, along with an upright piano, was the one object of any value that his mother had managed to bring to the projects. The other boys were only interested in tuning into the radio when their hero Joe Louis was fighting, but Bill enjoyed the comedy and the horror shows and memorized lines from them to share with his friends. He collected Jimmy Durante jokes and re-created the spooky sound effects and warnings from *Inner Sanctum* and *Lights Out* ("It . . . is . . . later . . .

than . . . you . . . think!").

Sometimes, though, the fantasies conjured on the radio were a source of pain. Once when his father was home, Bill heard a commercial for a popular brand of cereal that offered to mail a toy car to anyone who sent in a box top along with fifteen cents.

"Can I have fifteen cents?" he asked his father.

"We don't have it," his father snapped.

"Please, Dad, just fifteen cents!" Bill begged. "I'll pay you back someday!"

"Son, we don't have it!" his father snapped.

Bill asked again sweetly, and then started to plead tearfully, but still he kept getting the same answer: "We don't have it!" He stalked off to his room, cursing his parents under his breath and thinking, *Why did I have to be born to such losers?*

The toy car disappointment wasn't the only time Bill would be humiliated by how little money his family had. In their first years in the projects, before Anna arranged to have her husband's navy pay sent directly to her, she missed the rent deadline several times, and eviction notices were tacked on the door of apartment A. Other kids gathered around to gawk at them, acting as if they were waiting to see the Cosby family furniture thrown out on the street.

"Hey, Shorty, you're *really* poor, man!" his friends taunted. "You didn't pay the rent!"

73

When Bill joined the Boy Scouts, he didn't have enough money for a uniform, so he wore only the neckerchief. No one in the projects could afford to go on camping trips, so for field trips his troop assembled at six o'clock in the morning and took the trolley to Fairmount Park, where they picked sassafras until a mounted policeman ordered them to stop.

Although Bill loved bikes, he could only dream of owning one. He had an uncle Jack who owned a bicycle store, and for years he fantasized that he would someday inherit a used model. But his uncle only allowed him to ride bikes inside the store, until one day he ran into a glass showcase and cracked it.

"Junior, I was going to give you a bike," his uncle told him, "but since you just broke my showcase, you can forget about it!"

Bill was crestfallen. Then he thought: *He was never going to give me a bike!* Later he would recall it as an early lesson in the futility of expecting people to do things they aren't prepared to do — and the hypocrisy of people who insist that they *would* have done something for you only once they have an excuse not to.

To mask his shame over his family's poverty, Bill found playful ways of making fun of it. At Christmastime, Anna Cosby didn't have enough money for a tree. So Bill found a wooden crate and painted it orange. When his friends came over and there was nothing but cereal in the house to eat, he made them laugh by showing them how not to waste milk: when his bowl was almost empty, he poured water into it and slurped up the last drops.

Yet while his sense of humor made Shorty Cosby a popular boy in the projects, there were many things about his life at home that he kept private from even his best friends. They knew little of his tense and distant relationship with his father, whom they remembered seeing only a few times in the years that the Cosbys lived in the Richard Allen Homes. They had no idea how wounded his son was by a taunt he heard when one of the eviction notices was posted on the door of apartment A: "If your father sold all that wine he drank, you could pay your rent!"

As for Anna Cosby, Bill's friends saw her as another hardworking domestic, like many of their own mothers. They didn't know that, despite her long hours, she found time to run her own private finishing school inside their tiny apartment. Sometimes Anna's instructions would take the form of funny warnings: advising Bill not to play with his navel, she told him that it was going to pop out and let the air out of his body and leave him flying around the room like a punctured balloon. Showing him to eat grapes, she said that if he swallowed the seeds, branches would grow

75

out of his ears and the neighbors would hang laundry on them. Although her boys favored soul food — and Anna made a fine mess of chitlin's — she wanted them to appreciate more refined fare, so she taught them how to use soup spoons and brought home leftovers of lobster thermidor and Chateaubriand that she cooked for one of her employers.

His friends witnessed little of Bill's relationships with his younger brothers, who were still too small to spend much time playing outside. They didn't know about the resentment he felt toward his baby brother, Robert, whom he thought his mother spoiled. And they didn't see the mixture of affection and exasperation he had for his freckle-faced middle brother, Russell, who was seven years younger and had been born shortly after the family moved to the Richard Allen Homes.

While Robert slept in a crib in Anna's room, Bill and Russell shared a bed in the second bedroom, which made them very close but ensured that they would get on each other's nerves. At the kitchen table, they alternated between clowning and bickering. On some days Bill made Russell giggle by squirting food coloring in his eggs. On others they fought over helpings of scrapple, the mixture of pork scraps and cornmeal that Anna fried up in a cast-iron skillet. If one of the brothers thought the other had been served a better piece of scrapple, he would spit on it.

Bill's friends also had no idea what had happened to his illness-prone brother James. One day, on a rare occasion when he was well enough to go outside, Anna asked Bill to take him into the yard to get some sun. One of Bill's friends passed by and noticed the thin, pale child for the first time.

"Shorty, your brother sure looks sickly!" the friend said.

Before Bill could say anything in his brother's defense, he watched James's tiny right hand roll up in a fist and punch the other boy in the face.

It would remain his most vivid memory of James. But most of the images that stayed with him were of a still, sad-faced child who didn't respond to his older brother's most energetic efforts to cheer him up. Then one day in 1946, not long after he turned seven, James came down with strep throat and then developed rheumatic fever. It killed him within weeks, just a month short of Bill's ninth birthday.

Although Anna Cosby kept working around the clock and tried to maintain a brave face, the loss of her second child broke her heart. She also worried that it was one more reason that her talented first son wasn't doing well in school. Since his successful first-grade year, Bill had been increasingly bored by classwork and distracted by the stresses at home and his busy social life in the projects. His report cards were full of uneven grades and comments from teachers about how he would rather clown than learn.

Yet as he began sixth grade, Bill came home with news that gave his mother hope for turning around his lackadaisical attitude toward his schoolwork. He had a new teacher, he told her, a Russian woman with a reputation as a tough taskmaster.

"She's called Miss Forchic," he said glumly.

Miss Forchic? Anna thought. That name sounded familiar. And then she remembered the little girl she had befriended during her semester at Girls' High two decades earlier, the one who had always wanted to become a teacher: Mary Forchic.

The previous fall, Mrs. McKinney, Bill's fifth-grade teacher, had skipped her normal lessons one day so that her students could take a special test. She handed out sharpened pencils and notebooks full of brain-teasing questions. Called an aptitude test, it was based on methods of measuring an individual's "intelligence quotient" that had originally been developed at the turn of the century by French psychologists to detect children with mental retardation. Now public schools across America were starting to use IQ tests to identify students with advanced learning potential.

Several weeks later, Mrs. McKinney revealed the results to her class.

"Guess who is the brightest person in this school!" she announced. "Mr. Cosby!"

At first the news filled him with competitive pride — *I'm the smartest of them all!* he thought — but it didn't take long for him to see it as a curse. His gang had always made fun of the nerdy kids in their class, like Rudolph Robinson, whom they called "the philosopher." Now his friends starting calling Shorty an egghead, too, which meant he had to work even harder to appear cool outside of school.

Mrs. McKinney transferred Bill to her advanced class, which studied subjects such as world geography and music theory. But most of her lessons went in one ear and out the other. He was too busy wondering what all his friends in the "dumb class" were up to, as he gazed out the window and watched them playing in the schoolyard or boarding buses for field trips to the Philadelphia Zoo and the planetarium while the "smart class" was forced to stay inside doing extra work.

Even in the advanced class, Bill continued to play the fool. One day, Mrs. McKinney grew tired of his hijinks and decided to put him on the spot. She asked if he wanted to come up to the front of the class and perform for everyone's benefit. He had no idea what to do, but he wanted to get a laugh, so he launched into an impersonation that was a big hit with his friends. He stuck out his behind and wiggled his hips back and forth the way that old ladies walked around the projects.

Seeing that Bill wasn't afraid of an audience, Mrs. McKinney chose him to give a demonstration of public speaking. He decided to talk about the strategic battle for territory that he had every night with his brother Russell.

"I share a bed with my little brother, but he's not little enough," he began, and the other students laughed.

"He keeps touching me," Bill said, "but I don't like a bed that feels like a bus."

The laughter grew louder.

"Sometimes he does more than just touch me," Bill said. "He thinks the bed is a boxing ring, but he never goes to the neutral corner!"

The laughs grew even louder, and Bill felt like a surge of electricity was running through his body. Later, he would recall it as his first experience of the adrenaline rush that comes with performing before a live audience.

Yet apart from those brief, exciting moments, Bill left fifth grade with memories of boredom and restlessness and another disappointing report card. When summer came, he and his buddies were glad to be out of school, but they were old enough that vacation no longer meant playing stickball from dawn to dusk, until the Spaldeen disappeared in the darkness. At eleven years old, they started to have summer jobs, which earned them pocket money but gave them a taste of racial attitudes in Philadelphia in the late 1940s. Bill wangled a job for himself and Skeet Matthews shagging balls at an all-white golf club. To amuse the club members, the owner unleashed a dog named Tex that chased the boys under the driving range fence. With Bootsie Barnes, Bill got a job in the men's room at the Broadwood Hotel, where they handed out towels and pretended not to hear "nigger jokes."

As fall approached, the boys dreaded going back to school, because they had heard about the reputation of the two sixth-grade teachers. Their classrooms were right across from each other's, and they were both considered as tough as nails. One was the tiny lady with a Russian accent, Miss Forchic. The other one, Mrs. Patho, wore her hair in a severe, braided bun. The boys had heard that it was because she was Pennsylvania Dutch, although they didn't know what that meant.

Yet to their surprise, the boys found that they liked both teachers. They were very demanding, but also very patient and creative. Miss Forchic, in particular, went out of her way to find out what students were interested in and to connect those passions with their schoolwork. With the boys, she used batting averages to teach math. On Fridays, she brought in milk and cookies to reward the students for their hard work, something no other teacher had ever done for them.

What Bill and his friends didn't know was that Miss Forchic was making an extra effort partly because of him. When Anna Cosby had learned that her old friend would be her son's teacher, she arranged for a secret meeting. One afternoon after the children had gone home, they met in the schoolyard and discussed Bill's erratic ways, and Anna asked Mary to do whatever it took to "get him."

Miss Forchic started by giving Bill a new place in her classroom. Desks in the elementary school were assigned by alphabetical order. The "As" sat in the first row, the "Bs" behind them, and so forth. With a last name beginning with "C," Bill should have been at the end of the first row. But in Miss Forchic's class, he found himself at the front of the fifth row, between the "Rs" and the "Ss."

Miss Forchic began calling on him and watching to see when he wasn't paying attention. But instead of scolding him, she walked over to his desk and ran her hand through his curly hair. "You're going to be better than you want to be, young man!" she said.

One weekend she took Bill to a movie downtown. Afterward, she bought him a meal at a diner and brought him home in a taxicab. It was one of the first times he had been outside of North Philadelphia, and when he woke up the next morning he felt like it had been a magical dream.

"Shorty's the teacher's pet!" his friends teased him, and their suspicions were confirmed when Miss Forchic convinced him to try out for the school play. The rest of the boys had no interest in giving up precious time on the playground. But to their amazement, they watched as Bill stayed after class to rehearse with a girl named Betty Anderson. They learned dialogue from *King Koko for Kookoo Island* and lyrics from *South Pacific,* the Rodgers and Hammerstein musical that had just taken Broadway by storm. When the performance took place on the tiny stage in the school auditorium, Betty gave a rousing rendition of "I'm Going to Wash That Man Right Outa My Hair," while Bill played his parts with gusto. His friends were impressed: *Shorty can act and sing!*

Before sixth grade was over, however, Bill would have his first taste of a very different sensation. As a fifth grader, he had been made a crossing guard, a job that involved wearing a sash labeled "Safety Patrol" after school and helping younger kids cross the street at the corner of Eighth Street and Parrish. He liked the assignment because it allowed him to flirt with the girls in his grade, such as a classmate named Elaine who was almost struck by a car one day when he gallantly waved her across the street without checking to see that the light was red. Still, he did well enough that in sixth grade he was promoted to the head of the safety patrol, an honor that came with making a speech before the entire school.

"Come Thou, Almighty King!" the students sang at the opening of morning assembly. Then the principal invited the new head of the safety patrol to say a few words. But as soon as Bill looked out at the auditorium full of teachers and students, his mind went blank. He had memorized a speech, but he couldn't remember a word. Worse, the principal didn't come to his rescue. He just stood there with a smirk on his face.

Bill's heart pounded faster, and he felt as if he might faint. Minutes seemed to go by, although he couldn't be sure; it felt like minutes. Finally, he managed to spit out a short, halting sentence.

"I want to . . . thank you for . . . this great honor," he said.

Then he bowed awkwardly and retreated to his seat.

After the assembly was over, the principal offered him a piece of advice.

"Cosby, forget about ever speaking in public!" he said.

Bill would remember it as his first bout with stage fright, and it wouldn't be his last. He was relieved to get back to Miss Forchic's class, where he felt safe and supported and was excelling in all of his subjects for the first time since first grade.

At the end of the school year, Bill proudly brought home a report card full of As. When he showed it to his mother, she gave him a hug and said nothing about her secret meeting with his teacher. Anna felt hopeful that her son might finally be starting to fulfill her dreams for him. But she couldn't help but worry about a remark that Mary Forchic made in her assessment of his progress.

"William is a boy's boy, an all-around fellow, and he should grow up to do great things," she wrote, adding that there were still times when he "would rather be a clown than a student, and feels that his mission is to amuse his classmates inside and outside of school."

Then Miss Forchic added a prophetic warning. "I'm just afraid," she wrote, "as William moves to the seventh grade, that he will not be monitored and will then fall back on his old habits."

3
LOST IN GERMANTOWN

Starting in seventh grade, Bill no longer had a short stroll under the Ninth Street railroad tracks to get to school. Instead he arose at the crack of dawn to ride the trolley from Tenth and Parrish all the way to Susquehanna Avenue, three miles to the west. He walked another two blocks north along Twenty-Sixth Street until he reached a gray Gothic building on the corner of West Cumberland Street. It was called Thomas Fitzsimons Junior High School, and his mother had enrolled him there because after Mary Channing Wister Elementary, she didn't think the schools near the projects were good enough for her talented but undisciplined son.

The long commute wasn't the only change that put an end to the happy-go-luck existence that Shorty Cosby and his friends had known in the Richard Allen Homes. Looking back, most of the families who lived there in the 1940s recalled a critical difference between their community and the ugly reality of "the projects" that took hold in the coming decades. For their generation, the Homes were a way station, a place for working-class strivers to live until they saved enough money to buy a house or move to a nicer neighborhood. They were not yet the urban traps that ensnared future generations in a seemingly inescapable web of joblessness, teen pregnancy, drug addiction, and crime.

By the time Bill entered junior high, that exodus was under way, and some of his friends had moved on up from the Homes. Bootsie and Junior Barnes departed, as did Skeet Matthews and the family of an older boy named Joe Johnson Jr., who had become part of their circle. The Cosby family still lived on Parrish Street, but Bill now had fewer playmates to cavort with and less time to do it, since by the end of the fall it was almost dark when he finished his streetcar ride back from Thomas Fitzsimons.

He was juggling more odd jobs, too, to help his mother with expenses and to keep spending money in his own pocket. He shined shoes and bagged groceries after school and delivered newspapers in the morning. On the weekends, he tagged along after the milkman and the bread man as they made their rounds through the projects, pestering them to pay him a few dollars to help distribute their wares.

87

But the biggest change for Bill and his friends as they entered their teens was a new preoccupation with the opposite sex. To begin with, their nicknames started to change once they began hanging around girls. Bill would no longer go by Junior, except to his parents and grandparents, or by Shorty, unless it was in the company of his childhood buddies. Henceforth, he was known to his peers as Cosby, or "Cos" for short.

For Cos and his teen friends, what happened on the playgrounds of the Homes was now of less urgency than what took place every week at the recreation center. Every Friday night and at Wednesday evening "canteens," the rec center held a dance. Girls would line up on one side of the room and boys on the other. But asking a girl to dance was a risky proposition. If she said no, her friends would too, since they wanted no part of a suitor who had been rejected. So the boys looked for topics of conservation to impress the girls and help get them on the dance floor.

For Cos, the icebreaker was jazz. Most of the music his friends danced to was swinging R&B: "Well Oh Well" by Tiny Bradshaw; "Temptation" by Earl Bostic; and anything by Louis Jordan — "Caldonia," "Choo Choo Ch'Boogie," and his latest, the two-sided hit "Saturday Night Fish Fry." But Cosby was getting interested in the bebop jazz scene on nearby Columbia Avenue, spearheaded by local Philadelphia musicians such as John Coltrane and Jimmy Heath and Philly Joe Jones. He was studying how hipsters danced to the avant-garde music, with a step called the Bop, or Off-Time, because it was performed at one step to every two beats to allow dancers to keep up with the frantic eighth- and sixteenth-note pace of bebop.

At the rec hall dances, Cosby would ask girls if they knew about Off-Time and invite them on the floor to try the Bop. Because it had yet to acquire formulaic moves (as it would when it became another white teenage dance craze), the Bop provided a perfect vehicle for his creative imagination. Rather than sticking to the box step that he had learned in Anna Cosby's home finishing school or to the Lindy Hop and Charleston moves that all the kids knew, he made up the dance as he went along, jiving with his body and making goofy faces. From the moment he started getting laughs from the girls at the rec center, his versions of the Bop would become another of the amusing quirks for which Cos became famous among his friends.

In junior high and later in high school, he used jazz as a pretext to meet pretty girls. One of his favorite young musicians was saxophonist James Moody, who, while performing with Dizzy Gillespie, had improvised a variation on "I'm in the Mood for Love" that was so memorable that it became a standard of its own called "Moody's Mood for Love." When jazz singer Eddie Jefferson put lyrics to the serpentine tune, Cosby spent hours memorizing the lyric and mastering its disjointed rhythms and swooping high notes to impress his teenage crushes:

There I go, there I go, there I go, there I go
Pretty baby, you are the soul who snaps
    my control . . .

Yet if Cosby was learning how to approach girls, he was still self-conscious about his height — his growth spurt was still a year off — and about how little money he had. When it came time for the junior high prom at Thomas Fitzsimons, he couldn't afford to rent a tuxedo. He wore black slacks and a blue double-breasted suit coat borrowed from his father, underneath a raincoat. He didn't have enough cash for a taxi, and he was dreading what his date would say about riding the streetcars in her prom gown. Luckily, when Cosby showed up at her house, her mother took pity on him and slipped six one-dollar bills into his palm to pay for cab fare.

Discovering girls and losing after-school playtime only made it harder to swallow another new reality about junior high. At Mary Channing Wister Elementary, Cosby had always managed to do his class work in school. But at Fitzsimons, teachers handed out lengthy overnight assignments. They called it "homework," but as far as he was concerned, that was a contradiction in terms. *Isn't school for work?* he thought.

In eighth grade, his allergy to homework caught up with him when he took geometry for the first time. Although he could see the practical benefits of the addition, subtraction, and fractions, he didn't understand what use he would ever have for geometry. He never took home his textbook, and when asked why he hadn't done his homework, he trotted out a reliable alibi: a relative had died or fallen ill.

The geometry teacher didn't buy his excuses. "It seems these people are always dying when you are supposed to turn in your homework," he said skeptically.

The teacher's name was Benjamin Sapolsky, and he reminded Cosby of Miss Forchic. He was another Russian immigrant, a Jew, who had devoted himself to teaching in Philadelphia's inner city. He was small like her, at least for a man — no more than five foot seven. He wore the same sports jacket every day, and he bubbled with enthusiasm as he drew triangles and circles and geometric formulas on the blackboard. But he could also be stern and sarcastic, with Cosby in particular.

At the end of the fall semester, Mr. Sapolsky gave the class a final exam. It contained four problems, and he gave the students the entire period to solve them. Because Cosby had never cracked open his textbook, he had no clue what formulas to use. Nonetheless, he went to work trying to solve the first problem. Forty-five minutes later, he had a solution, but it had taken him twelve pages of calculations, and he hadn't touched the rest of the test.

When Mr. Sapolsky returned the test, the problem that Cosby had completed was marked "Correct." But there was a large F scrawled on the front, along with a note at the bottom that said: "See me after class."

"You know I failed you on the exam," Mr. Sapolsky said when they were alone.

"Yes, sir," Cosby said.

"But you got one answer correct," the teacher said. "I followed your philosophy, and you're a genius!"

"Thank you," Cosby said.

Mr. Sapolsky held up one of the twelve pages. "The problem is that you could have used just this much paper to give the correct answer if you had read the book."

"Mr. Sapolsky," Cosby pleaded, "I just want to play."

"So you don't want to *be* anything?" the teacher asked.

"Yes."

"What?"

"I don't know."

"You could be a lawyer."

"Yeah, but that's hard!"

In the spring, when the class moved on to Geometry II, Mr. Sapolsky handed out textbooks but passed by Cosby's desk without giving him a copy. "You don't need it!" he said facetiously.

Despite his uneven grades, Cosby's parents were convinced that his high IQ would make him a candidate for the most prestigious public high school in Philadelphia, Central High. An all-male counterpart to Girls' High, Central administered an admissions test to identify the brightest boys from across the city. Graduates prided themselves on being part of a unique meritocracy and being prepared better than anyone else by the time they got to college. They went on to become doctors, lawyers, judges, politicians, and even creative pioneers such as the painter Thomas Eakins, the architect Louis Kahn, and Larry Feinberg, better known as Larry of the Three Stooges.

Anna Cosby wasn't the only one who wanted her son to go to Central High. Despite his long absences, Bill Sr. became keenly interested in the prospect, in part because he had heard how much money the school's graduates earned. Friends remembered Cos grousing about how his old man had suddenly come out of the woodwork to pressure him to take the Central High exam.

For most of the years since its founding in 1836, Central High School had graduated two classes a year, one in January and one in June. So when Bill Cosby passed the entrance test and was accepted for the 1951–1952 school year, he became a member of the 204th class. His parents were thrilled to share the good news with his grandparents, other family friends, and his father's drinking buddies. But then Bill Sr. went back into the navy, Anna kept working from dawn to dusk, and no one was at home to make sure their son did what was required to stay there.

In the fall of 1951, just as Bill Cosby was about to enter Central High, another black student was trying to enroll in a new school more than a thousand miles away in Kansas. Linda Brown, a third grader, lived in an integrated neighborhood in Topeka where she had white playmates named Mona and Wanda and Guinevere. The day her father took her to Sumner Elementary, the all-white school seven blocks from her house, she thought that she was going to get to go to school with her friends. But as Linda sat outside the principal's office, she heard the sound of arguing. When her father emerged, he grabbed her hand, led her away and told her that she would have to go back to Monroe Elementary, the all-black school a mile away.

Linda's father, Oliver Brown, was a part-time clergyman and a welder for the Santa Fe Railroad. He had a childhood friend named Charles Scott who had grown up to become a lawyer. Scott was working for the National Association for the Advancement of Colored People (NAACP), and he had asked Brown to try to enroll Linda at Sumner Elementary as part of the civil rights organization's effort to contest the federal law allowing states to keep Negro students out of white schools. In the following months, the NAACP would put Oliver Brown at the head of a list of parents named as plaintiffs in a lawsuit against the Board of Education of Topeka that would slowly make its way to the US Supreme Court and challenge that "separate but equal" pretext for legal segregation.

At the time, Cos and his friends weren't paying any attention to the burgeoning civil rights struggle. They were more interested in developments in the jazz world. For them, the most exciting news of 1951 was that the coolest of all their favorite jazz artists, Miles Davis, was coming out with his own album. As soon as it was issued, they rushed to listen to *Blue Period* on the Prestige label, featuring Miles fronting a group that included Sonny Rollins on sax and Art Blakey on drums.

Once Cosby entered Central High, his mind also turned to football. He was still skinny, but he was beginning to shoot up, and he couldn't wait to play on the school's sprawling athletic fields and to wear its red and gold uniform.

"Don't play football until you're twenty-one years old!" Granddad Samuel had always warned him.

"Why, Granddad?" Cosby asked.

"Because your bones aren't set until you're twenty-one!" Samuel said.

Yet much as he revered Samuel, Cosby was a teenager now, and he thought, *Granddad's just trying to stop you from doing what you want to do!* He went out for the freshman team, and in the first game, he leapt over a defensive end to avoid a tackle, fell to the ground, and broke his left arm just below the shoulder. The fracture required a cast and put him out for the season.

Cosby was used to visiting his grandfather in Germantown, but after the accident Samuel came to see him, taking a trolley all the way to the Richard Allen Homes. He expected a lecture, but instead Samuel came over to the couch where he was stretched out and kissed him on the forehead. Then he pulled out the sock full of coins wrapped around his belt and placed a quarter in his grandson's hand.

"Get yourself some ice cream, June bug!" Samuel said, after all the times he had told his grandson not to waste the quarters on sweets. "It's got calcium in it."

The quarter ritual, coming after one of his

grandfather's stories, had always given Cosby a feeling of warmth. But now he had a very different sensation. He felt embarrassed. What Granddad Samuel didn't say — "I told you so" — was worse than if he had said it, and Cosby realized that he was getting a lesson in shame.

It took months for his shoulder to heal, but by the spring he was ready to try a new sport: track and field. He was a natural at the high jump, with a vertical leap that earned him a place on the varsity squad. He wasn't as talented a sprinter, but he was fast enough to compete in hurdles and to make the mid-distance relay team. As he lay awake at night, he no longer fantasized about being the next Jackie Robinson or Marques Haynes. Now he was Herb McKenley, the great Jamaican sprinter, running the anchor lap to win the gold medal in the 4×400 relays at the 1952 Olympics in Helsinki.

His freshmen year at Central High brought another big development in Cosby's life: his family moved back to Germantown. Now that their son had been admitted to the school of their dreams, Bill Sr. and Anna decided that it was their turn to move on up from the Richard Allen Homes. In ten years in the projects, they had saved up enough money to afford a down payment on a home in their old neighborhood. They searched the area and found a property selling for $5,000 at 6159 North Twenty-First Street, around the corner from Granddad Samuel's home on West Godfrey Avenue.

It was a narrow little house, with seven rooms packed onto two floors of less than nine hundred square feet each. The lone bathroom had no sink; to brush his teeth, Cosby had to sit on the toilet and use water from the bathtub. But the house had features that appealed to both of his parents. For Anna, there was a small formal dining room off the kitchen, columns on the front steps, a bay window in the living room, and a grape arbor in the yard out back. For Bill Sr., there was a basement downstairs where he could escape with his cronies to make homemade wine.

For Cosby, the move left him a short commute to school every day. His new house was less than a mile away from the Central High campus, with its five acres of land surrounding a massive limestone classroom building on a hilltop off West Olney Avenue. So he saw little of the studious white boys from Central who kept their noses buried in their textbooks as they rode the buses and streetcars back home. Instead, he got off the bus at the corner of Wister and Spencer to the sight of neighborhood bums who spent their days loitering outside the drug store across the street.

Cosby wasn't hanging out on street corners,

but he wasn't hitting the books like his classmates either. The courses at Central were more demanding than anything he had experienced at Mary Channing Wister or Thomas Fitzsimons, and the students, a majority of them Jewish, were the brightest the city had to offer. Every day, he was exposed to the names and ideas of the world's great writers and thinkers. But he struggled with rote assignments and found it far more interesting to make his classmates laugh. To add to his academic misery, he discovered that Benjamin Sapolsky, his eighth-grade geometry teacher, had followed him to Central High, and now Mr. Sapolsky was taunting him for his inability to learn trigonometry.

Instead of applying himself to his studies, Cosby played the class clown during the day and spent his after-school hours competing in sports and indulging his other passions. Now he was not only listening to jazz music but also trying to play the drums. He had started by banging on garbage can lids in the Richard Allen Homes and fooling around on a drum set owned by the Barnes family. Once he moved to Germantown, he saved up $75 from his part-time jobs and bought a used kit from a pawnshop. If he had cash left over at the end of the week, he would go to Wurlitzer's Music Store and take a lesson for $2.50 an hour. But mostly he tried to teach himself, by playing along to jazz records in his bedroom and imagining that he was Philly Joe Jones.

One weekend he even got a shot at a professional gig. A local musician named Groove Holmes was performing at a bar called Mickey's Playhouse. His regular drummer, Mickey Roker, couldn't make it one night, so he called up Cosby and told him to bring his drum set down to the club.

As soon as he got on the bandstand, he started dropping bombs like his hero Philly Joe. But Groove wanted a simple backbeat. "Come on, man," he kept hissing, until Cosby calmed down and started hitting the drums "on the two and the four."

"That's it!" Groove called out. "Leave it right there!"

But Cosby couldn't resist showing off, and soon he was back trying to play like Philly Joe or Art Blakey.

When the first set was over, Holmes handed him sixteen dollars and told him to go home. "Come back and get your drums later," Groove said.

Once Cosby paid off his drum kit, he set his sights on another pawnshop purchase: a used TV set. At Central High, he met people who owned television sets for the first time in his life, and as soon as he experienced the new marvel, he was hooked. At the homes of white classmates, he watched transfixed as the stars he knew from radio came to life before his eyes: Jimmy Durante, Jack Benny, the Lone Ranger! Even big movie stars — Martin and Lewis, Abbott and Costello, the leads in the pictures that played the Booker Theater or the Fairmount — were on television.

By the early fifties TV sets were getting bigger, with hulking consoles and square screens. No one wanted the original models from the 1940s anymore, the ones with the small round screens that looked like big radios. So Cosby bided his time until he found one of those old models, a Tele-tone, selling at a pawnshop for $50.

He saved up enough shoeshine and grocery clerk money to buy the used television, and from then on he spent dozens of hours every week with his face pressed against its tiny porthole. For the first time, he saw black faces on TV. He was a fan of *The Beulah Show*, the ABC show about the maid who, like his mother, worked for white families and often had more sense than they did. But he hated *The Amos 'n Andy Show* on CBS. *Would anyone ever believe any of these characters if they were white?* he thought as he watched the adventures of the hapless band of Negroes: Lightnin', who was slow in every way; Calhoun, the lawyer who never won a case; Kingfish, the con man who always got out-conned. Only Amos, the quiet cab driver, made any sense, but he rarely spoke. *Amos 'n Andy* on the radio had been bad enough, but on TV, with actual black actors playing the parts, it was if the show was making fun of all Negroes!

With so few black shows to watch, Cosby came to worship the white idols on the little screen. On *This Is Show Business,* he discovered Sam Levenson, a former schoolteacher who told funny stories about the quirky behavior of "VUPs," or "Very Unimportant People." He fell in love with *The Jackie Gleason Show* and *The Red Skelton Show* and *You Bet Your Life,* the game show where Groucho Marx made sharp-witted conversation with gullible contestants. He waited eagerly for Sunday nights and the *Colgate Comedy Hour,* which introduced him to silent movie clips of Buster Keaton and Charlie Chaplin and allowed him to master an impersonation of Jerry Lewis's high-pitched voice.

It was on Saturday night that his favorite program of all came on. Cosby adored *Your Show of Shows,* starring Sid Caesar, Imogene Coca, Howard Morris, and Carl Reiner. He was in awe of the comic ensemble's improvised skits and of the way Caesar transformed himself into all the double-talking incarnations of "the Professor." Along with his athletic fantasies, he later recalled, his fondest dream as a teenager was to be "Sid

Caesar's second banana."

Yet even more than his sports and his drums and his TV, Cosby's greatest obsession in high school was the "Down Cats." That was the name that he gave a group of friends who spent hours of free time listening to the latest jazz sides, cruising around in cars and looking for parties to crash. Cosby even designed Down Cats membership cards with a special logo and distributed them to the other members of the club: Andy Patterson and Joe Johnson Jr., his old friend from the projects whose family had moved to Germantown.

After school, instead of doing their schoolwork, the Down Cats would go "window shopping." They took the streetcar to Wanamaker's or one of the other department stores downtown and roamed the aisles imagining that they were rich enough to afford the kind of outfits they saw on their jazz heroes, like the polished cotton olive green Brooks Brothers suits that Miles and Blakey wore. If they had pocket money, they picked up what they called "odds and ends": a pair of socks or a belt or a tie that could be purchased for a dollar or two. Afterward, they went to a hamburger stand, where Cosby told funny stories in hopes that one of his friends would pay for his burger. Or they ate at Horn & Hardart, the automated diner that sold cheap meals out of a coin-operated machine and had no waiters to tip.

On the weekends, the Down Cats prowled. As Friday night approached, Cos would tell Joe Johnson to compile a list of all the house parties that would be taking place around the city. Then they would look for a friend with a car. Sometimes it was Eddie Ford, who had access to his sister's wheels. Sometimes it was Charley Wades, who had inherited an old jalopy from his father, although Wades was never their first choice, because he made them pitch in for gas money.

Eventually Andy Patterson inherited his father's beat-up 1946 Oldsmobile. It was a slow, noisy vehicle with a huge hole in the front passenger seat covered with an army blanket. If Patterson didn't warn his date, she could find herself with her rear end on the floorboard and the blanket wrapped over her head.

One rainy night, Cosby and Patterson were on a double date when the Olds ran out of gas. They pulled into a filling station and honked to get the attention of the attendant, who was inside the booth waiting out the storm. Wearily, the attendant put on a rain-coat and hat and came out to serve them. As he approached the Olds, he slipped on the wet ground and landed on his backside, and when he picked himself up he saw the four Negro teenagers laughing at him.

"Gimme nineteen cents' worth of regular,"

Patterson asked.

"Nineteen cents?" the attendant said.

Shaking his head in disgust, he put the gas nozzle back in its holder and walked back to the dry shelter of his booth.

On a good night, the Cats could hit half a dozen parties and be out until four o'clock in the morning. They had so much energy in part because none of them drank or used drugs. In Cosby's case, he avoided liquor because he saw what it did to his father, and he didn't want to end up like his old man. As for drugs, he was tempted to try marijuana only once, when he was offered a puff at a party. Accustomed to the smell of his grandfather's cigars, he was turned off by the weird odor and declined the hit.

Yet Cosby was such a cutup that people often assumed that he might be drunk or high. And while his friends thought Cos was the life of the party, not everyone was charmed. More than a few girls refused to date him because he seemed like a frivolous jokester, and some parents warned their daughters not to waste their time.

But if girlfriends came and went, there were always the Cats. On Sundays, they headed to the Showboat, the jazz club in the basement of the Douglas Hotel on Lombard Street. Between four and six o'clock in the afternoon, the Showboat featured a "jazz matinee" with a dollar charge for cover and a drink. It was prohibited to minors, so Cosby would paint a mustache on his lip to pass for twenty-one. Once inside he would order a Coke and nurse it for two hours, keeping his hand over the frosted glass so the bartender couldn't see when it was empty.

It was at the Showboat in 1954, when Cosby was seventeen, that he met the epitome of cool in person. Miles Davis was playing a matinee with his band, and during a break he went to rest on the stairs behind the bar. Seizing his chance, Cosby went over and sat down next to Miles. For several minutes, he debated with himself what to say: *We've got to say something hip . . . How about: "You are bad, man. Your playing is mean." . . . No, don't say that!*

"Everything going all right, is it?" Cosby said finally.

"Yeah," Miles answered.

Now what? Cosby thought. He couldn't think of anything clever, but he wanted to look cool to his friends, and it didn't look cool just to sit there.

After several more minutes of silence, he stood up.

"I'll see you later, Miles," he said.

"All right," Miles said.

As soon as Cosby got back to his seat, Andy Patterson demanded a report.

"What did he say?" Patterson asked.

"Oh, we were just talking," Cosby said.

"Naah, we were watching you," Patterson said. "You didn't say nothing!"

"Me and Miles . . ." Cosby said.

"Right, you and Miles," said Patterson. "What did he say?"

"He told me everything was fine and asked me where I lived," Cosby lied. "He told me he might come up and visit me sometime!"

At the time Davis had just started to tour again on the East Coast, after spending several years in his hometown of St. Louis kicking a heroin habit. He had begun recording again, too, and in 1954 he released his first album in three years, *Blue Haze* featuring Horace Silver on piano, Percy Heath on bass, and Art Blakey on drums. There was a jukebox in Germantown that played the six-minute title song divided into two parts: "Blue Haze, Part 1" and "Blue Haze, Part 2" — and the Down Cats listened to it so often that they could perform the whole tune, taking turns scatting the four parts. "Okay, you be Percy," Cos would say. "You be Horace. I'll be Miles."

To keep from being broke all the time, Cosby was spending more time than ever shining shoes. But the tip money ran out quickly, forcing him to put in even more hours boot blacking. By seventeen, he was on the move around the clock making time for everything — the sports, the jazz, the friends, the part-time jobs. The one thing he wasn't making time for were his studies. His grades had gone from bad to worse, and by his sophomore year at Central High, he had flunked so many classes that the school officials insisted that he repeat a semester. He was no longer in the 204th class, but in the 205th. When his grades didn't improve, he was moved down to the 206th class and forced to repeat a semester of tenth grade again.

Cosby was so embarrassed that he went to the school psychologist. He wasn't cut out for such a competitive academic environment, he pleaded. When he told his parents that the psychologist had recommended that he transfer to another school, his father was furious and his mother heartbroken. But Cosby hadn't given them much of a choice; at the rate he was going, it seemed that he might never graduate if he stayed at Central High.

As it happened, 1954 was also the year that *Brown v. Board of Education of Topeka* finally reached the Supreme Court. The previous fall, President Eisenhower had appointed a new chief justice of the Supreme Court — Earl Warren, the former governor of California — and Warren successfully stalled and cajoled until he persuaded all of his fellow justices to join him in ruling that segregating black students from white students violated their rights under the equal protection clause of the Fourteenth Amendment to the US Constitution.

Cosby still wasn't paying attention to what was going on in Washington, but his mother was, and she couldn't help but grieve at the irony. When the Warren Court handed down its unanimous decision in *Brown v. Board of Education,* it opened the way for millions of black children to go to the school alongside white children their own age. Yet Anna's bright son with the high IQ had already been given that opportunity, at one of the finest integrated high schools in the country, and he had squandered it.

Cosby transferred to Germantown High, the local school where more than half the students were black, compared with less than ten percent at Central High. He became the captain of the football team and track teams, although he wasn't allowed to play varsity basketball. The coach said it was because his grades weren't good enough, but among the Negro students it was assumed that the school deliberately limited their numbers on all the varsity squads so that more Irish, Italian, and Jewish kids could letter.

By the time Cosby made it to junior year, it was 1955 and most of his old friends were graduating. He was still struggling with his schoolwork and facing the prospect that he would be in his twenties by the time he got out of high school. So he decided to drop out. He took a full-time job at the shoe repair store and got extra work on the side fixing mufflers at an auto body shop. To keep his mother happy, he enrolled in a night school, but taking remedial courses alongside half-educated adults depressed him, and soon he stopped taking those courses, too.

By now, the Down Cats had dispersed, and Cosby was spending most of his free time hanging out with a friend from Germantown named Rookie Jackson. Rookie had a next-door neighbor named Raymond Travis, a man in his early twenties with a wife and young daughter. Travis took a liking to the boys and invited them up on his porch to play pinochle. Seeing how broke Cos was, he would lend him a few dollars now and then, and sneak him into drive-in movies in the trunk of his car.

Cosby became so comfortable in Travis's home that one day, for the first time in his life, he accepted his offer of a beer. But after taking a few sips, he felt a slight loss of control, and it unnerved him. He refused the rest of the beer, and he would never touch alcohol again. Although they never discussed the matter, his older friend sensed how ashamed Cosby was of his father, whom Travis remembered as a "wino" who hung out on street corners when he came home to Germantown. As far as Travis was concerned, that was about the worst embarrassment a man could visit on his family, and he couldn't help feeling sorry for his young friend.

Yet if Cosby was determined to avoid his father's bad habits, he had no other plan for his life. Outwardly, he maintained his usual cool, making everyone laugh. Inwardly, he felt aimless and full of self-doubt. He would later recall that he devoted so much of his teen years to sports and jazz because they were the only fields where he had seen Negroes with no money or family connections make it big. But now he knew that he wasn't talented enough to be a pro ball player or a famous musician. "As a kid in Philadelphia," he said, "I gravitated to athletics as kids instinctively veer to what's going to help them survive. By eighteen, I guess I knew I'd never make it as a professional athlete and I thought, *There goes my only chance of making any decent money.*"

"I had no backup plan," he recalled. "I had hit rock bottom."

Cosby did confide in one person, the man who had taught him so much about pride and shame. Granddad Samuel's advice was to keep his head high and not let anyone detect his inner turmoil. "If you put yourself in a compromised position," he said, "you're going to have to learn to act not embarrassed."

It was while he was working at the shoe

repair store at the corner of Germantown Avenue and Shelton Street that Cosby decided that something had to change. The owner had issued him a gray apron and cobbler's hammer, and he was working alongside two older black men putting new heels on worn-out shoes. It was raining outside, and he kept hitting himself on his thumb with the hammer, sending a sharp pain all the way up to his elbow. As he looked out the window, he realized that all of his friends were gone now, to college or to the military, and that if he didn't find a way out of Germantown, too, he might be stuck there for the rest of his life, like the old bootblacks in their stained aprons.

Cosby would later joke that he decided on which branch of the military to join by calculating the least unpleasant way to die. He didn't want to eat meals out of cans and perish in a foxhole like an army grunt. He didn't want to be shot down out of the air like an air force pilot. And the marines — well, everything about them seemed too difficult and deadly. Drowning in the ocean didn't sound so bad, however; besides, he would die with clean underwear, which would make his mother happy.

In fact, Cosby chose the navy because that was all he knew. Seeing his father in uniform was one of the few positive associations he had with Bill Sr., and he had heard his mother say how handsome she thought the dress whites were. So shortly before his nineteenth birthday, without telling Anna or anyone else ahead of time, he went to the enlistment center in Philadelphia and approached the recruiter on duty.

"So you want to join the navy to see the world?" the man asked.

"No," Cosby replied, "I just want to get off my block."

4
THE NAVY WAY

"Stand up!"

The RDC was hovering over Cosby, a lit cigarette dangling from his mouth. A few minutes earlier, he had turned on all the lights in the barracks and started to walk through the rows of bunks, banging the metal railings with a baton. Cosby had stuck his foot out from underneath his sheet, signaling that he was getting ready to get up. But that wasn't enough to satisfy the recruit division commander, the drill sergeant of the navy. He had made himself perfectly clear to the recruits of Company 217 when he welcomed them to the Naval Training Center in Bainbridge, Maryland, the night before. "Reveille will be at 0430 hours!" he told them. And now it was four thirty in the morning.

"Stand up!" the RDC barked again.

"Yes, sir," Cosby replied, groggily lifting himself from the bunk.

"Don't you sir me!" the RDC yelled.

"No, sir," Cosby said sleepily.

Then the RDC leaned into his face, the smoke from the cigarette rising from his nostrils into Cosby's eyes.

"I . . . am . . . not . . . your . . . mother!" he shouted.

That much was already clear. Cosby had only been in the navy one day, and he could see that it wasn't going to be anything like living at home with his mother or roving the streets of North Philly with the Down Cats. The night before, he had briefly turned on the charm the way he did back home. The new recruits had stayed up until one o'clock in the morning getting to know one another, talking about where they grew up and what sports they played. Cosby had joked that they were all lying when they bragged about winning the state championship, and the other men had laughed.

Yet the RDC appeared immune to humor. Cosby kiddingly suggested that the government could save some money by allowing him to skip breakfast, but the man didn't crack a smile.

"I want to see the base commander," Cosby said.

"About what?" the RDC asked.

"I know two fellows from my neighborhood who should be in the service," he said. "I'll get them if you let me out!"

The RDC didn't think that was funny either.

Anna Cosby had never forced her son to make his bed. At home in Germantown, she would tell him to do it, but when he ignored her, she would tidy up after him, because he was her baby. Now Cosby had to learn how to tend to his "rack" every morning and to do it the navy way, with the sheets tucked under the bunk in tight hospital corners. If the corners weren't perfect or he didn't do it fast enough, the RDC would rip off the sheets and shout: "Make it again!"

Cosby was used to playground insults, but the RDC had terms of abuse he had never heard before. "You two-hundred-pound sack of maggots!" he yelled at sailors who he thought were sloppy or not showing respect. At first Cosby fantasized about slugging the man, but he had heard about the brig and he didn't want to go there. Then he imagined schemes for getting out of the navy, but any hope of that was soon dashed, too.

One night he was assigned to base patrol in the wee small hours, from 0200 hours to 0400 hours. When he reported for duty in the cold and the dark, he was handed a wooden rifle and told to guard an empty clothesline. The next day, he wrote a plaintive letter to his mother. Could she contact the base commander and try to get him discharged? he asked. Instead, Anna wrote back to the commander telling him that her son needed to learn the value of discipline

116

and to keep on him.

Before long, Cosby realized that he was never going to be an exception to the navy's rules. His country "had him" now. So he learned to obey orders, to not talk back, to make his rack, and to do everything else that the recruit division commander asked. And the RDC rewarded him by making him the recruit chief petty officer in charge of helping to maintain order in the barracks.

As recruit chief petty officer, Cosby got to march at the head of his unit, holding a saber, at "pass in review," the last of training. He invited his mother to the ceremony, and as he passed her, he realized that it was the first time she had seen him graduate from anything since the eighth grade at Thomas Fitzsimons Junior High School.

"Company, eyes front!" he shouted, his chest bursting with emotion that he had finally given his mother a reason to be proud.

Cosby would come up with another set of wisecracks to explain why he decided to join the Hospital Corpsmen, the navy men who provided medical care to other sailors. He said he flirted with becoming a sonar technician, because he had seen them in the movies, wearing their headphones and listening for the *blip, blip, blip* of enemy submarines, and he thought they looked cool. But then he learned that submarines were sealed shut when they came under attack. He heard that hospital corpsmen got to wear a special insignia, and that the Geneva Conventions prohibited the enemy from firing on them. *Here we go!* he thought.

In fact, Cosby had a more serious motivation for joining the Hospital Corps. He didn't want to be a mess worker, like his father, and he was privately determined to outdo the old man. That meant developing a specialty, and tending to physical ailments was one task for which he felt qualified, after all the sports injuries he had suffered.

His next stop was the Naval Hospital Corps School, where he learned to give shots, draw blood and administer X-rays and also received extra training in physical therapy. Once he was certified as an HC third class, he was transferred to the Marine Corps base in Quantico, Virginia, where corpsmen served as "docs" for the marines. For a while, Cosby thought that he might die the death of a marine, after all, if he was assigned to one of their units in a foreign war. But instead, he received a navy deployment, which came as a relief except for the fact that his destination was so far in the middle of nowhere that he could barely find it on a map.

It was called Argentia, and it was on the edge of Canada — on the jagged coast of a peninsula that jutted out from the eastern end of the island of Newfoundland. The name meant "land of silver" in Latin, although herring had long proved a more reliable source of local income than the thin vein of silver ore that ran under an Argentian cove. The town might have carried on forever as a sleepy outpost of several hundred fishermen had Britain not taken up the lonely fight against Hitler in 1940. When Winston Churchill pleaded for Franklin Roosevelt's help, the tiny deepwater port with its convenient railroad connection to the main island was one of the colonial properties the prime minister offered in exchange for the loan of US warships under the Lend-Lease Act.

By the late 1950s, when Cosby arrived, Argentia was seen as a vital outpost in the global fight against the Soviet Union. Assuming the Russians would behave like the Nazis, who sent U-boats from bases in the North Atlantic to attack Allied ships, the US military had created an elaborate antisubmarine "barrier" made up of subs, ships, and airplanes along the Atlantic seaboard, all fed by a sonar-tracking network. In fact, the Soviets had redirected their naval strategy to defending against US nuclear warships, so few Russian subs were ever spotted in the waters off Canada. Still, the Cold War strategy kept hundreds of sailors stationed on the remote base, accompanied by squadrons of navy pilots who arrived every few months to "fly the barrier."

One of those airmen was a young black

pilot named Ronald Crockett. Crockett had grown up in a Colored neighborhood in northeast Washington, DC, and attended nearby Howard University for several years. But ever since he had heard about the Tuskegee Airmen as a teenager, he had fantasized about becoming a pilot. By 1955, the navy was accepting African Americans into its aviator-training program, so he dropped out of college to pursue his dream. He earned his wings in Hutchinson, Kansas, and was assigned to "Pax River," the Naval Air Station at Patuxent River, Maryland. Several times a year, his squadron was given the mission of flying up to Argentia for two and a half weeks to hunt for Soviet subs.

Next to flying, Crockett's greatest love was jazz. He had played piano in local trios in Washington, and he kept a phonograph and a collection of Blue Note Records in his barracks at Pax River. So he was intrigued one day when he was wandering through the base at Argentia and heard the sound of drums. He followed the sound to the rec room, where he was even more surprised to see another black serviceman sitting at a drum set, trying to teach a white sailor how to play in three-quarter time.

There was a piano in the other corner of the room, so Crockett sat down and started to play. One of his favorite records at the time was a new album that had just come out in

1956 called *Sonny Rollins Plus 4,* featuring
the tenor saxophonist playing with the Clifford Brown–Max Roach quartet. The album
had a song that Crockett particularly liked, a
jazz waltz called "Valse Hot." So he began
playing "Valse Hot" over the three-quarter
drumbeat, and without saying a word the two
musicians were performing their own private
two-piece gig.

Finally, Crockett got up from the keyboard
and went over to introduce himself.

"I'm Ron Crockett," he said.

"I'm Bill Cosby," said the drummer.

Until then, Cosby had been bored out of
his mind in Argentia. After he finished admin-
istering shots and handing out Band-Aids
and stitching up the occasional wound, there
was very little to do. The road to the nearest
city, Saint John's, was unpaved, and the
nightlife there was barely worth the bumpy
journey. At the base shop, the only albums
on sale were Chet Atkins records. So he spent
most of his spare time reading and daydreaming and writing to his family and friends in
Philadelphia, telling funny stories about his
navy life and correcting the grammar and
spelling in the letters that his younger brothers wrote back.

Now Cosby had a friend to keep him
company, a black friend who loved jazz as
much as he did. He and Crockett would stay
up past midnight talking about their favorite

Miles and Sonny and Blakey tunes and the local musicians that they had grown up listening to in clubs in Philadelphia and Washington. They relived their schoolboy sports heroics at Central and Germantown and Dunbar High School in DC, which Crockett had attended. They swapped stories about their time in the navy and laughed at the coincidence of two black men from the inner city finding themselves in one of the whitest, remotest places on earth.

Soon they were calling each other by their nicknames: Cos and "Stymie," which everyone called Crockett because with his broad forehead he resembled the character in *The Little Rascals*. Stymie was struck by how funny Cos was, and by how his sense of humor allowed him to get away with things that most other people, particularly black people, never could. In his barracks, Cosby would sneak up on white sailors as they were napping and pull their feet: they would snap awake angrily, and then smile when they saw who it was. "Oh, Cos!" they said with a smile. But the older man was also impressed with how observant his new friend was. For a twenty-one-year-old, Cosby seemed to have a particularly shrewd assessment of everyone on the base, and an extremely wise understanding of how people behaved.

Although Crockett was four years older, Cosby had a way of making their age difference disappear, just as he had with the old heads in the Richard Allen Homes. Cosby admired Stymie — a black pilot and officer! — but he never acted intimidated. They also shared a wry take on white racism. They would talk about it, but with a sense of bemusement rather than bitterness. And both were just as perceptive about the foibles of black people. Crockett talked about how difficult it was for other brothers in the navy to acknowledge his superior rank. He mimicked the slow and reluctant way that they saluted him, and Cosby chuckled with recognition.

The next time Crockett flew up from Pax River, he brought his phonograph and Blue Note albums. The two friends listened to the records over and over again, comparing their favorite solos with the bass-heavy "East Coast" sound. Crockett reported the latest news from the jazz world: Had Cos heard that Miles Davis fired Red Garland? Had he heard *Moanin'*, a new Art Blakey album whose title track would later become a private theme song for Cos and Stymie? By now, the two navy men were close enough that Crockett invited Cosby to stay with his family when he came to the DC area, an offer that he accepted for the first time soon after when he traveled to Washington to compete with the navy's track and field team.

As he had in high school, Cosby seized any opportunity to play sports in the military. At the Bethesda Naval Hospital, where he was posted briefly, he played guard and forward with the National Naval Center basketball team. At Quantico, he joined the Marines football squad. In Argentia, he got excused from duty to compete with the navy track team at the Penn Relays and other meets around the country. He looked forward to the travel and was proud of the personal bests he was posting: 6'5" in the high jump, 46', 8" in the long jump, and 10.2 seconds in the hundred-yard dash.

The athletic competitions also took Cosby to the Deep South for the first time and gave him a taste of Jim Crow. Because blacks weren't allowed to eat in white restaurants in the South, the football coach at Quantico, a Marine named Ben Moore, made box lunches for his integrated team to eat on the bus. The athletes hated the dried baloney sandwiches but came to look forward to Cosby's funny complaints about the food and his teasing of Coach Moore, whom he nicknamed "Box Lunch Benny."

When the teams did stop at restaurants, Cosby and the black athletes had to go through the back door and eat in the kitchen with the cooks and waiters. But they discovered that sometimes that indignity had its advantages. At one South Carolina diner, the black staff gave Cosby the run of the kitchen refrigerator, and he found all the fixings —

ham, salami, lettuce, tomato, and a long, crusted roll — to make a Philadelphia-style hoagie sandwich. As he got back on the bus munching the tail end of the hoagie, his white teammates eyed him with envy.

Cosby kept up the busy athletic schedule until the late fall of 1958, when he was abruptly sidelined by injury. He dislocated the left shoulder that he had broken at Central High, and this time he required surgery. His superiors at Argentia arranged for him to be treated at the Philadelphia Naval Hospital, so that he could be close to home while he underwent postoperative therapy.

When Cosby arrived at the striking Art Deco hospital, he was directed to a smaller, out-of-the way building that housed the physical therapy unit. It was called Ward P, and he was surprised to find that it was run by a woman. Her name was Lieutenant Jean Lamb, and he took an immediate liking to her. She was tall, friendly, and direct and, unlike some white navy officers, she seemed completely comfortable around him.

It wasn't an accident. Jean Lamb's first friend in the world had been black — a girl she met in elementary school in her hometown of Paris, Illinois. Her upbringing had also been similar to Cosby's in many ways. Her parents were working-class strivers — her father was a seventh-grade dropout who worked at the local water company, and her mother ran an antiques store out of their home — who dreamed of giving their daughter a better education than they had. Lamb had gone to UCLA with the intention of becoming a doctor, but she had to work two jobs to afford it, and eventually she concluded that it was more practical to become a physical therapist. She had gotten the inspiration to join the military from two high school teachers who had served as Waves during World War II and from the look of the navy uniform.

Cosby received preoperative therapy from Lamb's team and returned for rehabilitation after his surgery. While on Ward P, he noticed that they were having trouble keeping up with all the patients who came through. One day he asked if he could help out. He told Lamb about his training as a Corpsman and all the experience he had with physical therapy, and she happily accepted his offer.

With his arm still in a sling, Cosby became an unofficial member of the Ward P team, and as the time neared for him to return to Argentia, he approached Lieutenant Lamb with an idea. "I have a year left in my enlistment," he said. "Do you think you could get me transferred here?"

Bill Cosby wasn't Jean Lamb's only new recruit. At home, she had a miniature schnauzer she had named Sir Chief of Rainybrook, or Chipper for short. He was a frisky dog who could wreak havoc on the furnishings in the tiny apartment where she lived near the hospital. One day Lamb came home and Chipper had pulled the drapes off the windows and scratched much of the plaster off the walls. The dog could no longer be trusted to stay at home alone, she decided, so she asked the chief of orthopedic surgery if she could start bringing Chipper to work.

When Cosby showed up for duty as a PT technician, he and Chipper quickly turned Ward P into the most popular wing of the hospital. Between Cosby's sense of humor and the dog's antics, patients began to look forward to coming for treatment, and no one seemed to miss an appointment. Chipper ran from bed to bed, licking the hands of the patients and giving them a tennis ball to play throw-and-fetch. During amputee softball games outside, the dog retrieved balls and chased the wheelchairs around the bases. It wasn't long before the doctors realized that he could sniff out infections, too, and they started taking Chipper to weekly "stump inspections."

Before the evening meal every day, around four thirty in the afternoon, Cosby took a seat in the middle of the ward and told funny stories. Many involved Chipper, who sat at his feet and barked with delight. Cosby made the schnauzer the hero of his make-believe adventures, and the patients laughed so hard that Lieutenant Lamb worried that some of the stroke victims might have another attack.

Cosby insisted that Chipper could talk. He demonstrated how he was teaching the dog new phrases. He knelt down and put his face up to the schnauzer's snout and told the dog to repeat what he was saying.

"I want to go outside!" Cosby said.

"A-wa-woo-wo-wow-wie!" the dog barked.

"See!" Cosby said. "He's saying that he wants to go outside!"

Lamb was charmed by Cosby's comic imagination, but she was even more impressed with his bedside manner. He seemed able to get along with any kind of patient, no matter how difficult his personality or miserable his affliction. One of the amputees who visited the ward every week was a Catholic priest named Father Casey. He had lost both his legs to diabetes and was full of self-pity. "God, why are you punishing me?" the priest complained. Instead of wearing prostheses on both of his legs, he left one leg uncovered and tied his pants leg around it, so everyone could witness his misfortune.

Father Casey drank, which made matters worse. Some weeks he returned to the ward after a weekend bender and his stump was so swollen that he couldn't get it into his "bucket." He cursed so loudly that the whole ward could hear him.

Still, Father Casey never seemed to get mad at Cosby, who knew something about dealing with drunkards. The priest even let him get away with practical jokes that would have sent him into a fury if anyone else had tried them. One Monday, he arrived at the ward so drunk that he passed out, and while he was unconscious Cosby playfully untied his pant leg and tied the other side instead. When Father Casey awoke, he tried to put on his bucket but it didn't fit. He started cursing, until he realized that the prosthesis was meant for the other leg.

"Cosby!" he shouted, his ruddy Irish face breaking into a smile. "Did you do this to me?"

Another patient was a Marine Corps officer from Mississippi named Major Riggins. He was on Ward P as a result of a horrific accident: He had been sitting on a bench in Philadelphia's Rittenhouse Square, enjoying the view on a sunny day, when a mental patient on a weekend pass attacked him with a hatchet. The madman pierced the officer's skull and left him with severe nerve damage. The left side of his face sagged, and his eyelids drooped. Yet for all his infirmities, it was still unmistakable where Major Riggins came from. He talked with a deep Southern drawl that had become even more elongated as a result of the accident. So Lieutenant

Lamb didn't know what to expect when she asked Cosby to care for him.

But as the days went by, she could see them developing mutual respect and kidding affection.

"Yeess . . . sir!" Riggins said as Cosby led him through his exercises.

"Major, you can't say that to me," Cosby replied. "I'm a noncommissioned person."

"Weeell," Riggins said in his Mississippi drawl. "If you are, how come yoooou are givin' meee orders?"

"Because I'm the therapist and you're the patient," Cosby explained.

"Yeees . . . sir!" Riggins repeated, giving him a salute.

One day Cosby arranged to borrow an ambulance to take Major Riggins to a football game. The Washington Redskins, then an all-white team, were playing the Chicago Cardinals, whose star running back at the time was the black Olympic sprinter Ollie Matson. As Matson dominated his white opponents, Cosby silently cheered him on but worried what his guest might think.

Yet Major Riggins seemed to enjoy the spectacle, too. "That guuuy is tearin' these people up, Bill!" he said.

"Yes, and I'm happy to see it," Cosby said.

"Do yoooou know him?" Riggins asked.

The implication that black people all knew one another was the first reference that the

130

major had made to Cosby's race. But Cosby wasn't offended. *Riggins just slipped,* he thought. *Besides, it'll make a funny story.*

Although Ward P managed to remain free of racial tension, the same couldn't be said of the rest of the sprawling naval hospital. In one incident that became the talk of the place, a mulatto serviceman named Tony Reynolds had gone to a dance attended by both white and black Waves. Reynolds asked girls of both races to dance, and afterward some white sailors confronted him. Cosby never said anything to Jean Lamb, but she learned that he had intervened to mediate the dispute. Cosby was friendly enough with the white sailors to tell them to go easy on Reynolds, but frank enough with Reynolds to advise him to stick to "our women," at least in public.

As Cosby neared the end of his four-year navy enlistment, he confided in Lamb about his plans for the future. His work as a hospital corpsman and a PT had convinced him of what he should do with the rest of his life: become a teacher. He wanted to help kids, particularly the kind he had grown up with in North Philadelphia. He was thinking of combining that goal with his love of sports and going to college to get a degree in physical education. Then he would get a job as a gym teacher and coach in a junior high school, where he could have a positive influence on teenagers at the difficult and impressionable age when he himself had lost his way.

Cosby talked about how his four years in the navy had given him the discipline that he lacked as a teenager. "I'm not your mother!" the RDC had shouted on his first day of boot camp. But in many ways, the navy had been like a parent to him, instilling the kind of respect for authority, habits of punctuality, and hard work that his own parents never managed to teach him, because his father wasn't around and his mother was too busy working.

At the end of his tour of duty, Cosby experienced another epiphany. His superiors discovered that he had yet to serve aboard a ship, a requirement for getting discharged. So they arranged for him to sail on a dock landing ship called the USS *Fort Mandan* that was making a run to Cuba. On the way to Guantánamo Bay, the *Fort Mandan* encountered a fierce storm, so violent that baked beans spilled all over the mess and the normally imperturbable captain cursed at the top of his lungs. As the boat lurched on the open sea, Cosby had a sudden sense of things in life beyond his control. Then he thought: *If I survive, I have to get more serious about the things I can control.*

Tending to disabled vets who worked so hard to recover from their injuries had also made him ashamed of taking his own intellectual and physical gifts for granted. It was "a mental sin," as his Granddad Samuel would say.

Yet if Cosby intended to go to college, he had to overcome several hurdles. The first was finding a school that would take him. But he had a plan. While working at the hospital, he had been living with his mother on North Twenty-First Street and spending time around Temple University, the school located south of Germantown. He had decided that he wanted to go there, and when he asked Lieutenant Lamb for a letter of recommendation, she happily said yes.

The second hurdle was figuring out how to afford college. But Cosby had an idea for that, too. He was still on the navy track team, and they were about to participate in a meet at Villanova University where athletes from Temple would be competing. When the day arrived, Cosby went over to the Owls squad and introduced himself to a tall, wiry white man with curly brown hair who appeared to be their coach.

"My name is Bill Cosby, and I'm with the Navy team," he said.

"Gavin White," said the coach, extending his hand.

"I'm about done with my service, and I was wondering if you could help me get a track scholarship to Temple," Cosby said.

"How high can you jump?" White asked.

"Seven feet!" Cosby quipped.

"Well, I only take people who can jump five feet eight!" White said.

White could already tell that he liked the young jokester from the navy. He had also been watching Cosby and could see that he was a gifted athlete. He had the makings of a star high jumper, and he seemed well rounded enough to compete in several other events as well. So by the time their conversation was over, White agreed to recruit Cosby for an athletic scholarship to Temple — provided that he cleared one last hurdle.

Cosby had already taken correspondence courses offered by the navy and received his GED, the certificate that was supposed to be the equivalent of a high school diploma. But Temple also wanted to see a score on the SAT — the Scholastic Aptitude Test that by the early 1960s most American colleges required applicants to take.

As Cosby sat in a school auditorium in Philadelphia and gazed at the booklet full of multiple-choice questions on the SAT exam, he felt as if his entire wasted school career were passing before his eyes. His high IQ wasn't going to help him remember the vocabulary he needed to answer the reading comprehension questions and the formulas required to solve the math problems. *So this was what Mrs. McKinney was talking about!* he thought, remembering all the clowning and daydreaming he had done in fifth grade. Cosby was tempted to put down his pencil and walk away, but that would be the end of the new life plan. So he imagined himself playing poker in the navy and did his best to bluff his way through the exam.

When Cosby got the SAT results back, they were abysmal. He had scored a total of 500 points on the entire exam, barely more than half the average of all the students heading to college in 1960. Still, Temple was impressed enough with Coach White's recruiting report and Lieutenant Lamb's letter of recommendation that it awarded him a place in its Class of 1964. He was going to be twenty-three years old when he enrolled in the fall, a full four or five years older than most of the other freshman. But he was finally going to college, as Anna had always dreamed, and this time he was determined not to waste the opportunity.

Finish school this time, baby, Cosby thought. *Otherwise it's Horn & Hardart for the rest of your life.*

5

THE BAR AT TEMPLE

Cosby wanted to run the 220-yard hurdles.

He was already a high jumper, the best on the Temple track and field team. He was competing in the long jump, the triple jump, the javelin, the discus, and the shot put, sometimes scoring in as many as eight events. But now he wanted to run the hurdles, too, even though running was not exactly his strong suit.

"You're going to have to train with the sprinters," Gavin White warned.

"I'm ready," Cosby said.

"I'm going to make you run three-twenties!" Coach White said.

"I'm ready," Cosby said.

The Owls team worked out at Temple Stadium, ten miles from the main campus in North Philadelphia. It was a dilapidated facility with a worn-out track and rusting equipment, so White had to come up with his own clever ways to keep his team in tip-top shape. One was a training exercise he called "320s."

To push the 440 men to run faster and to increase the endurance of the 220 men, he designed a makeshift track that measured 320 yards. It went inside of the quarter-mile oval and around the long jump pit at the end of the field. When Cosby ran the route for the first time, he kept pace until he rounded the pit, and then he started huffing and puffing.

"What happened?" White asked.

"Rigor mortis set in!" Cosby said.

"Rigor mortis?" White said.

"Yeah, Riggie," Cosby joked. "He's a little man who jumped out of the pit with a plastic hammer and hit me in the knee!"

For someone determined to turn his life around, Cosby had come to the right place at the right time. He entered Temple University in the fall of 1960, just months before America elected a young president who would inspire the country with visions of a New Frontier. And Temple was an institution that specialized in fresh starts. It had begun its life in the late nineteenth century in the Grace Baptist Church, where Reverend Russell Conwell tutored poor locals who couldn't afford to attend classes during the daytime. He called them "owls of the night" that dreamed of becoming "eagles of the day." As the school expanded into a full-fledged university with thousands of students and a hundred acre campus, it kept Temple as its name and the owl as its mascot, and

Conwell's night owl metaphor remained a good description for working-class strivers the school attracted.

Eager to meet other black students, Cosby pledged the small Temple chapter of Omega Psi Phi, America's oldest Negro fraternity. He also pestered Gavin White, who coached the freshman football team in the fall, to let him join the squad. White tried to talk him out of it, since the head football coach, George Makris, wanted preference given to his own recruits. But Cosby wouldn't take no for an answer. "He was twenty-three years old, and he was almost crying!" White recalled.

Cosby made the freshman squad as a fullback and helped the team go undefeated. He wasn't fast enough to be a great rusher, but at 6'1" and 185 pounds now he could throw a ferocious cross-body block. "He loved to hit people," White recalled.

Cosby could also take a hit. After a particularly vicious tackle that left him stunned and feeling like "caterpillar fuzz," Coach White and the team's trainer rushed onto the field to see if he was all right.

"Ask his name!" the trainer said.

That's a stupid question, Cosby thought.

"Rumpelstiltskin!" he called out.

White shook his head and smiled. "He's all right!" he said.

When Cosby joined the track team in the

138

spring, he was the oldest man on the squad, despite being a freshman. On the first day of practice, he befriended a nineteen-year-old black sophomore named Don Council who came from Camden, New Jersey, and was Temple's best sprinter. Although Council was a wiry 5'8", Cosby thought he looked like the boxer Jack Johnson because of his shaved head, and that was the nickname he gave him: "Jack Johnson, Jack Johnson!"

Council quickly learned how competitive Cosby was. Before their first meet, he wanted to bet on which one of them could win the most events and be the first to amass the twenty-five points needed to secure a varsity letter. Driven by the friendly rivalry, they both surpassed that total in one day — Council running the 100, the 200, and the 440; Cosby high jumping and throwing the shot put, discus, and javelin. Council narrowly won both bets, and they continued the one-upmanship throughout the season.

"I just won the one hundred, what are you going to do about that?" Council would taunt.

Cosby would soon be back in Council's face: "Well, I just won the high jump! What else do you have?"

Cosby was so competitive, in fact, that when his athletic talent couldn't guarantee victory, he used his big mouth. Arriving at the Mid-Athletic Conference championship,

he discovered that meet officials had short-
ened the high jump apron by a few inches.
While his opponents were jumping, he stood
on the sidelines and shouted warnings about
the alteration. They became so rattled that
they blew their approaches, and Cosby won
the event with a jump of only six feet, two
inches.

Cosby was officially a day student and
couldn't afford room and board. But at
twenty-three, he thought he was too old to
live at home with his mother and brothers, so
he hid a mattress under the bed in Don
Council's dorm room. He snuck his seventy-
five-dollar drum set on campus and pretended to be a boarder so he could eat for
free at the cafeteria. He scraped together
another seventy-five dollars and bought a
used Dodge that he nicknamed "the Black
Rat." But the car had a mind of its own, and
he never knew when it would start. On days
when he couldn't rouse the Rat, he and
Council rode the subways, waiting until the
trains pulled into the station to jump the
turnstile and beat the fare.

Because Cosby was older, had served in the
military, and projected an air of maturity
when he wasn't clowning around, the younger
athletes looked up to him. They learned that
they could come to him for advice and count
on his discretion. Once they became friends,
Council confided a secret that he hadn't told

anyone else at Temple: the sprinter had a one-year-old daughter back in Camden who had been born to his high school girlfriend.

Coach White also came to rely on Cosby as a morale officer for the team. When they traveled to out-of-town meets, White brought along a bullhorn to give pep talks on the bus. When he finished, he turned the bullhorn over to Cosby, who told amusing stories about the teams the Owls were about to face or the competitions they had just completed. Although there were four blacks on the squad — Cosby, Council, a shot putter named Bill Lights, and a hurdler named Billy Rose — there was never a hint of racial tension, and White attributed it to Cos's ability to help everyone get along.

Cosby had always loved to tease people, and he found a willing target in White. He particularly enjoyed making fun of how straightlaced his coach was. White had grown up in Wissahickon, the Philadelphia neighborhood where Cosby went to the Boys Club as a teen. He had been an athletic star throughout his youth, from sandlot baseball and the Pop Warner football league to playing left halfback and quarterback for Temple. Yet even though he came from the streets of North Philly and been around jocks his entire life, he never swore, and Cosby ribbed him about it in front of the other players. "Coach never curses!" he said. "He's so clean, I'm

141

surprised he has children!"

Beneath all banter, both men were coming to see their relationship as more than athlete and coach. To White, Cosby seemed like a son, even though they were only twelve years apart in age. But Cosby had been too disappointed by his own father to be looking for a surrogate dad. In his mind, White was what he called an abolitionist.

It was a private term that he used for white people who went out of their way to help him. Just as the original opponents of slavery had helped free his ancestors, Cosby's abolitionists were helping him to liberate his potential. He thought of Miss Forchic as one, and would one day see Mr. Sapolsky as another. Lieutenant Jean Lamb was part of the club, and so were the white coaches Cosby had in high school. But none had been as meaningful as Gavin White, the man who had gotten him into Temple and was inspiring him with his clean-cut example, no matter how much he kidded him about it. Yes, "Coach" was an abolitionist, all right, even if his name *was* White!

During summer recess, White was surprised and touched to receive a letter from Cosby. The postmark was Los Angeles, California, of all places. Cosby had driven the Black Rat across country to spend his vacation there. In the mornings, he worked in a furniture store. When he was done around three o'clock in the afternoon, he drove to the University of Southern California track to watch the local athletes practice. He had made friends with some of them, and they had invited him to work out with them.

When White read the names, he was astonished. Charlie Dumas, a student at USC who had won the gold medal in the high jump in the 1956 Olympics! Ollie Matson, now with the LA Rams, and Dick Bass, another of the team's biggest stars! Wow, he thought, Cosby really had some kind of charisma to become buddies with guys like that!

Cosby said that his new friends were encouraging him to transfer out west. The Southern California Intercollegiate Athletic Conference was dangling a place at one of its member schools. But he felt homesick. "The weather is great here," he wrote, "but people stay in their cars all day, polluting the air." He had seen playgrounds in LA bigger than all the playgrounds in Philadelphia combined, but no one ever used them. All anyone wanted to do was go to the beach. He had made a lady friend, too, but even dating felt lonely. "My girl and I take walks at night, and we're the only ones on the street," he wrote.

So Cosby came back to Temple in the fall, and his summer workouts paid off when he made the varsity football team. But he was under George Makris's command now, and the head coach with the severe crew cut wasn't about to let a track recruit start in his sophomore year. So Cosby spent most of the season playing for Temple's "B squad" and sitting on the sidelines during varsity games.

During one game against Lafayette College, he was riding the bench when he heard a fan of the other team shouting insults at Coach Makris, razzing him about what a lousy team Temple had. The guy wouldn't shut up, and he was getting on Cosby's nerves. Whatever his personal feelings about Makris, he thought the coach was doing the best he could with a beleaguered franchise and none of the financial resources of bigger schools. Besides, the loudmouth was trashing Temple, too.

Finally, Cosby had heard enough. He turned to a white teammate who was sitting next to him on the sidelines.

"Let's get that guy!" he said.

Cosby and the teammate quietly got up from the bench and climbed into the stands. When the obnoxious fan saw the two muscular players coming after him, he fled down the stadium steps and out an exit. But he wasn't fast enough. Cosby and his teammate chased him down and beat him up, then turned around and went back to the game.

As the starting squad was going back on the field after halftime, they were coming into the locker room, sweating and looking agitated. Don Council, who was Temple's star halfback, shot his friend a what's-up look. Cosby glared at him as if to say: *None of your business!*

When some of his other teammates heard what had happened, they couldn't believe that he would be capable of such a thing. Not happy-go-lucky Cos! But it didn't surprise Don Council. He loved Cosby like a brother, but he knew that his friend had a temper, and that it could flare suddenly and sometimes violently, particularly when he thought he was being disrespected.

Council had seen evidence of Cosby's hot side the previous May, when the sprinter's older brother invited them to a Miles Davis concert in New York City. Davis was playing Carnegie Hall in a benefit to support the African Research Foundation, a group that provided medical care to countries declaring their independence from colonial rule. As Davis was settling into his solo on "Someday My Prince Will Come," a black man and woman walked onto the stage holding placards that read "Freedom Now!" and "Africa for Africans!"

Cosby recognized the protestors as the jazz drummer Max Roach and his girlfriend, the singer Abbey Lincoln. He didn't know what their beef was (it turned out that they thought the African Research Foundation was a CIA front), but as far as Cosby was concerned, what they were doing was wrong. Roach was another of his jazz heroes, but no one messed with Miles!

Cosby stood up in the audience. "Hey, Max, get the hell off the stage!" he shouted. "Don't go interrupting Miles Davis!"

By his second year at Temple, Cosby was feeling good enough about his own drumming to play with professional musicians. He applied for membership in Local 274 of the American Federation of Musicians and began to hang out at a recreation center at Pleasant Playground where local jazzmen jammed. As usual, he quickly made friends and developed a special bond with one in particular: a saxophonist named Tony Williams. Williams was almost a foot shorter than Cosby and several years older, but he too quickly came to forget about the age difference. After practice sessions, they took long walks through Germantown, talking about music and life, before ending up at the house on North Twenty-First for one of Anna Cosby's home-cooked meals.

Eventually, Cosby caught the attention of a top bandleader in town, a trumpeter named Charlie Chisholm. A Georgia native, Chisholm had moved to Philly in the early 1940s and become part of the early bebop scene. He formed a quintet called the Philadelphians, featuring four other well-regarded local musicians: Frank Gatlin on tenor sax,

146

John Gale on bass, "Sonny" Hoxter on piano, and Jimmy Griffin on drums. They had even cut enough material for an album, although they hadn't found a record label to release it yet.

At some point Jimmy Griffin had to leave the band, and Chisholm asked Cosby to fill in on the drums. Suddenly he was playing around the city and imagining the possibility of a career as a jazz musician. But he was stretched too thin, between his sports and his schoolwork, and he kept showing up late to practices and gigs. Then he would clown around on stage. Eventually Chisholm had had enough and fired him.

But as Cosby's sophomore year progressed, a new calling emerged that would eclipse his sports and his music. And yet again, it was made possible by an abolitionist.

"I want you to write about an experience of doing something for the first time," Cosby's Remedial English teacher told the class.

Now he had Cosby's attention. He liked the fact that the assignment left something to the imagination. He started considering the possibilities: His first touchdown? His first kiss? *No, too easy . . .* he thought.

Cosby had been placed on the Remedial English track because his SAT scores were so low. He worried that the classes would be full of rote memorization and grammar exercises, like the ones he hated in high school. But he was pleased to discover that his teacher had creative ways of making his class interesting. The key to English, he told the students, was writing: learning how to do it well and recognizing good writing when you read it. He gave the class the assignment of writing about a "first experience" to see what they could do with it.

Cosby decided to write about the first time he lost a tooth, when he was six years old. He remembered how he couldn't stop wiggling the tooth when it came loose, how he ran to look at the bloody gash in the mirror when it popped out, and how he lay awake wondering if the Tooth Fairy would visit the Richard Allen Homes. He started writing down his memories and turning them into a story. He wanted to make it as good as he could, because he wanted to impress his teacher but also because he was still worried about flunking out of Temple if he didn't get good grades. He wrote and rewrote and finished the assignment two days before it was due, something he had never done before.

A week later, the teacher passed back the graded papers but didn't hand one to Cosby. His heart sank. He became even more downcast as the professor described how predictable the essays were.

"But there was one exception," he said,

"and I want to read it to you. It's by Mr. Cosby, and it's about how he lost his first tooth."

Cosby couldn't believe it: no teacher had ever read aloud something that he had written! He became even more excited as the other students laughed at the wiggly tooth and the bloody stump and the image of the Tooth Fairy coming to the projects.

When the teacher handed back his essay, Cosby was thrilled to see that he had given it an A for content — along with a C minus in the margin for poor spelling and grammar.

Next, the teacher told the students to write an essay on a subject of their own choice. Cosby came up with story called "Procrastination, or the Perfect Point." Whenever he didn't feel like starting an assignment, he wrote, he sharpened his pencil. He liked his number 2s nice and pointy, but when he pulled the pencil out of the sharpener, something was always wrong with it. The lead tip was stubby or wobbly, or the wood wasn't perfectly shaved. So he kept sharpening to get a "perfect point" until there was nothing left but the eraser. And then he had an excuse not to do the homework!

Once again, the teacher read the story aloud, and the class loved it. Cosby got another A for content and his grade for grammar improved to B+.

Cosby eventually forgot the name of his

Remedial English teacher, but he would never forget how the man helped him think differently about his gift for humor. He had always known that he could be funny in a spontaneous, fast-on-his-feet way. But now he saw that he had a talent for developing comic ideas, and that he could make them better by writing them down. He started carrying a notepad and a number 2 pencil wherever he went, to jot down ideas and dialogue as soon as they popped into his head. Gradually he worked them into full-blown routines, with characters that he acted out like the ones in the Bible stories that Granddad Samuel had told him as a child.

He began to fantasize about a future as a comedy writer. He had read about Mel Brooks and Carl Reiner and the writers' room at *Your Show of Shows,* and he had heard about stand-up comics who paid for material. Maybe he could shop his routines to the white comedians who came through Philadelphia. He assumed that they would be white, since the only black comedians he had ever heard of were the ribald veterans of "chitlin' circuit" such as Redd Foxx, Moms Mabley, and Pigmeat Markham, who played at the Uptown Theater on North Broad Street.

Cosby went to work developing routines to sell. *Rhinoceros* had always struck him as a funny word, so he wrote a bit about a family that kept a pet rhinoceros. He wrote another one about a saber tooth tiger who lost one of his teeth and talked with a lisp. Remembering all the hours he had spent listening to *The Lone Ranger* on the radio as a boy, he imagined what would happen if the Ranger and Tonto got drunk and Tonto started talking back to his boss:

"You go to town, Tonto!"

"You go to hell, Kimosabe!"

One day in history class, as he was listening to a dreary lecture about the Revolutionary War, he thought: *What if wars began with a coin toss, like football games?* He took out his notepad and started fleshing out the idea. What if the Colonial Army had won the toss and elected to wear ragtag clothes and use guerrilla tactics while insisting that the British dress in bright red uniforms and march in formation like sitting ducks? What if a flip of the coin before the Battle of Little Bighorn had allowed Sitting Bull to set up his ambush of General Custer?

The first comedian Cosby approached with his material wasn't impressed. "This is not funny," he said after reading several pages.

"Wait a minute," Cosby said. "Let me show you how to do it."

He tried to act out a few lines before the comedian stopped him.

"It's still not funny," the comedian said.

Cosby decided to try the owner of the

151

Gilded Cage, a local coffee house, but he didn't laugh either. The negative feedback made Cosby feel like he was in the navy again, confronting the humorless recruit division commander. Disheartened, he threw the pages into a sewer grate before taking the trolley back to North Philadelphia.

Although his track scholarship had gotten him into Temple, Cosby had to pay $350 per semester in tuition, so he was still working part time. Some of his jazz musician friends played at a small nightclub called the Underground on North Broad Street run by a manager named Elwood Johnson. Johnson also managed a tiny bar next door called the Cellar, where Cosby took a job as a bartender.

Tending bar suddenly gave him a captive audience for his comic experiments. As he poured beer and mixed cocktails, he tried out the routines that he was writing in English class. He started getting laughs and bigger tips. When Elwood Johnson saw how popular he was becoming, he made Cosby a proposal. Johnson offered to pay him an extra five dollars a night if he would sit on a chair at the end of the bar and tell jokes so that everyone in the room could hear him.

At first there was little rhyme or reason to Cosby's routines. He would arrive at the Cellar with a manila folder full of handwritten notes, newspaper clippings, and copies of *Mad* magazine and leaf through them for comic inspiration. Sometimes he used one-liners lifted from other comedians, although he always credited the source in case any of the customers had heard them already. He pictured that material as punches in a boxing match: *Hit 'em hard and straighten 'em up . . . left, right, bam.*

But at other times, Cosby shared funny observations about things that had happened to him at Temple or that he had seen on the streets of Philadelphia. If the crowd laughed, he stretched out the story for as long as possible. His friend Tony Williams remembered one night at the Cellar when Cosby kept everyone in stitches for half an hour making fun of a local preacher from South Philadelphia named Bishop Johnson. He described the vain way the preacher dressed and imitated the pompous sermons in which he claimed that the voice of God had told him he would live forever.

In search of ideas, Cosby checked out the comedy records at the neighborhood store where he bought jazz LPs. One day he came across a new album called *2000 Years with Carl Reiner and Mel Brooks.* It featured the two writers from *Your Show of Shows* performing skits that they had started doing at dinner parties. Reiner would pick a character for Brooks to play, and Brooks would improvise responses as Reiner asked him questions. The album included Reiner interviewing Brooks as an astronaut, a psychiatrist, and a Peruvian with a New York accent named Fabiolo.

In the funniest of the routines, the one that inspired the title of the album, Brooks played a two-thousand-year-old man who had something to say about everything that had happened in the past two millennia, from his many offspring ("Over forty-two thousand children, and none of them comes to visit me!") to historical figures such as Joan of Arc ("Know her? I went with her, dummy, I went with her!").

Cosby fell in love with the album, and one night he invited his friend Joe Johnson Jr., one of the Down Cats, to his house in Germantown to play it for him.

"Joe, you gotta hear this record," Cosby said.

"Yeah, that's cool," Joe agreed.

"Man, I think we could do that!" Cosby said.

He suggested they form a comedy duo. Cos would play the Mel Brooks role, improvising in character, and Joe would be the interviewer. They started writing down ideas and came up with a routine in which Cosby played his idol Miles Davis:

"So Mr. Davis, how did you start playing the trumpet? What was your inspiration?"

"Mostly fear . . ."

After they had written enough material for a short set, Cosby went to Elwood Johnson and asked if they could try it out at the Underground. He also took Joe along to open mic nights at the Media Club, a jazz joint in West Philadelphia that was partly owned by a distant cousin, Del Shields.

After three or four performances, Johnson decided that the life of a stand-up comic wasn't for him. He could see that Cos was hooked, but he didn't see the attraction. Johnson hated the begging for auditions, the staying up late, the waiting around to perform, the patrons talking and ordering drinks and not paying attention during the act. Most of all, he hated the hecklers. For every patron who laughed at the routine, there was a drunk who took one look at Cosby in his black sunglasses and beret trying to sound like Miles Davis and shouted: "Get these damn kids off the stage!"

At the time, a black comic named Pop Foster was performing at the Underground. He was a veteran of the chitlin' circuit who was friends with Redd Foxx and an up-and-coming Negro comedian named Flip Wilson. Pop was also a drinker who could often be found sleeping off benders in the club's supply closet. One night, he was scheduled to perform but was nowhere to be found. At the last minute, Elwood Johnson asked Cosby if

155

he and Johnson could fill in. But when Cos called Joe, the Down Cat said he was no longer up for playing a straight man.

So Cosby went on stage and acted out the Miles routine by himself. He assumed the deep, smooth voice of a TV interviewer, then put on sunglasses and answered them in the spacey, raspy voice of a jazz hipster. He could see the audience was amused by the spectacle of a young black man in a collegiate jacket and tie jumping from one comic persona to another. They started to laugh, louder than audiences had ever done when he and Joe Johnson performed the bit.

There was a British couple at the Underground that night, and after the set they invited Cosby over to their table. They told him how funny he was and were surprised to learn that he was still a college student. They asked if he had ever performed outside of Philadelphia. When Cosby said he hadn't, they offered to put him in touch with a friend who owned a club in New York City called the Gaslight Café. It was a coffee shop in Greenwich Village where folksingers provided the entertainment and comedians were hired to amuse the crowd between musical sets.

Shortly afterward, Cosby's cousin Del Shields set him up with another gig acting as MC at a club called Woody's Bar. One of the performers was another Temple University student named Alix Dobkin, who wanted to be a folksinger and had a soaring soprano voice reminiscent of Joan Baez. Dobkin brought along a third Temple classmate named Herb Gart, who was hoping to become her manager. When they met Cosby and learned that he was thinking of trying to get a summer job in Greenwich Village, Gart offered to drive them to New York for an audition.

As Dobkin remembered it, they took the New Jersey Turnpike to the Village, where they searched the maze of stores and eateries on MacDougal Street until they found a small sign engraved "Gaslight Café" at the bottom of a narrow stairway. They went inside, parted a thick black curtain, and entered a dark room. A languid-looking man was sitting at a table in the back. He said he worked for the owner, John Mitchell, and that he would listen to their auditions. As Dobkin sang and Cosby told jokes, the man looked like he was about to fall asleep. But when they were done, he told them to come back in June and promised to give them work. It was only after Dobkin returned to the Village and got to know the scene better that she concluded that the man appeared so sleepy because he was stoned.

With a summer gig in New York to look forward to, Cosby went to work writing new material and practicing his comic delivery. After leaving the Cellar, he would head to

Lombard Street to listen to the bands playing at the Showboat or around the corner at Pep's, another jazz club at the corner of South and Broad. As he had done with the Down Cats in high school, he liked to take Don Council to the jazz matinee on Sunday, where a dollar still paid for the cover and a Coke.

One Sunday, Cosby and Council had been sitting at the Showboat for several hours when the bartender tried to get them to buy a second round.

"Okay, fellas, what'll it be?" the bartender said.

"Je ne parles pas a vous etes et non merci avec mon chien le cool jazz!" Cosby blurted out.

"Huh?" the bartender said.

Cosby let loose with more foreign-sounding double talk of the sort Sid Caesar used on *Your Show of Shows.* The bartender shook his head and walked away.

"He's not going to ask us again," Cosby whispered to Council. "He's too embarrassed to admit he doesn't understand what I'm saying!"

As Cosby grooved to the music, he thought about the ways comedy could resemble jazz. When Mel Brooks did his "2000 Year Old Man" routine, he was improvising in the way jazz musicians did, by playing off a familiar melody or chord structure. *That's what the material I'm writing down will be for me,* Cosby thought. *They'll be my theme and my chords.* But when he performed, he wouldn't repeat the routines word for word, as old-fashioned comics did. He would riff, so that his material always felt fresh, to his audience and to him.

He thought about how jazz was also about listening — how cats had to listen to each other and to the room. When he did stand-up, he wanted to feed off his audience the way a jazz soloist would, sensing when to swing hard and when to lay back, when to cut a riff short and when to take extra helpings. Some nights at the Cellar, he already had that sensation. After one performance, Tony Williams said that he felt Cosby was using all of his "five special senses," as though he were absorbing everything that was happening in the bar — the conversation, the clothes, the taste of the drinks, and the smell of the perfume and the cologne — as he decided where to go next.

Jazz was also about hard work. People who simply listened to the music might think it was purely spontaneous, but anyone who played it knew how much preparation was involved: the endless hours of playing scales, of transposing keys, of training hands and fingers to play with lightning speed or feathery touch. On the drums, Cosby would never match the best musicians in those clubs. But if he was going to be a comedian, he would have to master the same jazz discipline, the kind of work ethic that allowed those cats on the bandstand to make everything they did look effortless.

Most of all, jazz was about innovation. Cosby thought about his hero, Miles Davis, and all the times he had changed his sound and his sidemen. When Cosby was in the navy and heard that Davis had dropped Philly Joe Jones as his drummer, he thought it would be the end of him. *Well, that's it,* Cosby thought, *because Philly Joe kept that stuff together.* Then he heard the new drummer was a guy named Jimmy Cobb who had played with Sarah Vaughan, and he thought, *How you gonna have a cat who played with a woman singer play with Miles? Miles is gonna run him off the stand.* Cosby thought the same thing when Davis replaced Red Garland, the keyboard wizard from Philly, with a white pianist named Bill Evans. But it was that Miles group, including Evans and Cobb, which produced the immortal album *Kind of Blue.* It only goes to show, Cosby reflected, that audiences crave what they already know, but a true artist keeps moving on, keeps experimenting, keeps searching for the new thing that people don't know they want until they hear it.

Before he left for New York that summer,

Cosby would have another epiphany about where that experimenting could lead him. He was working at the Cellar one night and popped out for a quick meal at a Chinese restaurant. As he waited for his food to arrive, he noticed a table full of people who were having the time of their lives. He watched closely and saw that they were all listening to one person, an otherwise unassuming man who was talking with great animation. But the man wasn't telling jokes. He was recounting stories, acting out various parts as he went along. His friends nodded and chuckled, and when he got to the end of each story, they let out a huge laugh.

For weeks afterward, Cosby couldn't get that picture from the Chinese restaurant out of his head. *That's the kind of comedian I want to be,* he thought. *I want to be the storyteller whose friends all think he is the funniest guy in the world.*

6
"Noah" in the Village

The Gaslight Café had a tiny storeroom on the floor above the club, in the back. During the day, musicians killed time there with penny-ante poker games, and sometimes if the room was empty, a waiter and a waitress would lock the door for a quickie. The club's entertainment director, a part-time poet and humorist named Hugh Romney, later known as Wavy Gravy, kept a portable typewriter in the storeroom. When he wasn't using it, he lent it to his friends, who included a skinny folksinger who had arrived in Greenwich Village from Minnesota the year before, wearing a corduroy Huck Finn cap and playing Woody Guthrie songs on his Gibson guitar and Hohner harmonica.

One day in September 1962, Tom Paxton, a Gaslight regular, walked into the storeroom and found Bob Dylan typing feverishly.

"What do you think of this?" Dylan asked, handing Paxton several sheets of paper that contained an ode in the style of an Anglo-

Saxon border ballad.

Paxton was struck by the wild imagery: ". . . twelve misty mountains . . . six twisted highways . . . a clown who cried in the alley . . . a young child beside a dead pony."

"It's pretty good," Paxton said. "Are you going to put music to it?"

"Do you think I should?" Dylan asked.

"Yeah," Paxton said. "Otherwise it'll just end up in some literary quarterly."

Dylan was performing at another Village club, Gerde's Folk City on West Fourth Street, but he often came to the Gaslight to try out songs that he hadn't finished. Several days later, he showed up before closing time and gave the first performance of the ballad he had written upstairs, which he would record as "A Hard Rain's A-Gonna Fall."

The Gaslight Café storeroom where that groundbreaking song was written was also where Bill Cosby slept every night during that summer of 1962, while performing on the tiny stage downstairs.

When Cosby arrived in Greenwich Village in early June, it was a buzzing hive of young artists pushing the boundaries of their crafts. Having recorded a debut album of traditional folk anthems, Dylan was writing his own songs and tweaking his nasal delivery and rebel look. (When he wasn't using the typewriter at the Gaslight, he could be found sitting on the rickety steps outside, coating his curly locks with hairspray to make them stand up in a messy pompadour.) On the Gaslight stage, Paxton and another young talent, Buffy Sainte-Marie, were honing their sounds, borrowing from folk stars like Pete Seeger and the Kingston Trio but also from Mississippi John Hurt, a Delta bluesmen who was a regular at the club.

At the Village Gate at the corner of Thompson and Bleecker and the Half Note on Hudson Street, bebop pioneers John Coltrane, Ornette Coleman, and Charles Mingus were taking their music into new frontiers of modal and atonal "free" jazz that borrowed from Gregorian chants and avant-garde classical music. In the theater world, a neighborhood impresario named Joe Cino was turning over the floor of his coffee house, the Caffé Cino, to the first productions of an off-Off Broadway movement that would launch the careers of such innovative playwrights as Sam Shepard and John Guare.

On Bleecker Street, another ambitious impresario, Fred Weintraub, was turning the Bitter End into a showcase not only for folk musicians but also for a new generation of comedians who wanted their audiences to think as well as laugh. Mort Sahl, the droll political commentator, and Lenny Bruce, the profane social satirist, were Bitter End regulars. So were two novices named Woody Allen and Dick Cavett, both gifted but shy writers for late-night talk shows who were slowly and awkwardly turning their quirky observations into stand-up comedy.

Before Cosby could start honing his own craft, however, he had to deal with an unexpected setback. When he arrived at the Gaslight Café, he discovered that its ownership had changed hands. John Mitchell, the flamboyant entrepreneur who had built the club from scratch, had skipped town and left it in the hands of a Mississippi native named Clarence Hood. Hood, who had made and lost several fortunes in the lumber and orchard business, knew nothing about folk music, much less comedy.

When Cosby first saw Hood in his crew cut and top coat and heard his nasal Southern drawl, he thought: *What is this good ol' boy from Mississippi going to make of me?* To make matters worse, no one had told Hood anything about the earlier job offers for Cosby and Dobkin, and he wanted them to audition all over again.

So Cosby did a routine he had written about learning Spanish in high school. *"Grande es el burro!"* he recited. *"El burro es grande!"*

Hood was instantly smitten. "Bill, I'm telling you, you're going to be tremendous!" he said in a high-pitched voice. "I don't know how long we're going to be able to hold you!"

165

Herb Gart sensed an opportunity and offered Hood a deal: book Cosby and Dobkin just for one weekend, and if it went well, they would promise to stay for the rest of the summer. The gambit worked, and later Cosby learned another reason why Hood had been so welcoming: he was a long-time supporter of civil rights who, as Democratic committeeman in Mississippi, had been one of the few politicians in the state to support Harry Truman's efforts to desegregate the US military.

The Gaslight Café had started its life in the late 1950s as a "basket house," a coffee shop that served espresso and pastries and allowed Beat poets such as Allen Ginsberg to pass a basket for donations. The basement space was only big enough for a hundred people or so, and the ceilings were so low that Mitchell had to lower the floor by digging it up and leaving sacks of dirt on MacDougal Street. Eventually a black poet named Len Chandler began performing songs, too, and the club became a venue for novice folksingers, including a Cornell psychology graduate named Peter Yarrow, who struck up a friendship with the Gaslight's MC, Noel Stookey.

By 1962, Yarrow and Stookey had formed a folk trio with a friend named Mary Travers and released their first album on Warner Bros. Records. *Peter, Paul and Mary* was now at the top of the *Billboard* charts, the first folk

166

album to rise that far, and the Gaslight had become a destination not just for local hipsters and New York University students but foreign tourists, uptown professionals, and suburbanites from New Jersey, Long Island, and Westchester County.

Hood told Cosby that his job description was to keep the crowd amused between musical acts. He would get paid sixty dollars a week and, since he had no place to live and no money, he could crash in the storeroom above the club. The Gaslight stage was a tiny space against a brick wall, with no curtain or backstage, and the ceiling pipes leaked on artists while they were performing. If Cosby didn't get wet from the faulty plumbing, he was usually drenched in sweat from the summer heat.

Yet he got what he had come to Greenwich Village for: work, and plenty of it. He was on call every day from eight o'clock until four o'clock in the morning, performing twenty-minute sets between the folk acts. As he mounted the tiny Gaslight stage over and over again, he began to learn the little tricks of stand-up: how to deal with hecklers, how to get audience members involved in his act, how to respond to sudden noises or other unexpected events in the room. For the first time, he figured out what made an ad-lib funny: it wasn't just what he said, but how he set it up.

When Cosby finished work shortly before dawn, he would go to the downtown jazz clubs that were still open, looking for release and inspiration. Sometimes he would hop a cab for the short ride to the Half Note or the Five Spot Cafe; sometimes he would just wander the streets of the Village, listening for the sound of a jam session. One night he wandered into a new place and found Cedar Walton, Art Blakey's pianist, playing in a trio with bassist Buster Williams and drummer Ben Riley.

"How long are you going to play?" Cosby asked.

" 'Til death," Riley replied.

After returning to the Gaslight storeroom at sunrise to catch a few hours' sleep, Cosby spent the days reworking his routines. He added to the bits that had gone well the night before, cut down or eliminated ones that had bombed, and jotted down ideas for new material. In the late afternoon, he played pick-up basketball on the public courts around the corner on Fourth Street. Brimming with sweat, he returned to the storeroom and washed at the sink in the restroom. Then he put on a blazer and tie and a fake signet ring that he had bought from the jeweler next door on MacDougal Street and went downstairs to perform until four o'clock in the morning again.

Tom Paxton was impressed with how

quickly Cosby's act was evolving. Rather than sticking with the same routines, he was constantly experimenting with new material. He would do a twenty-minute bit one night and, if didn't work, it would be gone forever. Meanwhile, the stories that did work got longer and better: Paxton particularly liked one Cosby told about discovering in the navy that Jim Crow "wasn't so bad," when he had to eat in restaurant kitchens in the South and got treated like a prince by the Negro cooks.

As a musician trained to pay attention to acoustics, Paxton was also amazed at the effects Cosby created with the Gaslight's bulbous omni-directional microphone. Cosby played the mic as though it was a jazz instrument: mixing whispers and cries and shouts; tapping and thumping out rhythms; even swallowing the whole thing into his mouth as he created a one-man soundtrack to his routines. When Paxton found out that Cosby had barely ever used a professional microphone before, he was astonished.

In less than a month, word of Cosby's presence in the Village reached the *New York Times.* One of his football coaches at Temple knew an editor there and alerted him to the story of a black college student spending his summer working as a comedian. The *Times* had recently launched a new Culture department, and its associate editor, Arthur Gelb, was intrigued. He figured that it was the kind of story that would appeal to his bosses, Turner Catledge and Clifton Daniels, two Southerners who were devoting more and more coverage to the civil rights movement. So Gelb assigned one of his young reporters, Paul Gardner, to go to Greenwich Village and interview Cosby.

When Gardner was assigned a profile, he usually consulted the *Times* library of newspaper clips, but he could find nothing about Cosby. And the night Gardner went to the Gaslight, it was hardly packed. The crowd consisted of bearded bohemians, a few foreign tourists, and some college girls chatting about medical care for the elderly. Although Gardner enjoyed the act, he didn't come away with the impression that Cosby would be the next big thing. What did strike him, however, was that unlike Lenny Bruce or other political comics he had heard, there was nothing cutting or raw or raunchy about the act. Instead, Cosby wandered amiably from topic to topic, mixing a few mild racial jokes ("I used to live in a nice neighborhood, then two white families moved in") with stories about growing up in Philadelphia and a parody of Beat poetry:

Roses are red,
Violets are blue,
Grass is green,
And Dirt is brown.

Afterward, the two men sat on thatched barstools in the corner of the nightclub and talked. Gardner noted how preppy his subject looked in his plaid sports coat and rep tie. Cosby struck him as friendly but quiet, even a bit shy. He admitted that he hoped "to make it big" in show business but stressed that he wanted to earn his college diploma first. "My mother wants me to finish, and I suppose that's best," he said. Cosby talked about his impoverished childhood in the projects, but he didn't dramatize it. "I was happy when I finally got a job in a grocery store," he said. He also showed how much he was thinking about the new school of cerebral comedy. "Audiences don't go for cheap laughter," he said. "You need an education to be a comic today."

The next day Gardner went into the Times Building on West Forty-Third Street and told Gelb what he had, and the editor was impressed enough to assign the story six hundred words — a full-blown feature in those days. In Gardner's mind, the story was as much about a college jock from Temple trying to break into stand-up comedy as a piece about race. But that's not how it looked in the newspaper.

"Comic Turns Quips into Tuition" read the headline, followed by the subheads: "Bill Cosby, Student at Temple, Featured at Gaslight Café; Philadelphia Negro Aims His

Barbs at Race Relations."

Conjuring the image of an African tribesman, the opening paragraph described Cosby "hurling verbal spears at the relations between whites and Negroes." And while the story eventually noted that he "pokes fun at faith healers, fundamentalist preachers, Greenwich Village life, and international trouble spots," it dwelled on his racial material. In one bit, Cosby had pretended to be the first black president telling an old friend how it was going: "Yeah, baby, everything's fine, except a lot of 'For Sale' signs are going up on this block." In another, he told a stony-faced man in the audience: "You better laugh; I've got a club that's the opposite of the Ku Klux Klan." At the end of the story, he was quoted comparing himself to the hottest Negro comedian of the day. "Some people call me 'the Philadelphia Dick Gregory,' " he said, "but that's silly. I'm taller — and better looking."

When Herb Gart opened a copy of the *New York Times* on the morning of July 26, he was thrilled. Less than a month in Greenwich Village, and his friend and unofficial client was the subject of a feature story in the city's most prestigious newspaper! But Cosby was upset. He thought the story focused too much on the race angle. It had quoted a few black jokes at length and skipped over the more observational and conceptual humor

172

that he thought of as the heart of his act. What's more, he had opened up to the reporter, tried to show him how thoughtful he was, and he was pigeonholed as another angry Negro comic. His first experience with the press had already left him feeling misunderstood and mistrustful.

At first, Gart thought Cosby was being oversensitive. "Bill, have you looked in the mirror, lately?" he told him. But as they talked, Gart came to see just how serious Cosby was about the vision he had had in the Chinese restaurant in Philadelphia. He wanted to be not just another joke machine but a storyteller with his own distinctive voice, like his mother's favorite writer Mark Twain, whose memory was being revived at that very moment by a touring one-man play starring actor Hal Holbrook. Decades later, Gart recalled the conversation and said: "That was a lesson I learned from Bill. You are who you are. You ain't who they think you are. As long as you figure out who that is, you have a better chance of making it than if you pretend to be someone else."

Yet Cosby had to admit that the *Times* article, as distorted as he thought it was, had put a finger on something. He *was* trying to have it both ways — to develop his own style and to capitalize on Dick Gregory's popularity at the same time.

Cosby couldn't help but identify with Gregory, the St. Louis native who had become famous for his biting barbs at white racism. Not only was Gregory another black man trying to make it in the white comedy world; he was also a track and field man and military veteran. Cosby was proud to see how far the older comic had risen — all the way to the couch next to Jack Paar on *The Tonight Show,* a place no other Negro comedian had ever been. He also thought that Gregory's material — lines such as "I know the South very well; I spent twenty years there one night" — was very funny. But he knew in his heart that he didn't want to be Philadelphia's Dick Gregory, and reading the *Times* piece left him more determined to go in his own direction.

Several days later, he was killing time with a few other comedians at a Village coffee shop. The espresso machine was on the fritz, so they were drinking the bitter dregs of a pot that had been brewing since the morning. The other comics were ribbing Cosby about the *Times* article, and one of them said: "You know, if you turned white tomorrow, you wouldn't have any more material."

That does it, Cosby thought. *That stuff is gone.*

It was easier said than done, however. On some nights, his other material fell flat, and he went back to the race jokes just to get a laugh. His delivery was still a work in progress. Gart gave him recordings of performers he thought Cosby should study. One was Anna Russell, a Canadian comedienne who played the piano and gave comic lectures about classical music. Gart told Cosby to listen to her timing, how she rode the waves of applause and laughter. Another was an eccentric comic named Lord Buckley who was a master at creating comic voices: one minute he was a pompous aristocratic fop, the next a jive-talking hipster who called himself "the Nazz."

On rare nights off, Cosby tried to catch other comedy acts around the Village. He was excited to see Alan King, the cigar-puffing mocker of suburban life who was one of his favorite guests on *The Ed Sullivan Show.* He had written King a fan letter while he was at Temple, and King remembered it when Cosby introduced himself. He also went to see Lenny Bruce. He came away captivated by Bruce's improvisational brilliance but bothered by his nonstop use of profanity. When Cosby scanned the audience, he couldn't tell whether people were laughing at Bruce's material or at the shock of hearing a comic say "fuck" and "schmuck" and "cocksucker."

Although he was still developing his own voice, Cosby had made one important resolution already: he was going to work clean. It wasn't that he was unfamiliar or uncomfortable with swearing. After all, he had lived in the projects and served in the navy, and he could cuss with the best of them in private. But he had also grown up in Anna Cosby's house and competed for Gavin White's track team. Whenever he performed, he couldn't help imagining one of them, or his Granddad Samuel, in the audience. Besides, he thought swearing was often a crutch for comics who wanted to be like Lenny Bruce or Redd Foxx but weren't as talented. If he worked clean, he would know when his stuff stood up — and when it fell flat.

After the *New York Times* article, crowds started to grow for Cosby's performances, and talent scouts came out of the woodwork. Gart noticed Albert Grossman, the agent for Peter, Paul and Mary, showing up at the Gaslight. He didn't want to lose his client to a rival, so he reached out to an older manager named Len Rosenfeld, whose office he was sharing for the summer. They agreed that Gart would keep a percentage of Cosby's commission, but that Rosenfeld would take over managing his affairs. But that arrangement lasted only a few weeks, until the hustling owner of the Bitter End, Fred Weintraub, set his sights on Cosby. Weintraub decided that he wanted to represent the new toast of the *Times,* and he knew just the man to help him do it: another fiercely driven young manager on the Village scene named Roy Silver.

■ ■ ■ ■

For Roy Silver, there was also a Bob Dylan story before there was a Bill Cosby story. A college dropout and former accountant, Silver had come to the Village in his late twenties looking to get into the talent management business. With his dark suits, horned-rimmed glasses, and short-cropped hair, he looked like a salesman, and he behaved like one, too. As soon as Dylan arrived in New York, Silver started following him around, trying to get him gigs and pestering him to find out what he was writing.

One day in July 1962, Silver persuaded Dylan to show him a new song he had written based on a Negro spiritual called "No Auction Block for Me." Silver scribbled a makeshift copyright agreement on a piece of paper, got Dylan to sign it, and took him uptown to see Art Mogull, the head of a music publishing company called M. Witmark & Sons that was owned by Warner Bros. Records. Mogull was so impressed by the lyrics — lines like "How many ears must one man have before he can hear people cry?" — that he signed Dylan to a five-year publishing deal for one thousand dollars.

The next day, Silver was back in Mogull's office with a confession: Dylan already had a deal with another publisher, Leeds Music. "What are you talking about?" Mogull erupted. "You can't sign with two companies at the same time!" But by then, Mogull had decided that "Blowin' in the Wind" would make a terrific song for the next Warner Bros. album by Peter, Paul and Mary. So he gave Silver another thousand dollars to buy Dylan out of his Leeds contract, and then arranged for the folk trio's manager, Albert Grossman, to take over Dylan's affairs.

Asked about the episode decades later, Dylan remembered Roy Silver curtly. "He was kind of like a hustler type on the street, somebody trying to make a deal about this, a deal about that," he said. "He was a fast talker."

Within weeks of losing Dylan, however, Roy Silver had Bill Cosby as a client. When Fred Weintraub proposed that they team up to sign the young black comedian, Silver leapt at the opportunity. Cosby met with the two managers and came away impressed. He could tell they were operators, but they seemed more ambitious than Len Rosenfeld, the kindly older agent to whom he had been introduced by Herb Gart. He also liked the fact that Weintraub and Silver praised his observational humor and thought he should do more of it rather than emulating Dick Gregory.

Years later, Weintraub and Silver would maintain that Cosby didn't want to abandon his racial material initially and got furious at them for suggesting it. In a memoir, Weintraub would write that "as his managers, that's what we focused on: styling Bill's Everyman persona. He was resistant, at first. Not because he believed so strongly in his edgy, civil-rights-minded material, I think, but because someone else came up with a better angle for him." Silver told a *Life* magazine reporter that Cosby "threatened to punch me for making him change." But Cosby had a different recollection. He acknowledged early tensions with the managers but said it was over *how* they wanted him to change. Weintraub and Silver insisted that he come to the Bitter End during the day and practice new material in front of them before he performed it for an audience.

"Go up on stage and rehearse!" Silver commanded.

"That's not going to happen!" Cosby snapped angrily. "I don't work that way. I need an audience."

Impatient with Cosby's methods, Weintraub was soon barking out a suggestion or two and leaving Silver to do the real work of being his manager. Accepting that Cosby wouldn't rehearse, Silver suggested bringing a tape recorder to his live shows, so that they could analyze the results afterwards. Cosby liked that approach better, because it allowed him to remain spontaneous on stage and listen to the tapes afterward to study what had worked and what hadn't and to "find the funny," as he liked to put it.

Going back over one night's work, Cosby noticed a ripple of audience reaction when he talked about riding the subways in New York. *Subways . . . maybe there's something there,* he thought. But where was the funny? A few days later, he was talking to friend about how expensive it was to live in New York. *Could I do a bit about that?* he thought. Suddenly, he put the two ideas together: even if you were broke in New York, you could entertain yourself by watching the crazy people in the subways. *Now that's funny!* he thought. He went back to the Gaslight storeroom and started writing, and soon he had a full three minutes he could bring on stage downstairs:

"If you plan to come into New York any time soon," the bit began, "you don't have to bring a lot of money. You can get all the entertainment you want for fifteen cents, riding the subways. It's marvelous: They put a nut in every car! . . . I saw a three-act show from West Fourth Street to 125th Street . . . First act was a woman who went around condemning everyone. She was so great when she got off on Twenty-Third Street we gave her a standing ovation! . . . At Thirty-Fourth Street, she was replaced by two hundred high school kids who went through the car, cut up

180

the seats and the people . . . The ladies and the kids all did a high kickoff at Eighty-First Street, and on came two winos and a guy nudges me and says: 'These are the stars of the show! They come on every time.' They talked to each other and the play was entitled 'Incoherency' . . ."

With routines like "A Nut in Every Car," Cosby was learning how to take the funny observations that had always amused his friends and turn them into polished routines, with setups and development and punch lines. But as he played back the tapes of his performances, he realized that he was still missing the one thing all the top comics had: a signature bit. The comedians who were really big at the time, the ones who had hit record albums and appeared on late-night talk shows, had routines for which they were famous. Cosby's idols, Mel Brooks and Carl Reiner, had "The 2000 Year Old Man." The improv duo of Mike Nichols and Elaine May had "Mother and Son" and "$65 Funeral." Bob Newhart, the former advertising writer who had become the first comedian to top the *Billboard* charts with his albums, had his "The Driving Instructor" number.

So Cosby started working on a routine that he thought had the potential to become a trademark. He got the initial inspiration from the Bible stories that his Granddad Samuel had read to him as a child. He always thought

181

the tale of Noah was particularly memorable, with all the animals and the big boat with the strange name. He remembered the way that his grandfather told the story, acting out all the parts. So Cosby started writing a bit about how Noah might have reacted when God first talked to him:

"Noah!"

"Who is that?"

"It's the Lord, Noah!"

"Right! Where are you?"

"I want you to build an ark!"

"Right! What's an ark? . . ."

Cosby tried the brief bit out at the Gaslight one night, and it got an appreciative laugh. The next day, he wrote more. He thought the Biblical word *cubit* was funny, so he added a line where Noah asked: "What's a cubit?" Next, he added a reference to a hit TV show of the day: "Am I on *Candid Camera*?" Finally, he had an inspiration for ending the routine that came from his childhood in the projects: Noah tells God that if he really wants to punish mankind, he should just let it rain until the sewers back up, and this time it's God who answers: "Right!"

As Cosby slowly constructed the "Noah" routine, he worked on his delivery. He played back the tapes and fine-tuned the voices of God and the disbelieving patriarch. He measured the length of the comic pause before Noah answered ". . . Right!" He experimented with the Gaslight microphone to add a sound effect of Noah sawing wood in his workshop: *"Voomba . . . voomba . . . voomba . . ."*

It took him several weeks, but by the end of the summer Cosby had a full routine that was getting reliable laughs and applause. He was feeling so good about his progress as a professional comedian, in fact, that he briefly flirted with the idea of staying in Greenwich Village and not returning to Philadelphia for his junior year at Temple.

His friend Don Council talked him out of it. Council was visiting a brother who lived in Brooklyn and had come to see Cosby perform at the Gaslight.

"I'm thinking of staying here," Cosby confided after the show.

"You can't do that!" Council said. "We black guys have to show that we can graduate from college!"

So Cosby returned to Philadelphia, but managing his hectic schedule was now more complicated than ever. Roy Silver kept booking stand-up appearances on the weekends, and Cosby had his hands full with his schoolwork and playing football for the Owls. In November, Cosby was offered a Friday night date at Philadelphia's Town Hall that paid $250 — more than he had ever made — to open for Peter, Paul and Mary. But the Owls were scheduled to play an away game on

Saturday against the University of Toledo and the team was taking a bus to Ohio the day before. So Cosby asked Coach Mikras for permission to travel separately.

Mikras consulted with Temple's athletic director, Ernie Casale, who said he would talk to Cosby. When they met, Casale was blunt. He said he didn't see how Cosby could keep juggling his schoolwork, his athletic commitments, and a career as a comedian at the same time.

What about going to Toledo on Saturday? Cosby asked.

Casale said he couldn't permit it, because something might happen if he traveled alone. So Cosby nodded and replied that in that case, he would turn in his uniform and quit the football team.

When Cosby showed up at Town Hall for the engagement, however, he was informed that Peter, Paul and Mary didn't want an opening act. He was handed his paycheck and told he could go home. He was about to do so when the folk trio asked to speak with him. They apologized for the misunderstanding — they had never performed with an opening act, they explained, and didn't want to start now — but they said that Cosby was welcome to come on after them. So he stuck around, and he was delighted to find that most of the audience remained in their seats. And while he didn't exactly receive a standing ovation, he still got lots of laughs at his first big-time venue.

In his mind, he knew that the next step was now inevitable. But he was full of conflicted emotions: guilt toward his mother and coaches, anxiety about whether he was really good enough to make it, anger about all the arguments that he expected to get from people trying to talk him out of it. He couldn't bring himself to discuss the matter with Anna Cosby, so he confided in his friend Don Council.

"You don't need to do that!" Council said again. "You need to graduate!"

Cosby listened glumly until he had had enough of Council's lecture. "Get out of my face!" he snapped.

Finally, Cosby worked up the courage to tell his mother that he was going to drop out of Temple. He didn't want to get an earful from her, either, so he didn't ask her opinion; he simply informed her that he had made up his mind. Her reaction was precisely what he had feared. After everything that he had put her through — dropping out of high school, joining the navy, then finally getting into Temple and making the dean's list in his sophomore year — she couldn't believe that her son was going to leave only a year away from being the first member of the family to graduate from college. Cosby didn't stick around long enough to see it, but his brothers later told him that his mother went to her room and lay in bed for a week.

The next day, he was back at the Gaslight Café. Soon he was a regular at the Bitter End, too, where he was no longer the only comedian in the house but one of several on the bill. Cosby's material wasn't as brilliant as Woody Allen's, and his delivery wasn't as polished as that of other comedians at the club, but he outdid them all in likeability and natural rapport with the audience. Paul Colby, a booker for the Bitter End who would later purchase the club from Fred Weintraub, noticed that the other comedians even looked forward to following Cosby because he left the crowd in such a good mood.

By now, he had nailed "Noah," and it had become the trademark he imagined. After seeing him at the Bitter End, people would tell their friends: "You gotta hear this Bill Cosby guy. He has this bit about the Lord and Noah . . ." So he added more elements to the routine. He wrote a bit about what the neighbors thought of the ark. ("Get that thing out of my driveway!") He created another conversation with the Lord after Noah has spent weeks trying to round up a male and female of every species. ("Have you looked in the bottom of that ark? Who's going to clean that up?") Fed up with the difficult animals, Noah fumes that he's "sick and tired of this mess" and ready to "let all these animals out and burn down this ark and go to Florida!" Then it starts to rain and thunder, and he changes his tune: "It's not a shower, is it? Okay, Lord, me and you!"

Night by night, Cosby constructed another signature routine. It started with a word he thought was funny — *karate* — and the observation that there were a lot of karate schools in Greenwich Village. He added a few lines about what happens when you learn karate. (Your hand becomes "as big as a foot" and you develop "a smell that will kill you.") He acted out the various ways that karate students could subdue their attackers: by scaring them away with karate noises or by walking down a dark street, pretending to "act passive," then chopping an assailant to bits before "walking away, passively." Eventually he had a solid six minutes that always got laughs and added to his growing reputation as a Negro comic who could be funny without ever referring to his skin color.

By the spring of 1963, he was starting to get offers from clubs outside of New York and Philadelphia. The first was the Gate of Horn in Chicago, another folk joint where comedians filled in between musical acts such as Odetta and Theodore Bikel. The club's owner, Alan Ribback, had seen Cosby at the Gaslight Café and offered to pay him $75 a night for an entire week. When he got paid at the end of the engagement, he asked for it all in $5 bills and celebrated by throwing the bills in the air all over his hotel room.

Then in March, Silver secured Cosby a gig at a nightclub called the Shadows in Washington, DC. Cosby was thrilled about the money — $500 for the week! — and about the fact that Shadows was a jazz club, not another folk den. He was also looking forward to staying at the home of his navy buddy Ron Crockett instead of in another seedy hotel. But as he set out toward Washington, neither Cos nor Stymie had an inkling of the fateful encounter that their reunion would make possible.

7
Two Blind Dates

The scene was a familiar one in Catholic schools across America in the 1950s. A group of elementary school children in neatly pressed uniforms sat obediently at their desks, taking instruction from kindly but strict nuns trained in the Jesuit method of teaching. The only difference at St. Cyprian's Elementary-Middle School in Washington, DC, was that all the students were black — and so were all the nuns.

The sisters were members of an order whose origins traced back to the island of Haiti in the late eighteenth century. When a young black plantation worker named Toussaint L'Ouverture led a rebellion against the French colonial rulers of Saint-Domingue, as it was then called, thousands of freed Haitians fled to the United States, and many settled in and around Baltimore, Maryland. One was an idealistic woman named Mary Elizabeth Lange, who started a school in her home for black refugee children. Encouraged by a

French-born Catholic priest, Father Joubert, she took her vows and the name of Sister Mary, and with a group of other Colored nuns from Baltimore founded the Oblate Sisters of Providence, the first Catholic order in the world established by black women.

By the 1950s, the order had grown to as many as three hundred Oblate Sisters who ran orphanages and schools for black children in eighteen states. One was St. Cyprian's in Washington, DC, and it was there that a bright, mocha-skinned girl named Camille Hanks had her first formative educational experiences. From the nuns, Camille learned the rules, rituals, and rigorous academic standards familiar to most Catholic school students. (When her younger brother entered the school in third grade, he had trouble reading, Camille recalled, but "he was ready for Shakespeare by the end of his first week after our Sisters began shaping him up.") Camille also absorbed a gospel of black pride that the Sisters taught with sly disregard for the white male hierarchy of the church, which was still cool to the cause of civil rights for Negroes. "Can do and can be" were the mottos taught to the children of St. Cyprian's.

It was a creed that reinforced the messages that Camille and her three younger siblings had grown up with in her tight-knit, middle-class family in a black enclave of Silver Spring, Maryland. Her father, Guy Hanks, was a slender, light-skinned man whose ancestors were said to have acquired the family name from relatives of Abraham Lincoln's mother, who was born Nancy Hanks. He had graduated from Southern University in Louisiana and gone on to earn a master's degree at Fisk University in Nashville before becoming a research chemist at Walter Reed Army Medical Center. Camille's mother, Catherine, was a graduate of Howard University who ran a nursery. Their home was full of books and artwork celebrating African American history as well as recordings of classical music. For a while, her parents hoped that Camille might become a musician. But by the time she entered college, at the University of Maryland, she had decided to study psychology, and she would often say that it was their mutual interest in the study of human behavior that first attracted her to Bill Cosby.

Cosby originally went to Washington, DC, thinking he would be there for two weeks. Roy Silver had booked him at the Shadows, a small club at the end of a narrow alley in Georgetown. When he showed up the first night, he wasn't surprised to discover that he had to climb down a narrow flight of stairs to enter the club, since it was a joke among his comedian and jazz musicians friends that they always had to "go downstairs" to perform. His job was to fill in between sets for the main attraction, a folk trio called the Big Three that featured a female lead singer with a soulful voice named Cass Elliot. But his first couple of nights went well enough that Silver was able to extend the booking for two more weeks.

So for an entire month Cosby lived at the home of Ron Crockett on Bryant Street, and the navy pilot was able to witness the day-to-day realities of his friend's new life as a professional comedian. One was how hard he was working. After Cosby finished a night at the Shadows, his sports jacket was so soaked in sweat that he had to turn it inside out to make sure it dried by the next night. Another was the hovering presence of Roy Silver. When Crockett went to the Shadows, Silver was always lurking around. Cosby seemed a bit suspicious of his manager, particularly when he kept asking to borrow pocket money. "I thought it was supposed to be the other way around!" he joked. But he also seemed to crave Silver's professional opinion, and after the show he wanted to analyze how his performance had gone, routine by routine.

"So what did you think?" Silver asked Crockett.

"I'm the wrong person to ask," Crockett chuckled. "I start laughing as soon as Cos opens his mouth."

As much as Crockett enjoyed Cosby's act, he found his friend even funnier in person.

He was particularly charming and witty with Crockett's mother, who treated him like he was one of her own sons. If Cos could win over audiences the way he had won over Mrs. Crockett, Ron thought, he'd have it made.

For his part, Cosby was happy to have a trusted friend to spend time with after months in the strange, mostly white world of Greenwich Village. He and Crockett fell into their old routine, listening to jazz albums during the day and going to see whoever was jamming at the Bohemian Caverns after Cosby finished work. When they got hungry, they headed down U Street to their favorite restaurant, Ben's Chili Bowl.

Run by an immigrant from Trinidad and his American-born wife, Ben's was an old silent movie house that had been turned into a bustling diner famous for a sausage in a bun called a "half smoke," so named because it was made of equal parts smoked pork and smoked beef. At any time of the day or night, there was always a hungry crowd of college students, young government staffers, and curious tourists perched on red stools at the long counter or crowded around the vinyl-covered tables, happily munching on half smokes smothered in mustard, onions, and chili. Digging into his meal, Cosby declared that all he needed to be happy in life was "six half smokes and a good woman!"

As fortune would have it, his second wish

was also about to be granted. Crockett had enrolled at the University of Maryland in College Park, north of Washington. Coming out of a class one day, he struck up a conversation with an attractive coed who introduced herself as Camille Hanks. *This is someone Cos should meet!* he thought. He and Cosby were both fans of the exquisite jazz singer Lena Horne, and Camille could have been Horne's younger sister, with the same light skin, wide-set eyes, and elegant cheekbones. She also had an air of quiet intelligence about her that was as striking as her beauty. During their brief conversation, Crockett discovered that they had a friend in common named Eula Lam. So later that day, he asked Eula if she would introduce Camille Hanks to his friend Bill Cosby.

The next day, Cosby drove up to the University of Maryland campus and met Camille at a bowling alley where she was taking a physical education class. When he told Crockett about it later, he made fun of her awkward bowling moves, but Crockett could tell that he was smitten. They went on a double date to see Cosby perform at the Shadows, and afterward he sat with Camille in his car for several hours and told her his life story. They went out several more nights over the next week, often ending up at Ben's Chili Bowl. Crockett suspected that things were getting serious when Cosby invited Camille's parents to see his act. He seemed to be going out of his way to impress Guy and Catherine Hanks, to prove that no matter what they might have heard about show business, he was a hard-working professional who performed at reputable clubs.

What Crockett didn't know was that on the second weekend after they met, Cosby asked Camille to marry him. He did it at the Shadows, in a small vestibule off his dressing room, because he didn't want to be so forward as to invite her into the space where he changed his clothes.

Camille was startled. "We haven't known each other that long," she pointed out.

Cosby reminded her that he would be going back to New York soon and said he wanted her to come with him. But Camille was more practical, as the nuns had taught her to be. She wanted to see whether the whirlwind romance could survive his return to the exciting life of New York and all the enticements that awaited him there.

So without telling Crockett or anyone else, Cosby embarked on a long-distance courtship. Once he returned to New York, he called Camille on the phone almost every night. On the weekends, after working past midnight, he caught a few hours' sleep and then made the four-hour drive to Maryland. Now that he was bringing in real money, he had traded up from the Black Rat, his used Dodge, to an

MG convertible. But it didn't have a wind-shield, so on a cold or rainy day it wasn't an easy trip. He took Camille out to the movies, where they held hands and Cosby sometimes dozed off because he was so exhausted.

"That's when I fell in love with him," she recalled.

Bit by bit, they discovered qualities in each other that weren't immediately apparent. Cosby learned that Camille was not only lovely to look at, with a soft voice that melted his heart, but also perceptive and shrewd beneath her shy exterior. Although she was from "high cotton," as they said in the black world, she never reminded him of his humble origins or made him feel unworthy. He remembered a saying: that a man should look for a woman with "the three Bs" — beauty, brains, and breeding. Camille Hanks had all three.

Yet as fair as she was, Camille was very much a black woman, proud of her heritage and her people. She told Cosby how glad she was that he didn't engage in humor that caricatured Negroes. She was also impressed when he told her that he had asked the Shadows club to place ads for his show in the local black-owned newspaper, the *Washington Afro American.*

Camille saw that there was more to Cosby than the charming jokester who made her laugh and introduced her to the exciting nightclub life. From their first talk in his car outside the nightclub, she was struck by his sincerity. He opened up to her about his long-term dreams. After he had made enough money as a performer, he wanted to resume the plan that he had when he left the navy: to become a gym teacher at a city high school, where he could help young teens avoid the mistakes he had made at their age. In those serious moments, Camille was reminded of the calling to educate and uplift black youth that she had seen in the Oblate Sisters of Providence, and she was moved.

Once the spring semester was over, Camille went to visit relatives in New York so that she could meet Cosby there. When her parents found out that the two lovebirds were still seeing each other, they were furious. They didn't want their daughter dating a man who was seven years older, particularly one who worked in the seedy world of nightclubs. Her father was worried that she might not finish her education, while her mother made it clear that she didn't like the idea of Bill Cosby, period.

Catherine Hanks decided that she needed to do something to keep her daughter away from Cosby. So she sent Camille to stay for the rest of the summer with a grandmother who lived in rural Virginia in a house with no telephone.

When Cosby's family found out what was

happening, they were upset, too. Anna was angry that the Hanks family didn't think that her son was good enough for them, and she suspected that it had as much to do with where he came from as with what he did to earn a living. Camille's parents were behaving like the black "Old Philadelphians" who had snubbed her parents and in-laws when they first arrived from the South. Ron Crockett's mother was every bit as incensed, and she saw it as a case of "high yellow Negroes" looking down on a dark-skinned brother.

Unable to see his beloved, Cosby wrote Camille a long letter and asked Crockett to try to get to her. His friend drove to the Hanks home in Silver Spring and handed the envelope to Camille's mother, who gave him a withering look. When Crockett asked him several weeks later if he had heard back, Cosby didn't let on that he had, and that Camille had written to say that she thought it was best that they end the relationship.

"Maybe it's just not going to work out," Cos told Stymie.

In June 1963, Cosby was encouraged to see the first mention of his name in *Billboard,* the weekly bible of the recording and nightclub industry. He was back at the Bitter End, appearing with Cass Elliot and the Big Three. Noting the lack of racial content in his act, *Billboard* described Cosby as "singular among

Negro stand-ups in that he has apparently not given much thought to sit-ins." But it also made clear that he and the Big Three were secondary attractions next to the featured act of the evening, a popular folk duo called Bud & Travis that played spirited versions of Spanish folk songs. "Both are attractive acts," *Billboard* concluded, "but when Bud & Travis took the stage, they were unfairly dwarfed by comparison."

Cosby and Roy Silver were getting impatient for a breakthrough. They decided that it was time to reach for the ultimate stepping-stone for a rising comic: an appearance on *The Tonight Show.* Silver knew the talent coordinator for the late-night program, a former agent named Sheldon Schultz, so he called his friend "Shelly" up and invited him to come to the Bitter End.

When Schultz saw Cosby's act, he was impressed. It wasn't forty minutes of "killer," he thought, like the best comedians had. But there were at least fifteen minutes of good material, enough to boil down into the six or seven minutes that a comic got on *The Tonight Show.* More than anything, he was taken with Cosby's endearing, nice-guy persona. *This guy is adorable,* he thought. *TV viewers are going to love his ass!*

When Cosby came off stage, Silver brought him over to Schultz's table, where the booker told him how much he liked the act.

"Bill, I'm going to try to make this work," he promised.

As Schultz took a cab back to his East Side apartment, he decided that he would try to get Cosby on the show the following week. A young comic that talented, and a black one at that, wasn't going to remain undiscovered in the Village for long, and he didn't want *The Ed Sullivan Show* to get to him first. He also knew that his boss, Johnny Carson, would have the week off. The comedian Allan Sherman was scheduled to fill in, and Schultz figured it was a good time to try out Cosby without the risk of embarrassing Johnny if the guy wasn't a hit.

At the daily meeting of *Tonight Show* writers the next day, he made his pitch.

"I saw this black kid down at the Bitter End and he was fabulous," Schultz said.

"Yeah, I saw him," one of the writers said. "He's not so good."

Another writer who had been to the Bitter End also spoke up, declaring that Cosby wasn't ready for television.

Schultz kept pressing. "I guarantee you I can get seven minutes from him that will kill," he said, "I'll stake my job on it!"

He was confident because he had a good feeling about Cosby, but also because of the way *The Tonight Show* was run. Schultz had joined the show a year earlier when Jack Paar was still the host. Then the temperamental Paar quit abruptly, citing exhaustion, and NBC replaced him with the imperturbable game show host Johnny Carson. Carson was still under contract to ABC, so other celebrities filled in for six months. At Carson's encouragement, the producers used that period to create a system that all but guaranteed that he would be a success.

Bookers began interviewing guests in advance, so that all of Carson's questions could be scripted and he would know what answers to expect. Comedians were prepped to make sure that their routines would fit in exactly the amount of time they were allotted. The show was filmed "live to tape" at five o'clock in the afternoon before a studio audience, but by the time the cameras rolled, the only thing left to chance were Johnny's witty comebacks. He was a master at coming up with those lines, conducting what looked like unrehearsed conversations while he waited for a chance to get a laugh.

Eventually Schultz convinced the producers to take a chance on Cosby, and he called Silver with the good news. Cosby was booked for the following Tuesday, August 6, and would be paid $350, plus a 10 percent commission for Silver. Schultz said he wanted Cosby to do his "Karate" routine and to come two hours early to prepare.

When Cosby arrived at Schultz's office at

NBC's headquarters at Rockefeller Center, the booker asked him to sit down and talk out his "Karate" lines. But without standing up and moving around, Cosby thought the routine felt flat. Worse, Schultz didn't laugh. He didn't even crack a smile. He kept his head down, scribbling on a notepad. When Cosby was done, Schultz spent an hour giving him detailed directions about how to edit the routine — how to give it "a beginning, a middle, and an end" — and to make sure that it lasted no more than six minutes, allowing a minute for laughter and applause.

Schultz thought the meeting had gone well. He rarely laughed while prepping comics, because he had already seen their stuff and knew that it was good. His job was to make sure the bits worked for television. But his lack of response rattled Cosby. As he left the office, he seemed as nervous as a cat, so Schultz told him and Silver to take a walk around Rockefeller Center before reporting back for the show at five o'clock.

In 1963, *The Tonight Show* aired for an hour and forty-five minutes, starting at 11:15 p.m. on the East Coast. Cosby was scheduled next to last in the order of guests, so he had to wait for almost an hour and a half while three acts went on before him. First was Kaye Stevens, the flame-haired singer famous for running around with Frank Sinatra and his Rat Pack in Las Vegas. Next was Art Buchwald, the witty, cigar-chomping columnist for the *Washington Post.* Then there were a group of contestants from the "Miss International" beauty pageant. As Allan Sherman flirted with the foreign beauty queens, Cosby paced and fidgeted backstage.

Finally his turn came, and he heard Sherman say the words "Bill Cosby." He came out from behind the stage curtain and looked out at the small audience packed into NBC's Studio 6B. He began the "Karate" routine the way he usually did, keeping his hands in his pockets and casually observing how many karate schools there were in New York. He liked to ease into the bit, and normally it wasn't until he described the calloused hand that looked like a foot he got a big laugh. But this time, the audience howled as soon as he uttered the words "karate schools." He was startled for a second, but then he realized what was happening. He wasn't in the Village anymore. These weren't hipsters but tourists and white people from out of town. *Just the sight of a Negro talking about karate strikes them as funny!* he thought.

The next six minutes were a blur, but Cosby could tell it was going well. He felt loose, and the audience was buying the whole bit: his imitations of karate moves, the comic noises he made. A few times the laughter went on so long that he had to slow down and wait for it to end. When he finished, there was a gush of applause, and he looked over to see Sherman waving him to the desk. He was getting "called over" on *The Tonight Show*! It was his first appearance, and he was going to sit and have a conversation with the host the way only a handful of black comics — Dick Gregory, Nipsey Russell, maybe Redd Foxx — ever had before.

Listening backstage, Shelly Schultz had never heard anything like it. His instincts had told him that Cosby would be good, but not this good. He had seen first-time comics get laughs on *The Tonight Show,* but rarely affection. Affection took a while, until comedians had been on several times and the audience felt they knew them. But with Cosby, it happened right away. The words that had come to mind at the Bitter End popped back into Schultz's head, and this time he uttered them out loud.

"They love his ass!" he said.

Before taking his job at *The Tonight Show* Schultz had worked for the MCA agency in Chicago and learned the talent business from the firm's legendary boss, Lew Wasserman. He knew how show business worked, so he could predict what was about to happen next. And he hada feeling that Cosby and his manager weren't ready for it.

"The kid was terrific," Schultz told Roy Silver when the show was over. "But the shit is going to hit the fan, so you better be available!"

When *The Tonight Show* aired later that night, Cosby didn't see it. He was walking around Greenwich Village, eyeing all the people who were still on the street at midnight and silently cursing them for not being at home watching him on television. The next day, he decided to buy a cigar to celebrate. He walked into Dunhill, the most expensive smoke shop he knew, and purchased a green-leaf candela for sixty cents. As Cosby lit up in the store, he thought about his grand-father, who had taught him to smoke cigars. But this one tasted nothing like the stogies that Granddad Samuel kept behind the cellar furnace. As Cosby boarded a bus, still puffing away, the smell of the candela made him think that he had stepped in dog droppings on the street.

As Shelly Schultz had predicted, it wasn't long before Warner Bros. Records, the company that produced Allan Sherman's comedy albums, was on the phone to Roy Silver. Warner Bros. had been among the first labels to recognize the potential of long-playing technology, which was fifteen years old in 1963, to open up a lucrative new market for the recording industry. LPs, which allowed for twenty some minutes of material per side, were far more conducive to the spoken word than the old 78s, and their length and the marketing appeal of their album covers were making stars out of a new generation of comics who acted out skits and told stories rather than rattling off jokes. In 1960, Warner Bros. had released the first comedy album ever to top the *Billboard* chart with *The Button-Down Mind of Bob Newhart,* and Newhart's second effort a year later had been the first comedy album to win a Grammy Award.

Now Warner's latest star was Allan Sherman, whose specialty was making fun of the folk music craze by writing and singing Jewish-themed parodies of traditional ballads. With songs like "Sarah Jackman" (sung to the tune of "Frere Jacques") and "Harvey and Sheila" (to "Hava Nagila"), Sherman's first two albums for the label had briefly topped the *Billboard* charts. That month, August 1963, he was coming out with a new album, *My Son, the Nut,* featuring a spoof on camp songs called "Hello Muddah, Hello Fadduh," that would become an even bigger hit. So as soon as the Warner Bros. executives saw Cosby on *The Tonight Show* — on a night guest-hosted by Allan Sherman, no less — they determined to sign him to a record deal as quickly as possible.

Now that the record industry was knocking, Silver realized that Cosby needed the help of a talent agency. He called Sherman Tankel, a young agent he knew in the New York office of William Morris. Founded in the vaudeville era, Morris had been the first talent agency to become a major force in Hollywood, and now it was signing up scores of clients in the record and television industries.

As soon as Tankel met Cosby and watched a tape of his *Tonight Show* appearance, he agreed to take him on, at the firm's standard 10 percent commission rate. While Cosby was visiting the William Morris offices, he also met another of the firm's rising stars, a black agent named Wally Amos, and they would stay in touch for the next decade until Amos left the agency to found his own business selling chocolate chip cookies under the name of "Famous Amos."

Tankel went to work, and less than three weeks later, Warner Bros. had signed Cosby to a record deal. Reporting the news, *Billboard* confirmed how it had happened. "Cosby made a name for himself with his appearance on the Johnny Carson show a few weeks ago, when Allan Sherman subbed for Carson," the trade sheet reported. The label was in a rush to get the record out for the holiday buying season, so Silver had to work fast. He arranged for recording equipment to tape Cosby at the Bitter End, and he and Cosby started putting together a set that would showcase his best material and could be edited down to fill an LP.

The centerpiece would be the "Noah"

routine, plus the bits about Noah's neighbors and the "Me and You, God!" exchange. "Karate" was also a must. Cosby voted for the "Toin Coss" routine that he had written at Temple, as well as another conceptual piece about a smart cow trying to explain to a dumb cow what hoof-and-mouth disease was. For filler, he threw in two observational riffs on TV commercials that always got laughs: one about razor blade ads that he called "Little Tiny Hairs" and another about hair tonic called "Greasy Kid Stuff."

Capitalizing on the popularity of the "Noah" routine, Warner Bros. entitled the album *Bill Cosby Is a Very Funny Fellow — Right!* The cover featured those words in large pink type wrapped around a headshot of Cosby with his hand to his face, as if he were sharing a secret with the buying public. Underneath were the words "Produced by Allan Sherman," and on the back were liner notes written by the older comic.

"Bill Cosby's 'Noah' (the last three bands on side one) is a masterpiece, even though nobody has heard it yet," Sherman kvelled. He went on for several paragraphs before ending: "I don't know who you are; all I know is that you are one of millions of people who buy records and who made my life so crazy and wonderful during the last year. I want to return the favor. That's why I'm so proud and happy to introduce you to Bill Cosby. It isn't every day that we come into contact with greatness. The day you first listen to this album will be one of those days for you."

Those liner notes, the production credit on the album cover, and the appearance on *The Tonight Show* all added to the impression that Allan Sherman had "discovered" Bill Cosby. In reality, their pairing while Johnny Carson was on vacation had been as much of a blind date as Cosby's first encounter with Camille Hanks. Yet executives at Warner Bros. were shrewd enough to see a marketing opportunity. They could throw a bone to an established star by allowing Sherman to sponsor Cosby. Meanwhile, they could pitch Cosby to the audience that Sherman had already captured, particularly college students and suburban teenagers who loved Sherman's ethnic humor and might be open to embracing a young black comedian.

After *The Tonight Show* appearance, more clubs started calling. Alan Ribback, the owner of the Gate of Horn, offered Cosby a return engagement, this time to open for the popular folk trio the Tarriers. While Cosby was in Chicago, the owners of Mister Kelly's, the top jazz and comedy venue in the city, came to see his act. They were two brothers named George and Oscar Marienthal, and shortly afterward they contacted Silver to propose a week's booking at their club. They offered $750 — the most Cosby had ever made —

plus airfare to and from Chicago.

Cosby was over the moon. Mister Kelly's was a block away from the Gate of Horn, and during his previous visits to Chicago, he had walked past it almost every day and fantasized about performing there. All the big names in the comedy business had headlined at Mister Kelly's: Lenny Bruce, Shelley Berman, Jack E. Leonard, George Kirby, Mort Sahl, Dick Gregory, Jonathan Winters. The biggest were said to make as much as $2,500 a week! The Gaslight Café and the Bitter End were the minor leagues in comparison. Mister Kelly's in Chicago, the Hungry I in San Francisco, the Basin Street East in New York — those were the big leagues.

Mister Kelly's! Cosby thought as he packed his bags for Chicago. *Shorty's on his way now!*

8
"RIGGIE" IN CHICAGO

"Everything okay, Mr. Cosby?" the announcer asked as he stuck his head in the door of the dressing room at Mister Kelly's.

Lost in thought, Cosby looked up at the man's reflection in the vanity mirror and nodded silently.

"Just checking to see how you want to be introduced!" the announcer said.

Cosby frowned. "How about: 'Ladies and Gentleman, one of America's fastest rising young comedians," he said.

"Sounds good!" the announcer said. "We'll call for you in an hour."

Is it seven o'clock already? Cosby thought. He had been sitting in the dressing room for almost four hours. He was so excited about his opening night at Mister Kelly's that he had arrived at three o'clock in the afternoon, five hours before his first set. He had checked into his twelve-dollar room at the Hotel Maryland down the block on Rush Street and come straight over to get a feel for the space.

Mister Kelly's looked like other clubs that he had played, only larger. There was the same small stage, the same low ceiling, the same jumble of tables. But there was seating for two hundred and fifty people, about twice as many as the clubs in Greenwich Village. There were also photos lining the walls of all the great comedians who had performed there. Cosby took his time inspecting every face and every signature and soaking up the fact that he was about to join their company.

George Marienthal, the owner, came out from his office.

"Do you want to rehearse?" Marienthal asked.

"Never rehearse," Cosby said breezily.

So the club owner showed Cosby to his small dressing room.

Cosby started to sift through material in his head. He felt pumped up, the way he did before a big football game or a race at the Penn Relays. His mind went back to the nights he performed at the Gate of Horn, clowning around with the singer Oscar Brown Jr. and filling time between folk groups. Little did those espresso drinkers know that the next time he came back to Chicago, he would have a record contract with Warner Bros. and that he'd be playing the big room down the street!

Mister Kelly's! he thought. *I'm here! And I deserve to be here!*

212

But as the minutes ticked by, another voice entered his mind. *That's some swelled head you have!* it said. *You really think you're that good?*

The first voice talked back. *Yeah, I'm confident, but so what? You have to be confident to go out there and do what I do!*

For the next two hours, the two voices wrestled inside Cosby's brain, and gradually the second one got the upper hand. It wasn't a voice of doubt or fear, exactly, but of a kind of negative ego. It said: *I'm going to show you that you're no Jack E. Leonard!* It kept reminding Cosby that the people in the audience that night weren't going to be the earnest, sandal-wearing coffeehouse people who came to see him in Greenwich Village. These were sophisticated Chicago people, hard liquor–drinking people, blue serge and silk–wearing people, people who paid good money and expected to get big laughs. At Mister Kelly's, they were used to the best in the business, and they weren't going to cut a "likeable newcomer" any slack.

Finally there was another knock on the dressing room door.

"Come down and take your place," a stagehand said.

Cosby went backstage and listened to a jazz trio finish its set. Then he heard the announcer he had met earlier exclaim: "And now, ladies and gentleman, Mister Kelly's is proud to present one of the fastest-rising young comedians in America. Let's give a big hand to Mr. Bill Cosby!"

Cosby walked out on the stage, and his confident ego was nowhere to be found. All that was left was the negative ego. The room was half-full, and only about half of the people who were there clapped. Cosby started to do his routine, but he felt like he was reciting it, without any animation and energy. The crowd wasn't laughing, but they seemed too bored to heckle; instead, they kept talking as he droned on. Finally he walked off the stage to a patter of perfunctory applause. He looked at his wristwatch: His act was supposed to last thirty-five minutes, but he had sped through it in less than eighteen.

As he returned to the dressing room, Cosby felt like he was about to throw up. *That's it,* he thought. *I'm through. I'm going back to Temple.* He would finish his senior year, get his diploma like his mother wanted, and become a gym teacher.

There was knock on the door. It was George Marienthal.

"I'm very, very sorry for what just happened," Cosby apologized. "I don't want to be paid. I'm going back to the hotel. I want to thank you for this opportunity, but I'm not going back out on that stage."

"Good!" Marienthal said. "Because you stank!"

"As soon as I get the money, I'll pay you back for the plane trip, the hotel room, everything," Cosby said.

"You don't have to pay me back," Marienthal said. "Just take your things and leave."

Marienthal began to walk out, but then he turned around. "Do me a favor, though," he said. "When you get back to the hotel, tell them that I want Bill Cosby back here at eleven o'clock. Because Bill Cosby is funny, and he owes me another show."

Marienthal's sarcasm only made Cosby feel worse. He went back to the Hotel Maryland and sat on his bed, too depressed to move. Eventually he worked up the nerve to return to the club. The jazz trio was midway through its second set, and the crowd had grown bigger and louder. He went back to the dressing room and stared at the vase of flowers that the Marienthals had sent earlier in the day, which now seemed to mock rather than welcome him.

"Please set yourself!" a voice called out just before eleven o'clock.

He went backstage, and the announcer introduced him again: "Ladies and gentleman, Bill Cosby!"

Wait a second, Cosby thought. *Where's the rest?*

He walked out onto the stage and turned

to the announcer. "What happened to my introduction?" he asked.

The audience started to laugh, thinking it was part of his routine.

"When I came out for my first set," Cosby said, "you called me one of the fastest-rising comedians in America!"

"Yeah," said the announcer. "Did you see that first show?"

The crowd guffawed.

The laughter snapped Cosby out of his funk. He kept needling the announcer, making up jabs as he went along, and the audience ate it up. From there he was off, riffing on whatever came into his head, prancing around the stage. If he had been performing at a jazz club, the cats on the bandstand would have said that he was playing "out of his mind." Before he knew it, he was walking off to a loud round of applause, after a killer thirty-five-minute set. Except that when he looked at his watch, he saw that it hadn't been thirty-five minutes; it had been almost an hour. The female singer scheduled to go on next gave him a furious look.

The announcer came over to Cosby and congratulated him.

"Man, that was a great show!" he said.

"First time I've heard eighty percent of it!" Cosby said, still not quite sure what had just happened.

When he got back to the dressing room,

George Marienthal was there with more words of praise.

"So where's that guy who was here for the first show?" Marienthal asked.

"He's gone, man," Cosby said. "And I hope he never comes back again!"

The rest of his engagement in Chicago was a big success, and Roy Silver was soon booking Cosby into other prestigious clubs like the Hungry I in San Francisco, where Warner Bros. threw a party to celebrate his debut appearance in December. But the first night at Mister Kelly's had served as a wake-up call. For all of his apparent confidence, Cosby realized that those self-undermining thoughts, that voice of his negative ego, could creep up on him at any moment. He even gave it a name: "Riggie," after the imaginary gnome who came storming out the long jump pit and ambushed him during track practice at Temple. Riggie stalked all stand-up artists, he would tell younger comedians later on, and survival in the business required strategies to keep the little devil at bay.

The scare made Cosby realize that he had to keep coming up with fresh material. "Noah" and "Karate" might have been his ticket to television and a record contract, but they weren't enough to keep Riggie off his back, to prove that he was as good as he thought he was. Luckily, he had a sense of the territory he wanted to stake out next.

While he had been working on his first routines with Roy Silver over the previous year, he had been meeting with another Philadelphia native who had moved to New York and was trying to break into the comedy writing business.

His name was Ed Weinberger, and they had become friends at Central High, where the Jewish son of a butcher was another kid from the streets who liked to make people laugh. When they got together in the Village, they shared memories of their boyhood. Weinberger was astonished at how much Cosby remembered and how amusing his stories were. He encouraged him to write more routines based on his experiences growing up.

"Let Gregory do race and Winters do voices," Weinberger advised. "You do childhood."

Still, Cosby was no longer performing at the Gaslight Café, where he could change his act overnight. He was playing swanky clubs where his routines had to be tight. Audiences expected to see "Noah" and "Karate," and he had to keep giving them what they paid for, at least for a while. So he began to develop a method of introducing new material. He called it "loading the boat." He started by writing down a few lines and working them into his act to see what kind of response they got. If the audience laughed, he added more

218

lines and more voices and more sound effects, night after night, until he had a full-blown routine that was solid enough to replace one of the old ones.

That fall, Cosby began working on a new routine that began with six words: "I started out as a child." Maybe because it sounded so charmingly self-evident, that line always got a laugh. Then he added a bit about how he and his friends first discovered sneakers. He created a character named Rudy who was the first kid in the projects to own a pair, then added sound effects to show how fast the sneakers made Rudy run. Next he added a memory from his days working in the shoe repair shop, of the noise that rubber soles made when they came loose. He toyed with the microphone to combine the sound of flapping shoes and corduroy pants: *"Voom-voom-flap, voom-voom, flap . . ."* Eventually, he had a two-minute bit that was strong enough to become a fixture in his act.

Cosby was fleshing out several other ideas based on his life in the Richard Allen Homes that he had first scribbled down when he was enrolled at Temple University. One was about the trouble he would get into with his mother when he drank straight out of the water jar in the refrigerator. Another was about street football, which in his comic retelling involved a huddle where the quarterback used garbage scraps to diagram plays through a maze of

North Philadelphia streets. ("Cosby, you go down to Third Street, catch the J bus, have them open the doors at Nineteenth Street; I'll fake it to ya.") And then there was a bit that, by the time it was finished, Cosby would consider one of the best three minutes of comedy he had ever written:

"When I was a child, the grown-ups were trying to murder us," it began. "I have proof! We had a perfectly good playground, perfectly good! They tore down some houses, and we called it our playground. It had broken glass and rocks and bricks, but we never lost one kid. Maybe a little gash here or there, but that's all right . . . And then the grown-ups moved in the monkey bars. We lost one hundred twenty-four kids in one day! Kids were falling off the monkey bars like snowflakes! Broken arms, legs, everything! I made it my philosophy from then on to never play on nothing I didn't see no grown-ups playing on. You never saw grown-ups playing on no monkey bars! They would build them, but they wouldn't play on them! And the last thing they put up was the seesaw. An out-and-out attempt to kill us! They even got another kid in on the plot. There are a lot of kids who never had a chance to have a deep voice because of that seesaw!"

Slowly but surely, he was reloading his boat, and it was just in time, since after the hectic autumn in front of him the whole country would be familiar with his old routines and wondering what could be expected next from Bill Cosby.

On the hot, sunny Wednesday of August 28, 1963, more than two hundred thousand black Americans and fifty thousand of their white supporters descended on the nation's capital for a demonstration advertised as the March on Washington for Jobs and Freedom. Singing "We Shall Overcome" and other Negro spirituals, they poured forth from thousands of chartered buses and walked toward the Mall between the Washington Monument and the Lincoln Memorial. After a long afternoon of speeches and songs on the steps below the statue of the president who ended slavery, the nation's leading civil rights leader, Dr. Martin Luther King Jr., rose to speak.

King was almost finished with his prepared remarks when the gospel singer Mahalia Jackson called out from the crowd.

"Tell them about the dream, Martin!" she shouted.

King looked up from his written text and started to improvise. He drew on a metaphor that he had used in his church sermons, giving the image an urgency that it had never had before. "I have a dream," he cried, "that one day this nation will rise up and live out the true meaning of its creed . . . I have a dream that my four little children will one

221

day live in a nation where they will not be judged by the color of their skin but by the content of their character . . . I have a dream today!"

How significant was it that Bill Cosby's emergence as a national celebrity took place in the autumn of 1963, in the months after King's "I Have a Dream" speech? Or that 1963 happened to be the year when a series of brutal setbacks for the civil rights movement rattled America's conscience: the fire hose attacks on black protestors in Alabama; the murder of civil rights organizer Medgar Evers in Mississippi; the bombing of the Sixteenth Street Baptist Church in Birmingham that left four black school girls dead? Cosby never mentioned these events in his performances, and neither did the white TV hosts who competed to book him on their shows. But as the civil rights battle raged on, there was no question that a charming Negro comedian who got laughs without any reference to the "race problem" was a comforting figure to Americans who wanted to show that they were capable of judging a man not by the color of his skin but by the content of his comedy.

Cosby owed his meteoric rise to more prosaic factors as well, like the rivalry between evening TV show hosts. Although Jack Paar had quit *The Tonight Show* the year before, he now had his own program. Rather than see him defect to another network, NBC had created a weekly variety offering called *The Jack Paar Show* on Friday nights. As soon as Johnny Carson took over Paar's old desk, the two hosts were vying for guests and bragging rights to new discoveries. (Paar liked to boast that he had run a film clip of the Beatles months before they appeared on *The Ed Sullivan Show.*) Once Paar saw how well Bill Cosby had done on *The Tonight Show* with Allan Sherman, he set out to book him before Carson invited him back.

Cosby was honored by the invitation, because he respected Paar's intelligence. (He later remembered Paar as someone who "wouldn't want to play anyone cheap.") But he didn't like the long, saccharine introduction the host gave him when he first appeared on the show on Friday, September 27. As Paar built him up as "a promising young comedian who's kept every promise," Cosby stood backstage thinking: *Come on, Jack, we're doing comedy here! It's not your job to make them love Bill Cosby. I'll do that.*

Cosby came out from behind the curtain looking shy and awkward at first, with his hands tucked in the pockets of his tan suit and a goofy smile on his face. "I'd like to talk to you about the movies," he began, "because when I was a kid I used to go to the movies every Saturday. And the guys who scared me

223

the most were the monsters — Frankenstein and the Mummy and Wolf Man. I'd run home and jump in bed with my mother, because she'd protect me. Today, I look at my mother, she's only four foot one, and I think she'd have trouble trying to punch out Frankenstein . . ."

Suddenly Cosby exploded with physical energy. He crouched down and pumped his arms as if he was his mother trying to punch the monster in the knees. He imitated the lumbering walks of Frankenstein and the Mummy ("about the slowest guys in the world") and became the Wolf Man at a barbershop as the full moon appears. ("Aw, that's going to cost you an extra eight dollars!" . . . "Okay, but make it light around the legs, will ya!") Turning to movie Westerns, he hummed the ominous soundtrack music that should warn stagecoach drivers that an attack is coming. The TV camera zoomed in on Cosby as he whinnied like a confused horse, the close-up capturing the rubbery dexterity of his face.

The next Monday, Marty Litke, a diminutive man with a mustache who handled TV bookings for the William Morris agency, called Cosby and told him to come to his office in Midtown. When he got there, Litke had good news: Paar and his producers had liked Cosby so much that they wanted him back on the show again, the very next week.

Cosby was ecstatic, and thought of all the friends and family members who would have another chance to watch him on television. *The people in the projects are going to go crazy!* he thought. *I saw Shorty on TV!*

"They want to pay you four-fifty," Litke said, "but I told them seven-fifty or you're not coming."

"What?" Cosby blurted out. "Get them back on the phone!"

"Bill, you're going to get seven-fifty," Litke said firmly.

Cosby hadn't punched anyone in a long time, since his run-in with the fan heckling the Temple football team, but he had an urge to strike his agent. Was he going to blow this chance for a measly three hundred dollars? *Hell, I'd take six dollars for another shot at the Paar show!* he thought.

The phone in the office rang and Litke picked it up.

"That's more like it," he said.

"You're getting seven-fifty," he told Cosby.

"Okay," Cosby said, "but from now on let me handle the fees."

"From now on," Litke said, "you're not going to be in the room!"

So that's how it works, Cosby thought. *I do my thing, and they do theirs.* From that moment on, he decided to get out of the way and trust his representatives to handle his business affairs — until the day he learned

225

he couldn't.

When Cosby appeared on the Paar show that Friday, he performed the "Noah" routine for the first time on television, just in time to coincide with the arrival of his first comedy album. The first reviews for *Bill Cosby Is a Very Funny Fellow — Right!* were enthusiastic. *Billboard* included it in the magazine's "Pop Special Merit" picks for the week, and took note of the universal appeal of its humor. "Bill Cosby is a very funny fella," the short review concluded. "The comedian has a most engaging delivery and his bits, many of which are nicely timed for deejay play, all strike at those human frailties and peculiarities that make for the most penetrating kind of wit."

By the end of October, Cosby was on a plane to Los Angeles to appear on a weekly variety show on ABC called *Hootenany*. The program was hosted by Jack Linkletter and filmed before an audience of college students at a different campus each week. Cosby had been invited to perform at the University of California at Los Angeles as the lone comedian on a bill of folk acts of every size — from soloists Trini Lopez and Nancy Ames to duos Bud & Travis and the Dalton Boys, to Travelers 3, the Brothers Four, and the ten members of the Goodtime Singers.

Bounding onto a theater-in-the-round stage, Cosby announced that he was going to talk about football, since it was the season.

He drew a few hisses from the audience with a wisecrack about the UCLA Bruins. ("You don't have many roses this year, ha, ha," he said, referring to their 2–8 record, which gave them no chance of qualifying for the Rose Bowl.) But he quickly won back the crowd with his "Coin Toss" routine. He ended with a bit that he called "Locker Room," describing the pep talks that take place before football games. He conjured a coach exhorting his team ("Fight! Kill!") and players repeating after him. Then, just as they are about to storm onto the field, they discover that the locker room door is locked. The routine didn't have any more of a punch line than that, but it left wide smiles on the sea of young white faces.

Several weeks later, Cosby was invited to appear on *The Garry Moore Show*. The show was scheduled to air on Tuesday, November 26, and he was told to show up at the CBS studio on Friday the twenty-second for a dry run. But in the middle of the rehearsal, just after two o'clock in the afternoon, a producer rushed onto the set. President Kennedy had been shot and killed in Dallas, Texas, he reported. Gasps of disbelief and tears of grief filled the room, and the producers sent everyone home.

Cosby was supposed to perform that evening, but all the nightclubs in New York shut down. For the next two days, he sat in front of a TV set, like millions of Americans, stunned and saddened and wondering what the assassination would mean for the country. By Saturday morning, he felt so depressed that he had to turn the channel, and he watched *Tom and Jerry* cartoons for a while before switching back to the news. More than anything, he felt helpless, so he was relieved to get a phone call from his agents telling him that CBS planned to go ahead with *The Garry Moore Show* on Tuesday. At least it would give people something to smile about for an hour, Cosby thought, and give him something to do to take his mind off the tragedy.

At NBC, Johnny Carson was also looking for guests who could strike the right tone after the Kennedy assassination, and he thought of Cosby. He told Shelly Schultz to get him back on *The Tonight Show* as soon as possible, and he was booked for the following Thursday, December 5.

"He better be funny!" Carson said. "We still need funny."

"Don't worry," said Schultz. "You're going to love his ass."

To make certain, Schultz took extra time readying Cosby to do the "Noah" routine before his second appearance on *The Tonight Show*. The preparation paid off: Cosby gave his most polished late-night performance yet.

Afterward Carson invited him over to his desk, and their conversation got more laughs. Cosby was impressed with how smoothly Carson fed him questions so that he could "get his story off" — explaining where he came from and how he got started in show business. Carson was impressed, too, and afterward he was uncharacteristically effusive in discussing Cosby with his staff.

"Twice in a row, that doesn't happen!" Carson said, showing that he had paid closer attention to Cosby's appearance with Allan Sherman than he had let on at the time.

Yet along with viewers of *The Tonight Show, The Jack Paar Show,* and *The Garry Moore Show,* Bill Cosby was playing to another important audience in the fall of 1963. He kept hoping that once he was on television, Camille Hanks might want to see him again and her parents would accept him as a respectable catch.

When Cosby returned to Washington in the fall of 1963, he called the Hanks home, and Camille answered. The first thing that struck him was the softness of her voice. It told him that she still loved him and wanted him, and he later described it as the "most delicious sound I ever heard." He asked her out on another date, and as soon as she saw him again, she knew that she wanted to be his wife.

When Cosby returned to Greenwich Village, he went to the Conrad Shop, a small jewelry store run by an Austrian immigrant next door to the Gaslight Café on MacDougal Street. He bought the most expensive ring he could afford, a $250 diamond number that still had specks of coal in the setting. He drove his MG to Maryland and, before offering Camille the engagement ring, he went to her home to ask her father his permission.

"Come down to the basement," Guy Hanks said. "I want to talk to you."

When the two men were alone, Camille's father said: "Do me a favor. Take this girl off my hands. Because her mother is driving me crazy!"

Catherine Hanks may not have been happy about the wedding, but she didn't stand in the way. The only thing the family asked was that the couple complete the premarriage instruction prescribed by their Catholic faith. So for the next several months, Cosby drove his MG to Maryland every week to join Camille for pre-cana classes with the family parish priest, Father Carl Dianda, who was working out of a converted school basketball court in Olney, Maryland, because his church was under construction.

Camille's parents hosted the wedding and chose a Saturday — January 25, 1964 — for the date. Cosby was playing the Basin Street East, on a bill with the South African singer

Miriam Makeba, so he took a plane to Washington on Saturday morning after performing past midnight on Friday. Ron Crockett, whom Cosby had asked to his best man, picked him up at the airport and drove him straight to the ceremony and reception at the temporary church in Olney.

Two weeks later a brief, lighthearted item about the wedding appeared in *Jet* magazine, the weekly chronicle of the comings-and-goings of black celebrities. Cosby showed the *Jet* reporter the marriage certificate, which had mistakenly listed the newlyweds as both "WH" — for white. "You better keep it, honey; we might go down South!" he quipped to Camille, who sat demurely by his side. Cosby hammed it up for the *Jet* photographer, rifling through Camille's purse and joking about how his nineteen-year-old bride had already taken over his life. Within seventy-two hours after the wedding, he said, "I suddenly lost most of my closet space, and someone moved my toothbrush. A hanging nylon stocking almost killed me, too."

In fact, the wedding had been more awkward than *Jet* reported. Not only did it take place on a converted basketball court; all of the guests were friends and relatives of the Hanks family. Stymie Crockett was the only guest on the groom's side, and he kept wondering why no one from Cosby's family was there, not even Anna Cosby. Was it because she hadn't been invited, or because she was still angry about how Camille's parents had treated her son when he first met Camille?

As soon as the reception was over, Crockett drove the newlyweds back to the airport for a flight to New York. Camille had never flown before, and she grabbed Cosby's arm as the plane hit turbulence and her coffee spilled into the aisle. For their wedding night, he had rented the most expensive room at the Lexington Hotel — the Arthur Godfrey Suite, named after the radio host who played his ukulele in the Hawaiian Room. But whatever sleep the couple got was during the day, because Cosby gave his new bride a crash course introduction to his favorite music and his night owl ways.

Cosby was obsessed with John Coltrane, the Philadelphia saxophonist who was now fronting his own quartet and producing long, probing solos the likes of which no one had heard before, such as his thirteen-minute version of "My Favorite Things." Coltrane's quartet was finishing up a two-week engagement at the Half Note in Greenwich Village, and Cosby wanted to catch as much of them as he could. So as soon as he got offstage at the Basin Street East, he took Camille to hear Coltrane.

Cosby was friendly with the quartet's drummer, Elvin Jones, who came over to greet him on the first night they showed up. Jones had just gotten off the bandstand and was dripping with perspiration. When Cosby introduced Camille, Jones hugged her, and her dress got soaked in sweat.

The next night, Cosby waved to Jones from their table. Camille shot him a look as if to say: *Please, Bill! Not again!*

But that only brought out the devilishness in her new husband. "Hey, Elvin!" he called out, pointing to Camille. "Guess who's here? Come on over and say hello!"

Camille was learning quickly that being Bill Cosby's wife was going to require a game sense of humor and a lot of energy. Because his career was taking off so fast, he decided to take her on a working honeymoon. After the Basin Street East, he was scheduled to travel down the East Coast — first for a gig at Philadelphia's Academy of Music, then a stay at the Diplomat Hotel in Miami. Starting in May, Silver had booked a series of club dates on the West Coast and rented a houseboat in the Sausalito harbor for the couple to use as a romantic retreat. Now that Cosby was making good money, he traded in his beaten-up MG and put down $11,000 to buy a new sports car, a bright red Mercedes two-seater, to drive Camille across the country in style.

During the honeymoon road trip, Cosby sent Ron Crockett postcards documenting their adventures. He was particularly funny about the Mercedes sports car, which he turned into a character in his stories. He detailed its many mechanical breakdowns and its failure to protect against the fickle weather. He also chronicled his struggles with the stick shift, which he would soon take as inspiration for a routine about driving in the streets of San Francisco.

As the newlyweds made their way across America in the temperamental red roadster, Cosby thought about how far he had come in just a matter of months, since his August appearance on *The Tonight Show*. The TV gigs, the record album, the wedding, and now he was going to be performing "upstairs" at venues like the Crescendo in Los Angeles and Harrah's in Lake Tahoe, on a bill with Andy Williams! In a few months, he would make a triumphant return to Mister Kelly's in Chicago, to record his second album for Warner Bros. Entitled *I Started Out as a Child,* it would showcase the routines that he was creating about his boyhood in Philadelphia, from the bits about sneakers and street football and the water bottle to one called "The Giant," his first attempt to turn his painful memories of his father into a source of comedy.

But if Cosby thought that his rapid success would silence the voice of Riggie, he was wrong. Soon his surface coolness and bravado would be tested again, by an unexpected adventure that would bring two new abolitionists into his life.

9
"Sheldon's Folly"

It was a Thursday night, and Rob Reiner, Carl Reiner's sixteen-year-old son, had school the next day. But his parents were out for the evening, at a black-tie Hollywood affair, so Rob decided to stay up to watch *The Tonight Show.* He wanted to see Selma Diamond, his dad's former colleague on *Your Show of Shows* and the model for the female comedy writer Sally Rogers on his dad's new program, *The Dick Van Dyke Show.* The journalist Jimmy Breslin was also a guest, along with Perry Botkin, the guitarist on *The Beverly Hillbillies,* and a young black comedian named Bill Cosby.

When Carl Reiner and his wife Estelle got home around one o'clock in the morning, Rob was still downstairs in his pajamas, waiting to greet them.

"What are you doing awake?" his father asked. "You have school tomorrow."

"I just watched the greatest comedian I've ever seen!" Rob said excitedly. "His name is

Bill Cosby. Let me show you the routine he did!"

Rob started to act out "Noah," which had made such a strong impression on him that he already knew it by heart. As he imitated Cosby doing the voice of God and the befuddled carpenter, his father chortled.

"You're right!" he said. "That's very funny. Now go to bed!"

To himself, Carl Reiner thought: *Maybe this could be the guy that Sheldon is looking for.*

By the end of 1963, when Cosby appeared on *The Tonight Show* with Johnny Carson, Carl Reiner was in his third year as producer and head writer on *The Dick Van Dyke Show.* He had created the series about a TV comedy writing team and appeared as Alan Brady, the boss of Van Dyke's character, Rob Petrie. The executive producer of the show was Sheldon Leonard, the television impresario who with his business partner, the comedian Danny Thomas, had created *The Danny Thomas Show, The Real McCoys, My Favorite Martian,* and *The Andy Griffith Show.*

Reiner made inquiries and learned that William Morris, the same agency that represented both him and Leonard, handled Cosby. The firm's top TV agent on the West Coast, Norman Brokaw, told Reiner that his New York colleagues were very high on the young comedian and that he would be coming to the West Coast that summer. So when Cosby arrived in California at the end of his honeymoon road trip with Camille, Reiner made arrangements to see his act at the Crescendo Club and to greet him backstage.

Cosby was thrilled to meet Carl Reiner. Here was the man who had been Mel Brooks's straight man on the *2000 Year Old Man,* his favorite comedy album, and had worked alongside the great Sid Caesar on *Your Show of Shows,* his favorite TV program. He was even more excited when Reiner told him how much he liked his act and invited him to the set of the Van Dyke show the next day.

"I loved your show, man," Reiner said. "My producer, Sheldon Leonard, wants to see you. He couldn't be here tonight, but he loves your work."

The following day, the cast of *The Dick Van Dyke Show* was doing a read-through of their latest episode. Arriving on the set, Cosby couldn't believe that he was meeting the stars he had seen on TV: Van Dyke, Mary Tyler Moore, Morey Amsterdam, Rose Marie. But he played it cool. When Reiner told him how much his son had loved "Noah," Cosby acted out the routine. He told stories about growing up in Philadelphia and his cross-country trip with Camille, and his hosts loved them. Cosby kept hamming it up, thinking that he might land a guest appearance on the show, and Van Dyke recalled that the cast barely got any work done because they were laughing so hard.

Finally, Reiner introduced Cosby to Sheldon Leonard. He was a tall man with a large round face who Cosby recognized from his early career as a Hollywood character actor. Leonard had played the bartender in *It's a Wonderful Life* and Harry the Horse in *Guys and Dolls* and other minor roles that he had seen. Cosby was amused to see that he actually talked like a mobster, out of the side of his mouth, and that he was smoking a long, brown-leaf panatela cigar like the ones that Cosby had come to favor since his encounter with the smelly green-leaf candela in Greenwich Village.

After watching Cosby clown around, Leonard invited him to his office and shut the door. Instead of offering him a cameo role on *The Dick Van Dyke* show, he started talking in long, grandiose sentences about another project he was developing. It was a spy show that would have the Cold War intrigue of *Dr. No,* the James Bond film that had made a sensation when it came to America the previous summer. He planned to shoot it in exotic locations around the world, starting with Hong Kong.

The stars of the show would be two secret

239

agents who traveled the world disguised as international tennis players, Leonard explained. He paused for theatrical effect. "I intend for one of those agents to be black!" he said. "And I believe that you have the natural personality to play that role!"

At first, Cosby could only think about Hong Kong. Had he heard right? Was this white producer talking about taking him to *Hong Kong*? It took a second for the rest to sink in: that Leonard was proposing casting him in a prime-time TV drama. In his imagination, Cosby had pictured that if he succeeded as a stand-up comic, he might get cast in a movie one day. But he had never thought about a TV drama.

"Can you act?" Leonard asked.

"Are you high?" Cosby joked. "Didn't you see me when I did *Othello* in Central Park?"

Leonard smiled. "It doesn't matter," he said. "If you exhibit the same natural ability on television that I have seen you display as a comedian, you will be a success."

Cosby nodded, but he was still stuck on Hong Kong. *Hong Kong, man,* he thought. *I'm gonna see the original Chinese people, the ones I've read about!*

Leonard told Cosby that he wasn't ready to make an offer yet. He was still negotiating a deal with NBC and working to sign the white lead actor. So Cosby let Leonard know where he could be found for the next two months

— performing at Harrah's in Lake Tahoe and the Hungry I in San Francisco.

"Come see me do my thing sometime," he said.

"I shall be in touch!" Leonard promised.

Afterward, Cosby called Roy Silver to tell him what had happened.

"Don't let this cat off the hook," he told his manager, "because if he's blowing smoke, we're not going to let him get out of it."

In Sheldon Leonard's mind, he had spent a lifetime preparing for the bold experiment he described to Cosby. Born in the East Bronx, Leonard had joined a youth gang by the time he was ten. When his family moved to Belleville, New Jersey, he was the only Jewish kid in his school and endured taunts like, "Get away from me, you kike!" and "You smell like herring!" He learned to strike back with his fists, but also to escape into a fantasy world of *Tarzan* books and Horatio Alger stories.

Leonard's parents wanted him to be a doctor or an accountant, but he fell in love with acting in high school and as a college student at Syracuse University. After graduating, he sought his fortune on Broadway. When theater work dried up during the Depression, he headed west to work in motion pictures. Over the next decade, he appeared in more than sixty pictures playing parts that called for his imposing size and growling voice, mostly heavies with names like Blackie and Lefty and Pretty Willie.

To make extra money, Leonard began acting and writing for radio. A friend asked to adapt one of his stories for the new medium of television, but Leonard didn't like the results. So his friend suggested that Leonard try directing.

That led Leonard to William Morris, the talent agency that was expanding from movies to television and starting to "package" acting, directing, and producing clients to make new TV shows. An up-and-coming agent named Norman Brokaw got Leonard a job directing *Make Room for Daddy,* starring Danny Thomas. Soon the Jew born Sholem Labe Bershad and the Lebanese comedian born Amos Muzyad Yakhoob Kairouz formed a production company that created one hit comedy show after another.

By the early 1960s, Leonard was one of the best-known producers in television. On the set, he was an imposing taskmaster. He chomped on his cigar and barked orders out of the side of his mouth like the heavies he played in films. But his actors loved the way he fought with network executives and spared no expense on their comfort. Leonard also had a way of getting the best out of talented ensembles. A family man who had married his wife, Frankie, when he was twenty-four, he cherished playing the role of *paterfamilias*

242

on the "happy sets" he created. He managed the egos of stars such as Andy Griffith and Dick Van Dyke and helped the actors around them to shine. He was a patient mentor to child actors like Ron Howard, who played Griffith's son Opie. Leonard even had a way with animals, as he demonstrated when he directed several episodes of *Lassie.*

Yet after a decade working in Hollywood sound studios, he was getting restless. He was tired of three-room sets with their limited camera options: the wide shot, followed by a close-up, followed by another close-up. Leonard called it "the talking heads world of Jack Webb," after the star of fifties police drama *Dragnet.* Television screens, once thirteen inches in diagonal, were getting larger. The new twenty-one-inch models cried out for more interesting scenery and camera angles. So did color televisions, which were now on sale across America.

Network rivalry had also created an opportunity for the star producer. Envious of what he had done for CBS, where his hit comedies aired, NBC executives were pursuing him to develop a show. NBC was in the process of converting from black-and-white to all-color programming, the first network to do so. So Leonard pitched them on his ambitious idea of a spy series filmed on location around the world, arguing that it would be a perfect fit for NBC's "peacock" brand.

Leonard had an even more daring idea for his new show. For a decade, he had been struck by the heated response he got whenever a Negro appeared on one of his comedies. When Danny Thomas put his arm around a black character in one episode, he got hate mail: "If I wanted to see a white man make love to a gorilla, I would go to a freak show!" read one letter. After another episode, Thomas received dozens of irate postcards filled with racist language from across the South. As someone familiar with bigotry from his painful boyhood, Leonard saw TV's power to incite racism, but he was also thinking about how the medium could be used to combat it.

In the fall of 1963, he introduced race to *The Dick Van Dyke Show*. He championed a script called "That's My Boy??" and fought with NBC's censors to air it. The episode was a flashback in which Van Dyke's character, Rob Petrie, becomes convinced that his wife Laura has brought the wrong baby home from the hospital. After the Petries receive flowers and candy meant for a family named Peters, Rob suspects they were given the Peters boy by mistake. But when the Peters visit the Petrie house, Rob discovers that they're black. Van Dyke acts the flustered fool while Mr. Peters, played by Greg Morris, is a model of intelligent reserve.

Leonard received hundreds of angry letters

about "That's My Boy??" But he also got something he had never seen before: more than a thousand positive letters saying things like "how refreshing it was to see blacks played with dignity on TV."

After the success of the James Bond film, Leonard wasn't the only showman in Hollywood thinking about how to cash in on the espionage craze. Another producer named Norman Felton was shooting a pilot for NBC that he planned to call *Solo,* about the exploits of a spy named Napoleon Solo. Felton had offered the starring role to a handsome young TV actor named Robert Culp, who played a Texas Ranger in a show called *Trackdown.* But Culp found the script for Felton's pilot cheesy and passed on the project that would become *The Man from U.N.C.L.E.*

Instead Culp decided to come up with his own pilot. Under the tutelage of a *Trackdown* writer named Sam Peckinpah, he had begun to try his hand at penning scripts for television. He turned out a seventy-six-page story called "Danny Doyle," about a professional athlete who moonlights as a secret agent. A friend suggested that Culp send it to Carl Reiner, but when Reiner saw that it was a spy script, he passed it along to Sheldon Leonard.

"I like your idea, kid, but I like mine better!" Leonard said when he invited Culp to his office.

"Okay, I'll bite," Culp said. "What's yours?"

"Two American secret agents, working out of the Pentagon, go around the world on the professional tennis circuit, posing as a pro and his trainer," Leonard said. "And one of them is black."

Culp would later say that he felt as if a depth charge had gone off in his head. Raised in Berkeley, California, and trained as an actor in Off-Broadway New York, he instantly appreciated how artistically brave and socially powerful Leonard's idea could be. A Negro spy, working for the US government — that would truly be something new!

"You're right," Culp agreed. "Your idea *is* better!"

By now Leonard had decided that Culp was the man to play the white secret agent. He had the rugged good looks and bedroom eyes that Leonard was looking for, and his enthusiasm about working with a black costar clinched the deal. Leonard had also lined up one of the hottest writing teams in Hollywood, Morton Fine and David Friedkin, who had worked together in radio and television and had just written their first movie script, a powerful story about a Holocaust survivor called *The Pawnbroker.*

As the pieces of his puzzle came together, Leonard was closing in on a unique financial arrangement with NBC. The network was so eager to secure Leonard's services — and to have another James Bond knockoff — that it agreed to a "pay or play" deal that was unheard of in the history of television.

According to the contract Leonard signed in late June, he would be paid for eighteen episodes whether they aired or not. Because he couldn't afford to finance months of foreign shooting out his own pocket, NBC also agreed to lend him $8 million at no interest. The network exacted a steep price, however. It demanded an option for five full seasons as well as ownership of foreign rights and a hefty cut of future syndication deals. Inside NBC, executives referred to the venture as "Sheldon's Folly"–although some skeptics wondered if NBC might end up the fool.

By midsummer, Leonard was ready to make his final pitch. He flew to Manhattan to visit NBC headquarters in Rockefeller Center. In his luggage, he carried a printed analysis of the mail about the "That's My Boy??" episode of *The Dick Van Dyke Show.* Of some 1,960 letters, 1,782 praised the story and Greg Morris's character. Only 201 letters were negative, and the rest were neutral. If it were needed, Leonard planned to cite the analysis as proof that America was ready for a black hero.

The president of NBC was Robert Kitner, a Swarthmore College graduate who favored bow ties and a crew cut. He had worked as a reporter before becoming a television executive and was known for his keen journalistic instincts. Legend had it that Kitner had personally suggested that the network broadcast the transfer of JFK's assassin, Lee Harvey Oswald, to a county jail in Dallas on the Sunday after the murder, making NBC the only network on the scene when nightclub owner Jack Ruby shot Oswald.

"So how is the casting coming along?" Kitner asked.

"You know about Bob Culp," Leonard said. "You okayed him."

"Yes, he'll be fine," Kitner said. "How about the other part?"

"I haven't settled on anyone yet," Leonard said, "but I've got my eye on someone."

"Do I know him?" Kitner asked.

"No," Leonard said. "He hasn't been around much, but I've seen his work, and he's just what I want."

"Then why don't you make a deal with him?" Kitner said.

"Because he's black," Leonard said.

"What difference does that make?" Kitner asked.

"As of the moment, Mr. Kitner," Leonard said, "it makes no difference whatsoever."

Leonard kept a poker face, but inside he felt giddy. Decades later, he would say that it was as if "somewhere bells rang and trumpets roared." He didn't know quite how yet, but

248

he sensed that "the whole history of television had changed in that moment."

When Sheldon Leonard finally got back to Cosby, he was performing at the Hungry I in San Francisco. Cosby suggested that the producer and his two writers, Mort Fine and David Friedkin, fly up from LA to see his act. Doing his best to impress them, he invited the three men to spend the afternoon with him and Camille on the houseboat in Sausalito where they were staying.

Although Leonard was thirty years his senior, Cosby quickly sensed a kindred spirit. Remembering that the producer smoked panatelas, he offered him one and demonstrated how he liked to prepare cigars: by punching a hole in the tip rather than snipping it off. He was impressed by Leonard's eloquence and liked his dry sense of humor. And while his gruff side may have intimidated others, Cosby recognized it as the kind of tough exterior that a sensitive kid from a rough neighborhood has to develop.

Cosby also saw that Leonard was a man he could tease. One of the first things that he noticed about the producer was his hair. It was almost as kinky as black hair, and he wore it short and slicked back with pomade, like a brother! So Cosby started ribbing him about it, and Leonard grinned from ear to ear. Later, when Cosby made hair jokes in front of his wife and family, they couldn't believe it, because they knew how sensitive he was about the topic. But Cosby got away with it because he made Leonard laugh.

Leonard saw much of himself, too, in Cosby's streetwise manner and stories about growing up playing stickball in the projects. And he was even more impressed once he saw the performance at the Hungry I. As he watched Cosby command the club's small stage with its red brick backdrop, he checked off all the qualities he was looking for: good looks, physical agility, a quick wit, and an air of intelligence.

David Friedkin had a son named Gregory who was a student at the University of California at Berkeley, and the producers invited him along with several fraternity brothers to get a sense of how younger viewers might respond to Cosby.

"What do you think?" Friedkin asked after the performance.

"Cast that guy now!" Gregory said. "He's a winner. You'd be crazy not to cast this guy!"

After the show, Leonard asked to meet with Cosby, and Cosby insisted on bringing along Camille. They were both intrigued, but they wanted to hear more about the character Cosby would play. Bluffing more than a bit, Cosby said he wasn't fazed by acting in a dramatic role, but that he wanted to make sure that his character wouldn't be an eye-rolling black caricature like Stepin Fetchit.

"Will he carry a gun?" he asked.

"Naturally!" Leonard said.

"And when he's attacked, he'll be able to fire back?" Cosby said.

"He shall!" Leonard said.

"So he's not going to run and hide in the bushes?" Cosby said.

"Never!" Leonard said. "He will be a full-fledged secret agent on assignment for the United States government, with a license to kill!"

Satisfied by Leonard's answers, and with Camille's blessing, Cosby told Roy Silver to make a deal. The manager met with Leonard and didn't wait for an offer before throwing out the number he had in mind.

"Twelve hundred and fifty dollars a show!" Silver said.

"That's fine," Leonard responded, not letting on what he was thinking: that $1,250 an episode was a steal for someone of Cosby's talent, even if he had no experience as a TV actor.

Leonard told Silver that his writers were still working on a first script, and that he would be back in touch when it was ready. So for the rest of the summer, Cosby was left to ponder what he had gotten himself into.

He had a lot to gain from the TV series — but also a lot to lose at a time when his career as a comedian was just taking off. He was getting bookings across the country now, and at the end of May, he had even performed for the president of the United States. A producer named Richard Adler had invited Cosby to be part of "A Salute to Lyndon B. Johnson" at Madison Square Garden. Adler had assembled an all-star cast of "old guard" superstars like Gregory Peck, Gina Lollobrigida, and Mitzi Gaynor and "new guard" singers and comedians including Joan Baez, Allan Sherman, and Woody Allen. Cosby had found it an odd experience, watching people wait to laugh until the president laughed first. But Johnson did, and afterward he praised it grandly as "the finest assembly of talent gathered together anywhere, any time."

While Cosby was in New York for the gala, he was put up at the Hilton Hotel in the largest suite he had ever seen — two adjoining rooms costing fifty dollars apiece per night. Roy Silver told him that he could "order anything you want" from room service, so Cosby invited two friends from Greenwich Village, the white folksinger Shel Silverstein and a black Off-Broadway actor named Lee Weaver, over for lunch.

"We're in tall cotton now!" Weaver joked.

"I'll have the twenty-eight-dollar steak!" Silverstein told the waiter, who scanned the singer's beard and jeans with a look of disdain.

"That's a filet mignon for two," the waiter

said haughtily.

"That's okay, I'll have it for one," Silverstein said.

"Cosby, we're going to jail!" Weaver laughed.

Along with protecting his stand-up career, Cosby had to think about his reputation among his own people. In late April, he had been profiled for the first time in *Ebony* magazine. " 'Raceless' Bill Cosby" had put a positive spin on his decision to do comedy that made no reference to racial tensions, but it had noted that "by doing so he has left himself open to skeptics who would like to brand him as a deserter to the cause."

A month later, Cosby was welcomed into the ranks of Negro civil rights and show business aristocracy in a national closed-circuit TV concert to raise money for the NAACP. Called the "Freedom Spectacular," it honored Supreme Court justice Thurgood Marshall and featured the country's leading black entertainers — Sidney Poitier, Sammy Davis Jr., Duke Ellington, Nat "King" Cole, and Lena Horne — along with white supporters such as Ed Sullivan, Steve Allen, Tony Bennett, Elizabeth Taylor, and Richard Burton. Cosby's routine was seen by tens of thousands of black people who filled theaters and auditoriums in forty-five different cities, from Madison Square Garden in New York and the Masonic Temple in Jackson, Mississippi, to venues in Los Angeles, Kansas City, Philadelphia, Albuquerque, Baltimore, and Chattanooga, Tennessee.

Now that he was becoming famous, Cosby was fielding pointed questions about his views on race. In late July, he traveled to Chicago to appear at Mister Kelly's and to record his second comedy album, *I Started Out as a Child.* He agreed to an interview for *Jet, Ebony*'s sister publication, with Chester Higgins, a longtime reporter for black newspapers such as the *Pittsburgh Courier* and the *Louisville Defender.* They met at the London House, an elegant restaurant and jazz club, and at first Cosby appeared to be in a relaxed mood, leaning back in his chair and stretching out his legs. But he got more emotional as Higgins asked why he never mentioned the fact that he was black in his act.

"Well, I'm not trying to hide the fact I'm Negro," Cosby said. "I come out on the stage and man, there I am. You know I'm Negro. But everyone can sit back and enjoy me. They know after they've seen me once I'm not going to embarrass anybody. I don't tell ethnic jokes. I don't lampoon the Negro, the white man, the Jew. Nobody. I just tell jokes."

Higgins pressed. What about Negroes? Might they get the impression that Cosby was denying his heritage or ignoring hard racial realities? And what about white folks? Didn't they need to hear humor that exposed stereotypes and bigotry?

"Whoa!" Cosby blurted out. "I don't think that at all. Listen, I'm not trying to be a Negro comedian, nor trying to be something or somebody else. My stick is humor. So I try to be funny. I am trying to make people laugh. I think with all the racial tension on the outside, people appreciate coming in to see me. Some people may be disappointed because I don't tell racial tension jokes. But the majority, I believe, enjoy me because I don't."

Put on the spot, Cosby hinted at his political beliefs for the first time. "Of course, I have views on Goldwater," he said. "I'm highly aware of the Negro struggle for freedom. Ask me my private views, and I won't hesitate to voice them. But I feel it's time for the Negro to just be a comedian. And I aim to be one who tells funny stories that everyone can identify with."

So when Cosby arrived in Los Angeles at the end of the summer for his first reading with Robert Culp, he was in a testy mood. By now "Sheldon's Folly" had a name: *I Spy.* Although Leonard had sold the series without a pilot, he planned to film a "test script" in Hong Kong to get a feel for the setting and to have something to show the network. Fine and Friedkin had written a story called "Affair in T'Sien Cha" introducing the two main characters. The white spy, Kelly Robinson,

255

was undercover as traveling tennis pro. The black spy, Alexander Scott, nicknamed Scotty, was a multilingual Rhodes scholar who masqueraded as Robinson's trainer.

It was a hot August day, and Sheldon Leonard's office on the studio lot felt like a sauna. Cosby was dripping sweat and as self-conscious as he had ever been. He was used to telling funny stories in front of live audiences, but he hadn't performed from a written script since he was in grade school. He kept flubbing his lines, and each time he stumbled, he got angrier at himself. Riggie, his negative ego, was back with a vengeance, and it kept telling him that he didn't belong there.

Cosby never looked up from his script, but he could sense the eyes of the white TV professionals staring, judging. Culp tried to meet his gaze, but Cosby refused. He knew he wasn't in Culp's league as an actor, and he was furious that he had allowed himself to be put in such a humiliating position. The reading went on for three hours, and it felt like an eternity.

Culp watched the painful spectacle with a mixture of compassion and fascination. Although he looked like a Hollywood pretty boy, he considered himself a serious actor. He had studied drama at the University of Washington and method acting with Herbert Berghof and Uta Hagen in New York City.

He had first come to Hollywood for a bit part in *The Zane Grey Theater* and had decided to stay only once he and his second wife started having children and he realized that acting in television paid the bills better than performing on stage.

Despite Cosby's stumbles, Culp was impressed with what he saw. When he failed to deliver a line as written, he said something funnier and more natural. He seemed to have an instinctive ability to turn a line inside out and make it better. Culp had worked with hundreds of actors and saw in Cosby gifts that he didn't think could be taught: a lightning-fast mind and a spontaneous wit. He thought of a line that he had heard attributed to Sir Arthur Conan Doyle, the creator of Sherlock Holmes: "Mediocrity knows nothing higher than itself, but talent instantly recognizes genius." Culp thought of himself as possessing talent, but what he sensed in Cosby was genius.

Culp detected something else that drew him to Cosby. There were a few clumsy lines in the script that played up the fact that Scotty was black. "No, it doesn't rub off, and it's not war paint," Scotty was supposed to say when a Chinese boy touched his face. Every time Cosby came to one of those passages, he would mumble or reword the lines. *Man, he's doing that on purpose!* Culp thought. *He doesn't like the racial material, and he'll be damned if he's going to sell it.*

Cosby displayed "a very quiet, dry, humorous, and gentle contempt for the references to race that were in the script," Culp recalled. "He would get to a line that contained such a reference, and he would ad-lib it in another form, which indicated that he was hostile toward the line itself. This rang a bell with me, because I was hostile toward it, too."

When the reading was over, everyone sat in awkward silence. Finally, Fine and Friedkin went back to the office they shared on the lot, and Culp followed them.

"Do you know what we saw there?" he asked the writers.

"Yeah, a bad actor," Fine replied.

Culp said he saw just the opposite. He saw a natural. Anyone that quick — and capable of that kind of anger — could become a good actor. The problem was that the Scotty role, as written, didn't fit Cosby. It had been conceived as too much of a black servant. Kelly had most of the lines. That wasn't going to work, Culp argued. The humor would succeed only if he and Cosby were equals. "What you saw today doesn't matter a damn," he said as he walked out of the writers' office. "This is going to work. But these guys can't be Matt Dillon and Chester from *Gunsmoke.* It has to be fifty-fifty."

10
"TELEVISION'S JACKIE ROBINSON"

Cosby peered through the cracks in the boarded-up windows of Hong Kong's Peninsula Hotel. On the streets below, an October typhoon was blowing pedestrians around like cheap umbrellas. The tide was so high in Victoria Harbor that all the boats had been ordered off the water. On their second day in Hong Kong, Sheldon Leonard's *I Spy* crew was trapped indoors, and it looked like they would be there all week.

Leonard didn't like to be alone, so he kept inviting Cosby and Culp to his room — the lavish Marco Polo suite on the top floor of the hotel, where world leaders from Richard Nixon to the Maharajah of Jaipur stayed. They ordered scrambled eggs with caviar for breakfast and played cards and smoked cigars as Leonard told long-winded stories, and Cosby and Culp got to know one another better.

When the weather finally cleared, Leonard invited his two actors to dinner again, but

Cosby had another idea.

"Bob, I'm tired of eating with Sheldon," Cosby said. "We have to go to dinner by ourselves."

"Amen!" Culp said.

They went out onto the soggy streets, now teeming with thousands of people, and within a couple of blocks they saw more than fifty Chinese restaurants. Which to choose? Finally, they selected one at random and were greeted by a waiter who spoke broken English. Eager to sample the local delicacies, they chose a dish from every column on the menu.

"Order too much!" the waiter said.

"We're starved!" Cosby said. "We've been cooped up for days!"

One after another the dishes arrived: soup, dumplings, fried rolls, spare ribs, fish, chicken, beef . . . It was more food than Cosby had ever seen in his life. When the waiter brought out the glazed duck, the Americans' eyes glazed over. They were too full to take another bite.

"Can you find some poor people to give that to?" Cosby asked.

"You pay for duck?" the waiter asked.

"Yes, we'll pay for it," Cosby laughed. "We just can't eat it!"

Cosby and Culp were in Hong Kong for two weeks with a small traveling crew to film the outdoor scenes for the test episode of *I*

Spy. For Sheldon Leonard, it was a test of his complex production scheme. To shoot around the world, he had required approval from the union that represented television crews, the International Alliance of Theatrical Stage Employees. To get the IA on board, he offered a "one-third, two-third" guarantee. One third of the scenes for each *I Spy* episode would be shot in the field. Two-thirds would be shot back in Hollywood, using union crews, at a sound stage lot owned by Desilu Productions, the company owned by Lucille Ball and Desi Arnaz. Leonard planned to shoot footage for nine episodes in each new foreign city, which meant that nine scripts had to be written before each trip began.

Leonard had scouted some stunning locales in Hong Kong: the Tiger Balm Gardens, Aberdeen Harbour, an ancient village outside the city, and the busy downtown streets where Kelly and Scotty were to take a rickshaw ride. Yet as soon as shooting resumed, his well-laid plans started to go awry. Rather than lug tons of expensive gear on the trip, he had arranged to rent equipment from Run Run Shaw, the king of Asian filmmakers. But Run Run's cameras and lights were mostly run down, and they kept breaking.

Cosby was stiff and tentative in front of the cameras. He kept forgetting what he was supposed to say, and he had trouble responding naturally to the action around him. When

Culp was talking, Cosby looked as if he were getting ready to deliver his next line. He tried to take his cues from the experienced actor, asking what he should do and eavesdropping when the star and the director talked about how a scene should be played. But he felt awkward. "It was really weird, man," Cosby recalled. "It took weeks before I felt able to do my thing without feeling self-conscious."

Culp blamed the script. He believed that good writing makes for good acting, and he didn't think much of the dialogue. He thought that the best moments came when he and Cosby improvised.

In one scene, as they were racing up a flight of stairs in Tiger Balm Gardens, Culp pulled Cosby out of the way of a falling Chinese sculpture.

"Next time I'll take my chance with the statue!" Cosby quipped.

In another scene in which they are questioned by the local authorities, Cosby ad-libbed a description of the two spies as "the Green Hornet and his faithful valet Kato."

In a scene shot on the railroad tracks on the outskirts of Hong Kong, they riffed a run of teasing banter.

"You're not listening to me," Culp complained.

"No, I'm not," Cosby said.

"All right, you're fired!" Culp shot back.

By the time the crew flew back to Los

Angeles, Cosby didn't think that he had made much progress as an actor, but he was pleased to be developing a personal relationship with Culp and Leonard. When they were holed up at the Peninsula, they had gone window-shopping in the hotel's arcade. Leonard had bought a vicuna coat, but then had started to complain about all the tax that he would have to pay. So on the return, he tried to avoid customs duty by wearing the coat.

When they landed in Los Angeles, the temperature was in the nineties, and sweat was cascading down Leonard's wide brow as he waited in the customs line.

"Hey, Shel, you look warm!" Cosby called out from behind him. "Why don't you take off your coat?"

Leonard glared at Cosby as if he wanted to strangle him.

"Shel, you're sweating!" Cosby cried as Leonard approached the customs officer. "Take off your coat!"

Realizing that the jig was up, Leonard admitted that he had bought the coat in Hong Kong and offered to pay duty. But once they were past customs, he laughed and thanked Cosby for helping him avoid a smuggling charge.

Now that they were home, both Cosby and Culp felt even more certain that the test episode had been a flop. Culp focused his frustration on Fine and Friedkin. If their first script was any indication, he thought, the project was doomed. And he knew who would get blamed: Bill Cosby. So he decided to find out if what he had heard was true. He arranged to bump into Leonard and ask him if NBC had in fact agreed to a "pay or play" deal for eighteen episodes.

NBC had, Leonard replied.

Did Leonard intend to shoot all the episodes, no matter what?

"I'm going to make all eighteen, or die in the attempt," Leonard said.

"Thanks, boss," Culp said. "I just needed to know."

I've got it! Culp thought. He would take matters into his own hands and show everyone what *I Spy* could be. He would write four scripts for those eighteen episodes, but he wouldn't tell Leonard until he was finished. The only person he would tell was Cosby. He knew that the relationship between Kelly and Scotty would be the heart of the show and that the key to figuring that out was getting to know his costar better, to start hearing Cosby's voice in his head.

Cosby was back on the road performing a two-week engagement at the Latin Casino in Camden, New Jersey. Culp started calling the club, staying on the phone for hours every day as he threw out story ideas. He had committed to Cosby and the belief that they would be a successful team. He grew even more confident once he heard how funny Cosby was on the phone and how smart his responses were to Culp's story lines. He could sense that Cosby wasn't quite as committed at first but that he was slowly warming to the possibilities of their on-camera relationship.

In fact, Cosby did find Culp's daily phone calls odd at first. *Why does the cat keep saying that we have to be married?* he thought. It took a while for him to understand that it was just Culp's "actor talk." But the more he listened, the more he was encouraged that Culp shared the same up-lifting vision for his character that he and Camille had. They all wanted Scotty to be something new on television: a highly educated black man who was able to relate to people from all walks of life. Scotty would be a natural-born "educator" as well as a spy.

Cosby confided to Culp that he thought the test episode had been "horrible because of me." And talking to a *New York Times* reporter for a story for *I Spy,* he was humble about his new career. "If I have any potential as an actor, if I'm better than average, then I'd like to continue acting in movies and in television," he said. "If it doesn't work out, I can always be a comic."

He could afford to be philosophical, because his comedy career was going so well. His yearly earnings were approaching

265

$100,000 — more than he ever thought he'd make. The money came from concert fees and from payments for dozens of TV appearances in 1964, including return visits to *The Tonight Show* and *The Jack Paar Show* and spots on *The Ed Sullivan Show, The Andy Williams Show, The Jimmy Dean Show,* and a US version of the British satirical review *That Was the Week That Was.* His second album, *I Started Out as a Child,* was getting rave reviews. *Billboard* magazine listed it as a "Breakout" pick and predicted: "This Cosby album should be a sure hit, as Bill takes us into the zany, make-believe world of his youth . . . Bill, by virtue of talent and good national TV exposure, has become a top comic overnight. It's easy to understand why."

As the holiday shopping season got under way, Warner Bros. stopped releasing new albums and put all of its marketing muscle behind Cosby and a few other top artists. "Call your Warner Bros. distributors now!" an ad in the trade press urged record stores. "Let Bill Cosby crank up your customer count." Sure enough, by mid-December *I Started Out as a Child* was number 85 on the *Billboard* charts, the only comedy album to crack the Top 100.

For Christmas week, Cosby had accepted an engagement at the Shoreham Hotel in

Washington, DC, so that he and Camille could spend the holiday with the Hanks clan. Remembering the impoverished holidays of his youth, when a wooden crate had served as his Christmas tree, he bought hundreds of dollars' worth of gifts for his in-laws, for Camille — and for their unborn child. For the best news of all was that Camille was five months' pregnant. Cosby was so thrilled that he started to talk about his impending fatherhood in his stand-up act, telling his audiences that he wanted "sixteen sons."

Yet if Cosby hoped to spend the holiday taking his mind off his new acting career, *Variety* made that impossible. Two days before Christmas, on December 23, the weekly bible of the entertainment ran a preview of the coming fall television season with the banner headline: "Television's Jackie Robinson."

"Of the 88 proposed new evening programs for 1965–66 . . . one is far more notable than the rest," wrote George Rosen, *Variety*'s veteran TV and radio editor. "The certain standout is *I Spy,* an hour-long dramatic adventure series shot on location around the world and produced by Sheldon Leonard . . . Reason: it costars a Negro. For the first time in TV history, a Negro (albeit on a costar basis) will have his name atop the marquee of a continuing prime-time TV series. Negro comic Bill Cosby, teamed with non-Negro Bob Culp, will become 'Television's Jackie

Robinson.' "

Rosen noted that *I Spy* was the only new show with a regular role for a black actor, and that the NAACP and the Congress for Racial Equality were demanding that CBS and ABC do something about their lily-white lineups. As he put it with a pianistic flourish: "There are 87 'all-white' pilots plus one integrated *I Spy* to comprise the 88 keyboard on which will be played the new TV program melodies of '65–66.'"

Reading the *Variety* story, Cosby had mixed feelings. It made him anxious, because he wasn't sure he was up to the expectations raised by the comparison with Jackie Robinson. But it reminded him that he had a responsibility.

Growing up, he had always wondered why all the cowboys and other heroes in movies and on TV were white. *Where are the heroes for black kids?* he thought. If they were lucky, they might find one in a teacher or a coach or a minister, but at that age the role models who really counted were athletes and entertainers. For Shorty Cosby, the Brooklyn Dodgers great had been one of those heroes, so much so that he imitated his pigeon-toed walk. So if he had an opportunity to follow in those footsteps now, even by playing a fictional spy on TV, he had a duty to do the best job he could.

■ ■ ■ ■

Bob Culp was having a less merry Christmas. With four children under the age of seven, he and his wife Nancy were exhausted and barely speaking. As he worked on his *I Spy* scripts, he was all but living in his redwood-paneled study on the third floor of their Woodland Hills home.

On New Year's Day, Culp awoke early and checked the intercom system that allowed him to hear what was going on throughout the house. In each of his children's bedrooms, he heard crying. At the end of his rope, he punched the seven-ply wall next to the intercom as hard as he could, and a sharp pain shot up his arm.

Jeez, I just broke my hand, he thought.

While the rest of the family was still in bed, Culp drove to the hospital, where he was diagnosed with a fracture. He cursed himself for being so stupid, but he wasn't going to let hot-headedness stand in his way. He went back to the house with a cast on his hand, testily informed Nancy what had happened, and then locked the door to the third-floor staircase and started hunting and pecking with one finger.

Culp was working around the clock on two scripts. He wanted both to give Cosby as large a role as he had, and to feature other black characters as well. One story he had in mind was inspired by Olympic decathlete Rafer Johnson and the boxer Cassius Clay, who a year earlier had converted to Islam and changed his name to Muhammad Ali. Tentatively entitled "The Greatest," the story would feature a black Olympic star who grows so sick of racial conditions in America that he defects to China, where Kelly and Scotty are sent to bring him home.

Culp was even more excited by the other story he was writing. If he got it right, he was certain, it would change Bill Cosby's life. His new friend would never be seen as a true leading man unless he was allowed to "get the girl." But he was sure that the executives at NBC had no plans to let that happen, because they didn't want to invite a backlash from white viewers and advertisers.

If Scotty couldn't fall in love, however, he could show compassion. In acting school, Culp had learned that the two emotions were dramatically interchangeable. So he was writing an episode in which Scotty would develop intense feelings of compassion for a lonely, drug-addicted jazz singer he meets in Hong Kong. "Get ready for a Valentine's Day present!" he told Cosby in one of their daily phone calls, before sending him a special delivery package containing a script called "The Loser."

Several weeks later, Culp received the

phone call from Sheldon Leonard that he had been dreading.

"They want to replace Bill," Leonard said. He didn't say who "they" were, but Culp knew: the NBC executives.

"Okay, that's fine, no problem, replace him," Culp replied coolly. "They'll have to replace me too."

"Now don't get upset," Leonard said.

"Who's upset?" Culp said.

"Calm down," Leonard said. "I had to make the call.

"Just work on your tennis," Leonard told Culp. "Don't worry. I'll take care of it."

As soon as he hung up, the emotion that Culp had held in check came pouring out. *Replace Bill?* he thought. *Don't those stupid suits realize that the two of us are their only hope?* Culp knew the actors that might be hired to take their place, and he didn't think any of them could hold a candle to him and Cosby. *Just give us a shot at the scripts I'm writing,* he thought, *and we'll have a hit.*

Leonard, too, had been assuming for months that the front office would eventually turn on Cosby. He realized that the acting in the Hong Kong test episode was weak, so he had sent the executives only short rushes that showed off the exotic scenery. They liked what they saw well enough to approve the show for a debut in the fall. Leonard waited

271

to send the full episode of "Affair in T'Shen Cha" to headquarters until the week before Christmas, when no one would be around. So it wasn't until late January that the executives finally screened it, and not until February that they sent back a memo summarizing their reaction. "Unanimously disparaging," was the consensus — particularly about Cosby's performance.

But now Leonard had the ammunition he needed to fire back: Bob Culp's threat that if Bill Cosby was fired, he would walk, too.

Days later, Earle Hagen, the veteran TV composer who was writing the music for *I Spy,* was outside Leonard's office talking to his secretary, Skippy, when a call from New York came through the switchboard. Hagen watched as Leonard listened to the executive on the other end of the line.

"Bill Cosby is the guy I want for this part," Leonard said.

There was a pause.

"I don't give a goddamn if we lose the South," he said.

There was another pause.

"In that case, we don't do the show," Leonard said calmly, then he hung up.

Turning to Hagen and Skippy, he exploded: "This is 1965, and they're giving me this stuff about 'those guys are going to be living in the same room and using the same wash basin'!"

Ten minutes later, the NBC executive

called back.

When Leonard hung up this time, he was grinning like the Cheshire cat.

"Okay," he said. "We're on."

By sticking up for Cosby, Leonard was taking a noble stand but also assuming a huge risk. The fine print in his contract with NBC stipulated that if at any time he couldn't deliver shows on schedule, the network could take the show away from him. Culp was determined not to let that happen. By the end of March he had completed his four scripts, and they were all very good, if he did say so himself. He had been acting in TV dramas for a decade, and he had never seen a better-developed rapport between two characters. Now he just had to figure out how to break the news to Fine and Friedkin that he had been writing episodes for *I Spy* behind their backs.

The next day, Culp went to see Fine at his office on the studio lot. Acting as if it was no big deal, he handed over the script for his Olympic defector episode, which he had entitled "So Long, Patrick Henry."

"Where the hell did this come from?" Fine asked.

"Mort, read it," Culp said.

A few days later, Fine called him back. The script wasn't bad, he said. Sheldon had read it and "liked a few things." Then Fine reprimanded Culp for being so sneaky. If he was going to write as well as act, he had to follow the rules. The producers needed to see a three-page outline of a script before they could approve it.

"Well, I have another story in mind," Culp said. "I'll give you a few pages."

Over the next few days, he boiled down the story about Scotty's compassion for the junkie jazz singer to a three-page outline.

"It's interesting," Fine said when Culp showed it to him. "Good title: 'The Loser.' Go ahead, write it."

The next morning, Culp put the finished script on Fine's desk.

"You sonofabitch!" Fine said.

What Culp didn't know yet was that Fine and Friedkin needed his scripts badly. The timetable of "Sheldon's folly" required that they have eight more stories finished by the time they went back to Hong Kong in April. They had received dozens of submissions from some of the top TV drama writers in the business, but few had a good feel for the pairing of Kelly and Scott. So after making Culp sweat for a few days, Fine told him that all four of his scripts would be shot.

By the time Leonard took his cast and crew back to Hong Kong in April, NBC executives had changed their tune and were going out of their way to take credit for casting Cosby. In a seven-page ad in *Variety,* they touted *I Spy* as the network's top new show. They also granted access to Charles L. Mee Jr., a young Off-Broadway playwright, for a *New York Times Magazine* profile of their costar. After gushing about his stand-up act, Mee predicted that "when Cosby assumes his role as an undercover agent on television this fall, viewers will get some inkling of how it would be to see Thelonious Monk playing piano in the orchestra of Lawrence Welk."

Cosby played along with the marketing blitz, but he was already growing irritated at all the hoopla over his skin color. One day, a network publicist handed him a press release that breathlessly described him as "the first black performer to have a starring role in a regular dramatic series on American television."

Cosby took a drag of his cigar. "Is there one in England?" he asked dryly.

11
MR. CROSLEY AND MR. CUPS

Before boarding the plane back to Hong Kong in April 1965, Cosby and Culp went to check out the dressing rooms that they had been assigned on the Desilu lot. The rooms were side by side, separated by a small cubbyhole with enough room for one desk. So they agreed to hire a secretary to work for both of them. Already, they sensed that they liked and trusted each other enough that they didn't have to have any secrets.

They had discovered other things in common as well, apart from their subversive sense of humor. They had both been track stars in college: Cosby the Temple high jumper and javelin thrower, Culp a triple threat at pole vault, long jump, and high jump at the University of Washington. Both came from troubled families. Culp's father, Crozier, was a lawyer and a ladies' man who, in his son's words, "would give you the shirt off his back, as long as he had another one in the drawer." Like Bill Cosby Sr., he had joined the military to escape the responsibilities of marriage. And like Cosby, Culp identified with his long-suffering mother, who he described as a kindhearted woman whose only wish in life was to find a good man, but instead she had married Crozier Culp.

Days later they were back in Asia in the middle of a heat wave. Culp was spending the first day of shooting filming scenes of Kelly playing tennis. Leonard had commandeered a clay court on an estate on the outskirts of Hong Kong. But as Culp ran around under the blazing sun, the court disintegrated beneath his feet. After nine hours of shooting, he was caked in perspiration and red clay. He went back to his room at the Peninsula Hotel, soaked in a hot bath, and went straight to bed.

Hours later, he woke up with a hacking cough. He couldn't breathe. *I have to get to someone who can help me!* he thought. *I have to get to Bill!*

Culp rose to wake up Cosby in the next room, but before he could get to the door he passed out cold. When he awoke the next morning, he was spiking a fever. He was prescribed an antibiotic and dragged through a second day of shooting, but he wasn't feeling much better by the following morning, when they were to shoot a chase scene that involved running up a steep hill overlooking

Hong Kong.

Feverish and having trouble breathing, Culp kept pulling up short.

"I can't make it," he panted. "I can't do this."

"Sure you can," Cosby said. "I'll grab you from behind."

Cosby placed his hand under his partner's jacket and clasped hold of his belt. He positioned himself so that to the camera, stationed across a ravine, it looked as if they were running together. The next day, he did the same thing in a scene where bad guys chased Scotty and Kelly across the rooftops of Hong Kong.

As Cosby saw it, he was only returning a favor, since Culp was doing so much to support him as an actor. Not only was Culp offering him acting tips; if he thought Cosby wasn't ready to handle a scene, he fought with the director and writers to have it changed. Culp was the star of the show, the "I" in *I Spy,* and yet he was putting their on-screen relationship above everything else. So hoisting him around by his belt for a few days was the least Cosby could do in return.

Not that they ever waxed sentimental about their blooming friendship. As soon as Culp felt better, they went back to playful banter and insults, off-screen and on. And they did it with a kind of jive vernacular that was common among black and white hipsters but had

278

never been heard on prime-time television. Culp called it their "divine bullshit."

One thing they didn't share in common was their relationship with Sheldon Leonard. Culp remained respectful but wary of the boss, while Cosby was already treating him with the kind of teasing ease that he had established with Lieutenant Lamb in the navy and Coach White at Temple. One day, they were filming a scene on a ferryboat. The script called for Scotty to sound the ship's horn in an attempt to warn other boats off the water. Then a Chinese actor playing the ship's captain was supposed to say: "You signaled iceberg in Hong Kong Harbor!"

Instead, the line came out of the actor's mouth sounding something like: "You sell no raspberries ha-ka ha-ba!"

Leonard tried to break down the line for him: "You . . . sig . . . naled . . . ice . . . berg . . . in . . . Hong . . . Kong . . . Har . . . bor."

"You sell no raspberries in ha-ka ha-ba!" the actor repeated.

"Hey, Shel, he's making progress!" Cosby joked. "He got the word 'in.' That was clear as a bell!"

Watching the scene unfold, Culp kept waiting for an explosion, but he saw that Leonard didn't mind the needling, coming from Cos.

Day by day, Cosby was growing more confident as an actor. Leonard had hired a professional coach, Frank Silvera, to give him feedback. Culp had also offered advice from his method-acting guru, Herbert Berghof. "Don't try to feel a character's emotion," he said, "just try to think his thoughts; the rest will come naturally." But mostly Cosby was settling in his own style and rhythm, like a jazz musician finding his groove. He was gradually turning Scotty into a more reserved version of himself. If Kelly was an American James Bond, all sex appeal and slick charm, Scotty would be a black Dr. Watson, wise and wittily observant. As the show progressed, the writers incorporated details of Cosby's real life into Scotty's back story: he had gone to college at Temple University; he had been a star athlete; he was close to his mother.

Scotty also was a teetotaler, a rarity in an era when television was full of men drinking cocktails at all hours of the day and night. "My father drank, and it was my decision to play Scotty that way," Cosby told an interviewer.

He was now in almost every scene with Culp, which presented Leonard with another challenge: how to film men of such different complexions without the benefit of studio cameras and lights. Culp was even more pale than usual after months of writing indoors. Cosby was getting darker with every day in the Asian sun. Any makeup they put on melted in the ninety-degree heat. But the show's "location producer," an Egyptian named Fouad Said, came to the rescue. After the troubled first trip to Hong Kong, the young film school grad had persuaded Leonard to dispense with Run Run Shaw's bulky camera and audio equipment and use more portable gear that fit in a van he called the "Cinemobile." Said also proved to be a whiz at lighting, covering his small cameras with scrims and silks and gobos to adjust for the contrast in skin tones.

Cosby was having so much fun on his second trip to Hong Kong that his only regret was being separated from Camille, who was eight months' pregnant and couldn't travel. He had planned to return to Los Angeles in time for the delivery, but shooting fell behind schedule. So he was still in Asia on April 8, when he got word that Camille had given birth to a baby girl. Cosby was thrilled, even if it wasn't a boy. They named the baby Erika and told everyone that the E stood for "excellence."

He finally made it back to Los Angeles the next week, just in time to attend the Grammy Awards at the Beverly Hilton Hotel. The previous year, *Bill Cosby Is a Very Funny Fellow — Right!* had been nominated but lost to Allan Sherman's *My Son, the Nut.* This year, Cosby won Best Comedy Performance for *I Started Out as a Child,* just as he was now outselling Sherman and every other comic in record stores.

For Cosby, the Grammy vindicated the decisions he was making about where to take his comedy. He was still closing his nightclub act with "Noah," but he sensed that it was time to ease away from the routine. As Jonathan Winters had warned him, he was getting sick of it even if his audiences weren't. A few months later, Cosby would record his third album, at the Flamingo Hotel in Las Vegas, and its humor would be entirely personal and observational. The very names of the routines on *Why Is There Air?* reflected his new storytelling direction: "Kindergarten," "Shop," "Baby," "$75 Car," "Driving in San Francisco."

On the album cover, Cosby held a volleyball and wore a Temple T-shirt, looking like the gym teacher that he had once planned to be. For the back cover, Warner Bros. assigned its marketing director and crack liner note writer, Stan Cornyn, to capture Cosby's original style. "He shouldn't be funny, because he doesn't tell jokes," Cornyn wrote. "But he is funny . . . You identify with Bill's material . . . And when he talks about things we have all gone through, and then forgot, he just talks. No big setups. No knock-'em-dead ringers. And when he takes up a situation, like Kindergarten, he doesn't exaggerate. If anything, Bill underexaggerates. No topical jibes. No White House gags. Just plain ole Mankind on Review."

Cosby didn't have long to celebrate his Grammy. Soon he and Culp were back at the Desilu lot shooting interior scenes for the first *I Spy* episodes. One morning, they arrived at their adjacent dressing rooms at the same time. Cosby was wearing a new sweater, and Culp said how much he liked it. "Here, you can have it," Cosby said.

The next morning, Cosby admired the sports jacket Culp was wearing. Now a game of one-upmanship was on. Each man started to shop for elegant items of clothing that he would relinquish as soon as the other paid a compliment. The competition went on for weeks, until they decided that it had gotten out of hand and called it off.

After work, they were spending more time together, too. Culp was looking for any excuse not to be alone with Nancy, so he started inviting Bill and Camille to dinner. As couples, they hit it off, except when the two husbands started talking in their language of inside jokes and the wives couldn't understand what they were saying.

"You sell no raspberries in ha-ka ha-ba!" one of them would blurt out.

"We're not toying with you, Missa Brown!" the other would respond.

Now that Culp was earning a star's salary for *I Spy,* he had hired an Asian couple to help take care of his four children. When the Cosbys came over to the Culp house, the caretakers had trouble pronouncing their last name.

"Hello, Mr. and Mrs. Crosley," they said.

The Asian couple referred to Bob and Nancy as "Mr. and Mrs. Cups."

So another set of pet nicknames was born.

"Mr. Crosley!" Culp greeted Cosby every morning.

"Mr. Cups!" Cosby exclaimed.

Although they avoided earnestness at all costs, the two men did have one heart-to-heart in the summer before *I Spy* went on the air. Ever since the first awkward table read the previous summer, they had bonded over their dislike of contrived racial lines. "Watermelon jokes," they called them. So they were both upset at some offensive dialogue that made its way into a script called "Danny Was a Million Laughs," about an American mobster whom Kelly and Scotty are asked to guard before he is extradited to the United States to stand trial for racketeering.

Martin Landau, the young actor who would soon get a lead role in *Mission: Impossible,* played Danny Preston. In the story, he has a big mouth and a knack for offending everyone in sight. The script had Danny encountering Scotty in a hotel and mistaking him for a bellman. "Here you go, boy," Danny says, flipping Scotty a coin. "I'll put my shoes in the hall for you."

Cosby and Culp wanted the line cut. Instead, the writers suggested adding more dialogue to show how angry it made the two spies. They wanted Kelly to whisper: "We could disconnect every bone in his body!" Then Scotty would say: "Tell me about it."

But Cosby didn't think the comeback was strong enough, and when it came time to shoot the scene he improvised. "No," he said. "Work before pleasure!"

After shooting the scene, the actors went back to their dressing rooms and for the first and last time had a serious discussion about the social message of *I Spy*. They both said what each had been thinking, that the best contribution they could make to the race issue was to have Kelly and Scotty behave as though it didn't exist.

"Our statement will be a nonstatement," Culp said.

"Dead on, pard," Cosby agreed.

Ever since NBC announced that *I Spy* was coming, there had been speculation in the press about how many of the network's local stations would boycott the program. "Cosby in 'Spy' Puts NBC Dixie Affils on Spot" was the headline of a *Variety* story that identified local markets with a track record of rejecting TV shows with prominent Negro roles. The story recalled that an NBC variety show starring Nat "King" Cole had lost sponsors because of its failure to clear affiliates in the South, and that Southern boycotts had helped sink a CBS urban drama called *East Side/West Side.*

As the fall season neared, NBC executives fielded nervous questions from affiliates and advertisers. How big a role would Cosby have? Would he and Culp do things like share bathrooms and eat together in restaurants that would have been illegal in parts of the country until just a year earlier, before Congress passed the Civil Rights Act?

But a week before the show's premiere in late September, only four stations had refused to carry the show — in Savannah, Georgia; Birmingham, Alabama; Alexandria, Louisiana; and Daytona Beach, Florida. In all, 180 stations had agreed to air the program, representing "what amounts to full network clearance," the *New York Times* reported.

For the first episode of the season, Leonard had hoped to avoid any treatment of race with his lightweight test episode "Affair in T'Sien Cha." But when he sent the finished edit to Grant Tinker, NBC's vice president of programming for the West Coast, Tinker hated the corny plot and the wooden performance by Cosby. "Do you have anything else in the pipeline?" he asked.

As it happened, Leonard had just finished

postproduction on "So Long, Patrick Henry," Culp's edgy script about the black Olympic athlete who defects to Communist China. He was pleased with everything about it — Culp's writing, the performances from all the actors, the movie quality atmosphere created by director Leo Penn. He screened it for Tinker. The young executive, who was developing a reputation for his sophisticated eye, liked the layered story, with its mixture of drama and comedy and echoes of real-life events. "Let's take a chance," Tinker said.

The episode featured strong performances by two other black actors: Ivan Dixon, who played the treasonous athlete, and Cicely Tyson, who played his girlfriend. And for anyone who knew Cosby only from his comedy albums and talk-show appearances, it showed that he would not be playing for laughs on *I Spy.* Instead of expressing solidarity with his black brother, the script called for Scotty to be offended by his lack of patriotism. "The whole world's trying to keep bloody fools like you from selling themselves back into slavery," Scotty snaps at the defector. "But you did it anyway."

Although NBC executives agreed to make "So Long, Patrick Henry" the premiere episode, they were nervous about Cosby wielding a gun. The network censors handed down an edict: Kelly was to do most of the shooting, and if Scotty used his firearm, it

287

would never be on his own. The writers gave Culp a line of dialogue to explain why only he was returning fire. "I'll do it," Kelly says. "I have the silencer."

But the mischievous actors couldn't resist ad-libbing a jab at the censors.

"Can't you ever bring a silencer?" Culp said the next time they were in a gun battle.

"It ruins the lining of my suit," Cosby replied.

Once the premier episode was chosen, it was time for Leonard to approve the show's opening. He asked Earle Hagen, who had written the catchy themes for *The Andy Griffith Show* and *The Dick Van Dyke Show,* to compose very different music for *I Spy.* He wanted a jazzy theme song and an original score for every episode, as if it were a motion picture. The credits, too, looked more like a movie than a TV show. They opened with the name of the producer — "Sheldon Leonard presents . . . I Spy" — and ended with the names of the stars: first Robert Culp and then, in smaller type, Bill Cosby.

Yet as NBC mounted its final publicity blitz for *I Spy,* its black costar was getting far more attention than its dashing lead and inventive producer. *The Saturday Evening Post* gave the job of previewing the show to Stanley Karnow, normally a war correspondent for *Time* magazine. "For the first time, a Negro stars in a TV series — and he won't sing, dance or play the second banana," Karnow wrote. When Karnow asked Cosby how he thought America would respond to the show, Cosby was pensive but optimistic. "What we're doing will offend all sorts of bigots, and not just in the South," he predicted. "There are folks in Philadelphia who'll write in to say, 'How come you have a colored guy kicking a Caucasian?' Some will even object to seeing a Negro in the same room with a White. But it will balance out. The pros will outweigh the cons."

One pro became clear as soon as *I Spy* premiered on Wednesday nights at ten o'clock: viewers were curious. The first episode shot ahead of the *The Danny Kaye Show,* the previous leader in the time slot. Critics were also impressed. While some focused on the exotic footage of Hong Kong, most singled out Cosby's performance. "Bill Cosby, the comedian, is now the most unexpectedly proficient performer of the season," wrote Jack O'Brian in the *New York Journal-American.* In the *New York Daily News,* Ben Gross captured the essence of Cosby and Culp's "nonstatement" appeal. "Cosby is presented without any emphasis whatsoever on his race," Gross wrote. "His presence is merely taken for granted and thereby more is achieved for better racial relations than by a thousand propaganda exhortations."

By the third episode of the season, *I Spy* was not only holding its lead but developing a cult following. In "Carry Me Back to Old T'sing-Tao," Kelly and Scotty hunt down a Hong Kong gambling magnet who owes a million dollars to the IRS and fight off his thuggish sons-in-law, comically named Morton, Harold, and Turkey. Cleveland Amory of *TV Guide* raved about the episode, particularly the badinage between Cosby and Culp, who by now had perfected their jive shorthand.

After one fight scene, Culp coined a phrase that would become one of their trademarks.

"We did whup up on old Morton and Harold and Turkey," Cosby gloated.

"Indeed we did," Culp said. "I would share with you in the warmth and glory and wonderfulness of that moment were it not for the sadness of our government."

What viewers taken with the "wonderfulness" of that episode didn't know was that it had precipitated Cosby's first disagreement with Sheldon Leonard. The script called for a car chase scene in which Scotty's vehicle flips over. Filmed in the Hollywood Hills, it was too dangerous for Cosby to do himself, so the studio called the stuntmen's union, which sent over a white man in black face. When Cosby saw the stand-in on the set, he complained to Leonard.

"Hey, Shel," he said, "there are plenty of

guys in my old neighborhood in Philly who'd be happy to get the job!"

Conceding the point, Leonard ordered a search for a black stuntman, and Calvin Brown, an extra on *Gomer Pyle, USMC,* was hired to play Cosby's body double.

An episode entitled "Dragon's Teeth" produced more behind-the-scenes tension. The script called on an old girlfriend of Kelly's to kiss Culp and Cosby on both cheeks, in the French manner. When the NBC censors saw the dailies, they edited out Scotty's peck. Americans still weren't ready to see a white woman kissing a black man, they argued, even if it was an air kiss. Leonard wasn't happy but had to pick his battles, and he concluded that this one wasn't worth fighting.

On the fifth week of the new season, NBC aired Culp's Valentine's gift to Cosby. In "The Loser," Hong Kong drug dealers kidnap Scotty in an attempt to get back a heroin shipment that he and Kelly have intercepted. They take Scotty to a seedy nightclub and stash him in the dressing room of a jazz singer named Angel, played by Eartha Kitt, the black singer and activist famous for her flirtatious voice.

In his interactions with Kitt, Cosby displayed a wider range of dramatic emotions than he had ever shown before: anger at his confinement; contempt when Scotty realizes that Angel is a junkie who only cares about her next fix; then flickers of gratitude and sympathy when she helps him escape. In the final act, Scotty takes Kelly back to the nightclub to save Angel and reveals how much he cares for her. "I come from a long line of losers," he says, offering the first hint that Scotty's laid-back, scholarly persona might be a self-protective facade. "Whenever I see one, it hurts."

As the closing credits rolled, Bob Culp felt sure that "The Loser" had done for Bill Cosby what he hoped. By allowing Scotty to show such convincing compassion, it had proved Cosby could play love scenes, too. But as another gushing review in *TV Guide* testified, "The Loser" did more than that. It began to win Cosby a level of praise for his acting that would prove a tribute to Culp's tutelage but also a test of their flourishing friendship.

12
A WORLD OF "WONDERFULNESS"

When the *I Spy* crew arrived in Tokyo, Leonard put them up at the New Otani Hotel, a shimmering modern building in the Koichoi district. As Cosby was checking in, he took one look around and decided that he didn't like the low ceilings and narrow hallways and delicate furnishings. Everything about the place made him feel like an oversized American.

"Let's get out of here!" he suggested to Culp.

"What about Sheldon?" Culp asked.

"He can't run our lives completely," Cosby said.

So the two men and their wives hopped a taxi to the more spacious Hilton hotel nearby. When Leonard heard about it, he hit the roof. He was angry with his actors and worried about losing face with the owners of the New Otani, whom he was counting on to give him access to the hotel's rock garden to use as a scenic backdrop. He blamed Culp for the whole thing, even though it was Cosby who instigated the jailbreak.

"How could you do this to me!" Leonard shouted at his lead actor.

"It wasn't just me," Culp answered. "Bill was in on it, too!"

But by now, Culp had come to see that Leonard was so fond of Cosby that he was incapable of holding anything against him. The sense of injustice gnawed at him until he finally confronted his costar.

"Why does Sheldon always blame me?" Culp asked.

Cosby shrugged. "He can't help it," he said. "I'm the good son. You're the bad son. That's just the way it is. I tease him. He loves that. You push him. What do you expect, gratitude?"

"Yes, I do," Culp said.

"Good luck!" Cosby said.

Leonard had chosen Japan as the second foreign location for *I Spy* because, like Hong Kong, it offered an exotic backdrop for Cold War intrigue. In one of his grand gestures, he invited Cosby and Culp to bring their wives. Baby Erika came, too, which delighted her father but meant that he was putting in long days shooting only to return to the demands of caring for a four-month-old at the hotel. One night a crewmember named Michael Preece took pity on the new parents and offered to babysit. Bill and Camille went out to dinner but were so anxious about leaving the baby alone that they were back in forty-five minutes. "She's been sleeping the whole time," Preece reassured them.

Cosby fell in love with the food in Japan, but otherwise he and the rest of the crew found the locals difficult. Unlike the Chinese, who were curious but friendly, the Japanese seemed suspicious of the Americans. Locals kept creeping up behind the actors while they were in the middle of shooting. At a Tokyo nightclub where one scene was set, the building janitor thought that the TV crew had slighted him so he cut the power and locked the fuse box. The cabbies drove like maniacs, paying no attention when the Americans tried to use their few words of Japanese.

Still, Cosby would remember the trip fondly, if not for the Japanese welcome then for how it felt to travel the world as one of the stars of *I Spy*. It was something that he had never experienced as a black man in America: a sense of dignity. "When I go off on these overseas location trips with my wife and baby," he told a reporter after his return to LA, "I have a feeling which perhaps never occurs to a white performer. As an *I Spy* star, I'm part of the NBC team and as such I'm not deferred to really, but respected and protected. This is difficult to express — but that is an odd feeling for the average Negro."

As *I Spy* was premiering on television,

Cosby and Culp were back in LA shooting interior scenes for the Japan stories. One of them was a script that Culp had written called "Court of the Lion," about a Zulu nobleman who takes over a Japanese fishing village and forces the locals to help him ship industrial diamonds to the Chinese Communists. Leonard had agreed to let Culp direct the episode, so he was working around the clock to fine-tune the script and work out the filming schedule.

Seeing how fanatically Culp was preparing, Cosby couldn't help ribbing him. He would stick his head in the door of Culp's dressing room as he was poring over shot lists and start rattling off random numbers until Culp lost his train of thought.

Culp's perfectionism even produced a rare moment of friction between the two "pards." The script called on Scotty to deliver a long piece of dialogue that was vital for the exposition of the plot. Knowing Cosby's tendency to half-learn his lines and to rely on his improvisational skills, Culp stressed how important it was to follow the script as written. Offering a piece of acting advice that he had learned from his teachers in New York, he told Cosby to break down the dialogue into small chunks and work on "transitions" to make the delivery seem as natural as possible.

"You can't wing it!" Culp warned. "You

have to memorize it verbatim."

"No problem," Cosby assured him.

But on the night of the shoot, Cosby couldn't get through the soliloquy without flubbing his lines. Stagehands brought him the script to refresh his memory, and he thought: *Okay, got it!* Then as soon as the script was gone, his mind said: *Forget!* After multiple takes, Cosby became furious with himself. The voice of Riggie was back in his head, taunting him for his inadequacy as an actor and for letting his friend down. The number piled up, and Cosby got madder and madder. The shoot had gone for so long that he could hear the stomachs of the hungry crewmembers growling.

"I'm sorry!" he kept apologizing. "I'm sorry!"

"Forget it. Let's just get it," Culp replied patiently, until after thirty tries Cosby finally delivered a usable take.

Culp was upset, too, but he couldn't stay angry for long. He reminded himself of what Cos had done for him just a few days earlier. Culp was shooting a scene in Malibu in which Scotty was supposed to help the Japanese villagers collect oyster shells packed with diamonds. It was a cold, overcast day, and Culp was so obsessed with capturing the right light that he made Cosby stand in the ocean, in only a bathing suit, for several hours. Only later did he discover that Cosby was running a fever of 102 degrees, but that he hadn't complained because he didn't want to ruin his partner's first day as a director.

When the shooting was finished, Leonard forbade the compulsive Culp from ever directing again. "I need a live actor, not a dead director!" he said.

Still, Culp's writing and directing and a guest star performance by black comedian Godfrey Cambridge made "Court of the Lion" one of the most memorable episodes of the first season of *I Spy*. So was another Culp script called "The Tiger." Based on his original pilot for *Danny Doyle,* the episode involved a US spy who is taken prisoner by Vietnamese guerrillas and starred a stunning Euro-Asian actress named France Nuyen as the spy's half-Vietnamese daughter, Sam-Than MacLean.

In the story, Kelly and Sam fall in love, and it didn't take long for the same thing to happen to Bob Culp and France Nuyen. Soon Culp was spending nights at Nuyen's apartment in Beverly Hills rather than going home to his wife and kids. Everyone on the set could see what was going on, and Culp sensed that Leonard, in particular, disapproved. He knew how much the producer doted on his own wife Frankie and identified with other family men. It was another reason, Culp was convinced, that Leonard favored Cosby — because he saw how devoted he was to Camille and their baby. Yet again, Sheldon viewed him as "the bad son" and Cos as "the good son."

The tension over Culp's affair with Nuyen continued to hang over the cast's next trip in December, to Mexico. Once again Leonard invited Camille and Erika to come along, and he put up the Cosbys in style: in an elegant casita at the Las Brisas resort overlooking Acapulco Bay, with a pink Jeep to ferry them around the property. After work, they joined the rest of the crew for parties that "Fou" Said organized around the pool every night. But Bob Culp was lonely for Nuyen, and he kept nagging Leonard to let him write a script that would justify bringing her to Mexico.

One day Culp cornered Leonard in the Las Brisas parking lot to argue for casting Nuyen in another episode.

"No," Leonard said.

Culp kept pushing.

"No!" Leonard shouted, loud enough that everyone on the set could hear.

For Culp, it was the last straw. Until then, he had treated Leonard with respect, and he expected the same in return, since in his view *I Spy* was his baby as much as Sheldon's. The show had been sold to NBC partly based on Culp's star power, and he had written the scripts that had set its tone and made it a critical success. Culp saw them as equal partners, the artist and the producer. But

299

now Leonard was treating him like a child. *Well, he's not my dad,* Culp thought. *He wants to be everyone's dad, but he's not up to that job as far as I'm concerned!*

For the rest of the Mexico stay, Culp stopped talking to his boss. When Leonard approached, he stared down at the clipboard he carried around to jot down script ideas. If Leonard gave him instructions on the set, he refused to make eye contact. If Culp wanted something from Leonard, he found someone to act as a go-between. The rest of the crew called it "the Mexican standoff," and they were more grateful than ever for Cosby's ability to clear the air by making everyone laugh.

If Cosby was able to shrug off the tensions on the *I Spy* set, it was partly because he was so busy with the rest of his career. When he returned from Mexico at the beginning of 1966, he discovered that four months on prime-time television had propelled his earning power as a nightclub performer and record artist into a new orbit. An early inkling came when he went to perform at Texas Tech University. So many tickets had been sold that the concert had to be moved from the college auditorium to a town hall in Lubbock seating 7,300 people. In February, Cosby took a weekend away from *I Spy* to do two weekend concerts with Stan Getz, and the two Grammy winners drew a crowd of 4,000 in Portland and another 6,000 in Seattle.

Roy Silver was suddenly getting offers from promoters across the country to put Cosby in venues that seated thousands of people and where, at $5 a ticket, he could make $15,000 to $20,000 in one show. He could now gross close to $100,000 in one weekend, if he did double shows, and several times that if he took a week or two off and did a multicity tour. Remembering the girls who didn't want to date him because he was such a clown in high school, he couldn't help feel a sense of vindication. *Sold Bill Cosby short at a few bucks, and now he's worth a few hundred!* he thought.

Still, Cosby had no idea how long his hot hand would last. He knew that show business could be a fickle game and that you had to grab the money while it was on the table. So he told Silver to keep booking every single concert that he could possibly fit into his schedule during breaks from *I Spy*.

When he returned to Harrah's in Lake Tahoe in March, he was paid $20,000 a week. Driving up to the casino, he saw the name "Bill Cosby" at the top of the marquee for the first time. Bill Harrah had always been fond of him, but now the casino owner greeted him as a prince, putting him up in one of the ritziest suites at the resort. Feeling flush for the first time in his life, Cosby splurged by buying one of Harrah's private fleet of Rolls-Royces for $35,000.

Silver was recording the Harrah's concerts for another Warner Bros. album — the fourth in three years — so Cosby used the engagement to perfect two new routines that stretched longer than anything he had ever done. In one, he spun a long tale about having his tonsils taken out as a boy. It began with his excitement at being told that he could eat "all the ice cream in the world!" after the operation. Then it turned to hilarious panic as he and the other kids in the hospital saw the first patient wheeled out of the operating room: "We looked at each other and said: 'Ice cream, we're gonna eat ice cream!' . . . Oh, Johnson's back. Hey, Johnson, wake up! Hey, Johnson, how come your eyeballs keep waving around in the air? Nurse, that's ketchup in his mouth, ain't it? Please say it's ketchup because we'd hate to think that you KILLED JOHNSON!"

The other bit was inspired by Cosby's memories of listening to the suspense show *Lights Out* on the radio as a child. When he was five years old, the show's host, Arch Oboler, had broadcast a scary story called "Chicken Heart," based on a *Chicago Tribune* report that scientists had succeeded in keeping the heart of a chicken alive after removing it from the body. Oboler had created a frightening tale of a chicken heart that kept growing until it started to attack human beings and destroy entire cities. With the help of his trusty microphone (and his memory refreshed by an album of *Lights Out* classics released in 1962), Cosby created a spellbinding account of becoming so frightened that he smeared Jell-O all over the kitchen floor to protect himself from the monster.

Harrah's audiences howled as Cosby reached the climax of his "Chicken Heart" routine: "The chicken heart was kept alive in the laboratory in a vat, with a special solution, half blood, half sodium . . . *thump, thump* . . . One day, a careless janitor knocked the vat over . . . *thump, thump* . . . He went to get a rag to clean it up . . . *thump, thump* . . . The chicken heart grew, six foot, five inches . . . *thump, thump* . . . in search of human blood . . . *thump, thump* . . . The janitor came back, opened the door, the heart ate him, 'Waaaa!' . . . *thump, thump* . . . It moved into the hallway . . . *thump, thump* . . . Rang for the elevator . . . *thump, thump* . . . Fourth floor: 'Waaaa!' . . . Moved into the street, ate up all the cabs . . . *thump, thump* . . . The Empire State Building! . . . *thump, thump* . . . Ate up the Jersey Turnpike! . . . *thump, thump* . . . It's in your home state! . . . *thump, thump* . . . It's outside your door! . . . *thump, thump* . . . And it's going to eat you up! . . ."

"Oh no!" Cosby cried out in his child's voice. "I got my Jell-O, started smearing it all over the floor! 'Get out of here, chicken heart!' I set the sofa on fire! 'You won't come near smoke and fire and Jell-O'!"

Cosby called the album he recorded at Harrah's *Wonderfulness,* after the pet phrase that Culp had coined on *I Spy.* In a teasing tribute to Sheldon Leonard, he included a routine called "Niagara Falls" in which he imitated his boss telling a long-winded tale about his honeymoon. When the album was released a month later, it raced up the charts and lifted the sales of Cosby's three previous records. Within ten weeks, all four of his Warner Bros. albums were on the *Billboard* Top 100 list, a first for any comedian.

In mid-April, *I Spy* finished its first season in strong shape. It had won its Wednesday time slot every week and was the second most-watched drama on television. A ratings service called the Home Testing Institute that was beginning to measure viewership among specific "demographics" rated it the most popular show for viewers between the ages of eighteen and thirty-four. After months of profiles in magazines such as *Look* and *Newsweek* and covers of *TV Guide* and *TV Weekly,* Cosby and Culp were familiar faces in mailboxes and on grocery store checkout lines across America.

Then came the Emmy nominations. *I Spy* scored an impressive seven nods, including for the show itself, for Earle Hagen's music, for Fine and Friedkin's writing, for Eartha

Kitt's guest performance, and for Sheldon Leonard's directing. The last nomination came as a surprise, since Leonard was the producer of the show and had directed only the overseas shoots. But the television academy wanted to recognize his revolutionary "folly" of blending location and studio filming.

The last two nominations were for Bob Culp and Bill Cosby, both for Outstanding Actor in a Dramatic Series. Culp's nod was for his performance in "The Tiger," the Vietnam story that had launched his affair with France Nuyen. Cosby was nominated for "The Loser," Culp's script about Scotty's compassion for the junkie singer named Angel. In a category otherwise filled with ruggedly handsome white actors, Cosby was also up against David McCallum for *The Man from U.N.C.L.E*, David Janssen for *The Fugitive,* and Richard Crenna for *Slattery's People*.

Cosby was also invited to cohost the Emmy broadcast. In 1966, the awards were handed out at two ceremonies, at the Palladium in Los Angeles and the Americana Hotel in Manhattan. Cosby emceed the New York event, while Danny Kaye did the honors in Hollywood. Kaye began the broadcast by making a joke about *I Spy* beating his show on Wednesday nights. "I find it amusing," he said. "No, amusing isn't the right word. Interesting? No, that's not it, either. Damaging, that's what it is!"

When the stars of *Batman,* Adam West and Burt Ward, came on to present the award for best dramatic actor, Cosby was backstage in his hosting outfit, a black tuxedo with a white vest and bow tie. Camille was sitting in the audience, wearing a ribbon in her hair and a huge diamond ring. Cosby had invited his mother, too, as well as his father, who was dressed in a Brooks Brothers suit that his son had bought to clean the old man up for the occasion.

Culp was on the other side of the country at the Palladium, seated next to his wife. He told himself that he would be happy if either he or Cosby won, but he was worried about Nancy. If Bill got the Emmy, Culp thought, she wasn't going to take it well.

Adam West tore open the envelope.

"The winner is Bill Cosby!" he announced.

When Bob Culp heard the words, his mixed feelings melted away. All he felt was pride. No one else in the audience knew just how far Cosby had come in just one season. No one else knew how rocky his start had been, going back to his first nervous table read in Sheldon Leonard's office. No one else knew how important a role he, Bob Culp, had played in helping his friend grow as an actor, by giving him tips and writing scripts for him and developing such natural on-screen chemistry. Culp turned to Nancy, wanting to share his vicarious joy. But all he felt from her was fury.

When Cosby came back on stage in New York to accept his statuette, he spoke in a quiet, humble voice. "I have to thank a man who brought me into his office — that talks out of the side of his mouth — and was talking straight," he said, tipping his hat first to Sheldon Leonard. "He looked at me and said, 'I'm going to put you on television.' I said, 'Yeah, sure, fine. You call me, I won't call you.' "

"I would like to thank NBC for having guts," Cosby continued. Then, holding up his Emmy, he said: "I extend my hand to a man named Robert Culp. The guy took a comedian who couldn't do anything as far as acting is concerned, and he lost this because he helped me. That's the greatest thing a human being can ever do."

At the end of the first season of *I Spy,* Cosby was switching planes at O'Hare Airport in Chicago when he ran into his musical hero, Miles Davis. Excited, he reminded Davis of the first time they had met, when as a teenager Cosby had gone up to talk to him at the Showboat club in Philadelphia. Miles had no recollection of that encounter, but he did recognize Cosby from *I Spy* and said how much he liked the show.

"Thanks, Miles," Cosby replied, "but I just

hope they give me one woman to have a relationship with before the show is over! They're acting like black people don't go to bed or have love lives like white people do. I hope they just give me a love scene with one woman one time, just let me have a kissing scene just once!"

Around the same time, an attorney for the NAACP visited the show's head writer, Mort Fine, and posed the same question. "How come Cosby doesn't have a girl?" the civil rights lawyer asked.

Fine replied that he and David Friedkin were in the process of writing an episode where Scotty would finally "get the girl."

Because Leonard had gone almost a half million dollars over his budget for the first season, he decided to save some money by setting the first eight shows of season two in America. So over the summer of 1966, Cosby went to work in Las Vegas filming the romantic story that Fine had promised. Wanting to get maximum publicity for the episode, Leonard cast Nancy Wilson, the famous jazz singer, as Scotty's love interest: a songstress named Lori who is the sister of a missing black spy suspected in a string of murders of US agents around the world.

The first scene took place in a Las Vegas nightclub and called for Wilson to deliver a sultry rendition of "Angel Mine." Allowed to show sexual attraction for the first time,

Scotty shushes Kelly while she is performing. "Listen, I am watching a beautiful woman, my man!" he says. "Please do not bother me, or I will have you thrown out!" In the next scene, Scotty and Lori hug. At the end of the episode, they share a long good-bye kiss. "That is a definite arrivederci," he says as their lips part.

NBC chose "Lori" to open the second season of *I Spy,* and it drew a large audience: 40 percent of all viewers watching TV at ten o'clock on Wednesday night. To the network's relief, there was barely a peep of protest about two Negroes kissing on television. A reviewer for *Variety* dwelled on Wilson's limitations as an actress — "as with most beginners, she attacked the part rather than played it," he wrote — while viewers who wrote to NBC mostly wanted to know why the plot had been so confusing.

Heartened by the lack of controversy, NBC aired another Scotty love story two weeks later. When Cosby read the script for "Trial by Treehouse," by a young TV writer named Michael Zagor, he was impressed. Cosby was trying to improve his acting — he had bought a 16-millimeter projector and was screening *Casablanca, The Grapes of Wrath,* and *The Treasure of the Sierra Madre* at home — and he was pleased by the different emotions he would get to portray. "Hey, man, I like what you did," Cosby told Zagor, "and I'm even going to do some of your lines."

In the episode, Cosby got to cozy up to Cicely Tyson, who played a female agent named Vickie who pretends to be Scotty's wife while he is undercover as a factory worker. The script called on Scotty first to act annoyed at the uptight Vickie; then to show tenderness toward her young son; then to fall in love with her. Usually, *I Spy* episodes ended with Cosby needling Culp about his latest romantic escapade, but this time it was the other way around.

"The gentleness and sweetness of it!" Kelly teases after watching Scotty give Vickie a long good-bye kiss.

"You were peeking!" Scotty said.

"I never peek, my man," Kelly quips. "Leer a good deal, like the dirty old man that I am."

Everyone was so pleased with "Trial by Treehouse" that Zagor was assigned to write another love story for Scotty set in Italy, where Leonard took the cast in the summer of 1966. Traveling again with Camille and Erika, Cosby had a grand time eating pasta and seeing the sights of Rome, Florence, and Venice. Bob Culp, meanwhile, seized the opportunity to end his troubled marriage. Nancy Culp had planned to join him in Rome, but before she could depart he sent her a letter asking for his freedom, and soon news of the nasty split and of Culp's affair with France Nuyen was the talk of the Hollywood tabloids. "The Oriental Girl Robert Culp Left His Wife For," read a headline in *Screenland*. "Nancy's hands trembled that day when she put down a letter with an Italian postmark!" Within days, the Italian papers were also full of melodramatic stories about the visiting American TV star and his scandalous divorce.

The embarrassing publicity did nothing to improve Culp's relationship with Leonard. Their "Mexican standoff" had finally ended after Leonard visited Culp's dressing room and pleaded with him to cease the silent treatment. Culp agreed, feeling privately ashamed of how childishly he had behaved. But their interactions were still chilly, and the mood on the set remained tense. Culp continued to complain about any script that he hadn't written himself, and during the six weeks of shooting in Italy he and Cosby were constantly demanding rewrites and making up dialogue.

Leonard hadn't minded their improvising at first, but now he saw it as arrogant and self-indulgent. "What had started as harmless interjections became increasingly intrusive ad libs, often inconsistent with the story line," he recalled. "Eventually it reached a point where they were totally unacceptable." And once again, he blamed Culp. Leonard was convinced that the leading man had become jealous of Cosby and was trying to show that

he could be every bit as funny and spontaneous.

Yet some of the writers saw Cosby as the
greater culprit. A veteran script doctor named
Jerry Ludwig was particularly bitter. "Cosby
was the guy who was pissing on the scripts,"
he recalled. "He is gifted, I agree. But the
odds on someone standing there, on the hoof,
and coming up with something in the moment that is better than something that a
writer sat in a room for a month working on,
something that was reviewed by other writers, is unlikely. And sometimes they would
lose the point of what we were writing
about . . . They would encourage each other
to be bad guys — what I designate as being
bad guys."

Cosby had respect for at least one writer —
Michael Zagor — and he was pleased with
the Italian love story he produced for Scotty.
This time, Cosby got to play opposite Leslie
Uggams, the twenty-three-year-old singing
prodigy who was making her debut as a
dramatic actress. In "Tonia," Scotty falls in
love with the daughter of an American USO
performer who has been raised in Italy and is
being used as bait by the Communist Party
to entrap American spies. The director, Alf
Kjellin, encouraged Cosby not to hold back
in his scenes with Uggams. Resuming shooting after a lunch break one day, Kjellin called
out: "All right, now I want you to kiss her

hungrily!"

NBC would air "Tonia" right after New Year's Day of 1967, just as the Supreme Court was hearing arguments in *Loving v. Virginia,* the landmark case challenging state laws that banned whites and blacks from marrying. Against that backdrop, some viewers saw Scotty's love stories as conveying the message that the races should stick to their own kind. As one letter to NBC observed, "a romantic scene between White and White, and Negro and Negro, proved what most intelligent Civil Rights workers have been saying all along: 'Just because your sister goes to school with a Negro, doesn't mean he'd want to marry her (or vice-versa).' " Talking to the press, Cosby took pains to stress that his onscreen love life would not cross the color line. "As far as White women go, I want Scotty to be sterile," he told a reporter from *Newsweek.* "I believe in my women first."

Yet if a Negro actor "getting the girl" didn't spark the kind of protest NBC had feared, it wasn't just because of the changing mood of the country. It was also because of what viewers had come to think of the actor in question.

After watching "Tonia," a man from St. Petersburg, Florida, wrote a letter to Robert Sarnoff, the president of RCA, NBC's parent company. "Dear Sir:" the letter read. "I'm a White man, not that it's important, but —

I'm writing this in praise of Bill Cosby. I suppose you have other letters in his praise — but, if not, please read this one. Bill is a great guy — his acting and feeling on *I Spy* — Jan 4, 1967 — was great. I wish I could express myself better, but what I'm trying to say — Bill Cosby is a credit to all Americans. I know he's an actor, but such a kind, relaxed, wonderful guy — a great American. God bless him. I hope this helps all Negroes and Whites. This is a very modest letter — not proving a thing — but I would like you to show it to Bill."

13
BIGGER THAN *I* SPY

When *Ebony* magazine asked Bill and Camille Cosby to pose for the cover of its September 1966 issue, its readers found out several striking things about Cosby's twenty-two-year-old wife. One was how beautiful she was: smiling for the cover photo, she looked like a black Jackie Kennedy, as her husband beamed proudly behind her and sixteen-month old Erika sat on her lap, waving at the camera.

Another was what a devoted mother Camille had become. The magazine's photographer captured her taking Erika to visit the *I Spy* set, changing a diaper in a Las Vegas hotel room, and shopping for baby clothes with her mother-in-law Anna. Although the Cosbys had hired a cleaning lady, Camille said that they didn't want a nurse because she intended to raise the baby by herself.

The readers also learned what anyone who got to know Camille quickly discovered: while shy, she wasn't afraid to speak her mind. Camille admitted that her parents had initially opposed her marriage and that adjusting to Cosby's night owl schedule had been difficult at first. When they were newlyweds, he had tried to find people to keep her company while he was performing, but Camille had her own opinions about who was worth her time. "He used to introduce me to friends and say, 'Why don't you go out with so-and-so,' " she said. "But I just might not want to go out with so-and-so. Finally, I did meet people I liked and we would go out."

Camille described how much she enjoyed traveling with the *I Spy* cast and how happy she was that Cosby's shooting schedule in LA got him home in time for dinner. But she admitted that she was an introvert who found it hard to keep up with him on the weekends, when he liked to entertain friends at their house and go out on the town, sometimes hitting four or five clubs in one night.

She was candid about the various sides of her husband's personality. "He is a very considerate person," she said. "If he's going to be late, he always calls. He's very thoughtful; he remembers birthdays and anniversaries. He's a great father. He loves children, and he's always a very good family man to his mother and his brothers." But she also said that Cosby could be "temperamental" and "impulsive" and "moody" in private.

Did Camille ever think her husband would

be such a big star?

"I knew he would be as successful as he is," she replied, "but I really didn't think it would happen this fast."

And did Cosby try out his material on her?

"In the beginning he did," she said, "but when you're intimate with someone, it's hard to see them as funny."

What *Ebony* readers didn't learn from the story — unless they looked closely at the loose cut of the yellow dress that Camille wore in the photographs — was the real news in the Cosby family. Just weeks earlier, she had given birth to a second child, another girl named Erinn. The delivery came three weeks early, on July 23, and the baby's health was still fragile enough that the Cosbys didn't want to tempt fate by telling the world about the newborn. Yet in its own way, that undisclosed fact revealed another key to understanding Camille Cosby: the lengths she would go to protect her family's privacy.

For Cosby, meanwhile, the *Ebony* cover story was only the latest evidence that he was emerging as the breakout star of *I Spy*. Acknowledging that, Sheldon Leonard had given him equal billing in the opening credits, even though Bob Culp's contract stipulated that his name appear in larger type. (When Culp found out about it, he didn't object, although he saw it as one more sign of Leonard's favoritism toward Cos.)

Cosby had received a raise — to $2,000 an episode. His agents had wanted to push for more, but he refused. He didn't want to squeeze Leonard, because he knew how expensive *I Spy* was to make, and he was grateful that his mentor let him bring his family on the road and put them up in such style. He also saw that *I Spy* was increasing the value of everything else that he did, and that it was the sold-out concert arenas and the gold record albums that were making him rich.

For the Down Cat from North Philly, it felt good to be rich. It felt good to drive around LA in a Cadillac and a Rolls-Royce instead of a $75 used Dodge. It felt good to rent an eleven-room house in Benedict Canyon with a swimming pool and a sauna instead of living in an apartment in the projects or a row house in Germantown. It felt good to be able to afford the kind of threads he had fantasized about when he went "window-shopping" as a teenager, and to buy expensive furs and jewelry for Camille, so that she looked as fine as the finest Beverly Hills ladies when they went out on the town.

Most of all, it felt good to be able to put his younger brothers through school and to send his mother enough money so that she never had to work again. Instead, Cosby flew Anna Cosby out for long visits to Los Angeles, where she stayed at the house in Benedict Canyon and shared babysitting chores with Camille.

For Anna, the realization that the wayward boy she had raised in Philadelphia was now a big Hollywood star was still sinking in. "The only thing I had to give him was plenty of love, and oh, dear God, I gave him all I had," she told reporters. "But success comes from within, and Bill was determined to be something."

At times, Anna seemed disoriented by Cosby's fame, like the day he took her to the Desilu lot and introduced her to the star who worked next door.

"Mom, this is Andy Griffith," Cosby said.

"Oh my God!" Anna gasped — and she slapped Griffith's face.

"Andy, I'm sorry," Cosby apologized.

"I appreciate it," he said graciously.

Later, Cosby concluded that his mother must have "short-circuited" and forgotten where she was or that her son might know a white man as famous as Andy Griffith.

Yet as good as it felt to be rich, Cosby hated the idea that his friends would think that wealth had changed him, so he went out of his way to show that he was the same old Cos. On his lunch break on the Desilu lot, he hung out with the head writers for *The Dick Van Dyke Show,* Bill Persky and Sam Denoff, who had both had poor Jewish boyhoods in Brooklyn. They smoked cigars and played stickball with Spaldeens in the studio parking lot. When Cannonball and Nat Adderley, the jazz musician brothers, came to visit the *I Spy* set, Cosby sent out for a down-home soul food meal of barbecued ribs, ham, red rice and beans, cornbread, and sweet potato pie.

Although Cosby could easily afford season tickets now, he still took delight in sneaking into LA Rams football games under a hole in a fence at the Los Angeles Coliseum. He introduced the trick to his friend Anthony Quinn, and they used it to get into several games together, but Quinn never stopped worrying that they would get caught, even after they were on the fifty-yard line being greeted as famous celebrities.

"We're going to jail!" Quinn would complain. "They'll lock us up!"

"Tony, they're not going to take us to jail!" Cosby said.

"But Bill, I'm Mexican!" Quinn said.

"Aren't you part Irish?" Cosby said.

"Well, what good is that going to do me in Los Angeles?" Quinn said.

"The Irish part will get you *out* of jail!" Cosby joked.

"What about you?" Quinn said. "You're black!"

"Well, I'll just start yelling!" Cosby said.

Whenever he could, Cosby also made time for the inner-city school kids he had once dreamed of teaching. As part of a program called Operation Coolhead, he went to high schools in South Central LA and spoke to their predominantly black student bodies. He also liked to drop by USC and UCLA to work out with the track teams and kibbitz with undergrads. His friend Ron Crockett remembered one meeting in the fall of 1967, when a UCLA student asked Cosby about why he was doing *I Spy* rather than a more politically daring show like *The Smothers Brothers Comedy Hour.* He calmly puffed on his cigar and explained that he thought the best thing he could do for black people was to become successful enough that he could hire more of them.

Cosby also watched carefully for signs that his success might bother Bob Culp. Culp never displayed any resentment, but he did have moments of self-pity. Shortly after Cosby's Emmy win, they shot a scene where Kelly and Scotty are locked up together in a jail cell. The script called for Culp to pace around the room, but instead he kept lying on the bunk bed, staring at the ceiling.

Cosby kicked the bottom of the bed. "How can you just lie there?" he asked.

"Well, they wouldn't give me no award for pacing," Culp ad-libbed. "So I'm going for a new category. It's called Best Performance by a Leading Half-Wit While Lying on His Back in a Jail Cell, Looking at the Ceiling, Being Pitiful."

Luckily for Cosby, Culp was too wrapped up in his affair with France Nuyen to think about much else. In November, the *I Spy* crew traveled to Spain, and Nuyen came with them. Leonard had finally agreed to shoot the story that Culp had written for her in Mexico, "Magic Mirror," in which the character of Sam-Than MacLean returns as the mistress of a pro-Soviet strongman who is plotting to overthrow the Spanish government. Although Culp and Nuyen were both stricken with food poisoning when they arrived in Spain, they shot several steamy love scenes. But everybody on the set could see their romance was a stormy one. As they filmed a final scene in which Sam runs off with the general rather than staying with Kelly, Nuyen pointed to Culp and told the director: "Just keep that sonofabitch away from me!"

Cosby, meanwhile, had the time of his life in Spain. He had become renowned on the *I Spy* set for his appetite, and there were delicious Spanish meals to be had every night. Once again he had his family with him, including his mother and the new baby, Erinn, who was now healthy enough to travel. When they checked into their hotel room, the women took over all the closet space, and Cosby had to store his clothes with the wardrobe man. "It takes me two days to get a shower!" he joked.

Toward the end of 1966, Leonard took Cosby to film an episode of *I Spy* in Philadelphia. Called "Cops and Robbers," it was the story of a friend gone bad who kidnaps Scotty's mother and sister in hopes of trading them for secret microfilm that could be sold to the Russians. Jim Brown, the football star turned actor, was Scotty's treacherous friend. To portray Scotty's mother, Cosby suggested the stage actress Beah Richards, who later that year would star with Sidney Poitier in *Guess Who's Coming to Dinner?* After two years of working alongside Bob Culp and the many distinguished actors who guest-starred on *I Spy* — Boris Karloff, Carroll O'Connor, Gene Hackman, Jean Marsh, Michael J. Pollard, Sally Kellerman — Cosby had come to realize that the more he improvised, the more it helped to be paired with trained pros.

Returning to his hometown made Cosby realize how differently even old neighbors viewed him now that he was a star. One day he was visiting his mother in Germantown and ran into the father of a boyhood friend.

"Mr. Triplett, how are you?" Cosby called out.

"I'm fine, Mr. Cosby," the man replied.

"Mr. Triplett — it's Cosby!" he said.

By the beginning of 1967, Leonard was ready to begin shooting location footage for the third season of *I Spy*. He told his stars that they would be leaving for two months in Marrakesh and Greece in early April. So with a window of only a few months, Roy Silver booked Cosby into Harrah's in Lake Tahoe for a three-week engagement in March and arranged to record another album for Warner Bros.

After seven months as a father of two girls, Cosby returned to Harrah's with five very funny minutes about the difference between his daughters. He depicted his firstborn Erika as eager to please her parents and to let them sleep late. Then he described the baby Erinn: "Now the second one, Beelzebub, first, she come out of the shoot a month early, champagne in one hand and a cigarette in the other . . . 'All right, who's in charge here? You the ugly, what are you doing here?' . . . 'I'm your father' . . . 'Get rid of him, Momsy!' . . . 'What time have you been gettin' up in the morning?' . . . 'Oh, eight thirty' . . . 'Well, would you believe three thirty, for no particular reason. And this is the way I cry: WAAAA!'"

Cosby even turned his disappointment with still not having a male child into new material: "I asked my wife for sons. I looked at her and said, 'You will give me sons! Repeat after me!' . . . My wife tried to blame it on me: 'Well, you know, the male carries the determining factor, you see. He carries the Y and the X chromosome' . . . Yeah, bull! In my philosophy, it's the person's fault who last had it! I said: 'Camille, you were the last one with it. What happened?' "

Yet what everyone in the Harrah's audiences would remember most was an unforgettable new character in Cosby's comic world of childhood. He was introduced in a routine based on Cosby's memories of playing "buck, buck," the game where one team of kids lines up like a horse and members of the other team jump on their backs. Cosby slowly built up to the moment when it looked like his team would lose the "buck, buck championship of the world" and they had only one player left to put on the field.

"Come on out, Fat Albert!" he cried. "Fat Albert was the baddest buck, buck breaker in the world. Fat Albert weighed two thousand pounds . . . We put a little ramp down for him to walk on so he could build up steam, because he couldn't hardly walk fast, and he was coming — 'HEY, HEY, HEY!' . . . The ground was trembling . . . 'HEY, HEY, HEY!' . . . Trees falling over, buildings losing pieces of brick, parents taking their kids off the street . . . 'HEY, HEY, HEY! . . . The guys were saying, 'How come the ground's shaking?' . . . 'That's Fat Albert, coming for you' . . . 'HEY, HEY, HEY!' . . . And he turned the corner, and they saw one leg . . . 'Who's that?' . . . 'That's Fat Albert!' . . .

'HEY, HEY HEY!' . . . And they stood up: 'We give. He ain't falling on us!' "

Less than two months later, Warner Bros. would release *Revenge,* the second album recorded at Harrah's. (The title was based on another routine about Cosby's real-life experience of refrigerating a snowball to get back at Junior Barnes for spitting in his soda.) The record immediately shot to number two on the charts, joining Cosby's other four albums, which between them had now spent more than three hundred weeks in the *Billboard* Top 100. Six weeks later, *Revenge* was the top-selling album in America, and across the country teenagers were imitating Fat Albert's "HEY, HEY HEY!"

Meanwhile, Cosby's boyhood friends in Philadelphia were trying to figure out who Fat Albert was, since none of them remembered playing "buck, buck" with someone of his description. The guys who knew Shorty in the Richard Allen Homes could only recall a chubby Italian neighbor named Albert Vamachelli and another kid nicknamed "Fat Al" who lived to the east on Marshall Street. Johnny Baines, Cosby's best friend from his toddler days on Beechwood Street, suspected the inspiration was Albert Nichols, a local boy from Germantown who had been enormous even as a child and was now a 6'4" adult weighing close to four hundred pounds. Cosby never commented on the speculation for a good reason. Most of his characters were based on his childhood gang, including Shorty, which had been his own nickname. But now that they were also worth a lot of money, he didn't want anyone trying to claim a piece of the action. So he either created fanciful composites — like Fat Albert and Old Weird Harold, his make-believe best friend — or modeled his characters on people he knew he could trust, like his brother Russell.

Two weeks before *Revenge* was released, Cosby had received another piece of good news: he and Bob Culp had both been nominated for Emmys again. But neither of them had time to celebrate, since they were already in Greece with Sheldon Leonard, shooting a fake spy series in the middle of a real-life military coup.

Leonard's original plan for his sixth foreign trip was to film several episodes in Marrakesh, then to shoot a half dozen more in Athens and the Greek Isles. He had commissioned an eighteen-ton Greek cruise ship, the *Lena B,* to serve as a floating hotel and production center. But as the cast and crew were en route from North Africa, they learned that a junta of Greek generals had seized control of the government and called off scheduled elections. The country's airports were shut down and the *I Spy* plane had to land in Lisbon, Portugal.

For the next week, Leonard pleaded with Greek authorities to let him go ahead with his production plans. Losing $30,000 for every day he couldn't shoot, he argued that showing the splendors of Greece on American TV would be good PR for the new military regime. He said that it would help attract US tourists. But he got nowhere.

Finally, Leonard dispatched his location producer, a Greek American named Leon Chooluck, to sneak into the country with all the cash he could fit in his carry-on luggage. Days later, he looked out of his hotel window in Lisbon and saw the *Lena B* steaming into the harbor, carrying Chooluck and a new friend, a three-star Greek general, ready to take everyone to Athens and on to Mykonos, Delos, Crete, and Rhodes.

During the stay in Greece, Culp carried a clipboard wherever he went, writing in block letters on a legal pad with a mechanical pencil. He was putting the finishing touches on his latest script for *I Spy,* which he called "Home to Judgment." The story was based on Culp's grandfather, a "mountain man" who had walked west on foot as a young man and spent his life prospecting for gold. In the script, Kelly and Scotty are on the run from a team of assassins and take refuge in a farm owned by a tough old codger and his home-spun wife. Culp was pleased with the results, but the writing had kept him up all night for weeks.

Cosby was sitting next to him on a deck chair in the hot Mediterranean sun, taking a rest between scenes, when Culp finally wrote "THE END."

"I'm done," Culp said.

"Good for you," Cosby said. "What's next?"

"No, I mean I'm done with writing," Culp said.

"Come on, man," Cosby said. "You don't mean that."

"No, I mean it," Culp said. "I'm whipped. I don't have an idea left in me. I'm out. I'm toast."

Two and a half years of nonstop work on *I Spy* had taken a punishing toll on its leading man. Since the first trip to Hong Kong — between shooting more than fifty episodes, writing seven scripts, and directing "Court of the Lion" — Culp had had only twelve days of vacation. He knew because he kept track. At first, Cosby didn't think his partner was serious about the threat to stop writing. With his usual impishness, he tried to encourage Culp to keep at it. He left the clipboard on Culp's chair while they were shooting. He pointed the mechanical pencil at him and wiggled his eyebrows like Groucho Marx. But Culp didn't bite it. When he said he was done, he meant it.

Cosby and Culp were making their way

back from Europe when the Emmys were handed out in another joint LA–New York ceremony, and they asked Leonard to stand in for them. So it was their boss who accepted the award for Cosby when he won the Emmy for Outstanding Dramatic Actor for a second year in a row. This time, Cosby found it hard to be happy, because he felt so bad for Culp. "Bob and I are a team," he said when he got back to Los Angeles and had to face the press. "That's why I don't feel anyone should split us up and give an award to just one guy."

During a lunch break on the set soon afterward, Cosby came over to Culp and started to apologize.

"Don't!" Culp cut him off. "Don't you ever do that. This is for the show. This is for what we have done together. It couldn't be as important if it went any other way. It's got to be like this."

Cosby would feel even more embarrassed two months later when he went to see his friend Harry Belafonte perform at the Greek Theatre in Los Angeles. Calling Cosby on stage to take a bow, Belafonte made a crude joke at Culp's expense in front of thousands of people. "Two Emmys — don't be a greedy Negro!" Belafonte said. "Don't take it all away from Whitey!"

As if to prove that nothing could come between them, Cosby and Culp went out of their way to celebrate each other's birthdays that summer. On July 12, the day Cosby turned thirty, Culp surprised his pardner with a party on the Desilu lot. Dressed in pajamas for an *I Spy* scene, he was summoned to a soundstage next door where Culp was waiting with a collection of Cosby's Hollywood friends, including Lou Rawls, Martin Landau, Yaphet Kotto, Roman Polanski, and Sharon Tate. A month later, Cosby presented Culp with a special gift for his thirty-seventh birthday: a new Cadillac.

When Cosby gave Roy Silver a twenty-five-foot speedboat the next week, Army Archerd, the gossip columnist for *Daily Variety,* quipped: "Everybody's sending Cosby his birthdate." But Cosby figured he could afford to be generous. During his summer break from *I Spy,* he had gone on another standing-room-only concert tour across America. He was also launching a profitable sideline as a singer. Calling himself "Silver Throat," he was about to release an album for Warner Bros. covering soul classics like "I Got a Woman" and he was booked at the Whisky a Go Go for nine nights with the Watts 103rd Street Band.

While Cosby was making the most of his time off, Leonard was trying to figure out where to take *I Spy* next. He had visions of filming in China and the Soviet Union, but on a scouting trip to Moscow he discovered that his hotel room was bugged. When he returned to LA, a friend in Washington warned that he might not be able to get visas because the Johnson administration didn't want to look soft on communism. So at the last minute, Leonard decided to take the show to San Francisco. It would be the first time that a TV series filmed on location in the Bay Area, but even that shoot became a logistical nightmare. The Summer of Love had overtaken the city, and its streets were swarming with unruly "be-ins" and hallucinating hippies.

When the I Spy team came back to the Desilu lot, it was no longer the warm, welcoming place to which they had become accustomed. Lucille Ball had sold the facility to Paramount Pictures, which was now owned by the Gulf+Western conglomerate. There were accountants and efficiency experts crawling all over the place, questioning spending on everything from catering to office supplies. Leon Chooluck, the hero of the Greece shoot, returned to discover that his office had been taken away.

Relations between the stars and the writers of I Spy were more strained than ever. Culp's and Cosby's complaints were now a weekly ritual. As soon as new scripts were delivered to their homes on Sunday, they would phone each other with withering critiques. "What's this?" Cosby would ask. "It's the same lame plot as last week!"

On Mondays, Cosby and Culp would march into Fine and Friedkin's office and demand changes. The head writers would take notes but order few modifications. So Cosby and Culp kept rewriting and ad-libbing at will.

As Cosby and Culp saw it, they had nothing against writers, just bad writing. But they had created a vicious cycle: Because they were notorious for ignoring their lines, the best writers in Hollywood refused to work for *I Spy*. Or Leonard refused to pay top dollar for scripts he knew would be ignored. Now the show was attracting mostly second-string writers, making improvisation even more necessary.

Finally, Mort Fine and David Friedkin had had enough. They were tired of listening to whining from Culp and Cosby and watching material they had written or commissioned get tossed out the window. Three months into the third season, they informed Leonard that they wouldn't be back.

Fine and Friedkin may have seen other dark omens. For two years, *I Spy* had dominated the ten o'clock time slot on Wednesday nights. But when NBC announced its lineup for the 1967 fall season, it moved the series to ten o'clock on Mondays, opposite *The Big Valley* on ABC. NBC executives expected strong competition from that show, but not much from CBS's new offering, a variety show starring the comedienne Carol Burnett. But to everyone's surprise, Burnett was soon beating both dramas handily. *I Spy* was now fighting to stay in second place on Monday and to remain in the top fifty in the Nielsen ratings.

Leonard was also distracted by a new venture. After the first hit season of *I Spy*, NBC had offered him a new deal that allowed him to develop another series and guaranteed that the network would run it. That summer, while shooting in Italy, he had met a young Italian actor named Enzo Cerusico in whom he saw the kind of raw talent he had spotted in Bill Cosby. He began developing a series for Cerusico called *My Pal Tony*, in which the Italian would play a cop teamed up with the crusty veteran actor James Whitmore. But NBC wasn't crazy about the pilot and kept waffling about whether it would be on the 1968 schedule.

Finally, Leonard called the network's bluff. He demanded that NBC make good on his deal and air the new show. To make room for *My Pal Tony*, the network decided to sacrifice another program that was in its first season on Friday nights, a futuristic space drama that had attracted a young cult following but mystified executives at Rockefeller Plaza. But when word spread that *Star Trek* might be canceled, NBC was inundated with more than a million protest letters and confronted with picketers outside its offices in New York and Los Angeles. In a panic, the executives went back to Leonard and told him that they didn't have room for *My Pal Tony* after all. But this time, Leonard shocked them with his response. He told NBC to cancel *I Spy* instead.

For decades, Leonard would allow the world to believe that NBC had pulled the plug. But the reality was that he had reached the end of his patience. He knew the writing for the show had gone downhill, and he was weary of feuding with Bob Culp. He was also tired of all the effort required to scout and shoot in foreign cities. He loved Bill Cosby like a son, but he figured that his protégé was destined for bigger things anyway. With the storm clouds gathering overhead, he wasn't sure that he could navigate the show to a fifth season, which it would need to guarantee a lucrative deal for rerun rights and residuals. Syndication had always been the ultimate destination, but there was a real chance that he would go broke before he got there.

Cosby and Culp knew none of this in January 1968, when Culp's story "Home to Judgment" was televised. The part based on his grandfather was played by character actor Will Geer, who was just getting work again after more than a decade of being blacklisted for refusing to testify before the House Un-American Activities Committee. When they finished shooting, the costars agreed that "Home to Judgment" was the best episode of *I Spy* yet. Culp said he knew it because it embodied every lesson about writing and acting that he had learned in twenty years in the business. He said Cosby knew it because his instincts told him so, and Cos's instincts were rarely wrong.

Cosby would tell the two abolitionists who had changed his life very different things when he learned that *I Spy* would not be renewed in early March 1968. He phoned Sheldon Leonard and said he was disappointed. He felt good about the episodes in the works for season four, including more love stories for Scotty. He was proud of what his character had done for the image of the black man in America, and he worried about how quickly that effect might fade.

Yet to Bob Culp, Cosby admitted that he was ready for *I Spy* to end. Only they knew how much the last three years had taken out of them. They were both drained dry, so tired that they had even started to get on each other's nerves for the first time. Off the set, they were still tight — so much so that Culp asked Cosby to be his best man when he married France Nuyen. But at work they no longer ate lunch together every day, and they often skipped comparing notes before shooting a scene. They agreed that it was best to quit while they could still be proud of the show, and still "pards."

Exhausted, Bob Culp would take a break from acting before returning two years later in his first big movie role in *Bob and Carol and Ted and Alice,* the Paul Mazursky film about two couples who get carried away by the sexual revolution. But apart from that, Culp would never again achieve the kind of success and personal satisfaction that he had found working on *I Spy.* He would spend the next four decades much as he had the decade before meeting Leonard and Cosby, guest starring in TV dramas, making forgettable movies, and trying to develop new projects that never got off the ground.

Sheldon Leonard's career, too, would never be the same. He managed to pay off his $8 million debt to NBC when the show eventually did go into syndication. But the project that he had sacrificed the show for, *My Friend Tony,* was parked in the dead end time slot of Sunday night at ten o'clock and lasted half a season. He went on to produce a number of shows that he thought couldn't miss: *My World and Welcome to It,* inspired by the writing of James Thurber; *Shirley's World,* starring Shirley MacLaine; and *The Don Rickles Show.* All of them flopped. Word spread through Hollywood that Leonard had lost his touch, and after five years without a hit, no one would hire the former master of sitcoms to produce another TV show.

Yet for the rest of his life, Leonard had the satisfaction of knowing that he and Cosby had helped transform the racial landscape of American television. Four years after he had recruited the untested black comic and fought with NBC to make him the first black star of a TV drama, African Americans were everywhere in prime time. Many of them had guest-starred on *I Spy* before getting featured roles in other series: Ivan Dixon of *Hogan's Heroes;* Greg Morris of *Mission: Impossible;* and Nichelle Nichols of *Star Trek.* Soon there were Negro supporting actors on *N.Y.P.D., Ironside, Daktari,* and *Peyton Place.*

In the fall of 1968, two new series would debut featuring black actors (and close friends of Cosby) in leading roles. Clarence Williams III played Linc Hayes, the black crime fighter with the enormous Afro in *The Mod Squad.* And heartened by the reception that its viewers had given Scotty, NBC introduced another dignified, well-educated character who would help revise America's view of black people. This time she was a woman: a black nurse named Julia, played by Diahann Carroll.

With their "divine bullshit," Cosby and Culp had also revived and reinvented the "buddy genre." The press often called them a modern-day Bob Hope and Bing Crosby. For their part, they preferred comparisons to Stan Laurel and Oliver Hardy, and they often called each other Stan and Ollie. But after *I Spy* those partnerships seemed quaint. From then on, the buddy genre would be defined by hip, wisecracking banter, and, more often than not, by a white and a black partner.

But Bill Cosby wasn't looking back at the legacy of *I Spy* in March 1968. He was looking forward, over the vast entertainment kingdom that lay at his feet. In one realm, stand-up concerts, he embarked on a tour of twenty-four cities in January with his new musical sidekicks, the Pair Extraordinaire, and grossed between $35,000 and $45,000 at each stop. In February, they played an extended gig at the Frontier casino in Las Vegas that drew the biggest crowds that resort had seen since its opening.

In the second realm — television — Cosby was in negotiation with NBC for a new prime-time show and the network had just aired its first *Bill Cosby Special.* In the well-reviewed variety show, Cosby acted out his "Street Football" routine on the streets of Philadelphia, performed a "Fat Albert" dance, sang "Little Old Man" from his *Silver Throat* album, told stories about his daughters Erika and "Beelzebub," and confided to the studio audience how much he wanted to have a son one day.

In the third realm — record albums — Cosby was now one of top-selling artists of any kind in America. His five spoken comedy records and two song collections had sold more than six and a half million copies and accounted for more than half of all Warner Bros. album sales over the previous two years. And the label was about to release a seventh recording that would prove another huge hit, of a concert that included an electric performance of his longest and most memorable comic monologue yet.

The show had taken place on a Saturday night in Cleveland, the next to last stop on the monthlong tour. The Cleveland Public Auditorium was one of the largest venues Cosby had ever played, with more than ten thousand seats, and it was sold out. A boat show was taking place next door and parking was so tight that the eight o'clock show started a half hour late. After performing in twenty-two different cities in as many days, Cosby was exhausted. But when he walked onto the stage, taking his place on a wooden stool under a spotlight, he felt a surge of energy as he looked out at the huge crowd.

"This is a very, very beautiful place here, I must say," he began, gazing at the tiers of balcony seats that stretched back in a huge oval underneath a curved ceiling. "Is it all right, up top there? I'm talking to the one-dollar people up there!"

Cosby began with a long, funny description of the eating habits of his two daughters. Then he made his way through a bit about Adam and Eve and another one about playing basketball before he launched into the routine that he had been slowly building, night after night, for an entire month.

He set the scene: a bedroom in the projects where he and his younger brother Russell share the same bed. One night he accuses Russell of touching him on "my side of the bed." They make so much noise arguing that their father arrives to threaten them with "the belt." ("We had never seen the belt," Cosby said ominously, "but we had heard about it! The belt was nine feet long, eight feet wide, and it had hooks on it! It would rip the meat right off your body if it ever hit you!") When the boys jump on the bed until it breaks, their father pushes in the door and demands to know what is going on. ("Some man came in here and started jumping on the bed, Dad!" Cosby whimpered. "You should have seen him! He came in through the window, and he didn't have no shoes on, which is why you don't see no marks!") The boys get into a water fight, spraying each other with cheeks full of liquid from the bathroom sink, and their father punishes them by making them stand on the floor all night. ("I don't want you touching my side of the floor, neither!" Cosby hissed in the closing line.)

Stretching to more than twenty minutes, it was more than just a funny story. It was more like a brilliant one-man, one-act play, with Cosby acting out all three parts, manufacturing the sound effects of breaking beds and crashing doors and making the audience feel like it was in the bedroom with the two little boys and their exasperated father. When Warner Bros. executives heard the tape of the Cleveland concert, they knew they had a classic on their hands. Releasing it as an LP two months later, they turned over the entire B side to the bedroom routine and named the album after it. *To Russell, My Brother, Whom I Slept With* climbed quickly up the records charts and within a month was one of the top ten albums in the country.

As the spring of 1968 arrived, nothing could go wrong for Bill Cosby — or so it seemed. And in the back of his mind yet another idea was germinating. He had mused about it a year earlier to the reporter for *Ebony* magazine, as he held his daughter Erika in his arms and clownishly put her tiny wool cap on his head. "Someday I want to do a family situation comedy on television," Cosby said, predicting: "And it will be a hit because people want to see what goes on in a Negro home today."

1. Growing up in North Philadelphia, Cosby was a gifted athlete but a terrible student.

2. He flunked out of Central High and quit Germantown High despite captaining the football team.

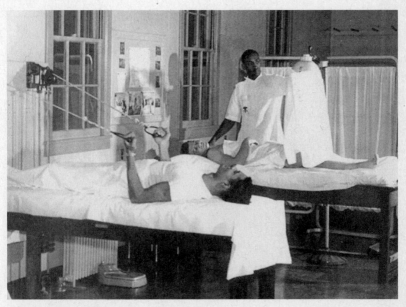

3. *He pulled himself together as a physical therapist in the navy and got into Temple University — barely — on a track scholarship.*

4. *While at Temple, Cosby began doing stand-up in Philadel-phia bars and clubs and went to Greenwich Village to perform at the Gaslight Café for a summer. 5. After he dropped out of col-lege, his first* Tonight Show *appearance led to a Warner Bros. Records contract that produced six top-selling comedy albums.*

6. Cosby's pairing with Robert Culp in I Spy, as secret agents traveling the world undercover as tennis players, made him the first black star of a TV drama. It also won him three straight Emmys.

7. *Martin Luther King Jr.'s assassination jolted Cosby and deepened his resolve to hire and support fellow blacks. But Cosby's plans were set back when manager Roy Silver (center) squandered his savings in a mismanaged production company.*

8. *Cosby was an early guest on* Sesame Street *and an original cast member of a spin-off for early readers,* The Electric Company, *along with Rita Moreno (front center) and Morgan Freeman (back right).*

9. Soon he launched his own educational Saturday morning cartoon show, Fat Albert and the Cosby Kids.

IT'S RICH, IT'S CREAMY, IT'S HERE!

10. In the seventies, Cosby costarred in three movies featuring predominantly black casts directed by his friend Sidney Poitier (above). 11. But with his TV and recording careers flagging, he supported his family performing stand-up in Las Vegas and around the country and building a new and increasingly lucrative sideline as an advertising pitchman.

12. *As he turned forty, Cosby collected a doctoral degree in education from the University of Massachusetts. 13. After the ceremony, he threw a garden party at his nearby estate and celebrated with his overjoyed mother, Anna (below), who had lamented her son's decision to drop out of college and once dreamed herself of becoming a teacher.*

14. Sitting for an Ebony *cover story with Camille and their five children in 1977, Cosby embraced his new identity as a middle-aged family man and turned it into comedy.*

15. *Seven years later, those routines became the basis for the Huxtables, the groundbreaking TV family of seven on* The Cosby Show.

16. *The* The Cosby Show *became known for Cliff Huxtable's quirky sweaters . . .*

17. . . . and its portrait of a stable, affectionate black marriage.

18. *But at the heart of* The Cosby Show *was the universally recognizable "loving war between parents and children," reflected in a family conference scene from the award-winning episode* Denise's Friend.

19. Cosby used the show to celebrate black culture, from the paintings on the wall to guest roles for musicians including jazz great Dizzy Gillespie.

20. *Stevie Wonder introduced future hip-hop innovators to "sampling."*

*21. Sammy Davis Jr. appeared in one of
his last roles.*

22. Alicia Keys appeared in one of her first.

Seeds were planted in the 1880s by the Rockefellers, and nurtured in the 1980s by the Cosbys.

Spelman College

23. By the late eighties, a record windfall from syndication had made Cosby America's highest-paid entertainer. He and Camille donated $20 million of their growing fortune to Spelman College, while quietly putting hundreds of African American students through college.

24. In the nineties, a remake of the game show You Bet Your Life flopped.

25. In a deal brokered by longtime William Morris agent Norman Brokaw, CBS offered the moon for Cosby.

26. The new sitcom reunited its star with Phylicia Rashad and paired him with legendary comedienne Madeline Kahn.

27. *After struggling with dyslexia, Ennis Cosby (above, in high school) was pursuing a doctorate in education when he was murdered in LA. 28. Below, his parents leaving New York on the day of Ennis's death.*

29. *Two months after Ennis' death, the Cosbys sought relief from their grief by traveling to South Africa to meet Nelson Mandela.*

30. *In 2004, Cosby sparked controversy with a fiery speech about responsibility in the black community, and then spread his message in a series of "callout" tours.*

31. Cosby's once estranged daughter Erinn (above center) —
along with daughters Ensa and Evin, wife Camille, and brother
Russell — cheered him on when he received the Mark Twain
Prize for American Humor in 2009. 32. Five years later, in his
midseventies, Cosby was still on the road performing more
than sixty concerts a year.

■ ■ ■ ■

PART TWO

■ ■ ■ ■

14
BLACK IS BEAUTIFUL

Cosby was at the University of Kansas on the evening of April 4, about to start the first of two shows at the Hoch Auditorium, when he heard the news. He immediately called Harry Belafonte, because he knew how close his friend was to Martin Luther King Jr. Belafonte confirmed what the bulletins on the TV set backstage were reporting: Dr. King had been shot at a motel in Memphis, and it looked bad, very bad.

Cosby started flipping through the channels, searching for new details. His mind raced with questions: *Who could have done it? And why?* But he didn't have much time to process what had happened, because he had to a show to do.

Most of the students and locals in the crowd didn't appear to have heard about King yet. They laughed as Cosby joked about the Kansas Jayhawks beating the Temple Owls and then eased into his Fat Albert routine. He felt mentally strong and focused enough on the task at hand to keep his thoughts from straying to Dr. King.

As soon as he got offstage, he called Belafonte again.

His friend was weeping. "Martin is dead," he said.

Cosby hung up the phone, stunned and not sure what to do next. His first instinct was to cancel the second show. But now feelings of depression and fear about what would happen next washed over him, and they made him recall the last time he had felt that way: when President Kennedy was assassinated. Cosby remembered watching TV in a daze over that long weekend, looking for anything to take his mind off the tragedy.

He could hear the hall outside filling with the audience for the second show. By now, most of them would have heard the news, too, and they would be just as down as he was. So he decided to try to lift their spirits for a couple of hours.

Yet as soon as he walked on stage again, all he could think about was Memphis. Words started spilling out of him: about how the world had lost a great leader; about how Dr. King had tried to sober up America from the drunkenness of racism; about the role that Kansas had played in the battle for school desegregation and as a stop on the Underground Railroad. He was struggling to find the right words and his tone and timing felt completely off.

After ten minutes, he couldn't go on.

"I came here to entertain," he told the crowd. "I entertained, but I can't forget. Now, it's getting to me. I've got to go be with myself alone. I humbly apologize for depressing you the last few minutes. Let's join hands together and keep cool."

As Cosby walked off the stage, the crowd stood to their feet, first clasping hands and then applauding. He thought to himself: *The ovation isn't for me. It's for Martin.*

As soon as he got back to his hotel room, Cosby called his agents and told them to cancel the five concerts he had left on his seven-city tour. He talked again with Belafonte, who was already helping Coretta Scott King prepare for the funeral the following Tuesday. On Monday, he was planning to accompany King's widow to Memphis, where she wanted to show support for the striking black sanitation workers who had brought her husband to the city and to the Lorraine Motel.

"I'll join you," Cosby said.

The next call he got was from Bob Culp.

"What are you going to do?" Culp asked.

"I'm going to Memphis to march with the garbage men," Cosby said.

"Not without me, you're not," Culp said.

Bad airplane connections delayed their arrival, and by the time they got to downtown

Memphis they were stuck at the end of a long line of protestors. As they approached the city square, they could hear Belafonte and Sidney Poitier giving speeches, but the crowd was too thick for them to get through. So they turned around and headed to Atlanta for King's funeral the following day.

The service was held at the Ebenezer Baptist Church, where King had first preached and where his father was the presiding minister. The sanctuary had enough space for about 70 VIPs in addition to the regular parishioners, and more than 425 were expected — including presidential candidates Robert Kennedy, Eugene McCarthy, Hubert Humphrey, Richard Nixon, and Nelson Rockefeller, top governors and members of Congress, as well as scores of the country's most famous entertainers. Belafonte and Poitier were close enough to the King family to get seats inside, but Cosby and Culp were part of a group that was driven by bus to a spot half a block from the church and told to wait to join the funeral procession as it made its way from the church to Morehouse College, where King had been an undergraduate.

Sitting at the back of the bus, Cosby gazed upon a Who's Who of black entertainers and athletes: Ray Charles, Aretha Franklin, Dizzy Gillespie, Lena Horne, Diahann Carroll, Ossie Davis and Ruby Dee, Cazzie Russell and other players from the New York Knicks. Aretha was sobbing; Culp sat glum and silent. Cosby kept telling funny stories to try to cheer everyone up. Seated next to him in the back, Stevie Wonder was at turns crying over Martin and chuckling at Cosby.

Finally, the funeral cortege turned the corner and came toward the bus in waves of mourners: first the pallbearers walking alongside the flag-draped casket pulled by mules, a symbol of King's support for the downtrodden; then Coretta Scott King in her veil clutching the hands of her four little children; then King's top civil rights lieutenants; then the politicians and other VIPs who had been allowed inside the church. The celebrities in Cosby's group got off the bus and took their place in the procession. More than two hundred thousand people thronged the three-mile route to Morehouse, and as the blazing sun and eighty-two-degree heat beat down on them, Cosby could see people fainting and hear voices calling for help.

He observed the mood of the crowd as it shifted from anger to grief to moments of levity back to anger again. At one point, word shot through the procession that the marchers were about to pass the offices of Lester Maddox, the segregationist governor who had refused to let King's body lie in state at Georgia's capitol.

"Did you hear what Maddox said about

Martin?" someone said.

"We should go up there and do to him what he'd like to do to us!" someone else said.

When the procession reached Morehouse, the Reverend Benjamin Mays, the former president of the college and a mentor of King's, gave the official eulogy and captured the mixture of grief and bitterness felt by every black person in the crowd.

"We all pray that the assassin will be apprehended and brought to justice," Mays said. "But make no mistake. The American people are in part responsible for Martin Luther King's death. The assassin heard enough condemnation of King and Negroes to feel that he had public support . . . It is time for the American people to repent and make democracy equally applicable to all Americans!"

Ever since he had burst onto the national scene five years earlier, Cosby had embodied the integrationist dream that King preached: a black comic in a Brooks Brothers blazer who could succeed without reference to his skin color, by making people of all races laugh at the things that they had in common, not the things that divided them. But King's murder would shake the faith of black Americans in that vision, and it would change the way Cosby looked at the world and at himself. He had always wanted to appeal to white audiences while making Negroes proud, but now his focus would shift more strongly toward that second, "black is beautiful" message.

When Cosby showed up for the Emmy Awards ceremony at the Palladium in Los Angeles on Sunday afternoon, May 20, he was no longer wearing the collegiate haircut and preppy glasses that had been his trademark since his days as a student moonlighting in Greenwich Village. Now he wore wire-rimmed glasses, a bushy Afro and a thick Fu Manchu mustache. And when he won his third straight Best Actor award for the last season of *I Spy,* he used the occasion to make the strongest political statement he ever had. Holding the golden statue aloft, he told the crowd: "Let the message be known to bigots and racists that they don't count!"

By this time, Cosby had made up the concerts he had canceled after King's assassination, grossing more than $100,000 for three nights work in Columbus, Ohio; Hartford, Connecticut; and Providence, Rhode Island. But he knew where he wanted to go next, and it wasn't to another 3,000-seat arena in Middle America. "When are you going to play the Apollo?" his friend Pete Long had been asking for years, ever since the one-time promoter for Billie Holiday and Miles Davis had gone to work for the legendary theater in Harlem. "Let people come see me at Madison Square Garden!" Cosby had replied cockily. But now, in the wake of King's murder, he knew it was time to make the pilgrimage to the mecca of black entertainment.

Cosby committed to a weeklong, two-shows-a-night engagement at the Apollo in June. He told the owners that he wanted to donate his fee to Betty Shabazz, the widow of Malcolm X, who had been struggling to raise six daughters since her husband was gunned down in the Audubon Ballroom. He assumed that he would be a big draw; two other big stars, Nancy Wilson and Dionne Warwick, had just played the Apollo, and they had people lining up for blocks down 125th Street.

But on Cosby's opening night, there were no long lines for his first show. After an hour of water-skiing videos and air force commercials that served as trailers, the hall was barely full. Backstage, as he changed from chinos and a leather jacket into a Carnaby Street tux, he overheard two stagehands who didn't know who he was.

"Is that him?" one asked.

"Yes, that the cat," the other answered.

"What's he going to do?"

"I dunno, maybe shoot some cats."

Walking onto the stage, Cosby noticed that a man in the front row was fast asleep.

The man in the next seat took off his hat and hit the dozer in the face.

"What the fuck you do that for?" the first man said.

"The motherfucker's here!" the second man said.

"Okay, but why the fuck did you have to hit me?" the first man said.

When the night was over, Cosby asked Pete Long why the crowd hadn't been larger. Long delivered a sobering analysis: many black folks in Harlem thought of Cosby as "the guy on the white TV show." They assumed that he was working for the Man, or, worse, that he might be a spy for the government, like one he played on television. So Cosby asked Long to put the word on the street that he was a brother who had grown up in the projects and gave his money to black causes and was friendly with Harry Belafonte and Malcolm X's widow. By the second night of his run, the Apollo was overflowing with blacks from the neighborhood and white fans who made their way uptown.

From Harlem, Cosby traveled to Washington, DC, for June 19 — otherwise known as "Juneteenth," the day that blacks celebrated the abolition of slavery. At the last minute, Coretta Scott King and her husband's successors had chosen the day to stage a march in support of the Poor People's Campaign, the push for economic justice that King had started before his death. The event was meant as a sequel to the March on Washington, and there were reminders of that day: the buses of protestors, the demonstrators holding hands in the Reflection Pool singing "We Shall Overcome." But this time the crowd was smaller, the event was less well organized, and the mood was as dark as the storm clouds that threatened overhead all day.

Cosby was one of a group of stars that entertained the protestors at the foot of the Washington Monument in the morning. He got a few laughs, but Ossie Davis captured the somber tone when he said: "We didn't come down here to sing and dance; we mean business!" And Eartha Kitt reflected the new theme of black pride as she sang the words of Oscar Brown Jr.'s "Brown Baby":

I want you to stand up tall and proud
And I want you to speak up clear and
    loud . . .

For the month of July, Cosby would spend much of his time helping Belafonte organize a benefit for the Southern Christian Leadership Conference, the civil rights organization that King had led, at the Hollywood Bowl in Los Angeles. He and Harry had been close before the assassination, as part of a foursome of friends that included Sidney Poitier and Sammy Davis Jr. (Cosby kept a picture of Poitier in his Beverly Hills office signed: "Me and you all the way because Sammy and

Harry have to get old someday.") But since King's death, Belafonte had been spending more time than ever with Cosby, partly because he was feuding with his old friend Poitier over an argument that the two obstinate West Indians had had on the eve of King's funeral.

The Hollywood Bowl benefit finally came together on July 17. Ralph Abernathy, King's successor as president of the SCLC, was there, and Belafonte had lined up Barbra Streisand and Herb Alpert and the Tijuana Brass to perform. Cosby warmed up the sold-out crowd of more than 17,000 people with the routine about sleeping with his brother Russell. After that, the plan was for Alpert to play a few numbers and then for the headliners to take over: Harry Belafonte followed by Barbra Streisand, each for fifty minutes.

But when Belafonte's turn came, he went on for an hour and a half, singing and recounting memories of Dr. King and their days on the front lines of the civil rights struggle. Backstage, Cosby could see Streisand getting more and more upset as she waited for her turn to go on stage.

"I'm not here!" Cosby joked to his road manager, Joe Gannon.

Earlier that month, Cosby had hosted an hour-long TV special on black history on CBS. Wearing a leather jacket and his new Afro, he opened the special in a classroom in suburban New York, talking to an integrated group of fourth graders about all the black inventors and pioneers whose names never showed up in the history books. He narrated a review of demeaning portrayals of blacks in movies and on television, from the sexual predators in *Birth of a Nation* to "happy darkies" like Stepin Fetchit and Bill "Bojangles" Robinson.

The special ended with a provocative look at a disciple of Malcolm X named John Churchville who ran a storefront preschool program in North Philadelphia. Churchville was drilling his young students in a gospel of militancy and black pride.

"When do you want your freedom, young man?" he asked a five-year-old named Michael.

"I want my freedom now!" Michael responded.

"How are you going to get you freedom?" Churchville asked.

"I will use any means necessary to get my freedom!" the five-year-old recited.

"Any means necessary?"

"Yes!"

Cosby appeared on screen again, looked out at the television audience, and offered a solemn commentary crafted with the help of CBS wordsmith Andy Rooney.

"That's kind of like brainwashing, or is it?" he said. "Can you blame us for overcompensating when you take the way black history has been lost, stolen, or strayed? When you think about kids drawing themselves without faces, and you remember the fine actors who had to play baboons to make a buck? I guess you've got to give us the sin of pride: Pride, *hubris* in the original Greek. There's three hundred years we've been in this American melting pot, and we haven't been able to melt in yet, and that's a long wait. Listen, we've been trying all kinds of parts to make the American scene. We've been trying to play it straight and white, but it's been bit parts. From now on, we're going to play it black and American, because we're proud of both. *Hubris!*"

When a *New York Times* reporter sat down with Cosby at the Old Tarrytown Road School to ask why he had agreed to host the black history special, his answers revealed how his priorities had shifted. "Nobody really wants to go around telling people that they're wrong," Cosby said, "But I have to do it, because my children, my wife, my people, are involved in whether America gets the message. For the past three years, *I Spy* has served two purposes. It's been good entertainment, and it has showed the races living and working together — and getting along. But there's a need for programs that go further. I just can't keep making the joyful noise."

While Cosby was honoring the memory of Dr. King, Roy Silver was driving a hard bargain. After months of tough negotiating, he thought he had finally won Cosby the new contract from Warner Bros. Records that he deserved. So he was stunned by a call he got in May 1968 from the label's president, Mike Maitland.

Silver had persuaded Maitland to pay Cosby a whopping $3.5 million to extend his contract with Warner Bros. for five more years. It was the biggest advance in the label's history, and as far as Silver was concerned, it had been earned. After all, Cosby had accounted for more than half of all Warner Bros. album sales over the previous two years and had brought in more than $30 million in revenue for the company.

But now Maitland was phoning to say that his bosses in New York had balked at the deal. They were the owners of Seven Arts, the small film production company that had shocked Hollywood by buying Jack Warner's entire film and recording empire two years earlier. Low-budget film guys, they were still getting used to the idea that the movie studio they had purchased was less valuable than the record business that came with it. They were too cheap to pay an artist that much money up front — no matter how impressive his track record.

Silver had a surprise for Maitland, too. Instead of doing what anyone who had known him in the past might have expected — keep haggling — he said that his client would walk. He would move to a new record label that Silver had just launched as part of a year-old production company that he was building with Bill Cosby's money.

When Cosby had moved to Los Angeles to star in *I Spy,* his manager had come with him. But Silver quickly discovered that the big shots in LA weren't club owners and managers; they were the deal makers who ran movie, TV, and record companies. So he set his sights on becoming a Hollywood mogul. And he found a willing partner in Cosby, who was looking for a way to shelter his growing earnings from "Sam," as he called the federal government, at a time when the IRS claimed 70 percent or more of all income over $200,000.

Taking $2 million of Cosby's money and using it as collateral to borrow $3.5 million, Silver and Cosby formed a production company called Campbell/Silver/Cosby. (Their third partner was a film producer named Bruce Campbell whom they brought in to get them into the movie business.) In just six months, Silver had embarked on an ambitious deal-making spree. He had signed a contract with the film division of "Warner 7" to produce five movies. He had launched the new record label, called Tetragrammaton, and hired his old friend Artie Mogull to run it. (A comedian on the new label named Murray Roman had suggested the odd title for the label, which referred to the four letters that spell God in Hebrew scripture.) And now that Warner Bros. created an opening to move Cosby to Tetragrammaton, the new production company — and Roy Silver — stood to be even bigger players in Hollywood.

For Cosby, meanwhile, the production venture promised another kind of clout: the power to put black people to work. Because the more he thought about it, the more convinced he was that creating jobs for brothers and sisters was the greatest personal contribution that he could make to the Black Power movement.

He had little taste for political activism. When Bobby Kennedy had entered the presidential race, he had added his name to a long list of Hollywood supporters in an ad that ran in the industry trades. But Kennedy's assassination in June, coming so soon after King's murder, had left him heartsick. Interviewed about the presidential contest by WGBH, the public television station in Boston, Cosby had dismissed Richard Nixon as a "pathological liar" and George Wallace, the third-party candidate, as a cynic who was "lying to white bigots" about how tough he would be on Negroes. In the fall campaign, Cosby had stumped briefly for Hubert Humphrey, but without much enthusiasm, and afterward he told reporters that he was swearing off politics.

Yet at least the WGBH interview had offered Cosby an opportunity to talk seriously about his political views. Dressed in another leather jacket and smoking a huge white pipe, he fielded questions from reporter Stewart Thomas for almost an hour without cracking a joke, and the station aired the entire discussion.

As for the rest of the media, Cosby was increasingly unhappy with the kind of coverage he was getting. Publications would send reporters to profile him, and he would talk to them about his views on race and society, and they would write stories in which he came off as little more than a talented jokester — or worse, an oblivious Uncle Tom. After King's assassination, Cosby had given a *Newsweek* reporter hours of his time, and the magazine had published a story headlined "Color-blind Comic" that made it sound like all he cared about was playing basketball and driving his Ferrari.

So on the anniversary of King's death, Cosby decided to let the public know what he thought about the racial strife convulsing America. He chose *Playboy* magazine to do it. He had become friendly with publisher Hugh Hefner, whose clubs he admired for their racial egalitarianism. He also thought the publication had smart articles and interviews amid all the pictures of naked women. Cosby invited a *Playboy* writer named Lawrence Linderman to join him on a concert tour of the Midwest and treated him to the most passionate discussion he had ever had with a member of the press.

He started by firing back at the rap that he was too color-blind. "White critics will write about Cosby not doing any racial material, because they think that now is the time for me to stand up and tell my audiences what color I am and what's going on in America," he said. "But I don't see these people knocking the black elevator man in their building just because he isn't doing anything for civil rights by running that elevator . . . The fact that I'm not trying to win converts on stage bothers some people, but I don't think an entertainer *can* win converts. I've never known any kind of white bigot to pay to see a black man, unless the black man was being hung. So I don't spend my hours worrying how to slip a social message into my act; I just go out and do my thing."

Asked about black militants Stokely Carmichael and Eldridge Cleaver, both of whom had rejected King's message of nonviolence, Cosby expressed sympathy for them. "I'm not in favor of raising guns, but I don't think Cleaver would be, either, if he thought there was another way to solve the racial situation in this country . . ." he said. "I can tell you that I don't believe in letting black people get pushed around when they're in the right. If a lot of black people no longer believe in nonviolence, it's because they've lost all faith and trust in the white man. Black people have lain in the streets, and they've let whites hit them in the head with everything from clubs to ketchup bottles. They let themselves be called niggers and have still somehow managed to walk tall and show that they still believe in nonviolence, that this philosophy makes them better than those who torment them. But they've taken all this abuse, and for what? How far has it really gotten them? Many intelligent and educated black people are tired, just plain tired, of being noble, of not striking back."

But Cosby warned that black violence would only play into the hands of white bigots who wanted an excuse to crack down on Negroes. He scoffed at the posturing of militants such as H. Rap Brown of the Black Panthers. "When Rap makes a speech and says we should get guns and use them on Whitey, it doesn't strike me as a cool move tactically," he said. "I, for one, would never let people know I was planning to shoot at them . . . This goes back to my street-corner days. Unless he's got another card to pull out, it's not the brightest cat in the world who stands around telling a guy, 'I'm going to get a gun and blow your head off.' "

In the end, Cosby told Linderman, blacks had to fight for their own empowerment — by pursuing education and seeking political and business clout. He cited Carl Stokes and Richard Hatcher, who had just been elected the first black mayors of Cleveland, Ohio, and Gary, Indiana, respectively. Instead of attacking white cops, Cosby argued for demanding black policemen in black neighborhoods. "Black cops may be hated as much or even more than white cops by a lot of people in the ghetto," he said, "but I still think it's advisable for at least two reasons: kids could grow up seeing black men in positions of authority, and ghetto streets wouldn't wind up in the charge of a scared white cat who thinks the answer to problems is to hit people in the head . . ."

Most of all, Cosby argued, black people needed good jobs that would give them self-respect and a stake in the system. And not the kind of "summer youth jobs" that had sprouted up in cities across the country since the riots that followed King's assassination. "White legislators think that as long as a kid's energy is spent and his time taken up, he'll be too tired to throw a bomb," he said scornfully. "But that's bullshit, because a kid's got more energy than a grown-up. And I know, man. I used to play basketball from nine in the morning until the sun came down!"

Welfare checks weren't the answer either, Cosby argued. "I'm in favor of a guaranteed *job;* no man, black or white, really wants to be given a paycheck or handed a loaf of bread or a book of stamps," he said. "Men want to work, and they want to be paid decent salaries."

For his part, Cosby said he intended to get rich enough that he could afford to quit show business and help black teenagers by becoming an inner-city schoolteacher. "I could no more sit on my ass and let that check come in than I could be paralyzed in a bed for the rest of my life," he said. "I've got to do something with my hands, my feet and my brain. To me, it won't make any difference if it's a job as a part-time schoolteacher, paying thirty dollars week — because I'll have that dividend check coming in every week. But I'll be working. Jobs are what the black man wants."

Cosby talked proudly about using his financial power to help his family and to assist other blacks in the entertainment business. "I feel I've really put together a hell of a one-man antipoverty program," he said. "I took my talent and I put it to work, and today, I've brought up, by the bootstraps, the economic conditions of a mother, a father, two brothers, aunts, uncles, grandfathers, and other family members, and then reached out to help close friends . . . The next step is to help out other black people. This doesn't simply mean giving them five hundred thousand dollars — although I give plenty. But to me, reaching out to black people means to open up my particular part of the industry. My production company will have black apprenticeship programs and will use black actors, directors, and stagehands. After they've demonstrated their talents, and people can dig them, they can then go on their own, which is why I tour with talented black performers like the Pair Extraordinaire and Leon Bibb. When they meet my audience, the people remember their names. So I don't feel guilty about having bread."

On April 9, around the time that Cosby was talking to the *Playboy* reporter, *The Second Bill Cosby Special* aired on NBC. Like the first variety hour a year earlier, it consisted mostly of staged versions of his stand-up routines, with Cosby acting out his "To My Brother, Russell" bit in a black box set and doing "Noah" in a shepherd's costume. But what many of the millions of white viewers may have missed was the powerful symbolism of the show's ending, when Cosby walked on stage and joined the Art Reynolds Singers in "Lift Every Voice and Sing," otherwise known in black America as "The Negro

National Anthem."

The black writer James Weldon Johnson had written the lyrics in 1900, on the anniversary of Abraham Lincoln's birth. Booker T. Washington, the head of the Tuskegee Institute, was visiting the segregated Florida high school that Johnson ran, and the poet wanted to honor him. Washington was just beginning the battle for which he would become known: to make blacks see that seeking their own educational and economic advancement was just as important as fighting the unjust white legal system. Now, seven decades later, Cosby found himself believing in those same priorities, and as he sang Johnson's words, he couldn't help hearing them as a call for self-improvement:

> . . . Sing a song full of faith that the dark
>   past has taught us,
> Sing a song full of hope that the present
>   has brought us,
> Facing the rising sun of our new day
>   begun,
> Let us march on till victory is won . . .

No, Cosby didn't feel guilty about having dough, because he was just living out Booker T. Washington's dream. He was setting an example of what black folks could accomplish with hard work and belief in themselves. With all the money he was making, he would soon be in a position to lift up others, too, by creating jobs in his industry and spreading the gospel of education.

What Cosby didn't know yet was that he had a lot more to worry about than feeling guilty about his money. Just weeks after *The Second Bill Cosby Special* aired and the May issue of *Playboy* hit the newsstands, he would learn that almost all of his hard-earned bread was gone.

15
BUST IN BEVERLY HILLS

"Call Roy," Cosby said to the twenty-four-year-old talent agent with the raspy Brooklyn accent who approached him for a job while he was performing at Mister Kelly's in August 1968.

It was all Jeff Wald needed to hear. A brash, down-on-his-luck New Yorker, Wald had moved to Chicago after washing out of the mailroom at William Morris in Manhattan and racking up hundreds of dollars in unpaid parking tickets. He brought along his wife, a struggling Australian pop singer named Helen Reddy, and her five-year-old daughter, and landed a job booking acts for Mister Kelly's. But Reddy's career was going nowhere in Chicago, and Wald couldn't get used to winter in the Windy City.

So when Cosby showed up at Mister Kelly's, Wald cornered him to see if there might be a job at his new production company in Los Angeles. Cosby told him to call Roy Silver, who was noncommittal. "If you're ever out here, get in touch," he said.

Wald took that as an invitation. The next day, he, Reddy, and her daughter got in their car and drove straight to the West Coast, and Wald went directly to the offices of Campbell/Silver/Cosby.

Wald had never seen anything like it. He had heard the stories about the LA lifestyle from people at talent agencies and advertising firms who were heading west in the late sixties, and the production company's olive-colored headquarters on North Canon Drive, with the Mercedes-Benzes and Cadillacs parked out back, seemed to epitomize everything that he had been told. When Wald rang the doorbell, a butler welcomed him into an opulent, wood-paneled lobby decorated with expensive antique furniture. There was food laid out in the reception area prepared by a full-time chef. Everywhere Wald turned, attractive young women in miniskirts and go-go boots buzzed about, answering phones, fetching papers, and offering guests drinks or, if requested, freshly rolled joints.

When Wald was ushered in to see Roy Silver, Cosby's manager looked down on him from behind an elevated mahogany desk, like a king addressing one of his subjects. Gone were the accountant's horned-rimmed glasses and dark suits that Silver had worn in his Greenwich Village days; now he sported stylish wire rims and a Zapata mustache and dressed in turtlenecks or open-necked neon-colored shirts. As he conducted business, he kept snapping his fingers to summon underlings and signal impatience that his bidding wasn't being done faster.

In a year since launching Campbell/Silver/Cosby, Silver had leased the two-story building in Beverly Hills and hired eighty employees to work on all the record, movie, and TV deals he had in the works. By the fall of 1968, he was bragging to the press that the company would soon be making $50 million a year. He also continued to take on new clients as a manager, including the oddball singing sensation Tiny Tim and a buxom aspiring actress named Carol Wayne, who spent a suspiciously large amount of time in Silver's office. But he didn't have much time to devote to management anymore, so after a brief job interview, he hired Jeff Wald to do that day-to-day work for him.

Wald's first big assignment was to look after Herbert Khaury, the curly-haired, beak-nosed singer known as Tiny Tim. After years of struggling as a novelty act in Greenwich Village, Khaury had gotten his big break with guest appearances on *Rowan and Martin's Laugh-In* and *The Tonight Show*. Now he was singing "Tiptoe Through the Tulips" to the tune of $5,000 a night at Caesars Palace and concert halls across the country. In person, Wald found Khaury extremely conceited and unpleasant, and he couldn't believe that he would prove a great long-term investment for Cosby's company. But for the moment he was happy to accompany Tiny Tim to London, where he performed to a sold-out crowd at the Royal Albert Hall.

Silver came on the trip to London, too, to promote Tiny Tim's concert but also to score the coup that he hoped would put his new record company, Tetragrammaton, on the map. The label had recently had its first commercial hit with a debut album from the British rock band Deep Purple. Emboldened by that success, Silver was now stalking much bigger prey: John Lennon.

The previous May, the Beatle had met the conceptual artist Yoko Ono at an art exhibit and taken her to his home studio to record several reels of experimental music. By dawn, they had made love and taken nude photographs of themselves. Lennon had turned that recording session into *Two Virgins,* its cover featuring a photo of the naked couple. But the band's American label, Capitol Records, was refusing to distribute it, so Silver went to Britain to buy the US rights for Tetragrammaton — without consulting Bill Cosby.

On the trip back to New York, Silver smuggled the nude images of Lennon and Ono past customs by hiding them amid the lingerie in his wife's luggage. To avoid charges of pornography, he chose a picture of the couple shot from the rear for the US cover and supplied record stores with brown paper bags to wrap the album. But that didn't deter the police. By January 1969, copies of *Two Virgins* were being confiscated across the country, including thirty thousand impounded in New Jersey alone.

The headlines further weakened already lackluster sales, and *Two Virgins* never made it past 124 on the *Billboard* charts. Yet Silver and Mogull kept snapping up one act after another. They signed the Turtles ("Happy Together") and sent them to play at Tricia Nixon's coming-out party at the White House, where the band members snorted cocaine in the Lincoln bedroom. They kept making bets on obscure American acts that they thought would be the next big thing, such as a San Fernando garage band called Quatrain and a psychedelic rock group called Summerhill.

Around the Campbell/Silver/Cosby headquarters, rumors swirled about the troubles in the film division as well. Its chief, Bruce Campbell, was an artistic soul who hung photographs from the ceiling of his office and passed out Cosby's money to his favorite *auteur* directors, including $300,000 to Orson Welles for unspecified projects. Yet there was little to show for it, and staffers compared

Campbell to an insecure student who didn't want to hand in any papers for fear of being graded.

The one film that the company did have in production had turned into a nightmare. *The Picasso Summer* was based on a Ray Bradbury short story about a burned-out San Francisco architect who flees to Spain to commune with Picasso. Silver had bought the film rights for $25,000 and lined up an impressive international cast of actors and filmmakers: Albert Finney and Yvette Mimieux to costar, Michel Legrand to compose the music, and an Oscar-winning French director named Serge Bourguignon to direct. But now Bradbury and the director were at each other's throats, and Picasso, who had originally agreed to make a cameo appearance, had pulled out, forcing the filmmakers to film furtively around the artist's Spanish estate.

Yet in spite of all the signs of trouble, Roy Silver continued to project finger-snapping confidence, and Bill Cosby was rarely to be seen. He was either on the road performing or working on the one Campbell film in which he was slated to star — a remake of the movie *Here Comes Mr. Jordan,* in which he was to play a black boxer who comes back to life as a millionaire.

When Cosby did show up at the office, it was usually to recruit players for an exhibition basketball team that he fielded to raise money for local high schools. Or he would drop by with Lew Alcindor, the star center for the champion UCLA basketball team, to play chess. But mostly his empty office served as a prop on the tour of the premises given by the miniskirted assistants, who showed visitors the leather barber chair, the dented twenty-gallon trashcan, and the framed copy of the Emancipation Proclamation that Cosby kept on display as a reminder of his roots.

The only time that Jeff Wald caught more than a fleeting glimpse of Cosby was when he was assigned to accompany him on a trip to New York. Cosby didn't say a word during the flight, so Wald assumed that he was another stuck-up star who couldn't be bothered to interact with low-level employees. But when they got to the Warwick Hotel in Manhattan, Cosby invited Wald to watch a Knicks game in his room. Cosby still didn't engage in small talk, but after the game he announced that he was going out to meet some friends and asked if Wald wanted to come along. As they arrived at the Hippopotamus nightclub, Wald was dumbfounded to discover that Cosby's friends were Harry Belafonte and Sidney Poitier.

"If you don't mind, I'm going back to the hotel," Wald said, feeling self-conscious about his slovenly dress and Brooklyn accent. "I feel like the guy wearing brown shoes at a black-tie event!"

Observing Cosby during the rest of the trip, Wald couldn't get over how different he was from other celebrities he had met. Cosby wasn't needy for attention like Richard Pryor. Pryor had been performing at Mister Kelly's on the night of Martin Luther King's assassination, and he had insisted that Wald drive him around the burning streets of Chicago as he wept and got high on marijuana. Nor did Cosby display any of the arrogance that had already infected a star as minor as Tiny Tim. The next day, when they flew to Buffalo and rented a car, Cosby didn't complain when an Avis attendant asked for his autograph and then demanded two pieces of identification. Yet as affable as he could be, Wald thought, Cosby had an air of self-containment that said: *Don't fuck with me!*

As the winter of 1969 dragged on, Wald and other staffers at CSC finally saw signs that Cosby was starting to pay attention to what was going on behind the doors of their posh headquarters. One day in February, they learned that twenty-nine staffers had been fired, mostly secretaries, marketers, and accountants hired by Silver. Then they heard about what had happened when Bruce Campbell screened a rough cut of *The Picasso Summer* for his two business partners. When the lights came up, the writer, Ray

Bradbury, turned to the French director, Serge Bourguignon, and shouted: "Fire that man!"

Then Cosby stood up and addressed the entire room in a disgusted voice.

"I don't need you people to waste my money," he said. "I can waste it myself!"

"Bill and I are building something big here!" Roy Silver boasted as he looked down from his lofty desk at Ron DeBlasio, a young trainee in the television department of William Morris. William Morris had just given out Christmas bonuses for 1968, and DeBlasio wasn't happy with his reward, so he had come to Silver's office to see if there was a job at Campbell/Silver/Cosby.

By the end of the interview, Silver had hired DeBlasio to join his management team, alongside Jeff Wald. And within weeks, DeBlasio was on the road with Bill Cosby, who was embarking on a thirty-five-day tour of college auditoriums, concert halls, and sports arenas across the United States and Canada. Recognizing a fellow street-smart city kid in the young New Yorker, Cosby took the young manager under his wing, and DeBlasio learned several telling things about his new boss.

The first was how Cosby "wrote" his material on his feet — by building new bits night after night, loading the boat until it was full.

During this tour, he was developing a routine about why people shouldn't take God's name in vain. He began with a few lines about how God was too busy dealing with all the crises in the world — from the Vietnam War to the race riots — to have time to answer selfish individual prayers. The next night, he added a few more lines about how instead of asking for God's help, people should call on Cosby's friend Rudy, because Rudy had all the time in the world. Next, he conjured the voice of a man praying to Rudy at the craps table: "Oh, Rudy, please make me that hard eight!" Within a few weeks, he had a solid ten minutes on God and Rudy.

Another discovery came when Cosby performed in Philadelphia. Instead of putting himself up in a hotel, he stayed with his mother in Germantown, and he invited De-Blasio to join them. The young manager was flattered by the invitation and charmed to discover how sweet and welcoming Anna Cosby was. But he couldn't get over the tiny dimensions of the house, which felt like a cramped furniture storeroom. And he was alarmed to see the number of people who showed up at the doorstep to hit Cosby up for cash or try to sweet-talk him into sketchy business ventures.

"Scratch Philly, man!" Cosby said as they left the city, betraying how hurt he felt that so many of his childhood friends now had their hands out for money.

The most revealing thing DeBlasio learned during the monthlong concert tour was how much Cosby had come to distrust Roy Silver. He was now demanding that Silver send him all of the company's contracts before they were signed, and he started asking DeBlasio to review them.

"What do you think of this?" he would ask. "Do you think it's necessary?"

At other times, Cosby revealed how concerned Camille was about the company. "She keeps asking me: what are we doing here?" he said. Or he complained that Silver was out of his depth. "Ronny, Roy is just a PR guy," he said. "That's all he ever was."

DeBlasio realized how strained the relationship was getting one day when he brought Cosby five contracts and he approved only one. Then he heard that Cosby was moving his office from the CSC headquarters to the Warner Bros. TV lot, where he was working on a new sitcom.

What DeBlasio didn't know was that Cosby had asked his agent at William Morris, Norman Brokaw, to launch an investigation into what was going on inside the offices on North Canon Drive. Brokaw was the head of William Morris's TV division, the man who had brought Sheldon Leonard and Danny Thomas together and who had started to represent Cosby when he moved to LA to star in *I Spy.* He was also part of William Morris royalty: his uncle, Johnny Hyde, had built the agency's West Coast business with his partner, Abe Lastfogel. Brokaw had started in the mailroom at fifteen years old and worked his way up through the radio department to TV. He was a slight, dapper man whose courtly manner belied a shrewd head for business. And like the other abolitionists, he had become particularly fond and protective of Cosby, who teasingly referred to Brokaw as "the Coach."

Reviewing the Campbell/Silver/Cosby books, Brokaw became increasingly alarmed. Not only had Silver spent the entire $2 million that Cosby had originally invested in the venture; he was siphoning off more money from other accounts and plowing all of his client's new earnings into the production company. The money wasn't just financing the dozens of record and film projects Silver had launched; it was also fueling his own lavish lifestyle — his first-class travel and meals, the opulent parties he threw at the Beverly Hills office, and the copious quantities of marijuana and cocaine that Silver was consuming and passing around wherever he went.

"Bill, there's been some pilfering going on," Brokaw told Cosby when he presented him with the results of his inquiry. "You only have fifty thousand dollars left in the bank."

"Fifty thousand dollars?" Cosby asked, making sure that he had heard right.

"Fifty thousand dollars," Brokaw repeated gravely.

Ever since Cosby had started making big money, he had always known that he wasn't as rich as everyone assumed. The previous year, he had earned what sounded like a fortune at the time — $2 million. But from that sum, he had to pay Silver's management fee, a 10 percent commission to William Morris, his accountant bills, and the tab for the acts that appeared with him on the road, such as the Pair Extraordinaire. Federal and state taxes also took a huge bite, big enough that in 1967 Cosby had to take out a temporary loan to pay the $833,000 bill he owed to "Sam."

Other money went to keeping up the appearances of a Hollywood star. There was the $500,000 brick mansion in Beverly Hills (designed by a black architect, Paul Williams) that his friends called "the Cosby Hilton," with its thirty-one rooms, pool and cabana, and staff of servants. There were the expensive imported cigars, along with the dozens of gold- and silver-plated ashtrays and humidors that he kept in a room that Camille called "Cosby's Dunhill." There were the three or four luxury cars that Cosby owned at any given time. (At that moment he had a Ferrari, a Cadillac, a 1934 Aston Martin, and an Excalibur roadster that he had bought for his wife; he had sold his Rolls-Royce back to Bill Harrah because he felt self-conscious driving it around Los Angeles.)

Now he faced the prospect that he could end up broke, and he couldn't think of anything that would be more humiliating. He would have to face his mother, who had wanted him to stay in school and get his college degree rather than dropping out and trying to make it as an entertainer. Camille would have to face her parents, who had always had their doubts about their up-from-the-streets son-in-law. He and his mother and brothers would have to face everyone back in Germantown and the Richard Allen Homes, who would read the headlines about Shorty Cosby going bust.

So when Brokaw urged Cosby to fire Roy Silver and sever all ties with Campbell/Silver/Cosby, he knew he didn't have a choice. But he did it more in sorrow than in anger. Cosby was a loyal man by nature, and part of him still felt grateful to Silver. After all, Silver had believed in him from the start, back when he was a college kid practicing at being a comedian in a Greenwich Village cellar. He had encouraged Cosby to find his own voice and helped build the recording and concert career that was the cornerstone of his success. If Roy hadn't had such grandiose visions of being a Hollywood big shot, Cosby thought, if he hadn't alienated so many people, if he had been content to stick to what he was good at — being the "PR guy" — he could have continued to get rich on Cosby's commissions, and Cosby would still have the fat nest egg that he had hoped to amass by his midthirties.

In spite of everything that had happened, Cosby wanted to be fair to Silver — and to give him an incentive to keep his mouth shut. He told Brokaw to let the manager keep a cut of all the record albums they had made together and related projects still in the works. The only exception, he specified, was anything having to do with Fat Albert, around whom he was planning TV specials and a chain of fast-food restaurants.

Cosby also told Brokaw that he wanted to make sure that Ron DeBlasio and Jeff Wald landed on their feet.

Not long afterward, Brokaw phoned the two young managers. "I want you guys to come down here," he said, summoning them to the William Morris headquarters.

When they got there, Brokaw shut his office door. "You both have William Morris blood in your veins," he said. "We know the right way and the wrong way to do business, and Roy Silver is doing the wrong thing. We're going to get rid of him. And if you guys want to have careers in this industry, you should leave now. Don't go down with the ship."

Then Brokaw handed the young managers an envelope containing $30,000. "That's a loan to help you start your own company," he said.

DeBlasio and Wald didn't know whether to feel grateful or petrified. They didn't know the first thing about running their own business. But they both had mouths to feed, and neither of them wanted to make an enemy of Norman Brokaw or Bill Cosby.

The next day, they went into Roy Silver's office to tell him that they were quitting to form their own company.

"Who the fuck do you think you are?" Silver scoffed. "None of the acts will follow you!"

(In fact, they did: within months, DeBlasio and Wald lured away Tiny Tim, Deep Purple, and the Turtles. Soon they scored a big success on their own when they convinced the comedian George Carlin to shed his preppy attire and start dressing like the "hippy dippy weather man" he made fun of in his act.)

As the crisis unfolded, Cosby remembered his Granddad Samuel's advice: "If you put yourself in a compromised position, you're going to have to learn to act not embarrassed." So on Saturday, May 11, he was in New York City, hosting a benefit at the Waldorf-Astoria hotel and offering no hint that he was about to divorce his business partners.

The event was to raise money for the Free Southern Theater, an organization that staged plays in barns and cornfields in black communities across the rural south. Among the eight hundred attendees was an integrated cross-section of Hollywood royalty, including Sidney Poitier, Harry Belafonte, Lena Horne, Duke Ellington, and Muhammad Ali and white movie stars Jack Lemmon, Gregory Peck, Ava Gardner and Lauren Bacall. For the first time in its history, the Waldorf kitchen was attempting to cook soul food, and its waiters were serving the meal family style, at long tables set with picnic cloths.

Cosby wasn't impressed with the Waldorf's version of fried chicken, black-eyed peas, and collard greens, and he feasted on the fare for laughs. "That's not soul food!" he shouted as he came on stage, as the crowd roared in agreement. "Even though you have a grease ring around your mouths, that's not how soul food tastes. We should have had pizza!"

Two days later, *le tout Hollywood* picked up the Monday edition of *Variety* to see a banner front-page headline: "Cosby, Silver, Campbell Split." The trade reported that Cosby was leaving the production company and terminating his deal with Tetragrammaton Records. Roy Silver tried to make it sound like the government had forced the breakup. He told reporters that the Securities and Exchange Commission had declared it a conflict of interest for him to run the company and still manage Cosby's career. Cosby's spokespeople kept the details vague,' saying only that he was leaving Campbell/Silver/Cosby but might participate in future projects.

Cosby was more blunt when he spoke to *Variety*. "I no longer have anything to do with them," he said about his former business partners. "That's it, simply."

Without Cosby's money and name behind it, Silver's grandiose bid to become a Hollywood mogul imploded. By December, when another production company named Filmways looked at purchasing the company, it was reported to be $1.3 million in the red and losing as much as $2,000 a week. That deal never happened, and Tetragrammaton filed for bankruptcy a year later. Meanwhile, Warner Brothers shelved the release of *The Picasso Summer* and later sold it to television. And the only Bruce Campbell film to survive from his original five-picture deal was *Johnny Got His Gun,* a dark antiwar movie directed by once blacklisted screenwriter Dalton Trumbo, which won critical acclaim but was never a commercial hit.

Fortunately for Cosby, he was still a hot enough commodity that it didn't take long to start replenishing his bank account. By the end of May, he had signed a seven-year deal with MCA Records for more comedy albums. (The only album he had released on the Tetragrammaton label, a hastily assembled recording of two live shows at Harrah's called *8:15 12:15,* sank without a trace, the first flop he had experienced since his record career started.) His concert bookings were still strong, and he was able to take control of the new half-hour situation comedy that he was developing for NBC.

But Cosby walked away from the crash of Roy Silver's production company bruised, embarrassed, and more wary than ever. From then on, he would stick to the business of Bill Cosby — projects that he conceived and that he controlled. He would form his own production company called Jemmin, Inc. (named for the way his Granddad Samuel pronounced the word *gentleman*), and he would staff it with loyal long-time associates. After Silver, he would never hire another manager; from then on "the Coach," Norman Brokaw, would oversee every aspect of his career.

Cosby would also turn over supervision of all his professional and personal finances to the one person he knew he could trust: Camille Cosby, who had studied accounting as well as psychology at the University of Maryland. For the rest of his career, Cosby

387

would insist that all checks relating to any aspect of his business be personally signed either by him or by his wife. As credit cards became a universal method of payment, he refused to use them, saying that he didn't see why he should pay fees or interest or entrust strangers with his financial information. Instead, he carried rolls of hundred-dollar bills, or he left his cash at home, and let business associates pick up his restaurant and travel expenses.

Shortly after the collapse of Campbell/Silver/Cosby, Cosby ran into Don Council, his buddy from Temple University. "I was a fool," he confided. "Bill Cosby makes the money; Bill Cosby should count the money. Camille can count, too, so she's going to handle the bread!"

Although few outside of Cosby's inner circle knew about the increasingly strong hand that his wife was taking in his professional career, Jeff Wald would get a hint of it several months after leaving Campbell/Silver/Cosby. He was at a charity event when out of the blue Camille Cosby, whom he had never met, came over to speak to him.

"You did the right thing," she said quietly. "Bill doesn't forget."

Yet for all the turmoil in his professional life, Bill Cosby would remember the spring of 1969 as a season of personal joy. For it was on April 15 of that year that he was granted the wish he had been making for five years, since his wedding night, the one that he had shared with millions of fans who bought his albums, attended his concerts, and watched his prime-time TV specials. Camille finally gave him a son.

His name was Ennis William Cosby. His parents chose another first name beginning in E for "excellence," like his sisters Erika and Erinn, and the middle name William in honor of his father, in the family tradition. And this time, when his mother and father allowed *Ebony* magazine to photograph them for another cover story, they did nothing to hide their latest newborn. They proudly posed for a family portrait with their three adorable children in the courtyard of their Beverly Hills mansion. For the cover shot, Cosby held Ennis in his arms, talking to his two-month-old boy as though he were already a little man.

16
MORE SITUATION THAN COMEDY

Quincy Jones was in the booth of his recording studio, listening to the jazz orchestra he had assembled to create music for *The Bill Cosby Show*. Sitting in the room outside were some of the best jazz artists to be found in Los Angeles in the summer of 1969, the top cats playing at Shelly's Manne-Hole or the Lighthouse Cafe in Hermosa Beach. As soon as they arrived in town, Jones would invite them to jam for Cosby's new show, and they would show up — even at eight-thirty in the morning, after playing all-night gigs — stars including Oscar Peterson, Milt Jackson, and Cannonball Adderley. But as Jones monitored this morning's session through his earphones, something sounded off. A frenetic honking noise came through his "cans," like the bleating of a wounded animal.

Jones looked out into the studio and there, sitting at the back of the orchestra, was Bill Cosby, trying to play a bassoon.

For an amateur, Jones thought, Cosby had

a genuine gift for music. He couldn't read a score, but he was a natural conductor: he could stand in front of a group of professional musicians and get a good sound by using facial expressions and body language. But a bassoon, a double reed instrument — please! He wasn't ready for that.

"Hey, Bunions, what's that?" Quincy asked Cosby, using the private nickname they had for one another.

"Coltrane!" Cosby said.

Jones told him to surrender the bassoon and handed him a cowbell.

"Try this," Jones said.

"Okay, Bunions," Cosby said.

"Q," as his friends called him, was one of the most sought-after composers in Hollywood, the creator of memorable soundtracks for such hit movies as *The Pawnbroker* and *In Cold Blood.* Now he was experimenting with something different for *The Bill Cosby Show:* improvising a new score for each episode. Once his pick-up orchestra of all-star musicians had gathered, Jones handed them a hastily scribbled theme and called them to take unrehearsed solos.

When Cosby's turn came, he hit the cowbell and shouted out a stream of nonsense words. Or they sounded like nonsense words; in fact, they drew on childhood memories of the way Granddad Samuel talked, in the dense patois of the black rural South.

"Aw, Lawd!" he cried out. "I'm gonnna get me some raggetts and some rolls and some greasimessin', he he, he! Every day! Long as I'm away!"

Cosby scatted a few more lines and then a two-word coda popped into his head.

"Hickey Burrrrr!" he sang, blubbering his lips. "Hickey Burrrr!"

Quincy Jones loved the spontaneous riff, so he and Cosby decided to use it as the theme song for the new show. Never mind that it had nothing to do with the sitcom's premise or characters, like every other theme on television. Cosby was the boss, the executive producer of the *The Bill Cosby Show,* and for the moment that was all that mattered.

As the fall of 1969 approached, NBC executives were counting on Bill Cosby's debut in a comedy series to be one of the big hits of the new TV season. They awarded him one of the week's most coveted time slots: eight thirty on Sunday nights, sandwiched between *The Wonderful World of Disney* and *Bonanza.* Even without a pilot, focus group research indicated that Cosby was so well known and well liked that his show would beat both of its competitors, *The Ed Sullivan Show* on CBS and *The FBI* on ABC. Banking on a huge audience, Procter & Gamble signed up as the exclusive sponsor for the entire first season, at a cost of $125,000 per episode.

For the June "press tour" that NBC hosted to introduce its new TV lineup, the network trotted out Cosby to emcee a huge party on the Twentieth Century-Fox lot. It was a gorgeous evening without a cloud in the sky, and he was in rare form, charming the crowd and putting them in stitches with his standup material. Sitting in the audience, the West Coast programming chief, Herb Schlosser, leaned over to Mort Werner, the visiting New York–based head of all NBC programs, and congratulated him on what a big star they had on their roster.

"This guy is Bob Hope, only black!" Schlosser said.

Yet what Cosby was busy cooking up on the Warner Bros. lot in the spring and summer of 1969 wasn't the kind of time-tested sitcom recipe that the network executives and advertisers expected. Instead, he was stubbornly dispensing with all of the usual ingredients: the formulaic gag lines, the goofy sidekicks, and the laugh track that was now *de rigueur* on every TV comedy of the day. In fact, what he was confecting wasn't a conventional sitcom at all. It was a lot more situation than comedy.

At first, when Roy Silver was involved, Cosby had agreed to a fairly conventional premise for his new series. His character would be a married detective in San Francisco who fought crime by day and struggled to raise two kids by night. But Cosby was determined to film on location, like his mentor Sheldon Leonard, and as the financial woes of his production company mounted, he agreed to change the setting to Los Angeles. Then he decided that he wanted to play a high school gym teacher, like the kind he had planned to be before he left Temple University. In a compromise, he agreed that his character would be a gym instructor who moonlighted as a detective.

But once he broke with Silver, Cosby concluded that the detective angle was "a bunch of crap," as he put it to a TV reporter named Tom Mackin who interviewed him as he was shooting the first season. In the end, he settled on a show about a gym instructor named Chet Kincaid who would have everyday adventures and mishaps with which everyone could identify. "Sure, this is a comedy show, but it's a show with reality," he explained to Mackin as he waved his panatela and plucked bits of brown leaf from his tongue. "It's going to be honest all the way."

Since forming Jemmin, Inc., Cosby had tightened the inner circle around the show to a handpicked creative team that shared his disdain for television clichés. Ed Weinberger, his friend from Central High School, was the head writer and co-executive producer, along with Michael Zagor, the only writer for *I Spy* that Cosby respected apart from Bob Culp.

394

The producer was Marvin Miller, an associate producer on *The Picasso Summer* who had earned Cosby's trust when he learned that Miller had grown up in North Philly and attended Benjamin Franklin High School.

Together, the Philadelphians were drawing inspiration from their boyhood memories and their love of classic films. They sprinkled the show with references to their hometown: the high school where Chet Kincaid teaches would be named Richard Allen Holmes, after the housing project where Cosby lived as a boy. They envisioned each episode as a little movie with its own style and cinematic allusions and allegoric messages, usually disconnected for anything that preceded or followed it. They also prided themselves on shooting like a movie crew — often on location and very quickly, fast enough to film most episodes in two and a half days.

Months before it aired, Cosby and his collaborators were speculating about all the people their show would confound. To Macklin, he predicted that his quirky take on a gym instructor's life would upset some teachers. "Oh, we'll get letters," he said. "I'll tell them that Chet Kincaid, my character, is not a perfect human being. He makes mistakes. Some of his methods in the classroom are unusual. He's not too bright sometimes." Marvin Miller was bracing for all the people who would say that Cosby's character wasn't black enough. "There will be no racial overtones or messages, and we may expect protests from the militants," he told *Variety* columnist Jack Hellman.

In fact, Cosby did have racial messages he wanted to convey with his new show, but they were subtle. On the one hand, he wanted to show how much black people were like everyone else, just focused on making it through the day. Chet Kincaid would be a regular guy trying to get from point A to point B when some unexpected encounter or misunderstanding veers him off course — a ringing phone in a public booth that he can't resist answering, for instance, or a brother who shows up to stay with him after he's had a fight with his wife.

Yet while making Chet Kincaid an amiable Everyman, Cosby wanted him to be unmistakably black. Not only would he be allowed to have a love life; he would be a ladies man, romancing a series of beautiful black women. His apartment would be decorated with African American art and photos of black musicians and athletes. His family members would be played with earthy authenticity by black stage actors who Cosby personally recruited: Lillian Randolph as Chet's home-remedy-peddling mother; and Lee Weaver, his old friend from Greenwich Village, as the brother, a garbage man named Brian. (In the episode where Brian leaves his wife, he and

Chet fight over sharing a bed, an inside-joke reference to Cosby's "To Russell" routine.)

When Chet did have an experience with racial overtones, Cosby's goal was to show that a black man doesn't always have to be angry. Looking back at the show, he recalled that one of its messages was: "I want the same thing you do. I don't want an *angry* hamburger. When I get on the bus, I want a seat; I don't want an *angry* seat."

For the pilot episode, Cosby chose a story in which Chet runs afoul of the police. "The Fatal Phone Call" was a comedy of errors in which Chet goes for a jog and gets pulled over by patrolmen who think he fits the description of a robbery suspect. But the only person who can prove his innocence is a white mechanic Chet has just angered by telling his wife that he has gone to a pool hall (after he answers that call in the public phone booth). As the police push Chet into the back of their patrol car, he quips sarcastically, "I can understand it, especially with my face." But in the end, the mechanic saves the day by coming to the station to vouch for Chet.

An episode called "The Gumball Incident" dealt with the criminal justice system. Mistakenly accused of breaking a gumball machine, Chet volunteers to go to prison rather than admit to something he didn't do. After posing for a mug shot and spending a day in a jail cell with an amusing drunk (played by

397

the character actor Tom Bosley), Chet's stand on principle is vindicated when his accuser has a change of heart. Another episode called "Rules Is Rules" was a lighthearted parable about fighting the system. Chet has run out of valve needles to inflate basketballs, but when he tries to requisition a new one, he wanders into the high school's Kafkaesque maze of bureaucratic red tape. When he finally prevails and gets his valve needle, Cosby proclaims that he is "a man who went up, fought the establishment, and won!"

When it came to casting, Cosby was determined to employ a broad mix of actors, and not to stick them in stereotypical roles. "I'm tired of seeing a Chinese hired to run a laundry or a Mexican hired to act silly," he told Macklin. "In the classroom of my show we're going to mix up all the races. You'll see every type: Japanese, Mexican, Indian, Negro, even white." The adults would be diverse, too; of the forty actors with recurring roles in the first season, fifteen were black, at the time a record number for a prime-time show.

Cosby took special pleasure in showcasing black guest stars who had rarely if ever been seen on television. One was Mantan Moreland, a veteran of the chitlin' circuit and "darky" roles in B movies. Cosby invited Moreland to guest star with Jackie "Moms" Mabley — another chitlin' circuit comedian who had been introduced to TV by *The*

Smothers Brothers Comedy Hour — as Chet's quarrelsome Uncle Bowie and Aunt Edna.

When it came time to shoot an episode called "Lover's Quarrel," the director let Moreland and Mabley improvise, and their war of insults was so hilarious that Cosby couldn't get through more than a few lines without cracking up.

In one scene, Chet was supposed to be teaching his aunt and uncle how to be nicer to one another.

"Now pretend that it's morning," Cosby said to Moms. "You just got up. Now what do you do?"

"I tell him he snored so loud until it rattled my teeth!" she ad-libbed.

"Then you should keep them in the glass farther from the bed!" Moreland shot back.

Cosby started hooting and couldn't stop. After several minutes, he gave up and walked away from the camera. "Just cut me out of the scene!" he told the director as he wiped the tears of laughter from his face.

Another guest star was the distinguished black actor Rex Ingram, who had played the escaped slave Jim opposite Mickey Rooney in the film version of *The Adventures of Huckleberry Finn.* In "A Christmas Ballad," Ingram played a curmudgeonly Christmas tree salesman whose hard heart is softened when Chet recruits him to play Santa Claus for the kids at a community center. (Cosby jokingly referred to the story as "Frank Capra in twenty-two minutes.")

When the shooting was over, Ingram came over to Cosby and shook his hand. "I want to thank you," he said, "because this is the first time I've got to play a part where I'm just a man, not a black man."

Several weeks later, Ingram died of a heart attack, and Cosby couldn't help wondering if in some karmic way the seventy-three-year-old actor felt "ready to go now," having left the moving performance in *The Bill Cosby Show* as his epitaph.

Cosby managed to recruit some memorable white guest stars as well, and one in particular. When Marvin Miller reported that Henry Fonda had agreed to appear on the show, Cosby was so excited that he called Camille, and she made a rare appearance at the studio to meet the legendary actor. In "The Elevator Doesn't Stop Here Anymore," Fonda is a repressed English teacher named Mr. Richards who gets stuck in the school elevator with Chet and a cleaning lady named Mrs. Wochuk (played by Elsa Lanchester). To pass the time, he and Chet play children's games, and Cosby and Fonda joust at Twenty Questions and Simon Says. As in the *I Spy* days, Cosby rarely stuck to his script, but for this occasion he made an exception. He was so worried about embarrassing himself in front of Henry Fonda that he had his lines written out on cue cards.

If filming the whimsical stories and creating the funky music for *The Bill Cosby Show* was a groove, as Cosby would have put it in those days, the politics of the show were another matter. From the first day of shooting, he waged several pitched battles behind the scenes.

The first was over his desire to use the show as a training ground for blacks in Hollywood. While NBC preferred white directors such as Coby Ruskin, Ralph Senensky, and Jay Sandrich, Cosby kept pushing to give black directors a shot. One was Ivan Dixon, the actor who had guest-starred in the first episode of *I Spy.* He had gone on to a starring role in *Hogan's Heroes,* but now he was starting a career as a director, and Cosby arranged for him to oversee three episodes. Another was an intriguing black filmmaker named Melvin Van Peebles who had just arrived in Los Angeles after a decade making movies in France; he would direct the last episode of the first season.

But when Cosby tried to hire blacks for other production roles, he ran afoul of the Hollywood trade unions. On the first day of shooting, he showed up at the Warner Brothers lot with nine friends from Philadelphia whom he wanted to put to work behind the cameras. Union officials informed him that only its members could work on the show. When Cosby asked what it took to get into the union, they confronted him with a catch-22: you had to pass a special skills test, but to prepare for the test you had to train alongside an existing union member. And during that period, both the veteran worker and the trainee had to be paid.

As news of the standoff spread, Cosby was told to back off by many of his industry friends, but one person urged him to persevere. "Roll the dice!" Camille said, and she gave her husband permission to use their personal bank account, which they were still replenishing after the Campbell/Silver/Cosby debacle, to help fund the extra cost of the training. Over the next two years, the Cosbys would be successful in getting union cards for forty-eight new black members.

Along the way, however, Cosby continued to meet resistance from older union members who were worried about losing their jobs. He even encountered wariness from some of the black technicians he was trying to help. After a hairdresser named Hazel Washington completed her sixteen weeks of training, Cosby kept asking if she had taken the test, and each time she told him that she hadn't gotten around to it.

"Hazel, you have to tell me what you're doing!" he said.

"If I take the test, I'm going to lose my friends," she said.

"You mean those white people?" Cosby asked.

"They're my friends," she said.

"So you're never going to take this test?" he asked.

"No, Mr. Cosby," Hazel said.

The experience rattled Cosby and made him realize how much it was still "a time of contradictions" for black people, of new opportunities but of continuing mistrust and self-doubt. Or as he put it: "You could, but you couldn't."

An even bigger fight was over the laugh track. By the 1960s, television had given up on early experiments with filming TV comedies such as *I Love Lucy* in front of live audiences. Now all sitcoms were "single-camera" productions; one camera shot footage from multiple viewpoints over multiple takes, and then that was edited to make the action look as if it were happening at once. But a CBS sound engineer named Charley Douglass had come up with a substitute for an audience: a machine full of taped laughter that could be mixed in the editing room to sound like live spectators.

By the late 1960s, the secretive Douglass, who had a monopoly on the technology, was driving his "laff box" from a padlocked garage in San Fernando Valley all over Hollywood. He provided canned laughter and "titter tracks" for single-camera shows at all three networks and helped "sweeten" the laugher on variety shows that were filmed before an audience. Opinions about Douglass's invention were mixed: some critics thought the laugh track was the height of fakeness; others argued that it helped viewers feel like part of a larger community. But television executives only cared about their research, which showed that laugh tracks boosted ratings.

NBC executives wanted *The Bill Cosby Show* to have a laugh track from the beginning, and they became more adamant once they saw the first rough cuts. The episodes — about Chet losing sleep because his neighbor has a new dog that barks, or helping a shy girl at a community center, or substituting for the algebra teacher — had amusing moments, but there were few obvious laugh lines, and no attempt to tell viewers what they should consider funny. Cosby also wasn't the volcano of comic energy he was in his nightclub act or on his comedy albums. Instead, he was more like the laid-back figure he had played on *I Spy.* But now he didn't have Robert Culp as a foil, just a cast of fellow teachers and neighbors who weren't particularly funny themselves.

NBC kept pressing for the laugh track, and Cosby kept refusing. As he recalled, his response was: "No, you're not getting one! I want people at home to laugh at what they want to laugh at. I don't want someone pressing a button and you've got 'Good morning Jack! Ha, ha ha!' This is sedating your audience! Viewers don't even have to pay attention. They just sit there and hear people laugh for them!"

When *The Bill Cosby Show* premiered in mid-September, its initial ratings were strong enough to keep the executives off Cosby's back. For its first several months, the show ranked in the top ten in the Nielsen ratings, reaching as high as number three one week. Among new shows that season, only *Marcus Welby, M.D.* on ABC was a greater success.

Critics didn't quite know what to make of the show. Jack Gould, the respected television critic for *The New York Times,* found the premiere "beset by too many hurried co-incidences," but he noted that "if anyone can minimize the viewer's awareness of easy contrivances, it is Cosby, a good man to have around." *Variety*'s daily and weekly editions had completely different takes: the former praised the show's "gentle humor" and hailed it as a "welcome relief to TV comedy"; the latter dismissed it as "frail and contrived" and "short on humor and even shorter on story."

As Marvin Miller had predicted, Black Power advocates criticized Cosby for not being sufficiently militant. "Cosby . . . has a new image this season, but to call it honest, to refer to it as a show with a black man in situations that actually portray the black experience, would be to state an untruth," black literary historian Faith Berry wrote in the *New York Times*. ". . . Anyone expecting something about black athletes, Afro-American history, community control of schools, teacher strikes, the black family, the black neighborhood, the busing of school children, or 'soul culture' will not find it — unless some changes are made."

Other black commentators rose to Cosby's defense. Responding to Berry in the *Times,* the prominent African American journalist A. S. "Doc" Young praised Cosby for opening doors for black actors and technicians and providing a model for a "strong and self-sufficient" celebrity and businessman who didn't have to "beg" for influence. "Bill Cosby is not Malcolm X or Dr. Martin Luther King or Stokely Carmichael," Young wrote. "Is it fair or right to demand that he become a carbon copy of any of them, or for that matter, of anyone else? Bill Cosby is Bill Cosby, and he is something special. He is an original, a one of a kind."

To the outside world, Cosby's show still looked like a success by the end of its first season. Although its ratings had fallen off after the first months, it earned the number eleven spot in the Nielsen rankings for the year, making it NBC's third most successful offering after *Rowan and Martin's Laugh-In* and *The Wonderful World of Disney*. Come Emmy season, it picked up four nominations: for best comedy, best new series, best comedy actor for Cosby, and best music for Quincy Jones's funky soundtracks.

Yet as soon as shooting for the second season began in May 1970, the war between Cosby and the network over the show's offbeat scripts and lack of a laugh track erupted all over again. A sign of the feuding came in June when Marvin Miller, Cosby's producer, told *Variety* that he was looking for "tighter scripts" and more "guests of stature" — a clear signal to unhappy executives that he was trying to push Cosby for changes. But Cosby dug in his heels, and by the time the season started, he had had enough. In September, he told friends in Hollywood that he planned to quit the show — "voluntarily," he insisted — at the end of the season.

Looking back, Cosby would maintain that he broke up with NBC before the network could break up with him. He was convinced that the executives had tired of his defiance and decided to get rid of him. "Word kept coming back from these people: 'You've got to put on a laugh track,'" he recalled. "And I said: 'I don't have to and I don't want to.' Well, they became angry, and to this day I believe they said: 'Okay, this guy, we want to get rid of him. He's finished. He's got a two-year contract. We'll let it roll, and then we're going to just cancel the show.' "

Whatever the causes, the falling out between Bill Cosby and NBC quickly became a self-fulfilling prophecy. With a star whose heart was no longer in the show, a network that had lost faith in it, and a public that was scratching its head over what to make of it, ratings for *The Bill Cosby Show* plummeted in the second season. Although the shows on either side of it, *The Wonderful World of Disney* and *Bonanza,* remained in Nielsen's top fifteen, Cosby fell out of the top thirty. With those numbers as cover, NBC had all the justification it needed not to try to get him back for a third season.

Whatever qualms NBC might have had about pulling Cosby off the air were also assuaged by its latest success. In the fall of 1970, *The Flip Wilson Show* debuted and instantly rose to the top of the ratings to become the number-two show on TV for the next two seasons. After *I Spy* and *Julia,* NBC executives liked to think of themselves as leaders in integrating prime-time television, and now they had a new black star, one who had no problem playing for easy laughs by dressing in drag and squealing "The devil made me do it!" And though the variety show was filmed before a live audience, Wilson had no objections if the network wanted to "sweeten" his soundtrack with extra whoops and titters from Charley Douglass's "laff box."

Yet when NBC executives looked back at the failure of Bill Cosby's first sitcom, they wouldn't cite the clash over canned laughter as the problem. Herb Schlosser, the former West Coast programming chief, would recall the magical night in the summer of 1969, under a star-filled sky on the Twentieth Century-Fox lot, when Cosby did such a memorable job emceeing NBC's press tour party and everyone marveled at how charismatic and larger than life he was.

"He was bigger than Chet Kincaid," Schlosser concluded. "The audience expected Bill Cosby."

17
FAT ALBERT'S NEW HOME

Ever since the Roaring Twenties, when car trips first became a popular form of vacationing, one of the most popular motoring destinations in America has been a mountain road in northwestern Massachusetts called the Mohawk Trail. As drivers make their way along the scenic route, they hit a stunning stretch that twists up the Hoosac Range above North Adams, makes a heartstopping hairpin turn, then winds down through a forest east of Charlemont and snakes along the Deerfield River into the valley town of Shelburne Falls. There, amid quaint shops and the second oldest bowling alley in America, are rocks along the riverbank etched with glacial potholes formed at the end of the last Ice Age and an arched onetime trolley bridge that has been planted with thousands of flowers by the Shelburne Falls Area Women's Club.

Driving those picturesque roads in the summer of 1971, Bill and Camille Cosby found their dream house. It was a two-story, fifteen-room white farmhouse on a looping bend southeast of Shelburne Falls, a quarter mile from Bardwell's Ferry Bridge, a red iron expanse with wooden planks and trusses shaped liked convex lenses that straddles the Deerfield River. The owner was a local farmer and carpenter named Cointon McCarthy who had bought the property and 180 surrounding acres from a local family that built the house in 1842 and maintained it for five generations. Smitten by the charm of the property and the tranquility of the setting, the Cosbys paid $65,000 for the house and twenty-one acres, allowing McCarthy to keep farming the rest of the land. The deal closed in August, and by September, the Cosbys had sold their mansion in Beverly Hills, said good-bye to Jack Lemmon and their other movie star neighbors, and moved their three small children to a new home a universe away from the glitz and glamour of Hollywood.

The story of how Bill Cosby made that improbable move had begun two years earlier with another abolitionist, an educational reformer named Dwight Allen. A Stanford University graduate, Allen had made a name for himself as a young professor there in the early 1960s, pioneering a training technique called "microteaching." At the age of thirty-seven, he had been hired away by the University of Massachusetts at Amherst as dean of its School of Education. The year was 1968, and Allen began shaking up that institution in the spirit of the times. He challenged rigid, classroom-bound methods of instruction, announced a mission to combat racism in the profession, and launched a program to recruit graduate students who hadn't finished college but had shown a commitment to the cause of education in their professional careers.

When Bill Cosby came to perform on the U. Mass campus a year later, an instructor at the education school helped out as a stagehand. The next day, he walked in to Allen's office and suggested that Cosby might be a candidate for his program for midcareer professionals. Allen was intrigued by the idea and wrote Cosby a letter. Shortly afterward, Cosby invited him to New York City for a meeting.

Over lunch, Allen told Cosby how much he liked his comedy albums and *I Spy* and how he could see the theme of education running through his work. Flattered, Cosby poured out his ideas about using television as a tool to reach young people, as he had tried to do by creating a sitcom based on the life of a high school gym teacher.

"Would you like to put those ideas down on paper?" Allen asked.

"Yes!" Cosby replied enthusiastically.

Allen invited Cosby to visit the U. Mass

campus, and he immediately felt at home there. Like Temple University, he could sense that it was a "step school," a place where strivers who might not have the means or credentials for more elite institutions went to improve their minds and their prospects. He saw black, Hispanic, and Asian faces; he heard about two students in the education program who had done time in prison. He discovered that one of the school's rising leaders was black, a geologist named Randolph Bromery, who would become the school's chancellor a year later. Walking the leafy grounds, picturing himself pursuing the dream he had given up when he left Temple, imagining how his mother would react when she heard that he was going back to school, Cosby couldn't help but feel the hand of fate.

When he returned to LA, he told Camille about Allen's offer and raised the possibility of moving the family to Massachusetts. Camille was instantly supportive of the idea, for three reasons. One was financial. Although few outside of their inner circle knew it, her husband's income had declined precipitously since his split with Roy Silver. In the late sixties, with Silver pushing for top-dollar bookings across the country, Cosby had been able to earn $2 million in five months of touring; now he would have to be on the road nonstop to make that much. As their new circumstances had sunk in, he and Camille had begun fretting about whether they could still afford life in "the Cosby Hilton," with its thirty-one rooms and fleet of expensive sports and luxury cars in the garage.

One night, they had discussed their finances as they sat in the living room of the Beverly Hills mansion.

"How important is all of this to you?" Cosby asked, pointing at all the rooms and expensive furniture. "Do you need all this stuff?"

"I'm your wife," Camille responded. "I want what you want."

"Do you think we could live on seven hundred fifty thousand dollars a year?" he asked, naming the sum that he had calculated that he could now earn comfortably.

"Of course," she said, thinking how much more that was than she had ever imagined her husband would make when she married him.

"Okay," Cosby said. "Then we'll find a way to get out of here and survive on what we can make as a business, with me making the money and you watching it."

Camille's second worry was for her family's safety. When the Cosbys had first moved to LA, they had rented a house in Benedict Canyon and become friendly with a couple that lived nearby, the movie director Roman Polanski and his starlet wife, Sharon Tate. So they had been particularly horrified the previous summer when Tate, just two weeks away from giving birth to a baby boy, had been brutally murdered in her home by followers of the bizarre cult leader Charles Manson. If such an unthinkable thing could happen to Tate, they asked each other, how could anyone in Los Angeles feel secure, particularly a celebrity family?

Since Richard Nixon had taken office, the Cosbys had also been under surveillance by the government. The IRS had audited their tax returns, FBI agents had visited their home several times, and they had heard noises that made them suspect that their phones were tapped. (Several years later, when Congress held hearings into the Watergate scandal, Cosby would learn that he was on a "master list" of political opponents kept by Nixon aides Charles Colson and John Dean. Since Cosby had always stayed away from politics in his humor, he concluded that he had made the so-called enemies list because of his support for civil rights causes and his refusal of several invitations to attend events organized by the Nixon administration.)

Camille's third concern was about the culture of Hollywood. A stickler for privacy, she resented being on the maps of celebrity homes that had nosy tourists gazing through her bushes at all hours. Still shy and modest, she had grown weary of the demands of the industry's club-hopping social life. Most of all, she worried about the effect of Los Angeles on her children and her husband. She didn't think it was a wholesome environment in which to raise her growing daughters and infant son. And decades later, she would confess to the pain that her husband's "selfish" behavior caused her in their LA years, as he indulged a roving eye.

Cosby thought the move would be good for his family, too, but for him it also represented a matter of identity. It was a chance for the Down Cat from North Philly to go back to the part of the country where, deep down, he knew he belonged. In the jazz terms, Cosby had always thought of himself as "East Coast," a lover of hard bebop rhythms and a heavy backbeat, not the breezy West Coast sound. From his first trip there, as a Temple freshman on summer break, he had never gotten used to the lack of street life in Los Angeles or to the fact that the seasons never changed. Although Shelburne Falls was a far cry from Philadelphia or Greenwich Village, it had its own earthiness and authenticity. It would also bring him closer to the friends and family he had grown up with and the bustling Eastern cities where he felt most at home.

When Cosby returned to Hollywood in September 1970, as the second season of *The Bill Cosby Show* was starting, he told friends and reporters that he planned to move to

Massachusetts. He would become a teacher, he said, and limit his show business career to performing enough concerts to provide for his family.

While the Cosbys looked for a permanent new home, they leased a house in the town of Petersham, a forty-minute drive away from Amherst, and Cosby started commuting back and forth to Los Angeles. "All I want is a parking space," he told Allen, pledging to attend classes with all the other students. But as soon as Cosby set foot on the U. Mass campus, fans and autograph seekers besieged him. To Allen, it became clear that treating him like an ordinary student wasn't going to work. So they devised a traveling tutorial. For each course that Cosby needed for his master's degree, he was sent a reading list. Once he finished it, he paid to have a U. Mass professor fly to wherever he was performing and meet with him every day, from one o'clock until four in the afternoon, until he logged the number of class hours required to complete the course.

As if to confirm that it was time for a change, the winter and spring of 1971, as the Cosbys were making the transition to Massachusetts, brought another bitter taste of the fickleness of Hollywood. Before his break with Roy Silver, Cosby had been preparing to star in his first movie, a remake of *Here Comes Mr. Jordan,* and he had lined up the

417

promising young filmmaker Francis Ford Coppola to direct. But Silver owned the rights to the story, and the collapse of their production company brought an abrupt end to the project.

Instead, Cosby decided to pursue another longtime dream: to make a family Western with a black hero. He commissioned a script entitled *Man and Boy* from two veteran screenwriters, Harry Essex and Oscar Saul. It was a heartwarming story of a black homesteader named Caleb Rivers who sets out to recover a stolen horse with his son Billy. Cosby enlisted his friend Quincy Jones to compose the score and his sitcom partner Marvin Miller to produce.

But every Hollywood studio they approached passed on the project. Some declared the story too old-fashioned; others, too boring. In one meeting, a studio executive yawned, drummed his fingers, and cleaned his teeth. Another studio executive insisted that there had been no black gunslingers (until Miller presented him with a book called *The Negro Cowboys*). Still others objected to the casting choices: Cosby wanted the bad guy to be black, too, but also to be friendly with a white villain.

To Cosby, the excuses cloaked an underlying message. "They just didn't want to see that many black people in a cowboy picture," he said.

418

Friends in the industry advised Cosby to cut his losses, warning that making a film without studio support was folly. The rejections only made him more obstinate. "There were just enough no's that I didn't like," he complained, "the kind of reasons given that are why black actors don't act, black directors don't direct, and black writers don't write as far as the screen is concerned."

One night, he was venting his frustration when Camille offered her two cents.

"If you believe enough in the picture," she said, "why don't you go ahead and put the money on it?"

Cosby got Marvin Miller on the phone. "Go ahead tomorrow with plans for the picture!" he said.

Cosby fronted $350,000 to start production while Miller continued to look for additional financing. "Let's shoot until we have to stop," he told the twenty-five actors and forty technicians he took into the Arizona desert to begin filming. The production crew included a black cameraman, lighting expert, and associate producer, and the integrated cast featured Gloria Foster as Caleb's wife, a child actor named George Spell as his son Billy, and the stage veteran Douglas Turner Ward as a villain named Christmas.

Although several potential backers emerged, Cosby kept rejecting them because he thought they were trying to take advantage of

419

him. One wanted 60 percent ownership in exchange for a third of the financing; another demanded 2.5 percent of the gross for five years. (As Cosby put it, "He just wanted to be able to sit around and tell his friends that he owned two and a half percent of Bill Cosby.")

After three weeks of production, at a cost of $12,000 a day, Cosby had run through almost all of the money that he had invested. Through a friend, Marvin Miller made contact with a mobile home builder from Long Beach named John Crean. Crean had never financed a film before, but Miller flew him to Scottsdale to watch a day of shooting. The businessman was impressed with the production and the G-rated script. The next day, he agreed to put up another $500,000, enough to allow Cosby and Miller to complete the movie and to cover postproduction costs.

Yet even after *Man and Boy* was finished, Cosby couldn't find a big studio to release it. Eventually he turned to Leavitt-Pickman Film Corporation, an independent distributor that specialized in art house flicks. The movie played briefly in several cities, then disappeared. In a lukewarm review, critic Roger Ebert praised Cosby's "marvelously open, easy, honest presence" but complained that "the movie lacks structure and disciple, and we're left hanging too often while plot points are shoveled in."

As Cosby was struggling to make his pet project, meanwhile, so was another black filmmaker — Melvin Van Peebles, the director who had returned from France to film an episode of *The Bill Cosby Show.* Since then, Van Peebles had made a comedy called *Watermelon Man* that had been a box office hit. Columbia Pictures was dangling a three-picture deal, but Van Peebles was determined to shoot an underground movie without studio interference. It was the story of an orphan, raised in a whorehouse and nicknamed Sweetback by the prostitutes, who is framed for murder and flees from police and escapes across the Mexican border.

Van Peebles had pulled together a rag-tag crew to shoot *Sweet Sweetback's Baadasssss Song* and had cast himself in the lead role to save money. But he didn't have enough cash to begin production. Remembering how friendly and supportive Cosby had been when he directed the sitcom, he took a chance and picked up the phone.

"Bill, I'm making a film, and I need some bread," Van Peebles said.

"How much do you need?" Cosby asked.

"Well, it's going to cost five hundred thousand," Van Peebles said.

"That's not what I asked you," Cosby said.

"Fifty thousand," Van Peebles said. "I need fifty thousand more."

"You got it," Cosby said.

With that extra investment, Van Peebles scrambled to shoot the movie in nineteen days. He disguised it as a porno flick to get around union rules, performed his own stunts, and brought guns on location in the Mojave Desert to protect against vandals and union vigilantes. Without a marketing budget, he promoted the film by prereleasing the soundtrack by an as yet unknown band called Earth, Wind and Fire and by touting its X rating as a racist conspiracy. ("Rated X by an all-white jury" read the movie posters.) As soon as the movie opened, at first in two theaters in Detroit and Atlanta, it became a cult phenomenon. Within weeks it was packing movie houses in black neighborhoods across America, often with fans who came back to see it multiple times.

Sweet Sweetback's Baadasssss Song went on to gross more than $15 million, making it one of the most successful independent films up to that date. By showing the Hollywood studios that films aimed at black audiences could be profitable, it also paved the way for a wave of blaxploitation movies over the next decade.

Cosby had helped make it all possible, but he never demanded production credit or an extra share of the profits. "Cosby didn't want an equity part," Van Peebles recalled. "He just wanted his money back."

By the time Van Peebles's film became a hit and *Man and Boy* proved a disappointing flop, Cosby was moving on to other things. He was reuniting with Bob Culp for a detective film, *Hickey and Boggs,* directed by Culp and written by then novice screenwriter Walter Hill, and developing a poignant made-for-television movie called *To All My Friends on Shore* about a financially strapped carhop who discovers that his son is dying of sickle-cell anemia. After a year of searching the Massachusetts countryside for a permanent home, the Cosbys had bought the farm in Shelburne Falls, and Camille had embarked on a $375,000 renovation to fix up the main house and turn two barns into a study for her husband and a home for her mother-in-law Anna.

Now that Cosby was out of favor at NBC, CBS was after him to star in a weekly variety show. Through his agents, he sent word that he would jump networks on two conditions. He asked to shoot the variety show in New York, so that he could stay close to his new home in Massachusetts. And inspired by two educational programs for children on which he had started to appear, he pushed CBS to buy a Saturday morning cartoon show based on his most famous comedic character, Fat Albert.

In the early months of 1970, *Sesame Street*

had just launched and its exhausted creator, Joan Ganz Cooney, was hoping to have some time to recover from the hectic debut. Yet several weeks after her revolutionary learning program for young children went on the air, she got a call from her partner at the Children's Television Workshop, Lloyd Morrisett, with an idea for another show. Morrisett told Cooney that the Nixon administration was launching a campaign to improve national literacy and that federal funds might be available for a TV program aimed at teaching reading.

Cooney assigned her *Sesame Street* producers, Dave Connell and Sam Gibbon, and Gerald Lesser, a Harvard education professor, to come up with a concept. After consulting experts in the field, they proposed a show aimed at students who hadn't learned to read properly by the second and third grades, the pivotal years after which catching up becomes much more difficult. It would be based on state-of-the-art research on decoding, the practice of teaching reading by helping students detect underlying patterns behind words and sentences.

To appeal to the six- to nine-year-old age group, the producers suggested a format that would be different from *Sesame Street*. It would be funnier and hipper, featuring real actors rather than puppets. If the original concept for *Sesame Street* was a kind of

Laugh-In for toddlers, the model for this show would be the cheeky sketch comedy hour *The Carol Burnett Show*. To drive home the ensemble concept, they suggested the title *Easy Company* — until someone came up with the image of a lightbulb, and they changed the name to *The Electric Company*.

Connell and Gibbon pitched Cooney on the idea of getting Bill Cosby to star in the show. They thought he might be interested because of his commitment to education, and they pictured him giving the show instant credibility with elementary school kids and their parents. To their delight, he said yes. Cosby knew their work from *Sesame Street* after appearing on several early episodes, and his children loved that show. His appetite for creating children's television had also been whetted by a special he had done for NBC called *Bill Cosby Talks to Kids About Drugs* that had received widespread praise.

Taking the job would test his new plan to live on $750,000 a year, however. The Children's Television Workshop was offering only $77,400 and insisting that Cosby be on set in New York City two days a week for half a year. That would limit his concert bookings and mean that he would have to spend most of his weeks off on the road. But after talking with Camille — and warning his agents at William Morris — Cosby decided to make the sacrifice. After all, he thought, having the flexibility to do work like *The Electric Company* was one of the reasons he had left Hollywood.

He also liked the multiracial ensemble that Cooney's team was pulling together, and he was eager to work with two of them in particular. One was Rita Moreno, the spirited Puerto Rican actress and singer who had won an Oscar for playing Anita in the movie version of *West Side Story.* The other was Morgan Freeman, a tall, elegant black actor who, although a month older than Cosby, was struggling to make a name on the New York stage while appearing in the soap opera *Another World.*

Once production started, the other actors on *The Electric Company* were charmed by Cosby but astonished at his relaxed attitude toward their grueling schedule. In all, they had to shoot 180 episodes for the first season, enough for a new show every day of the school year. Each episode included anywhere from five to eight skits, with different scripts, costumes, sets and "green screen" special effects. Rita Moreno recalled putting in punishing twelve-hour days and spending nights prerecording songs and memorizing new dialogue.

Yet Cosby would show up for his two shooting days with no preparation, usually just off a red-eye flight from Las Vegas or another concert venue. He saw scripts for the first time on cue cards, but mostly he improvised. Although his methods made for more disorder on an already chaotic set, the producers couldn't argue with the results. Cosby came across as utterly present and at ease on camera, whether playing sketch characters like the Ice Cream Man or William Wadsworth Wordsmith or talking to children, a format for which he displayed a particular gift.

As the ringleader of the ensemble, Cosby also helped foster an atmosphere of creative anarchy that added to the show's energy and kept the cast and crew on their toes. Conscious of how careful they had to be about language on a children's program, the actors took glee in telling bawdy jokes off-camera and saying naughty things to make one another "break" during tapings.

In one skit written to feature words with the letter B, Cosby played a milkman who was trying to buy flowers for his girlfriend.

"How about some flowers for my girl?" he said to Moreno, who played a shopkeeper. "You don't have any bluebells? You don't have any blushing violets? You don't have any blooming things?"

"All gone!" Moreno said.

"I know what," Cosby deadpanned. "I'll get her Tampax."

Moreno laughed so hard that she fell over backwards.

Given the show's modest pay and time-consuming demands, Cosby spent only one full season on *The Electric Company,* but that was enough to help establish it as the most successful program for school-aged children in the history of television. Within two months, almost a quarter of all US public and private elementary schools — more than eighteen thousand — were using the program. In urban areas, the penetration rate was as high as 70 percent. After the first year, the Educational Testing Service published a study finding that the show had produced a measurable jump in reading skills across all racial and economic categories. It had also made kids look forward to going to school: one South Dakota elementary school showed *The Electric Company* at nine o'clock in the morning and saw its tardiness rate drop from eighty incidents a week to virtually zero.

While his stay on *The Electric Company* was brief, it also served as a reminder of what America loved about Bill Cosby. He may have mystified TV viewers as the laid-back bachelor Chet Kincaid and failed to find a movie audience as the honorable but crotchety frontiersman Caleb Rivers. But children and their parents instantly recognized the Cosby who did funny voices and made goofy faces, who ad-libbed brilliantly and made everyone feel like a kid at heart.

In the spring of 1972, as his twenty-six-week commitment to *The Electric Company* was ending, Cosby proudly collected a master's degree in education from the University of Massachusetts. He was starting to talk with Dwight Allen about how he could earn a doctoral degree when another twist of fate presented an opportunity. Filmation, the animation company that had created the *Archie* cartoon shows, called William Morris to see if Cosby would help them create a Saturday morning show based on Fat Albert and the other childhood characters in his stand-up routines.

It wasn't the first time the idea of a Fat Albert show had come up. When Cosby signed his post–*I Spy* deal with NBC, it included a commitment to several Fat Albert specials. For the first one, he had hired an idiosyncratic illustrator named Ken Mundie, who mixed cartoon and filmed images and drew with grease pencils straight onto animation cels. Notoriously secretive, Mundie worked out of a padlocked studio next to a strip club in Santa Monica and refused to send his work to a printer, instead using a homemade dryer built with bicycle wheels. But Cosby liked Mundie's original style, and he became heavily involved in the project. He wrote the script with his friend Ed Weinberger, recruited local children to do voices, and showed up at Mundie's lab in the wee hours to check on what the illustrator and five assistants were up to. When the special aired in November 1969, however, critics and viewers were flummoxed. *Variety* complained that it belonged in an "art film house," and NBC dropped plans to do any further Fat Albert specials.

Yet the NBC special had helped Cosby expand his conception of the Fat Albert character. In the story he and Weinberger wrote, Fat Albert, sick of his friend's fat jokes, decides that he doesn't want to play with them anymore. After the young Bill character goes to his house to apologize, Fat Albert comes out to help them win the big football game against the toughs from across town. In Cosby's mind, the story was a parable for the plight of black children who encounter bigotry and low expectations but who, if given a chance, can become heroes — on the sports field and in life. As he told Dwight Allen, "Fat Albert" was really another way of saying "Black Albert."

When Cosby met with Lou Scheimer, the head of Filmation, he was pleased to discover that Scheimer embraced his vision for Fat Albert. Scheimer flattered Cosby by describing him as a modern Aesop, a fable spinner who disguised allegories about race and other social issues as children's stories. Now that *Sesame Street* and *The Electric Company* had introduced educational children's programming to public television, the two men agreed that it was time for what Scheimer called "a pro-social show" on the commercial airwaves.

When Scheimer pitched the concept to NBC, however, the network passed. The focus on education wouldn't work, the executives said. Scheimer got the same dismissive response from ABC. That left CBS, where an ambitious young programmer named Fred Silverman was in charge of Saturday mornings. Silverman professed to like the "pro-social" idea and agreed to buy the cartoon show, although Scheimer suspected that it was mostly a concession to get Cosby to agree to host a nighttime variety show.

With Dwight Allen's blessing, Cosby now had a dissertation project: the creation and study of *Fat Albert and the Cosby Kids*. Having learned his lesson from the NBC special, he decided to focus on the big picture rather than trying to micromanage the project. Filmation could handle the details of script writing and illustration. Cosby would concentrate on the overall tone of the show and the elements that would give it educational value and make it a unique viewing experience.

First were the characters, which Cosby wanted to defy stereotypes and reflect genuine child psychology. Inspired by his love of music, he suggested that the show revolve around a Junkyard Band of six friends from a city housing project who each played a different instrument. Far from an object of ridicule, Fat Albert would be the intelligent leader of the gang, who summoned the boys with his call of "Hey, Hey, Hey" and acted as a wise problem solver and peacemaker. Rudy would be a hustler with "an Adonis feeling about himself," as Cosby put it, always thinking that he was slicker than he was. Russell, modeled after his younger brother, would be a pint-sized truth teller who deflated Rudy's pretensions with the ultimate putdown: "No class!"

Other characters would be identified by the kind of nicknames that Shorty Cosby and his friends gave each other in the Richard Allen Homes. There was awkward Weird Harold, buck-toothed Bucky, slow-witted Dumb Donald, and Mushmouth, so called because of a speech impediment that caused him to end every word with "ibya." At the center of the group was Bill, a cartoon version of Cosby himself, whom he thought of as a "nine-year-old narrator for *Our Town.*"

The second key was creating stories with a message. Cosby wanted each episode to tackle a real problem confronted by young people, and to leave kids at home with a lesson about how to deal with it. Sometimes Cosby proposed the themes himself — about the value of good study habits, for instance — but mostly he left the Filmation writers to come up with them, in collaboration with a

432

black education professor from UCLA named Gordon Berry. As the show developed, it would tackle provocative topics such as shoplifting, venereal disease, and gun violence — subjects that no other Saturday morning cartoon show would touch.

The third key was the voices, which Cosby knew from his comedy albums would be essential to establishing the warmth and humor of the show. He volunteered to be the voice not only of Bill and of Fat Albert but also of Mushmouth and of a recurring character named Mudfoot Brown, a wise old beggar who liked to use reverse psychology on the boys. Later, he added a character called the Brown Hornet, who starred in a show-within-a-show based on one of Cosby's favorite childhood radio programs, *The Green Hornet.*

By creating a character named Bill Cosby and a brother named Russell, he cleverly left the impression that the rest of his cartoon friends were real, too. In fact, they were all inventions or composites — with one other exception. Cosby based Mushmouth on a boy with a speech impediment he had known in the projects, and once the show was on the air he decided to repay the inspiration. One day Cosby came up to Lou Scheimer and handed him a piece of paper with an address in Philadelphia. "The money you pay me for voices, I want it to go here," he said, and for the next year Cosby's checks for the show

433

went to the real-life Mushmouth.

The new cartoon show launched in the fall of 1972, along with the program that CBS really wanted, *The New Bill Cosby Show.* Hoping for a big hit, the network hired the man who created *Laugh-In,* George Schlatter, to produce the variety hour. Cosby surrounded himself with a talented group of regulars such as Lola Falana, and he invited some of the funniest comics he knew to appear on the show, including Buddy Hackett, Don Knotts, Lily Tomlin, and Richard Pryor.

In one particularly memorable episode of *The New Bill Cosby Show,* Groucho Marx made what would be his last appearance on TV. Cosby had first met the man he considered one of his professional idols in the midsixties, when he was a rising comic and Marx was guest-hosting *The Tonight Show.* He tried his best to trade Groucho joke for joke that night, but afterward he realized that it would have been funnier if he had played the straight man. So this time, when he invited Marx to be a guest on his variety show, he resolved to let Groucho get all the laughs.

Groucho was in his eighties by then. His wit was still as sharp as ever — but not as quick. So when they did an interview in front of the studio audience, Cosby told the producers to give him as much time as he needed to think up his responses and to edit out the pauses later. On air, the result was a vintage stream of witty Groucho comebacks.

"You smoke cigars, I see," Groucho said.

"Yeah, I like 'em," Cosby said. "This mostly comes from the first time that I saw you and I figured, gee wiz, I would like to smoke cigars."

"Well, you know it's a handy thing to have for a comedian," Groucho replied, "assuming you *are* a comedian."

Cosby chuckled at the insult and the audience roared.

"There's one question I wanted to ask you," Cosby said. "You've known all the truly great names in comedy. Now, how would you classify me?"

"You?" Groucho said.

"Yeah," Cosby said.

"You'd come right after Nixon," Groucho said. He wiggled his eyebrows and added: "And so would I, if I had a chance."

"Do you believe in life after death?" Cosby asked.

"I have serious doubts about life before death," Groucho quipped. "I also believe in death during life, and so does everyone watching this show."

After the taping, Cosby handed Marx a fistful of Cuban cigars from his dressing room. Along with Groucho's excitement at looking like his old self on TV again, it cemented a new friendship. "Cosby is one of the most talented people in show business — especially after he gave me the cigars," Groucho would later say. The next year, Marx asked for Cosby to be the emcee at a lavish party he threw in his own honor after winning an Oscar for lifetime achievement. (He held it at Hollywood's predominantly Jewish Hillcrest Country Club, where Groucho belonged in spite of his famous joke about not wanting to join any club that would have him as a member.)

As it turned out, Groucho's putdown of *The New Bill Cosby Show* would prove prophetic. Although the variety hour had some high points, it was crippled from the start by two handicaps. CBS had eventually insisted on filming the show in Los Angeles, so Cosby was wearing himself out flying back and forth to Massachusetts. Even more fatally, the network had scheduled the show on Monday nights, opposite a two-year-old juggernaut on ABC called *Monday Night Football.*

When Russell Cosby heard about the time slot, he gave his brother a pitying look. "You better be funny!" he said.

Cosby wasn't funny enough, and the CBS variety show lasted only one season. Meanwhile, *Fat Albert and the Cosby Kids,* the cartoon show that began as an afterthought for CBS, went on for thirteen years and 110 episodes, was nominated for an Emmy Award, and was named by *TV Guide* as the best cartoon show of the 1970s.

For the next decade, Filmation would send producers to record Cosby doing the voices for Fat Albert, Bill, and Mushmouth wherever he could find time: backstage in Las Vegas, in hotel suites, or at local radio stations as far away as Alaska. Once a year, Cosby would also visit Filmation headquarters to film "wraparounds" for the beginning and the end of the show. It was always a big event at the studio, as illustrators and writers gathered round to witness their star in action. "This is Bill Cosby comin' at ya with music and fun, and if you're not careful, you might learn something before it's done!" Cosby chimed again and again, changing into different outfits as an assistant held a cigar so he could take puffs between takes.

One year, the Filmation staff was charmed to see Cosby bring his six-year-old son Ennis to the studio. They remarked on what a handsome boy he was becoming, with his round face and curly little Afro. Then Ennis waited outside the recording booth while his father laid down the voices for a new show.

"Hey, hey hey!" came the familiar shout from the booth.

When Cosby stepped outside, Ennis rushed over to him and hugged his leg.

"Dad!" he said excitedly. "You're Fat Albert!"

Cosby beamed. *Man, this is it!* he thought. *New best friend in the whole world!*

18
Playboy of the West

In the 1970s, the largest hotel in Las Vegas was the brand-new Hilton International, a sleek Y-shaped behemoth that investor Kirk Kerkorian had constructed on the site of an old racetrack and sold to the famous family of hoteliers. In addition to more than 2,000 rooms, 1,000 slot machines, 100 keno seats, 21 blackjack, 12 craps, and 7 poker tables, it had an eight-acre deck off the third floor that housed a 350,000-gallon swimming pool, an eighteen-hole putting course, and four illuminated tennis courts where, whenever Cosby was in Las Vegas, he could be found every afternoon between two and four, enjoying a match or taking lessons in his favorite new sport.

As he was playing tennis on the Hilton deck on a sunny July afternoon in 1972, Cosby rushed the net in the middle of a point and the ball flew past his racquet.

"That was caused by your bum left shoulder!" a familiar voice called out.

438

Cosby stopped and peered over to the sidelines. There, wearing sunglasses but unmistakable, with her tall bearing and curly brown hair, was Jean Lamb, the physical therapist who had treated his dislocated shoulder when he was in the navy and become his commander on Ward P of the Philadelphia Naval Hospital.

Thrilled to see her, Cosby leapt over the net and they shared a warm hug.

"How are you?" he asked. "What are you doing here?"

Lamb explained that she was in town for a physical therapists' convention at the Hilton. As soon as Cosby got off the court, she told him about everything that had happened to her since they had last seen one another. The navy had sent her to graduate school in Minnesota, where she first learned that Cosby had become a big star when she was frying eggs one night and turned on *The Tonight Show.* Later she was transferred to Oakland, California, where she was planning to retire with the rank of captain. She had also wed and now went by her married name, Jean Heath.

"And how's Chipper, the talking dog?" Cosby asked, remembering the miniature schnauzer that she had once brought to work.

Chipper was alive and well at fifteen, Heath reported. And he had inspired the career that she planned to pursue after leaving the navy, as a dog breeder.

"That's great!" Cosby said. "Can I help? Do you need money for a kennel?"

"No," she said, "but how would you like to co-own a show dog?"

Cosby had no idea what that involved, but it sounded like a fun adventure. After meeting Chipper, he had always had a soft spot for schnauzers; when he lived in LA, he had bought one named Vallie that became a favorite of his children and his mother. And Cosby hadn't forgotten how much he owed his old boss, for her kindness and help in getting him into Temple University.

"Sure," Cosby said. "Let's do it."

Captain Heath already had a dog in mind. She had been breeding part-time for half a decade, beginning by renting Chipper to stud. Hoping to start a new breeding line, she had paid to impregnate one of Chipper's female offspring, a puppy named Timber. When Timber couldn't conceive, she had applied the stud fee toward purchase of another female breeder dog — or "brood bitch" — named Misty.

The day that Heath arrived in Las Vegas, Misty had given birth to — or "whelped" — a new litter. The friend who oversaw the birth called Heath to report that the batch included one male puppy, and he popped out with his head cocked and an expression that seemed to say: "I'm the one." If this puppy was that special, Heath had plans to train him to compete in dog shows and then put him to stud producing a new generation of show-worthy schnauzers.

That night Cosby invited Heath to see his show at the Hilton, and over the coming weeks, he called her in Oakland to check up on their puppy.

"I have a great name for our dog!" he suggested. "Fat Albert!"

"You can't name a miniature schnauzer Fat Albert!" Heath said.

"Sure, you can!" he said.

Over the next few years, the puppy grew into a stunning specimen, with a dark, salt-and-pepper coat, white legs, and a regal "headpiece." Three years later, Heath phoned Cosby to report that the schnauzer had won enough points at dog shows to earn the title of champion — Champion Fat Albert.

"That's great," he said. "What's next?"

Heath told him about another dog she was handling named Champion Shlosshaus's Jo-Jo-Dared, or Jo-Jo for short, a red Lakeland descended from four generations of Best in Show terriers. Jo-Jo had "finished his championship" in just eight shows, and Heath was hoping to buy breeding rights to put him to stud.

"Go!" Cosby said.

With that began a thirty-five-year partnership, with Cosby acting as financier and cheerleader, and Heath serving as breeder and trainer. Together, they would raise over two hundred championship dogs, including two more generations of "Best in Show" Lakeland Terriers descended from Jo-Jo and the top-winning Lakeland of all time, named Champion Black Watt Awesome Blossom. Eventually, Cosby and Heath would have a Best-in-Show Terrier at the sport's most prestigious event, the Westminster Kennel Club show in New York City: a Dandie Dimont with the literary name of Champion Hobergays Finneus Fogg and a fuzzy ball of white hair almost as big as the Afro that Cosby wore in the seventies.

Heath also furnished Cosby with dogs for his family and friends. Two months after their reunion in Las Vegas, he called her to say he wanted a surprise birthday gift for his mother. Heath suggested a miniature schnauzer named the Admiral that was especially handsome but too big to show (at all of fifteen inches). So Cosby sent two first-class tickets to Los Angeles, where a limousine picked up Heath and the dog at the airport and drove them to his brother's house. When Anna Cosby saw her gift, she got down on the floor and began to play with the dog, and tears flowed as she remembered her old dog Vallie and realized how happy she was to have a new schnauzer. *I'm already ahead of the game with this investment,* Cosby thought.

Yet for Cosby, betting on Jean Heath's dogs wasn't just a way to help out an old friend. It was another example of the gambling spirit that overtook him whenever he traveled to Las Vegas in the mid-1970s.

In his late thirties now, Bill Cosby was leading two lives at once. One was his East Coast existence. There, he was the family man of Shelburne Falls and the doctoral candidate of the University of Massachusetts. He was the earnest would-be educator who financed, directed, and starred in a fifty-minute documentary film for public television called *A Day at Graterford,* in which he traveled to a prison outside of Philadelphia to profile three convicted killers who had turned their lives around through the power of learning. He was the devoted son of Temple University who gave a concert to raise funds for student scholarships in honor of the school's beloved white gymnastics coach, Carl Patterson, after he passed away suddenly.

The East was also where Cosby sought to emulate a new inspiration, the poet Carl Sandburg. Cosby had discovered Sandburg in 1973, as he was driving to a concert in Denver. He was listening to the car radio and heard Sandburg recite a poem called "Laughing Corn." Cosby's ears perked up at the opening lines, which were full of images of humor:

443

There was a high majestic fooling
Day before yesterday in the yellow
    corn . . .
The ears ripen in late summer
And come on with a conquering
    laughter . . .

Cosby liked the way Sandburg's poem made the corn and the birds and the wind and the rain and the sun come alive. It reminded him of the personification in his comedy routines, where he gave everything from car engines to his own body parts minds and voices of their own. Cosby was especially taken with the end of the poem, which reminded him of Camille, of their life together on the farm in Massachusetts, and at all the ways that she acted as his sounding board and adviser:

Over the road is the farmhouse.
The siding is white and a green blind is
    slung loose.
It will not be fixed until the corn is husked.
The farmer and his wife talk things over
    together.

Cosby didn't know much about Carl Sandburg, but he was intrigued. He researched the details of the poet's life and came away struck by how similar they were, despite the surface differences between a black descendant of slaves and a white son of Swedish immigrants. Sandburg had grown up poor, in a three-room cottage in Illinois. He had left school and worked as a milkman, a bricklayer, and a farmworker before enrolling in college, dropping out, and joining the military. He landed a job as a reporter in Chicago and began writing children's books such as *Rootabaga Stories,* much as Cosby had first made a name for himself telling tales of childhood. Yet that wasn't the end of Sandburg's achievements: he went on to become one of America's most revered poets, a biographer of Abraham Lincoln, and a three-time winner of the Pulitzer Prize.

To Cosby, Sandburg's story seemed like the ultimate testament to human potential. It showed the power of education to change people's lives, no matter where they came from or what their stage of life. And it served as a beacon as well: a suggestion of what Cosby himself might still be capable of as he grew older, if he didn't lose faith in himself.

Yet if self-improvement was a leitmotif of Cosby's life on the East Coast, on the West Coast it was self-indulgence. When he visited Los Angeles now, it was usually without his family; his children Erika, Erinn, and Ennis were in school in Massachusetts, and by 1973, Camille had a new baby at home, another girl named Ensa. In LA, Cosby was free to spend his evenings hanging out with celebrity swingers and comely bunnies at Hugh Hefner's Playboy Mansion. When the sun came up, he could feed his voracious appetite for tennis. He played for several hours every day and became an avid participant in the new craze for celebrity tennis tournaments. Between 1973 and 1975, he hosted three of the events himself (donating the proceeds to Cedars-Sinai Medical Center and Jesse Jackson's Operation PUSH), and participated in dozens of others hosted by everyone from his comedian pal Alan King to actor David Janssen of *The Fugitive.*

Cosby had also found a second playground in Las Vegas. It was ironic, because he had disliked the city when he first performed there in the 1960s. After an early run at the Flamingo, he told a reporter from the *Los Angeles Herald-Examiner* that he couldn't stand the "gimme" attitude of the hotel workers, who expected lavish tips and free gifts from visiting stars. When the casino held a hastily scheduled press conference to allow Cosby to explain his remarks, he doubled down.

"I don't take back anything I said!" Cosby snapped when a reporter waved the article at him.

After several more testy exchanges, he abruptly ended the session.

"Any more questions?" he asked.

"Yes, Mr. Cosby," a reporter answered

snidely. "Can you give me an album?"

But that was before the Las Vegas Hilton came along. It was before the new top hotel on the Strip started spending millions to lure headliners to fill its nightclubs and keep its 2,000 rooms and 30,000 square feet of casino space full. Once the Hilton raised the ante on "Vegas money," no star was too big to resist it. Not Barbra Streisand, who played the black-tie opening of the Showroom, the largest of the hotel's three theaters. Not Elvis Presley, who chose the Hilton to debut a new act, complete with a sequined white jumpsuit and cape and dramatic intro music from Richard Strauss's *Also Sprach Zarathustra.* And certainly not Liberace, who was said to earn between $75,000 and $100,000 a week for an over-the-top act during which he drove a Rolls-Royce limousine, a Mercedes Excalibur roadster, and a 1930 Model A Ford onto the stage.

For Cosby, still working to rebuild his fortune after the Roy Silver debacle, the Vegas money was too good to pass up. During the seventies, he returned to the Hilton again and again, at least twice and sometimes as many as four times a year. He shared his bill with a succession of musical acts, from Ike and Tina Turner to Nancy Wilson, Leslie Uggams, Ben Vereen, and Sha Na Na. The singers kept his show fresh — and left Cosby with only an hour's worth of material to come up with for each show.

For the casino crowd, he was filling that hour not just with charming tales of childhood but two more grown-up routines that he honed during his stints in Vegas.

He called the first one "The Dentist." Using a variation of his Mushmouth voice, he did a hilarious ten minutes playing a patient trying to communicate with mouth full of Novocain while his dentist drills his teeth:

"Wait a min-ibyi!"

"What's the matter?"

"Smuck!"

"What?"

"Smuck! There is smuck coming out-ibyi of my mouth-ibyi!"

"I don't understand."

"Fire!! Do you understand-ibyi da fire! There's a fire in my mouth-ibyi and the smuck is combing out-ibyi and my face-ibyi is hanging on the floor-ibyi!"

The second routine was about gambling. After several years in Vegas, Cosby could do a whole hour on casino psychology. How gamblers lie to themselves ("I'll only bet with the money in this pocket!"). How they suddenly become devout ("God, get me even, and I'll never gamble again!"). How they listen to the wrong kind of music ("You ought to be listening to James Brown! Get up! Get on up!").

Cosby even brought the audience into the

bit, inviting someone on stage to play keno. He'd ask the volunteer to give him a dollar and write a number on a piece of paper with a crayon. Then he would announce that it was the wrong number and ask the volunteer for ten more dollars to play again. "That's keno!" he said as the audience roared in recognition. "You have to be an idiot to play that game! I mean, what do you expect from a game with crayons? Keno is a Korean word for 'idiot with crayon!' "

In fact, Cosby's jokes helped the gamblers laugh away their sorrows and go back out to wager more money. The hotel knew that, which was why Barron Hilton himself would show up at the act and hoot appreciatively at the gambling jokes. It whetted Cosby's appetite, too: after his second show was done, he could often be found playing blackjack or craps into the wee hours, betting thousands of dollars as well-liquored men and flirtatious women egged him on.

On one of those nights, Shelly Schultz, the talent agent who had first put Cosby on *The Tonight Show* happened to be in Las Vegas. He saw Cosby dressed in a tuxedo at the craps table and approached to say hello.

Cosby waved his cigar. "Let's have din-din!" he said.

Din-din! What the fuck is that? Schultz thought. He wondered what had happened to the adorable-ass kid from Greenwich Village and was so upset by the change in Cosby's behavior that he never called him.

Then there was the other self-indulgence that Cosby permitted himself while he was out west, one that would abruptly come back to haunt him in the summer of 1975.

It was a strange, anything-goes season in America, as the aftermath of Watergate hung over Washington, disco fueled the sexual revolution, and cocaine overtook marijuana as the hipster drug of choice. Even Cosby was making tame attempts to capture the licentious zeitgeist: he had a routine about the difference between people who were high on coke and on grass, and he was recording parodies of Barry White make-out ballads. At the end of that summer, the culture of excess also presented him with an unexpected professional opportunity. Elvis Presley, bloated and strung out on drugs, canceled a two-week run at the Las Vegas Hilton after only five nights. Cosby, who was scheduled to begin his own engagement in mid-September, agreed to take over and suddenly he found himself booked at the Hilton for an entire month.

Two years earlier, Cosby had spotted a tall, striking twenty-year-old brunette in a hotel nightclub in Los Angeles. She could have passed for white, but when they started chatting, Cosby discovered that she had Negro and Indian blood. Her name was Shawn

Berkes, and she told him that she had come to LA from her childhood home in Idaho and was supporting herself doing secretarial work. Cosby invited her to dance and then asked for her phone number. Later he called and arranged for her to come to Las Vegas, where he was performing, for what he described as a "rendezvous."

Now, finding himself alone in Vegas for a month, Cosby called Shawn Berkes again. He invited her to join him for another rendezvous at the Hilton. But when Berkes arrived at his suite on the thirtieth floor, she had a surprise. She reached into her purse and pulled out a photograph of a fourteen-month-old baby, a little girl with curly hair and olive skin named Autumn. "This is your daughter," Berkes said.

Cosby said he didn't believe it. If he was the father, he demanded to know, why hadn't Berkes informed him about the pregnancy? Why had she waited fourteen months after the birth to say anything? And why did Autumn have the last name of another man, a fellow named Jackson? But he couldn't be certain Berkes wasn't telling the truth, since they had made love around the time that the baby would have been conceived. And he didn't want to risk a scandal that could jeopardize the life he was working so hard to build on the East Coast. So he listened as Berkes tearfully pleaded that she only wanted what was best for the child; that she would keep the secret and wouldn't tell Camille; that she wasn't just trying to get money from him.

Cosby suspected otherwise, and he would soon be proven right. For the day when his West Coast life caught up with him was only the start of a saga that would go on for more than two decades, well beyond the day several years later when he told his wife about Shawn Berkes and began doing everything he could to win Camille's forgiveness.

It was only ten minutes into the screening of *Uptown Saturday Night,* and the head of the production company, First Artists, had fallen asleep. Sidney Poitier, the director and costar, glanced around at the other white executives in the room, who were barely cracking a smile at the antics of three of the funniest black men on the planet: Bill Cosby, Flip Wilson, and Richard Pryor. At the end of the comedy about two black working stiffs who go on a hunt for a stolen lottery ticket in Harlem, there was dead silence in the room. Finally Ted Ashley, the head of Warner Brothers, the distributor for the movie, turned to Poitier and asked a few perfunctory questions about how the movie would be scored. "Well, I don't understand all of it," Ashley confessed as he left the room. "I'm not as familiar as I'd like to be with the milieu. But I wish you luck with it and thanks for letting us see it."

The other suits followed, but a minute later Leo Greenfield, one of the Warner Brothers executives, came back. He looked Poitier in the eye. "I'll tell you what I think about your picture," Greenfield said. "It's going to be a hit. It will do at least nine or ten million dollars. With the exception of Ashley, those guys are too fucking scared to comment, because they don't know."

Poitier had screened the movie for the executives only as a courtesy, because they had to release *Uptown Saturday Night* whether they liked the film or not. Five years earlier, when he was one of the biggest movie draws in America — the Academy Award winner of *Lilies of the Field* and the matinee idol of *To Sir, with Love* and *Guess Who's Coming to Dinner* — Poitier had banded with Paul Newman and Barbra Streisand to form a new production company designed to allow the Hollywood stars to make their own passion projects.

Naming the company First Artists, the stars entered into a revolutionary new financial arrangement with Warner Brothers. They agreed to forgo the million-dollar fees they would normally command and instead take a piece of the gross — 25 percent of the profit made by the studio. In exchange, Warner Brothers committed to financing and distributing three films for each of the stars, as long as they kept the budgets under $3 million. Over the next few years, the deal would help Streisand make *Up the Sandbox* and *A Star Is Born* and Newman to produce *The Life and Times of Judge Roy Bean.*

Poitier's initial First Artists project, a romance called *A Warm December,* flopped at the box office. But he had high hopes for this second one, a takeoff on blaxploitation films such as *Shaft, Super Fly,* and *Hammer.* Poitier had gone to all of those movies and cheered with the raucous audiences as Richard Roundtree, Fred Williamson, and Jim Brown beat up on cartoonish white villains. But eventually he came to see those low-budget revenge films as suffering from the same problem as his noble films of the 1960s: they didn't connect with the real lives of black Americans.

Poitier started to conceive a comedy that would turn the genre around by casting ordinary guys as the heroes. And while he was at it, he set out to involve more black talent, in front of and behind the camera, than had ever worked on a Hollywood film.

While they were vacationing together with their wives in the Bahamas, Poitier approached his friend Bill Cosby. Cosby immediately said yes — provided that he got costar billing. Harry Belafonte, Flip Wilson, and Richard Pryor signed on over the phone without seeing a script. Knowing how tight Poitier's budget was, they all agreed to work for a fraction of what they made giving live concerts. Poitier rounded out the all-black cast with Calvin Lockhart, Roscoe Lee Browne, Jill Kelly, and Rosalind Cash. He commissioned a script from a young black playwright, Richard Wesley, and hired hundreds of black extras and a crew that was a quarter black. By the time production began on the MGM lot in November 1973, the *Amsterdam News* estimated that more than 1,300 African Americans were working on it in one way or another.

For a change, Cosby liked Wesley's script, which was full of funny street lingo but never stooped to vulgarity. It was a tale of two regular Joes, a steelworker named Steve Jackson (played by Poitier) and a cab driver named Wardell Franklin (played by Cosby), who sneak out of the house to go to a swanky speakeasy. When the place is robbed, Jackson loses his wallet, but later finds out that it contains a winning lottery ticket. They go "uptown" in search of the ticket, an odyssey that brings them into contact with a collection of eccentric ministers, politicians, and gangsters.

"This is the funniest script I've ever read," Cosby told *Jet* magazine, applauding the fact that it made no attempt to push "social overtones" onto the audience. "The characters in the story are not concerned with who is keeping them down — or blaming white people," he said. "The only message is that married men shouldn't sneak out and gamble while their wives are asleep."

Once the cameras were rolling, Cosby still took his usual ad-libbing liberties. As Wardell, a bluffer who talks the two protagonists into and out of trouble, he showed more of his North Philly street-corner side than he ever had on screen before. And compared with his subdued, self-conscious dramatic acting in *Man and Boy,* he seemed utterly relaxed and confident doing pure comedy.

While Poitier's own acting was often stiff, he got some very spontaneous and funny performances from his supporting cast. Belafonte did a hilarious Marlon Brando imitation as the gangster Geechie Dan. Roscoe Lee Browne captured the unctuousness of a "poverty pimp" politician. Reprising the Reverend Leroy routine from his TV show, Flip Wilson delivered a raunchy sermon on the theme of "Loose Lips Sink Ships." And in the funniest scene in the movie, Richard Pryor played a twitchy, paranoid private eye named Sharpeye Washington.

Pryor would spend only a day on the MGM lot filming the scene, but it represented an important reunion for him and Cosby. The two men had first met a decade earlier, when the painfully nervous aspiring comic from Peoria, Illinois, arrived on the Greenwich Village scene at the age of twenty-three. Cosby was just becoming a star, appearing on television and recording his first albums, and Pryor modeled himself after him. He adopted Cosby's collegiate look, his clean-cut style, his subject matter — stories of childhood — and even some pet phrases like "Looking good!" He began to show up on the TV programs that had given Cosby his first national exposure, from *The Tonight Show* to *The Ed Sullivan Show.* After Cosby moved to Los Angeles to film *I Spy,* Pryor did, too, and by the late sixties Cosby was getting reports from friends about how much of Pryor's act seemed to borrow from his material and mannerisms.

One day in early 1969, when Ron DeBlasio was working for Campbell/Silver/Cosby, Roy Silver called him into his office. "Mr. Cosby says that Richard Pryor is doing his stuff," Silver said. "We're going to get him in here and talk to him."

When Pryor arrived for the meeting with Cosby's manager, his eyes darted apprehensively around the room. Silver did most of the talking, scolding Pryor for imitating Cosby and pointing out that Cosby had only become a star after he stopped trying to be another Dick Gregory. Pryor made no effort to defend himself, and DeBlasio sensed that the lecture was resonating with a private struggle that was already going on inside the comedian's head.

Soon afterward, Pryor vanished from the LA and Vegas club scene. He moved to Berkeley, California, and for several years performed only in small clubs and spent time hanging out with Bay Area intellectuals, poets, and Black Panthers. Gradually, he developed a new act that was as different from Cosby's as it could be. Drawing on a troubled childhood growing up in a brothel run by his grandmother, it was full of biting observations about race relations and the differences between the social and sexual behavior of whites and blacks. Unlike his earlier act, it was also laced with "motherfuckers" and other curse words and an almost gleeful use of the word "nigger" — not as a racial epithet but in the way black people used the word among themselves, as a term of self-mockery and teasing endearment.

In 1972, Pryor resurfaced on the Hollywood scene with a touching performance as Billie Holiday's accompanist Piano Man in *Lady Sings the Blues,* the biographical film starring Diana Ross. In early 1974, he returned to San Francisco to record a stand-up album at the Soul Train Club. Entitled *That Nigger's Crazy,* the album was released by Stax Records and won the Grammy Award for Best Comedy Album in 1975. Signing

458

with Warner Bros., Cosby's original label, Pryor made two more records in the next two years — *Is It Something I Said?* and *Bicentennial Nigger* — that earned two more Grammies. His movie career took off as well, with concert films and a series of buddy movies costarring Gene Wilder that cemented Pryor's place as the hottest comedian of the late seventies and early eighties, just as Cosby had dominated the 1960s.

Pryor's rise inevitably brought rumors of friction with Cosby, who was said to be jealous of his success and disapproving of his use of profanity. In fact, they never stopped being friends or admiring each other's work. Cosby told intimates that he couldn't condemn Pryor's use of foul language because, like Lenny Bruce, he possessed a truly original comic voice. During his visits to Graterford Prison in 1974, he told the inmates that the comedian he would most like to see have his own TV show was Richard Pryor. (Pryor later got a show on NBC, but he clashed so bitterly with network executives that it was canceled after four weeks.) Using a jazz metaphor, however, Cosby told the prisoners that he and Pryor were playing two completely different beats. "He's talking about one and three," he said, "and I'm talking about two and four."

Pryor, meanwhile, was grateful that Cosby's manager had pushed him to develop his own style. After he reemerged on the national scene, he hired Ron DeBlasio, Cosby's former protégé, as his manager. He confessed to De-Blasio that Silver's intervention was the best thing that had ever happened to him. When Pryor toured with Gladys Knight and the Pips in the mid-seventies, the Cosbys went to check out his new act. After the concert, they visited him backstage, and Camille was particularly effusive. DeBlasio had never seen Pryor look so happy. "He was like a little kid again," he recalled.

Cosby and Pryor would appear together in another movie a few years later, playing two bickering doctors on an ill-fated vacation to Beverly Hills in a film adaptation of Neil Simon's *California Suite.* In *The New Yorker,* film critic Pauline Kael argued that casting black actors in the roles had "racist over-tones" and made them look like "dumb blacks who don't belong in a rich, civilized atmosphere." Cosby was so insulted that he bought ad space in *Variety* to publish a letter disputing the charge and proudly comparing his work with Pryor to great comic duos of the past.

"Are we to be denied the right," Cosby wrote, "to romp through hotels, bite noses, and in general, beat up on one another in the way Abbott and Costello, Laurel and Hardy, Martin and Lewis, Buster Keaton and Char-lie Chaplin did — and more recently as those actors in the movie *Animal House*? I heard not cries of racism in those reviews. If my work is not funny — it's not funny. But this industry does not need projected racism from critics."

Yet if Cosby enjoyed working with Pryor on *California Suite,* he was alarmed at his physical condition. By 1978, when the film was shot, Pryor had suffered a minor heart attack, and his spindly frame and jumpy behavior betrayed how much cocaine he was using. Cosby urged Pryor to get help and continued to reach out after he set himself on fire freebasing the stuff two years later. As Pryor's decline continued, Cosby would privately compare the comedian to another group of geniuses he both revered and lamented: the great jazz musicians who had let drugs destroy their God-given talent.

When *Uptown Saturday Night* came out in 1974, however, Cosby and Poitier were proud to have Pryor on the roster of black actors who could claim credit for its success. As Leo Greenfield had predicted, the film proved a commercial hit, making almost $7 million in its first year of release, more than any of the blaxploitation films except for *Shaft.* A year later, Poitier and Cosby would team up to film a sequel called *Let's Do It Again,* in which they played two more regular guys trying to save their Masonic lodge by concocting a boxing promotion scheme. While less memorable than *Uptown,* it earned twice as much at the box office.

In 1977, Poitier and Cosby returned in a second sequel called *A Piece of the Action.* But this time the reviews and the box office were tepid. The blaxploitation craze had run its course, and even black audiences weren't flocking to films with all-black casts. Hollywood studios were moving away from movies with small budgets and modest returns in favor of such blockbusters as *Jaws* and *Star Wars.* The kinds of films that Sidney Poitier, Paul Newman, and Barbra Streisand had formed First Artists to make were no longer in fashion. Once Warner Brothers fulfilled its commitment to the actors, the company folded, and the string of Poitier-Cosby buddy movies came to an end.

By the time *A Piece of the Action* was released, Cosby had also seen yet another TV show fail. In the fall of 1975, he did a one-hour variety special for ABC, and the network found it promising enough to give him a weekly show called *Cos* the following season. They hired one of the hottest variety producers in the business, Chris Bearde, who had created *The Sonny and Cher Show* for CBS, and lined up some of the network's biggest stars as guests: Lynda Carter from *Wonder Woman,* Gabe Kaplan from *Welcome Back, Kotter,* and Cindy Williams from *Happy Days* and *Laverne & Shirley.* But the ratings for the premiere were abysmal, and they got even worse the following week.

Two days after that second episode of *Cos,* on Tuesday September 28, Muhammad Ali boxed Ken Norton for the third time to retain his heavyweight crown. Cosby was a friend of Ali's and had attended many of his earlier fights, but filming the variety show in LA prevented him from attending the bout in Yankee Stadium. So instead he went to the Playboy Mansion, where Hugh Hefner had installed closed-circuit television and invited hundreds of Hollywood celebrities to watch the fight.

Another guest at the mansion that night was the comedian Tommy Smothers, who had a fraught history with Cosby. In the late 1960s, when he and his brother Dick were hosting *The Smothers Brothers Comedy Hour,* Tommy had chided Cosby for not coming out against the Vietnam War and taking a more public stance on civil rights issues. Cosby didn't appreciate the criticism and started refusing to talk to Smothers whenever they ran into one another.

The previous spring, Smothers had appeared on *The Tonight Show* when Cosby was filling in for Johnny Carson. He had made fun of the way Cosby introduced his guests, suggesting that it sounded arrogant and dismissive. After the show was over, according to Smothers, Cosby had muttered an angry threat.

"Maybe I'll knock you upside the head one of these days," Cosby said.

"Yeah, go ahead and try," Smothers replied.

So Cosby was not amused to see Smothers coming toward him as he chatted with Hugh Hefner on the night of the Ali-Norton fight. And he became even more annoyed when he heard what Tommy had to say.

"I liked your show!" Smothers said. "It was a really good effort."

Later, Smothers would insist that he was trying to say something nice to clear the air between the two men. But to Cosby's ear, it sounded like he was mocking him, since the word was out that *Cos* looked like a flop. "A really good effort" struck Cosby as a particularly condescending compliment, coming from the star of one of the most famous TV variety hours of all time.

Cosby didn't answer Smothers and instead glared at him as if to say: *Buzz off!* Smothers didn't budge. He stood there, waiting for an answer, as Cosby grew more and more enraged.

"Well, fuck you!" Tommy said finally, and then walked away.

Cosby was so furious that he couldn't control himself. He slipped around Hefner and punched Smothers in the head from behind, so hard that the smaller comedian fell to the ground. "C'mon, I'll kick your ass!" he shouted at Smothers as Hefner intervened to separate the two men.

The sucker punch at the Playboy Mansion was immediately the talk of Hollywood. By Thursday, it was the lead item in Army Archerd's must-read gossip column in *Daily Variety*. "There was a knockdown during the Ali-Norton fight — but it wasn't at Yankee Stadium," Archerd reported. "The haymaker was landed by Bill Cosby, 6'1", 180 lbs., on the left cheek of Tommy Smothers, 5'8", 150 lbs. The short-lived preliminary event (more exciting than the main bout) took place at Hugh Hefner's place, where he closed-circuited the fight for an SRO showbiz crowd . . . A dazed Smothers was still asking yesterday, 'Why did he do it? Did he explain it to you?' We were waiting at press time for Cos to return our call . . ."

Later his publicist would insist that Cosby tried three times to get Smothers to quit bothering him. "When he wouldn't stop," he said, "Bill tried other means to get him to stop." But privately, Cosby realized that the outburst had made him look foolish and reinforced the worst stereo-types about thin-skinned celebrities and angry black men.

When Camille heard about the incident, she was mortified. And two months later, when *Cos* was canceled after only nine episodes, she couldn't help but feel relieved.

She was sorry for her husband that another TV show hadn't worked out. But she didn't regret that he would be coming home from Los Angeles, which she continued to view warily as a city of oversized egos and unhealthy influences.

Yet if the Tommy Smothers fight and the cancellation of *Cos* were sources of embarrassment, Cosby did have something to feel proud of that fall. After four years of hard work, he finally handed in his doctoral thesis. In 242 pages, it explored how three children's programs that he had helped launch — *Fat Albert and the Cosby Kids, The Electric Company,* and *Sesame Street* — could be used as teaching tools in urban schools. It was hardly a breezy read, as suggested by its laborious title: "An Integration of the Visual Media via 'Fat Albert and the Cosby Kids' into the Elementary School Curriculum as a Teaching Aid and Vehicle to Achieve Increased Learning." But it more than satisfied the requirements for Cosby to collect his doctorate in education and to earn the title of "Dr. William H. Cosby Jr."

Shortly after his humiliating retreat from LA, Cosby also became the patriarch of his family. Three years earlier, Bill Cosby Sr. had died, his lifetime of hard drinking taking its toll at the age of sixty-one. Then in February 1977, Samuel Russell Cosby, the grandfather who had taken his father's place as Cosby's role model, passed away at the age of ninety-five. As Cosby looked forward to his fortieth birthday in July, there was another reminder of his family responsibilities at home in Massachusetts: a baby girl named Evin, born that summer. And now that Cosby had time to spend with his older children, he observed the unmistakable signs that Erika would soon be a teenager and that her sister Erinn and brother Ennis wouldn't be far behind.

There was no question about it, Cosby thought: he was officially entering middle age. And as the winter snow blanketed Shelburne Falls, it occurred to him that rather than fight it, the time had come to embrace this new season of life.

19
THE ART OF JELL-O

On a sunny May morning in 1977, Cosby awoke at his Massachusetts estate and donned the regalia it had taken him seven years to earn. He zipped on the floor-length robe with the burgundy sleeves and black velvet panels. He wrapped the satin hood edged with white cording around his neck. He placed the black mortarboard with the gold tassel on his head and inspected himself in the mirror. *This is what it's about!* he thought. The long tutorials on the road, the three months he had taken off to write the thesis, the times he had turned down honorary degrees from other colleges and universities. "The first degree I'll get is my own!" he had vowed stubbornly during all those years.

When officials at U. Mass had asked Cosby to give the commencement address that afternoon, he had declined that invitation, too. He didn't want to draw attention to himself, he told them. Not today. Today, he wanted to be in the crowd with his fellow students, waiting his turn to step forward and accept a diploma from the school's chancellor, Randolph Bromery. "At the end of the day, I'll be Dr. Bill," he told them. "But not before."

Cosby wanted to set an example of humility for his children, but most of all, he knew that it was what his mother would expect. This day was for her, too. And as soon as the ceremony was over, Anna Cosby pushed passed a security guard and sat in her son's lap. He could see that she had been crying. "If she was dead, she would have gotten up to come here today!" he joked. "Her tears mean so much."

Then Anna repeated the words of wisdom that she had dispensed — and he had ignored — so many times. "Now you have something to fall back on!" she said.

For Cosby, the contents of that leather binding stood for more than just a diploma. As he turned forty, it represented a standard that he had to live up to, in his professional and personal life. Shortly after the graduation ceremony, he appeared on another *Ebony* cover, this time headlined "Dr. Bill Cosby — Comedian, Actor, Author, Philosopher, Educator — and FAMILY MAN." For the cover, Cosby posed with Camille and their five children: Erika and Erinn, ears pierced and on the cusp of puberty; Ennis, a gap-toothed eight-year-old ringer for the young

469

Michael Jackson; four-year old Ensa, already a natural ham like her father; and one-year-old, angelic-looking Evin. For the story, they allowed a photographer inside their Massachusetts home for the first time, where he shot images of Cosby playing backgammon with his kids, cutting a birthday cake in the kitchen, and leafing through psychology texts in his study.

Cosby was eager to project another grown-up image to the readers of the magazine: as a tough businessman who had learned his lessons the hard way. Making a rare reference to Bill Cosby Sr., he told the *Ebony* reporter that he was thinking about making a film about a character who reaches his late fifties without saving any money — someone, he said, "who happens to be what I see my father as being." Cosby talked bluntly about what he had learned from the failure of his production venture with Roy Silver and the struggles that he had seen other black celebrities have with money. "The problem is, most of us come from a low economic background where money is used to just pay bills," he said. "We are stunned when we realize that we can make a lot of money. We have no idea how the system works that is going to pay us so much money, so we leave off the most important part — protecting that money."

It was learning to view himself as a corporation, Cosby said, that had helped him rebuild the fortune he had lost in Hollywood. His talent was "the product," and he had to "watch dollars coming in" and "watch dollars going out." And as it turned out, most of those dollars hadn't come from TV, not with three prime-time flops in a row and a modest income from *Fat Albert and the Cosby Kids.* Nor had they come from movies, since Cosby had all but worked for scale to make his friend Sidney Poitier's low-budget films. If Bill Cosby was entering middle age as a wealthy man, it was thanks to his relentless stand-up schedule — the frequent trips to Las Vegas and a nationwide tour every summer — and his increasingly lucrative sideline as an advertising pitchman.

The idea that a black man could become one of the most effective spokesmen in advertising history was hardly obvious when Cosby first pictured himself doing commercials. In the 1950s, *The Nat "King" Cole Show* had lasted only a year on NBC, and the singer had blamed its demise on lack of sponsor support, declaring that "Madison Avenue is afraid of the dark." But as Cosby waited for *I Spy* to go on the air in 1965, he was looking to become a more recognizable face and name. As a cigar lover, he had noticed the White Owl ads with the slogan "We're going to get you!" He liked the catchy line and thought he could deliver it in a funny way. So he asked Norman Brokaw to approach White Owl with the idea of using him as a pitchman.

His inspiration came at an opportune moment. Madison Avenue was beginning to look for playful ways to tap into the sixties zeitgeist. The ad men at J. Walter Thompson, White Owl's firm, saw that using a black comedian as a spokesman could be a distinctive marketing gimmick, and they were vindicated when Cosby's TV ads boosted sales. "Sooner or later, you're gonna try a White Owl, and then we got ya!" he teased, wiggling his eyebrows. "We're gonna get you! You know we're gonna get you!"

More than cigars, the product that Cosby had always dreamed of selling was Jell-O. Growing up, he had watched the greatest comedians of their eras become spokesmen for the brand: Jack Benny in the forties, Lucille Ball in the fifties, and Andy Griffith and Jim Nabors in the sixties. "Those are acts I want to follow!" he told Brokaw, asking his agent to pitch him as the face of Jell-O for the 1970s.

Again, Cosby's interest in Jell-O came at an auspicious moment for the brand. After World War II, the popularity of the powdered gelatin and pudding mixes had soared as Americans moved to the suburbs and looked for cheap ways to feed their families. But starting in the late fifties, sales had slumped as women entered the workforce and no longer had the time to make the time-consuming original recipes.

Now Jell-O's ad agency, Young & Rubicam, was plotting a new strategy: appeal to mothers through their children. The idea was to show that kids craved Jell-O so much that mothers had to buy it, and the agency realized that Cosby could be just the celebrity to do that, given his popularity with young fans of *Fat Albert and the Cosby Kids* and *The Electric Company.* In 1974, it began rolling out the first of what would become dozens of "Bill Cosby with Kids" campaigns, in which Cosby made children giggle with delight at the thought of Jell-O treats while announcers lectured their parents: "If you have kids, you have to have pudding!"

The Jell-O commercials were so effective that other brands came after Cosby. In 1975, Del Monte recruited him as the voice of its "Mom Brings Home Del Monte" campaign. A year later, Brokaw got a call from the chief of marketing at Ford Motor Company. Ford's board of directors had decided that it was time for the car giant to have a black spokesman. But when Cosby heard the offer, he was offended by its patronizing tone. "The marketing people got so involved with the question of whether or not they were going to accept Bill Cosby, the black," he recalled, "that they forgot to ask the black if he wanted to do it first." Only when his William Morris agents argued that the offer was too good to pass up — "with great balls of sweat rolling down their heads," Cosby joked — did he accept Ford's business, and its money.

As Cosby's renown as a pitchman grew, so did his reputation for clashing with the people who made advertising. As always, he preferred to ad-lib rather than to recite ad copy word for word. Young & Rubicam allowed him do that in his early Jell-O spots, but soon creative directors were demanding that he follow their scripts and dismissing his suggestions. At one Jell-O shoot in Lake Tahoe, Cosby refused to use the word *hunger,* arguing that hunger was too profound a condition for a dessert snack to satisfy. He kept substituting the word *appetite,* and the disagreement escalated into a tense confrontation.

Cosby was notoriously demanding about the kids in the Jell-O commercials. He thought they should reflect an array of races and ethnicities, and he would protest if he didn't get the "rainbow" he wanted. He had little time for the kind of spoiled behavior that was all too common among child models and their stage parents, and more than once he had an offending brat thrown off the set. Working with children also reinforced what he saw as one of the most annoying traits of overbearing creative directors: their insistence on endless takes. Cosby had an expression for his distaste for wasting time on a shoot. "I'm not lonely!" he'd say, suggesting that he could be doing better things. And as far as he was concerned, there seemed to be a lot of lonely people in the advertising game.

Cosby made no excuses for his impatience with the Madison Avenue culture. Deep down, he believed that he understood the products he was selling better than most of the executives who oversaw the accounts. After all, he had grown up sneaking ten-cent cigars with his Granddad Samuel, fighting with his brother Russell over the last dish of Jell-O Pudding (Cosby liked to put his in the refrigerator to make a "hard top"), and getting served Del Monte fruit salad out of a can by his mother. "Once I believe in the product, I aim to sell it, and that is what I think I do better than anybody," he boasted to a reporter for *Advertising Age* in 1976.

And no one could argue with Cosby's results. Once he became the spokesman for Jell-O, the brand began to pull out of its twenty-year slump. At General Foods, the company's parent, a creative young marketing director and part-time poet named Dana Gioia joined the Jell-O team and used Cosby to introduce two new, ultra-convenient product lines. One was Jell-O Jigglers, a concentrated gelatin snack that could be cut into decorative shapes and eaten with your fingers. Another was Jell-O Pudding Pops, prefrozen popsicles made out of pudding that generated $100 million in sales in the first year after Cosby introduced them in 1979.

That same year, Coca-Cola recruited Cosby for a huge ad campaign called "Have a Coke and a Smile." The soda giant was under assault from "the Pepsi Challenge," a marketing blitz that showed the rival soda winning taste tests and being favored by consumers caught on hidden camera. Cosby and Bob Hope were hired to record "tags" at the end of the new Coke commercials. Hope delivered his as written, while Cosby improvised and came up with something much better. "I saw you!" he said, his face capturing playful conspiracy. "I saw you! You're smiling!"

Coke and its ad agency McCann Erickson were so impressed that they enlisted Cosby in a counterattack against the Pepsi Challenge. They had him shoot scores of commercials tailored for markets where Pepsi had cut into Coke's market share. In one spot, he pretended to spy on people choosing Coke rather than Pepsi; in another, he stood next to a Pepsi vending machine, mocking the competition. "If you're number two," he said impishly, "you know what you want to be when you grow up. Yes, Coke is it. You're nodding, yes?"

In his account of the campaign, John Bergin, a top McCann Erickson executive, recalled Cosby as being "inconceivably arrogant" during the shoots and described numerous "blow-ups." But Bergin conceded that Cosby was "brilliantly entertaining in his ridicule" and that "magic happens when the camera starts." After two years of Cosby's ribbing, Pepsi called off its challenge, and Bergin acknowledged "our greatest weapon has been Bill Cosby when we have used him."

Clare Bisceglia, a Coke marketer assigned to work on the commercials, had a different recollection. She said that Cosby always gave the ad directors what they wanted before offering suggestions about how to make it better. Only when the agency people chafed at what they saw as second-guessing from "talent" did things get tense. Bisceglia, meanwhile, marveled at Cosby's onscreen magic as well as his stamina: he could knock off twenty-five ads in a day, when others might take eight hours to produce one usable spot. As they traveled the country shooting ads and making promotional appearances, she was impressed with how "low maintenance" Cosby was compared with other celebrities she had worked with: he always traveled alone, dressed in sweat clothes and sneakers, with no publicist or other posse (and, as usual, no cash).

While helping to stave off Pepsi, Cosby was also playing a behind-the-scenes role in persuading Coke to take a historic step. He threw his support behind Jesse Jackson's campaign to get the soda giant to allow black businessmen to buy one of its bottling plants. When Coke finally agreed in 1983, Cosby joined the first black investors to take advantage of the opportunity. They bought 36 percent of the Coca-Cola Bottling Company of New York and effectively took control of one of its subsidiaries, the bottling plant in his hometown of Philadelphia.

In the 1980s Cosby would add Texas Instruments, Kodak Film, E. F. Hutton, and the US Census bureau to his list of advertising clients. When *Black Enterprise* magazine published a cover story on African American pitchmen in 1981, writer Stephen Gayle reported that the deals earned Cosby more than $3 million a year. Gayle explained that so many companies were eager to use him because of his sky-high "Q scores" — the focus-group research on public perception of honesty and likeability. As Coke's chief of public relations, Anthony Tortorici, put it: "The three most believable personalities are God, Walter Cronkite, and Bill Cosby."

As early as 1977, Cosby's career as a pitchman had changed the manner in which he lived and the way he thought about the future. It had helped him become a substantial property owner: after buying more than 200 additional acres surrounding his Massachusetts farm, he had purchased a brownstone in Manhattan and a new home in Los

Angeles, in the Pacific Palisades hills. (He referred to the LA residence as "the house that Jell-O built.") The ad earnings allowed the Cosbys to vacation every summer in the south of France — at the Hotel du Cap in Antibes, a retreat so exclusive that it took payment only in cash. When Cosby went to pay up and check out one summer, he discovered that Coke had already picked up the entire bill for the stay.

Thanks to the riches that he had amassed as a pitchman, Cosby began his forties with the kind of financial security that he never could have imagined in his youth and that had slipped through his fingers in his early thirties. He could now think about more than satisfying his personal needs and building a nest egg for his family. He could start to invest in a lasting legacy.

"David Driskell? This is Bill Cosby."

At first Driskell thought the phone call was a joke. What would Bill Cosby be doing contacting an art history professor? And how would he have known where to call? It was September 1977, and Driskell had arrived at the University of Maryland only six months earlier, after years of teaching at Fisk University. Driskell assumed that it must be his brother-in-law, who liked to do imitations of famous people.

"I have your book," Cosby said. "I understand that it's the Bible of black art!"

"Well, thank you . . ." Driskell replied, as it dawned on him that he really was talking to Bill Cosby.

"My wife, Camille, and I would like to invite you and your wife to our home in Massachusetts in late November," Cosby said. "We'd like to discuss our art collection."

"That's very kind of you," Driskell said, "but our family usually stays close to home around Thanksgiving."

"I see," Cosby said. "Is your wife at home? Can I speak with her?"

Driskell fetched his wife, Thelma, and watched as she listened to the voice on the other end of the line. He saw her eyes widen and her head nod.

"Oh, yes we can!" she said.

So it was that David Driskell — a forty-six-year-old black painter, curator, and scholar who was emerging as one of America's foremost authorities on African American art — came to spend three days in rural Massachusetts in November 1977, discussing how to help two very enthusiastic art buyers become world-class collectors.

As Bill and Camille Cosby showed Driskell around their home, the professor was impressed with the works already hanging on the walls. The Cosbys had begun acquiring art in the late sixties, when they were living in Los Angeles. In 1967, they had visited the

Heritage Gallery and discovered the work of Charles White, a black artist from Chicago who specialized in black-and-white drawings etched in charcoal and Chinese ink. The Cosbys bought a nude, and twelve days later they were back to purchase a White drawing called *Cathedral of Life.* Eventually they acquired a total of eighteen Whites, including a portrait of Cosby that Camille commissioned. Called *Bill,* it was a somber-faced, barrel-chested depiction that would remain her favorite likeness of her husband because she thought it captured his serious, reflective side.

Over the next decade, the Cosbys pieced together an eclectic collection that included many of the usual favorites, including Rembrandt, Renoir, Matisse, and Picasso. They took particular pleasure in buying the work of black artists and of white artists who captured African American themes, such as a 1940 Thomas Hart Benton painting of a black father reading to his boy called *The Bible Lesson.* But now that the Cosbys could afford to do more than dabble, they wanted an expert to help them build a collection that was not only valuable but historically significant.

For three days — over meals, late-night conversations, and brisk walks through the New England countryside — Driskell quizzed the Cosbys about how their partnership would work. He wanted to know how much leeway he would have, and to make sure that they shared the same tastes. Driskell was so pleased by their response that it startled him when Cosby briefly reminded him who would be the boss.

"I just want to warn you," he said. "Certain times, I will say no."

"Why?" Driskell asked.

"Because it's my money!" Cosby said.

Over the next three decades, Driskell would help the Cosbys acquire hundreds of pieces, including major works by leading black Modernists such as Jacob Lawrence, Romare Bearden, Faith Ringgold, and Elizabeth Catlett. But in the early years, the couple still favored nineteenth- and early-twentieth-century Realists and early Impressionists. So Camille was excited to receive a phone call from Driskell in the fall of 1981 with news that Sotheby's was auctioning off a rare work by Henry Ossawa Tanner, a black artist from Pittsburgh who had gone to study in Paris in the 1890s and become a significant figure in the Impressionist salons.

Entitled *The Thankful Poor,* the painting portrayed an old black laborer and a young boy reciting grace over empty plates. It bore a striking resemblance to Tanner's most famous painting, *The Banjo Lesson,* which depicted the same man teaching the boy how to play the banjo. Tanner had donated *The*

Thankful Poor to the Philadelphia School for the Deaf, where it sat in a basement for half a century before the school discovered the painting and decided to sell it to raise money.

The auction was scheduled for December, and Camille told Driskell that she wanted to buy the painting as a Christmas gift for her husband. She had plans to be in Los Angeles, so she dispatched Driskell to Sotheby's with instructions about how much she was willing to pay. Driskell hung back for the first round of offers before jumping in, and soon he was competing with two other bidders. One dropped out, but the other, a New England art dealer, kept going.

Finally the auctioneer reached the limit that Camille had set. "Two hundred and fifty thousand!" he called out.

Driskell raised his paddle, and the competitor folded.

When Driskell called Camille in LA to tell her, she was elated. Then he gave her more news: the price she had paid — $250,000, plus a $35,000 commission — was the most that had ever been paid by a private buyer for the work of a black artist.

Several weeks later, Camille presented *The Thankful Poor* to her husband on Christmas day. He was thrilled, and he later phoned Driskell to thank him — and to have some fun pulling his leg.

"Now what about the companion piece?"

Cosby asked.

"Which one?" Driskell replied.

"The one with the banjo!" Cosby said.

"Oh, you mean *The Banjo Lesson,*" Driskell said. "I'm afraid it's not for sale. It's part of the permanent collection at Hampton University."

Cosby knew that, but he couldn't resist the punch line.

"How much is Hampton?" he asked.

With Driskell's help, the Cosbys would gradually acquire the most valuable private collection of African American art in the world. But they went out of their way not to draw public attention to it, keeping most of their purchases confidential and declining to loan out the art to galleries or museums. When pressed, they insisted that they bought the art for their own enjoyment — and for the edification of their children.

Always a champion of education, Cosby was now focused on what his own five children were learning as they got older. He quizzed them about their grades and report cards, and he wanted them to know things they weren't likely to learn in the Massachusetts public schools or the private prep schools they attended for high school. Most important was the story of their people — the black history that Cosby had once described on TV as "lost, stolen, or strayed." And what better way to teach their children about their heritage, he and Camille believed, than to surround them with artwork that told the African American story and testified to its capacity for genius?

Another subject was money. Once Erika turned twelve, Cosby began taking her to concert dates to show her how he made a living and to explain the fundamentals of his business. He showed her box office receipts and how he calculated his gross and his net. "I don't ever want my children to feel that what I'm doing is magical," he explained. "I'm not a magical person. I'm an artist, and I want them to see me making my sketches . . . I don't want them to think that I get up in the morning and go to the set and things just jump out of my head, because if that is what they think, then they are going to fail."

In fact, Cosby never really worried about Erika failing in life — not his conscientious oldest daughter. But to his dismay, he couldn't say the same for her younger brother, Ennis.

From the time he was born, Ennis Cosby, the only boy in the family, had been the apple of his father's eye. When he was a toddler, Cosby had regaled Dick Cavett and his TV guests with accounts of teaching his son to say "my main man!" Whenever Cosby came home to Massachusetts, he make a point of spending one-on-one time with Ennis, taking

485

him for a drive in one of his sports cars or to get a hamburger at the McDonald's in Greenfield, the next town over from Shelburne Falls.

Once Ennis was old enough, Cosby started taking him on the road, just the two of them. They would hang out together during the day, and then Cosby would leave him in the hotel room at night while he performed.

"Lock the door and wait until I come back," Cosby explained one night when they were in Cincinnati.

"Okay," Ennis said.

Cosby gave him a stern look. "If anybody knocks on the door," he said, "you call down to the desk and tell them somebody is knocking. But don't open the door for anybody!"

"Okay, Dad," Ennis replied.

Half an hour later, Cosby was on stage, in front of four thousand people, when he saw a small head of curly hair bob down the center aisle. When Ennis got to the front rows, he perched himself on the arm of an aisle seat. Cosby looked down and thought: *Eeennnnis!* He interrupted the performance to ask an usher to take his son backstage, and as soon as the concert was over, he went to scold him.

"Why?!" Cosby asked, his voice full of exasperation.

Ennis gazed adoringly at his father: "You're funny!" he said.

Yet as charmed as he was by his son's sweet

nature, Cosby was increasingly frustrated with how badly Ennis did in school. The older he got, the more he struggled with taking exams and completing homework assignments. For a while, Cosby thought the problem was with the local elementary school in Massachusetts. Boys there often teased Ennis about his famous father, and at eight he got into a fistfight with a bully who called him names. So for junior high, the Cosbys enrolled Ennis at the Eaglebrook School in nearby Deerfield that fed graduates to the famous academy next door and other New England prep schools. But at Eaglebrook, Ennis's academic struggles — and his attitude toward school — only got worse.

After a teacher reported that he wasn't handing in his homework, Cosby confronted his son and demanded to know what was going on.

"I was robbed!" Ennis said. "I was on my way to school, and a man with a gun took my homework."

"And he didn't take your money?" Cosby asked skeptically.

"He didn't want my money," Ennis pleaded. "Just my homework!"

It was the kind of fib that Cosby might have considered funny if it had come from anybody but Ennis. After all, he had made audiences laugh for years with his "To Russell" bit about "the man who came in through the window and broke the bed!" But Cosby wasn't the least bit amused to see his own son lie to his face, and he was determined to teach him never to do it again. He took Ennis out to one of the barns on the property and gave him a spanking.

"Do you promise not to lie again?" Cosby said.

"Yes!" Ennis said, sniffling back tears.

"Good!" Cosby said. "Then go back to the house."

As Ennis moved toward the barn door, Cosby hit him again.

Ennis stared at him in shock.

"I lied!" Cosby said. "Do you want me to lie to you again?"

"No!" Ennis whimpered.

For a while, Ennis started to work harder and got his homework in on time. But even when he applied himself, he did poorly on exams, and it took him forever to complete assignments, particularly when they involved reading. Gradually his attitude toward school shifted from frustration to indifference — which was even worse, as far as his parents were concerned.

One night, Cosby returned home in the middle of a concert tour for an overnight stay. As soon as he saw Camille's face, he knew that something was wrong.

"Ennis says he's not going to college!" Camille said.

"What?" Cosby said.

"You go talk to him!" she said.

Cosby went to Ennis's room and didn't come out until the next morning. In an emotional voice, Ennis insisted that he wanted to be "regular people." Regular people didn't go to college, he said. Regular people didn't want to be celebrities or doctors or lawyers. Regular people didn't care about being rich; they just wanted an apartment and a car.

As Cosby listened to his son's speech, he grew more and more agitated. If Ennis was serious, he shot back, then his mother and father were going to make a list of what regular people did and didn't do. Regular people had to clean their own rooms and wash their own laundry because they didn't have maids. Regular people ate only home-cooked meals because they couldn't afford chefs or fancy restaurants or takeout food. Regular people had to watch their phone bills, so they couldn't afford to make long-distance phone calls to the girlfriends they met at camp.

Back and forth they went until five o'clock in the morning, when Cosby had to leave for the airport. He hadn't slept and was still dressed in the clothes he had arrived home in the night before. But when he phoned Camille to check in that night, she had good news. "Regular people came to talk to me,"

489

Camille said. "Regular people said that regular people don't want to be regular people anymore."

As he had done with his difficult childhood, Cosby was coming to grips with the frustrations of being a middle-aged man and father by transforming them into humor. By the early eighties, the physical toll of aging became a major theme of his comedy act. "Life begins at forty when your body calls a meeting with the brain and tells it what it's not going to do anymore!" he joked. He did routines about his deteriorating eyesight, his losing war with intestinal gas, and his failing memory. ("You find yourself walking into rooms and forgetting what you went in for," he complained, "or standing around after a shower and trying to remember where you've put the deodorant, or getting into a car and driving off and then forgetting where you're going. And your family is no help because they keep moving things on you . . .")

In a comic essay for *Ebony* entitled "Bill Cosby Talks About Middle Age — and Other Aggravations," Cosby even talked about how aging had affected his roving eye for women. "One of the most important things when you turn forty is that you weigh things thusly," he wrote. "You look at the enjoyment you may get from a given activity, and then you look at the amount of work that may have to go into it . . . for example, sex with a young beautiful woman who has plenty of energy." He described a forty-plus man contemplating "the amount of seating and digging and crawling you're going to have to do . . ." before concluding ". . . it's not worth it." In a picture that accompanied the story, Cosby stood on a diving board, smoking a cigar, looking over his shoulder wistfully at a bikini-clad, mocha-skinned beauty. "One of those things you want but are glad you can't have," the caption read.

(Cosby didn't tell *Ebony* readers about another step that he had taken to prove that he was serious about cutting back on his womanizing ways. He told one longtime girlfriend that he wanted to put an end to their relationship, and then he invited the woman and her mother, who had always disapproved of her daughter being involved with a married man, out to dinner to celebrate. "I'm very happy to be here," the mother told Cosby, "because I always thought you had more sense than that!")

The *Ebony* essay ended with a story about the expression "peace of mind." When he was young, Cosby wrote, he would hear old people say that the thing they wished for most in life was "peace of mind." Are they crazy? he thought at the time. What about a car? Then he painted a picture of what happened when he and Camille found a summer camp that would accept all five of their children:

"We were supposed to mail the check, but instead we drove the check over, accompanied by a lawyer and a notary public. On the day the bus came to pick up the children — my wife and I had, on our own, hired a backup bus to make sure they got there — after they loaded the last child onto the bus, we watched it disappear, and finally we walked back onto our property and headed toward the house. We could *hear* our property. We had never heard our property before. We noticed that the birds were coming back. My wife's face began to twitch and tremble, and I said: 'Dear, are you having a stroke?' She said, 'No, I think I'm going to smile.' I said, 'What do you think it is?' And she said: 'Peace of mind!' "

Through the late seventies and into the early eighties, Cosby reloaded his boat with new family material, as he continued to give as many as a hundred stand-up concerts a year. In the rest of his time, he discovered new opportunities to indulge his love of jazz. In 1979, Hugh Hefner decided to re-create an experiment he had first tried in *Playboy*'s early days in Chicago: putting on a jazz festival. He took over the Hollywood Bowl, hired George Wein, the creator of the Newport Jazz Festival, to book the musicians, and invited Cosby to emcee. The first outing proved such a success that Hefner made it an annual event, and for the next thirty-two years, Cosby would spend a weekend in June presiding over the two-day celebration of California sunshine and good vibrations.

The same year, Cosby was responsible for a small but memorable milestone in jazz history. He was a guest on *The Tonight Show* and he persuaded Johnny Carson to book Sonny Rollins, the legendary saxophonist. Rollins had met Cosby while performing at the Village Gate in the early sixties, and they had gotten to know each other over the years; but Rollins was shy, so they never became close. Still, Rollins had always respected Cosby, as much for the example he set on *I Spy* as for his comedy; he likened it to what Charlie Parker had done for jazz musicians, showing that a black man could be a star without "Tomming." So Rollins was flattered when Cosby called him out of the blue, said that he had seen him on a public television show performing with the singer Garland Jeffreys, and promised to get him on *The Tonight Show*.

On the day of the broadcast, Rollins attended a morning walkthrough at the NBC studio in Burbank and was told he would have eight minutes at the end of the show. Carson's producers assumed that he would play for a couple of minutes and then join the other guests on the couch. But Cosby pulled Rollins aside and told him not to worry about Johnny and just play. So that's what Sonny did: donning a wool cap, he came out from behind the colorful striped curtain and blew eight minutes of unaccompanied free jazz — the first time a solo of that kind and length had ever been seen on network television. As he was playing, Rollins could see the producers fuming and the musicians in the house band smiling. He walked off the stage without saying a word or looking at Carson, who had a stunned expression on his face. Backstage, the Spanish singer Charo told Rollins she couldn't believe what she had heard. "Ah si!" she said. "How you play like that?"

Of all his connections to the jazz world, the one Cosby still couldn't get over was that he had become friends with his boyhood hero, Miles Davis. On Thanksgiving Day, 1981, he even hosted Davis's wedding to the actress Cicely Tyson at his home in Shelburne Falls. Reverend Andrew Young performed the ceremony, and the guests included Dizzy Gillespie, Max Roach, and Dick Gregory. In his autobiography, Miles recalled the wedding as a warm occasion but described himself as having a look of "almost-death" on his face, the result of decades of drug abuse and chain-smoking and a harbinger of his real death a decade later at the age of sixty-five. (Cosby liked to tell the story of visiting Miles backstage in southern France in those last years and seeing Davis's reaction to the throng of French fans lined up outside his dressing room. "They've come to get what's left," Miles rasped, cool as ever.)

By 1983, Cosby had spent enough time on the road perfecting his family man material that he was ready to record it. But he had little appetite for making another comedy album, after bouncing from label to label in the seventies and never matching the success he had with Warner Bros. in the sixties. Instead, he decided to make a concert film — a new medium that ironically had been made popular by Richard Pryor, the comic who had once modeled himself after Cosby.

Four years earlier, Pryor had electrified the comedy world with a filmed version of his profane and wildly funny club act called *Richard Pryor: Live in Concert.* In 1982, he had returned with a second concert film, *Richard Pryor: Live on the Sunset Strip,* that was an even bigger commercial and critical success, winning particular acclaim for Pryor's painful but hilarious account of almost burning himself to death free-basing cocaine. Cosby went to see the films and thought they were hilarious, but what he envied most were the close-ups of Pryor's face. In many ways, Pryor had learned how to use his face by watching Cosby — how to pull an audience into a long, funny story by acting out all of its characters — but now Pryor had beaten him to putting that dimension of a live stand-up performance on the big screen.

Cosby set out to produce a concert film that would show what the original master could do with his face. His company Jemmin negotiated a distribution deal with Twentieth Century-Fox and arranged to film a series of concerts at the Hamilton Place Theatre in Ontario, Canada. Cosby decided to begin with several time-tested bits built around his talent for funny faces, walks, and impersonations: "The Dentist" routine; the one about getting stoned versus getting drunk; and another one about "Jeffrey," a brat he had once endured on an airplane flight.

Halfway through the film, Cosby segued into his new material on the trials of parenthood. "My wife and I have five children," he announced, his eyes full of exasperation, "and the reason why we have five children is because we do not want six!" He did a couple of minutes on how cute he and Camille thought their children's "poo poo" was until it started to smell. He described the constant squabbling between his kids, and how they were always tattling on one another. He reenacted the day when he fed his children chocolate cake for breakfast and Camille hit the roof when she found out. "Parents aren't interested in justice — they want QUIET!" he exclaimed, as the parents in the audience roared in recognition.

"I am not the boss of my house," Cosby confessed, his face capturing the exhaustion of a father who has been worn down by all the daily battles in his household. "I don't know how I lost it. I don't know where I lost it. I don't think I ever had it. But I've seen the boss's job and I don't want it!"

When the executives at Fox saw Cosby's film, they thought it wasn't edgy enough to win the kind of mass audience that had flocked to Pryor's movies. They shunted it to Fox's International Classics division and slated it for limited release along with films like *Eating Raoul.* A harsh *Variety* review compared the film to watching home movies. (Over the opening credits, Cosby had run a montage of photos of his children and sung a whimsical song called "Just the Slew of Us.")

Bill Cosby: Himself lasted in theaters for only a matter of weeks before it was relegated to Home Box Office, the new cable movie channel. But because HBO had such limited inventory at the time, it began running the film at all hours of the day and night, whenever it needed to fill airtime. And it was there, on the twenty-four-hour programming wheel of cable TV, that a new generation of aspiring stand-up comedians rediscovered Cosby, and far from dismissing his retro humor, marveled at his mastery of the form they were struggling to learn.

Jerry Seinfeld, a twenty-nine-year-old from Long Island, was laboring to write two- and three-minute routines that could survive in New York comedy clubs. He was astounded to see Cosby sustain funny ideas for ten, fifteen, sometimes twenty minutes. He was even more impressed that Cosby had the confidence to do it *sitting down,* giving up the fundamental power move of standing up in front of an audience.

Ray Romano, a twenty-six-year-old Queens College dropout who was trying to figure out how to break into comedy, was struck at how Cosby managed to be such a loveable grouch. How could he complain so openly about his wife and children, Romano wondered, and still come off as a caring father and husband?

Larry Wilmore, a black LA native who had dropped out of California State Polytechnic University to try his hand at stand-up, couldn't believe that Cosby dared to bring clean comedy back *after* Richard Pryor. Pryor was supposed to have changed all the rules with his raunchy, confessional material. But here was Cosby talking about getting a sore mouth from going to a dentist, not performing oral sex — and making it just as funny. As a member of the generation that associated Cosby with the childhood world of Fat Albert cartoons, Wilmore was stunned to see him so convincingly capture the world as seen through the eyes of adults. When Cosby described taunting his children with the same threat Bill Sr. had used on him — "I brought you into this world, and I can take you out!" — Wilmore thought, *That could be my dad!*

In a business that still judged movies by their box office, Cosby couldn't help but be disappointed by the performance of his concert film. But he responded the way he usually did to professional setbacks: he looked around for a new project. By the fall of 1983, he had found one: trying to help Sammy Davis Jr. make a comeback.

Ever since they had first met in the early sixties, Cosby had had a soft spot for Sammy. He looked up to the multitalented song-and-dance man both as a remarkable performer and as an example of a black man willing to outwork any white man at his craft. When Davis drew fire from the Black Power crowd for marrying a white woman and hugging Richard Nixon, Cosby defended him. "He just wants to be loved," Cosby explained. "That's his psyche. Sammy Toms for everyone!"

In the seventies, Cosby had watched Sammy's hard living take its toll. His manager had dumped him, and he was all but broke. In 1980, Cosby reached out to Davis and suggested that they develop a show together. They tried it out at Harrah's, and then at Caesars Palace, and found that they enjoyed each other's company and on-stage chemistry. But Sammy was struggling to hit notes and had stopped trying to dance, and he could sense Cosby observing him and growing more and more alarmed.

After an early show one day, Cosby appeared in Davis's dressing room. He pointed at his friend's distended belly.

"What the fuck is wrong with you?" Cosby said.

Davis took a sip of the vodka and Coke on his dresser and fingered his paunch.

"Age, babe," he said. "I'm not fighting it. Grow old gracefully, they say."

"You're drinking all the time now," Cosby said.

Sammy saw a look on Cosby's face that he had never witnessed before. As he described it in his autobiography: "That wonderful, caring face that looked like it had been run over by every kind of trouble and sadness in the world, but still remembered how to smile, was frowning."

"Whatever you're doing," Cosby said, "don't end like this."

Now Cosby was trying to make sure that didn't happen. He put together a show with Sammy called *Two Friends,* and secured a two-week run at the Gershwin Theater on Broadway. Yet even after weeks of advance press and promotion, the show was a bust: only slightly more than half of the available tickets were sold, and the first six nights

500

brought in only $213,632. Every day that Cosby looked at the empty seats at the Gershwin, he grew more upset — about his inability to deliver for Sammy, about his friend's sorry condition, but also about the thought that the years were slipping away for him, too, the years when he was supposed to be pushing himself to new heights, like his inspiration Carl Sandburg.

Norman Brokaw was used to getting middle-of-the-night phone calls from Cosby. He had seen his favorite client in every kind of mood during those conversations, and he could tell that he was in a particularly somber and reflective state the night he called from New York in the middle of the Broadway run with Sammy Davis Jr.

"I think I'm ready to try another TV show," Cosby said. "Can you get on it?"

20
"MEET YOUR NEW FAMILY"

Marcy Carsey and Tom Werner were desperate. After rising through the ranks at ABC, the two young programming executives had quit their jobs to form an independent production company. They had sold their first venture, a show about a trend-crazed housewife called *Oh Madeline,* to their old network, but ABC had canceled it after one season. The two partners were working in a one-room office above a shoe store and had taken out second mortgages on their homes to keep the company afloat.

Carsey, a blunt blonde from New Hampshire, and Werner, a genial preppy from Manhattan, liked working together in part because they shared the same sense of humor. But their jokes were getting increasingly morbid. Leaving the office to pick up her dry cleaning one day, Carsey mused that it might be cheaper to abandon her clothes than to keep paying the cleaning bills.

It didn't help that many in the TV business

thought the entire mission of Carsey-Werner Productions was completely out of date. The two programmers had made their names at ABC in the late seventies developing the situation comedies *Taxi* and *Soap*. But now it was 1984, and the conventional wisdom in Hollywood was that sitcoms were dead. *Dallas, Dynasty,* and other prime-time soap operas sat atop the ratings charts, and only a handful of comedies were in Nielsen's top thirty.

Making their venture even more challenging, the two producers insisted on a unique approach to creating comedies. Most other TV production companies started their development process with a catchy premise or a cleverly written pilot. Carsey and Werner preferred to find comedians with strong personalities and build around them. It's what they had done with a hyperkinetic young talent named Robin Williams on *Mork & Mindy* and tried to do with Madeline Kahn, the zany comedienne famous for her roles in Mel Brooks movies, in *Oh Madeline*. But now that show had failed, and Carsey and Werner needed to find another comedian around whom to create their next show.

The head of the television department at William Morris, a gruff-talking Brooklyn native named Larry Auerbach, had helped Carsey and Werner put together the deal of *Oh*

Madeline, so they set up a meeting to see if he could help them.

"Who you got?" Carsey asked when they gathered in Auerbach's office.

What am I running, a grocery store? Auerbach thought.

"Well, there's Bill Cosby," he said. "Norman says he may be ready to do another TV show."

Carsey and Werner perked up. Several times in the past, they had inquired about Cosby's availability, but his agents had always said the timing wasn't right.

"You know how much we love Bill Cosby!" Carsey said.

"Yes, but he wants a *lot* of money," Auerbach said. "I don't know if you can afford him for a half-hour show."

When Auerbach told them how much, the producers swallowed hard. Per episode, it was enough that they would have to pay Cosby more than $1 million per season if the show succeeded. The producers had always said they were "betting on themselves" when they went independent, but that kind of money would mean betting the company. They told Auerbach that they needed time to think about it, and they decided to refresh their memories of Cosby by going to see him perform in Las Vegas.

Sitting in the audience at the Las Vegas Hilton, Carsey and Werner were reminded of everything they loved about Cosby. They had been teenagers when his first comedy albums came out and *I Spy* went on the air, and he still had the wonderful delivery and expressive face they remembered. But they also saw something new and, to them, even more exciting. As young parents — Carsey with two young children, Werner with three — they thought Cosby's new material on parenthood was extremely funny and remarkably true to life.

"What's missing on TV?" was a question they often asked themselves as they searched for ideas. And when it came to sitcoms in the early eighties, what was missing was the old *Father Knows Best* sense that parents were in charge. From *Silver Spoons* to *Webster,* the family comedies of the day revolved around improbably precocious children manipulating hapless adults. Now Cosby was painting a picture that was still common across America but nowhere to be found on the TV dial: of parents who loved their children but were determined to retain control of their own households.

Returning from Vegas, Carsey and Werner decided to take the plunge. They called Auerbach and asked if he could set up a meeting with Cosby. Shortly afterward, they were invited to dinner with the two William Morris agents at "the house that Jell-O built," Cosby's home in the Pacific Palisades.

When they arrived, Cosby greeted them at the door, a big cigar in hand as usual. He apologized that Mrs. Cosby couldn't join them and explained that she was at home in Massachusetts with their children. Still, Carsey could feel Camille's presence in the house. Among the many works of art on the walls was one that struck Carsey in particular, a portrait of the Cosbys sitting under a tree. Camille was posed elegantly on her knees, her back straight, her eyes fixed forward with a regal air. Her husband was sprawled casually on his side, a mischievous expression on his face. Carsey gazed at the portrait and reflected on what it said about the couple's relationship: the obvious reverence that Cosby had for his wife, but also the interesting commentary on how personalities complemented one another.

Cosby ushered his four guests — Carsey, Werner, Auerbach, and Brokaw — to the dinner table, and they didn't get up until past midnight. At first, Cosby said that if he was going to return to television, he wanted to do an hour-long drama. He threw out the concept of a high-rolling New York City private eye who ate at the '21' Club.

Politely but firmly, Carsey and Werner made the case for a half-hour comedy. "That's what we know how to do," Werner said. "If you really want to do a drama, we're not the right people."

506

Carsey started to make the argument for a show about family, based on the strong point of view reflected in Cosby's comedy routines. It would be about the loving "war between parents and their children" in which the authority of the mother and father was constantly tested but never broken. Flattered by the respect the producers showed for his stand-up material, Cosby warmed to the idea.

Yet when it came to the profession that Cosby's character would have on the show, he and the two producers had very different notions. Cosby thought it would be funny for the character to drive a limousine. He pointed out that it would allow him to tell stories about all the people and situations he encountered on the job, and give him a flexible schedule so he could be at home during the day to interact with his children. Cosby also liked the idea of a contemporary, two-career marriage, and proposed that the wife be a plumber or a carpenter. A woman who was handier around the house than her husband: that would be a clever role reversal. And she would be Latino and speak Spanish, so that when they had an argument, her husband wouldn't be able to understand what she was saying.

Cosby was talking with such forcefulness, pointing his cigar and using a "this is how it should be!" tone of voice, that for a while all

Carsey and Werner could do was sit back and listen.

Carsey heard two voices inside her head. One was saying: *Do whatever he wants! He's Bill Cosby, for God's sake! You need him, and you need this show!* But another was saying: *He's Bill Cosby! Even if he throws you out of this house, you need to tell him what you really think. You owe that to yourself — and to him.*

Finally, Cosby finished talking, and the producers sketched out their vision. They imagined a working couple, too, but they felt strongly that both should be college graduates. As Cosby had proven in his stand-up act, the war of wits between parents and children was even funnier if the parents thought of themselves as highly intelligent people. Making the character a limo driver would bring economic issues into the show, which would be a distraction from the dominant theme of family. Laying on more respectful flattery, Carsey and Werner told Cosby that they envisioned a simple show with minimal plots that would do what he did best: find the universal humor in everyday human experience.

For several hours, the conversation went back and forth, with Cosby continuing to muse about the limo driver and the handywoman, and Carsey and Werner arguing with increasing firmness for their concept.

"Hey, chauffeurs make good money!" Cosby insisted. "The guy will own his own car, meaning he'll be free to be at home at all kinds of weird hours — especially when his wife is working."

Finally, shortly before one o'clock in the morning, Cosby said the words that made Marcy Carsey think that she might be getting someplace.

"I think my wife would agree with you," Cosby said.

As it turned out, he was right.

"You will not be a chauffeur!" Camille said when he briefed her on the meeting.

"Why not?" Cosby asked.

"Because I'm not going to be a carpenter!" Camille said.

"What's the problem?" he said. "Is there something wrong with being a chauffeur or carpenter?"

"Bill, of course, there's nothing wrong with those occupations — I'd be stupid if I thought that," she said. "But nobody's going to believe that *you're* a chauffeur. Your image has always been Temple University, college, grad school. Nobody's going to believe it when you put on a uniform and stand beside a car and start polishing it. And people are going to laugh in your face when they see me with a hammer!"

Camille rarely got so adamant about casual things, so Cosby could tell that she was taking the decision about his next TV role very seriously. It was as if she was saying that he hadn't come this far — fighting for the dignity of the Alexander Scott and Chet Kincaid characters on his previous shows, creating the role model of Fat Albert for kids, earning a doctorate in education — to fall back on the stereotypes conjured by a black chauffeur and a Latina handywoman. More quickly than her husband, she also understood that once he had brought her and their children into his comedy routines, viewers would assume that the show was based at least in part on their real life.

As usual, Cosby trusted Camille's judgment, but he also didn't want to live with her displeasure. At one point, she told him that the limo driver idea was so crazy that he should see a psychiatrist and bring back a note. He knew he wasn't going to win the argument, so he got back to Brokaw and told him to inform Carsey and Werner that he would drop the chauffeur idea and agree to the more upscale professions. It was quickly decided that his character would be an obstetrician — a job that Cosby suggested because it reminded him of the medical counseling he had done as a physical therapist in the navy — and that his wife would be a lawyer.

Now Carsey and Werner had to figure out how to make the numbers work. And the financial hurdles they faced were far different from the ones that had confronted Cosby's first boss, Sheldon Leonard, when he set up his production company with Danny Thomas in the 1950s. In those days, production houses could get networks to fund most of the cost of creating new shows in exchange for giving them a large cut of syndication: the profit that would eventually be made by selling rerun rights to local TV stations. But all that had changed in the 1970s when the Federal Communications Commission issued new "financial interest and syndication" rules ("syn-fin" for short) that barred networks from having an ownership stake in the programs they aired.

When networks bought programs now, they were purchasing only the right to air the shows once or twice and sell commercials during those broadcasts. In essence, they were paying a licensing fee, and it rarely covered the cost of creating a new show. As a result, production companies had to engage in what was known in the business as "deficit financing" — taking a loss in the short term in hopes that they would come out ahead after syndication. But if a show never got to that point — because the network canceled it before there were enough episodes to qualify for syndication, or because it wasn't attractive to local stations — the production company could take a big loss.

Carsey and Werner were willing to go on the hook themselves, assuming enough risk that if they failed they would have to go back to working for other people. But that still wasn't going to be enough, given Cosby's salary demands. So Larry Auerbach proposed a way of getting additional funding: sell off a stake in future syndication immediately, before the show went on the air.

After the syn-fin ruling, the networks had created separate companies to handle syndication deals. One of them was Viacom International, a spin-off from CBS that sold rights to shows including *I Love Lucy* and *All in the Family.* Auerbach called his contacts at Viacom and quickly negotiated a deal that gave Viacom control of syndication down the road in exchange for the extra money that Carsey and Werner needed to get the Cosby show off the ground.

Next the producers had to find a network prepared to add a new situation comedy to its roster. And Cosby hadn't made life any easier by insisting that he would do the show only if a network committed to at least six episodes, not just a pilot. Because Carsey and Werner had a "first look" deal with their old bosses at ABC, they went to Lou Ehrlich, the head of the network's entertainment division. But with hits like *Dynasty* and *Hotel* and Monday night football, Ehrlich didn't see the point of taking a risk in the defunct realm of sitcoms. Knowing that it would kill the deal, he said he would only negotiate for a pilot and not the six episodes that Cosby demanded.

Auerbach and the producers went next to NBC, the network that had the most history with Cosby. Not only had he gotten his start on *The Tonight Show* and *I Spy,* but Grant Tinker, the programming executive who had helped get *I Spy* off the ground, was now president of the network. After running a production company with his wife, Mary Tyler Moore, for a decade, Tinker had returned to NBC and empowered an ambitious young head of programming named Brandon Tartikoff. Together, they had continued to invest in comedies, launching two smarter-than-average sitcoms — *Cheers* and *Family Ties* — and keeping them on the air despite low ratings. NBC was also the network most inclined to take new risks, given how badly their current shows were doing: in the previous season, the network had had only one show in the Nielsen top twenty, the schlocky adventure series *The A Team.*

Sure enough, Tartikoff was intrigued when he took a meeting with Carsey, Werner, and Auerbach. He had seen Cosby's parenting routines on *The Tonight Show* and *Bill Cosby: Himself,* and they had struck a nerve with him, too, as the father of two young daughters. But Tartikoff had his own idea about the

513

format for the show. He envisioned a retro homage to the comedies of the 1950s, when Jack Benny or George Burns and Gracie Allen would start each show by telling jokes from their stand-up routines before going into character.

Carsey and Werner listened politely before pleading their case yet again. They wanted realism, they told Tartikoff, and they worried that reminding viewers every week that Cosby was a comedian and that his TV character was an act would undercut the show's appeal. Eventually, Tartikoff saw their point and relented, and everyone agreed on the concept that the two producers had pushed from the start: "the war between parents and children" as told through the life of a middle-class black family.

Tartikoff approved negotiations toward a deal, but talks quickly stalled. Word came back that NBC's head of business affairs, John Agoglia, had taken the deal off the table because of Cosby's financial demands and his desire to shoot the show in New York. There were whispers about his three-show losing streak and the possibility that NBC affiliates who had memories of *The Bill Cosby Show* would be less than enthusiastic about his return to prime time.

By now, however, Cosby had become invested in the new show, and Carsey and Werner felt that they had given him their word. They were running out of time to get a place in the fall lineup: if one of the networks didn't commit soon, the show might be slated as a midseason replacement, a fate that was sure to dull Cosby's enthusiasm and make the financial gamble for Carsey-Werner Productions even riskier.

Auerbach called his contacts at CBS, who agreed to take a meeting. When word leaked back to NBC, suddenly its deal was back on the table. The network agreed to meet Cosby's demands and promised him the creative control he wanted. But they still had to show their affiliates and advertisers how this Bill Cosby show was going to be different from his previous flops. It was March by now, too late to make a fully scripted half-hour pilot. So Tartikoff asked for several scenes, fifteen minutes or so, to include in the "upfront" show that he was putting together to introduce NBC's fall season. And he wanted the "presentation" in a matter of weeks, by the end of April.

"Please God, help me be quiet," Phylicia Ayers-Allen prayed as she awoke in a Los Angeles hotel room on a Monday morning in late April 1984. She had flown in from New York the night before, leaving her family on Easter Sunday, after being called for her last audition for Cosby's new show. She got dressed, climbed into the car that had been sent for her, and soon found herself in an office suite in a nondescript Hollywood building where a group of children and two other women were seated in the lobby.

When Ayers-Allen introduced herself, a production assistant led her down a hallway and opened the door to a small office.

"This is a room where you can be quiet," the assistant said.

I hope that's an omen! Ayers-Allen thought.

Not long before, the elegant actress with the high cheekbones and refined diction would never have imagined herself auditioning for a TV sitcom. Her dream had always been to be in theater, from the time she was a Howard University student taking the train on weekends to see the Negro Ensemble Company in New York City. After graduating, she had joined the ranks of that fabled troupe. By the late seventies, she was waiting in the wings as the understudy for leading black female roles on Broadway: Dorothy in *The Wiz,* then Deena Jones in *Dreamgirls.* But when the actress who played Deena, Sheryl Lee Ralph, left the show, Ayers-Allen didn't get the part. She was bitterly disappointed, and in frustration she turned to television, taking the part of a female defense attorney on the daytime soap opera *One Life to Live.*

When she heard that casting agents were looking for an actress to play Bill Cosby's wife in a new sitcom, Ayers-Allen was intrigued. She had met Cosby when she was in college at Howard, when he had come to campus to perform. She asked him a question for the school newspaper, and his answer didn't just make her laugh but made her think. She had learned to respect the force of comedy as an art form from one of her favorite teachers at Howard, a Greek literature professor named Frank Snowden. During class one day Snowden had polled his students to find out if they preferred tragedy or comedy, and they had all dutifully voted for tragedy. "Ah, what a shame!" Snowden said. "Tragedy appeals only to the emotions, but comedy appeals to the mind."

Still, Ayers-Allen viewed the Cosby role as a long shot. Sheryl Lee Ralph, the actress for whom she had understudied on Broadway, was also auditioning for the part. They both made it through two callbacks and were told they were among three actresses chosen for a final audition in Los Angeles. Ralph was already going around town acting as though she had the part sewn up, so as Ayers-Allen boarded the plane, she told herself not to hope for too much. At least she was getting a free trip to California — even if she did have to travel on Easter weekend.

She hoped that she had one small thing in her favor. The casting agent had tipped her off that Cosby was looking for an actress who spoke Spanish. No one knew why, but he seemed fixated. As it happened, Ayers-Allen had learned the language as a child growing up in Texas, and her family had lived in Mexico for a brief time. But it had been years ago, and her Spanish was rusty. So she asked her son's babysitter, a young woman from the Dominican Republic, to help her bone up. When she got home from the soap opera, they would make conversation so that Phylicia could relearn a few phrases and practice the rhythm of the language.

The production assistant returned and escorted Ayers-Allen to a conference room. Seated around a table were several important-looking white people and Bill Cosby, wearing sweatpants and sneakers and smoking a cigar. He asked her to read a few lines with him. While Phylicia did her theater-trained best, Cosby was mumbling. But she sensed him watching her face — looking, he would later tell her, for that special "angry mother look in her eyes," the one Anna Cosby had given him as a boy and that he had seen so often in Camille.

When the reading was over, Cosby asked Ayers-Allen to say a few words in Spanish, and she rattled off one of the phrases she had practiced with the babysitter.

He didn't seem impressed. "Say something else," he said.

She recited another rehearsed line, and this time his face lit up.

"That's what I'm talking about!" he said.

The production assistant escorted Ayers-Allen back to the silent office, and she waited for what seemed like an eternity. Finally, the door opened and in walked Jay Sandrich, the man who had directed her final screen test.

Sandrich had been all business before, but now he was smiling.

"Come meet your new family!" he said.

For Bill Cosby, Marcy Carsey, and Tom Werner, the month leading up to that moment had been a mad scramble. Although NBC had agreed to accept a presentation of their new show rather than a full-blown pilot, network executives wanted to know who the writers would be. Carsey and Werner had called all around town but couldn't get any big names to commit to the project. Some of the writers they approached still bore scars from working on *I Spy* or had heard the scuttlebutt about Cosby's disdain for most TV scripts. Others were reluctant to get involved with a show that was being thrown together at the last minute and didn't stand much of a chance in the era of extinct sitcoms.

On a Thursday night, Tartikoff's deputy, Warren Littlefield, called Carsey and warned her that if she didn't have a head writer by the following Monday, he would push the new show out of the fall lineup and into the dreaded no-man's land of midseason replacements. Pulling out her Rolodex, Carsey came upon what she would describe as her "Hail Mary pass." As a young page working for *The Tonight Show,* she had met Ed Weinberger. She knew that he was a friend of Cosby's and that they had worked together on his first sitcom. She had an old number, so she dialed it. To her relief, Weinberger answered the phone. When Carsey described the idea of Cosby in a family comedy, Weinberger liked it. He said he would help write the presentation on one condition: that Michael Leeson work with him. Leeson had been a top writer on *Taxi,* and Carsey knew him from her ABC days. She agreed, Leeson signed on, and by the weekend she was able to call Littlefield with the good news.

"What?" said the impressed programmer. "You got Weinberger and Leeson!"

To direct the minipilot, Carsey and Werner had one name in mind: Jay Sandrich. A protégé of Sheldon Leonard's who cut his teeth working on shows like *The Danny Thomas Show* and *The Dick Van Dyke Show,* Sandrich had come into his own directing virtually every episode of *The Mary Tyler Moore Show* during its seven-year run in the seventies. Carsey and Werner had gotten to know him as a director on *Soap,* the offbeat ensemble comedy they helped develop for ABC. A small, slender man whose serious manner belied his expertise at comedy, Sandrich was known for handling actors with a deft touch while keeping a firm hand on the production tiller. He was also an ace in the editing room, where footage from the three or four cameras used on most sitcom sets was mixed. The use of reaction shots and laughter from an audience or a laugh track were almost as important to TV comedy as the quality of the writing and acting, and Sandrich was a master of making the juggling act look effortless.

At first, Sandrich wasn't interested. The citizen in him liked the idea of a show that would paint a positive picture of black family life, but the perfectionist hated the idea of doing a test episode without a finished script. He had a reputation as "the king of pilots," the guy you wanted in the director's booth to make your first show look as good as possible, and he didn't want to compromise his standards. Only when Carsey and Werner assured him that the presentation wouldn't air on television — that it was just meant to give the network a feel for the show and to whet the appetites of advertisers and affiliates — did he agree to come on board.

Next came the most important piece of the puzzle: casting the members of Cosby's TV family. He and his producers wanted a "character-driven" rather than a "story-driven" show, so it was essential to find actors who would jell but also have distinct personalities. Once Cosby bought into the idea of a family much like his own, he was also looking for very specific traits that he had seen in his own wife and children. He told Carsey and Werner that for each part he wanted to see three finalists, who would be flown to Los Angeles in early April to read with him.

By now it had been decided that Cosby would play a doctor named Clifford Huxtable. (The first name would be changed to Heathcliff after several episodes.) He would be married to a lawyer named Clair, and they would have four children, two girls and two boys. So with only weeks to spare, Carsey and Werner put out calls to casting agents across the country to scout for young actors to play the Huxtable children.

Originally, Cosby had decreed that none of the children should be younger than ten or eleven. He knew from making his Jell-O commercials how difficult it could be to get younger children to learn lines and follow directions. "We'll be shooting for the rest of our lives if we have a little kid!" he warned. But Carsey and Werner took the opposite lesson from those ads: Cosby was too good with little kids *not* to have one on the show. They urged him to at least meet with a few candidates for the youngest Huxtable child, who they envisioned as a boy of six or seven named Rudy.

As Tom Werner was reviewing casting tapes, he came across a commercial for Del Monte canned corn featuring an adorable little girl with pinked-bowed braids, dancing eyes, and a gap-tooted smile. "You sure do know about 'trition!" she said to a kindly local grocer in the ad. Werner thought: *We've got to audition this kid!*

From the day she was born in Newark, New Jersey, Keshia Knight Pulliam had loved to coo and smile. Her mother, Denise, saw the makings of a child model and took her to a talent agency when she was five months old. By eight months, Keshia had appeared in a Johnson & Johnson ad in *Ebony* magazine, and by three years old she was a veteran of *Sesame Street.* But Jay Sandrich didn't realize just how young she was until he directed her screen test.

"How old are you?" he asked.

"Five!" Keshia said proudly — although that was barely true, since she had just celebrated her birthday in early April.

"Can you memorize lines?" Sandrich asked.

"Yes!" Keshia said confidently.

Sandrich noticed that she kept gazing away from the camera, transfixed by the TV monitors on the wall.

"What are you looking at?" he said.

"How can you make me on the TV?" Keshia asked.

When Cosby saw the audition tape, he had

to admit that the little girl was "all personality." And when she read with him, he saw that she was very intelligent — smart enough to learn lines and follow directions, despite the fact that she was barely five years old. So instead of a boy, he and the producers agreed to cast Keshia Knight Pulliam as the youngest Huxtable child.

"But what will her name be?" someone asked.

"What's wrong with Rudy?" Cosby said. "That works for a girl, too."

Casting the eldest of the four Huxtable children (a fifth, a college student named Sondra, would be added later) went quickly when Cosby met a fifteen-year-old actress from Los Angeles who came to her audition with makeup on only one side of her face. Cosby took one look at Lisa Bonet and thought: *That's the character!* He wanted Denise Huxtable to be hip, fashion-conscious, and a bit flaky — just spaced-out enough that the audience might wonder if she was on drugs, although she wouldn't be. Bonet, the biracial daughter of a black opera singer and white schoolteacher who had been born in San Francisco, exuded those qualities just by being herself. Cosby was also struck by Bonet's exotic beauty — like Camille, she had Lena Horne's combination of light skin, delicate cheekbones, and piercing, wide-set eyes. When she was brought in to read with him, he loved the naturalness of her delivery, which had none of the stagey quality he hated in most child actors.

When Cosby met the three finalists for the third Huxtable child, he also declared a clear winner. He envisioned Vanessa Huxtable as a "young old soul" — a child who could read her siblings and outwit her parents, but whose intelligence would fly out the window as she became obsessed with social popularity and appealing to boys. Cosby sensed that personality type immediately when he met Tempestt Bledsoe, a ten-year-old from Chicago. Bledsoe didn't have much experience as an actress — she had appeared in a few commercials — and she was astonished when she made it through five local callbacks and was asked to fly to LA. When Cosby read with Bledsoe, he was taken with the intelligent tone of her voice as well as its high pitch, which he thought would be perfect for a girl who was at turns a whiz and a whiner.

For the Huxtable boy, Cosby wanted someone who looked like Ennis, who had just turned fifteen, and had shot up to more than six feet tall. He also wanted another natural actor, not a showy wise-ass. On the last day of casting, however, he still hadn't found anyone he was happy with. Then a young stage mother named Pamela Warner appeared with her son, Malcolm-Jamal. Named for Malcolm X and the jazz pianist Ahmad

Jamal, the thirteen-year-old was also from New Jersey — Jersey City, north of Newark — and had been raised by his divorced mother. She had enrolled him in acting classes at the age of nine, moved to LA to help him break into show business, and brought him to the audition after getting a last-minute call from a casting agent the night before.

Warner was ushered in to read with Cosby, and he began to deliver the lines he was given to read in the precocious, wise-aleck tone he had heard so often on TV. Hearing laughter around the table, he thought: *I've got this!* Then he looked up and saw a stony expression on Cosby's face.

"Stop right there!" Cosby said after a few minutes. "Now let me ask you a question. Would you talk to your father like that?"

"No," Warner replied sheepishly.

"Well, I don't want to see that on this show," Cosby said. "I want you to go out in the hallway and work on those lines again. And when you come back, I don't want to see a TV kid, I want to see a real kid."

When Warner returned, he delivered his lines with a naturalness that impressed everyone in the room. Cosby smiled and thought: *Just like Ennis! Nailed it!*

The choice of Phylicia Ayers-Allen to play Clair Huxtable completed the casting, and as she was brought in to meet her new TV family, she hugged each of the children. Suddenly the spirit moved her to ask them to hold hands and pray. "May the Lord watch over thee and me while we are absent from each other," she recited, invoking a prayer she had learned as a child growing up in Houston.

They would be absent from each other only until the next day, when they gathered for one day of rehearsal before taping the presentation before a live audience. Ed Weinberger and Michael Leeson had finally delivered a script, but it was hardly a full-blown story, just a few scenes built around bits from Cosby's stand-up act. As the rehearsal began, it seemed as though Cosby didn't recognize his own material. He kept mumbling and flubbing lines. The child actors were all over the place, stumbling over dialogue and struggling to find the right tone and attitude. Only Ayers-Allen seemed remotely ready to face an audience the next day. It took the ensemble more than an hour to get through fifteen minutes' worth of material.

Afterward, the producers and director huddled to assess their options.

Sandrich was deeply worried. "Maybe we should postpone," he said.

Carsey and Werner reminded everyone that Cosby was only available for another day — after that, he was leaving town for a concert gig — and that it would be very expensive to start all over again with another live audience.

"In that case, we better go ahead," Sandrich said. "Bill comes alive before an audience. I'm not going to do this without one."

To save money, Carsey and Werner had decided to film the presentation on the set of their canceled sitcom *Oh Madeline.* It was meant to be the living room of a suburban white couple, not a black urban family. The furniture was all off-white, and the walls were adorned with bland landscape paintings. But it would have to do. After sending out invitations to a free TV taping at the last minute, the producers also had no idea what kind of audience to expect.

On the day of the taping, Cosby arrived at the studio wearing a beige sports jacket and a brown argyle vest, and as soon as he heard the crowd, he perked up. Speaking to the audience from the director's booth, Sandrich told them that the performance was about to start, and Bill Cosby and Phylicia Ayers-Allen came on stage as Cliff and Clair Huxtable and opened with a line pulled straight from Cosby's stand-up act.

"Remind me why we have four children?" she said in a cross voice.

"Because we didn't want to have five!" he said.

The audience burst into laughter, and from then on, Cosby was a different man. The distracted mumbler from the day before was gone. Suddenly he was the Bill Cosby of his stand-up act and his comedy albums: expressive, energetic, and effortlessly funny. One after another, the actors playing the Huxtable children appeared on stage, and he seemed utterly at ease with each of them: affectionate with little Rudy, skeptical with manipulative Vanessa, at once exasperated by and protective of free-spirited Denise. "How ugly is he?" he asked upon learning that a boy had come to call on his daughter, and the crowd roared again.

The final scene called for Cliff to go up to Theo's messy room to talk to him about his dismal report card. It was based almost word for word on the tense, nightlong argument Cosby had with Ennis about his son's desire to be "regular people." The only embellishment was a visual conceit that Weinberger and Leeson had added for television: Cliff would give Theo a lecture using Monopoly money. He would hand Theo three hundred dollars and then snatch bills away to show how quickly the money would go once Theo paid taxes, bought food and clothes, and took a girlfriend out on a date.

To make sure they had enough footage for the upfront, the producers filmed two live performances of the seventeen-minute presentation. The first one took place in the afternoon, and the audience was filled with young people who didn't have day jobs or were playing hooky from school. They laughed during Cliff's Monopoly speech but responded even more strongly when Theo stood up to give his impassioned response.

"You're a doctor and Mom's a lawyer and you're successful and everything and that's great," he said. "But maybe I was born to be a regular person and have a regular life. If I were a doctor, I wouldn't love you less, because you're my dad. And so, instead of acting disappointed because I'm not like you, maybe you can just accept who I am and love me anyway, because I'm your son."

Cosby had thought that the audience would see through the ridiculousness of Theo's speech, but instead they burst into applause. For a moment, he thought: *Maybe I'm in trouble here; they're sympathizing with the boy rather than the father.* He had to restrain himself from putting a few choice curse words in Cliff's mouth. But instead he channeled his exasperation into his comeback line.

"Theo!" Cosby snapped. "That's the dumbest thing I ever heard in my life! It's no wonder you get *D*s in everything. Now you are afraid to try because you're afraid your brain is going to explode and it will ooze out of your ears. Now I'm telling you, you are going to try as hard as you can and you're going to do it because I said so, and I'm your father."

Then he added another line from his comedy act, the one he had always attributed to Bill Cosby Sr. "I brought you in this world," he said, "and I will take you out!"

Cosby's outburst got enough laughs to make the scene work, but he still came away feeling that it hadn't played the way he expected.

That evening, far more adults were in the audience, many of them arriving from work. This time, there was dutiful applause when Theo delivered his "love me for who I am" soliloquy. But as soon as Cosby let loose with "That's the dumbest thing I've heard in my life!" the crowd went wild. They hooted and hollered and jumped to their feet to give him a standing ovation. The applause was thunderous, and it went on for several minutes.

Sandrich thought someone was playing tricks on him. "Who turned on the applause sign?" he asked, running out of the control booth.

"Not us!" said Carsey and Warner. The three stood watching as the crowd continued to cheer. Between them they had seen hundreds of sitcom episodes shot before live audiences, and none of them had ever witnessed anything quite like it.

Watching the jubilant audience reaction, Carsey felt a sense of vindication. It suggested that she and Werner had been right about what was missing on TV. Those whooping adults were tired of seeing parents get bossed around by smart-alecky kids. They were ready for a father who stood up and said: *I'm right, and you're wrong!* They were rooting for the parents to take back the household.

Sandrich sensed something even more profound. He was struck by the contrast between the way the Monopoly scene had played in the afternoon and the way it was playing now. The younger crowd had seen it from the son's vantage. Now this older crowd was identifying with the father's point of view. If *The Cosby Show* could pull off that trick on a regular basis, he thought — portraying family life in a way that both children and parents could relate to — then it was sure to be a hit.

Cosby, meanwhile, was doing what he had done for twenty years: not analyzing the audience's reacting so much as reading its mind. As he sensed what the crowd was thinking and feeling, he thought: *We've got it! We've got a show!*

Later, NBC executives would insist that they also knew from that moment that they had a winner on their hands. Yet even after seeing how well the presentation went over with the live audiences, they weren't ready to confirm a place on the fall schedule. "We have a lot of good pilots this year," they told Carsey and Werner. It wasn't until the upfront, when the network officially announced its fall lineup, that they confirmed that *The Cosby Show* would be part of it.

NBC slated the show for eight o'clock on Thursday nights. It was hardly a vote of confidence, since the drama *Magnum P.I.* on CBS had dominated the time slot for years. But at least it was the first show of the night, in the leadoff position where baseball fans Carsey and Werner believed it belonged. Now all they had to do was to put the first half dozen episodes together in less than two months before the season started, a challenge that had been made all the more daunting by the final demand Cosby made in agreeing to return to television.

On the set one day, Cosby would joke with Jay Sandrich that he insisted on filming the show in New York City because Camille wouldn't permit him to return to Los Angeles after the trouble he had gotten into at "Hugh Hefner's place." But the truth was that, for all his cigar-waving bravado, Cosby was still haunted by his three failed TV shows since *I Spy.* And in an era when sitcoms were getting "test pattern ratings," as he liked to joke, he could hardly be confident that this outing would succeed.

As he quipped to Marcy Carsey about the decision to shoot in New York: "At least if I get canceled, I won't have to fly home."

21
THE SERFS OF FLATBUSH

It was Earl Pomerantz's first call to Bill Cosby, and he was nervous. The thirty-nine-year-old TV writer had worked for some of the biggest names in the business, from Mary Tyler Moore and Valerie Harper to Bob Newhart, but he still got self-conscious dealing with stars. And he never was good on the phone. Still, Marcy Carsey and Tom Werner had hired the curly-haired Canadian to be the head writer of *The Cosby Show* after Ed Weinberger and Michael Leeson refused to relocate to New York, and they wanted him to place a courtesy call to his new boss.

Pomerantz had heard about the debate over what Cosby's character would do for a living, and he agreed with the decision to make him a doctor. But he was bothered by the idea of making the wife a lawyer, so he decided to lobby Cosby to consider another profession, like a college professor.

Cosby's reply was terse. "I'm a doctor and my wife is a lawyer," he said.

Pomerantz pressed on, warning about the danger of "status overkill."

There was a long silence on the other end of the line.

"I'm a doctor and my wife is a lawyer," Cosby repeated.

Okay, case closed! Pomerantz thought, getting a first taste of the suspicion of journeymen TV writers that Cosby had harbored ever since his *I Spy* days.

Their face-to-face meeting came a few days later, when Pomerantz and Tom Werner were invited to dinner at the house in the Pacific Palisades. When they got there, they discovered that the other guests, mostly from the advertising world, were all black. During the meal, jazz played in the background, and Cosby challenged Pomerantz to identify the musicians. Pomerantz didn't have a clue — at least until he heard Dr. John — but the black guests had no problem playing the parlor game. He sensed that Cosby was toying with him, giving him a taste of the way black people feel when they are outnumbered and culturally intimidated by white people.

At the end of the meal, Cosby handed out cigars, but he didn't offer one to Pomerantz, who decided that this was a snub too far.

"I want a cigar!" he piped up.

Cosby took him downstairs to a room stocked floor to ceiling with his favorite cigars: Royal Jamaicans, Hoyo de Monterrey double coronas from Cuba, Ashton Maduro No. 60s from the Dominican Republic.

"Which one do you want?" Cosby asked.

"Just give me one that isn't too big for my face," Pomerantz said, trying and failing to make the new boss laugh.

Before leaving, Pomerantz asked to see Cosby's doctoral dissertation on *Fat Albert and the Cosby Kids.* Cosby didn't seem thrilled by the request, but he went upstairs and returned with a leather-bound volume that he handed over with what struck Pomerantz as an odd comment, at once defensive and competitive. "You don't have to sit down to be a writer!" he said.

Pomerantz wanted to talk about the scripts he had begun writing, but Cosby put him off, saying that they would talk when they got to New York. Their next contact came during a last LA press junket, where reporters quizzed Cosby skeptically about why he wanted to return to the moribund world of sitcoms. "We have thirteen televisions in our house," Cosby replied. "It was either do a show I was willing to watch, or throw them all out."

Afterward, Pomerantz introduced his wife to Cosby, who couldn't resist another dig at the anxious writer.

"I hope your husband can write," he said, "because he certainly can't talk."

Pomerantz had other worries beside his

chemistry with Cosby. He was still scrambling to find other writers to be part of his team. Most of the trial scripts he was receiving were full of the kind of contrived plot lines and one-liners that Cosby hated. Some Hollywood veterans whom he had hoped to recruit refused to move to New York; others weren't affordable on the tight budget Carsey and Werner had provided. By the time shooting was about to start, Pomerantz had hired only two female writers, Korby Siamis and Caryl Miller, on short-term contracts, and a young writer whose audition script stood out from the others: a twenty-eight-year-old Stanford grad named John Markus.

It wasn't until he flew to New York, however, that Pomerantz discovered just how tight the budget for *The Cosby Show* would be. On the plane from Los Angeles, he sat in first class, courtesy of the Writers Guild of America, which had negotiated that perk for its members. Meanwhile, Tom Werner sat in economy, because he didn't want to waste his own money, alongside Markus, who had traded in his first-class ticket to pocket the refund. During the flight, an attendant kept bringing Pomerantz notes from his colleagues in coach.

"Any steak left over?" one note said.

"Did you get your hot cookie yet?" said another.

When Pomerantz arrived at the apartment

that had been rented for him in Manhattan, near the United Nations, there was no toilet paper in the bathrooms. He also discovered that he would have a very long commute to work. The only state-of-the-art TV production facility in New York City, the Kaufman Astoria Studios in Queens, was booked, so Carsey and Werner had arranged to shoot *The Cosby Show* on a dilapidated soundstage on the edge of Flatbush, on the southern end of Brooklyn.

The Vitagraph studio was almost a century old, and it looked it. Built at the end of the nineteenth century, the block-long complex on East Fourteenth Street between Locust and Chestnut Avenues had once been the largest movie production house in the world. Many classics of the silent film era, from *Vanity Fair* to *Uncle Tom's Cabin,* were shot there, and a huge smokestack emblazoned with the Vitagraph logo still loomed down the block. But as the surrounding neighborhood became an enclave for ultraorthodox Jews, the studio had been sold a religious girls' school that took over most of the property, leaving a small sound stage next door whose only tenant by 1984 was the soap opera *Another World.*

For office space, Carsey and Werner had rented two apartments above a kosher fish market with the ironic name of Twentieth

Century Fish. They took over one apartment, to do business and to shower after flying in on the red eye from Los Angeles on Monday mornings. They turned over the other apartment to Pomerantz and his team, who soon would be spending many nights working without making it home. "So, are you married?" asked a Jewish woman in a printed housecoat every time she saw Pomerantz in the elevator. On Fridays, the smell of chicken soup and gefilte fish filled the hallways. Adding to the gypsy working conditions, the writers had to decamp to a temporary office space every weekend, because the elevators stopped operating in Flatbush, and all the stores closed down for Shabbat, the Jewish Sabbath.

Inside the drafty soundstage, ancient lights hung from the ceiling and the production equipment was decades out of date. The cameras were old RCA models that didn't automatically correct for shifts in light and color like their modern Japanese counterparts, so shooting kept getting interrupted while the cameras were adjusted. Sometimes they broke down and couldn't be used again until they were repaired overnight. In the early weeks of shooting, Carsey and Werner repeatedly complained to Brandon Tartikoff, who put them off because he didn't want to tell his bosses at RCA, NBC's parent company, that their cameras weren't good enough. Then Tartikoff visited the set and was so appalled by how many times filming ground to a halt that he told the frustrated producers that they could order new Japanese cameras.

The fact that none of the NBC cameramen assigned to the show had any experience with sitcoms didn't make life any easier. Most came from *Saturday Night Live* or NBC Sports, and they weren't wild about having to travel to the middle of nowhere in Brooklyn to shoot an outmoded sitcom. And even when everything else was functioning, the arcane rules of New York City's craft unions could stop production at any moment.

The first episode scheduled for production in Brooklyn ended with a funeral for Rudy's pet goldfish. The script called for the Huxtable family to gather around a bathroom toilet to remember the dead pet before it was flushed down the drain. But as the set was being prepped, the show's designer, Garvin Eddy, noticed that there was no paper dispenser next to the toilet. Worried that the TV audience might notice, Eddy asked a man from the prop department to install a dispenser in the wall.

No sooner had the prop guy gone to work than the shop steward assigned to the show walked over to stop him.

"He can't do that," the steward said.

"Why not?" Eddy asked.

"That's a square hole," the steward said.

"Yeah, so, it's a square hole," Eddy said.

"Well, he can't cut a square hole," the steward said. "Someone from the prop department can only cut a round hole, not a square one."

Eddy frowned in disbelief. "Are you kidding me?" he said.

"No," the steward said. "If you want a square hole, you have to call the scene shop in Manhattan and get them to send a carpenter."

So Eddy lost several hours of work while the union sent a carpenter authorized to wield a saw all the way out to the southern tip of Brooklyn.

The neighborhood was such an unlikely location for a big network production that the local bank became suspicious. In order to facilitate payments to suppliers, Carsey and Werner set up an account at a local branch of Chemical Bank. By the time they arrived in New York, they were using it to make deposits and to cut checks worth tens of thousands of dollars a week. Bank officials in Manhattan noticed all the activity at their sleepy Flatbush branch and sent an inspector to investigate. The inspector became even more leery when he arrived at the address listed on the account — the tiny apartment above Twentieth Century Fish. He wouldn't leave until Carsey and Werner took him to the studio to see where all the money was going.

Inside the creaky old studio, however, a very different world from the one outside was coming to life. By the time shooting began in the summer, Cosby hadn't just bought into the notion that it should be about a prosperous black family. He now envisioned a *very* prosperous family. To save money, Carsey and Werner instructed Garvin Eddy to build a set in Los Angeles and ship it to New York. They told him that they wanted the Huxtable home to look comfortable but not too ostentatious. But when Eddy consulted Cosby, it became clear that he pictured something grander. He wanted the Huxtables to live in an elegant brownstone furnished with antiques and tasteful artwork, much like the town house that he and Camille owned on Manhattan's East Side.

Eddy wasn't sure about the idea. "Do you think America is going to believe a black family living in that kind of place?" he asked. "Will that be a problem?"

"I don't care," Cosby said. "That's what I want."

It was all Eddy needed to hear. He had long since developed a philosophy about his job: when he got different instructions, he went with the money. This was Cosby's show, so he would follow Cosby's orders.

For the next month, Eddy shopped for

542

antique furniture and rugs and paintings by African American artists, according to Cosby's detailed instructions. Meanwhile, NBC's West Coast scene shop constructed a classic sitcom set, with a living room, a kitchen, and another area that would serve as a bedroom for the parents or the kids, as well as modular space that could do extra duty as a hallway, front stoop, or backyard. The set was shipped and assembled in Brooklyn, and Eddy nervously awaited the verdict of his producers and star.

"Oh my god, it's too nice!" Jay Sandrich said as soon as he saw the set. "They're too rich!"

Carsey and Werner didn't venture an opinion, but Eddy could tell that they were concerned.

Then Cosby appeared. He began to walk around, running his hands over every piece of furniture, leaning over to inspect the rugs, turning over the objects on the tables and desks, and gazing at the paintings on the wall.

"He's not liking it at all!" Sandrich whispered.

Eddy couldn't tell, but he would remember it as the longest ten minutes of his life.

Finally, Cosby walked over to him and nodded approvingly.

"It's exactly right," he said.

Thank God! Eddy thought.

Cosby had another specific request: that all

the flowers on the set be real. When Eddy pointed out that viewers wouldn't be able to tell the difference, Cosby said that it wasn't for them. It was for the cast and crew, to help them feel like it was a genuine home. Privately, he was also taking a page from his mentor Sheldon Leonard and his first-class-all-the-way gestures. So each morning, even on rehearsal days, a van carrying freshly cut flowers would arrive in the bowels of Brooklyn to make a delivery to the Vitagraph studio.

Unbeknownst to Earl Pomerantz and the other writers, Cosby was taking another step to ensure the realism of the show. A decade earlier, he had made the acquaintance of a Harvard Medical School psychiatrist named Dr. Alvin Poussaint at a Chicago fundraiser for Jesse Jackson's Operation PUSH. Cosby was being inundated with requests to appear in documentaries about children and education, and he wanted help vetting them. He asked Poussaint if he would read the scripts and give him critiques drawing on the physician's expertise: child psychology and the influence of racial experience on the psyche of young minorities.

By 1984, Poussaint hadn't heard from Cosby in a while, so he was surprised to answer the phone and hear a familiar voice getting right to the point.

"I want you on my staff!" Cosby said.

"What do you mean, 'your staff'?" Poussaint asked.

"All the writers on my new TV show are white," Cosby said. "I'm worried that none of them has any experience with black families or black people."

Cosby asked Poussaint if he would read the scripts and offer his professional guidance. In his usual rambling way, he touched on all the things he wanted Poussaint to look out for. He wanted the children to speak in a believable way, not in contrived one-liners. ("No words that would never come out of the mouth of a sixteen-year-old!" he said.) He wanted disputes within the family to be settled by talking, not by shouting. He wanted Cliff and Clair Huxtable to forge a united front as parents but still have romance and physical affection in their relationship, to "give black folks a model of a strong two-parent household." And he wanted the smallest details of the family's life to reflect black reality, not a white writer's idea of black reality.

Cosby also told Poussaint to keep an eye out for dialogue that sounded disrespectful. "Sitcom writers like to use a lot of put-down humor," he warned. "I don't want any of that."

Earl Pomerantz had signed a contract with Carsey and Werner to write six episodes, in addition to fleshing out the presentation to create a pilot. What he didn't know was that as soon as he delivered the scripts to Cosby, Cosby sent them to Poussaint for a second opinion. And after reading the first few critiques, he asked the psychiatrist to be even tougher on the work of the show writers.

"I can sense that you're holding back on scenes that are supposed to be funny," Cosby said.

"Perhaps," Poussaint admitted.

"Well, don't," Cosby said. "Your job is to check reality. My job is to make it funny."

As soon as shooting began in New York, Cosby resumed his hazing of Earl Pomerantz. Several additional scenes were required to flesh out the presentation that had been filmed in LA. (No one wanted to reshoot the Monopoly money scene between Cliff and Theo because it had been so magical.) In one of the scenes, based on a Cosby stand-up routine about his own experience with Camille, Cliff was to comfort a nervous father waiting for his wife to give birth. At the table read on their second day on the job, Cosby asked Pomerantz if he wanted to play the part of the expectant father.

Pomerantz didn't know what to say. He wasn't an actor.

"What if I mess up?" he asked.

"Bases loaded," Cosby said. "Two outs. Bottom of the ninth."

Pomerantz read the part, and afterward

everyone agreed that it would be better to hire a professional actor.

Pomerantz shrugged off the latest bit of aggressive teasing as work began on his "Goodbye, Mr. Fish" episode. He was proud of the script, which he based on a story he had written for *Taxi* about a goldfish that dies while his owner is away. In this version, he wanted to show how attached little children become to their pets but also how quickly they can forget them. In his script, Rudy is thrown into depression when her goldfish Lamont passes. When her older siblings mockingly suggest a funeral, Cliff makes them go through with it, but then Rudy loses interest in the middle of the ceremony and leaves to watch TV.

When Carsey, Werner, and Pomerantz had met with Brandon Tartikoff to go over the first six scripts, Tartikoff wasn't happy with any of them. He didn't understand what was so funny about a dead goldfish, and he wondered what a scene involving a toilet was doing in a family comedy. He was similarly cool about the premises for the next three episodes, which involved Vanessa sneaking out to see a scary movie against her parents' wishes, Cliff being disappointed when Theo doesn't make the football team, and Denise trying to make a knockoff of a designer shirt for Theo when his parents refuse to pay for a "Gordon Gartrell" original.

"So what's the sixth week?" Tartikoff asked impatiently.

Werner started to describe a script that Pomerantz had written called "Breaking with Tradition."

"The grandfather comes over for dinner and talks to Denise about her choices for college," Werner said.

Tartikoff frowned. "Is that all that happens?" he asked.

Still, Carsey and Werner had stood up for the scripts, and Cosby seemed satisfied. As the first week unfolded, "Goodbye, Mr. Fish" appeared to withstand what was shaping up as a grueling production process. Most sitcoms were shot in five days, allowing three days for table reads and rehearsals before a day of "blocking" and a final day of taping. But because Cosby intended to keep performing stand-up on the weekends, he decreed a four-day schedule. Most stars also gave feedback on scripts before the table reads began, but Cosby informed the writers that he wanted to hear the words before offering an opinion, meaning that they wouldn't get his "notes" until the first read on Monday. (Cosby also wanted to give Alvin Poussaint time to weigh in — a weekly ritual that the writers would only learn about later in the first season.)

After the first table read, everyone had notes about the goldfish script — the star, the producers, the director, the NBC executives who sat in — but Pomerantz chalked that up to first-week jitters. He and his writers stayed up all night making changes, which were received well the following day. For the next two days, everyone stuck to the revised script as the cast did a second table read and then rehearsed on set so that Sandrich could figure out how to position his four cameras. The child actors worked hard to memorize their lines, and Cosby was hitting his, too, if not with much enthusiasm, as if he were reserving his energy for game day.

On Thursday, Pomerantz arrived at the Vitagraph studio wearing a new black blazer with gold buttons that Werner had urged him to buy for taping days. The schedule called for two performances before a live audience — one at 4:30 in the afternoon and another at 7:30 in the evening — so that Sandrich could choose the best takes from each taping to edit the show that would appear on the air. Pomerantz was so excited that he came out to welcome the audience and even got off a joke that made them laugh.

Then the performance started, and Pomerantz's mood shifted from excitement to bewilderment. Cosby wasn't reciting the dialogue that had been written for him. Sometimes he was reworking it; sometimes he was embellishing it; sometimes he was making up new lines entirely. As they scrambled to keep up with him, Ayers-Allen and the children were changing their dialogue as well. And the more the audience laughed, the more Cosby improvised.

Pomerantz felt like he was watching a *Twilight Zone* version of his script. Before the personal computers became commonplace, TV writers dictated scripts to secretaries, who typed up clean drafts for the cast and crew. Because no other sitcoms were shot in New York in 1984, the secretaries for *The Cosby Show* came from soap operas, law offices, and *Captain Kangaroo,* and for a moment Pomerantz wondered if they had somehow rewritten the final draft before handing it out.

During the break before the second taping, Carsey, Werner, Sandrich, and Pomerantz went to Cosby's dressing room to give him notes. Cosby had taken off his shirt, making Pomerantz feel even more intimidated as he eyed his athletic physique. Everyone else praised the first taping and offered only minor suggestions for the next performance, mostly about details of timing and movement.

The visitors were about to leave when Cosby pointed at Pomerantz.

"I want to know what *this* guy has to say," he said.

Pomerantz took another glance at Cosby's muscular chest. *This guy could beat me up for what I'm about to say,* he thought, but he plunged ahead.

"I really wish you'd learn your lines," he said.

There was dead silence in the room. Pomerantz glanced around at his coworkers, who were looking down at the floor. He would later compare it to the whooshing sound you hear when you hold a seashell to your ear.

Finally, Cosby spoke. "A doctor would never say some of those lines!" he snapped, and he continued fulminating until Carsey and Werner hustled Pomerantz out of the room.

Before the second taping began, Cosby called Pomerantz back to his dressing room.

"Sorry about before," he apologized.

Then he eyed Pomerantz's black blazer.

"You look like a doorman!" he said.

Things got worse for Pomerantz the next week. He had gone over the third episode with Carsey and Werner the week before, but at the Monday table read Cosby ripped it apart. He slammed the dialogue for not being funny, which he considered his area of expertise. Channeling the feedback he had received from Dr. Poussaint, he criticized it for not "ringing truthful." Another comment revealed who else was offering her opinion behind the scenes. "Camille and I were talking last night . . ." Cosby said.

The writers pulled another all-nighter to produce a "page one rewrite" — a complete overhaul of the original script. But by camera rehearsal on Wednesday, Cosby was already changing the rewritten lines, and at the two tapings on Thursday, he changed them again, riffing on the script as though it were no more than the theme to a jazz tune.

Afterward, Pomerantz went to Werner to complain.

"I don't know why you're not defending me," he said.

"It's not working for Bill," Werner said.

"But I thought you liked the script," Pomerantz said.

"Yes, but this is Bill's show and Bill's vision," Werner said.

"Well, I can't work this way," Pomerantz said. "You're going to have to choose."

"Then you better pack up and leave," Werner said.

From then on, it was clear that Pomerantz wouldn't be sticking around after his six-show commitment. Over the next month, he became even more desperate to leave as he worked round the clock, falling behind on new scripts as he rewrote old ones. He told himself that he only knew one way to write comedy — in a linear, logical fashion — and that he could never adjust to Cosby's "jazz talking," let alone his relentless perfectionism and his hostile needling.

Even though they drove him crazy, however, Pomerantz had to admit that Cosby's notes and improvisations made the shows better. He also came to see why Cosby was so tough on writers: because he considered himself one, too, after so many years creating spellbinding monologues on stage. One day, Cosby called Pomerantz into his dressing room to pitch an idea for a new episode. Instead of summing up the premise in a few sentences, the way most TV writers would have, he started narrating a story, acting the parts of all the characters as he went along.

"It that a story?" Cosby asked.

"It's half a story," Pomerantz replied.

So Cosby immediately started narrating an entire second act, as a captivated Pomerantz took notes and remembered what Cosby had said when they first met: "You don't have to sit down to be a writer!"

When Marcy Carsey informed Cosby that Pomerantz would be leaving, he shrugged. "Either we peel them off, or they'll peel us off," he said, summarizing the writers-are-expendable philosophy he had first absorbed from Bob Culp. Still, he wasn't above making a magnanimous gesture before the shell-shocked head writer departed. On Pomerantz's last day on the job, he was taking a final walk around the set when John Markus came over and handed him three cigars. "These are from Cosby," Markus said. "He said, 'Tell Earl he's an honest man.' "

Left without a showrunner after only seven weeks, Carsey and Werner scrambled to find a new one. They set their sights on Elliot Schoenman, another rising talent who had made a name for himself on *Maude* and was now writing for *Cheers,* the struggling sitcom that would air on Thursday nights after *The Cosby Show.* At first the Paramount executives who produced *Cheers* refused to let Schoenman out of his contract. But Marcy Carsey phoned them and, in her clipped Yankee accent, delivered the kind of blunt message for which she was becoming famous on the Cosby set. "Look, we're holding up your night," she said. "If we go down, the whole house of cards on Thursday nights is going to come down with us. I need Elliot, and I need him tomorrow!"

Schoenman arrived in Brooklyn two days later and immediately started working the kind of brutal hours that had burned out Earl Pomerantz. The two female writers hired on short contracts had departed, leaving only John Markus, so Schoenman brought in two more junior writers with unconventional backgrounds, a former seminary student named Carmen Finestra and an aspiring playwright named Matt Williams. But they were still understaffed, and Cosby's demanding routine had them working seven-day, hundred-hour weeks. One night, Schoenman passed out in the middle of writing a joke and had to be taken home in a taxi by one of the secretaries. The next day, the other writers had two questions for him: "Are you all right?" and "Do you remember the joke?"

The punishing routine eventually became too much for Schoenman, too, as it would for dozens of other writers who came and went over the life of the show. For many of them, it was only once they had escaped what sometimes felt like indentured servitude to a capricious comedic master that they appreciated how much they had learned from him and how dramatic Cosby's influence had been on the sitcom genre.

As Schoenman would later put it, before Cosby there were three variations on the script-driven school of TV comedy: the Norman Lear school of *All in the Family* and *Maude;* the Mary Tyler Moore school, exemplified by her and Bob Newhart; and the Garry Marshall school, which he named after the creator of *Happy Days* and *Laverne & Shirley.* Cosby would single-handedly create an entirely new genre, one that eschewed the classic "setup, joke, setup, joke" structure of the other schools and ushered in a new naturalistic style, one that he summed up in the mantra: "Tell the truth first. The funny will come."

Yet as the show's debut drew near in the early fall of 1984, none of that was clear to the skittish network executives. "NBC never stopped being nervous until the show was on the air," recalled Tom Werner. After the taping of "Goodbye, Mr. Fish," Tartikoff demanded to see an early edit and he still wasn't happy with the uneventful plot. From then on, Carsey and Werner started to play a game that they called "hide the rough cut." They would promise to send a tape, conveniently forget, and then pretend that it had gotten lost in the mail. They told their assistants to answer phone calls from the NBC suits by telling them that the producers were in a meeting.

Tartikoff responded by assigning one of his deputies, a twenty-seven-year-old programming whiz named Garth Ancier, to babysit the launch. But with each taping he attended, Ancier became antsier. Not only did Cosby play fast and loose with the script; the children kept cracking up and losing their place. The show was supposed to be twenty-five minutes long, but the tapings took forty minutes or more. "This is a disaster," Ancier told Carsey. "How is this going to work? How are you going to cut this show?"

But Jay Sandrich wasn't worried. The director had figured out that when it came to editing — or "cutting" — the show, he had two aces up his sleeve. One was the fact that he had two Thursday tapings to work with. When he went into the editing room, he could slice and dice to capture the best moments from each performance. The second was Phylicia Ayers-Allen. While Cosby was riffing and the child actors were losing their place, she always managed to keep her cool and stay in character. It was her theater training, Sandrich realized, and it proved invaluable. It meant that any time he had to patch together footage of Cosby from different tapings, he could cut to a reaction shot from Clair Huxtable.

Most important, the director had Cosby's confidence. Any other TV star with his name on the show would have demanded to see a rough cut every week. But once Cosby was done shooting, he was off to another stand-up gig. "I'm not lonely!" he announced as he left the set, repeating the phrase he used to warn advertising men that he wasn't going to let them waste his time. Cosby didn't feel competitive with Sandrich, as he did with the writers, because he knew that the director had a completely different job. It was to keep the trains running on time and to produce a finished product that reflected Cosby's voice and vision, and he trusted Jay to do that.

The show's debut finally came on Thursday, September 20, a week before the official start of the new 1984 fall season. Since NBC was in the ratings cellar, it decided to get a jump on the competition by launching seven shows early, including *The Cosby Show* and another newcomer called *Miami Vice*. Simply titled "Pilot," the first episode consisted of the three scenes that had been shot for the presentation and three more scenes filmed in Brooklyn, along with additional footage that had been hastily assembled in LA for the opening credits — of the Huxtables clambering out of a minivan and playing softball in a park.

In his upfront pitch to advertisers, Tartikoff had predicted that *The Cosby Show* would be "a strong second" to the drama *Magnum, P.I.* in its Thursday time slot. But virtually everyone in the TV world considered that a stretch. "This sitcom will lose to CBS's *Magnum, P.I.,*" predicted David Bianculli in the Sunday edition of the *Philadelphia Inquirer* after watching an advance tape of the pilot, before pleading with network executives to give the show time. "It's too funny, and Cosby is too good, for NBC to dump it," Bianculli wrote.

Other TV critics also reviewed the show as if they were trying to save it from an early grave. The *New York Times,* the *Washington Post,* and the *Los Angeles Times* all declared it the best new sitcom of the season, using superlatives like "funniest," "most entertaining," "classiest," and "most humane." Vindicating Carsey and Werner's sense of what was missing on television, the reviews applauded the show's realism and honest depiction of the war between parents and children. In the *Montreal Gazette*, Mike Boone used the word "credible" and called the Monopoly scene "a delightful confrontation."

Yet a funny thing happened on the way to second place. Not only did *The Cosby Show* immediately shoot past *Magnum P.I.* in the ratings; the pilot was the most watched TV show of the week with 21.6 million viewers. Carsey and Werner had always hoped that America would want to welcome Bill Cosby back into their living rooms. They had crossed their fingers that the strong critical buzz would help. But given the show's late launch and difficult birth, they never expected it to do so well so quickly. Nor did anyone else. Not the nervous executives at NBC. And not Cosby himself.

The next week, as he was in the middle of rehearsal, Carsey and Werner appeared on the Flatbush set and pulled him aside.

"Bill, you're not going to believe this," Carsey said. "The show last week was number one!"

"You mean in our time slot?" Cosby asked.

"No," Carsey said. "For the week."

"You're kidding," he said. "You mean we beat *60 Minutes*?"

"Yes," she said.

"Call Camille!" he said.

22
THE MASTER AT WORK

Jay Sandrich didn't know what else to do. Cosby wanted to do a show for the "teeny-weenies," as he called them — the kids in the audience around the age of Rudy, the youngest Huxtable child. His writers had taken the note and produced a script called "The Slumber Party." At the beginning of the episode, Rudy can't get any of her siblings to play with her so she asks her father if she can invite some friends to sleep over. Cliff agrees, forgetting that Clair has to work late, so he ends up having to look after Rudy and six of her little girlfriends by himself.

According to Cosby's instructions, the casting directors had hired a multiracial group of child actors to play Rudy's friends. They included Hispanic twins, a Japanese girl, and a biracial four-year-old with curly hair named Alicia Cook who would later take the stage name Alicia Keys when she became a professional singer. But the little girls couldn't follow directions. The writers had created a scene in which Cosby would talk with the kids the way he did in his commercials, but the girls started reciting their lines before he could ask the questions. Sandrich decided that staying on script was hopeless. He told Cosby to make something up and see if he could get the kids to play along.

Cosby decided that the way to make the scene funny was to milk it for as much visual humor as possible. He also wanted to get the girls laughing, because if they laughed, the audience would find it impossible not to laugh with them.

He started with a sight gag, bundling up the kids in winter coats and hats and marching them into the living room as if they were a navy regiment.

"Company halt!" he ordered. "About face! As fast as you can, take off your clothes. And after you take off your clothes, go to bed!"

The girls giggled as they stripped off their bulky coats. "But we just got here!" they protested.

Next, Cosby sat the girls down on the living room couch and had each of them bring him a folded note.

"It says here that you're a compulsive gambler and wanted by the police!" he joked as he opened the first one. He quizzed another girl about her dimples and reached out to "put them in my pocket." When the twins came to talk to him, he asked if they knew a song. They whispered to each other and began to recite a hand-clapping chant called "Uno Dos-ee-a-say."

"I met my boyfriend at the candy store . . ." they twins began, clapping and slapping each other's hands.

"Wait, wait!" Cosby interrupted. "What boyfriend?"

On the couch, Keshia Knight Pulliam and the other girls were giggling uncontrollably.

"I don't have a boyfriend!" one of the twins answered.

"You don't have a boyfriend?" Cosby said. "But you just said you met him at the candy store!"

"It's just a game!" said the twin.

"Honest?" he said. "Okay, go ahead."

The girls started clapping again. ". . . He brought me ice cream, he brought me cake . . ."

"Wait a minute!" Cosby interrupted again. "How old is this boy?"

Now the other girls were bouncing up and down on the couch with laughter.

"Two!" the twin answered.

"Two?" Cosby said. "He's two years old and he's got money for ice cream and cake!"

"The Slumber Party" marked the first appearance of Peter Costa, a young actor who played a chubby boy named Peter who lived across the street from the Huxtables. Costa would become one of Cosby's favorite bit players because he could get laughs without saying anything; the joke was that Peter never talked, he just answered by shaking his huge head. (Eventually, Costa's mother would demand that he get lines, at which point Cosby decreed that he wasn't funny anymore and he rarely appeared again.)

The script called for Peter to follow the girls into the house, so Cosby constructed another sight gag around him. He announced a game that, in a winking reference to his famous stand-up routine, he called "buck, buck, horse." The object was to see how long the children could stay on his knee as he bounced them around. He asked each of the girls to go first. ("Here comes my wife!" he ad-libbed as Alicia Cook approached, because she looked so much like a young Camille.) When Peter's turn came, Cosby played the bit for all it was worth, his face contorting in mock pain as he flailed the pudgy boy around and the girls on the couch howled with amusement.

He ended the improvised scene by announcing "Monster time!" and chasing the squealing children around the room as he made his Wolf Man face, the one with which Shorty Cosby had first entertained his friends after the Saturday matinees in North Philly.

With so much unscripted footage, Sandrich had his work cut out for him piecing together a coherent twenty-three-minute episode. But when he screened the final edit, he had to admit that it was "hysterically funny." And once again, he could only marvel at the magic that Cosby was able to pull out of his mind and body at a moment's notice.

By the time "The Slumber Party" aired, at the end of March, *The Cosby Show* was indisputably the hottest new program of the 1984–1985 TV season. It had remained the top show in its time slot every single week and become the third most-watched show in all of television. It was the first NBC offering to crack the top ten in several years and the first comedy to rank so high since the late 1970s, when *Three's Company* was going strong on ABC and *M*A*S*H* aired its record-breaking final episode on CBS. By the spring, only the prime-time soaps *Dynasty* and *Dallas* had more viewers. And starting the next fall, *The Cosby Show* would rise to the top of the ratings and stay there for five consecutive seasons, joining *All in the Family* as the second show in history ever to achieve that distinction.

The Cosby Show was also showered with TV's highest honors in its maiden season, including three Emmys. It won for best comedy series, best writing (for the "Pilot" episode), and best directing (for Sandrich's work on an episode called "The Younger Woman," an allegory about prejudice in which Cliff and Clair assume the worst about a younger woman that one of their white friends is dating). Cosby might well have won for best actor, too, but he refused to be considered. Publicly he said that the three Emmys he had won for *I Spy* were enough, but privately he was haunted by the memories of competitiveness and guilt he had felt toward Bob Culp and he didn't want to relive those emotions. (When another black actor, Robert Guillaume, won the award, he began his acceptance speech: "I'd like to thank Bill Cosby for not being here." And some in the industry would blame its star's snubbing of the Emmys for the fact that *The Cosby Show* didn't rack up more of them in subsequent years.)

But *The Cosby Show* was already more than another hit TV show. It had become a sacred ritual in millions of American homes: a time when everyone could gather around the TV set and laugh at situations that resonated with their own lives — as if, fans would frequently tell Cosby, he had been spying on *their* families. In its first season, a quarter of all US households with TV sets tuned in every Thursday night, and over the next two seasons that percentage would grow to more than a third, representing an average of 30 million viewers or more. (In the third season, 65 million people would watch an episode called "Say Hello to a Good Buy" that had no advance hype and only the still unknown comedians Sinbad and Gilbert Gottfried as guest stars.) *The Cosby Show* would soon be number one in every demographic as well — with men and women, young and old, black, white, and Hispanic.

It also represented a remarkable comeback for Bill Cosby, whose previous TV show had been canceled after nine weeks and who hadn't been seriously considering a return to prime time until less than a year before *The Cosby Show* premiered. Yet if he hadn't anticipated the opportunity that would allow him, like his inspiration Carl Sandburg, to push himself to new heights, he was unquestionably prepared for it. For in each of the ingredients that made the show such a hit, there were traces of every major event in Cosby's professional and personal life over the previous twenty years — all the successes, but also all the failures.

From his early days as a stand-up comedian and recording artist, he brought the gifts that had first made him a star: the jazz-influenced style of improvisational storytelling; the flair for comic voices and sound effects; the remarkably rubbery and expressive face. But now that he was older, he commanded those gifts in a way that was at once more effortless and more virtuosic, like the Frank Sinatra of the Capitol Records years compared with his crooner years with Columbia. With age, Cosby had also acquired an ease with self-deprecation, allowing him to play Cliff Huxtable as a loving father and wise doctor who had foibles that made him only more relatable: a sneaky addiction to food that was no longer good for him, a vanity about his fading athletic abilities, and a propensity to act as childish as his own children.

From his years on *I Spy*, Cosby brought a lesson that he learned at the feet of Sheldon Leonard but proceeded to forget in his first solo TV forays. Leonard preached that whoever the star was, a show rose or fell on the strength of its ensemble. That principle had been the key to *The Andy Griffith Show* and the *The Dick Van Dyke Show,* and it's what had made *I Spy* work, too, when Bob Culp realized that the show would be a bigger hit if he shared the limelight with his novice costar. Now it was Cosby's turn to play the star soloist who could also be a master accompanist. Week after week, he would be the clown in one scene and the straight man in the next, allowing his TV family members or one of his talented guest stars to get the laughs.

After fighting to "get the girl" on *I Spy*, Cosby now had the power to control the message he wanted to convey about sexual attraction. He used it to make the Huxtables perhaps the most physically affectionate married couple, black or white, that had ever appeared on television. When their children weren't around, Cliff and Clair could be found slow dancing to jazz ballads, snuggling on the living room couch, and lying together in bed at the end of an episode, engaging in verbal foreplay that left no doubt what was going to happen once the lights were out and the credits had rolled.

(To Cosby's disappointment, the romance quotient was dialed back after the second season, when Phylicia Ayers-Allen married Ahmad Rashad, the sports broadcaster and former pro football player. Phylicia Rashad would be pregnant for much of season three, forcing Sandrich and the set designers to limit the bedroom scenes and come up with numerous strategies to hide her swollen belly. Cosby would jokingly tease Rashad that she "didn't kiss the same" after her marriage.)

From *The Bill Cosby Show,* his ill-fated first sitcom, Cosby had learned that the audience wanted him to be more than cool and bemused; they expected him to be *funny.* But he still believed in the philosophy behind the quiet scripts for that earlier show — that the "situations" in situation comedy should be subtle and realistic rather than broad and contrived — and this time around he was determined to make the naturalistic approach work, no matter how crazy it drove his writing staff.

After his disastrous business experience with Roy Silver, Cosby continued to insist on veto power over anything that had his name and reputation attached to it. But after struggling to build his own production empire at Jemmin, he had an appreciation of how hard it was to juggle the business and creative ends at the same time. So he was ready to accept his partnership with Marcy Carsey and Tom Werner, who took care of countless financial, administrative, and personnel details and freed Cosby up to focus on the creative content of the show.

From his academic studies at the University of Massachusetts, and from all the scholars he had befriended over the previous decade, Cosby had acquired sophistication about concepts in education and child psychology that he would bring to bear on the show, with the help of Alvin Poussaint. From his work in commercials, he had developed an ability to *sell* to an audience, as well as a peerless talent for relating to kids on camera. But more than anything, it had been Cosby's decision to cut back on his playboy ways and devote himself to his wife and children once he turned forty that gave him a sixth sense for the most powerful quality of *The Cosby Show:* its uncannily realistic depiction of family life.

Once Cosby bought into the idea of making the Huxtables an upscale family like his own, he became liberated to bring the smallest details from his own life into the show. He began to see Clair Huxtable as a doppelgänger for Camille Cosby — elegant and refined, but also tough and bossy when necessary with her children and her husband. Because the soft-spoken Camille often communicated her displeasure with sharp looks rather than harsh words, Cosby wanted to see the same characteristic in Clair.

"You've done a lot of work in theater," he commented to Phylicia Ayers-Allen one day early in the first season.

"Yes, how did you know?" she replied.

"Because you always come in on cue," he said.

"Yes!" she said with a smile, thinking she was being complimented.

Cosby shook his head. "I want you to try something different," he said. "I want you to look at me before you deliver your lines, and trust that your audience will be with you."

From that hint was born what the actress called "the Clair stare," which she would later recognize when she saw Camille interact with her husband. As the show progressed, Cosby's wife would also become the inspiration for numerous other plot twists, such as the broken toe that Clair suffered soon after Camille fractured hers.

Many of the changes that the Huxtable children would undergo as they grew older came directly from Cosby's observations of his own children — in particular his son Ennis, whom he used as inspiration for virtually every nuance in the evolution of Theo's character. The Huxtables came to resemble the Cosbys so much, in fact, that once the shooting was under way it didn't feel right to him with just four children. His own fifth child, the first-born Erika, was attending Wesleyan University, so he suggested adding a fifth child who would also be an oldest daughter who was away at college.

Another casting search was made and one of the finalists was a twenty-one-year-old teen model from Newark, New Jersey. But when she arrived for her audition, Jay Sandrich discovered a problem. Before meeting with Cosby, Carsey, and Werner, the actors had to sign contracts indicating that they would be available to appear whenever the show needed them. This girl glanced at the legal forms and shook her head.

"I can't sign this contract," she said.

"Why not?" Sandrich asked.

"I want to be a singer," she said.

"Yeah, so?" he said.

"I can't be in every show because I may be on tour," she said.

"Well, if this show is successful, it could help your singing career," Sandrich said.

"Yes, but I'm going to be on tour," the girl repeated.

"And who told you you could sing?" he asked skeptically.

"My mother and my aunt," she said.

"Well, you can't sign the contract if you can't do every show," Sandrich said.

"Then I won't sign it," the girl said.

So the candidate from Newark was sent home. And it wasn't until a few years later that Sandrich realized that she wasn't kidding when she said she wanted to be a singer. In fact, the real reason Whitney Houston refused to commit to *The Cosby Show* was that she was under contract to someone else: hit maker Clive Davis of Arista Records, who was grooming her to be the next queen of pop music.

The part of Sondra Huxtable went to a twenty-six-year-old stage actress named Sabrina Le Beauf. Cosby chose her because he thought it would be funny to have one child who *wasn't* funny — "a stiff," as he put it — and Le Beauf, a product of Catholic schools, had an earnest streak that he recognized from Camille's side of the family. At the same time, Cosby wanted to underscore his favorite theme of education by showing America a black family with a child at Princeton. But once La Beauf was cast, she had little to do at first. "Have you forgotten about me?" she asked Cosby. He apologized and admitted that he associated her so much with Erika that he thought she really *was* away at college. He started urging the writers to give Le Beauf a bigger role, and by the second season they discovered a way to do it: by creating a relationship with a boyfriend named Elvin, played by Geoffrey Owens, who would become one of Cosby's favorite cast members because of his ability to get laughs by playing a chauvinistic dunce and setting up Rashad and the other women in the family to put him in his place.

As the show developed, Cosby insisted on a big role for the Huxtable grandparents, wanting to reflect the influence that his own grandparents had played in his life. He named Cliff's parents after his mother (Anna) and brother (Russell) and took pride in casting the black stage veterans Earle Hyman and Clarice Taylor to play them. Like his Granddad Samuel, he made Russell Huxtable a long-winded storyteller who pulled quarters out of his pocket to give to his grandchildren.

Before long, Cosby was treating his TV children almost as if they were his own kids. He teased Lisa Bonet and Tempestt Bledsoe about their taste in clothes and music and engaged Malcolm-Jamal Warner in competitive games of chess and pick-up basketball. Despite his early misgiving about having such a young member of the cast, he came to relish his relationship with Keshia Knight Pulliam. At times he patiently took her aside to give her acting instructions and slapped her five when she nailed it. "My sister!" he would shout. At others, he devilishly stole her lines until she cried out to Sandrich: "Tell Mr.

Cosby to stop that!" At all times, Cosby kept on top of the young actors about their schoolwork, which they completed with the help of private tutors. Calling them into his dressing room, he would interrogate them about their grades and give them parental lectures about the importance of education.

Cosby began to mingle his own life and his new TV life so thoroughly, in fact, that by the middle of the first season, the producers and director started to notice something telling. When they were discussing scripts, he would sometimes slip and refer to his character as Bill instead of Cliff.

"Apples aren't funny; oranges are," Cosby told Jack Gelbart. "So get me oranges!"

Gelbart was the "inside props guy," and the man who spent more time with the star, week in and week out, than anyone else on the set of *The Cosby Show.* He was the keeper of the Zippo, who held a lighter at the ready for Cosby to smoke a cigar whenever he wasn't in front of a camera. (The insurance company wouldn't allow Bics, because they were known to explode.) He was the personal caterer who dispatched town cars at all hours to pick up Cosby's favorite hoagie sandwiches, all the way from a joint called the White House on the boardwalk in Atlantic City. And he was the heavy who ran interference when Cosby left the studio and didn't want to be bothered by autograph seekers.

"I hear the guy's a real asshole!" people would shout out when they saw Gelbart wearing his swag jacket from *The Cosby Show.*

"On any given day, anybody can be an asshole!" Gelbart would growl back. He knew that Cosby needed his "private time," and he stood ready to shoo fans away whenever the boss gave the signal.

Most of all, Gelbart was the provider of funny fodder — the props that Cosby would request for specific episodes or to keep around the set for comic inspiration. The stout Brooklyn native had ended up a prop man by accident, because he was a stage electrician by training. He lived around the corner from the Vitagraph studio in Flatbush, and when he heard that Cosby was making a sitcom, he was intrigued, having seen him give a performance at the Playboy Club in Manhattan. So he applied for a job as head of the props department, and when he was hired he was told that the producers needed him for the even more important job of staying at Cosby's side at all times.

When it came to props, Cosby was always very specific about what he was looking for: precisely nine strawberry shortcakes for an episode about Clair's forty-sixth birthday, for instance, or the amusing oranges for the fruit bowl in the kitchen rather than the boring apples. (Once he asked Gelbart to put a

DustBuster on the living room set. During a taping, he held it to his head and warned: "Don't come any closer!" The rest of the cast cracked up, but the moment was deemed a little too dark to put on air.)

Then again, Cosby had specific ideas about everything: the set design, the lighting, the wardrobe. One week, he showed up on taping day wearing a crazy-quilt wool and leather sweater by the Dutch designer Koos Van Den Akker that a friend had given him. It got so much reaction from viewers — some loved it; others hated it — that he decided to make sweaters one of Cliff Huxtable's signatures. Over the coming seasons, he would wear scores of funky designs, including some that he considered works of art and others he deliberately chose for their tackiness.

His edicts became so legion that Gelbart and the rest of the crew presented him with a T-shirt emblazoned "Bill Knows . . ." The teasing implication was that when it came to production details, Bill thought he knew everything.

Cosby trusted his prop man so much that he started inviting him to table reads and asking his opinion afterward. And what Gelbart saw there was how Cosby knew writing, too, not in the conventional way that most TV writers understood it, as the ability to come up with one-liners, but as a knack for figuring out hooks that allowed him and the rest of the cast to "find the funny."

During the second season, Cosby wanted to do a show about kids keeping secrets from their parents. The writers came up with a provocative script called "Denise's Friend," in which Denise asks Cliff to see a girlfriend who is suffering from a delicate medical condition and doesn't want to tell her mother and father. Cliff examines the friend and discovers that she has an untreated bladder infection, but then he wants to know if his children would come to him and Clair under similar circumstances.

The problem with the script, however, was that it wasn't very funny.

After a disappointing Monday table read, Cosby huddled with the producers and Jay Sandrich and made a suggestion.

"Why don't we have a family conference?" he said.

A family conference? they thought. *Well, okay . . .*

After some quick restaging and rewriting, the cast gathered to shoot a new scene.

As it eventually aired, Cliff asks his kids to assemble in the living room so that he can deliver a loving message: if you're ever in trouble, you should feel free to come to your parents for help.

"Okay!" the kids say, jumping up from the sofa and thinking the talk is over.

"No, no, no, wait a minute!" Cliff says. "Sit

577

down!" He wants them to consider a serious hypothetical. What if one of them got pregnant?

"Hey, I know it's not me!" Theo says, eliciting a big laugh from the audience.

"Okay, let's say it *is* you!" Cliff shoots back, drawing an even bigger laugh. "What would you do?"

Theo admits that he would confide in his friend Cockroach first. "I'd be afraid that you would get mad!" he tells his father.

"Mad? I'm not going to get mad!" Cliff fumes, his tone and face conveying just the opposite. "I'm telling you that I wouldn't get mad! Now when I say I wouldn't get mad, I wouldn't get mad, do you understand! . . . Let's get this straight: *Dogs* get mad. Human beings get *angry*!"

Testing their parents, the children start posing hypotheticals of their own. Sondra asks: What if Vanessa was secretly dating a seventeen-year-old boy? Theo wonders what would happen if he drove Cliff's car without asking and brought it back with a ding.

"Okay, Mom, I've got one for you," Denise says. "Remember when I spent the night at Jeanette's house a couple of weeks ago?"

"Yes, I do," Clair says.

"Okay, well, I didn't spend the night at Jeanette's," Denise says. "I spent it at Tommy Watkins's!"

Clair looks like she's about to burst a vein

in her temple.

"Are you *angry*?" Denise says, and now the audience is cheering and clapping.

"Ask your mother!" Cliff says haplessly.

"I was just kidding!" Denise says. "I made it up, I did. It was a joke!"

With one suggestion — "Why don't we have a family conference?" — Cosby had produced a scene that allowed the cast to find the funny. It was also a microcosm of everything that made *The Cosby Show* special. Theatrically, it played like a jazz ensemble piece, giving Cosby the lead solo ("Mad? I'm not going to get mad!"), then allowing Rashad and the child actors to have their share of lines and laughs. When Jay Sandrich won a second Emmy for the episode, he would tell his wife Linda that he deserved it mostly for the job he did in the editing room. Comparing his work on *The Golden Girls,* where he worked on hiatus weeks, and *The Cosby Show,* he would say that the first was "about directing actors" and the second was "about shooting and editing."

As Sandrich had observed while filming the pilot, the family conference scene also managed to show the point of view of parents and kids at the same time. Like many of the most memorable episodes of *The Cosby Show* — about Theo's earring, or Denise's first car, or Vanessa's forays into dating — it captured the tension between a child's quest for independence and a parent's protectiveness and desire to set limits. It also conveyed the core message that Cosby wanted to drive home about healthy families: that they love and support one another despite their flaws and disagreements. As he put it in one interview: "The parents make mistakes, the kids make mistakes, but . . . the people show great love and respect for one another."

The scene was also an example of how Cosby's mind worked, and why *The Cosby Show* was more than just a showcase for his skills as a comic actor and observer of human behavior. It was a weekly laboratory for his endlessly creative, if often seemingly off-the-wall, ideas for what could be funny.

Week after week, Cosby would make suggestions that at first would have the writers and producers scratching their heads but would turn out brilliantly once they were "put on their feet." In one instance, he proposed doing a show about a kitchen appliance. *A kitchen appliance?* his colleagues thought. *How are we going to get a half hour out of a kitchen appliance?* What emerged from that idea was an uproarious episode called "The Juicer," in which Rudy and her friend Peter make a holy mess with Cliff's new kitchen toy, and Cliff learns a lesson in responsibility when Clair points out that none of it would have happened if he hadn't left the juicer plugged in.

Another week, Cosby decreed that he wanted to do a show on how different generations dance. The result was "Jitterbug Break," an episode that ends with a joyous dance-off between Denise and her friends demonstrating hip-hop moves and the Huxtables and another older couple strutting their dance hall stuff. (Close watchers of cameo appearances would note that one of Denise's friends was the young Blair Underwood and that Judith Jamison, the director and former lead dancer for the Alvin Ailey American Dance Theater, played the wife in the older couple.)

Sometimes the ideas sprang directly from experiences in Cosby's life, like Camille's broken toe or "Back to the Track, Jack," an episode where Cliff competes against old rivals from his college days. (To keep in shape, Cosby ran in the senior Masters competition at the Penn Relays every year.) Sometimes they would be pretexts for broad slapstick, like "Mr. Sandman," an episode where Cliff's competitiveness gets the better of him as he tries to show that he can tap dance. And sometimes they were so subtle that only a comic as gifted as Cosby could have pulled them off: in "Full House," Cliff comes home after a long night at the hospital and spends an entire episode searching the house for a quiet place to read the newspaper.

Sometimes Cosby's ideas were too outlandish or impractical to go anywhere. "The Huxtables go to Kenya!" he proposed, and Carsey and Werner had to explain all the financial and legal reasons why that wasn't feasible. And sometimes his mind raced so fast that no one could understand *what* he was talking about. But sometimes, a nugget of an idea was enough to lead to a deep pocket of comic gold.

When Cosby was asked to name his favorite episode of *The Cosby Show*, he would choose one that started with his desire to pay tribute to two of his comic idols. One was Buster Keaton, who had introduced him to the wonder of silent comedy as a boy growing up in Philadelphia. The other was W. C. Fields and his short films of the 1930s. Cosby had always loved a parody of Canadian Mountie movies called *The Fatal Glass of Beer*, in which Fields keeps trying to leave his log cabin in the midst of a blizzard. "It ain't a fit night out for man nor beast!" Fields repeats each time he opens the door, as snow and wind pelt him in the face.

In "Cliff's Wet Adventure," it's Thanksgiving, and Dr. Huxtable keeps forgetting items that he was supposed to buy for the holiday meal. Again and again, he goes back to the store in a driving rainstorm. Cosby asked the set and lighting designers to give him "the works" — simulated rain, wind, and flying leaves. During the tapings, he dressed in a long green raincoat and floppy brown hat that became more and more drenched each time he went out. When he came back into the house, his body language and facial expressions had the audience roaring before he ever opened his mouth.

For a final sight gag, Cosby asked Gelbart to get him a wet paper bag and score the bottom with a razor blade. When he returned with the last item — a dozen eggs — the bag broke and the eggs splattered all over the floor. The audience exploded. But Cosby was just as proud of the episode's closing moment. When Clair tells Cliff to put his sopping clothes on the stoop before he sits down to dinner, he opens the front door and the sun comes out — a silent ending worthy of a Buster Keaton classic.

But Cosby's most famous "find the funny" idea came the day he told the writers that he wanted to do a show where the Huxtables lip-synced.

Lip synced? Hmm, they thought. *Well, that might be funny . . .*

They went to work and came up with a story called "Happy Anniversary." To entertain Cliff's parents on their wedding anniversary, the Huxtables decide to perform a karaoke dance number. Cosby chose the music: Ray Charles's 1958 version of the R&B classic "(Night Time Is) The Right Time," a record he had first heard in the navy. Knowing her background in dance, he asked Phylicia Ayers-Allen to choreograph the rest. She blocked out a routine where Clair and the four daughters would stand at the bottom of the living room staircase, shimmying like the Raelettes. Theo would come down the stairs wearing a sports jacket and fedora, mouthing the first verse. Then, when backup singer Margie Hendricks started her blues shouting, little Rudy would take over.

"BAAABY!" Keshia Knight Pulliam wailed on the day of the taping, managing to look remarkably blues-stricken for a six-year-old, the bit becoming funnier as the lyrics got raunchier. "OH HOLD ME TIGHT! . . . NIGHT TIME IS THE RIGHT TIME TO BE WITH THE ONE YOU LOVE!"

On the second blues chorus, sung by Charles, Cosby jumped in. "Baby!" he began coolly. "Baby!" Baby!" Then as Ray let out a fourth "WHOA, BAAABY!," Cosby's face twisted into an over-the-top wince, one eye closed and the other bulging. Meanwhile, Earle Hyman and Clarice Taylor were pointing and slapping their knees with laughter, and so was everyone in the studio audience and in homes across America.

The rest of the episode provided a showcase for the veteran stage actors who played Cliff's parents. If "Slumber Party" had been a show for the "teeny weenies," this one was for the retiree crowd. It began with the parents turning down Cliff's gift of a European vacation, as Hyman and Taylor captured the way old people get set in their ways. It ended with the couple deciding to go off on a cruise after all — in secret. But when Sandrich saw what the cast had done with the "(Night Time)" song, he knew that it would make the episode a classic. To make sure no one forgot it, he edited the show to replay the entire number a second time as the credits rolled.

Sure enough, *TV Guide* would later name "Happy Anniversary" one of the hundred greatest TV shows of all time, and it would still be remembered a quarter century later. *Saturday Night Live* would spoof it in a skit that imagined Barack and Michelle Obama, Hillary Clinton, and Joe Biden as the lip-syncing Huxtables.

"Happy Anniversary" was the third episode of the second season, and it probably did more than any other show to cement *The Cosby Show* at the top of the Nielsen ratings, where it would stay for the next five years. Like the adult kids that Cosby joked about, Americans had moved in with the Huxtables, and they weren't going anywhere, at least not on Thursday nights. So universally loved was the show that only one complaint continued to dog it, a criticism that annoyed Cosby to no end and showed how little members of the media and many viewers knew about black history.

23
"It's Not an Invention"

Phylicia Rashad was doing a round of press interviews at NBC headquarters in Rockefeller Center, and three white reporters in a row had asked her the same question: Were the Huxtables a realistic depiction of a black family?

Finally, she had had enough.

"What time is it?" she asked the third reporter.

The man glanced at his watch.

"No, I mean what time is it?" she asked. "How many African Americans do you know?"

Rashad proceeded to inform the reporter about her own family. Her father, Andrew Arthur Allen, was a Houston dentist who had had a thriving practice, even in the days of Jim Crow. Her mother, Vivian Ayers, was a poet who had been nominated for a Pulitzer Prize. Although they divorced when Phylicia was young, they devoted themselves to the academic and cultural education of their

586

children. Her mother brought home the novels of Ralph Ellison and Richard Wright and the poems of William Blake from her part-time job in the Rice University library. She taught Phylicia and her older brother Tex and younger sister Debbie to read music in elementary school, and took them to the theater and to movies such as *Carmen Jones,* so they could see Dorothy Dandridge, a genuine black movie star. Phylicia and Debbie had both attended Howard University, where they took Greek and performed on stage, and Tex had studied composing at the University of North Texas on his way to becoming a professional jazz musician.

Two prosperous black professionals who were determined to see that their children went to college and appreciated the finest in black art and culture? It was "truthfully, quite realistic," Rashad lectured the embarrassed reporter. "It is not an invention now, and it was not an invention in my father's time!"

The family that Bill Cosby had married into — the Hankses of Silver Spring, Maryland — were another precursor to the Huxtables. And so was the Washington, DC, family of one of the women who served as a model for Clair Huxtable. When Rashad went north to Washington DC, for college, her father encouraged her to look up his best friend from dental school, Dr. Flavius Galiber. When she did, she met Galiber's charismatic wife Yetta, the director of a handicapped services organization and mother of four attractive, fun-loving children. Phylicia was welcomed into a home full of laughter and learning and reverence for black culture.

Yet Cosby and Rashad were both aware of a historical irony: the advances of the civil rights era had paradoxically led to a decline in families like the Hankses and Galibers. Growing up in Houston, Rashad had viewed black doctors and lawyers and their families as pillars of the community, and seen education as the key to succeeding in that self-contained world. "Everywhere I looked, I saw myself reflected in people with positions of authority," she recalled. But desegregation, for all of its benefits, had brought side effects that eroded the foundations of that way of life: white flight that weakened the economies of urban areas where many middle-class blacks lived; competition for employment in the larger white world that was more open but less secure. Gradually, black communities had fewer prosperous two-parent homes and more of the struggling, single-parent households decried by Daniel Patrick Moynihan in his 1965 report on "The Negro Family: The Case for National Action." So with the Huxtables, Cosby was in many ways simply resurrecting an old black bourgeois ideal that had existed under segregation.

When Cosby would complain to Alvin

Poussaint about the criticism that "the Huxtables aren't real," the psychiatrist would point out that the naysayers weren't just ignorant of black history. They were upset that *The Cosby Show* wasn't addressing problems such as crime and poverty faced by many inner-city blacks, or the more subtle forms of racism encountered by well-to-do African Americans. The critics believed that the show gave whites "a pass" on racism and reinforced the notion, increasingly in the air during Ronald Reagan's presidency, that blacks no longer needed special legal protections or government programs and that they could be every bit as successful as Cliff and Clair Huxtable if they were only willing to work hard enough.

Some of the criticism was downright insulting. The *Village Voice* scoffed that "Cosby no longer qualifies as black enough to be an Uncle Tom," and in *New York* magazine his sitcom was described as "*Leave It to Beaver* in blackface." But the case against *The Cosby Show* also got a more thoughtful hearing on the op-ed page of the *New York Times*. In a piece entitled "TV's Black World Turns — But Stays Unreal," one of the nation's leading African American scholars, Henry Louis Gates Jr., faulted Cosby for offering a misleading picture of conditions for black Americans as a whole. "As the dominant representation of blacks on TV," he wrote, "[*The*

Cosby Show] suggests that blacks are solely responsible for their social conditions, with no acknowledgment of the severely constricted life opportunities that most black people face . . . The social vision of *Cosby* . . . reflecting the miniscule integration of blacks into the upper middle class (having 'white money,' my mother used to say, rather than 'colored' money) reassuringly throws the blame back on the impoverished."

While Cosby refrained from addressing these attacks in public — the furthest he went was to complain to *Jet* magazine about "neo-liberals" who questioned the authenticity of the Huxtables — he raged against them in private. He accused African American intellectuals who dared to suggest that the image of the Huxtables was somehow making things *worse* for black people of being "poverty pimps": the derogatory term for hustlers who pretend to represent the interests of poor people to the wealthy white establishment so that they can profit as middlemen.

For a black pundit who wanted to get published in a newspaper or booked on television, Cosby complained, there was no better ploy than to attack a fellow black. Besides, he groused, where were the critics demanding that the *white* shows on TV grapple with racism? He also had psychological objections. White people didn't like being told that they were bigots, so rubbing their noses in it was just an invitation to change the channel. And for African American viewers, didn't it do more good to use the power of television to project a positive image of black life rather than another portrayal that made blacks look like victims?

Cosby had artistic arguments as well. Privately, he was as committed to contesting racism as anyone: he denounced it in *Playboy* and other publications; he made generous contributions to organizations dedicated to fighting it; and it was a regular topic of conversation with friends and family around his dinner tables in Massachusetts and Manhattan. But as he told Poussaint, *The Cosby Show* was a *comedy,* and he didn't want to trivialize serious problems by trying to make them funny.

Cosby would also tell the black writers that he brought on to the show that he wanted them to stay away from hot-button issues because he didn't want to date *The Cosby Show.* He envisioned it living on in reruns like *I Love Lucy* or *The Honeymooners,* and he thought a lack of reference to political or social controversies helped make those shows timeless. His show was not just about a black family, he reminded the writers, but about the universal experience of family, and he wanted people of all backgrounds to be able to identify with it twenty or fifty years in the future.

Yet as stubborn as Cosby was about staying away from negative stereotypes of African Americans, he was as determined to use his new platform to celebrate black culture. First was his beloved jazz music, which received more attention on *The Cosby Show* than it ever had or likely ever will again on prime-time television. Cosby decided to make Cliff's father a retired jazz musician, and his first suggestion for the part was his old friend Dizzy Gillespie, the legendary trumpet player.

"Dizzy's hilarious!" he told Sandrich.

"But can he act?" Sandrich asked.

"I don't know," Cosby said.

Skeptical but willing to try, Sandrich brought Gillespie in for an audition.

"Can you memorize lines?" he asked.

"Nope," Dizzy replied.

"Well, maybe a smaller part would be better," Sandrich said.

"Sure, man!" Dizzy said.

Instead, Gillespie became the first celebrity to make a guest star appearance. In "Play It Again, Vanessa," he portrayed Vanessa's music teacher, Mr. Hampton, whom the Huxtables hire to give her private lessons before a clarinet recital. The episode leads up to a scene at Vanessa's school, where Mr. Hampton ushers a student who has just mangled Rimsky-Korsakov off the stage before leading the student orchestra in a squeaky medley of Ellington's "Take the 'A' Train" and Gershwin's "Rhapsody in Blue."

"That was Bobby Tucker, on the bassoon, giving you his rendition of 'Flight of the Bumblebee,' " Dizzy was supposed to say, but he kept cracking up and flubbing the line, forcing a patient Sandrich to shoot "pickups" until two o'clock in the morning.

On the week of the first season finale, the young actors who played the Huxtable children didn't know what to make of a petite, elderly lady wearing thick glasses and a headscarf who was hanging around the set all week. That all changed when they shot the scene for "Cliff's Birthday" where he discovers that his surprise gift is going to a nightclub to hear Lena Horne. As Horne, now elegantly dressed and made up, serenaded Cosby with a soulful rendition of "I'm Glad There Is You," the children grew quiet and transfixed. And their newfound respect for a jazz legend was evident as they shot a final scene where Cliff takes his children backstage to meet "Miss Horne."

In the second season, Cosby devoted an entire episode to jazz. In "Play It Again, Russell," Cliff's father has a crisis of confidence about getting back together with his old band. The show culminated in a jam session that introduced thirty million viewers to some of the music's greatest living artists: Art

Blakey on drums, Jimmy Heath on alto sax, Percy Heath on bass, Tommy Flanagan on the piano, Tito Puente on congas, and Slide Hampton on the trombone solo that Earle Hyman pretended to play. It also allowed Cosby to do a favor for Bootsie Barnes, his old friend from the Richard Allen Homes, who had become a professional sax player and was invited to sit in with the all-stars.

Numerous other episodes featured moments that jazz aficionados would savor: Cliff and Clair cuddling to John Coltrane's "In a Sentimental Mood" or Big Maybelle's "Candy"; Cliff challenging a guest to recite the lyrics to "Moody's Mood for Love," the song that Cosby had memorized to impress girls in high school. But his most memorable nod to the music came each week during the opening credits. Cosby had composed the theme song, "Kiss Me," with his longtime musical collaborator Stu Gardner, and every year they came up with a new jazz arrangement for the tune: first straightahead, then Latin, then smooth, then orchestral, then rhythm and blues, then urban.

While making clear that Cliff favored jazz, Cosby also showcased other forms of black music. In season six, Rudy's friend Kenny drops by the house to meet a visiting singer named Riley Jackson, played by B. B. King, and joins the King of the Blues in an over-the-top rendition of "How Blue Can You

Get?" As the Huxtable kids grow older, they bring their music — reggae and rap — into the house. In fact, a future generation of hip-hop artists would credit one episode of *The Cosby Show* in particular with having had a transformative influence on their nascent art form.

In "A Touch of Wonder," a limo carrying Stevie Wonder sideswipes Denise's car. To make amends, Wonder invites the Huxtables to his recording studio. After shaking Stevie's hand, Cliff leaves to deliver a baby. (Cosby would often sit out scenes with famous guest stars so as not to upstage them.) Wonder uses a Synclavier, a recording technology that was less than a decade old at the time, to capture sound bites from the family and digitally alter and mix them. Decades later, "Questlove" Thompson of the Roots would say that he and many influential hip-hop musicians first became interested in the possibilities of "sampling" by watching that episode.

Now a world-class art collector, Cosby used the show to celebrate African American painters. By the mid-eighties, with David Driskell's help, he and Camille had become regular customers at Sotheby's and Christie's, and that experience became the basis for an episode called "The Auction." Clair sets out to reclaim a painting by her "great uncle Ellis" that has passed out of the family, and Cliff buys it back in an amusing bout of hypercompetitive bidding. The episode revived the reputation of a painter named Ellis Wilson who had died a pauper's death without ever having sold any of his work for more than $300. From then on, a framed print of Wilson's *Funeral Procession* hung in the Huxtable living room, while the real painting became part of the permanent collection at the Armistad Research Center at Tulane University.

The Cosby Show put living black artists on the map, too. One was Varnette Honeywood, a painter in her midthirties who was selling note cards and posters in Los Angeles in the early 1980s when Camille Cosby stumbled upon her work. Camille started buying pieces for the family collection, and when Cosby placed one on the walls of the Huxtable home, the value and demand for Varnette Honeywoods shot up overnight. Her success was particularly gratifying to the Cosbys because of the wholesome images of everyday African American life that she liked to portray. As Cosby told a *Washington Post* reporter in a profile of the artist: "You can depict segregating, starving, and homelessness, but in Varnette's work you can see teenagers doing homework, a family cooking a meal, girls doing their hair."

While publicly resisting pressure to do so, Cosby injected politics into *The Cosby Show* as well, but always at a time and in a manner of his choosing. In January 1986, almost two decades after he had walked off a stage in Lawrence, Kansas, overcome by grief at the assassination of Martin Luther King Jr., King's birthday was observed as a national holiday for the first time. Cosby decreed that he wanted to acknowledge the holiday, and the episode that aired the week before ended with the Huxtables putting aside squabbles over grades and borrowed clothes as the stirring cadences of King's "I Have a Dream" speech emanated from their living room TV set.

Although it may have seemed relatively innocuous to most viewers, that simple acknowledgment of America's racial past was enough to elicit irate letters from some viewers. The negative mail only made Cosby determined to return to the theme. The following October, he devoted a full episode to "The March," a story in which Theo writes a report on the famous 1963 protest, and his grandparents sit him down to tell him what it was actually like to be there.

Cosby also broke his no-topicality rule to make subtle but recurring references to the uprising against apartheid in South Africa. In the pilot episode, observant viewers noticed an "Abolish Apartheid" sign on the back of the door to Theo's bedroom. It was still there as taping began for season two, but at the last minute NBC executives sent word that they wanted it removed, arguing that the network couldn't be seen to be taking sides in a dispute that had commercial implications for advertisers and sponsors.

Less than a half hour before the Thursday taping was scheduled to start, Cosby called his producers into his dressing room and told them that he would walk off the set if they let the network have its way. "There may be two sides to apartheid in Archie Bunker's house," he seethed to Harry Waters, a *Newsweek* reporter who was working on a profile. "But it's impossible that the Huxtables would be on any side but one. That sign will stay on that door, and I've told NBC that if they will want it down, or if they try to edit it out, there will be no show."

The sign stayed.

When Sondra Huxtable gave birth to twins on the show, Cosby suggested naming them Nelson and Winnie, after South Africa's most famous political prisoner and his wife. And after Mandela was released and negotiations to end apartheid began, Cosby invited the South African singer and activist Miriam Makeba to appear on the show. Before singing "Kwazulu," the tribal song she had made famous in the 1960s, Makeba delivered an eloquent ode to the beauty of Africa and to "hard obstacles" that "will only disappear when people work together."

With Alvin Poussaint's encouragement,

Cosby eventually found a way to address the kind of social and economic troubles that the Huxtables never seemed to face. In season seven, he introduced a new character, a less well-to-do teenage cousin of Clair's who comes to live with the family after her mother moves to California to care for her grandmother. Plot twists involving Pam Tucker, played by Erika Alexander, would include pressure to have sex with a boyfriend, worries about affording college, and a community protest over supermarkets charging discriminatory prices in minority neighborhoods.

At first, Cosby chafed at one quibble he heard from some African American viewers. Blacks were "a people of the book," they asked, so why was there never any hint of religion on the show? In fact, he had come to so associate the Huxtables with his own life that he felt it would be disingenuous to have them go to church, since he had stopped doing so regularly after leaving North Philadelphia and Corinthian Baptist. But eventually he relented with an episode called "The Storyteller," in which Cliff's ninety-eight-year-old aunt, Gram Tee, visits the Huxtables and insists on taking the family to services. To make the experience as authentic as possible, Cosby filmed on location at St. James Presbyterian Church in Harlem, known for its thirty-six-stop organ and magnificent choir, which was led on the show by gospel singer Mavis Staples.

As he had done throughout his TV and movie career, Cosby pushed to hire blacks behind the cameras. One was Samuel L. Jackson, then a struggling theater actor who stood in for Cosby during run-throughs. Cosby insisted on an integrated writing staff as well. He brought in Matt Robinson, a childhood friend from Philadelphia who had worked on *Sanford and Son* and *Eight Is Enough,* and kept him on even as he developed advanced Parkinson's disease. Later he would go out of his way to mentor two apprentice African American writers: Erich Van Lowe and Lore Kimbrough, who had started writing TV spec scripts while working as a Pacific Bell technician.

Another early black recruit for the writing staff was a promising young black author Cosby first heard about from his friend Roscoe Lee Browne. Susan Fales was still an undergraduate at Harvard, but she had written clever spoofs of French theater and a takeoff of *Lifestyles of the Rich and Famous.* Cosby asked to meet her, and as soon as she graduated, he hired her as a writing trainee. "We need to grow our own!" he said, and he took to schooling her in his street-smart approach to comedy. The biracial daughter of a WASP investment banker who married the black actress Josephine Premice, Fales had attended Manhattan's Lycée Française and grown up amid the kind of rich society that wouldn't be caught dead in a comedy club. So Cosby assigned her to "warm-up" duty — greeting the audience before tapings — to force her to learn how to read a crowd and think fast on her feet.

One night, a woman in the audience was complaining about how long it was taking for the show to begin.

"You should be grateful to be here!" Fales snapped.

Cosby, who was watching from the wings, later pulled her aside.

"Never, ever, tell an audience that they should be grateful!" he scolded.

After surviving a year's tryout, Fales finally saw one of her own scripts produced at the beginning of the third season. In "Mother, May I?," Vanessa gets into trouble by starting to wear makeup despite Clair's orders that she is too young. But before Fales could rise further in the ranks of his show, Cosby asked her to take on a new project, one that grew out of what was by far the biggest cause he chose to promote with his power as America's most successful TV star.

Cosby loved Temple University, no question about it. Even after dropping out, he went back frequently to visit, and when he became a big star he did everything he could to repay the school that had helped give him his start.

He spoke at commencements, he served on the board of trustees, he raised money, he helped recruit coveted students and athletic coaches. Still, the older he got, the more Cosby reflected on what had been missing at Temple, at least in his time: a strong network of black students. He had become buddies with the few blacks on the track team and his Omega Psi Phi fraternity brothers. But they were few and far between. And as Cosby got older and made friends who had gone to historically black colleges and universities (or, HBCUs) such as Howard, Morehouse, and Spelman, he couldn't help but envy the lifelong bonds of friendship and support that they had established there.

By the mid-eighties, Cosby's own children were starting to make decisions about where they would go to college. In the fall of 1983, his eldest, Erika, had enrolled at Wesleyan University with the intention of studying art and art history, an interest fueled by her parent's collecting. But to the dismay of Erika and her parents, she discovered that there was virtually no teaching about African American art or artists at the otherwise famously artsy Connecticut institution. By 1984, as Cosby went to work on his new sitcom, he was thinking that an HBCU might be a better experience, socially and academically, for the next two children to go to college, Erinn and Ennis.

As an education advocate, Cosby was also aware that these venerable institutions, long the pinnacle of academic aspiration for African Americans, were under threat. It had been more than a century since freed slaves who didn't have access to white colleges had started to found their own: Lincoln University and Wilberforce University before the Civil War, then roughly a hundred more after Emancipation. But with the advent of desegregation and affirmative action, the HBCUs were losing applicants to predominantly white colleges. A decade earlier, they had accounted for a third of all black college graduates; now that number was dropping fast, and only the increase in black women attending college was keeping their enrollments up. They were also struggling with fund-raising, as wealthy blacks gave more money to the integrated colleges where their children went (or where their parents hoped they would go).

It was against the backdrop of those personal reflections that Cosby decided to champion the cause of HBCUs by making them a central thread in the Huxtable story. In the sixth week of the first season, he introduced a fictional black college called Hillman. Granddad Russell drops by the Huxtable house and quizzes Denise about where she wants to go to college. She's planning to look at Princeton, where her older sister Sondra goes, but her grandfather wants her to consider Hillman, which is his alma mater and where Cliff and Clair met. At first, Denise rolls her eyes at all the nostalgia — until Granddad informs her that at Hillman boys outnumber girls.

Eventually, Denise decides to maintain the family tradition, and Hillman figures in numerous episodes in the first three seasons. Roscoe Lee Browne would win an Emmy for "The Card Game," playing a Hillman professor named Dr. Foster who visits the Huxtables and engages Cliff in a hilariously competitive game of pinochle. Cosby was so pleased with that episode that he suggested another that would demonstrate Browne's prowess as a theater actor. In "Shakespeare," Dr. Foster is staying with the Huxtables when Granddad Russell drops by with a friend who teaches theater at Columbia, played by Christopher Plummer. Hearing that Theo is studying *Julius Caesar* and finding it a snooze, the three distinguished thespians set out to show him how dramatic the play could be by reciting its most famous speeches ("The fault, Dear Brutus . . ." "Age, thou are shamed," and "Young Cassius has a lean and hungry look . . .").

The Cosby Show was the highest rated show on television at the time, but NBC executives still "freaked out," as one writer put it, when they learned that Cosby wanted to do a show that contained five minutes of Shakespeare soliloquies. The suits demanded that the episode be held out of the third-season lineup, and only agreed to air it the following season on a Thursday in late October when ABC was broadcasting the fifth game of the 1987 World Series. Yet in spite of that competition and another momentous event that week — the "black Monday" stock market crash that saw the Dow Jones Industrial Average lose almost a quarter of its value in one day — the program held up in the ratings, vindicating one of the tenets that Cosby reminded his writers and producers of on a regular basis: "When an audience trusts you, they will stay with you."

Cosby may have temporarily lost the Shakespeare battle, but he was about to win a larger war in his campaign to promote the virtues of black education. In the finale of season three, the Huxtables go to Hillman to visit Denise and celebrate the retirement of the school's revered president. The episode was filmed on location at Spelman, the distinguished HBCU in Atlanta. And it served as what's known in television lingo as a "backdoor pilot," because Cosby had persuaded NBC to move forward with a spin-off show based on life at Hillman College.

A few years earlier, that green light would have been unimaginable. In the early eighties — with sitcoms considered dead, few African Americans anywhere in prime time, and the politics of Ronald Reagan in the ascendant — none of the big three television networks would have gone near a show based on life at a black college. But by 1986, *The Cosby Show* had become not only a juggernaut but a launching pad, lifting NBC's entire Thursday night lineup of comedies into Nielsen's top ten. The two shows that followed it — *Family Ties* and *Cheers* — were number two and three in the ratings, and the show that came next, *Night Court,* was number seven.

Any comedy that followed Cosby seemed destined to be a winner, and NBC was eager to use his coattails to produce a new hit. Marcy Carsey and Tom Werner had the leverage to insist on producing the show, and Cosby had the clout to dictate what it would be. And so it was that in the spring of 1986, NBC announced that when it came back for its fourth season *The Cosby Show* would be followed by a new sitcom called *A Different World.* It would be set at Hillman College, and it would give Cosby another vehicle to employ talented black actors, writers, and producers and to show the world both the variety and the universality of black experience.

For Cosby and everyone else involved, there was another, more commercial motive as well. They were eager to cash in on the surprise stardom of Lisa Bonet, and her huge appeal with younger television viewers in particular. When Bonet had been cast as Denise Huxtable three years earlier, few would have predicted that she would become the show's breakout star, least of all the sixteen-year-old herself. The product of a troubled mixed marriage — her father, a black opera singer named Allen Bonet, had divorced her mother, a Jewish schoolteacher born Arlene Litman, when Lisa was young — Bonet had grown up thinking of herself as somewhat of an ugly duckling. At Reseda High School, which she attended before taking up acting full time, she was shy and eccentric and often found herself without a date at school dances.

All that changed the instant *The Cosby Show* went on the air. Overnight, young viewers became obsessed with Lisa Bonet. When junior writers on the staff went out with her in public, fans gawked at the actress, shouted greetings, and hounded her for style tips. Boys thought she was gorgeous in a particularly exotic way, with her light skin and doe eyes and Rasta-braided hair. Girls loved her bohemian sense of fashion, which every week produced funky clothing choices that Bonet made herself, often with little input from the wardrobe department. And young people of both sexes related to her utterly real teenage demeanor, the laconic mixture of sweetness and sarcasm that captured the ironic detachment that was becoming a hallmark of Generation X.

Besides providing a vehicle for Bonet, Cosby had another one of his novel situational ideas for *A Different World.* He wanted Denise to have a white roommate, to show what it would be like for a white person to navigate a predominantly black environment, a reversal of the situation in which black people so often found themselves. Carsey and Werner spotted a talented up-and-comer to play the role: Marisa Tomei, then twenty-three years old and starring in the daytime soap opera *As the World Turns.* They also made a daring hire to oversee the sitcom, which was to be filmed in Los Angeles. Ann Beatts was an edgy comedy writer who had cut her teeth at the *National Lampoon* and *Saturday Night Live* and conceived the short-lived cult hit *Square Pegs.*

From the start, however, Beatts didn't seem to know what to do with the new show, and the first season became a muddle. Tomei's character came off as a whiz one week and a ditz the next. More white students were cast, so it wasn't clear whether Hillman was a black college or not. And Lisa Bonet seemed to want to be anywhere but on the set of her own TV show. Charmingly flakey in New York, with her colorful outfits and a habit of walking around barefoot on the set, she became increasingly difficult when she moved back to LA, at one point during the first season of *A Different World* hiding from producers by locking herself in the bathroom.

Phylicia Rashad flew out to LA to make a guest appearance toward the end of season one and came away deeply concerned. When she got back to New York, she knocked on the door of Cosby's dressing room door and asked if she could speak to him in private about the spin-off.

"It's not up to your standards," she said. "It doesn't represent you."

Cosby listened gravely and asked if Rashad had any suggestions.

She did. She recommended that Cosby bring in her younger sister, Debbie Allen, to fix the show. Although Allen had begun her career dancing on Broadway, she had learned the ins and outs of television as an actor and choreographer on *Fame.* As a graduate of Howard University, her sister argued, Allen had the right experience and sensibility to create a fictional black college that would be realistic and also make for good television.

Soon after, Cosby asked Allen to fly to New York and invited her to lunch at his Manhattan town house with Susan Fales, the apprentice writer from Harvard.

Allen told Cosby that if she was going to tackle the spin-off, she wanted the freedom to deal with the kind of real-life problems that students at HBCUs confronted — issues ranging from stereotyping within the black community to sexism and sexually transmitted diseases.

"All right," Cosby replied.

Fales was stunned. After all the times she had heard the boss lecture his writers about keeping *The Cosby Show* timeless, she couldn't believe that he was so quick to understand the virtue of making *A Different World* topical. Still, the prospect of tackling contemporary themes excited her, and she came away from the lunch realizing that the man she respectfully referred to as "Mr. Cosby" wasn't as much of a traditionalist as she had thought.

The next season, Debbie Allen moved swiftly to put her mark on *A Different World*. She eliminated the Tomei character as well as most of the other white student roles. She made Jasmine Guy and Kadeem Hardison, who played the spoiled debutante Whitley Gilbert and the ingratiating nerd Dwayne Wayne, the stars of the show. She added more black characters of different backgrounds, personalities, and skin colors — accentuating class and cultural tensions within the black community rather than between blacks and whites. She took her writers to Morehouse, Spelman, and Clark Atlanta University to meet with students, a road trip that became an annual tradition. Bit by bit, she championed scripts that took on highly contemporary and controversial topics: date rape, domestic violence, sexual harassment in the workplace, AIDS, hate crimes, use of the "n word," and even the history of black slave ownership and "mammy doll" collecting.

Allen's task in remaking the show was made more urgent by the abrupt departure of Lisa Bonet. Midway through the first season, Bonet had decided to try to prove herself as a dramatic actress by taking a part in a movie called *Angel Heart* directed by the British filmmaker Alan Parker. The role called for her character, a young voodoo practitioner named Epiphany Proudfoot, to have sex with a private eye played by bad-boy actor Mickey Rourke, and the scene was so explicit that Parker had to cut parts to get an R-rating. The performance shocked many of Bonet's fans, and it displeased Cosby and Carsey and Warner enough that they were all too happy to honor her request to leave *A Different World* to pursue more film acting.

It turned out to be only the beginning of their headaches with Bonet. The following November, she made tabloid headlines by eloping to Las Vegas with rock star Lenny Kravitz. Four months later, she was pregnant. At that point, Cosby and his producers couldn't even take her back in the role of Denise, so she was written out of the show for a year with a plot twist that had Denise dropping out of Hillman to travel to Africa. Once Bonet gave birth to a baby girl named Zoe,

Denise returned to *The Cosby Show* as the bride of a naval officer she had met during her voyage. That story line also allowed Cosby to introduce a new "teeny weenie" to the show, now that Keshia Knight Pulliam was growing up, a winning child actress named Raven-Symoné who played Denise's stepdaughter, Olivia. Bonet came and went in episodes over the next two years, but eventually Cosby became so annoyed and disappointed by her moodiness and lack of professionalism that he fired her.

With Bonet gone, Debbie Allen began to transform the Hillman of *A Different World* into a hip, contemporary HBCU that in many ways resonated with black viewers even more than *The Cosby Show* did. For four years after she took over as director and supervising producer, the spin-off was the highest rated show on television in the African American demographic, as well as number three or four in the overall Nielsen ratings. Even more gratifying for Cosby, it began to drive a dramatic spike in applications and enrollments at America's real HBCUs, a renaissance that he and Camille were determined to sustain by making history in another dramatic and unexpected way.

24
"A Vein of Gold"

Johnetta Cole was about to meet with the senior staff at Spelman College to prepare for becoming the school's president — the first African American female to hold that post in the 107-year history of the country's leading black women's college — when the phone rang in her office on the Atlanta campus.

Cole's assistant put her hand over the receiver. "I know you're heading to the meeting," she said, "but you may want to take this call. It's Bill Cosby!"

"Does the sun rise in the east?" Cole said.

"Dr. Bill!" she greeted Cosby, using the nickname she had used for him ever since he received his doctorate, in the days when Cole was still a professor at the University of Massachusetts. "How are you?"

"Oh, I'm doing pretty good," he said. "Camille and I were just watching you on television."

Cole laughed. "Dr. Bill, you're pulling my

leg again!" she said. "I watch *you* on television."

"No, no, no," he said. "Camille and I were watching you. You were on TV with Henry Ponder, the president of Fisk."

"Oh, you're right!" Cole said. "We taped that discussion a while ago. I remember now."

"Camille and I were wondering," he said. "Could you use twenty million dollars at Spelman?"

"I don't know what to say!" Cole said. "I remember when you and Camille gave a million and a half to Fisk, and it saved that place. And now you're telling me that you want to give *two* million to Spelman!"

"Girl!" Cosby said. "Can't you hear? I said *twenty* million!"

Cole was astonished. Twenty million dollars was almost half the size of Spelman's $42 million endowment. Several weeks later, when she announced the gift at a black-tie dinner celebrating her investiture, the crowd of two thousand gasped in awe and then stomped their feet and shouted for joy as though they were praising a miracle on Sunday morning. No private donor had ever given anything close to that amount to any of America's 112 black colleges and universities.

While Cosby's name made the story front-page news in the *New York Times,* everyone present at the dinner could see that Camille

Cosby was the driving force behind the gift. Cole announced that most of the $20 million would go to build a new campus hub called the Camille Olivia Hanks Cosby, EdD, Academic Center, a 69,000-square-foot complex of classrooms, research facilities, and archives devoted to subjects dear to her heart: humanities and women's studies, as well the Spelman Museum of Fine Art. Four million dollars would go to pay for visiting "Cosby Scholars" in fine arts, humanities, and social sciences. Rising to address the well-heeled crowd, Camille made it clear that she also viewed the donation as a challenge to other well-to-do African Americans — like the ones in the room — to do more to support HBCUs.

When Cosby spoke, he choked back tears. He rarely cried in public, but he was seized by a boyhood vision of Germantown, of all the black "jemmin' " in his old neighborhood who never had a chance to go to college. Then he pulled himself together and got a laugh by addressing the question that was on the mind of everyone in the room: How damn rich *is* Cosby that he can give away that much money?

"Mrs. Cosby and I have been blessed," he quipped, "because I found a vein of gold in the side of a mountain."

By the mid-eighties, that vein had turned into a gold mine. In 1987, *Forbes* magazine would rank Cosby as the highest-paid celebrity in America over the previous two years, with an income of $84 million. It included his seven-figure annual salary for *The Cosby Show,* the millions he continued to make as a pitchman, and the fees from as many as a hundred stand-up concerts a year. (In addition to Las Vegas and Tahoe and his other familiar haunts, he was now breaking box office records at Radio City Music Hall.) He had become one of America's most bankable authors, too: his book *Fatherhood,* a slender meditation on parenting written in collaboration with Ralph Schoenstein, had spent fifty-four weeks at the top of the *New York Times* bestseller list and earned him a $2 million advance for his next book, *Time Flies,* a humorous take on aging.

And all that was before the strike that *Forbes* estimated would push Cosby's fortune close to half a billion dollars: his take from the most lucrative syndication deal in television history.

Traditionally, local TV stations didn't consider buying rerun rights to a network show until it had aired for at least three seasons, proving its ratings appeal and building a large inventory of episodes. But syndication buzz for *The Cosby Show* began almost as soon as it went on the air. The interest was so intense partly because so few comedies were coming up for sale, after the sitcom drought of the early eighties. Local stations

616

loved comedies because they could run in any market or time slot, and their half-hour formats made them easy to schedule. But the frenzy was also the result of a particularly aggressive sales campaign mounted by Viacom International, the distribution company that had bought the right to syndicate *The Cosby Show* from Marcy Carsey and Tom Werner.

Even though reruns wouldn't be available until 1988, Viacom kicked off the campaign two years ahead of time, in the fall of 1986. It created an "off-network" auction, selling blocks of reruns to whichever NBC, ABC, or CBS affiliate in each market made the highest bid. With "hope and fear" marketing, it touted how much *The Cosby Show* could help a local station — or hurt it if a competitor got the show. Cosby himself appeared in more than twenty ads and tacked on personalized greetings to more than a hundred stations. By the time the reruns began airing, they had been sold into 165 local markets, covering 94 percent of all US TV viewers.

In all, the rights to the first three seasons of reruns netted more than $600 million. The haul was so enormous that it inevitably led to a legal dispute between Viacom and Carsey and Werner. The producers, convinced that they deserved a bigger cut than had been originally negotiated and worried about the implications of a debt-financed hostile takeover of Viacom by corporate raider Sumner

Redstone, filed suit in US District Court to protect their interests. Larry Auerbach from William Morris stepped in and brokered a deal in which Viacom kept a third of the early syndication revenue — still a huge return on a relatively small investment — while Carsey-Werner Productions split the rest between themselves and their star.

Three years after betting their company on Bill Cosby, the syndication deals made Marcy Carsey and Tom Werner personally wealthy and professionally positioned to launch a half dozen more sitcoms over the coming decade. And Cosby walked away with an estimated $166 million, a down payment on syndication royalties that would drive his personal worth higher and higher in the mid-nineties.

The Cosbys had long been generous philanthropists, but they were now in a position to take their giving to another level. In addition to the donation to Spelman, their gifts to HBCUs in the 1980s included $1.3 million to Fisk University, a combined $1.3 million to Howard, Florida A&M, Central State, and Shaw, and another $1.5 million divided between Maherry Medical College in Nashville, Tennessee, and Bethune-Cookman University in Daytona Beach, Florida.

While Camille enjoyed the strategy and recognition involved in public philanthropy, Cosby took even greater pleasure in giving away his money in spontaneous and anonymous ways. Whenever he met or heard about promising black high school students, he started offering to pay their way through college — a practice that would eventually lead to several Cosby-funded scholarship programs and hundreds of grateful graduates. As a generation of jazz musicians reached old age with little savings or insurance, Cosby footed their medical and funeral bills. After the wife of Jack Gelbart, his trusted inside prop man, suffered her second miscarriage, Cosby called him into his dressing room and handed him a blank check.

"We're going to have a baby!" he said, and he proceeded to pay for top specialists as well as visits to an expensive expert in Chinese herbal medicine until Gelbart's wife gave birth.

In addition to his financial generosity, Cosby relished the opportunity to use his command of TV's most popular program to thank and support longtime friends. Ever since the *I Spy* years, Cosby had gone out of his way to show gratitude to Sheldon Leonard. Whenever Leonard visited New York, reservations were waiting at the city's finest restaurants. One summer, Cosby paid for Leonard to stay at the Hotel du Cap and surprised him by dressing up as a bellman to take his bags to his room. Cosby and *I Spy* producer Fouad Said, who had gone on to make a fortune as an investor, hosted an annual wedding anniversary party for Leonard and his wife, Frankie. (One of them produced a favorite Cosby story: Frankie stood up to acknowledge the toasts and said, "If I knew I was going to live this long, I would have had my tits done!")

Once *The Cosby Show* launched, Cosby invited Leonard to be his second guest star after Dizzy Gillespie. In an episode called "Physician of the Year," Cliff is honored by his hospital. Leonard played Dr. Wexler, a former mentor whom Cliff selects to present him with the award. As a sign of respect, Cosby turned over his dressing room to his real-life mentor for the week so Leonard would be as comfortable as possible.

When Robert Culp was shopping a new TV pilot, Cosby wielded his clout to get NBC to consider it. "Bobby, I'm a two-thousand-ton elephant," Cosby said. "Let's go!" The series never materialized, but Culp did a guest turn on his show, playing a navy buddy of Cliff's. When Cosby persuaded his ailing friend Sammy Davis Jr. to make an appearance, Davis received an Emmy nomination for his portrayal of the illiterate grandfather. Davis died of throat cancer a year later, and for most of the next season Cliff Huxtable could be seen wearing a large pin inscribed with the letters "SD."

The list of guest stars from Cosby's professional past included Nancy Wilson and Leslie

Uggams, his *I Spy* love interests and Las Vegas night club partners; Rita Moreno from *The Electric Company* and Emmy cohost Danny Kaye, who played the Huxtable family dentist in one of his last appearances. In addition to famous musicians (Betty Carter, Placido Domingo), Cosby hosted numerous sports stars, from basketball's Bill Bradley, Dave DeBusschere, and Walt Hazzard to baseball's Frank Robinson and Olympic gold medalist Valerie Brisco-Hooks.

Every week, he would celebrate the week's guest stars as well as other friends and members of the cast and crew with a special ritual. In its fourth season, the show had moved from the dowdy Vitagraph studio to the much more spacious Kaufman Astoria Studios in Queens. Taking advantage of the new digs, Cosby hosted a sit-down dinner in his dressing room between tapings on Thursday. While directors and producers tried to give him notes before the second performance, he held court, offering his companions catered gourmet food and a selection of fine wines from his private collection (which Cosby continued to refuse to touch himself).

It was while trying to help a friend, in fact, that Cosby had one of his periodic outbursts of violent temper, the one time it flared on the set of *The Cosby Show*. Toward the end of the first season, he decided that he wanted to create a show for his friend Tony Orlando, with whom he had bonded when they were both headlining casinos in the seventies. As a poor kid growing up in New York's Hell's Kitchen, Orlando had attended a community center called the Hudson Guild, and Cosby envisioned the singer playing the director of a modern-day refuge for inner-city kids. With Hollywood's writers' union about to go on strike, Cosby himself penned much of the script for an episode called "Mr. Quiet" that was intended as a backdoor pilot for the new series.

During Wednesday's camera rehearsal, things weren't going well, and Cosby began to take out his frustration on a sound technician who he thought wasn't doing his job correctly. Cosby grabbed the technician and looked as if he was going to take a swing at him until Ahmad Rashad, who had begun dating Phylicia Ayers-Allen and was visiting the set, stepped in to restrain him. The next day, Orlando nailed the taped dress rehearsal but betrayed his nerves during the evening performance, and the pilot never went any further. Afterward, he felt so depressed about having let down his friend Cos that he retreated to his condo in Palm Springs and didn't come out for a month.

For his female costar, meanwhile, Cosby did another favor by turning her into a nightclub performer. During the first season, he came up to Phylicia Ayers-Allen on the set one day and relayed a message from Camille. "The boss says I'm supposed to take you to Atlantic City!" he said. "So get it together!"

Phylicia had performed in musicals on Broadway but had never done a nightclub act, and she had only weeks to prepare. For help, she reached out to the top black musical director on Broadway, Harold Wheeler, who would later oversee the music for several Academy Awards shows and TV's *Dancing with the Stars.* She was such a hit that Cosby made her a permanent part of his concert act, flying her when the show was on hiatus to Las Vegas, where he now commanded more than $300,000 for a week's work. She had to bow out for a couple of years when she became Phylicia Rashad and had a baby, but at the end of season six, Cosby took her to Vegas again, waiting until a musicians' strike was resolved to do another weeklong run at the Hilton.

Cosby's most extravagant gestures were reserved for "the Boss" herself. Once the *The Cosby Show* became a hit, he started throwing an annual "I Love My Wife" party. For the second one in 1986, he flew forty family members and friends to New York City for several days. The guests included Camille's parents; best man Ron Crockett and his wife; and celebrity pals like Anthony Quinn, Julius Erving, Geoffrey Holder, and their spouses.

Cosby hosted a black-tie dinner at Twenty:-Twenty, a restaurant owned by his East Side neighbors, the singer-songwriters Nick Ashford and Valerie Simpson. He treated everyone to a cruise around Manhattan and a visit to the boutique of Koos Van Den Akker, the Dutch designer who had created some of Cliff Huxtable's wildest sweaters, where the guests were invited to pick out originals for themselves. For a birthday gift, he presented Camille with another car to add to their collection: a jet black Rolls-Royce along with the services of a chauffeur whenever she was in New York City.

The celebrations could be spur of the moment as well. While they were rehearsing one day, Cosby casually invited Rashad over for dinner and told her to come to his East Side town house at six o'clock. She assumed they would eat there or go to a nearby restaurant, but when she arrived, Cosby was waiting in another car.

"We have to meet Camille!" he said. "Follow us!"

Soon they were crossing the George Washington Bridge and pulling into the Teterboro airfield in New Jersey.

"Hurry up, we have to meet Camille!" Cosby repeated as they boarded his private plane.

A half hour later they set down at a small airport in western Massachusetts, where Camille was waiting. She greeted Rashad with a warm hug, and then Cosby instructed both women to get back on the plane.

The aircraft took off again and landed an hour later in Chicago. Another car was waiting to take them to a French restaurant in town, where several other friends were waiting at a corner table. The group enjoyed a cozy meal with lots of laughter, and then Cosby's plane flew everyone back east after midnight, in time for a few hours' sleep before he and Rashad went back to work on *The Cosby Show* in the morning.

By 1987 Cosby began making plans to present Camille with his biggest gift yet: a magnificent new home in New York City. It was one of the most elegant town houses on Manhattan's East Side, a half block from Central Park and ten blocks north of their brownstone on Sixty-First Street. Built at the turn of the century, it had six stories and 12,000 square feet of elegant rooms for Camille to decorate with her beloved Shaker antiques and works from their ever-growing art collection.

Before Cosby could spring the surprise, however, it blew up on him. Wanting to fix up the town house before he gave it to Camille, he had assigned the family's financial manager, Mary Waller, to oversee a renovation. One day Camille wanted to use the family's private jet and found out that Waller had taken it. She confronted the aide, who told her about the town house and claimed that the travel was related to the renovation. But Camille was suspicious and launched an investigation. The Cosbys subsequently fired Waller and took her to court, claiming that she had been flying around on her own business, as well as siphoning off funds from a company petty cash fund to pay for personal expenses, including jewelry, a Range Rover, a private chef, and work on her house in Connecticut. She disputed the charges and tried to protect her assets by declaring bankruptcy. The incident produced a flurry of embarrassing headlines — and left the Cosbys once again feeling burned by a member of their inner circle whom they believed had betrayed their trust.

While Cosby usually seemed to be having the time of his life with the power and wealth that *The Cosby Show* had brought him, occasionally coworkers would catch him in a melancholy mood. He would call writers into his dressing room and muse about creating a show about the life of a struggling black coal miner or of a woman who has to piece her life back together after her husband divorces her. Once he talked to Jay Sandrich about shooting an episode where Dr. Huxtable loses a baby in delivery. He described Cliff sitting on the front porch of his Brooklyn brownstone, lost in feelings of regret and self-doubt. But he never mentioned it again, and a script was never written.

Given Cosby's intense code of privacy, only family members and close associates knew about the various private dramas that he was coping with during the heyday of *The Cosby Show.* One was a bitter dispute with one of his oldest friends, Harry Belafonte. On the surface, it was over two movie projects. In the mid-1980s, Camille had secured the rights to make a film about Winnie Mandela, the activist wife of Nelson Mandela. At the same time, Belafonte began working on a separate movie about Mandela himself, and he urged Cosby to persuade his wife to drop her project. According to Cosby, when he refused, Belafonte began trying to sabotage Camille's film. The showdown grew so ugly that the two men stopped talking to one another.

Yet at least one associate of both men detected another source of tension. Over the years, the associate had seen Belafonte become increasingly bitter about money. He appeared to resent the fact that at the height of his fame, big stars only made a fraction of what their counterparts would earn in future decades. According to the associate, he found it particularly galling that his old friend Cosby, who had been in a similar financial league when they first met in the 1960s, was now a multimillionaire in the 1980s, making the "big money" that Belafonte privately complained that he had missed out on.

Closer to home, Cosby was dealing with the declining health of his mother. Ever since her son had become a star, "Anna P.," as her friends called her, hadn't had to spend another day cleaning other people's houses. She had donated her tiny row house in Germantown to the church and moved into a manicured estate that Cosby bought for her in the more upscale Philadelphia neighborhood of Elkins Parks. When she visited Massachusetts, Anna had her own guesthouse, and when she wasn't looking after her grandchildren she liked to go bowling in Shelburne Falls or accompany Jean Heath to dog shows where Cosby's terriers and schnauzers were competing.

Once Anna reached her seventies, however, she became increasingly frail. She wasn't able to travel easily, so she would stay behind in Shelburne Falls when the rest of the family decamped to New York City. In 1987, Camille got an urgent call from a Massachusetts hospital where Anna had gone for minor surgery. She was suffering from blurred vision and weakness on her left side. Camille called Cosby at the studio and, knowing that he had a show to finish, volunteered to fly back to Shelburne Falls to find out what was wrong.

"I'm going to look after Mom," she said.

When a specialist examined Anna, he found that she had suffered a minor stroke. An X-ray of her heart revealed that one of her arteries was almost completely blocked. It threatened to close up at any minute, so the doctor ordered immediate surgery. Anna was being wheeled into the operating room as Cosby was beginning his first Thursday taping, and through the entire performance he couldn't stop worrying about her. When Camille called him between shows to tell him that the operation had been a success and that Anna was all right, he broke down in tears.

Cosby was sobbing with relief that his mother hadn't died or suffered a worse stroke, but also with gratitude toward Camille. He started blubbering the word "lucky" — how "lucky, lucky, lucky" he was that she had married him, that she had stayed with him despite his indiscretions, that she was there to care for his children and his mother and help guide his professional and financial decisions. Remembering the moment, Cosby would say that he had a vision of God looking down on him as a young man and realizing that if he was to be successful, he would need someone like Camille by his side. So God commanded Camille: "Now, you fall in love with him!"

Cosby and Camille were becoming even

closer as they grew older, which made another drama all the more vexing. He had long since confessed his liaison with Shawn Berkes to his wife, and after a tense period they had agreed to work harder on their marriage and had moved on. But Berkes, who was married to another man now and went by the name of Shawn Thompson, continued to hit Cosby up for money. "Bill, I need two hundred dollars," she would say when she called him. "I don't mean to bother you, but I'll pay you back." She never did, and over the years he had sent her more than $100,000, including payment for two rehab stints as she tried to kick a drug habit.

After *The Cosby Show* began, she started phoning Cosby at the studio.

"Tell her not to ever call here again!" he would tell his assistant. But a half hour later, she would be on the phone again.

"Shawn Thompson just called," his assistant would say. "She said, 'Does that mean forever?'"

Thompson told Cosby that her daughter, Autumn Jackson, a teenager now, wanted to meet him. He responded by inviting Autumn to a taping of the show, and he even agreed to place a photograph of her on the set so that she could see it on TV. But he took the occasion to tell her that while he would offer financial support and advice — particularly if she went to college and stayed there — he did not believe that she was his child. "I am not your father," he said, "but I will be your father figure."

An even bigger drama was unfolding around Cosby's daughter Erinn. In his early comedy routines, he had jokingly referred to his second-born as "Beelzebub" because she was so much wilder than her older sister Erika. Now entering her twenties, she was more than living up to that description. At fourteen, she had gone away to boarding school and started drinking alcohol and smoking pot. By the time she enrolled as a freshman at Spelman College, she was snorting cocaine and blowing off her schoolwork. When she took courses, she would show up to the first day of class and then stop going. In the middle of her sophomore year, she informed her parents that she intended to drop out.

They responded by telling her that if she left college, she would be on her own. Without naming Erinn, Cosby described the situation in another candid *Playboy* interview with Lawrence Linderman, the journalist to whom he had unburdened himself in the late sixties. "We let the child go," Cosby said. "No one's getting kicked out of the house, and we're not pulling away the safety net. We have phone numbers, and the person is to call any time there's any trouble. But we're also saying, 'This is your idea, and you're going to have to earn the right to be on your own. You get no money from us toward your support.' "

As far as Camille was concerned, the daughter who had grown up to look so much like her — with a beautiful round face and delicate light skin — could no longer be trusted. Camille "iced her," as one family friend put it, and decided that Erinn needed to learn to grow up the hard way. Cosby, meanwhile, viewed the situation from the perspective of someone who had to scrape bottom himself a few times before he turned his life around. "It's disheartening," he told Linderman. "However, when I look at my own life and some of the choices I made when I was young — you just never know."

For the next two years, Erinn lived in New York, crashing with friends and spending most of her time partying. One fall night in 1989, she went to a nightclub with a girlfriend and ran into a male friend who was with Mike Tyson. Shortly before midnight, they decided to go somewhere else to talk, and when they got into Tyson's car, it started toward New Jersey.

Tyson said he was throwing a party at his estate. He didn't say much else, except to ask Erinn what her father thought of him.

"He supports your fights," she said.

When they arrived at Tyson's estate, dozens of cars were parked outside. But inside, the house was empty. Tyson showed Erinn around, and as she was inspecting the memorabilia in his trophy room, he closed the door and came at her. She screamed. When a member of the household staff opened the door, Erinn darted out of the room, found her girlfriend, and ran away.

When Erinn told her parents what had happened, they were furious. "I'll handle it," Cosby said, and the next day he loosed his lawyers on the heavyweight champion. They informed Tyson that he would face charges unless he sought psychiatric counseling. Tyson agreed, but when he ran into Erinn at another nightclub several weeks later, he cursed her father for making him go into therapy. The boxer honored the agreement briefly, then stopped going to his sessions, and several years later he was convicted and sent to prison for raping an eighteen-year-old beauty contestant in an Indianapolis hotel room.

Cosby demanded that Erinn seek treatment as well. Once in therapy, she wrote a letter to her parents confessing that she had developed a $200-a-day cocaine habit that she was trying to kick. But after consulting Alvin Poussaint and other experts, the Cosbys decided that it was still too early to back off their tough-love stance. Her father told Erinn that he would pay for rehab but that she wouldn't be welcome back into the family until she straightened herself out for good.

As usual, his representatives did everything they could to keep the scandal out of the press. But in October 1989 the *National Enquirer* tracked Erinn down in Boston, where she was living with a cousin after spending five weeks at the Edgehill Newport Hospital in Rhode Island. "Looking back," she told the reporter, "I can't believe how Dad managed to go on with his show every week, portraying America's favorite father while having a daughter like me causing him so much pain . . . People see Bill Cosby as a super dad, but I'm proof that drug and alcohol tragedies can happen even in the most loving families."

Even after reading those contrite words, Cosby wasn't ready to accept Erinn back into his life. "Tough love is the only way of dealing with this," he told the *National Inquirer* when it reached him for comment. "We love her and want her to get better, but we have to take a very firm, very tough stand that forces her to realize that no one can fix things for her. She has to beat this on her own."

Two months later, Cosby granted one of his rare extended interviews to Lawrence Christon, a feature reporter for the *Los Angeles Times*. Meeting with Christon over several days in the art-filled den of his Manhattan town house and in his dressing room at the Kaufman Astoria studio, he showed yet again how much more outspoken he was in private than anyone would have guessed from his TV persona. In a rambling polemic, he railed against everything from how violent American society had become to what he called a new form of slavery: keeping poor black people uneducated. He also talked about how conscious he was of his race, no matter how successful he had become. "Living in this world, with this color of skin, there is no total rest, period," he said, stroking his face. "There is no total comfort. Period."

When Christon returned to Cosby's town house the next morning, he brought up the *National Enquirer* story about Erinn. Sipping an espresso, Cosby issued a harsh indictment of his daughter. "We have four other children," he said. "This particular daughter appears to be the only one who is really very selfish . . . She's twenty-three now. She's never held down a job, never kept an apartment for more than six months. She uses her boyfriends. She wants the finer things, but she can't stand anybody else's dirt . . . It's going to take her hitting rock bottom, where she's totally exhausted and at that point where she can't fight anymore. Right now we're estranged. She can't come here. She's not a person you can trust. You think you're not a good parent because you don't answer the call. But you can't let the kid use you."

Until that point, the rift in the Cosby family hadn't gotten much coverage beyond the tabloid press. But now the word *estranged,* coming from Cosby's mouth in the pages of the *Los Angeles Times,* made the story fair game, and it got picked up around the country and became grist for newspaper editorials and letters columns.

To some observers like William Raspberry, the black columnist for the *Washington Post,* the peek into Cosby's real life, while startling, was not inconsistent with the lessons he tried to teach on his show. "I hope Cosby will go on being Cliff Huxtable, model husband and father . . ." he wrote. "But I hope he will go along his path of 'tough love.' There are valuable lessons in that, too, chief among them the limits of what even the most loving of parents can do."

To others, the interview provided an unsettling glimpse at the judgmental, sometimes pitiless side of Cosby's personality. "I felt stunned and sad when I read what Bill Cosby had to say about his daughter in Lawrence Christon's December 10 article," a reader named P. Lucius Sladek Jr. wrote to the *Times.* "One of the loneliest experiences a human being can have is to be the recipient of blame and condemnation by a parent."

But if his second daughter was a cause of public embarrassment and private pain, 1989 would also bring good news to the family — news that, as far as Cosby was concerned, was worth as much as all his riches, which according to *Forbes* now included $4 million a month in syndication revenue from *The Cosby Show*. After years of tormenting his father with his academic struggles, Ennis Cosby had finally discovered the cause of his learning difficulties — a breakthrough that gave him and his parents new hope and provided an uplifting final chapter to the story of the Huxtable family.

25
ENNIS AND THEO

While his father was becoming the most popular TV star in America, Ennis Cosby was attending a low-key Quaker boarding school in the rolling hills of Bucks County, Pennsylvania. Founded in the late nineteenth century, George School was one of the oldest coed private schools in the country and a pioneer of integration. The first black student enrolled in 1940, and graduates included such civil rights aristocracy as Julian Bond, the future chairman of the NAACP, and Donzaleigh Abernathy, the daughter of Ralph Abernathy, Martin Luther King's top lieutenant. But for Ennis, George School's supportive academic environment was as much a draw as its history of championing black equality. Unlike pressure cookers like Deerfield Academy, the elite prep school near Shelburne Falls, George School was a place where activities such as community service and the arts were considered just as important as acing tests.

Arriving as a freshman in the fall of 1983,

Ennis quickly became a popular figure on the small campus. He got involved in musical theater and performed in a student-written revue, singing two songs that were fitting for a Cosby: a jazzy solo called "George School Blues" and a satirical number making fun of "Big Men on Campus." ("Big Men on Campus / A not exclusive group / You really need few talents / To Fool the Nincompoops!") As an upperclassman, he became a leader of SAGE, Students Associated for Greater Empathy, an organization of peer counselors who helped other students get through personal crises such as drug and alcohol addiction, eating disorders, date rape, and sexually transmitted diseases.

By the time Ennis was a sophomore, he had shot up to six feet three inches and grown as handsome as he was tall, his boyish smile and gentle eyes framed by a broad forehead and square jaw. A gifted athlete like his father, he played almost every sport at George School — football in the fall, basketball in the winter, and lacrosse and track and field in the spring. When Cosby was in the Philadelphia area, he would often pay a surprise visit to the George School campus to cheer Ennis on — and give his teammates so many pointers they would joke that Mr. Cosby thought *he* was the coach. But Cosby liked to describe Ennis as a "gentleman athlete," not like the boys of the Richard Allen Homes who would stay out on the battered playgrounds of the projects for seventeen hours in 102-degree heat. "Ennis has sense!" he chuckled.

Ennis grew to love the George School campus, with its red brick buildings, sloping lawns, and trees that turned brilliant colors in the fall, like the ones he had grown up among in Massachusetts. He particularly cherished the spirit of the place, the emphasis on community and spiritual reflection that was at the heart of the school's identity. Like most students who hadn't been raised in the faith, he even came to look forward to Quaker religious observance. Every Sunday, several hundred boarding students would gather for an hour of silent prayer on the wooden benches of the school's Meeting House, a structure built by Philadelphia Quakers in 1812 that had been moved brick by brick and truss by truss to the George School campus.

It was at George School that Ennis learned the traditional term of address that those early Quakers used for one another: "Friend." He loved the sound of the greeting, so old-world and so intimate at the same time, and he adopted it as his own. "Hello, Friend!" he would say cheerfully as he passed students in the dorms, saw professors outside of class, and greeted the staff who tended the grounds and served meals in the cafeteria. It didn't matter who you were or where you came from, you were "Friend" to Ennis Cosby.

Still, Ennis's academic struggles persisted while he was at George School, and so did his father's frustration. At his New York studio, coworkers grew accustomed to walking by Cosby's dressing room and overhearing his distressed phone calls. "You can do it, son!" he would say. "You just have to try harder!" Whenever Ennis came to New York, his father instructed the family valet, Cameron Cooper, to take him to museums and Broadway plays to try to stimulate his intellectual curiosity. The valet described it as "Mr. Cosby's plan" for his son. "Every evening he had things Ennis should do," Cooper recalled. "Some nights were reading, some nights were listening to jazz."

At the same time, Cosby wasn't above making professional fun of his son's travails and suggesting to the world that Ennis's real problem was that he wasn't willing to work hard enough. He summed it up in a story that he told in his nightclub act and repeated for the readers of *Playboy.*

When Ennis was fourteen, according to the story, he approached his father with a look that made Cosby suspect that he was going to ask for something.

"Dad," he said, "I was talking to my friends, and they think that when I'm sixteen and old enough to drive, I should have my own car."

"Fine," Cosby replied. "You've got wonderful friends. I think it's terrific they want to buy you a car."

"No, Dad!" Ennis said. "They want *you* to buy the car."

"What kind of car did you have in mind?" Cosby asked.

"Gee, Dad, I think it would be really nice to have a Corvette," Ennis said.

"Look, son, a Corvette costs twenty-five thousand dollars," Cosby said. "I'd like to buy you a Corvette — but not when you don't do your homework and you bring home D's on your report card. So I'll make you a deal: For the next two years, you make every effort to fulfill your potential in school, and even though Corvettes will then cost about fifty thousand dollars, I'll buy you one. And I won't even care if you *do* bring home D's. If your teachers tell me you tried as hard as you could, and that you talked to them every time you had a problem with your work, well, if a D was the best you could do, I can't ask any more of you. Just give a hundred percent effort in school for the next two years, and you've got yourself a Corvette."

In Cosby's account, Ennis grew very quiet.

"Dad," he said, "what do you think about a Volkswagen?"

When it came time for Ennis to apply to college, his mediocre grades ruled out the Ivies, but several Quaker colleges like Haverford showed an interest, based on his athletic ability and leadership activities. Cosby advised him instead to apply to Morehouse, the all-male black college that had graduated generations of distinguished African Americans from Martin Luther King Jr. to the filmmaker Spike Lee. Cosby confided his own mixed feelings about having been one of few blacks at Temple University and how much he envied the bonds forged by his friends who had gone to HBCUs.

Ennis took his father's advice, but in his freshman year at Morehouse he could manage no better than a 2.3 grade point average. He was trying as hard as he could, but getting nowhere. He shared his despair with friends, and in his sophomore year one of them asked if he had ever been tested for dyslexia.

When Ennis shared that possibility with his parents, they arranged for him to undergo a battery of tests at Landmark College, a school in Putney, Vermont, forty miles north of Shelburne Falls, which specialized in learning disabilities. The diagnosis came back positive: he had indeed been suffering all along from the disorder that makes it difficult for otherwise intelligent people to understand what they are reading or to decode how information has been organized. That summer, he spent several months at Landmark taking classes designed to help dyslexics develop strategies for reading and studying. When he returned to Morehouse, his grades began to improve.

During his junior year, Ennis spent three days a week as a student teacher at Dean Rusk Elementary School, near the Morehouse campus in southwest Atlanta, one of the city's blackest and poorest neighborhoods. He was assigned to a third-grade class of twenty-four students taught by a female teacher. After just two weeks, she told him that she had noticed that the boys in the class, particularly the ones who didn't have fathers at home, performed better when he was around. Thrilled to be making a difference, Ennis started volunteering his services to the school's special education classes as well. Suddenly he was hooked. He had found a calling: teaching.

He set his sights on attending graduate school to get advanced degrees in education. As he did more research into the teaching profession, he discovered that it was growing more female than ever, which only made him more excited about the kind of impact he could have, particularly with boys and kids with learning disabilities. But Ennis wanted to go to a top school, so he buckled down in his senior year. He deployed all the study skills that he had learned at Landmark: taking elaborate notes in class, outlining study plans on his computer, breaking his homework into manageable chunks instead of leaving it to the last minute. By the time he graduated in the spring of 1992, he had made the Dean's List and been accepted into his dream school, Columbia University's Teachers College.

Cosby was thrilled about Ennis's breakthrough — so thrilled, in fact, that he decided to share it with his 30 million viewers. Two months after Ennis's summer at Landmark, *The Cosby Show* ran an episode in which Theo Huxtable discovers that his long struggles with schoolwork are the result of dyslexia. "Theo's Gift" starts with Theo studying for a Greek mythology exam and impressing Cliff with his command of the Icarus story. But when he gets his test back, he has gotten a C and he doesn't know what to do.

"Another one of my lousy C's!" Theo laments to his parents. "I'm sick of killing myself for loser grades! . . . I'm sick of being stupid!"

Cliff and Clair try to suggest that he might have been overconfident. Then they tell him that they will be satisfied as long as he does his best. But Theo makes it clear that pleasing his parents isn't enough anymore.

"That's not the point!" he protests. "*I'm* not satisfied, Dad!"

The family visits a learning specialist who suggests the possibility of dyslexia, and Cliff wants instant results. "Dyslexia!" he exclaims, glad to have a name for what ails his son.

645

"Now fix it!" The specialist explains that dyslexia, which she describes as "a different kind of mind," is a complicated disorder that can take many forms, and that Theo will need to take diagnostic tests to see if any apply to him.

"You guys, I'm dyslexic!" Theo exults when he gets the results back, and Cliff and Clair erupt in cheers.

But Cosby wanted to share more than just the happiness that he and Camille had felt when Ennis had delivered the same news to them. He also wanted to blow the whistle on himself for having suggested for so long that the problem was a character flaw in Ennis, rather than a mental "glitch," as the script called it.

When Theo delivers the news to his sister Vanessa, she turns on Cliff.

"To think all these years Dad called you lazy!" she says.

"I know!" Theo says, thus turning "Theo's Gift" into a parable as much about a father's miscomprehension as a son's.

From that point forward, Theo's growth in self-confidence and maturity, entirely borrowed from what happened to Ennis after his dyslexia diagnosis, became the dominant theme of the last three years of *The Cosby Show*. By season seven, Theo is within striking distance of making the Dean's List — if he can keep from getting distracted by a beautiful exchange student played by Vanessa Williams. In the eighth and final season, he turns down the prospect of a corporate job in San Francisco and decides to go to graduate school to become a teacher dedicated to helping kids with learning disabilities — just as Ennis was planning to do at Columbia.

When Ennis received his diploma from Morehouse in the spring of 1992, it was one of the proudest days of his father's life. And it came just weeks after *The Cosby Show* ended with an episode celebrating Theo Huxtable's college graduation. "And So, We Commence" begins with Cliff scheming to get more tickets for the ceremony and ends with him and Clair alone together, after all the children have left the house, savoring everything that Theo has accomplished in the eight years since he came home with all D's on his report card and his father called his sermon about just wanting to be regular people "the dumbest thing I've heard in my life!"

But the final episode didn't end there. As Cosby moved to embrace Phylicia Rashad in what was supposed to be the closing shot, he added one last bit of inspired improvisation.

"I'm going to dance you out of the studio," he whispered.

And so he did, waltzing Rashad off the set, past the live audience and out a side door of the Kaufman Astoria Studios as everyone rose to give a standing ovation to the show that had made so much television history and put Bill Cosby back on the top of the entertainment world.

When asked why he chose to end *The Cosby Show* after eight seasons, Cosby gave a simple answer: the premise had run its course. After all, what was the point of prolonging a show about the comic "war between parents and children" when the children were all grown up? But he and his producers were also aware that by 1992, the social and political environment that had made Americans so receptive to his gentle family comedy had changed. A war in the Persian Gulf had sobered the public mood. After a seven-year boom in the mid-1980s, the US economy had slumped into a nasty recession, and the privileged life of an upper-middle-class black family no longer seemed quite so charming.

A nationally publicized police scandal had also reminded the country of the kind of racial tensions that never seemed to touch the Huxtables. In March 1991, a burly, unarmed black parolee named Rodney King had refused to heed a traffic stop in Los Angeles and led police on a high-speed car chase. When the cops pulled him over, they assumed King was resisting arrest and beat him into submission using clubs, Taser guns, and the sharp points of their boots. A nearby resident filmed the flogging on his camcorder, and when the footage was released to the media, it ignited an uproar over racial profiling and policy brutality. The policemen involved were put on trial, but on April 29, 1992, they were acquitted by a predominantly white jury, a verdict that so enraged blacks in Los Angeles that thousands took to the streets firing guns, looting stores, and setting fire to cars and buildings.

As it happened, the last episode of *The Cosby Show* was scheduled for the next night, April 30. With the streets of his city in flames, Tom Bradley, the black mayor of Los Angeles, issued a curfew and urged everyone to stay home to watch the finale. Cosby asked the local NBC affiliate for a few minutes before the two-part episode to call for an end to the violence. But the appeals from two of the most powerful black men in the country had little effect on the angry protestors in the streets. The riot raged on for four more days, leaving fifty-two people dead, as much as $1 billion worth of property destroyed, and Americans once again confronting the limits of the progress that they had made in race relations despite the popularity of *The Cosby Show.*

The television landscape had shifted as well. In the mid-eighties, Australian newspaper mogul Rupert Murdoch had started buying up local stations in some of America's largest cities and leveraging them to launch a fourth national TV network. Among the first shows he broadcast on the Fox network was *The Tracey Ullman Show,* a sketch comedy hour starring the British comedienne that featured a cartoon short about a dysfunctional family called the Simpsons. In 1989, Fox spun the animated feature off into a separate show on Sunday nights. In its first season, *The Simpsons* became so popular with young fans and media trendsetters that Fox decided to add to the buzz by shifting the show to Thursday night at eight o'clock, pitting its ironic upstart about a clueless dad named Homer and his bratty children against NBC's sentimental powerhouse about a model dad named Cliff and his loving kids.

At first, the move brought out the street fighter in Cosby. At one of his concerts before the season began, he saw a member of the audience wearing a Bart Simpson T-shirt, asked if he could have it, and wore it on stage for the rest of the show. He boasted to the press about hiring four new female writers and predicted that their touch as well as the addition of the cousin Pam character would help retain his younger audience. But as soon as the season started, *The Cosby Show* slipped from its number one spot in the ratings for the first time in six years. Suddenly Cosby wasn't in such a playful mood. When *Enter-*

tainment Weekly published a cover story suggesting that he was feeling the heat from *The Simpsons,* he sent the magazine's editor, Jeff Jarvis, a tart one-sentence letter. "Dear Jeff," it read, "Where are the flowers for my funeral?"

On Wednesday nights, meanwhile, NBC was broadcasting another edgy comedy with a tiny but avid audience called *Seinfeld.* The star, Jerry Seinfeld, had grown up on the South Shore of Long Island listening to Bill Cosby's comedy albums and taking them as inspiration for his own brand of observational humor. But the spirit of his show couldn't have been more different from his idol's. It wasn't about a tight-knit, upwardly mobile family, but instead a group of single slackers who drifted from job to job and had far too much time on their hands.

"No hugging, no learning," was how Seinfeld's writing partner, a darkly funny stand-up comedian Larry David, described the motto of the show, in mocking contrast to sentimental sitcoms like *The Cosby Show.* But in another sign of the shifting zeitgeist, the year *The Cosby Show* went off the air, *Seinfeld* spiked in the ratings and broke into the Nielsen top forty. Soon it became the new number-one comedy in America, as dominant in the ironic decade of Bill Clinton as *The Cosby Show* had been in the folksy decade of

Ronald Reagan.

Still, Seinfeld would always acknowledge a debt to Bill Cosby, and not only because of the early influence of his comedy albums. Cosby had proven that the "situations" in situation comedy didn't have to be broad and contrived to work, setting an example that Seinfeld and David took to ironic extremes with their "show about nothing." Two decades later, Larry David launched his own show, *Curb Your Enthusiasm,* using scripts only as outlines and allowing his actors to make up many of their lines as they went along. Soon the improvisational method that Bill Cosby had used for thirty-five years became the hot sitcom format of the new century.

By the 1990s, a more obvious impact was already evident. *The Cosby Show* had validated Marcy Carsey and Tom Werner's approach of building sitcoms around stand-up comedians and enshrined it as a new gospel of program development at all four television networks. Once *The Cosby Show* began to slip in the ratings, the show that took its place atop the Nielsen charts was another Carsey/ Warner production for ABC called *Roseanne,* a show about a working-class mother based on the sarcastic comedy act of Roseanne Barr. Along with *Seinfeld,* two of the other most popular comedies of the decade would be *Home Improvement* on ABC and *Everybody Loves Raymond* on CBS, two shows about family life based on the ordinary guy humor of comedians Tim Allen and Ray Romano, respectively. (Two writers for *The Cosby Show* Matt Williams and Carmen Finestra, would help create *Home Improvement* and would frequently credit the experience with teaching them to look for what was truthful before what was funny.)

In the annals of the National Broadcasting Company, it would be written that Cosby singlehandedly revived the network, and that was hardly an exaggeration. The year before he returned to television, NBC had only one program in the Nielsen top twenty. The instant success of *The Cosby Show* ended the losing streak and allowed network chiefs Tinker and Tartikoff to create a "must-see TV" strategy of stacking other comedies on Thursday nights. Soon those shows — *Family Ties, Cheers, Night Court,* and *A Different World* — were all top ten shows in their own right. By the mid-eighties the network was on a roll with dramas as well, with the hits *L.A. Law, Miami Vice,* and *Baywatch.* When General Electric purchased NBC in 1986, it was buying the hottest ratings and advertising franchise in television. By the 1989–1990 season, the network had eighteen of the top thirty shows, and won the overall network ratings battle every single week for more than a year, a feat never achieved before or since.

Looking back thirty years later, former NBC president Herb Schlosser would pay tribute to Cosby by calling him one of the three most important figures in the eighty-five-year history of the network, along with Bob Hope and Johnny Carson. But Schlosser would be even more struck by the cumulative influence that Cosby had on race relations in America by bringing such a positive image of black family life into tens of millions of US homes every week for eight years.

Even before it went off the air, scholars were examining that social impact. In 1992, Sut Jhally and Justin Lewis, two professors from the University of Massachusetts, published a study based on extensive focus group interviews with white and black viewers of the show. On the one hand, *Enlightened Racism: The Cosby Show, Audiences, and the Myth of the American Dream* confirmed the fears of Henry Louis Gates Jr. and others that the Huxtables had given whites a distorted view of overall black progress. But on the other hand, the study found that both blacks and whites were grateful to have had a show that portrayed African Americans in such a dignified and constructive light. (Jhally and Lewis also found that black viewers saw the charge that the Huxtables weren't authentic as "faintly ludicrous," given the show's constant invocation of African American history and culture.) No less an authority than Coretta

Scott King would concur with that verdict, calling *The Cosby Show* "the most positive portrayal of black family life that has ever been broadcast."

Less studied at the time, but perhaps as profound, was the show's influence on America's image around the globe. Viacom International had moved to secure overseas broadcast deals almost as soon as the show premiered. *The Cosby Show* first aired in the Caribbean, becoming an instant hit. By 1986 it was among the top ten TV shows in the Philippines, Indonesia, Hong Kong, and Australia; by 1988, it was number one in Lebanon. It was slower to catch on in Europe, partly due to competition from BBC comedies and other local programming, but eventually it scored big in Scandinavia. When they traveled abroad, the show's actors would hear passionate tributes from fans of all nationalities, identifying with the theme of family and admiring how people of all races interacted in the Huxtable household. As Phylicia Rashad put it, "We made America look *good* to the rest of the world!"

The show's impact was particularly meaningful in South Africa, where it became a touchstone in the battle over apartheid. When *The Cosby Show* began airing on South Africa's TV4 in 1986, it swiftly became the top-rated show among whites, many of whom took it as proof that South African blacks were not the equal of cultured "first world" blacks like the Huxtables. But it was just as popular with black South Africans who had access to television; they saw it as exploding the myth of racial inferiority on which apartheid was built and took encouragement from it to intensify their struggle.

From a business standpoint, the show helped create an international market for dozens of other "black shows" from America. And just as *I Spy* had done two decades earlier, it led US network executives to rethink their assumptions about the appeal of African American actors and programs. Encouraged by Cosby's success, NBC launched two more sitcoms featuring black casts in 1985 and 1986. Both were made possible, ironically, by the abrupt cancelation of the previous king of black comedies, *The Jeffersons* — a decision that CBS announced in the summer of 1985 without explanation and without alerting the actors. That allowed NBC to fast-forward a pilot about inner-city life called *227* starring Marla Gibbs, who had played the Jefferson's sassy maid Florence. A year later, the network snapped up Sherman Hemsley, who had played George Jefferson, to star in *Amen,* about a deacon in a black church in Philadelphia.

Both shows enjoyed solid ratings, further encouraging NBC to green-light another show about an inner city kid who goes to live with his rich aunt and uncle in Los Angeles. Produced by Cosby's friend Quincy Jones, *The Fresh Prince of Bel-Air* would run for six seasons, prove a huge hit overseas and in syndication, and make a star out of rapper Will Smith, another black performer with easygoing charm and crossover appeal. In a further example of Cosby's trailblazing influence, in 1990 the upstart Fox network launched a sketch comedy show called *In Living Color,* written by and starring two African American brothers, Keenen and Damon Wayans, and featuring a multiracial who's who of future superstars including Jim Carrey, Jamie Foxx, and Jennifer Lopez.

Yet if an entire generation of comedians and black actors owed their big breaks in large part to Cosby, one was determined not to show any gratitude. Eddie Murphy was barely out of his teens when he joined the cast of *Saturday Night Live* and became an overnight sensation, helping to revive the slumping sketch show with his street-wise takes on Mr. Rogers and Gumby. Like Cosby, he had had a difficult childhood, having been forced into foster care after his father died, and like Jerry Seinfeld he viewed Cosby's comedy albums as an important early influence. But Murphy was more inspired by the profane comedy of Richard Pryor, and as his career took off — vaulting him to movie stardom with the films *48 Hours* and *Beverly Hills Cop* — his sold-out stand-up concerts became increasingly raunchy.

In 1987, Murphy released a concert film, *Eddy Murphy Raw,* in which he used the word *fuck* 223 times. In one of his riffs, he described receiving a phone call from Cosby, who was upset that Ennis had seen Murphy's act and had heard so much cursing. According to Murphy, he called Richard Pryor to tell him about the lecture, and Pryor dismissed Cosby as a "Jello-O Pudding eatin' motherfucka" who should stay out of other comedians' business. "Have a Coke and a smile and shut the fuck up!" Murphy described Pryor as saying, in mocking reference to Cosby's commercials for the soda giant.

Indeed, Cosby had called Murphy one night from Lake Tahoe to take issue with his act, but he insisted that it was to chastise the younger comic for the way he treated his fans and bragged about how much money he made. And he publicly denounced Murphy as a "very nasty, nasty liar" for his account of what Pryor said.

Cosby felt certain that it was a lie, because Pryor had called him to deny it. One day the phone rang at his house and he recognized his friend's voice on the line.

"Bill, the thing that Eddie is saying, I didn't say that," Pryor said.

"I didn't think you did," Cosby replied.

If Cosby regained the Midas touch in the

1980s that he lost in the 1970s, however, the decade also brought several reminders that not everything he did turned to gold. After the blockbuster third season of *The Cosby Show,* he spent the summer in San Francisco making a fanciful movie about an aging spy named Leonard Parker who comes out of retirement to battle a mad scientist plotting to destroy the human race by fomenting a rebellion of pet animals. Cosby had conceived the whimsical story, but when he saw the rough cuts of *Leonard Part 6,* he immediately recognized that it didn't work. Before it came out, he urged his fans not to go see it, and the movie bombed.

The flop was an embarrassment not only for Cosby but also for David Puttman, the opinionated Englishman who had just taken over Columbia Pictures. Puttnam had personally recruited the director, a whiz kid named Paul Weiland who had shot funny commercials in Britain but never made a movie before. Weiland, who would go on to direct several successful films and the iconic BBC sitcoms *Blackadder* and *Mr. Bean,* blamed Cosby for the failure, suggesting that success in TV had swelled his head. "When anyone gets into that position, they are surrounded by sycophants and no one tells them the truth," he said. "But Cosby just wasn't funny. I couldn't tell him directly. I'd say it feels slow, and he'd say, 'You worry about construction, let me worry about funny.' "

Other Columbia executives who watched the fiasco unfold attributed it to a clash of comic sensibilities. Cosby envisioned a film that reflected his Mark Twain aesthetic of humorous storytelling, while the director and the studio head had a more British, over-the-top, satirical vision. "They didn't get each other at all," recalled Clare Bisceglia, the former Coke marketing executive who had moved over to work for Columbia Pictures after it was acquired by the soda giant. "You can call it a lot of good intentions gone bad, but it was a very bad fit."

After the blockbuster sales of his first book, *Fatherhood,* Cosby's success as an author also dwindled. His second book, *Time Flies,* soared to the top of the bestseller list but didn't stay there long, and eventually half of the print run went unsold. Still hoping for another jackpot, Cosby's publisher, Doubleday, doubled down on a third book called *Love and Marriage,* this time paying a $3.5-million advance despite plans to print only 850,000 books. As reports spread that Doubleday had eaten a $1.5-million loss, an ugly blame game broke out, with Cosby and the publisher faulting the other for not doing enough to promote the book.

Once *The Cosby Show* went off the air, meanwhile, *A Different World* was left to fend for itself. Continuing to reach for social

660

relevance, Debbie Allen opened the sixth season with two episodes in which Whitley and Dwayne, now married, go on their honeymoon to Los Angeles and get caught up in the 1992 riots. NBC executives hated the idea and tried to talk Allen out of it, but she dug in her heels, and even cast the controversial rap singer Sister Souljah as a militant LA resident. ("The great-great-grandchildren of slaves will never have equal protection under the law or be invited to the table of brotherhood," Souljah tells Whitley in one line from the original script.) Without Cosby's lead-in, the ratings fell off swiftly, and the network, worried about protecting "must-see Thursdays" but perhaps also aiming to teach Allen a lesson, started moving the show to other nights and time slots.

Before canceling *A Different World* at the end of the season, NBC executives began showing up on the set to look over Debbie Allen's shoulder. One week they were in the control room, and Susan Fales overheard them talking about Bill Cosby. They were laughing and rolling their eyes and joking about the man who had rescued their network "as though he was some kind of crazy uncle," she recalled.

Wow, Fales thought. *People in TV sure have short memories. Once you're out of the game, it's amazing how fast they can lose respect for you.*

■ ■ ■ ■

PART THREE

■ ■ ■ ■

26
A GIFT MARKED TIFFANY

On the day that Cosby's mother died, during the last season of *The Cosby Show,* other cast members noticed that he seemed unusually quiet. Phylicia Rashad didn't want to pry, and she sensed that he didn't want anyone else bothering him either. When a stagehand said he was going to ask the boss about a production detail, Rashad held him back. "I don't think this is a good time," she said.

But word eventually got out, and people started appearing in Cosby's dressing room to offer their sympathies.

"I'm sorry to hear about your mother," the first visitor said.

"It's okay," Cosby said.

"You only get one, you know," the visitor said.

The words — conjuring up the finality of his loss, but also his mother's uniqueness — hit Cosby hard. He was still pondering them when a female producer appeared in the doorway.

"Sorry about your mother," she said.

"Thank you," Cosby said.

"You only get one, you know," she said.

As Cosby headed toward the set, a stage-hand gave him a sad look.

"I lost my mother, too," he said.

"Yeah," Cosby nodded.

"You only get one," the stagehand said.

Cosby thought: *Once was enough, but I've got to put an end to this!* So when the next colleague approached him with a look of condolence, he started talking first. "My mother's gone, man!" he said. "And I had the most wonderful time with her! Let me tell you a story: One time we were sitting on a bed watching TV. I was drinking a bottle of 7-Up, and she thought she'd be slick and grab it from me while I wasn't looking. She threw it back as fast as she could, and all the bubbles exploded up her nose, and she started coughing, and I laughed so hard! I still remember that!"

"Yeah," the stagehand said, smiling with amusement but also relief that Cosby had alleviated his anxiety about saying the right thing.

Carrying on without the doting presence of Anna P. wasn't the only personal challenge that Cosby faced as the charmed life of *The Cosby Show* came to an end. Given his fierce code of privacy, he didn't discuss a second one even with close friends, but Alvin Poussaint had seen clues. When he visited the estate in Western Massachusetts, Cosby was no longer taking his sports cars out for spins on the country roads. He had also stopped playing tennis — the sport that had once consumed hours every day — on the professional-quality court on his property. When Poussaint asked why, Cosby deflected the question. "I'm through with that," he said tersely.

During a Christmas visit to Shelburne Falls in the early nineties, Poussaint finally put the pieces together. He had bought Cosby a copy of *The Encyclopedia of Jazz* as a gift. When Camille unwrapped it, she glanced at the huge volume, then at her husband.

"Look, Billy," she said. "Alvin got you this encyclopedia!"

There was something about the way Camille looked at Cosby, and the tender tone of her voice, that made Poussaint think: *He's never going to read the book.* It was the physician's first confirmation that his friend's eyesight was starting to fail.

Cosby was suffering from a rare form of glaucoma that had already robbed him of peripheral vision in one eye. He had consulted specialists, undergone operations, and experimented with acupuncture and Chinese medicine, but nothing seemed to do much good. Over the next twenty-five years, the vision in the first eye and then in the other would slowly but irreversibly deteriorate, as Cosby proudly deployed his other senses and the power of his mind to compensate — a feat he managed so convincingly that it would be more than a decade before most people who worked with him or saw him perform could tell that anything was wrong.

At the time *The Cosby Show* ended its eight-year run, however, Cosby was still perfectly capable of watching television, and he didn't like what he saw. He was particularly upset about a new program that had begun to air showcasing young stand-up comics. After everything that Cosby had done to demonstrate that it was possible to get laughs without talking dirty or demeaning his race, it drove him crazy to watch the black comics on HBO's *Def Comedy Jam* use the censor-free environment of cable television to revel in the use of profanity and repetition of the word *nigger.* And it drove him even crazier that a young interracial audience was flocking to the show.

"*Def Comedy Jam* is like the *Amos 'n Andy* of the nineties," he complained to the readers of *Ebony.* "They say 'niggers,' and we are laughing, just as we laughed at 'Amos 'n Andy' in the fifties. But we don't realize that there are people watching who know nothing about us. This is the only picture they have of us other than our mothers going to work in their homes and pushing their children in carriages and dusting their houses . . . And they say, 'Yeah, that's them. Just like we thought.' "

On the broadcast networks, Cosby's success had helped pave the way for more than half a dozen "black shows." But with the exception of *A Different World* and *Here and Now* — a new sitcom that he had championed, starring Malcolm-Jamal Warner as a counselor at an urban community center — he thought they all went for cheap laughs and trafficked in clownish stereotypes that gave white people an excuse to look down on black people and gave African Americans little to direct their sights upward.

On October 3, 1992, less than sixth months after he waltzed Phylicia Rashad out of the Kaufman Astoria Studios, Cosby arrived at Disney World in Orlando, Florida, to be inducted into the Academy of Television Arts & Sciences Hall of Fame. His fellow honorees were cable television news pioneer Ted Turner, Dinah Shore, Andy Griffith, and Sheldon Leonard, the now eighty-five-year-old producer who had done so much to turn Griffith and Cosby into stars. "Sheldon discovered both Bill and me," Griffith said in his genial remarks to a black-tie crowd of five hundred TV luminaries. "Bill was a young comic. I was an out-of-work comic. So it worked out good for us."

When Cosby rose to speak, he put an end to the industry self-congratulation. Pounding his hand on the lectern, he launched into a tirade about the portrayal of blacks on TV. "I'm begging you all now!" he pleaded. "Stop this horrible massacre of images that is being put up on the screen now! . . . It isn't us . . . I don't know where they get these people from. Drive-by, I guess. Writers drive by and see people on the street, and I don't know if these people are sad because *Amos 'n Andy* won't come back, but ladies and gentlemen, really and truly, *The Cosby Show* should have shown these writers something about our own people . . . 1992, ladies and gentlemen, 1992, and we've got African Americans on TV, women throwing their hands on their hips and saying, 'Honey, why don't you!' . . . None of these images happen to be the kind of people that you can imagine graduating from college, that you can imagine working beside you in a steel mill and seriously thinking about their family, about their life, about their contribution to making a better United States of America and the world."

In the days after that speech, Cosby grew even more upset and determined to do something dramatic to stop the "massacre of images." Three weeks later, he dispatched Norman Brokaw, who was now running the William Morris agency, on a confidential trip to New York. His mission: to communicate to

Bob Wright, the president of NBC, that Cosby wanted to buy the entire network.

Cosby had reason to think that Wright might listen. By the early nineties, NBC had suffered a steep, rapid fall from its position during the *The Cosby Show*'s run, falling into third place in the network ratings race. Jack Welch, the president of General Electric, was famous for demanding that GE be either number one or number two in all of its businesses, so rumors were swirling that the conglomerate might dump NBC. Cosby had read reports that his old boss Brandon Tartikoff, now running Paramount Pictures, and Barry Diller, who had just quit as head of the Fox network, were sniffing around. He told Brokaw that he wanted to be in the hunt, too.

"We've been hearing about all these different people buying NBC," he said. "I want you to tell NBC we're seriously interested."

In his account of their meeting, Brokaw laid out for Wright both how and why Cosby proposed to buy NBC. Despite its recent slump, the network had a book value of close to $4 billion — far more than Cosby could afford on his own, even as one of the wealthiest entertainers in America. But he was proposing to line up other investors and contribute a good chunk of his personal fortune, which now surpassed $300 million and was growing by the day as total syndication revenue from *The Cosby Show* neared $1 billion and Cosby continued to get a healthy cut. In his discussion with Wright, Brokaw stressed the "warm feelings" that Cosby had about NBC, having started his TV career with *I Spy* and returned to create the most financially successful show of all time (a not-so-subtle reminder of how much NBC owed him). Most of all, he emphasized Cosby's desire to ensure a home for "quality television."

Wright responded that NBC was not for sale. When news of the meeting got out, spokesmen for the network poured cold water on it by suggesting that the talks had never gone very far. But Cosby didn't let the matter rest. He made a surprise visit to a meeting of NBC affiliate stations, giving a rousing five-minute speech in which he invoked the network's storied past and vowed "to see this peacock fly again." The following year, he retained the investment firm Goldman Sachs for strategic advice about pursuing NBC. But ultimately he couldn't find enough partners, and GE started to see more long-term value in NBC once it acquired the cable business news network CNBC and woke up to the profit potential of cable television, with its lower programming costs and revenue from both advertising and operator fees.

Still, the media coverage of the NBC bid continued to infuriate Cosby. Much of it made the idea sound like "the attack of the killer ego," as one story put it, rather than a legitimate business proposition pursued by a serious financial player. Just how offended Cosby was became apparent a year later when he was promoting a new show and a *TV Guide* reporter name Lisa Bernhard brought up the matter.

"What you have to understand is, I wasn't the only one," Cosby explained, alluding to Tartikoff and others who considered making a play for NBC. "[But] I was the only one as far as the press was concerned . . . The excitement of it was this entertainer, who is African American, was out to try and raise money to run a network. And then it comes down to, 'Can he run a network?' Well, what is the question *really*?"

He looked Bernhard in the eye and repeated the question. "What is the question, *really*?"

Bernhard replied that media reporters tended to think of TV executives as businessmen in suits rather than entertainers.

"They're *white*," Cosby said. "That's the issue. What makes an entertainer any dumber than some executive? I mean, can you even tell me why they keep saying TV is the way it is, and now an entertainer decides to try and run a part of the network, and he's going to do worse? You tell me I can't run a network? Bring me an old wreck that's beat up and say, 'You can't run this?' The question should

673

be, 'Why would you *want* to?' "

Yet if Cosby couldn't own a network, he was still determined to fight what he called TV's "recycling of mediocrity" with his own work. As *The Cosby Show* entered its last season, he had pitched Marcy Carsey and Tom Werner on a new project: a remake of the old Groucho Marx game show *Your Bet Your Life.* Long before he met his idol, Cosby had listened to Groucho's program on the radio as a boy and watched it on television as a teenager. He had always imagined himself in the format: a host who engaged amateur contestants in witty conversation before they competed for prize money by answering trivia questions.

Carsey and Werner liked the idea, too, for creative and financial reasons. They saw it as drawing on two of Cosby's greatest strengths: his natural ease with people of all ages and backgrounds and his ability to be funny on his feet. They also viewed it as an opportunity to put Carsey-Werner Productions into the syndication business, with a venture that they could sell themselves to local stations without having to share the spoils, as they had been forced to do with *The Cosby Show* as a result of the deal with Viacom International.

Many local TV executives saw *You Bet Your Life* as a can't-lose proposition. For one in particular, it looked like the answer to his prayers. As the president of the CBS stations group, presiding over the local affiliates owned by the parent network, Johnathan Rodgers was one of the highest-ranking African Americans in the TV industry. But his five "urban market" stations — in New York, Los Angeles, Chicago, Philadelphia, and Miami — were all losing to ABC, whose prime-time and afternoon programs (particularly *The Oprah Winfrey Show*) did better with city dwellers than CBS's offerings.

Rodgers was convinced that Cosby's new vehicle could be the key to holding local CBS viewers past the evening news into prime time. Although distributors usually courted programmers, Rodgers did the wooing. He invited Bob Jacobs, the head of syndication for Carsey-Werner, to his home base of Chicago and wined and dined him at expensive restaurants. He shrugged off the fact that the show didn't have a pilot, just a clip reel that mixed scenes from *The Cosby Show* with old footage of Groucho. Flying his general managers to Chicago, he issued a "mandate" that they all buy *You Bet Your Life* for their stations.

But as soon as it debuted in September 1992, it was clear that Cosby's game show was in trouble. Selling the program to 137 local stations, Jacobs had predicted that it would achieve audiences similar to *Wheel of Fortune* and *Jeopardy.* Those shows had ratings of 12 and 10, respectively — representing 12 percent and 10 percent of all households with televisions. Yet in its first week, *You Bet Your Life* managed only a 4.7 rating, a lower percentage than reruns of *The Cosby Show* were getting.

Realizing that his stations had a problem, Rodgers flew to Philadelphia to meet with Cosby and his producers. Cosby turned on the charm, and Rodgers was as entertained as the rest of the live audience by the playful way he had tweaked the original format. He had hired the striking actress Robbi Chong as his announcer and replaced one of Groucho's signatures — a toy duck that descended from the ceiling when a contestant said "the magic word" — with a stuffed goose dressed in a Temple University sweatshirt. But home viewers continued to find the program slow and hokey. By winter, Rodgers threw in the towel and allowed his restive station managers to replace *Your Bet Your Life* with other shows, and by June it was such a nationwide flop that Carsey and Werner shut down production.

Searching for what had gone wrong, Rodgers did more research into Groucho's original show. What he discovered was a rigged format. It turned out that the questions and answers and Marx's seemingly off-the-cuff comebacks were all scripted in advance. Cosby, meanwhile, was improvising, as he always did. And while he was often funny, he never achieved the volume of laughs per minute or the kind of rapid-fire timing that Groucho was remembered for, particularly since the daily pace didn't allow for the kind of artful editing of his riffs that Jay Sandrich had done on *The Cosby Show*.

Watching the show at home in Shelburne Falls, Camille Cosby detected another problem. Her husband prided himself on featuring likeable contestants, many of whom came from Philadelphia, where the show was produced, and talked about the good works they did in the community. But often those same contestants couldn't answer the trivia questions. And Cosby couldn't bring himself to make fun of them as Groucho would have done. Instead, he tried to find ways to score laughs while not making the contestants look bad or compromising his own nice-guy image.

"My wife felt that the people damn near served as buffoons," Cosby recalled. "She thought it was embarrassing to like people and then hear a question that was very simple, and these people were struggling to answer. I really tried to be as tender as I could. I think I gave respect to quite a few of them. But it was uneasy and embarrassing, and people didn't want to see it anymore."

After the failure of *You Bet Your Life* and *Here and Now* — the earnest Malcolm-Jamal

Warner vehicle that survived only half a season — Cosby's next attempt at a TV comeback was an hour-long drama. He still had enough clout with executives at NBC to sell them on *The Cosby Mysteries,* a show in which he would play a forensic expert who quits the police force after winning the lottery but keeps getting dragged back to solve difficult cases. Naming his character Guy Hanks, after Camille's father, Cosby pitched it as a show driven by vivid characters and smart stories rather than needless violence. He recruited a promising supporting cast: Dante Beze — later known as Mos Def — as Hanks's young sidekick, and Cosby's old pal Rita Moreno as his whacky, health food–obsessed housekeeper. Carsey and Werner hired two of the best crime drama writers in TV, David Black from *Law & Order* and William Link from *Columbo* and *Murder, She Wrote.*

But *The Cosby Mysteries* languished in the ratings and was canceled after eighteen weeks. Cosby was proud of several episodes, particularly a story called "Camouflage" about a young boy who accidently shoots his best friend, a gifted honors student. Believing that viewers still associated Cosby with the eight o'clock time slot, however, NBC had scheduled the show at that hour on Wednesday nights, violating every programming rule about when viewers liked to watch hour-long dramas. The show came and went so quickly that it would be remembered largely as the butt of jokes, from a parody on *Saturday Night Live* to a line on *The Simpsons,* the Fox show that mischievously continued to bait Cosby. (Hearing that *The Cosby Mysteries* has been canceled, Homer Simpson laments: "That show had limitless possibilities!")

Yet two months after *The Cosby Mysteries* went off the air, a major shakeup in the power structure of Hollywood created another opportunity for Cosby to bounce back. A young programming executive in a big hurry took over another struggling network and made one of his first calls to Cosby's agents at William Morris.

On the surface, Les Moonves and Sam Haskell couldn't have been more different. Moonves was a restless, gravel-voiced Jew from Long Island who had been a student actor at Bucknell. Haskell was a courtly Southern WASP who had grown up in a small town in Mississippi, gone to Ole Miss, and married his college sweetheart, a local beauty queen. But as they each moved to Los Angeles and started to rise through the entertainment business — Moonves as a programming executive, Haskell as a talent agent — the two men formed the kind of friendship that gets forged in the trenches of Hollywood deal making. They met for lunch or dinner almost every month, and Moonves was a regular at Haskell's annual Christmas party.

When Moonves was named president of entertainment for CBS in the summer of 1995, he reached out to Haskell for help in making his first big move. For almost a decade, the network had been relentlessly cutting costs under the reign of investor Larry Tisch. While the stock price had risen, the once dominant home of *Dallas, M*A*S*H,* and *All in the Family* had plummeted to third place in the prime-time ratings and developed a reputation in Hollywood's creative community as a cheap and unsupportive place to work. So Moonves was determined to do a deal that would start rebuilding his roster of programs and send a signal that CBS was prepared to spend big money to get big talent.

"Sam, this is the Tiffany network," he told Haskell. "I need to rebuild it, and to do that I need a show with America's most beloved guy. What do I have to do to get Bill Cosby?"

Moonves knew that Haskell would have to talk to his boss, Norman Brokaw, who still handled his favorite client personally. Brokaw reported back that both he and Cosby liked the idea of a new sitcom — but they wanted to test the waters with the other networks. He authorized Haskell to sound out NBC and ABC as well and to review the bidding with Cosby.

"Deputy Dawg!" Cosby greeted Haskell when he called to report the results, using the teasing nickname he had given the agent because of his Southern accent and role as Brokaw's trusted lieutenant.

Haskell laid out the options as dispassionately as he could. All three major networks had shown interest in the idea of a new Cosby comedy. NBC was intrigued, despite the disappointing performance of *The Cosby Mysteries*. ABC was, too, and Marcy Carsey and Tom Werner liked that scenario, given their personal history at the network and the success of *Roseanne*.

"So what do you think?" Cosby asked.

"If all things are equal financially," Haskell said, "I believe we should be at CBS, because you will be the most important person in Les Moonves's stable. There's something to be said for that."

Moonves wanted Cosby so badly that he made sure all things weren't equal. He made a preemptive bid that he knew neither of the other networks would match. He offered a virtually unheard-of buy of forty-four episodes, enough for two seasons. He also agreed to foot all the production costs, so Carsey and Werner wouldn't have to deficit-finance. Including Cosby's salary, that came to more than $1 million per episode — double the cost of the average new sitcom. He even promised to buy several other shows that Cosby might do in the future — a side deal that eventually led to a three-year run for a remake of *Kids Say the Darndest Things,* the legendary daytime show originally hosted by Art Linkletter.

Cosby opted to take the Tiffany network's silver, and by December 1995 he and Moonves were ready to unveil the new project to the world. Holding a press conference for TV reporters, they announced that in the tradition of *All in the Family,* the show would be based on a British sitcom. This time the model would be *One Foot in the Grave,* a comedy about a security guard who is forced to take early retirement and keeps getting into funny scrapes because he has too much time on his hands. They had hired Richard Day, a veteran of the Carsey-Werner shows *Roseanne* and *Cybill,* as head writer, and planned to shoot the show at the final home of *The Cosby Show,* the Kaufman Astoria Studios in Queens.

Far from skirting questions about how much he had paid to land Cosby, Moonves boasted about it. The deal, he said, demonstrated "CBS's commitment to put their money where their mouth is."

Cosby addressed the issue with a joke. Reminding reporters that CBS no longer broadcast National Football League games because Fox had outbid it for the rights, he crowed: "The $400 million goes to us!"

Happy to be back on familiar terrain, Cosby threw himself into the planning of every aspect of his new sitcom. But by April, when he was due to shoot the pilot, he had decided that it had two major problems.

One was Richard Day's scripts. Producing story lines for Cosby's character — Hilton Lucas, a laid-off airline worker — the head writer kept trying to capture the tone of *One Foot in the Grave*. In that show, the protagonist is a bitter curmudgeon who takes out his anger at the world in comically vindictive ways. But as he tried Day's character on for size, Cosby found it too much of a departure from the amiable image that he had spent thirty years cultivating. When Day dug in his heels, Cosby fired him and replaced him with a staff writer, Dennis Klein.

Day didn't go quietly. Venting to the *New York Post,* he insisted that Cosby had signed on to do an "edgy, dark absurd" comedy but had "lost his nerve because he'd had a lot of success with a very lovable persona." Klein, the new head writer, was trotted out to dispute the charge, telling the paper that Cosby was still committed to portraying "an interesting, odd, very angry character." But later, when he was asked about it directly, Cosby replied with his usual bluntness and confirmed Day's account. "Yes, that's correct," he told Greg Braxton, an entertainment reporter for the *Los Angeles Times*. "If the critics complain that Bill Cosby's got such a nice image he's afraid that he can't do evil things like this Englishman — well, that is correct. And that is nothing to be ashamed of if you're in show business."

The second problem was with the actress who had been cast to play Ruth Lucas, Hilton's long-suffering wife. Cosby had first met Telma Hopkins when she was a singer in Las Vegas, backing up his friend Tony Orlando as one of the duet called Dawn. Since then, she had become a successful TV comedienne, with featured roles in *Gimme a Break* and *Family Matters*. But once they went into rehearsal together, it became clear that Hopkins couldn't keep up with Cosby's ad-libbing. She could deliver memorized dialogue but got completely thrown when he went off on a comic tangent.

"I can't do this," Hopkins admitted to the show's executive producer, Joanne Curley Kerner. "I have to learn lines."

So with days to go before the pilot shoot, Cosby decided that he had to find someone else to play Ruth Lucas. And he chose the one actress he knew could be counted on to keep waltzing while he Bopped.

Phylicia Rashad was in Hartford, Connecticut, at the time, rehearsing for a play called *Blues for an Alabama Sky*. It was a

Friday, and the director had given the cast a long weekend off. She was doing errands in a chauffeured vehicle when the car phone rang and the driver told her that a producer from Los Angeles was on the line.

"Bill needs you to do his new show," the producer said.

"When?" she asked.

"Now!" the producer said. "We'll send a plane!"

Cosby got on the line and pleaded for her help. "This is a very emotional moment," he said.

Rashad flew to LA and walked straight into blocking rehearsals for the pilot. By Monday, Marcy Carsey was announcing to the trade press that Cosby had found a new Ruth Lucas, and Tom Werner was touting the reunion of "our Fred and Ginger."

When the pilot was previewed for entertainment critics, however, it met a cool reception, and Cosby and his producers continued to tinker. Originally the opera singer Audra McDonald had been cast to play Hilton Lucas's married daughter. But soon she was replaced, too, and T'Keyah Crystal Keymáh was hired to play a daughter who is single. Weeks before the pilot was scheduled to air, scenes were being reshot, and Cosby and his writers were tussling over how dark the comedy should be. One plot line — about Hilton looking after his daughter's pet turtle

— was lifted straight from *One Foot in the Grave.* In that show's over-the-top rendition, the turtle gets run over by a car and is incinerated in a garden bonfire. In Cosby's tamer version, the turtle emerges only slightly singed after Hilton mistakenly throws it into a leaf burner.

Yet as Les Moonves had hoped, America was eager to sample Bill Cosby in a new comedy. On Monday, September 16, more than a quarter of all Americans watching television tuned into the first episode of *Cosby,* the best debut for a sitcom since *The Cosby Show* twelve years earlier. The premiere even beat *Monday Night Football* on ABC, and lifted CBS to an overall win for the night.

The reviews were promising. John J. O'Connor, the venerable TV critic for the *New York Times,* wrote that the show was on a "positive track" and particularly praised the casting of Madeline Kahn as Hilton's sarcastic next-door neighbor. David Zurawick of the *Baltimore Sun* contrasted the show's working class milieu favorably with the upper-class world of the Huxtables. "Cosby deserves tremendous credit," he wrote, "for the risks he is taking with audience expectations in trying to create a sitcom and character that connect with the place where many audience members really live."

Cosby was genuinely surprised — and wary. Carsey and Werner had deliberately tried to play down comparisons with the instant success of *The Cosby Show*. They saw the new show as targeted to a smaller, older audience and were keenly aware of how much more crowded the TV landscape had become with the advent of the Fox network and so many cable channels. For *Cosby* to come out of the gate so strongly only meant that it might look as if it were fading later, and sure enough the falloff began in the following weeks. Some viewers went back to football; others gravitated toward a new family comedy on NBC called *The Jeff Foxworthy Show*. By October, *Cosby* was down to two-thirds of the audience that had tuned in for its premiere.

For Moonves's tarnished network, however, that qualified as an extra-base hit, if not a home run. *Cosby* remained CBS's highest-rated weekday program through the fall and trailed only three of the network's weekend shows, *60 Minutes, Touched by an Angel,* and *Walker, Texas Ranger.* More important for Cosby, it was in the Nielsen top twenty — meaning that unlike his previous two flops, it had every chance of surviving into a second season. At the Kaufman Astoria Studios, he was back in a familiar groove: bouncing scripts at the Monday table reads, clowning around with Phylicia Rashad and Madeline Kahn during blocking rehearsals, entertaining studio audiences on shooting day, and hosting his gourmet-catered dressing room dinners between tapings.

For the rest of the Cosby family, it was a happy time, too. Now in her early fifties, Camille had emerged as a public figure in her own right. A decade earlier, she had gone scuba diving on vacation and emerged from the water to find the coloring stripped from her hair. She had decided to leave it gray and then had cut it short so that she wouldn't have to straighten it so often. As she was photographed publicly with her new look, she received hundreds of letters applauding her for having the confidence to provide a model of natural, middle-aged beauty for black women.

Once her youngest child, Evin, was in high school, Camille had gone back to school. In 1992, she had proudly donned her own robes and collected a doctor of education degree from the University of Massachusetts. For two years after that, she had traveled to Harlem's Apollo Theater every week to conduct interviews for a book on the effect of television on the way African Americans viewed themselves. She had also become a stage and film producer, acquiring the theatrical rights to *Having Our Say*, the bestselling autobiography of Sadie and Bessie Delany, two black sisters who had lived into their hundreds and witnessed a century's worth of black history.

The two oldest Cosby girls were grown up now and living on their own. From Wesleyan, Erika had gone to the University of California at Berkeley to study art and embark on a career as a painter. Since the tabloid headlines about her troubles with her parents, Erinn had ended a brief marriage and moved to Miami Beach. Although still estranged from her parents, she kept a low profile, promoting parties and working in a gift shop. The two youngest daughters were still in school and happy to be associated with their famous parents and their work. While attending college, Ensa had assisted Camille with her book on television. Inspired by her stylish parents and their fashionable friends, Evin had transferred from Spelman to the Fashion Institute of Technology, in New York City, and in her spare time she liked to hang out at her dad's studio and help out in the wardrobe department.

The future looked particularly bright for Ennis Cosby. A year and a half earlier he had received his master's degree from Teachers College, as his beaming parents sat in the front row for the graduation ceremony. Now he was a couple of years away from becoming the third "doctor" in the Cosby household. Living in his parent's old brownstone in the East Sixties, he steered clear of the New York celebrity scene and focused on his teaching and research. Down the block on

Second Avenue, the staff at the Chicken Kitchen, where Ennis bought takeout meals, had no idea who their customer's father was. At the Adams Tobacco shop, where he got his morning newspapers, the fellow behind the counter called him "big man" only because of his height.

Sheena Wright had been a classmate of Ennis's at George School and now was a fellow graduate student at Columbia. She was amazed at how the shy, gangly kid she had known in high school had matured into a confident young man who talked about "living his dream" of becoming an educator. Ennis couldn't wait to get on the crosstown bus every week to work with dyslexic kids at P.S. 163, a grade school on West Ninety-Seventh Street. When he was assigned to tutor one student for a year to fulfill one of his requirements, the two hit if off so well that Ennis continued to work with the boy for two additional years.

In an essay for his course work, Ennis discussed the strengths he thought he could bring to his chosen profession. He loved kids, he wrote, and kids responded to him. He could be "stern on good morals and manners," but he also knew how to bond with young people. More than that, he had a belief in "chances" and not "quitting" born of his own learning struggles, as well as an understanding that "learning is a slow process, and patience is a very good quality in a teacher."

Beyond the impact he could have on individual students, Ennis declared, he had ambitions to shake up the field of special education based on the lessons he had learned as "a victim of the system." "I also feel that special education programs need to be changed," he wrote. "I just want all students to have an equal opportunity. I have a lifetime to devote to making the school system more balanced in any way I can."

What Ennis didn't mention was that his parents were planning to help him pursue that goal. As a gift when he earned his doctorate, they were going to give him enough money to start his own school. His grandmother Anna might have been forced to abandon it when she left Girls' High to become a maid; his father might have sacrificed it by dropping out of Temple University to go into show business; but after three generations, Ennis Cosby was finally going to fulfill the Cosby family dream of becoming a teacher.

In the meantime, he had already helped turn around the life of one grateful student: his uncle Russell Cosby. The kid brother who had been the inspiration for Cosby's early comedy routines and the "Russell" of his Saturday cartoon show had grown up to work for Delta Airlines in Atlanta, first as a baggage handler and then as a customer service rep. But he had always harbored a secret shame: he barely knew how to read. He had faked his way through his first years of school in North Philadelphia by studying the pictures in books, but once he had to decipher words alone, he got hopelessly lost. By fifth grade he was placed in a class for "slow" students.

"Russell, how do you spell *sky*?" other kids taunted him.

He couldn't answer.

"You don't know how to spell *sky*?" they said. "Man, you're dumb!"

His older brother tried to keep his spirits up. "Russ, you'll be all right," Cosby would tell him. But Russell felt backward and embarrassed, and he would hide his books for the "slow" class in a paper bag. Eventually, he transferred to a vocational school to study interior design and then dropped out in eleventh grade and went to work.

At Ennis's master's degree ceremony from Columbia, Russell saw a seventy-two-year-old man walk to the stage and accept a diploma. When Russell remarked on it later, Ennis urged him to go back to school to complete his own education. He could afford to, his nephew pointed out, now that he was fifty-two years old and the three children he had raised with his wife, Clemetene, were grown. Russell confessed that he was ashamed to try because he could only read at a third-grade level, but Ennis kept after him. He suggested that his uncle visit Landmark College and get tested for learning disabilities.

"Unc, you can do this!" the six foot three graduate student said, looking down at his father's freckle-faced brother and rubbing his curly head of hair.

When Russell took his nephew's advice and went to Landmark, he discovered that he, too, suffered from dyslexia. Relieved to find out that he wasn't stupid after all, he enrolled at Florida A&M University with the goal of earning a college degree by the time he turned sixty.

Over the Christmas holiday, Russell and Clemetene visited Shelburne Falls, as usual, and Ennis quizzed his uncle about how his studies were going. Once again, they told the story of how they had solved the Cosby mystery of learning troubles — and now everyone in the family could laugh about it.

"Ennis, I want you to change this shit around!" Cosby told his son when they talked about the school he was going to start. "No more talking about learning disabilities! We're talking about learning *differences*! Disability means something's not there. You've got something there, it's just that . . ."

"They've taken over!" Ennis interjected, using one of his funny metaphors for dyslexia: the brain occupiers. "There's a stupid demonstration going on up there!"

As the family celebrated Christmas, Ennis was also eager to talk about his upcoming trip to the West Coast, where he planned to spend a couple of weeks before returning to Columbia for the spring semester. His best friend from George School, Phil Caputo, had visited New York in the fall and come to the set of *Cosby,* and now Ennis was going to visit Caputo in LA, where Phil was starting a career as a lawyer.

Returning to work after the holiday, Cosby felt full of renewed energy and excitement to be back doing what he loved. On January 16, 1997, he had just returned from collecting a People's Choice award as America's favorite TV comedy actor for his new role of Hilton Lucas, and, as usual, he was one of the first people to arrive at the Kaufman Astoria Studios. As he prepared to shoot an episode called "Lucas Platonicus," he was looking forward to performing some Buster Keaton–style physical comedy in a bit where Hilton tries to install a satellite dish on his roof.

By midmorning, Cosby was on the set planning the bit when he saw his producer, Joanne Curley Kerner, walk toward him looking like she had something to tell him.

"Can we just finish this scene?" the director asked, so Curley Kerner stood by waiting. But Cosby noticed that her body language seemed tense, and that he she had a stricken look on her face.

27
NIGHTMARE OFF THE 405

Joanne Curley Kerner considered herself a tough Irishwoman, but this was the hardest thing she had ever had to do. She certainly didn't want to do it front of everyone on the set.

"Can I speak to you in your dressing room?" she asked.

"Okay," Cosby said.

"There's been a killing in Los Angeles," she said as soon as the door was closed. "Ennis may have been involved. He may be dead."

At first Cosby just looked stunned. Without saying anything, he put on his winter coat, as if to say that he was ready to go — now! — to get on his private jet and fly to his boy.

But Curley Kerner told Cosby that the police wanted him to stay put. They didn't know what the motive for the shooting was, and they were worried about his safety. Reporters had been calling all morning and were swarming outside the studio and around his homes in Manhattan and LA. Arrangements needed to be made to sneak him out of the Kaufman Astoria Studios so that no one would see him.

The chief spokesman for the LAPD, Commander Tim McBride, had been assigned to brief Cosby on the case. A call was put through, and McBride walked him through everything the police knew so far.

At roughly one thirty in the morning LA time, a middle-aged woman had flagged down a police patrol car near the Mulholland Drive exit to the 405 San Diego Freeway. She was frantic and said that she had a friend who had been shot. When she led the officers to a nearby access road called Skirball Center Drive, they found Ennis's dead body, a single bullet wound in his head. He was lying next to a green Mercedes convertible registered to Cosby Productions, and he had been changing a flat tire. The trunk was open, the emergency lights were blinking, and a tire iron was found close to the body.

Cosby was trying to concentrate on what the police officer was telling him, but his mind and emotions kept drifting. Grief and disbelief were swirling in his head like oil and water, unable to cohere. *How could this have happened?* he thought. *To Ennis? On his vacation?*

Cosby gathered himself and asked if there were any suspects.

The witness had seen someone, McBride said. But she was badly shaken, in a terrible state. She couldn't describe the suspect clearly. She said that Ennis had called her on his car phone and asked her to come help him change the tire by shining the lights of her vehicle so that he could see in the darkness. As she sat in her Jaguar, waiting for him to finish, a man tapped on her window and flashed a gun. Panicked, she drove off, but then she quickly turned around and came back to see that Ennis had been shot and the suspect was fleeing on foot.

Was it a robbery? Cosby asked, feeling heartsick at the thought of the $130,000 Mercedes 600SL convertible that Ennis had been driving. It was registered to his company, but it was his wife's car, another gift. Cosby recalled that Camille had warned Ennis not to drive the Mercedes while he was in LA, because she was worried that he might be the victim of a carjacking — an epidemic in the city at the time — or of profiling by cops suspicious of what a twenty-seven-year-old black man was doing behind the wheel of such an expensive vehicle.

Robbery might have been a motive, McBride said. But nothing appeared to be missing. Ennis still had a Rolex watch on his wrist and three twenty-dollar bills in his pocket. There was nothing to suggest that he had tried to resist a holdup. The only object in his

hand was a pack of American Spirit ciga-
rettes, as though he had been about to offer
his killer a smoke.

What about the witness? Cosby asked. How
did she know Ennis?

McBride said that it was unclear, since she
was in such fragile condition. So far the
police who questioned her had learned only
that she was a forty-seven-year-old white
woman named Stephanie Crane who described herself as a screenwriter. She said
that she had met Ennis at a party soon after
he arrived in town and that they had struck
up a conversation about learning disabilities.
That night, he called her to ask if he could
come to her house to continue the conversation. She lived on an affluent street in Sherman Oaks, less than two miles from where
Ennis was found, so he was only minutes
from his destination when his tire went flat.

(Later Cosby learned that Stephanie Crane
was also part of a show business family. Her
father, Harry Crane, was a comedy writer
who had created the sketch for Jackie Gleason that led to *The Honeymooners;* Cosby
remembered seeing him at Nate 'n Al's of
Beverly Hills, a deli that was a writers'
hangout back in the sixties.)

After Commander McBride finished his
briefing, he shared a personal detail. He had
lost a child, too, a daughter who had perished
in a hit-and-run accident when she was

sixteen. McBride talked about how he had coped with her death, and how he had helped other families whose children had been taken far too early. Cosby stayed on the phone for twenty more minutes, and McBride sensed that he was searching for a way to process his devastation, by thinking about other parents who had suffered similar tragedies.

In fact, those close to Cosby knew that he had a difficult time with death. He was always there for his friends when they were dying, but not always after they were gone. Dizzy Gillespie was one example. When the jazz giant had fallen ill with pancreatic cancer a few years earlier, Cosby had called him every day, had gone to visit Dizzy in the hospital, had sat by his bedside, and told him funny stories to try to keep his spirits up. But he hadn't gone to the funeral. "I don't like to see people horizontally," he told Alvin Poussaint and other friends at the time.

But now he was going to have to bury Ennis — his only son, his prince! He was going to have to comfort Camille, who would be suffering a mother's grief, the pain of losing the baby she carried and raised to be a man. He would have to be there for Ennis's sisters, for the rest of family, and for their dearest friends.

Cosby thought about Granddad Samuel, who had died exactly twenty years earlier. If there was ever a time when he needed to be strong like his grandfather, and not weak like his father, it was now. He needed to be strong for his own family, but also for the millions of people who now saw him as part of their families, as a result of everything he had come to stand for since he left North Philadelphia.

While Cosby was still at the studio talking to the police, Ed Lewis arrived at the family town house on the Upper East Side. The publisher of *Essence* magazine had become friends with the Cosbys after his wife, Carolyn, bonded with Camille during a parents' weekend at Spelman College. The Lewises were part of the inner circle, dining regularly with the Cosbys in New York and visiting Shelburne Falls for the holidays.

Lewis had heard about Ennis from Maxine Waters, the black congresswoman from South LA. Knowing that she was a friend of Cosby's, the police had called her office to ask how to reach him. Waters declined to give them a number. She thought someone close to the family should break the news in person, so she phoned their mutual friend Lewis.

By the time Lewis got there — eleven thirty that morning — Cosby had already reached Camille, and they had spoken to the LAPD together. Now she was secluded behind locked doors, stunned and crying, struggling to understand what had happened to her baby. Lewis didn't want to disturb her, so he waited, as members of the house staff passed by him in tears. After an hour he left, and when he walked out onto the street a phalanx of TV satellite trucks and dozens of reporters was stretched down the block.

At the Kaufman Astoria Studios, Curley Kerner arranged for a car to drive under the back of the soundstage so that Cosby could escape without being seen by the reporters. As he drove into Manhattan, he knew that he couldn't escape the media thronged in front of his house. He didn't want the images on the evening news or in the morning papers to be of police shooing the press away or of a remote celebrity walking by without saying a word. He knew he had to give them something, one sentence that expressed what he was feeling and told the world what Ennis had meant to him.

When the car pulled up to the town house, Cosby climbed out, put his key in the front door, and then turned to face the reporters.

"He was my hero," he said quietly, and then he went inside.

The rest of the day was a blur of tearful hugs, anguished phone calls, and tense consultations. Cosby's publicist called from LA to offer condolences and brief him on an alarming media development. Before Ennis's body could be removed from the crime scene, a picture had been taken of it from a local news helicopter. The station, KTLA, had decided that the image was too bloody to air, but the footage had been picked up by CNN and run across the country at the top of the cable network's early-afternoon broadcast. The network was besieged by hundreds of angry phone calls, as well as appalled protests from CNN's own staffers, and less than a half hour later anchor Bobbie Battista had come on the air to apologize to CNN's viewers and to the Cosby family.

The media circus made it obvious that there was only one place where Ennis could be buried in privacy. Cosby started making arrangements for the body to be flown to Massachusetts so Ennis could be laid to rest on the family property in Shelburne Falls, in the fields where he had played as a child. Still, when Cosby called back Ed Lewis to thank him for his visit, he was still struggling to accept his son's fate.

"I can't believe it," Cosby kept saying. "I can't believe. This could not have happened!"

That evening, Willie Williams, the Los Angeles chief of police, got through to Cosby, and they too talked about other parents who had lost their children. They discussed a seventeen-year-old black girl who had been shot that same day when she got caught in a gang battle as she was riding home from school in South Central LA. Cosby asked for the number of Corie Williams's mother and later called her several times to offer comfort.

"If we ever thought this was a special man," Williams said at a press conference after the call, "that conversation more than confirmed it."

Throughout the day, thousands of people had phoned CBS, Cosby's new network, his old home at NBC, and talk radio shows across the country to express their shock and sorrow. By nightfall, when the country's leading newscast, *NBC Nightly News,* came on, more than fifteen and a half million viewers tuned in to learn the details of Ennis Cosby's death — an audience that wouldn't be rivaled again for eight years, until the last broadcast of anchor Tom Brokaw. The following night, millions more turned to *Larry King Live* on CNN, where a tearful Phil Caputo remembered his best friend from George School.

Watching *Larry King* in Shelburne Falls, the Cosbys agreed about how they would start to honor their son's memory. The next day, they announced that they were creating a charity to support education for learning disabilities, and that they had asked Phil Caputo to run it. They named it the Hello, Friend/Ennis William Cosby Foundation, and over the next decade it would help bring tens of thousands of new books into city classrooms and put hundreds of kindergarten, first-grade, and second-grade teachers through a two-year "Cosby Scholars" program aimed at creating leaders in special-needs education.

Once two days had passed and the finality of Ennis's death had sunk in, Cosby began reflecting back on his years in the navy, to the amputees and brain-damaged patients he had treated at the Philadelphia Naval Hospital. He remembered how full of despair and self-pity some of them were when they first arrived on Ward P. He also recalled what he thought at the time, as an energetic young man with his life ahead of him, about what he would do if he ever suffered one of their disabilities. *I would kill myself,* he thought. But then he watched as, day by day, those patients came to accept their fate, to embrace life again, to carry on. Now it was going to be his turn to begin the long, painful process of accepting the unthinkable.

Cosby saw a very different response in Camille. As soon as she came out of her initial shock and grief, she focused on finding the killer. She talked about wanting that *thing* to pay. Her mouth barely moved when she said it, that's how angry she was. She was sure that someone knew who had done it, and she was furious that they didn't come forward. Observing the difference between the ways they were struggling with the news, Cosby was reminded of the time he and Camille were watching Ennis play football in high school and he was the target of a particularly vicious tackle. Cosby had started talking about what Ennis could have done differently, how he should have planted his feet and lowered his shoulder. Camille's reaction was: "He just hit my boy!"

Still, Cosby knew that he was going to have to be careful about dealing with the LAPD. He wanted to find the killer as much as Camille did, but he wanted to make sure that it was the "shaw 'nuff" person, as his friend Dizzy might have said, not some suspect pulled in off the streets because of the pressure for fast results in a high-profile case. He also wanted to make sure that the prosecution was airtight — no misplaced blood samples, none of the kind of flaws in the case that had allowed Johnnie Cochran to get O. J. Simpson off. He thought of the old saying: just because you can smell the cake baking doesn't mean it's ready to eat. He knew how sensitive the LAPD was about its reputation, particularly in dealing with racial cases, ever since the Rodney King affair, and he wanted them to feel that he had faith in them. Even if he hired his own private detective to work on the case (which he eventually would, investigator to the stars Gavin De Becker), he would make sure that he didn't get in the way of the cops.

Yet if Cosby understood that he had to be patient, it wasn't getting any easier as each day passed without a break in the case. By Saturday, the LAPD had released a sketch of a suspect, based on the information they had received from Stephanie Crane. It depicted a white man with an angular face and a scowling expression, wearing a knit wool cap. Flyers described the man as being of average height and between his midtwenties and midthirties in age. Scores of 911 calls had come in describing cars and people in the vicinity of the murder scene in the hours around the shooting. But when McBride and other LAPD officers briefed the Cosbys, they admitted that despite "lots of leads, and lots of directions," they still had no hard evidence.

Mark DeJackome, the chief of the tiny three-man police force in Shelburne Falls, could still picture Ennis as a boy. He remembered how Ennis raced through town on his bike, how he played in the town basketball league, and later, as a teen, how he called out "Hello, Friend!" to people on the street. DeJackome also knew how grateful the whole community had been when the Cosbys, at Camille's suggestion, had bought up 1,500 acres in addition to the 236 acres on their estate to keep away the developers. So the police chief didn't have to be asked twice to come to their assistance now, by deploying his men to block off the road to the house so Ennis could be laid to rest in peace.

Ennis's body had arrived in Massachusetts on Saturday, aboard a chartered cargo plane. (Cosby originally wanted to send his private jet but was told that it was too small to hold the casket safely.) A commercial flight from Los Angeles to Hartford, Connecticut, brought Russell Cosby, who had flown out to California to help deal with the arrangements; Ennis's friend Phil Caputo; and Howard Bingham, a photographer who had first met Cosby in the 1960s when he accompanied Muhammad Ali to the *I Spy* set and who had remained a trusted friend for three decades.

The last family member to arrive was Erinn Cosby. Although she had barely seen or spoken to her parents over the past decade, she flew in from Miami on Sunday morning to be with them in their time of grief. As soon as she appeared at the house, Howard Bingham, who had had a soft spot for Cosby's second child since she was a baby, shouted out her name, and she rushed over to give him a hug.

"Erinn, you have to get your act together," he whispered in her ear.

"I am," she whispered back.

The burial took place later that day, on one of those cold New England afternoons when the snow crunches underfoot. Besides Bingham and Caputo, there were only family members: Cosby and Camille and their four daughters, his brother Russell and his wife, Camille's mother and siblings and their spouses. There was no minister, because as far as they were concerned, Ennis was already blessed. And there would be no trip to a cemetery. Cosby had filed papers with the town to have an herb garden on the property designated as a funeral plot, so that when Ennis went home, as they said in the spirituals, he could stay home.

The mourners gathered in a renovated barn where the casket lay in state. Together, they carried it down a small hill to the herb garden, where the backhoe that had dug the plot loomed in the background. They lowered the casket and joined hands as Cosby began to eulogize his son.

"We now want to give praise to God for allowing us to know Ennis," he began, his voice cracking. "Not for giving him to us, but just for letting us know him. Now please bow your heads and give praise to God, and when you're finished with your prayers, bring your heads up."

Everyone prayed in silence for several long, solemn minutes.

As heads began to lift, Cosby said: "Now if you want to say something to Ennis, please say it."

His daughter Ensa went first. She addressed the casket and tried to express her feelings, but she was struggling to find the right words, and she kept breaking down crying. "Ennis, I'm just sounding like myself, aren't I!" she said, and everyone in the circle laughed.

Next Evin, the youngest, spoke up. "I would like to say something," she said. She began telling a story, but then she interrupted herself. "Yeah, but Ennis, I know that you know that I'm lying!" she said, and everyone laughed again.

As they went around the circle, everyone added a funny story or comment to Ennis, and the laughter continued. Cosby looked over at Camille's brother Guy, the namesake of her late father, who had a puzzled expression on his face. *He must think this family has some sort of psychiatric problem,* Cosby thought. But then he saw Guy start to nod, as he realized that they were remembering Ennis the way he would have wanted to be remembered, with a smile.

Finally, the circle came around to Cosby again. He talked about Ennis's great-great-grandfather, Zack Cosby, who had been born a slave but lived to be a proud, free farmer. He talked about Ennis's great-grandfather Samuel Russell Cosby, who had brought the family to Philadelphia and become a factory worker. He praised Ennis's grandparents for the sacrifices that they had made to make his own success possible.

"Each generation has built a step for their children to climb higher," Cosby said. "But Ennis, man, when your turn came, you said, 'Dad, this step you built, do you mind if I build it a little bit higher?' And I said, 'Help yourself, man, but you've got some children following you!' "

He pointed to a spot nearby. "Also, Ennis," he said, "we're going to put down a tree . . ."

"Yes, Ennis, a pine tree," Camille chimed in. "We're going to plant a pine tree and light it every Christmas, and on your birthday!"

"And our anniversary is coming up . . ." Cosby added.

"And for my birthday, too . . ." Camille said.

"I'd like it for my birthday, too . . ." Cosby said.

Ennis's sisters started to join in: "And on my birthday!" . . . "And mine!" . . . "And mine."

Cosby chuckled. "All right, Ennis," he said, "just to celebrate, we're going to turn the lights on the pine tree *off* on your birthday!"

Just as the last words of remembrance were being spoken, a car pulled into the Cosby estate. It was carrying Michael Merchant, a Chicago native who was one of Ennis's best friends at Morehouse. Merchant had been serving in the Peace Corps in Africa, deep in the countryside, when the awful news reached him. He immediately took the first ride he could find to the nearest big town, four hundred miles away: jumping into the back of a farmer's truck with the animals. It took him another three hundred miles to reach an airport, where he boarded a single-engine

711

plane for the first leg of his flight to Massachusetts. As Merchant joined the circle of mourners, hugging Ennis's parents and sisters, Cosby recalled what he had told his son when he was applying to college: if you go to Morehouse, you will make friends for life. He had, and now Cosby had those friends to keep Ennis alive in his heart.

After lowering the casket into the ground, the mourners made their way back to the barn, where snacks and warm drinks had been laid out. As they walked up the hill, Cosby turned to his brother Russell.

"Don't you feel light?" Cosby asked.

"Yes, I feel light," Russell said. "Man, this is kind of strange."

"Yeah, we went down this hill feeling like slaves," Cosby said, "and we're coming back up feeling like free people."

Then his mind made one of its sudden leaps, and he thought of a New Orleans jazz funeral. He pictured the band playing solemn dirges to the graveyard, then breaking into upbeat stomps once the body was "cut loose," as the procession and the second line filled the streets with joyful dancing.

"Russ, we did the New Orleans funeral without knowing it," Cosby said. "But we did it without the band."

At the barn and later inside the main house, there were more memories of Ennis, enough to keep everyone laughing and crying into

the night and to deflect Cosby's thoughts
from what was coming the next day, when
the press would find out about another
private drama that was sure to put his name
back in the headlines.

28
THE TRIALS OF "JOB"

After a week in Shelburne Falls, Cosby couldn't stay away any longer. He was convinced that it's what Ennis would have wanted. He could hear his son's voice in his head: "Hey, Dad, you have to go back to work, man!"

Six days after the burial, Cosby had his chauffeur drive him back to New York City. He went first to an appointment with his acupuncturist, and then headed toward Queens, where he planned to camp out at the Kaufman Astoria Studios because reporters were still lying in wait at his Manhattan town house.

Shortly before midnight, Cosby's chauffeur stopped at a red light and a Jeep sedan pulled up alongside the car. There were four people inside, and Cosby could tell that they recognized his face in the window. The driver gave him a thumbs-up, but he didn't smile, and the other passengers remained grim-faced.

Usually, Cosby would play a little game

with people who recognized him in public. He would see them pointing, or saying "It's Bill Cosby!", and he would look away coyly, as though he was embarrassed by the attention. Then he would turn around and give them a thumbs-up and a big smile, and everyone would laugh. But when Cosby returned the thumbs-up from the driver of the Jeep, he and the other passengers just stared at him with pitying looks.

Struggling to fall asleep that night, Cosby couldn't get the picture of the sad faces out of his head. It made him think of a routine he had once heard from Lenny Bruce: A vaudeville comedian arrives at the theater one night certain that he is going to be a big hit. He sits through the spinning plates and the bouncing dogs until there is just one more act before he is scheduled to go on. A quadriplegic war veteran with an eye patch rolls onto the stage in a wheelchair and sings "My Buddy," the tearjerker ballad. After that, the comedian doesn't stand a chance, and he bombs.

Now, Cosby realized, he was both of the figures in that story. He was the comedian, but he was also the tragic figure who made people too sad to laugh.

This isn't right! he thought. *I may be hurting inside, but I'm an entertainer. My job is to make people happy!*

On Sunday, Cosby awoke with another day

to go before shooting resumed. He tried to distract himself by watching sports on TV. The New York Knicks were playing the Miami Heat at Madison Square Garden, and pregame coverage of the Super Bowl had begun, with the Green Bay Packers set to meet the New England Patriots that evening.

As Cosby flipped back and forth between channels, he kept thinking about Ennis — about all the Knicks games they had attended and all the Super Bowl Sundays they had shared. On the spur of the moment, he decided that he wanted to tell the world what had been on his mind all night: that it was okay to laugh again. Reaching for the phone, he called Andrew Heyward, the president of CBS News. Would Dan Rather, the network's evening news anchor, be available to come out to Queens? he asked. Because Cosby was ready to grant his first interview since Ennis's death right away, that afternoon.

Rather was at the Knicks game that Cosby had been watching when Heyward tracked him down. He immediately left and headed to Queens, picking up a camerawoman along the way. When Rather arrived at the studio, he was carrying his own sound equipment, and Cosby teasingly asked if he was part of the crew.

While he was being interviewed, Cosby wanted viewers to be able to see an image of his son in the background. He had chosen a portrait of Ennis, wearing sunglasses and academic robes, on the day of his master's degree graduation from Columbia. Joanne Curley Kerner, who came to the studio to help out, suggested that Cosby and Rather talk on the living room set of *Cosby,* next to an armoire where the portrait of Ennis could sit. Because the interview had been arranged in such a hurry, Rather was still wearing his off-duty clothes — jeans and work boots and a black flannel shirt — and Cosby was dressed casually in brown corduroys and a green sweater.

Cosby told Rather that he wanted to tell the story of his son's burial, but that he wasn't sure if he could get through it without choking up. But he didn't use those words. Instead, he used his pet name for his negative ego — Riggie — the one based on the private joke he had shared during track practice with Coach White at Temple. "I get to a certain point when I tell this story, and I haven't been able to control it," Cosby said. "It's like running the four hundred meters and you reach the three-hundred-meter part and Riggie jumps out and says, 'Whap!' "

He managed to get through the story, his voice cracking once, as he described the laughter during the burial. Then he recalled the day his mother died, and how he had shared funny memories to keep people from feeling sorry for him.

As Cosby was telling that story — about all the people who told him "You only get one" — Rather remembered a detail he had read about Ennis, one that had jumped out at the anchor because he, too, had only one male child.

"In terms of a son, you only got one," Rather said. "Is that the reason you told me that story?"

Rather suspected that the question might get to Cosby, but he was unprepared for what happened next. They were standing at this point in the interview, next to the portrait of Ennis. Cosby smiled, wrapped Rather in a bear hug, and then planted a big kiss on the cheek. "Thank you!" he said, his eyes glistening with tears.

Rather asked several questions about the police investigation, pressing Cosby on whether he trusted the LAPD, but Cosby didn't take the bait. Cosby quoted a line from *Julius Caesar* to suggest that the LA cops had been unfairly tarnished by the Rodney King case. "It's like Shakespeare," he said. "When you die, the bad lives after you, and the good is interred with your bones. So it was with the LAPD. One big, big case, for so many years, and America sees this as potential for whatever . . . I have the confidence in them that they're doing everything that they can do."

After several more questions about the

murder probe, Rather started to bring up the other story about Cosby that had been in the news all week. Curley Kerner, Cosby's producer, had thought it would be off limits. But Rather had seen an opening at the beginning of the interview, when Cosby had looked him in the eye and invited him to ask "anything you want. You go ahead; I'll just give it."

"Let me change gears very quickly," Rather said, with a nervous cough. "There's a sidebar story, as we say in the press, running concurrently. Are you sensitive about talking about that? Does it make you angry to talk about that?"

A week earlier, the private drama that Cosby had tried to keep hidden for more than two decades had burst into the open. Two days after Ennis's murder, Autumn Jackson had been arrested on extortion charges for trying to get Cosby to pay $24 million to prevent her from telling the world that she was his out-of-wedlock daughter. Her arraignment and bail hearings had revealed that Jackson had conspired with a shady character named Jose Medina, a former real estate broker claiming to be a filmmaker. They were threatening to sell the story to the *Globe* tabloid and to share it with Cosby's bosses at CBS and companies that used him as an advertising pitchman. But when they arrived in New York City to receive what they thought had been a payoff negotiated by Cosby's lawyer, FBI agents had arrested them for extortion.

When news of the arrest first broke, Cosby's spokesmen insisted that he barely knew Jackson. They admitted that he had paid for Autumn's college tuition for a year and set up a fund for other expenses, but they described her as just one of the hundreds of young people Cosby had helped put through school. Other reports revealed further details about Jackson and her mother, the former Shawn Berkes. After Autumn had dropped out of college in Florida, she and her boyfriend had gone to live with Shawn in California, but she had kicked them out of the house when the boyfriend refused to get a job. Living out of her car, Autumn had started working as a desk clerk at a Holiday Inn in Burbank, where she met Medina and they began to hatch the extortion plot.

So far, however, much of the mainstream press had remained circumspect about the story. On Thursday, *People* magazine had published a poignant story with the cover line "A Death in the Family" that included only one paragraph about the Jackson arrest. Reflecting on the loss, the Reverend Jesse Jackson told *People* that it reminded him not of Noah, the Biblical figure once associated with Cosby, but of a very different figure from Scripture. "When Bill Cosby had the tailwind at his back," Jackson said, "doing no wrong in records, movies, and television, you didn't think it possible that he could be Job. But he and his family are facing a sudden storm. How they handle it is really the ultimate way one's character and strength are measured."

Then two days before the Rather interview, there had been another dramatic turn in the Jackson story. A man had stepped forward to say that he was Autumn's father. He was the Jerald Jackson, a forty-seven-year-old truck driver whose name was on her birth certificate and who, with his light skin and angular features, bore a striking facial resemblance to the young woman. Jackson told a *Daily News* reporter that in the early seventies, he had a fling with Autumn's mother, who still went by her maiden name of Shawn Berkes, when he was a "street person" and she was eking out a living doing secretarial work in LA. "I don't have any doubts about the paternity," Jackson said. "I'll take a blood test to prove it."

When Rather asked about the truck driver's account, Cosby said that he wanted to believe it, too. Why else would Jackson have come forward? he asked. But when Rather pressed for a categorical denial, he got an answer he wasn't expecting.

"Is there any possibility that you are the father of this child?" Rather asked.

Cosby sighed and looked up at the ceiling. "There's a possibility," he said. "I mean, if you said, 'Did you make love to the woman?' the answer is yes. 'Are you the father?' No, the father's name [on the birth certificate], I had nothing to do with it. I didn't call her and say, 'Put that man's name down.' "

Suddenly Rather had a scoop on his hands. Until then, neither Cosby nor anyone speaking for him had even conceded that he knew Autumn's mother. Now he was admitting that he had had sex with her, and that he could in theory be the father. As Rather calmly pressed on, Cosby revealed more details of his long entanglement with the two women: how he had learned of Autumn's existence after phoning Shawn Berkes for a second "rendezvous" in Las Vegas; how he had sent money to Shawn and Autumn in exchange for their silence but also with advice about how to improve their lives; and how he had told his lawyer to have Autumn arrested after she threatened him with public embarrassment.

"I didn't get a happy ending," he said, "In school, out of school . . . try this, try that, working the games . . . Something snapped, and when it snapped, I realized, there's a point of no return."

Did Cosby have any regrets? Rather asked.

Cosby answered with a shrug and a rueful smile. "What do I regret?" he said. "It's academic. I regret the thought, and then the execution, of the rendezvous."

A few minutes later, when Rather ventured that the public might not care that much about a dalliance, Cosby suggested why he was voluntarily confessing to something that his handlers had spent all week trying to suppress.

"As an entertainer, I want to be known as a fellow who — not only was he honest, he took the hit himself," he said soberly. "You're not going to find me running around talking about: 'How many entertainers do you know who . . . ?' or 'You can't go on the road without . . .' That's not it, man. It was *my* choice."

Rather returned to the subject of Ennis's murder, and Cosby gave more candid and emotional answers. When the anchor asked if there might be racial unrest if the killer turned out to be white, Cosby snapped: "It will never happen in my eyes, because they'll have to kill *me*! Not over my son's death. You're not going to play this bullshit game. No sir! And it is bullshit. There's no other word for it, no other word. It's bullshit!"

Rather ended the interview by asking if there was anything viewers could do to help Cosby and his family deal with their loss. Cosby responded by issuing a long and impassioned plea for "dignity," not just in responding to Ennis's death but in the way Americans behaved and treated one another. "Dignity!" he kept repeating, as he invoked the example of Nelson Mandela and pointed out the effect that merely putting on a suit and tie or a military uniform can have on a young person's self-image.

None of that, however, was in the excerpts from the interview that CBS released the next day, on its morning show and Rather's evening news broadcast. There were only clips of the most sensational news: Cosby's comments on the murder investigation and his admission that he had had sex with Autumn Jackson's mother and that it was "possible" he was the father. Over the next few days, other media outlets pounced on the Jackson revelations. Just as he once had in talking about his "estrangement" from his daughter Erinn, Cosby had legitimized the story. Now it was grist for newspaper head-lines, TV magazine reports, and op-ed and talk radio debates about the irony of TV's ultimate family man confessing that he had cheated on his wife.

In the *New York Times,* columnist Frank Rich saw a tale of schaudenfraude for the tabloid era. "This American syndrome — of ascribing extrahuman attributes to celebri-ties . . . and then reacting with shock and even rage when the more complex human re-ality is inevitably exposed — is nothing new," Rich wrote. "But what has changed in our faster-paced media age is the lag time be-tween the idealization and the debunking of our icons. What used to take years, even decades, now takes days. But however compressed, the script remains predictable. The melodrama of Bill Cosby and his accuser will play out in the press, on talk shows, and perhaps a televised trial, long after the truly disturbing story of Ennis Cosby's unsolved murder has disappeared from the evening news."

Yet as Cosby's twin trials made their way from the headlines into the criminal justice system, they didn't play out quite as predictably as Frank Rich expected.

On the Wednesday after he interviewed Cosby, Rather walked into an audio booth in the CBS News studio to record the script for his piece. The "track" he read into the microphone indicated *60 Minutes* that roughly two-thirds of the story scheduled to air the following Sunday would be devoted to Cosby's comments about his son's death and the murder investigation, and the other third to what he had said about the Autumn Jackson case. With an eloquent flourish that summed up Cosby's confessional tone, Rather concluded the piece by suggesting to viewers that what they had seen was "not just an interview but part of his healing."

Yet viewers never saw the interview. Two days later, CBS News announced that *60 Minutes* had killed the story. Immediately, questions were raised in the trade press about whether Cosby or his representatives had managed to get the story suppressed. In fact, Norman Brokaw had complained to Les Moonves, the CBS entertainment chief. But the president of the network, Peter Lund, initially refused to interfere in the decisions of the news division, particularly over a story that promised to produce huge ratings in the first week of February "sweeps."

What had scuttled the piece were internal politics within the news group. Don Hewitt, the fiercely competitive executive producer of *60 Minutes,* had never particularly liked Rather, going back to the days when the anchor was a correspondent for the newsmagazine. Hewitt was also upset that Cosby's most newsworthy statements had already aired on other CBS programs, including Rather's evening broadcast. Once Cosby's statements about Jackson and her mother became fodder for the likes of the *New York Post* and the tabloid TV program *Hard Copy,* Hewitt persuaded Heyward that appearing to add to the hysteria would tarnish the reputation of his program. Explaining the decision to kill the *60 Minutes* piece, Heyward told the *New York Times:* "We did the right thing in terms of immediately releasing the news from the interview. [But] it became a tabloid, feeding-frenzy kind of story. We didn't see any way to avoid the perception that we were somehow adding to this hype, or somehow exploiting this tragedy."

Meanwhile, the sensationalistic coverage of the Rather interview had enraged a central figure in the drama: Camille Cosby. She was furious that the press was paying so much more attention to the Autumn Jackson case than to her son's death, and she issued a statement chastising the media and defending her husband. "All personal negative issues between Bill and me were resolved years ago," she declared. "We are a united couple. What happened twenty-three years ago is not important to me except for the current issue of extortion. What is very important to me is the apprehension of the person or persons who killed our son."

The next week, Camille was infuriated when the *National Enquirer* ran a cover story alleging that she was sedated and on the verge of a nervous breakdown. Writing an op-ed piece in *USA Today* to dispute the charges, Camille shared more details of the inner workings of her marriage. She and Cosby had been nineteen and twenty-six years old when they wed, she pointed out. "We had to mature, we had to learn the definition of unselfish love, and we did . . . [But when we] committed to each other wholeheartedly years ago, our marriage became healthy and solid."

Camille was so upset with the *Enquirer* that she wanted no part of the paper's self-promotional attempts to become part of the investigation. When the tabloid offered to pay $100,000 for information leading to the conviction of Ennis's killer, the Cosbys announced that they didn't want the help. Yet as it happened, the *Enquirer*'s bait produced the first big break in the case, when a man named Christopher So contacted the tabloid to report he had met someone who was bragging that he had shot Bill Cosby's son.

The suspect's name was Mikail Markhasev. He was a pale, skinny eighteen-year-old Ukrainian immigrant who lived with his mother in North Hollywood, worked at a garden supply shop nearby, and had served six months for aggravated assault in a juvenile detention camp. Markhasev had showed So where he ditched the murder weapon, and when police searched the area, they found a knit cap containing a strand of the Ukrainian's hair wrapped around a .38 caliber handgun. Ballistic tests matched it with the bullet that killed Ennis, and in early March police arrested Markhasev and charged him with "murder with special circumstances," a classification that carried the possibility of the death penalty if he was convicted.

It would take more than a year, however, for Markhasev to go to trial. In the meantime, the extortion case against Autumn Jackson moved forward swiftly. The week after her arrest, her boyfriend, Antonay Williams, pleaded guilty to assisting the plot by doing research on Cosby's endorsement deals. Police seized damaging evidence from a room at the Holiday Inn in Burbank. Knowing that the defendants didn't have enough money to drag out the case, Cosby's lawyers pushed for a speedy trial, and they got a break when the judge instructed the jury to ignore Cosby's sexual history and to consider only the question of whether extortion had been committed.

During the brief trial, neither Autumn Jackson nor her mother testified, while Cosby took the stand for half a day. He admitted that he had initiated the relationship with Shawn Berkes, and he was blunt about how his feelings toward both women had soured as they kept trying to extract money from him. "You and your mother have never given me a happy moment for what I have given," he recalled telling Jackson over the phone. A week later, the case went to the jury, and after less than three days of deliberation it found Autumn Jackson guilty of extortion and later sentenced her to a twenty-six-month jail term.

Although Cosby felt vindicated, he was angry and embarrassed about the damage the case had done to his reputation. Once the verdict was handed down, he announced that he would take a DNA test to clear up the paternity issue. He had a blood sample drawn, and so did Jerald Jackson, the LA truck driver. Offered the opportunity to prove the truth once and for all, both Autumn Jackson and her mother refused to take the test.

When Mikail Markhasev went on trial a year later, Erinn Cosby sat in the courtroom every day alongside her sister Erika. Ever since Ennis's death, Erinn had not left her family's side, and now they were fully reconciled. She, Erika, and Ennis's friend Phil Caputo were determined to see his killer face justice, but the case for the prosecution didn't go quite as well as they hoped. Under cross-examination, Stephanie Crane admitted that she had initially picked another man, not Markhasev, out of a lineup. Christopher So, the *National Enquirer* tipster, turned out to have a prior conviction for embezzlement. And Michael Chang — the friend to whom Markhasev had bragged about killing Ennis, according to So — refused to testify at the last minute, telling authorities that he was afraid for his life.

Yet if other witnesses proved shaky, Markhasev managed to indict himself with his own words. Prosecutors played secretly recorded tapes of the young Ukrainian boasting about doing drugs and being a killer. They produced self-incriminating notes in Markhasev's handwriting that had been found in his jail cell. "They got a lot on me," one read, "the quete [slang for 'gun'], a beanie, other witnesses . . ." In another scribble, Markhasev referred to a "robbery gone bad." When the case went to the jury after three weeks, the panel of six men and six women zeroed in on that evidence, and in less than six hours they found Markhasev guilty of attempted robbery and first-degree murder.

Under California law, the twin convictions could have sent Markhasev to join the prisoners awaiting execution on San Quentin's Death Row. But Bill and Camille Cosby asked the court to exclude that option because of their philosophical objection to the death penalty. The Cosbys had attended one day of the trial, so that they could look their son's killer in the eye, but they stayed away for the verdict because they wanted it be a moment for solemn justice, not celebrity gawking. Erinn and Erika were there, however, and as the verdict was read, they wept silently, their bodies trembling with sorrowful relief.

A month later, Markhasev was sentenced to life imprisonment without the possibility of parole. The Cosbys were gratified by the trial's outcome but still upset with the way it had been covered in the media. Camille was particularly disturbed that the press had played down evidence suggesting that Markhasev targeted Ennis because he was black. During the trial, it had been revealed that the Ukrainian's previous assault conviction was for stabbing an African American man at a gas station. And when Christopher So took the stand, he testified that Markhasev boasted: "I killed a nigger. It's big. It's all over the news." But in stories about the testimony, most news organizations either didn't mention the slur or censored the word *nigger.*

In her grief, Camille Cosby had come to see larger forces behind her son's murder. A week after the verdict, she wrote another op-ed column for *USA Today,* this time arguing that Markhasev had been brainwashed by the persistent racism in American culture. "Presumably, Markhasev did not learn to hate black people in his native country," she wrote, before ticking off a list of particulars, from the necessity for the Voting Rights Act to the faces of the slave-owning Founding Fathers on the nation's currency, which showed that "racism and prejudice are omnipresent and eternalized in America's institutions, media, and myriad entities." Pointing out that Ennis had been shot in a wealthy white neighborhood, Camille concluded that "all African Americans, regardless of their educational and economic accomplishments, have been and are at risk in America simply because of their skin colors."

Commentators who had known Camille only as Bill Cosby's elegant, press-shy wife were startled to learn the strength of her private views. In the *Philadelphia Inquirer,* black columnist Linda Wright Moore applauded her frank expression of thoughts that most African Americans voiced only privately. White pundits, meanwhile, attacked the piece as ungrateful and smacking of reverse bigotry. "What can be said," conservative polemicist David Horowitz asked on Salon.com, "about a mother who exploits the tragic death of her own son to deliver a racist diatribe against a nation that has showered her with privilege, making her family wealthy and famous beyond the wildest dreams of almost everyone alive, including the very objects of her hate?"

Startled by the vehemence of the reaction, Camille sent a follow-up letter to *USA Today* saying that she welcomed a spirited debate about her social interpretation of Ennis's murder. Within a month, however, Markhasev was sentenced, and the media moved on to other crime stories, having largely ignored clues that, according to one longtime Cosby associate, offered a specific explanation for the killing.

During the trial, prosecutors had established that Markhasev was a hardened delinquent and a heavy drug user. Witnesses had testified that on the night of the murder he had gone with two friends to a park-and-ride lot near Skirball Center Drive that was known as a meeting point for drug transactions. In his prison notes, Markhasev had written that "I went to rob a connection, but obviously found something else." And when Stephanie Crane had arrived on the scene to help Ennis change his flat tire, she was wearing a mink coat that she had thrown on because it was such a cold night. Instead of a freak accident or a targeted racial killing, the clues suggested, Ennis Cosby's murder may have been a tragic case of mistaken identity by a cocky thug hoping to rob two wealthy parties in a drug deal.

Of all the explanations for his son's death, however, there was one that Bill Cosby would not accept. He heard the suggestion that it was God's will from many devout, well-meaning people after the killing, but he refused to believe it. Instead, Cosby detected the hand of the other antagonist in the Book of Job.

"You know, God called for Ennis because God wanted Ennis," one woman said.

"No, he didn't," Cosby answered. "God wouldn't do that to Ennis, because he knew what he was going to do. And he didn't need Ennis with all those souls up there. The man who pulled that trigger was riding with Satan."

29

A DEATH IN THE TV FAMILY

On Monday, January 27, the first day that the full cast and crew of his CBS show went back to work, Cosby asked them to gather on the soundstage of the Kaufman Astoria Studios. He thanked them for their notes of sympathy, and he told them that he intended to carry on as an example to all the viewers who had suffered their own personal tragedies. He said he knew that everyone in the room had bills to pay, and that he wasn't going to let them down.

Then he shared the story of the four people in the Jeep he had seen on his way back from Shelburne Falls. He described how shaken he was by their pitying faces, and he pleaded with his colleagues not to treat him differently than they had before. "If you see me being quiet, you'll understand," he said. "But my job is to make people laugh, and I like my job. But I can't do my job if everybody around me is looking sad."

With his son's killer then still on the loose

and the press chasing the Autumn Jackson story, Joanne Curley Kerner had decided she needed to "hide Bill." In Manhattan, scores of reporters remained camped outside his town house. But Cosby was holed up in Queens, in a makeshift apartment that had been constructed behind his dressing room. On his first week back on the job, he finished filming the episode that had been interrupted and rehearsed a Valentine's Day show that was taped on Friday, a day later than usual, before a live audience that was brought in under armed guard.

On Saturday, Cosby flew to West Palm Beach to perform stand-up. Camille had pleaded with him to cancel the concert, fearing that his emotional state was too fragile. When Cosby insisted, she asked Alvin Poussaint and his wife to travel with him, to make sure that he would be all right. As they talked on the way to Florida, Poussaint saw that his friend's decision to perform was more than a question of professionalism, of making good on a date that had been booked since the summer. It was a matter of identity. "I have to find out if I can still be funny," Cosby said.

For the first fifteen minutes of the concert, he wasn't funny at all. Poussaint became worried as he scanned Cosby's weary face and listened to his weak voice. The mostly white, elderly Palm Beach residents delivered a standing ovation when he walked on stage, many wiping away tears. "Please, sit down," Cosby responded, making a downward gesture with his hands as he sat in his chair in the middle of the stage. "Big deal, coming back," he began softly. "But we're going to get on with this business . . ."

He began to ramble in a voice that could barely be heard at the back of the 2,200-seat theater. He talked about Ennis and how "blessed" he had been to have a child who understood his "teachings." He recalled the numbness he had felt after Kennedy and King were assassinated. He described the stress of dealing with the grief of his fans as well as his friends and family. "I have to give them a release because that's what I do for a living," he said feebly. "I don't sing . . ."

His voice trailed off, and people in the audience glanced nervously at one another, wondering if he had lost his way.

"I do sell pudding," he added finally, and there was a ripple of laughter. His face relaxed, and his voice firmed. He started talking about Camille, and the sense of wonder he had felt when Ennis and his other children were born. "No man can match deliverance," he said. "I'm not going to talk about superiority because women win every time, because women are smarter."

This time laughter came gushing forward, as though Cosby had found the key to a door that was holding it back. His riffs began to flow, time-tested routines about marriage and the navy, as he pranced around the stage and rolled on the floor acting out his stories. For the next ninety minutes and through a second two-hour concert, the release continued, for the fans and for Cosby.

Cosby also started a new ritual in Palm Beach, one that he would continue at every concert he gave from that day forward. He wore a sweatshirt embroidered with Ennis's favorite greeting: "Hello, Friend." Soon he began asking promoters to have "Hello, Friend" sweatshirts made up and placed across the back of his chair wherever he performed. For people in the audience who had heard about his son, it seemed like a touching tribute, but it was more than that. He was giving the memory of Ennis a physical presence, so that he could carry it with him wherever he went.

At work and at home, he made the memorials even more concrete. In his office at the Kaufman Astoria Studios, he hung a huge "Hello, Friend" quilt. On the *Cosby* set, he asked the prop department to place a photo of Ennis downstage, where the TV cameras could sometimes catch it. For his homes in Shelburne Falls and Manhattan, he commissioned paintings of Ennis to hang on the walls and sculptures and busts to place where everyone could see them. And several times a day he talked to the likenesses, as though they could hear him, delivering the latest news of family and friends.

A few years later, *Newsweek* reporter Allison Samuels was summoned to Cosby's town house for an interview. Entering the elegant foyer, she was startled to see a life-size bronze statue of Ennis standing in the middle of the marble floor. She sat down with Cosby, and as they were talking he took a phone call from Ennis's friend Michael Merchant, who had gone to law school and just passed the bar exam.

When Cosby got off the phone, he stood up and walked to the foyer.

"Ennis, Michael passed on his very first try," he said, "Isn't that something? That's a Morehouse man for you! Nothing can stop you!"

Then Cosby kissed the statue on the forehead.

Three weeks after the Palm Beach concert, George Wein announced the lineup for the upcoming Playboy Jazz Festival that summer. When the concert promoter first heard about Ennis's death, he expected that Cosby might back out. But when the two men spoke in mid-February, Wein became the latest friend to see how desperately he was clinging to work as a way of coping with his son's murder.

"How can you go on?" Wein asked.

"If you had a job in a factory and your son

was killed, you would have to go to work," Cosby replied. "My job is making people laugh."

By the time *Cosby* finished shooting for the season in March, however, he badly wanted to get away — and to take Camille away, too. Through his friend Randall Robinson, founder of the activist group TransAfrica, he reached out to Nelson Mandela, who had been elected president of South Africa two years earlier, and Mandela invited them to visit his country. Relieved to escape from the press and the stress of the murder investigation, Camille brought along her mother and her sister for a three-week tour of South Africa's cities, shantytowns, game parks, and Mandela's presidential residence. (Cosby would later joke that the only sight he did his best *not* to see, in the company of all the women in his family, were the bare-breasted female dancers who greeted them at the airport.)

For Cosby, the high point of the trip was a private tour that Mandela gave him of the Robben Island jail where he had been held for eighteen of his twenty-seven years as a political prisoner. Mandela recalled how watching *The Cosby Show* together helped him become friends with his white guards. He also explained how the jailed activists from the African National Congress used the show to teach illiterate criminal prisoners to read, by tracing words they had heard the Huxtables speak in the limestone dust while they were breaking rocks. When Mandela passed away fifteen years later, Cosby would issue a statement recalling how gracious and comforting the great leader had been to him and his wife in the difficult period after their son's death.

At times in those early months, however, Ennis could still be a raw topic. For the executives at Jell-O, Cosby's personal crises had come at an awkward time: as they were about to mark the brand's hundredth birthday. A yearlong celebration had begun a week before Ennis was murdered and the Autumn Jackson case made headlines. Grace Leong, Jell-O's publicist, scrambled to cancel or postpone the planned events involving Cosby. But in March, she received a phone call from his publicist, telling her that Cosby was too attached to the Jell-O brand to sit out the festivities and that he wanted "to engage."

"I just don't want to talk about Ennis," Cosby told Leong when she called to brief him on ten back-to-back interviews she had lined up in early April. "So here's what I need. A green sweater embroidered 'Hello, Friend.' I'll wear it and no one will ask."

Leong thought it was a shrewd idea, but she didn't want to take any chances. Before the interviews began, she reminded each of the reporters: *Ennis is off-limits!* Still, one of them brought up the subject anyway, and Cosby blew up. But he didn't attack the reporter; he lashed out at Leong.

"I told you, no questions about that!" he snapped. "I'm ending this interview!"

Cosby stormed out of the room, leaving the reporter empty-handed and Leong full of confused emotions — sympathy for his pain, but also mortification that he had dressed her down so publicly. *I was only doing what you asked!* she thought. She had heard stories about Cosby's temper, but she had never experienced it. In fact, she had always loved working with him, so she decided to tell him how hurt she was.

But before she could say anything, Cosby apologized to Leong first. "I had to make you look like the bad guy," he explained sheepishly. "I have a reputation to protect."

Gavin White, Cosby's Temple University track coach, was a tough jock who rarely cried. But he had wept the day Cosby phoned to tell him about Ennis's burial. White was moved that his famous recruit considered him part of the extended family and that Cosby wanted him to know that he had been a good father to his son. As they spoke, White reached for an envelope and scribbled down his words: "No guilt here . . . Did all the right things with him . . . Nothing to say we failed as parents." White noted the number of references to humor — laughed "at the graveside" . . . "laughter after the ceremony" — and Cosby's insistence, even in those first days, that Ennis's spirit had not died with him. "We buried him at the house — as alive as he has ever been," he said.

White was even more touched three months later when Cosby agreed to be the best man at his second wedding. White knew that his friend felt indebted to him and that he was crazy about his fiancée Rose. Cosby had been so pleased when the two started dating that he sent them on a three-month cruise on the *QE II* and even arranged for separate suites since they weren't engaged yet. But that was one thing — particularly since Cosby was one of the entertainers on the cruise, coming aboard to perform when the ship docked in Hawaii. It was another for him to drive out to the Philadelphia suburbs where White had retired and spend all day at the Bensalem Country Club participating in the ceremony and patiently schmoozing with everyone at the reception.

So White didn't know what to say a few years later when a reporter for the *Philadelphia Inquirer* called him for comment on a bizarre story he was writing about Cosby. Ever since his mother had died, Cosby had relied on a friend named Gladys Rodgers to take care of the house he had purchased for Anna in Philadelphia. Gladys was the ex-wife of Guy Rodgers, a Temple basketball legend and onetime point guard for the Philadelphia 76ers, and she had become so close to the Cosbys that she often vacationed with them. But now there had been a sudden rift. The Cosbys had evicted Rodgers from the Elkins Park property, telling the press that she had allowed her son to move in and to keep a gun on the premises without their permission.

Rodgers told a far stranger story. She claimed that after Ennis's death, the Cosbys had fallen under the influence of an eccentric British spiritual adviser named David Kirby, who referred to himself as "Lama." According to Rodgers, Kirby had come to the house dressed in a purple and white robe and wearing an amulet around his neck to perform what he called a "spiritual cleansing." He had lit a fire, tossed seeds and floor sweepings into it, and rolled dice to conduct a "fire reading." Then, Rodgers claimed, Kirby had persuaded the Cosbys that she was the one guilty of sorcery. She said Kirby had accused her of engaging in rituals involving blood and feathers and candles in a bid to gain control over the house. Her "witchcraft," Kirby said, was the real reason the Cosbys were throwing Rodgers out.

Gavin White had known Gladys Rodgers as well as the Cosbys for decades, so he wasn't about to get in the middle of the dispute. "As far as I know, he's the same old Bill," he replied when the *Inquirer* reporter asked if

Cosby was losing his grip.

Still, like many of his old friends, White had noticed that Cosby had become more withdrawn in the years after Ennis's death. He mostly communicated by phone now, and he and Camille had stopped entertaining as much at their homes in Massachusetts and Manhattan. White knew from the experience of losing his first wife, Doris, what grief could do to a soul. He had only started to recover from his own loss once he met his second wife, Rose, and he could sense that Cosby was still searching for a path to take him out of his suffering and give his life new purpose.

The first time Ray Romano was introduced to stand-up comedy was when he was eleven years old and listened to a Bill Cosby album. It was *To Russell, My Brother, Whom I Slept With,* and Romano went wild for it. He loved Cosby's uproarious stories and his cool, conversational style and he thought to himself: *I'd like to try that someday!* But as a middle-class Italian kid growing up in Queens, Romano didn't have the first clue about how to become a comedian. He graduated from Hillcrest High and pumped gas and delivered futons before landing a job as a teller at the Williamsburg Savings Bank. Comedy remained a distant dream until, as Romano entered his midtwenties, he saw the concert film *Bill Cosby: Himself* on HBO and was inspired all over again.

The next year, 1984, Romano worked up the courage to go on stage during an open mic night at a New York comedy club. He got enough laughs to keep at it, and for the next five years he did stand-up on the side until he won $10,000 in a competition, enough to quit his day job and go on the road. Six years later, after a few successful appearances on *The Tonight Show,* he was cast in a new CBS sitcom called *News Radio.* But after two days, the producers decided that Romano's laid-back style didn't match the rapid pace of the show, and they fired him.

By this time Romano had appeared on David Letterman's show on CBS, and Letterman liked him. The late-night host asked his production company, Worldwide Pants, to try to create a show for Romano. The producers put the comic together with an LA comedy writer named Phil Rosenthal, another young father who, when he heard Romano's funny stories about his kids and parents, thought to himself: *This is like early Bill Cosby!* Together they created a pilot that impressed Les Moonves enough that he agreed to pick it up for his first season at CBS. But the show was such a long shot that he parked it in one of the network's worst time slots, on Friday nights at eight thirty, where for six months it struggled to stay in the Nielsen top 100.

Yet one influential fan spotted *Everybody*

Loves Raymond on Friday nights. Cosby would watch it while he was hiding out in the Kaufman Astoria Studios, and it reminded him of the kind of show he had always tried to create: built around family, finding humor in everyday situations rather than contrived plots.

In the early months of 1997, he picked up the phone and called Sam Haskell, "Deputy Dawg" at William Morris. "I want to talk to Les Moonves about Ray Romano," he said. "See if you can get him on the phone right now."

Haskell tracked down his friend Moonves, and he and Cosby both got on the line.

"I love this man, Ray Romano," Cosby said. "You put him behind me on Monday nights, and that show will work. We're compatible."

In early April, Moonves moved Romano to eight thirty on Monday nights. His ratings began to pick up. *Everybody Loves Raymond* finished the season at number 84 in the Nielsen rankings, and the next season it rose to 35. The following year, Moonves moved it back a half an hour, to nine o'clock, and it drew a bigger audience than *Cosby,* finishing the season just out of the top ten.

Originally, Moonves had hoped to build Monday nights around Bill Cosby and Ted Danson of *Cheers* fame, another former NBC star whom he had hired in a lavish deal to star in a new sitcom called *Ink.* But *Ink* lasted only one season, and now *Raymond* was the anchor for the night — sturdy enough that Moonves used it to float yet another new New York–based sitcom, *The King of Queens,* between *Cosby* and *Everybody Loves Raymond* at eight thirty.

If Cosby was pleased to have helped Ray Romano, he still wasn't satisfied with his own show. By the end of its first season *Cosby* was a respectable success, but it wasn't a hit. At times, Hilton Lucas seemed to be a truly distinct character (and one, in his more prickly moments, who was much like the real Bill Cosby). But at others, the pairing of Cosby and Rashad made it hard not to think of Cliff and Clair Huxtable. Often, the most memorable moments came from two supporting players: Doug E. Doug as Griffin, the goofy former foster child who moves back in with the Lucases, and the character actress Madeline Kahn as their eccentric neighbor Pauline.

In an indirect way, Kahn had helped pave the way for *The Cosby Show* a decade and a half earlier. Only when Marcy Carsey and Tom Werner failed to make *Oh Madeline* a success did they set their sights on Bill Cosby. Still, like most students of comedy, Carsey and Werner viewed the petite redhead with the high-pitched voice as a singular talent. They also thought she had a broader range than she had shown in over-the-top roles in

Mel Brooks movies, such as the bawdy saloon-keeper Lili Von Shtupp in *Blazing Saddles*. Cosby agreed, and in casting Kahn as Ruth Lucas's best friend, he gave her a chance to show off her ability to move effortlessly between dry sarcasm, touching vulnerability, and broad slapstick.

In a recurring joke, Hilton would ask Pauline if she loved him, and Kahn would find a droll way to avoid answering the question. ("I think Marcel Marceau said it best . . ." she quipped in one episode, making a mime face.) She also had a knack for getting laughs by playing absurd situations straight — when Pauline tries to teach Hilton how to meditate, for instance, or when she tells Ruth that she had an imaginary sister. In an episode called "Dating Games," Ruth and her catty sister Deborah (played by Rashad's real sister, Debbie Allen) compete over who can find the best match for their daughters. Inspired by their trash talk, Pauline asks Hilton to teach her how to trade insults, and the spectacle of tiny, squeaky-voiced Kahn "playing the dozens" is priceless. ("That's what you get," Pauline taunts Deborah, "for being all up in your daughter's Kool-Aid without knowing what the flavor is!")

Most weeks, however, Cosby continued to gripe that the scripts didn't do him justice, and now he was complaining on Kahn's behalf, too. Before long Dennis Klein quit, leaving even more junior writers to carry a heavier load. Carsey and Werner were having difficulty attracting new writers, particularly ones based in LA who weren't willing to uproot their families and move to New York after everything they heard about how grueling and precarious working for Cosby could be.

Joanne Curley Kerner, the line producer, found herself caught in the middle. The writers would complain to her that Cosby only wanted things his way, but she saw things differently. She knew that he had high standards and firm rules — "stories, not jokes;" "no put-down humor" — but she had also seen that he respected people who were prepared to be honest with him.

"I've decided the only way I can be executive producer of this show is never to disagree with Bill!" one temporary head writer complained.

No, that's the kiss of death! Curley Kerner thought.

But if Cosby was willing to take criticism from Curley Kerner, it wasn't just because she was candid with him. It was also because he could count on her loyalty. He knew so because, as he had done with so many in his inner circle over the years, he had extended a thoughtful personal gesture that would make her forever grateful to him.

Curley Kerner had moved her family from

Los Angeles to take the job on *Cosby*, and her teenage daughter, Lizzie, was miserable. Lizzie missed her friends in California, and she found herself hazed and shunned at the Convent of the Sacred Heart, the all-girls school in Manhattan where her mother enrolled her.

"How's it going with Lizzie?" Cosby asked one day, doing his usual checking up on the educational progress of his colleagues' children.

"The girls at her school are being bitches," Curley Kerner replied bluntly.

Cosby chuckled. "Okay, tell her to bring some of them to the show," he said. "Then we'll invite them backstage."

Once the girls at the Convent of the Sacred Heart heard about the lucky group that got to go to the taping and meet Bill Cosby, no one made fun of Curley Kerner's daughter anymore. The next year, Lizzie was elected to the student council, and Cosby had two more lifelong defenders.

As *Cosby* approached its third season, Curley Kerner was encouraged to hear about the new head writer who was joining the show. His name was Tom Straw, and, like her, he had worked on another Carsey-Werner sitcom called *Grace Under Fire,* starring the mercurial comedienne Brett Butler. If Straw had managed to survive Butler, Curley Kerner thought, he could handle Cosby.

Straw, too, had almost turned down the job. When Tom Werner called him to make the offer, he said that he was burned out after *Grace.* Privately, he also wasn't sure what it would be like to work with Bill Cosby. He was such a huge fan of Cosby's work — he could recite long passages of dialogue from *I Spy* from memory — that he worried that getting to know the man up close might be a disappointment. Yet he had watched episodes of *Cosby,* and it broke his heart to see some of the things that his idol was doing to get laughs — gags like Hilton accidentally gluing a rag to his teeth. So he promised Werner that he would fly to New York to meet with Cosby.

Straw recalled hearing the unmistakable voice first, as he was sitting in the waiting room of Cosby's Manhattan town house.

"Where is he?" Cosby called out, appearing in the doorway wearing silk lounging pajamas.

He sat down next to Straw and got right to the point. "So how are we going to work together?" he asked.

"Whatever idea serves the show best wins," Straw said.

Cosby smiled and shook Straw's hand, and the mutual audition was over.

"You bring me a good story, and I'll kill myself to make it funny," Cosby told his new head writer, and Straw set out to do just that. He told his staff to stop trying to come up with one-liners and focus on smart situations. After Monday table reads, he brought them onto the set, where Cosby could try out new ideas before scripts were rewritten. Instead of rolling his eyes at his star's scatter-shot ideas, Straw encouraged them, and soon Cosby was bringing more of his own experiences to the show. Sometimes the results could be poignant — such as an episode that he suggested after running into an old high school buddy from Philadelphia who was now homeless — and sometimes they could be as funny as anything that he had done on *The Cosby Show.*

"The Episode Episode," a show that aired two months into the third season, was a promising example. A story about Hilton's high cholesterol and Ruth's attempts to put him on a health food diet, it was taken directly from Cosby's own life. Now sixty-two, he had blown up close to 250 pounds after decades of soul food and daily bowls of rigatoni puttanesca at his favorite New York restaurant, Bravo Gianni, and Camille was after him constantly to lose weight and eat better. Much of the dialogue in the episode was improvised, as in a dinner scene where Ruth serves Hilton steamed halibut while Griffin eats a bacon cheeseburger.

"I'm a descendent of people from Virginia!" Cosby protested, conjuring up his own family roots. "We are the land of the oink eaters!

My people drank grease! They lived on lard! Oink! They ate sausage, bacon, ham, fatback, pork every day of their lives, three times a day!"

"Yes," Phylicia Rashad responded dryly, "and most of them did live to be at least twenty."

Cosby leaned back and traced a finger over his lip. "But they all died with a wonderful grease ring around their mouth!" he beamed.

A week later, Cosby and Madeline Kahn would give two more very funny performances in "Judgment Day," another heavily improvised episode about Hilton's decision to force a court battle over a spilling incident at Pauline's coffee shop. ("So sue us now!" a triumphant Pauline shouts at the actress playing the plaintiff after the case was dismissed. "Sue us now!") But two weeks after that, viewers would begin to notice something different about Kahn: she was wearing a silver blond wig.

As the third season of *Cosby* began, Madeline Kahn had been diagnosed with ovarian cancer. By November, she had begun chemotherapy treatments that made her trademark curly red hair fall out. She wouldn't go public with the news until the following season, when she was forced to quit the show. But her illness cast a pall over *Cosby* just as it was starting to regain momentum, dispiriting the cast and crew, forcing the writers to work around the Pauline character, and mystifying viewers who had become accustomed to Kahn's delightful flights of fancy. Despite Tom Straw's best efforts, the ratings continued to sink through the third season. The next fall, *Cosby* was moved from its Monday night slot so that CBS could pilot new, younger shows around *Everybody Loves Raymond* and *The King of Queens.* Once its fans no longer knew where to find it, the show dropped out of the Nielsen top forty and kept falling.

Madeline Kahn died on December 3, 1999, at the age of fifty-seven, four weeks after making her last appearance on *Cosby.* Three weeks later, Cosby scrapped the planned script and devoted a show to her memory called "Loving Madeline." Appearing as themselves, Cosby, Rashad, and three other members of the ensemble shared stories of Kahn's energetic and encouraging presence while clips played of her most memorable scenes. "This truly was, for her, family," Cosby said, his weary face etched with all the sadness he had endured over the previous three years. "Every person here [on this set] and every person that no one can see right now, all realize that this is family."

Then Cosby paid Kahn what for him was the highest compliment he could give to a fellow comedian. He compared her to his idol Jonathan Winters. "Madeline reminds me of

Jonathan," he said, "because so many people will say: 'Ah, there truly is a genius who stands alone!' "

Cosby was too proud and competitive to want to carry on with a show that was no longer in the top fifty, particularly one that had been clouded by so much death and tragedy. So he was the one who called Les Moonves and told him that he thought *Cosby* should be canceled after its fourth season. Moonves could hardly protest, given the show's low ratings and high cost, and he was grateful that Cosby was making the call rather than forcing him to embarrass a TV icon. "I'm going out with the class of 2000," Cosby told reporters. "I wish we could have done better for CBS."

Yet as far as Moonves was concerned, Bill Cosby had done enough. Looking back on *Cosby* a decade later, he would give it credit for communicating the message he had hoped to send as a newly minted network entertainment boss: CBS was back in business. Moonves would also recall how Cosby helped find an audience for *Everybody Loves Raymond,* a show that continued for nine seasons and played a pivotal role in making CBS the number-one network in prime time by 2002, a position it would retain for most of the following decade.

Meanwhile, Cosby still had a development deal with CBS. Once again, as he did in the

1970s, he had used the leverage to launch a children's television show. After Ennis's death, Cosby had started to publish a series of children's books about the adventures of an inquisitive five-year-old called Little Bill. Drawing on input from Alvin Poussaint and other child psychologists, the simple stories were intended to help kids up to the age of ten learn with how to cope with social challenges like making friends and confronting bullies. Cosby gave his fictional character Ennis's favorite expression — "Hello, Friend!" — and commissioned illustrations from Varnette Honeywood, the artist he made famous by hanging her works in the Huxtable living room. Now Cosby took advantage of the fact that CBS's parent company, Viacom, also owned a children's cable network. Working with Nickelodeon, he developed *Little Bill* into a TV series for the network's second channel, Nick Jr.

Teaming up with his former dean at the University of Massachusetts, Cosby also embarked on a quest to put education reform on the national agenda. Dwight Allen had become a professor at Old Dominion University in Virginia, and he was writing a book that called on the US government and America's booming technology companies to make an unprecedented investment in rebuilding crumbling schools, putting computers in classrooms, reforming curricula, and increasing teacher salaries. Cosby agreed to join Allen as the coauthor, and in the fall of 2000 they published a 150-page electronic book, dedicated to Ennis, entitled *American Education: The 100 Billion Dollar Challenge.*

Over the summer of 2001, Cosby and Allen received word that *American Schools* was a finalist for an e-book award at the prestigious, international Frankfurt Book Fair in October. They had hopes that a win might generate enough media curiosity that they would be invited to write op-ed pieces and go on television to discuss their reform ideas. But on the second Tuesday in September, Al Qaeda terrorists flew hijacked airplanes into the World Trade Center and the Pentagon and took almost three thousand lives, and the country become so consumed with the fallout from the 9/11 attacks that any chance of starting a national conversation about education was lost.

If 2001 was a year of national trauma and professional disappointment, however, it did bring an important moment of personal closure for Cosby and his family. In early February, they learned that Mikail Markhasev had sent a handwritten letter to California prosecutors confessing to the murder of Ennis Cosby and asking to withdraw his attempt to overturn the sentence of life in prison without parole. "Although my appeal is in its beginning stages, I don't want to continue with it because it's based on false-hood and deceit," he wrote. "I am guilty and I want to do the right thing . . . More than anything I want to apologize to the victim's family. It is my duty as a Christian and it's the least I can do after the great wickedness for which I'm responsible. This is way over-due and although my apology is too late, it's still the right thing to do."

California prosecutors were stunned, par-ticularly since Markhasev had nothing to gain legally by dropping his appeal. "This is an extremely rare event," said Kyle Brodie, the deputy attorney general who received the one-page letter. An LA city prosecutor could only conclude that "it falls in the category of confession is good for the soul."

As Cosby saw it, Markhasev's soul was none of his concern. The confession wasn't going to bring Ennis back or lessen the grief that he felt every day over losing his only son. So he instructed his publicist to tell reporters that he had no comment. Still, at least he and Camille could rest assured that their boy's killer would never go free again. Markhasev would spend the rest of his life in California's Corcoran State Prison, and now there could never be any doubt in anyone's mind about who was responsible for the evil that took Ennis away.

It had been a long, hard five years since Cosby turned sixty. His hair had thinned, his face had aged, and his eyes had begun to lose their youthful luster as his vision continued to dim. He was starting to look old, and on many days he *felt* old. But in June 2002, as he was about to turn sixty-five, he received a phone message that revived his spirits. A White House aide called to inform him that he had been selected as one of twelve annual recipients of the Presidential Medal of Freedom, the award that Harry Truman had created to honor civilian heroes of World War II and that had been revived by John F. Kennedy to recognize outstanding contributors to America's cultural life.

"You can't reject it, and you can't not accept it," the aide said, inviting Cosby to a ceremony at the White House but making it clear that he would receive the award whether he attended or not.

Cosby didn't have to think twice. He would attend the ceremony, no matter what he thought of the policies of the president who would be giving him the medal. And when he was asked for his guest list, he included not only Camille and other members of his family but the man he gave credit for making his success possible: Gavin White, the track coach who had helped him get into Temple University.

On July 9, three days before his birthday, Cosby proudly walked to the front of the White House East Room, dressed in a beige double-breasted suit. The twelve honorees were lined up in alphabetical order, so Cosby took his place next to Hank Aaron, the legendary Atlanta Braves slugger. Aaron was the first recipient to receive a medal from George W. Bush, and when he returned to his place, Cosby leaned over to take a close look at the medallion.

"William H. Cosby Jr.!" a military guard called out next.

Cosby didn't expect to hear his full name, and he had a flashback to grade school.

"Present!" he said.

Everyone in the room laughed, and Cosby walked to the president's side as the military guard read his citation: ". . . From television to film, from stand-up comedy to bestselling books, Bill Cosby's good-natured humor has always appealed to our common humanity, helping to bring people together through laughter. The United States proudly honors this truly outstanding American . . ."

Bush took the medal — a white enamel star surrounded by golden eagles — and began to pin it around Cosby's neck, but he couldn't get the clasp on the ribbon to fasten.

"Hold still!" he whispered, his face pressed close to Cosby's cheek.

After several more seconds, Bush pulled the ribbon away and started to fiddle with the clasp. Before he could try again, Cosby snatched the medal from the president's hands and returned to his seat, as everyone in attendance cracked up again.

For David Letterman's producers, it was too good a moment to pass up. When Cosby appeared on the talk show several weeks later, they played a clip of Bush's fumbling and Cosby delivered a humorous play-by-play. Then, as the audience laughed, a pensive expression came over Cosby's face. All of a sudden his mind was elsewhere, a half century back in time, seeing the faces not just of Gavin White but of Mary Forchic and Benjamin Sapolsky and Jean Lamb Heath and his remedial English teacher at Temple . . .

"A very, very honest moment," Cosby started to say, his thoughts bursting forth in emotional fragments. "The people of Philadelphia . . . all of the people who looked at me when I was a kid . . . and saw more in me than I saw in myself . . . I wanted to thank them . . . of all races, colors, and creeds."

The audience burst into applause, and as it died down Letterman told them what Cosby was planning do with his Presidential Medal of Freedom. Over the next year, he was going to lend it to each of the schools he had attended, so that each one could put the medal on display for a month as an inspiration to the students who were there now.

Then Cosby added: "The message that goes with it — for Fitzsimons Junior High School, Central, Temple, and U. Mass — is: 'Pay at-

tention to what old people are telling you
about yourself!' "

30
PROPHET OF POUND CAKE

The event was billed as a celebration. The heads of the NAACP and Howard University "invite you to the *Brown v. Board of Education* 50th Anniversary Commemoration — Honoring the Heroes of the Landmark Decision," the invitation read. The black-tie gala in Washington, DC, on May 19, 2004, boasted ex-presidents Clinton, Bush, and Carter, as well as Nancy Reagan as honorary chairs, and IBM, UPS, Sodexho, and Wachovia Bank as corporate sponsors. In the audience was a Who's Who of the African American establishment, including civil rights veterans (Andrew Young, Vernon Jordan, Julian Bond), business leaders (Richard Parsons, Frank Savage), and athletes and artists (Hank Aaron, Spike Lee, opera singer Jessye Norman). And there to be saluted was Cissy Marshall, the Hawaiian widow of the man who had argued the historic case before the Supreme Court, as well as two survivors of Thurgood Marshall's legal team, one black

(Judge Robert Carter) and one white (Jack Greenberg).

Yet as he sat in the audience at Constitution Hall, Bill Cosby was in no mood to cheer. He had come to accept an award for his educational philanthropy, and he was seated next to his friend L. Douglas Wilder, the former governor of Virginia. As one luminary after another spoke, Wilder noticed that Cosby was growing increasingly agitated.

"Doug, when are they going to hit the number?" he kept repeating in an angry whisper.

Listening to the rosy tributes to civil rights battles of the past, Cosby couldn't stop thinking about two men. One was Washington, DC,'s chief of police, Charles Ramsey. Riding in a cab earlier that day, Cosby had heard Ramsey on the radio talking about the city's crime rate and its roots in the breakdown of families. If the district was to have any hope of bringing down violence, Ramsey had argued, it had to start with parents taking responsibility for their own children.

The other man was Kenneth Clark, the black psychologist whose research had played a pivotal part in winning the Brown case. Along with his wife Mamie, Clark had conducted a series of studies using dolls to examine how black youth perceived themselves. The Clarks showed children white dolls with blonde hair and brown dolls with black hair and asked which they liked better. Overwhelmingly, the black kids saw the white dolls as "prettier" and "nicer," and the preference was even stronger among those attending segregated schools than those going to integrated schools.

As the *Brown* litigation made its way through the courts, the Clarks wrote briefs and appeared as expert witnesses, describing how forced segregation inflicted permanent psychological damage on black children. When the Supreme Court ruled, Chief Justice Earl Warren alluded to the findings of their so-called doll studies in his majority opinion. The US Constitution was not consistent, Warren wrote, with an educational system that burdened black children with "a feeling of inferiority as to their status in the community that may affect the children's hearts and minds in a way unlikely ever to be undone."

Clark was too ill to attend the Brown anniversary event. At eighty-nine, he rarely left his home north of New York City and was only a year away from dying of cancer. But Cosby knew what he would have thought had he been present, because he and Camille had spent so much time with him. After Clark's beloved Mamie died almost two decades earlier, the Cosby estate in Western Massachusetts had become a second home for the lonely widower. Clark was such a frequent visitor to Shelburne Falls that the Cosbys called one of their guesthouses "Ken's Cabin."

Over countless meals at the Cosby dinner table, the slight, puffy-eyed psychologist had chain-smoked Marlboros and poured out his heart about how discouraged he felt after a lifetime of fighting for equal rights. He was heartsick that more progress hadn't been made toward his dream of a fair, integrated society, and he blamed both the persistence of white racism and the refusal of many blacks to stop seeing themselves as victims. As the conversations extended into the night, he and Cosby would egg each other on with wistful stories of the black world which they had once known — a world of no excuses, of pressure to be "twice as good to get half as far," of parents and teachers who "stayed on" their youth to speak proper English and learn correct manners and make the most of their educations.

While Cosby shared memories of Anna P. and the other watchful mothers of the Richard Allen Homes, Clark told a story about his own mother, Miriam. When he was in tenth grade, he had told her that the black kids in his Harlem high school were being encouraged to transfer to vocational school. "Mama" Clark responded by storming into the school and confronting the guidance counselor. "I don't give a damn where you send *your* son," she said, "but mine isn't going to any vocational school!"

In Constitution Hall, the long night of speeches was drawing to a close. Doug Wilder had just finished delivering his remarks, and he was descending the steps to the stage as Cosby came up to receive his award.

As they passed each other, Wilder could see Cosby muttering under his breath.

"You still got this?" Wilder asked.

"You'll see," Cosby nodded.

Cosby had been placed at the end of the program with the hope that he would say a few words of thanks and deliver a line or two that would leave the crowd laughing. But he wasn't about to leave the stage without getting off his chest what he had been thinking all night: that the "Heroes of the Landmark Decision" would be horrified at what was happening in parts of black America fifty years after their historic victory.

"Ladies and gentlemen, I really have to ask you to seriously consider what you've heard, and now this is the end of the evening, so to speak . . ." Cosby began. "I heard a prize fight manager say to his fellow who was losing badly, 'David, listen to me, it's not what *he's* doing to you. It's what you're *not* doing.' "

The crowd laughed, because they expected Bill Cosby to be funny, although shrugs and puzzled looks suggested that many in the hall weren't sure what he was driving at with his prizefighter story.

Seeming to sense that, Cosby started over again. He pointed to the balcony where the veterans of the *Brown* battle were sitting. "Ladies and gentlemen," he said, "these people, they opened the doors, they gave us the right, and today, in our cities and public schools we have fifty percent dropout rates. In our own neighborhoods, we have men in prison. No longer is a person embarrassed because they're pregnant without a husband. No longer is a boy considered an embarrassment if he tries to run away from being the father of a child . . ."

The audience was with him now, clapping at the last two lines, so Cosby plunged ahead. "Ladies and gentlemen," he said, "the lower economic and lower middle economic people are not holding up their end in this deal. In the neighborhoods that most of us grew up in, parenting is not going on. In the old days, you couldn't hooky school because behind every drawn shade was an eye. And before your mother got off the bus and to the house, she knew exactly where you had gone, who had gone into the house, and where you got whatever you had and where you got it from. Parents don't know that today . . ."

Cosby was on a roll, riffing as he had in his youth, when he tried out new material on the fly rather than improvising on routines that he had built and polished night after night. The eye-behind-the-curtain line had gotten a laugh, and another image popped into his head, of parents visiting their children in prison. "I'm talking about these people who cry when their son is standing there in an orange suit!" he exclaimed. "Where were you when he was two? Where were you when he was twelve? Where were you when he was eighteen, and how come you don't know he had a pistol? And where is his father, and why don't you know where he is? And why doesn't the father show up to talk to this boy?"

He was preaching now, and his mind raced to the way black people turned to religion to drown their sorrows. "The church is only open on Sunday," he said. "And you can't keep asking Jesus to do things for you . . . God is tired of you. God was there when they won all those cases. Fifty in a row. That's where God was because these people were doing something. And God said, 'I'm going to find a way!' I wasn't there when God said it . . . I'm making this up. But it sounds like something God would do."

That line got another big laugh, as Cosby turned to the man he had been thinking about all evening. "I'm looking and I see a man named Kenneth Clark," he said. "I have to apologize to him for these people because Kenneth said it straight. He said you have to strengthen yourselves . . . Those of us sitting out here who have gone on to some college or whatever we've done, we still fear our parents. And these people are not parenting. They're buying things for the kid: five-hundred-dollar sneakers — for what? They won't buy or spend two hundred fifty dollars on Hooked on Phonics!"

There was more applause, as Cosby circled back to the youth in the orange prison suits. "Looking at the incarcerated — these are not political criminals!" he fumed. "These are people going around stealing Coca-Cola! People getting shot in the head over a piece of pound cake! Then we all run out and are outraged: 'The cops shouldn't have shot him!' What the hell was he doing with the pound cake in his hand? I wanted a piece of pound cake just as bad as anybody else! And I looked at it, and I had no money. And something called parenting said if you get caught with it, you're going to embarrass your mother. No! You're going to get your butt kicked. No! You're going to embarrass your mother. You're going to embarrass your family . . ."

Now Cosby no longer seemed to be exhorting black parents but criticizing black youth. He made fun of the way they dressed and the names they went by. "Are you not paying attention, people with their hat on backwards, pants down around the crack?" he asked.

"Isn't it a sign of something when she's got her dress all the way to the crack . . . and got all kinds of needles and things going through her body? What part of Africa did this come from? . . . These people are not Africans, they don't know a damned thing about Africa. With names like Shaniqua, Shaligua, Mohammed, and all that crap . . ."

Next it was the way some black kids talked. "Forget telling your child to go to the Peace Corps!" Cosby fulminated. "It's right around the corner! It's standing on the corner! It can't speak English! It doesn't want to speak English! I can't even talk the way these people talk: 'Why you ain't where you is no' . . . You used to talk a certain way on the corner, and you got into the house and switched to English. Everybody knows it's important to speak English except these knuckleheads!"

By now the applause and laughter was growing sparser, and it was clear that Cosby didn't know what he was going to say next. He went off on a tangent about a kid killing someone over pizza and trying to hide out in North Carolina. He went off on another about women having babies so young and men having sex with so many women that a man might end up sleeping with his own grandmother. There was another about how Black Muslims — with their "bean pies" — weren't afraid to police neighborhood streets, and what Christians could learn from them.

When Cosby heard himself talking about orange suits again, even he realized that he had gone on long enough.

"So, ladies and gentlemen, I want to thank you for the award," he said, getting his biggest laugh of the night, one of relief as much of amusement after his long tirade. Then he continued for several more minutes, before he found his way back to his starting point.

"Therefore, you have the pile-up of these sweet beautiful things born by nature raised by no one . . ." he said. "You all wonder what that's about? You're probably going to let Jesus figure it out for you. Well, I've got something to tell you about Jesus. When you go to church, look at the stained glass things of Jesus. Look at them. Is Jesus smiling? Not in one picture. So tell your friends: Let's try to do something. Let's try to make Jesus smile. Let's start parenting. Thank you, thank you."

Finally, after twenty minutes, Cosby left the stage, to applause and cheers but also more than a few stunned expressions in the crowd.

Doug Wilder had loved Cosby's speech — *Everything he's saying is right on time!* he thought — but it became immediately apparent that the evening's hosts were not amused. While Cosby was speaking, Wilder noticed

Kweisi Mfume, the chairman of the NAACP, squirming in his chair. During a troubled youth, Mfume had fathered five children out of wedlock with several different women, and although he became an attentive father later on, he seemed visibly discomforted by Cosby's lecture on parenting. Returning to the stage after Cosby finished, Ted Shaw, the head of the NAACP Legal Defense Fund, departed from his prepared remarks to remind the crowd that not all the problems of poor black people were self-inflicted.

When Wilder saw Patrick Swygert, the president of Howard University, after the event, Swygert complained that Cosby had delivered "the right message, but at the wrong time."

"When the message is right," Wilder shot back, "the time is always right!"

Despite the presence in Constitution Hall of several reporters, there was nothing in the newspapers about Cosby's rant the next morning. It wasn't until three days later that a brief item appeared in "Reliable Source," the gossip column of the *Washington Post.* "Bill Cosby was anything but politically correct in his remarks Monday night at a Constitution Hall bash commemorating the 50th anniversary of the *Brown v. Board of Education* decision," it read. "To astonishment, laughter, and applause, Cosby mocked everything from urban fashion to black spending

774

and speaking habits." The item quoted some of the most vivid lines from the tirade, including his image of black youth getting shot in the head for stealing "a piece of pound cake."

Suddenly Cosby's speech was news. And because the event hadn't been filmed, and there wasn't a recording or transcript yet, the focus was on what the *Post* had reported: the critical things he had said about black criminals and black youth. On Washington's WOL-AM radio station, the call-in lines to a show hosted by Joe Madison were jammed with listeners wanting to weigh in. On op-ed pages across the country, columnists gave their two cents. On his Fox News show, Bill O'Reilly hosted a debate that showed how much he and other white conservatives were relishing the opportunity to use Cosby's words to support their own view that individual responsibility, not more government help, was the key to addressing the woes of the inner city.

Among African Americans, reaction broke down along political and generational lines. While some older blacks fretted about Cosby airing the community's "dirty laundry" in public, many applauded him. Colbert King, the sixty-five-year-old Pulitzer Prize–winning columnist for the *Washington Post,* thanked Cosby for reminding black folks of the traditional values that had guided them in the past, lamenting only that he hadn't said the same about whites and middle-class blacks. Civil rights veterans Jesse Jackson, Al Sharpton, and Julian Bond took issue with Cosby for not talking about the social and economic hurdles faced by poor blacks but said that they agreed with him about the need for personal responsibility.

Younger blacks were far less charitable. They blasted Cosby for blaming the victim by criticizing poor blacks and lampooned him as a once admirable role model who had grown out of touch with age and wealth. Ta-Nehisi Coates, a twenty-nine-year-old columnist for the *Village Voice,* was particularly caustic. In a piece mockingly entitled "Ebonics! Weird Names! $500 Shoes!," he called Cosby "the patron saint of black elitists." In another column entitled "Mushmouth Reconsidered" several weeks later, Coates went further, describing the once-cool inventor of Fat Albert as "proving no more insightful than your crotchety old uncle, standing on the corner shaking his cane, ranting at no one in particular: 'Damn kids!' "

Another black critic was even more sweeping. Michael Eric Dyson, a forty-five-year-old academic who had made a name for himself as a TV pundit and author of provocative books about Malcolm X and Martin Luther King Jr., took on Cosby as his next subject. Within a year of the "Pound Cake Speech," as it had come to be called, Dyson rushed out a book with the polemical title *Is Bill Cosby Right — Or Has the Black Middle Class Lost Its Mind?* Placing Cosby in a tradition of upper-class black "Afristocrats" who looked down on the "Ghettocracy," Dyson criticized him for everything from a lack of understanding of social forces afflicting the poor, to factual errors (black dropout rates had never reached 50 percent) to personal hypocrisy in preaching about parenting after the Autumn Jackson mess and his struggles with his daughter Erinn.

Dyson's book drew a wide range of reviews, from raves for his synthesis of black intellectual history to pans of his overromanticizing of criminal elements in black culture. Yet none focused on the biggest flaw in his choice of Cosby as a target: the lack of any attempt to understand the circumstances of the Pound Cake Speech or the context of Cosby's personal story. Dyson treated his remarks as though they were a well-thought-out social analysis, rather than an off-the-cuff, impassioned riff from an entertainer used to winning over audiences with jazzlike storytelling and comic exaggeration.

Like much of secondhand debate over Cosby's harangue, Dyson also failed to appreciate its larger point. As inartful and sometimes cruel as his descriptions might have sounded — particularly when quoted out of context — Cosby hadn't initially set out to give a speech condemning black youth. Instead, he was laboring to illustrate what happened to young children — "these sweet beautiful things born by nature," as he had put it — if they grew up without love and discipline in the home and weren't taught the history of black struggle. It was a speech, such as it was, aimed not at young people but at their parents.

And in making that larger point, Cosby wasn't speaking from the perspective of a wealthy fat cat who didn't understand "these people." In fact, he understood them all too well, because he had once been in danger of becoming one of them — an aimless, undisciplined youth who might never have made it off the streets of North Philadelphia. If Cosby kept repeating the word *embarrass,* it was because he knew that at times only his fear of embarrassing his mother and grandparents had kept him on the straight and narrow. When he asked, "Where is the father?" it was because he knew what it was like to grow up with a dad who wasn't around and who, when he was, cared more about getting drunk than spending time with his children. To know Cosby's life story was to see that the emotion that poured out of him in Constitution Hall wasn't aristocratic disdain but the opposite. It was the passion of a self-made man who saw the forces that had eventually turned his life around — the discipline he learned in the navy and the personal attention he got from his grandparents and from the abolitionists — as the keys to salvation for his entire race.

For a while after the speech, Cosby seemed taken aback by the criticism and made several attempts to stress that he wasn't talking about all black parents or black youth. But as the incoming fire mounted, he went back on the offensive. Appearing at the annual conference of Jesse Jackson's Rainbow/PUSH coalition, he answered blacks who were upset at him for airing dirty laundry. "Let me tell you something," he said, "Your dirty laundry gets out of school at two thirty every day! It's cursing and calling each other 'nigger' as they're walking up and down the street. They think they're hip. They can't read. They can't write. They're laughing and giggling, and they're going nowhere."

Cosby also addressed the charge that his focus should be on white racism. "There is a time," he said, "when we have to turn the mirror around. Because for me it's almost analgesic to talk about what the white man is doing against us . . . It keeps you frozen in the hole you're sitting in."

Speaking to a reporter the next day, he shot back at criticisms of his harsh tone. "You can't get me to soften my message," he said stubbornly. "If I had said it nicely, then people wouldn't have listened!"

Once Michael Eric Dyson's book came out, Cosby focused much of his private anger at him. To friends, he denounced Dyson as a poverty pimp, his pet epithet for opportunists who profited by posing as champions of the poor. When the book made the bestseller lists, he fumed that it was only because the name "Bill Cosby" was in the title.

Dyson would discover firsthand exactly what Cosby thought of him in March 2006, when he was in midtown Manhattan attending the premiere of Spike Lee's new movie, *Inside Man.* As the author and his wife were leaving the Ziegfeld Theater, they passed by a restaurant and saw Ed Lewis, the publisher of *Essence,* sitting at a table near the window. Dyson, who had written for the magazine, waved at Lewis. Then he noticed that Camille Cosby was seated next to Lewis, and that across the table, with his back to the window, was her husband.

As Dyson looked on, Cosby turned his head enough to glance sideways out the window, then raised his right arm in the air and stuck out his middle finger.

"Thank you!" Dyson mouthed, blowing a sarcastic kiss.

The next day, Dyson was taking an Amtrak train back to Philadelphia and heard that Cosby was on board. He decided to see what would happen if he tried to introduce himself. This time Cosby shook the writer's hand and invited him to sit down. He apologized for the night before, explaining that it was a birthday dinner for Camille and that he wasn't happy about being interrupted. Then he spent the rest of the hour-long ride trying to convince Dyson that his book was wrong and that the author's own life story proved it. Cosby recited details of the Detroit native's misspent youth: how Dyson had joined a gang when he was fourteen and how he had only pulled his life together after a local minister took him under his wing.

"And that minister, you wanted to be like him!" Cosby said, leaning toward Dyson's face as the train pulled into Thirtieth Street Station. "They put a body on you!"

For Cosby, it was more than a turn of phrase. By 2006, he wasn't just decrying the crisis in the inner city. He was putting a body on it — his own body. For decades, he had quietly visited inner-city schools and jails in his spare time — in Watts in the 1960s, or at Graterford Prison in the 1970s. But now that he was nearing seventy and didn't have a weekly TV show to shoot or a million-dollar pitchman's image to protect, he had decided to practice what he preached with a three-front crusade to address the evils he had assailed in the Pound Cake Speech.

The first were face-to-face meetings with inner-city parents and children that Cosby described as "call-outs." When he wasn't jetting around the country giving stand-up performances for six figure fees, he was making free appearances in poor black communities, from the slums of Philadelphia and Newark to Cincinnati and Milwaukee to rural pockets of the South such as Greenwood, Mississippi.

Two years earlier, the phone had rung in the office of Stanley Battle, the president of Coppin State University, a financially strapped black college in the heart of West Baltimore, the crime- and drug-infested neighborhood that was becoming known to millions of Americans as the bleak backdrop to the HBO series *The Wire.*

"Bill Cosby's on the phone!" his assistant said.

"Yeah, right!" Battle said.

To Battle's amazement, it was Cosby, calling to inquire about the financial plight of Coppin State and to ask for the educator's help in arranging a tour of West Baltimore. He wanted to meet with local schoolchildren and with men from the neighborhood, so he could talk to them about parental responsibility. Since then, Cosby had returned three times, and in the summer of 2006 he came back again, visiting three elementary schools in one day and presiding over a gathering entitled "Fatherhood Works" at the Heritage United Church of Christ in Northwest Baltimore.

On a hot August night, an overflow crowd of men and women packed the pews of the brick colonnaded church on Liberty Heights Avenue to hear Cosby speak. "This is a great evening, because we're calling on men to come claim their children!" he shouted out, dressed in one of the athletic hoodies he wore to the call-outs. "You cannot be a man if you haven't claimed your child! And some of you have three, four, five of them. You have more children than you have jobs!"

The crowd laughed, and for the next two hours Cosby kept them alternatively cheering and listening intently as he finished his motivational speech and answered questions. He exhorted the men in the audience to stay involved with their kids, whether or not they were married to the mothers. He urged the women to give the "baby daddies" a place in their children's lives. And he warned everyone in the room not to expect handouts. They had to take advantage of the resources available in the community, no matter how meager. "It is there *for* you," Cosby repeated at each stop, "but it won't come *to* you!"

The second front in the crusade was focused on men and women who hoped to teach the children Cosby was trying to help. At Temple University, he launched a yearly series of "fireside chats" with students at the College of Education who planned to work in inner-city schools. With humorous lectures

783

and role-playing, he prepared them for what they would confront in urban classrooms.

"When most of you decided you were going to teach, you also felt you were going to save people!" Cosby said, kicking off one session. "Then you met 'people' and they didn't appear to want to be saved! As a matter of fact, they looked at you as if you were some sort of evil thing! You're in your twenties, you've had Psych 1, Psych 5, Abnormal Psychology, and after your first day, you go home and cry because you let a six-year-old kid put you in the toilet!"

The line got a big laugh, but then the master of stand-up turned serious as he tried to demonstrate how much authority and passion the aspiring teachers would need to project to get through to their pupils.

"This is your class!" Cosby said, taking a chair and sitting in front of one of the Ed School students as though he was facing a teacher at Mary Channing Wister Elementary. "We want to know: why we gotta know this?"

The woman said she would tell the kids that even if they wanted to be ballplayers or movie stars, they need a good education first.

"That's not an answer!" Cosby shot back. "Why are you *standing . . . up . . . there*? Because if you can't tell me why you *love* what you're teaching, it's not going to come *here* [he pointed around the imaginary classroom]!"

The third front was a book that Cosby was writing with Alvin Poussaint, laying out their diagnosis of the underclass epidemic as well as prescriptions for treating it. Published in 2007, *Come On, People: On the Path from Victims to Victors* combined testimonials from the shout-outs, "life lessons" of black role models from Harriet Tubman to Wynton Marsalis, and detailed advice about everything from child rearing and education, to healthy eating and financial management.

When the book was published, Cosby embarked on a TV tour that alerted millions of white viewers to his crusade for the first time. Appearing on *Meet the Press* with Poussaint, he heard moderator Tim Russert recite the alarming statistics from the book: "In 1950, five out of every six black children were born into a two-parent home. Today that number is less than two out of six."

After a rambling attempt to summarize his argument, Cosby drove it home in the way he knew best: with a vivid example. When Russert pointed out that he had been faulted for not putting more blame on institutional racism, Cosby zeroed in on a favorite example of the critics: the nation's discriminatory drug laws. "If you say my black child is going to do more time for selling crack cocaine than your white child for selling cocaine," he said, "then I'm going to tell my black child: 'DON'T SELL IT!' Here what's happening, son! It's the same as warning your kid that the Ku Klux Klan is coming! Don't tell me you can't help it! . . . This is part of love!"

When he appeared on *The Oprah Winfrey Show* to promote the book, Cosby had a chance to flesh out the aborted story with which he had started the Pound Cake Speech. It was a parable about a prizefighter named David. For the first few rounds of a title match, David is winning. But then he changes his style of boxing, and he begins to lose. After several rounds of getting badly knocked around by the other fighter, he returns to his corner and gives his manager a bewildered look.

"David, it's not what *he's* doing," the manager says. "It's what you're *not* doing!"

If that story had been on Cosby's mind on the night of the *Brown v. Board of Education* event, it was because he saw it as a metaphor for the civil rights movement. In the early rounds of the struggle, black people had fought one way: with dignity, disciple, erudition, and self-respect. Then they had changed the way they challenged the system, and all of a sudden they weren't moving forward anymore; they were falling backward. Yet in Cosby's worldview, the fight wasn't over. So if blacks were going to gain the upper hand again, they needed to stop complaining about what their opponents were doing and focus on what they were *not* doing.

By 2008, as the presidential race heated up and America flirted with the possibility of electing a black president, it was still hard for many observers to believe that Bill Cosby, the nonthreatening comic Everyman, had become a modern-day Jeremiah, an aging prophet of racial decline and redemption. Some doubters dismissed him as a deluded egotist; others continued to point out that his message was at odds with some of his own past personal behavior. Yet in the four years since the Pound Cake Speech, at least one critic had come to see Cosby in a different light.

After Ta-Nehisi Coates called Cosby "the patron saint of black elitists" in the *Village Voice,* he got an earful from his father. W. Paul Coates was a former Black Panther and Vietnam War veteran who had founded a black publishing house and raised his family in West Baltimore. He shared many of Cosby's views about black cultural decline, and he told his son that he should take the man more seriously. Ta-Nehisi listened. After taking a job at *Time* magazine, he arranged to follow Cosby on a visit to a Connecticut prison and a tour of Detroit. He came away deeply impressed with how powerfully blacks of all ages and walks of life, and black men in particular, were responding to the call-outs. But then Coates left *Time,* and the five-thousand-word freelance piece he wrote about Cosby got rejected from several magazines.

Finally, in 2008, *The Atlantic* agreed to publish the piece. The magazine's editors gave it the provocative title "This Is How We Lost to the White Man" — a quote from one of Cosby's call-out speeches. As much an essay on black culture and history as a feature story, it compared Cosby to Malcolm X and placed him in a long tradition of the "organic black conservatism" that still could be found in "black barbershops, churches, and backyard barbecues" across America.

"From Birmingham to Cleveland and Baltimore," Coates wrote, "at churches and colleges, Cosby has been telling thousands of black Americans that racism in America is omnipresent, but that it can't be an excuse to stop trying. As Cosby sees it, the antidote to racism is not rallies, protests, or pleas, but strong families and communities. Instead of focusing on some abstract notion of equality, he argues, blacks need to cleanse their culture, embrace personal responsibility, and reclaim the traditions that fortified them in the past. Driving Cosby's tough talk about values and responsibility is a vision starkly different from Martin Luther King's gauzy, all-inclusive dream; it's an America of competing powers, and a black America that is no longer content to be the weakest of the lot."

Thanks to the Cosby piece, Ta-Nehisi Coates got a full-time job at *The Atlantic,* where he blossomed into one of America's most original commentators. And unlike Dyson and other pundits, he managed to put his finger on the personal key to understanding Bill Cosby's crusade. It was the same key that explained the childhood universe he had created on his early comedy albums and the vision of family that he had painted on *The Cosby Show:* Cosby was still in mourning for the kind of firm but loving guidance that had wished for as a child but never fully received.

"People told me I was bright, but nobody stayed on me," Cosby told Coates over lunch in Greenwich Village on a cold, rainy day in August 2007, thirty-five years after he had started his career there and a month after his seventieth birthday. "My mother was too busy trying to feed and clothe us . . . [So] If you looked at me and said, 'Why is he doing this? Why right now?,' you could probably say, 'He's having a resurgence of his childhood.' What do I need if I am a child today? I need people to guide me. I need the possibility of change. I need people to stop saying I can't pull myself up by my own bootstraps. They say that's a myth. But these other people have their mythical stories — why can't we have our own?"

31
"THE COSBY EFFECT"

In Shelburne Falls, the fourth of November 2008 was the kind of sunny, crisp autumn day that had enchanted Bill and Camille Cosby ever since they moved to western Massachusetts. Fall foliage season was beyond its peak, but there were still lively patches of red and yellow and orange leaves on the trees as they drove into the village to vote. They parked their car and walked to town hall, and even in that modest polling place, they could feel the tingle of history in the air.

When Cosby's turn came, he ducked behind the curtain and told a joke. "How do you spell *plumber*?" he called out, eliciting the expected response from everyone waiting in line.

Then he reached into his pocket and pulled out three photographs. Six decades earlier, when Bill Cosby Sr. and Anna Pearl Hite Cosby moved into the Richard Allen Homes with their two young sons, who could have imagined that one of them would live to witness this moment? Neither of his parents had survived long enough, nor had sickly little James, but Cosby still wanted them there, at least in spirit.

"And now we're going to vote," he whispered, as he held the images of his parents and his brother in one hand and with the other cast his ballot for the first black president of the United States.

Cosby and Camille drove back to their house, past the gravesite of the other family member who should have lived to see this day, and spent the rest of the afternoon and evening watching election coverage on TV. Night owls that they both still were, they were prepared to stay up until the wee hours, but by the time the last polls closed, the race was over. Barack Obama had won a decisive victory over John McCain — 297 to 155 in the Electoral College and a 3 percent margin in the popular vote — and at the stroke of eleven o'clock in the east, all the networks declared him the winner.

Fifteen minutes later, on the Fox News Channel, anchor Chris Wallace was analyzing the social significance of the outcome with Karl Rove, the political adviser who had done so much to put the incumbent Republican in the White House.

"Now, for the next four years, we're going to have an African American president, and African American First Family," Wallace said, as the split screen showed a jubilant crowd awaiting Obama's victory speech in Chicago's Grant Park.

"Right . . ." Rove said.

"What's that going to do to people's conceptions about race?" Wallace asked.

"Look," Rove responded, "we've had an African American First Family for many years, in different forms. *The Cosby Show* was on. That was America's family. It wasn't a black family. It was *America's* family."

Rove wasn't the first commentator to draw the connection. During the campaign, a young Hispanic writer named Alisa Valdes-Rodriguez had coined the phrase "the Cosby Effect" in a blog arguing that cultural rumblings often foreshadowed seismic political shifts. It had happened before in America's history of race, she pointed out, when the Harlem Renaissance prefigured the civil rights movement by thirty years. On Election Day, Valdes-Rodriguez had observed living proof of her theory as she stood in line to vote at the University of New Mexico. She had overheard two graduate student supporters of Obama, both white, discussing how much they wanted to be part of the Huxtable family when they were growing up.

Five days after the election, the *New York Times* picked up the theme in a piece headlined "Before Obama, There Was Bill Cosby." Talking to reporter Tim Arango, Alvin Poussaint focused on the young voters who had flocked to work for Obama and who had formed such an important part of his winning coalition. "There were a lot of young people who were watching that show who are now of voting age," Poussaint pointed out.

When Cosby was asked about the theory several days after Obama's victory, his first instinct was to downplay it. "This isn't something that happened just because of a TV show," he said, praising instead the deftness of the candidate's campaign. Then he thought about it for a minute and decided that there was one impact of *The Cosby Show* that he wanted to emphasize. "It's what people have done with themselves by watching that show and believing in it," he said.

As far as Cosby was concerned, that was the point that Rove and all the other pundits were missing. They saw "the Cosby Effect" as something that he had done to alter the views of white people about black people. And there was no question that Cosby could claim an important share of credit for that gradual sea change, from the crossover appeal of his early comedy albums to the sympathetic impression he had made on millions of whites with his children's television shows, his commercials, and his historic sitcom. As he himself put it: "I would not be surprised with the comfort level of people looking at a family and not being afraid of them, and not holding them to some strange old thoughts of a nation." But the effect that Cosby had always cared about even more was the one he hoped to have on his own people, on their self-esteem and belief in what they could accomplish in the world.

A third of a century earlier, in the summer of 1971, a memorable milestone on the road to Obama's victory had taken place at the Sheraton Park Hotel in Washington, DC. Three thousand of America's most powerful African Americans had gathered to attend an inaugural fund-raiser for the newly formed Congressional Black Caucus. Cosby was one of two guest speakers, and after the actor Ossie Davis delivered an eloquent address praising the thirteen black members of the House of Representatives, he came to the stage to deliver some lighter entertainment.

"I think you niggers need to check yourselves out!" Cosby said within seconds of taking the microphone. ". . . I say, Good evening, niggers, because that's what a lot of you are going to be when you leave this room!"

The crowd gasped and exploded with laughter, thinking that the famously clean Cosby, the comic known for never using profanity and disdaining the "n word," was letting loose for their benefit.

"I mean, the white people sitting there, too!" he continued. "Niggers come in all colors! You think I'm lying? Ask Martha

Mitchell tomorrow morning!"

At the mention of Mitchell — the wife of Richard Nixon's US attorney general and a frequent subject of colorful press coverage for her boozy, loosed-lipped utterances — the audience went wild, clapping and shouting their approval.

"Now I know it's warm in here . . ." Cosby said, "but we're going to entertain you. So I want all of the men in here, if you feel so, please take your jacket off, and loosen up your tie . . . Doesn't make any difference what you look like when you leave here, because you know what they're going to say about us anyway!"

The audience was giddy now, so giddy that it didn't realize that Cosby wasn't merely playing them for laughs when he joked about how many of them had taken a nap after dinner, or stolen each other's tables, or given each other "the half-hour handshake" during Davis's speech. But then all of a sudden, his tone grew serious.

"You gotta tighten up your ship, tighten up your game," Cosby said. "Because it just doesn't end here . . . And you have to stop blaming white people. You can't blame the Jews who own the stores . . . There ain't but seven of you in here who can run a store! . . . And how many of you are going to tell your children about what you saw tonight? Only thing we can remember from when we were kids was watching Joe Louis knock somebody out. You understand what I'm saying? And somehow our children still believe that you get to be a doctor by being one on television, and that an architect has to be white to draw buildings . . . It's got to start with the youth, *our* youth . . . You can't blame white people, because who are you looking at? . . . So when you leave here, it depends on just how long it's going to take you before you go back to being a nigger."

Now there was dead silence in the room, as the well-heeled crowd finally understood what Cosby *was* saying. And in his mind, it was what he had been saying ever since: if black people wanted respect, they had to respect themselves first, and behave accordingly.

It's what had eventually won Cosby over to Obama. At first, he had his doubts about the aloof mixed-race law professor from Hawaii, wondering how well he understood the experience and problems of most Americans. But he had been swayed by Obama's dignity and eloquence, and he was even more taken with Michelle Obama and her family. The Robinsons of Chicago's South Side, the water plant worker with multiple sclerosis and his working wife who put two kids through Princeton: they were the kind of black folks Cosby loved. He also loved what he had heard about Obama's mother, the white anthropologist who woke her young son up at four thirty in the morning to help him with his homework; and about Obama's grandparents, the army vet and bank officer who kept close watch over "Barry" when he was a drifting, pot-smoking adolescent.

Over the course of the campaign, Obama had also impressed Cosby by addressing some of the same tough-love messages to black audiences that he had been delivering in his call-outs. "Too many fathers are missing, too many fathers are MIA!" Obama had admonished a largely black congregation at Chicago's Apostolic Church of God the previous Father's Day. "They've abandoned their responsibilities; they're acting like boys instead of men . . . Nowhere is it more true than in the African American community. We know that more than half of all black children live in single-parent households — half! — a number that's doubled since we were children. We know the statistics: that children who grow up without a father are five times more likely to live in poverty and commit crimes, nine times more likely to drop out of school, twenty times more likely to end up in prison . . . Some of this has to do with a tragic history, but we can't keep using that as an excuse. Some of it has to do with the failures of government — and those failures are real — but we can't keep using that as an excuse . . . We need families to raise our children. What makes you a man is not the ability to have a child — any fool can have a child — it's the courage to raise a child that makes you a father!"

Yet if Cosby was encouraged by Obama's words and proud to see a black family in the White House, he was appalled by the state of the country. Everywhere he went to perform, he saw the crushing impact of the financial crash of 2008 on the kind of middle-class Americans who attended his concerts (or didn't come now, because they could no longer afford the tickets). And he was heartbroken over what had become of the neighborhoods where he had grown up and others like them. When Cosby went back to Germantown, parts of it were like a bombed-out war zone. In the decades after he moved out, the Richard Allen Homes had turned into such a squalid, drug- and gun-infested slum that the city of Philadelphia bulldozed it to the ground in 2003. In its place were new garden apartments with fewer units and stricter residence requirements; but that had only pushed the poorest residents of the homes into more hopeless projects or back onto North Philly's worst streets.

Even with an African American president, the gap between the life of well-educated, middle-class blacks and blacks trapped in the urban underclass kept widening. And no city in America embodied the disparity more than

New Haven, Connecticut. At prestigious Yale University, hundreds of black faces could now be seen among the students whose degrees would all but guarantee them a place in the national elite. Less than a mile away, a predominantly black neighborhood called Newhallville had one of the highest crime rates in the country and a dropout rate that saw only a third of its children finish high school and less than 5 percent go to college.

This time, it was Stanley Battle who called Bill Cosby and invited him to Newhallville. The former president of Coppin State University in Baltimore had become interim president of Southern Connecticut State College in New Haven, and he asked if Cosby would speak at the college and join him in a call-out tour of the local schools and neighborhoods.

On a cool, cloudy day in late November 2010, Cosby gave a pep talk to excited students at the King/Robinson Interdistrict Magnet School and then ventured out into a section of Newhallville that was home to a drug gang called R2 BWE Black Flag, or "R2" for short. For months, residents had stayed locked inside for fear of being robbed or getting caught in gun battles between R2 and the nearby R1 gang or "red flag" and "blue flag" bangers from the Bloods and the Crips. But as word spread that Bill Cosby was visiting their neighborhood, hundreds of locals poured into the streets.

Dressed in a white "Hello, Friend" sweatshirt and a Southern Connecticut State baseball cap, Cosby marched to the corner of Read and Shelton, the heart of the gang's turf. ("R2" stood for the west side of Read Street; "BWE" stood for "Beef with Everybody.") Walking alongside him, Battle was struck that it was a doubly brave thing for him to do, given his limited field of vision. But Cosby never sought physical assistance; he only asked Battle to make sure that no one walked directly in front of him when he was on the move. Nor did he ever mention Ennis, although Battle couldn't help thinking: *This man knows what it means to try to save just one life.*

As Cosby stopped to chat with a group of women, a food pantry worker named Lillian Morrison informed him that it was her birthday. She was turning seventy, and she was already a great-grandmother.

"So much stuff happens at the park on Bassett [and Shelton]," she said. "I'm afraid to let my kids and grandkids go there; there are bullets flying."

Cosby put his arm around Liliane and turned to address the growing crowd. "This is your neighborhood!" he shouted. "Your children should be able to play right *here* without worrying about a bullet! . . . We want our seventy-year-olds to be able to walk at night, *here,* without worrying about being hit in the head, money taken that she's got to have for her medication!"

"I'm a cancer survivor," Morrison whispered. "Sixteen years."

"Sixteen-year cancer survivor!" Cosby called out. "But she may not survive where she lives! Let's make some sense, people! Let's put some pride in ourselves!"

"We'll be back!" he shouted as he marched on, and to the surprise of many of the residents, he made good on his promise. He returned to Newhallville three more times over the next two years, the following April with an NBC *Today* show crew in tow. The cameras followed Cosby as he walked the streets carrying a banner that read "Safe Passage for Our Children," but he shooed them away when he went into a private meeting that he had requested with gang members.

As Battle watched Cosby interact with the bangers, selected from a court-ordered diversion program for fifteen- to twenty-one-year-olds who had been involved in gun incidents, he was struck by how hardened they seemed. When Cosby asked one young man why his arm was bandaged, the kid replied coolly that he had been shot three times as if it were nothing. But Battle also noticed that unlike the adults on the street, Cosby never lectured them; he just asked them to tell him their stories. *These kids aren't looking for salvation, and he knows it,* Battle thought. *They just want someone to listen to them.*

Among the bangers was a particularly tough case, a girl who had been sexually molested and who would never let anyone touch her. Cosby took her aside and started talking to her, and all of a sudden she was sobbing and hugging him.

Looking on, the adult supervisor who had brought the kids to the meeting had tears in her eyes. "That's a miracle," she whispered to Battle.

Cosby told the gang members, too, that he would return, but as he left he couldn't help wondering how many of them would still be alive when he got back. For he was all too aware of another factor that made the lives of today's poor urban black kids very different from the world that he had grown up in, one that was always on his mind when he talked to parents about watching over their children. It was also the first thing that Cosby thought of a year later, when he heard news reports from Florida about a black teenager in a hoodie who had been shot to death by a suspicious neighborhood watchman as he walked home from a convenience store after buying a snack of Skittles and Arizona watermelon fruit punch.

Across the country, Americans debated whether George Zimmerman had stalked and killed Trayvon Martin because he was black.

But Cosby saw something other than racism at play. "Without a gun, I don't see Mr. Zimmerman approaching Trayvon by himself," he said when a reporter from the *Washington Times* asked him about the case. "The power-of-the-gun mentality had him unafraid to confront someone."

Although it wasn't a planned statement — the interview was supposed to be about an upcoming concert at the Kennedy Center — Cosby's remarks immediately became part of the raging media debate over the meaning of the Trayvon Martin story. Advocates of gun control seized on them as support for their cause. Other commentators read them as another instance of Cosby finding an excuse not to denounce racism. Still others assumed that he was preoccupied with the gun issue because of what had happened to Ennis.

That was true, of course — Cosby couldn't help but think of Ennis — but the Trayvon Martin case also reminded him of another sobering experience. It had happened in the late 1960s, when he and Camille were living in Los Angeles, after the Manson family's gruesome murder of their friend Sharon Tate. Cosby had become so worried about the safety of his wife and three young children that he decided to buy a gun. He applied for a license, purchased a revolver, and hired an off-duty police officer to teach him how to use it properly.

When they got to the shooting range, the officer offered Cosby a word of caution. "Once that bullet comes out," he said, "you can't call it back."

Cosby bought a holster to carry the gun around with him. But soon his mind started playing tricks. He had paranoid fantasies about what people might try to do to him. Then he imagined how he would respond, and he realized that his first impulse would no longer be to stay calm and try to talk himself out the situation. Now that he had a gun, he was going to let them know it! And once he pulled it out, well, who knew what might happen? Before long, all Cosby had to do was see people across the street to start imaging what he would do if they tried to start some foolishness.

After seven months, he couldn't take it anymore. He was sick of what carrying the pistol was doing to his head. So he put it in a locked drawer in his house and let the license expire. And when he and Camille left Los Angeles and moved their family to the Massachusetts countryside, Cosby sold the gun and donated the money to charity.

The news of Robert Culp's death came as a shock. Cosby hadn't been in regular contact with his old friend for a while, but when they did talk, it was always as though no time had passed — as if, he joked, Culp had just gone across the street to pick up a loaf of bread. On the phone, they didn't have to introduce themselves: it was just a "Hey" on the other end of the line, or "How ya doin', pard," in the raspy cowboy accents they liked to imitate in the *I Spy* days. When they got together, Culp looked dapper for a man in his late seventies. Unlike Cosby, who had only a fringe of gray hair left, he still sported a silver mane. Culp had kept in good shape, too, by taking daily walks in Runyon Canyon, the 160-acre park full of hiking trails and dog runs a short distance from his apartment in the Hollywood Hills.

On Wednesday morning, March 24, 2010, Culp had set out on one of those walks. As he entered the canyon, he clutched his chest and fell to the sidewalk. A passing jogger spotted him and called 911, but by the time police and paramedics arrived, he was gone.

Cosby was booked to perform that weekend in Florida, but as the concert approached, all he could think about was his old partner and everything that they had accomplished together. So that Saturday night, as he walked onto the stage at the Ruth Eckerd Hall in Clearwater, he decided that his usual routine could wait.

"I want to take this time to talk about my friend Bob . . . Culp," Cosby said as he placed the "Hello, Friend" sweatshirt over his chair. "When I was hired to do *I Spy . . .*

people were writing . . . that I was the Jackie Robinson of television drama. And I say to you, if this is true, then Robert Culp has to be . . . Eddie Stanky . . . Pee Wee Reese . . . those men who stood beside Jackie and put their arm around him."

The crowd applauded at the mention of *I Spy* and clapped again as Cosby invoked the man who had broken baseball's color barrier and the white Brooklyn Dodger teammates who befriended him and defended him against racist taunts.

"Racism is a waste of time! . . ." Cosby continued, reciting the line he had first heard from Granddad Samuel. "And Bob's contribution in *I Spy* was *very* valuable, in terms of civil rights in this country, the United States of America. He played a wonderful part — and never asked a question."

So many of Cosby's professional abolitionists were gone now, the people who had helped him get his start in show business. Sheldon Leonard had passed away in that awful January 1997, days before Ennis's murder. Clarence Hood and Alan Ribback, the coffeehouse owners responsible for his first bookings at the Gaslight Café and the Gate of Horn in Chicago, were gone, and so were their clubs. And Roy Silver — Silver had died of a brain tumor in 2003 so broke that he would have been homeless if a former girlfriend hadn't let him sleep on her couch.

After failing as a talent manager and a restaurant owner, Silver had lost most of his friends and barely knew his children, so he was astonished one day to pick up the phone and hear the voice of his most famous client on the line for the first time in more than thirty years.

"Guess who I got a call from?" an audibly moved Silver said when he phoned Ron De-Blasio to tell him the news. "Cos called!"

But Dick Gregory was still hanging on, a decade after surviving a nasty battle with lymphoma: Gregory, the comedian who had been Cosby's early model, and then his inspiration to develop an original style of his own. So Cosby was particularly touched when Gregory showed up to pay homage to him as he accepted the lifetime achievement award named after his very first influence, Mark Twain, the one whose stories his mother Anna had read to him as a child.

Cosby had turned down the Mark Twain Prize for American Humor twice before. The first recipient, in 1998, was Richard Pryor, and Cosby had been so upset at all the profanity in the tribute show that he told the Kennedy Center, which presented the award, that he wanted no part of it. But a decade had passed, and Cosby had mellowed, and when he was offered the prize for a third time in 2009, he accepted.

Before the televised ceremony, Cosby was

greeted backstage by his two favorite members of the Obama family: Michelle and her mother, Marian Robinson. Then as the First Lady took her place in the presidential box, Cosby, Camille, three of their daughters, and his brother Russell sat in another box directly above the stage and watched as Jimmy Heath and Wynton Marsalis serenaded them with jazz and three generations of comedians described the debt they owed to Bill Cosby.

Dick Gregory recalled what it had been like to be the first black comedian to perform in a white nightclub. It was 1961, and Gregory was a twenty-nine-year-old post office worker moonlighting at a black club in Chicago called Roberts Show Bar. Hugh Hefner came in one night and liked Gregory's "That's okay, I don't eat colored people" routine so much that he booked him at the Playboy Club. Gregory's career took off, but for years he was invariably referred to as a "Negro comedian."

"My brother," Gregory said as he looked up at Cosby's box, "I came out here tonight to thank you for what you was able to do . . . When Bill broke through with *I Spy* and all of the brilliance, all of the wisdom, from that day on they dropped the word 'Negro' off my name!"

Jerry Seinfeld remembered his first Bill Cosby album. It was 1966, and he was another twelve-year-old Jewish kid growing up in the Long Island suburbs. Like count-less other boys in Massapequa, he had a crew cut and wore Keds sneakers and T-shirts with horizontal stripes. Then one day he bought *Why Is There Air?* and brought it home to play on the portable turntable in his room. Legs crossed, he sat on the floor and listened to the album over and over again.

"I completely lost my mind," Seinfeld said. "In comedy, people very casually use the word *hysterical.* They don't mean it literally, because the real meaning of the word hysteri-cal is not something a person wants to be. It means an out of control, almost convulsive state of emotional breakdown. I became *hys-terical* listening to *Why Is There Air?* It really was the singular, most powerful event of my entire childhood."

Chris Rock told the story of being turned on to Bill Cosby by none other than Eddie Murphy, the same Murphy who later turned imitating and mocking Cosby into one of his trademarks. It was the mid-eighties, and Rock was a high school dropout from Brooklyn starting to perform stand-up in Manhattan comedy clubs. Murphy took him under his wing, and one day he gave Rock *To Russell, My Brother, Whom I Slept With.*

"He said, 'If you really want to be a come-dian, you need to listen to this album,' " Rock said. "And to this day, whenever I meet a comedian I like, I make sure that they have that album."

Between the tributes, the audience was taken on a trip back in time. On a huge screen across the back of the stage, big enough that Cosby's failing eyes could make it out, they watched some of his most memorable routines through the decades. They saw Cosby in his twenties, performing "Noah" on *The Jack Paar Show.* They saw him in his thirties, sporting a huge Afro and smoking a big cigar on *The Dick Cavett Show.* They saw him on *The Tonight Show* in his early forties, explaining what "a conniption" was: what Camille had the day she discovered Cosby feeding their kids chocolate cake for breakfast. (As that clip played, Camille leaned over and gave her husband a playful poke in the ribs.) They saw Cosby in his fifties, performing a bit about George Washington's father. And they saw him in his sixties, still making an audience howl with the "Dentist" number.

At last, the time came for Cosby to come to the stage to accept his award. He had already been there a decade earlier, when he was one of the recipients of the annual Kennedy Center Honors, but this time the night belonged to him and he wasn't going to be rushed. "This is all right!" he said after walking on to the music he had specifically requested for his entry, the Central High

School fight song. "Even my wife said I was funny!"

Then Cosby came out from behind the podium, leaned against it, and started telling tales about the improbable journey that had brought him to that night. He told the story of what a terrible student he was in elementary school and how his mother conspired with Miss Forchic to stay on him. He told the story about the grief he got from Mr. Sapolsky, the math teacher. He told stories about his days as a penniless college student trying to make it in Greenwich Village. He told so many stories that he got a big laugh when he said, "I'm taking my *time* to thank everybody!"

Finally, after thirty minutes, he began to wrap up. "And I just want you to know that each and every time I plant my feet, if it is to perform for you, you're going to get everything I have!" he vowed. But he couldn't finish without mentioning one of his favorite memories of the evening, watching his appearance on *The Dick Cavett Show* in the winter of 1973.

Cosby was a regular guest on Cavett's show in those days, but this night was special because he was on with Jack Benny. Jack Benny, whom he had first heard on the radio when was a boy in the projects! Jack Benny, whom he had watched on TV as a teenager to learn the art of comic timing! He had so much respect for Benny that when Cavett brought him on, he didn't even try to needle the host the way he usually did, because he didn't want to compete with his hero.

"You haven't picked on me this time," Cavett remarked.

"No, because Jack is here," Cosby replied. "He did you in pretty good."

Cavett had seen Cosby talking to the band before the show, so he started to ask about his interest in music.

"You wanted to be a jazz musician at one time," Cavett said. "That's a new one on me."

"Oh, that may be a new one on you," Cosby said, "but I was very serious about that."

He started to tell Cavett about his teenage dreams of becoming a jazz drummer. He described the $75 drum set he bought from the pawnshop and the $2.50 lessons he took at Wurlitzer's music store. Then he told the story of the day he tried to sit in with the professionals at the Showboat Club in Phila-delphia.

It was an open bandstand night, and Cosby, convinced that practicing along with record-ings of bluesy jazz numbers in his bedroom had given him all the chops he needed, took over the drum chair, pulled his blue-tipped sticks out of his back pocket, and started fid-dling with the keys on the snare as if he actu-ally knew how to tune the thing. When Cosby looked up, he saw that Sonny Stitt, the famed alto sax player, had joined the bandstand. *Oh boy, I'm going to play with Sonny Stitt!* he thought.

Stitt turned around to address the band. "Let's play some jazz!" he said. "I'm tired of just the blues!" Then he called out "Cherokee," the name of one of the most famous, and fastest, tunes in the bebop repertoire.

By now Cosby wasn't just telling Cavett the story. He was launched on one of his brilliant comic improvisations, reenacting every thought and sound and movement of the experience as if it were happening at that very moment. And for once, comedy and jazz were coming together, as Cosby riffed about riffing — or, as it turned out, about his inability to riff.

"Now wherein we had been doing *boom — de — booom, boom — de — boom,* in 'Cherokee' you have to play *dit-dit-dit-dit-dit-dit,*" Cosby explained, his arms frantically demonstrating the difference between a blues and a bebop rhythm. "And I had never played that fast before! . . . I was in a panic where this thing is starting to tighten up [he pointed to his right shoulder] . . . Meanwhile, the left hand is frozen. I want to do something hip, you see, because that's the hip part of the hand, but the dudes in my brain are saying: 'NO, WE CAN'T HANDLE THAT!' Now rigor mortis starts to settle into my forehead, and when your hand gets tired, you can't grab anything! [He picked up a lighter from the table and let it fall from his trembling hand.] The muscles here are saying: 'WE'RE NOT PLAYING ANYMORE!' . . ."

By this time, Jack Benny was doubled over with laughter, his head listing so far toward the floor that it was almost in Dick Cavett's lap. Cavett was pointing at Benny and looking into the camera, as if to say to the audience at home: *Can you believe this?*

Cosby was still going. "So now I start hitting with the shoulder," he said, "and this leg, I put it on automatic spasm . . . and I'm going like this — *dit* — *dit* — *dit* — and nobody's started playing yet!"

Now Benny lifted his head up, slapped his knee, and laughed so hard that he almost tumbled over backward.

On *The Dick Cavett Show* thirty-six years earlier, Cosby had been so busy telling his story that he only sensed what was going on next to him. But that night at the Mark Twain Prize ceremony, watching the clip on the huge screen, he had finally been able to savor a dream come true for Shorty Cosby of the Richard Allen Homes.

"This honor tonight is wonderful," he told the audience as he ended his acceptance speech. "And I'm especially happy that you saw Jack Benny fall out of his chair!"

EPILOGUE:
THE LONG-DISTANCE RUNNER

Even when Cosby isn't on the road now, he surrounds himself with reminders of how hard he's worked and how far he's come. In his study in Shelburne Falls, he keeps an old vaudeville megaphone emblazoned with the words "Helluva Hired Hand." Above the doorway is a sign that reads "Himself, Himself" — a playful commentary on self-invention. And on the mantle above the fireplace, keeping watch over him, are two urns containing the ashes of the women who first conspired to push him to fulfill his promise.

Over the years, Cosby had kept in touch with Mary Forchic, his sixth-grade teacher, but they hadn't seen each other in a while when he got a call one day from a Washington, DC, policeman.

"Do you know a Mary Nagle?" the policeman asked.

It took Cosby a few seconds to remember that Miss Forchic had married and divorced a man named Nagle.

"Yes, I do," he replied.

"Well, she died recently, and we've had her in the morgue for two days," the policeman said. "No relatives have come to claim her, and we saw your name and phone number in her address book."

The policeman informed Cosby that Miss Forchic had been living alone when she passed away in a predominantly black neighborhood in the nation's capital. Someone had taken all the money and checks from her apartment, but calls to her family members had gone unreturned.

"There's no one else to claim the body," the policeman said. "Do you want to decide what to do with it?"

So Cosby had Miss Forchic cremated and arranged for her remains to be sent to Massachusetts. Then he put them in an urn on the mantel in his study, next to the one containing the ashes of his mother Anna.

"Miss Forchic still scares me!" he jokes when he tells the story. "I'm afraid to open that urn!"

Cosby's study has become part of his stand-up act, too. When he gives a performance in Cerritos, California, that will be shown on Comedy Central and released under the title *Far from Finished* — his first major concert film since *Bill Cosby: Himself* — most of the ninety minutes is about material about husbands and wives. Or more precisely, it's devoted to how wives rule the roost. Cosby tells the story of how Camille "gave" him the study, because it's always "the wife's house." He describes a funny war of wills in which Camille turns the thermostat in the room down, and Cosby screws up all his remaining male courage to assert his right to keep the room at the temperature he likes.

The stories about the study and the thermostat get laughs wherever Cosby goes now, because so many of the couples that attend his concerts identify with what they say about longtime relationships: that they are just as much about the little things as the big things. Ask their close friends what has kept Bill and Camille Cosby together all these years, through so many ups and downs, so much triumph and tragedy, and they talk about the deeply held values and interests they share in common: the passion for family, for education, for black history and black art. But only the two of them know all the other quirks of compatibility that have now seen them all the way to their fiftieth wedding anniversary, as the lights on the pine tree near the herb garden twinkled with approval.

As he's done so often over the years, Cosby has plotted a playful surprise for the day of the anniversary, January 25, 2014. He leaves instructions in Shelburne Falls for Camille to board their single-engine plane (they've sold the larger G4 because they don't use it enough anymore to justify the expense) for an undisclosed destination. "If she asks any questions," he tells everyone involved in her transportation, "tell her: 'I'm sorry I don't speak English!' " As Camille looks out the window of the plane, she can't tell where it's headed because there is so much snow on the ground. When it lands at a suburban airfield a little more than an hour later, Catherine Hanks, now in her nineties, and Camille's sister are waiting for her.

"What's going on?" Camille asks her sister.

"I'm sorry, I don't speak English," her sister says.

"Come on, Mom," Camille says. "You can tell me."

"No hablo inglés!" Catherine says, using the Spanish she has practiced for weeks.

The three women climb into an awaiting car, and gradually Camille begins to recognize the Maryland roads she took to pre-Cana classes. Finally, they arrive at the school in Olney where she recited her wedding vows, on the basketball court on which her congregation met in that winter of 1964 while their church was under construction.

Assembled inside are Camille's four daughters, her three grandchildren, and dozens of siblings, cousins, nephews, and nieces who Cosby has invited for the occasion. As soon as she walks through the door, they rush to greet her. In his minute-by-minute planning, Cosby has estimated that it will take Camille forty seconds to cross the room, but there are so many hugs and kisses that it takes more than four minutes. At last she reaches the far end of the basketball court and sees the three men standing there: Father Carl Dianda, the priest who married her, now seventy-eight and retired; the best man, Ron "Stymie" Crockett; and her mischievous husband of fifty years.

"Hello, Father Dianda," Camille says, smiling and tearing up at the same time. "Hello, Stymie. And *hello,* Bill!"

Father Dianda addresses the room: "Is there anyone in this group who feels that these two should not be wed? Speak up now."

"Too late!" everyone shouts in unison.

Then the grandchildren and young nieces and nephews chime in with the refrain that Cosby has scripted especially for them.

"Cha, cha, cha!" the children call out.

From there, Cosby takes Camille to San Francisco, to relive their honeymoon trip across the country, and the rest of the year will be full of more sentimental journeys. But as always, it will also be packed with more concerts, more graduation speeches, and another lifetime achievement award — the Johnny Carson Award for Comedic Excellence at the American Comedy Awards, an honor that Cosby relishes because of the role that Carson and *The Tonight Show* played in launching his career.

When Cosby returns to Massachusetts, he retreats to his study to enjoy his favorite forms of relaxation: listening to jazz and watching old movies. Camille has given him a gift of a huge flat-screen TV that he can watch with his limited vision, and often she joins him in front of it, as they continue the ritual that they began a half century ago, when Cosby would drive from Greenwich Village to the University of Maryland on the weekends to take his sweetheart out to a matinee.

Cosby is a fan of Turner Classic Movies, one of the few cable channels that show the kind of black-and-white films he loves. Once he called up the TCM's veteran host, Robert Osborne, to tell him how wonderful he was. Osborne responded by inviting Cosby to be a guest programmer. One of Cosby's selections was Buster Keaton, of course — the silent classic *Steamboat Bill, Jr.* Another was his favorite Charlie Chaplin talkie, *Monsieur Verdoux.* And a third was the movie Cosby considers perhaps the greatest of all time, *The Treasure of the Sierra Madre,* with its grizzled performances by Humphrey Bogart and Walter Huston, and its eternal themes of fellowship, greed, and survival.

When the subject turns to movies during one of his road trips, however, Cosby mentions a more surprising favorite. He's talking about how a man's perspective changes with age, and it makes him think of a British film from the 1960s, *The Loneliness of the Long Distance Runner.*

Directed by Tony Richardson, one of the avant-garde European directors of the time, the movie tells the story of an angry, confused youth from the working-class Midlands named Colin Smith. When Smith, played by Tom Courtenay, robs a bakery along with some of his mates, he gets sent to a British "borstal." The governor of the reform school discovers Colin's talent for running and grooms him to compete in a big race against a local school. But at the last minute, just as Colin is about to win the race, he decides that he's had enough of being manipulated by older authority figures. Just yards from the finish line, he stops in his tracks and the other racers rush past him. As the film ends, Colin is back laboring in the reformatory's machine shop.

When the movie first came out, it was considered a classic of the "angry young man" school of British filmmaking, an allegory of social alienation and defiance. Cosby had seen it at the time, when he was single and struggling to establish an original comic voice in Greenwich Village, and he thought the message was groovy.

"I thought, this is great!" he says. "Not

another traditional ending!"

Twenty years later, Cosby saw the film again. He was in his early forties now, married with five children, working nonstop to rebuild his fortune as a nightclub performer and advertising pitchman.

"This time, I thought, why doesn't the guy want to win?" Cosby says. "He was far enough ahead in the race that he could have walked to the finish line and still made his point!"

But recently Cosby had watched *The Loneliness of the Long Distance Runner* again on TV one night, and this time he had a completely different response to the ending.

"I turned to Camille," Cosby says. "I said, 'He's already made one mistake. Now he's making another. He doesn't understand his responsibility to himself. That boy *deserves* to stay in the reformatory!' "

As Cosby finishes the story, a sweet, contented smile spreads across his face.

"And Camille agreed with me!" he says.

ACKNOWLEDGMENTS

I was nine years old when I discovered *Wonderfulness,* my first Bill Cosby album. It was a sad time in my childhood: my parents had divorced three years earlier, and my mother had taken my younger brother and me all the way across the country, from Los Angeles to Massachusetts. My father, who was black, was barely in contact with us, and there were no other African Americans in the small college town where my mother, who is white, found a full-time teaching job. So that album, with its sidesplitting "Tonsils" and "Chicken Heart" routines, and the handsome young comedian joyously riding a go-cart on the cover, filled two voids. It brought me both laughter and another black man to admire. After my mother purchased our first TV set, I found Cosby in *I Spy.* I begged her to let me watch and she agreed, despite her disapproval of Cold War espionage shows and the show's ten o'clock airtime, past my bedtime.

We eventually got several more Cosby albums, and, like millions of other children of the sixties, I listened to them over and over again, laughing until I cried. As a teen, I loved his hip, laid-back gym teacher character in his first sitcom, *The Bill Cosby Show* (as well as its funky theme music), and I kept watching cartoons on Saturday largely because of *Fat Albert and the Cosby Kids.* Then in my late twenties, I became a huge fan all over again when *The Cosby Show* debuted on NBC on Thursday nights. My girlfriend and I were just about to get married, and over the next eight years, as we became parents to two children, it offered a never-to-be missed weekly treat and a model for the kind of home we hoped to create with our own kids.

Yet my interest in Cosby wasn't just personal. As a journalist with a special interest in matters of race, I was fascinated to see him emerge in his midsixties, after a career built on nonracial comedy, as a fierce and controversial critic of self-destructive trends in the black community. When Barack Obama was elected president, I agreed with pundits who argued that *The Cosby Show* had prepared the national psyche for an African American family in the White House. Once I became a television executive, I grew even more conscious of the medium's profound social impact and of the ways that Cosby had transformed it several times in his career —

first integrating prime time, then helping to launch educational children's programming, then reviving the sitcom, opening doors each time for fellow comedians and people of color in the entertainment business. As a parent, I felt for him when he lost his only son and confessed estrangement from one of his daughters. If anyone deserved an in-depth study of the life and man behind the public image, I thought, it was Bill Cosby. So I decided to undertake one.

People ask if this is an "authorized" biography, and at first it was anything but. As an executive at NBC News and CNN, I had greeted and chatted with Cosby several times, but I didn't know him well. So I reached out to his friend and adviser Dr. Alvin Poussaint of the Harvard Medical School, who had been a source of mine since I began reporting for *The Harvard Crimson* as a college student. Poussaint agreed to speak to him on my behalf, but he called back to report that Cosby wasn't interested in helping me. He wouldn't try to block the book, I was told, but I shouldn't expect any cooperation.

I persisted anyway, interviewing Cosby associates and friends who would talk to me, and digging into the parts of the story that I could reconstruct from books, articles, and archived interviews. I stayed in touch with Cosby's publicist, David Brokaw, to let him know that I was still working away and hoping that the ice would thaw, and eventually it did. First, Brokaw sent me a few articles Cosby thought I should see. Then I received word that he wanted to speak to me. Finally, more than a year into my reporting, Cosby called me. We had several long phone conversations, and I spent a weekend traveling with and interviewing him in airports, on planes, in cars, and backstage before his concerts — about fifteen hours of one-on-one time, by far the most access he has given any prospective biographer. Just as helpful, he supplied me with names of important people in his life about whom I would not otherwise have been aware and who would not have talked to me without his permission. Without Bill Cosby's help, this would have been a different and less revealing book, and I am deeply grateful to him.

Still, most of what appears in these pages was independently researched and reported. Along with countless discussions with fans and followers of Cosby, I conducted more than sixty in-depth interviews with his close personal and professional associates, all of whom agreed to speak on the record with no ground rules. Wherever possible, I sought multiple sources and contemporaneous documentation for all of the scenes I have reconstructed. I remained wary of gossip and faulty memories, and the fact that Cosby is a professional storyteller whose accounts of his own life needed to be checked. Throughout, I applied a simple test: If I was confident from my own legwork that I could describe events as they actually occurred, I included them. If I wasn't, I didn't.

For the generous amount of time they made available for interviews, I am particularly indebted to L. Douglas Wilder, Stu Gardner, Johnny Baines, Bootsie Barnes, Skeet Matthews, Joe Johnson Jr., Raymond Travis, Jean Lamb Heath, Ronald Crockett, Diane Fearon, Donald Council, Tony Williams, Gavin White, Tom Paxton, Paul Gardner, Sheldon Schultz, Steve Bershad, Ron DeBlasio, Jeff Wald, Joe Gannon, Herb Schlosser, Ken Mundie, Dwight Allen, Joan Ganz Cooney, Grace Leong, Clare Bisceglia, David Driskell, George Wein, Sonny Rollins, Marcy Carsey, Tom Werner, Jay Sandrich, Phylicia Rashad, Alvin Poussaint, Susan Fales-Hill, Jack Gelbart, Johnathan Rodgers, Joanne Curley Kerner, Tom Straw, Ed Lewis, Howard Bingham, Allison Samuels, Stanley Battle, Al Shrier, Eddie Anderson, Kathleen McGhee Anderson, and Sheldon Pavel. I also relied on interviews that scores of newspaper and magazine reporters have done with Cosby over the years, as well as taped interviews commissioned by the Archive of American Television (a treasure trove for students of the medium) with Leslie Moonves, Larry Auerbach, Malcolm Jamal Warner, Garvin

Eddy, Quincy Jones, and, most invaluably, Sheldon Leonard and Robert Culp.

Of the hundreds of book and periodical sources I consulted, I want to acknowledge *Cosby: The Life of a Comic Legend,* a short biography written from secondary sources twenty-five years ago by Ronald L. Smith, for offering a useful guide to what was already known about Cosby's life and career and what gaps needed to be filled. I could not have done justice to Cosby's historic first foray into prime-time TV without the help of an encyclopedic, episode-by-episode guide compiled by Marc Cushman and Linda J. La-Rosa entitled *I Spy: A History and Episode Guide to the Groundbreaking Television Series.* Two *Playboy* interviews with Cosby, conducted sixteen years apart by Lawrence Linderman, were a gold mine, as was Oprah Winfrey's interview with Cosby's notoriously private wife, Camille. For any student of influential African Americans in the last half of the twentieth century, the magazines *Ebony* and *Jet,* now archived by Google Books, remain an indispensable resource.

Jeff Fager, Vicki Gordon, and Ann Fotiades at CBS News were kind enough to allow me to watch and make use of a never-aired, two-and-a-half-hour interview that Dan Rather did with Cosby ten days after his son, Ennis, was killed. Along with his colleague Kim Harjo, David Brokaw was cheerfully helpful in providing me with contact information for people in Cosby's world and offering insights into a man he has studied since he was a boy and his father, Norman Brokaw, was Cosby's agent and closest business adviser. At Simon & Schuster, I am grateful to Jonathan Cox, Lisa Healy, Patricia Romanowski, Elisa Rivlin, Michael Accordino, and Maureen Cole for everything they did to help the book sing and sell, and at Janklow & Nesbit Associates to Bennett Ashley and Stefanie Lieberman for their legal counsel.

Five years ago, Lynn Nesbit, my literary agent, and Alice Mayhew, my editor, took a gamble on an author who had never written a book when he presented them with a family memoir that he had completed on spec, with no advance or promise of publication. They had faith in me again when I proposed to write a book about Bill Cosby without any guarantee that he would cooperate. As all of their authors will attest, they are simply the very best at what they do.

For their friendship and support during the writing of the book, I am grateful to Henry and Celia McGee, Jonathan Alter and Emily Lazar, Shahnaz Batmanghelidj and Roddy Klotz, David Conney, Laura Levine, Farrell Evans, Holly Peterson, Renee Edelman, Mandy Grunwald, Geraldine Baum and Mike Oreskes, Bob Spitz and Becky Aikman, Meryl Gordon and Walter Shapiro, Diane

Terman and Marshall Felenstein, Mitch and Sarah Simms Rosenthal, and David Corvo and Michele Willens. My children, Rachel and Matthew, listened patiently to my Cosby stories and didn't seem fazed when their father spent a year at home writing. As always, their mother, Alexis Gelber, was my first and best reader, as well as my most enthusiastic cheerleader.

I have dedicated this book to my mother, Jeanne Theis Whitaker, and to my late grandmother, Edith McColes Whitaker. When I started out as a child, both of them made me feel that I would grow up to do worthwhile things, even when I was listening to comedy albums and watching TV spy shows instead of doing my homework.

COSBYOGRAPHY

TELEVISION SHOWS

I Spy, NBC, 1965–1968.*

The Bill Cosby Show, NBC, 1969–1971.

The Electric Company, PBS, 1971–1977.

The New Bill Cosby Show, CBS, 1972–1973.

Fat Albert and the Cosby Kids, CBS, 1972–1984.

Cos, ABC, 1976.

The Cosby Show, NBC, 1984–1992.**

You Bet Your Life, Carsey-Werner Productions, 1992–1993.

The Cosby Mysteries, NBC, 1994.

Cosby, CBS, 1996–2000.

Kids Say the Darndest Things, CBS, 1998–2000.

* Cosby won the Emmy Award for Outstanding Lead Actor in a Drama Series all three seasons.
** The show won the Emmy for Outstanding Comedy Series in 1985, but Cosby refused consideration for an individual Emmy in each of its eight seasons.

Little Bill, Nick Jr., 1999–2004.
Fatherhood, Nick at Night, 2004–2005.

COMEDY ALBUMS

Bill Cosby Is a Very Funny Fellow — Right!, Warner Bros., 1963.

I Started Out as a Child, Warner Bros., 1964.★★★

Why Is There Air?, Warner Bros., 1965.★★★

Wonderfulness, Warner Bros., 1966.★★★

Revenge, Warner Bros., 1967.★★★

To Russell, My Brother, Whom I Slept With, Warner Bros., 1968.★★★

200 M.P.H., Warner Bros., 1968.

It's True! It's True! Warner Bros., 1969.

8:15 12:15, Tetragrammaton, 1969.

Sports, UNI/MCA, 196.9★★★

Live: Madison Square Garden, UNI/MCA, 1970.

When I Was a Kid, MCA, 1971.

For Adults Only, MCA, 1971.

Inside the Mind of Bill Cosby, MCA, 1972.

Fat Albert, MCA, 1972.

My Father Confused Me . . . What Must I Do? What Must I Do?, Capitol/EMI, 1977.

Bill's Best Friend, Capitol/EMI, 1978.

Bill Cosby Himself, Motown, 1982.

Those of You With or Without Children, You'll Understand, Geffen, 1986.★★★

★★★ Winner of the Grammy Award for Best Comedy Performance/Recording.

Oh, Baby!, Geffen, 1991.

COMPILATION ALBUMS

The Best of Bill Cosby, Warner Bros., 1969.

More of the Best of Bill Cosby, Warner Bros., 1970.

Bill, MCA, 1973.

Down Under, Warner Bros., 1975.

Cosby and the Kids, Warner Bros., 1986.

At His Best, MCA, 1992.

20th Century Masters, The Millennium Collection: The Best of Bill Cosby, MCA, 2001.

The Bill Cosby Collection, EMI, 2001.

CHILDREN'S ALBUMS

The Electric Company, Warner Bros., 1971.★★★★

Bill Cosby Talks to Kids About Drugs, UNI, 1972.★★★★

MUSIC ALBUMS

Silver Throat: Bill Cosby Sings, Warner Bros., 1967.

Bill Cosby Sings Hooray for the Salvation Army Band, Warner Bros., 1968.

Badfoot Brown and the Bunions Bradford Funeral and Marching Band, UNI, 1971.

At Last Bill Cosby Really Sings, Partee, 1973.

Bill Cosby Is Not Himself These Days, Rat Own,

★★★★Winner of the Grammy Award for Best Recording for Children.

Rat Own, Capitol/EMI, 1976.

Disco Bill, Capitol/EMI, 1977.

Where You Lay Your Head, Verve, 1990.

My Appreciation, Verve, 1991.

Hello, Friend: To Ennis, with Love, Verve, 1997.

Quincy Jones & Bill Cosby: The Original Jam Sessions 1969, Concord, 2004.

Quincy Jones & Bill Cosby: The New Mixes, Concord, 2004.

Bill Cosby Presents The Cosnarati: State of Emergency, Turtle Head, 2009.

Keep Standing (with the Hilton Ruiz Ensemble), Turtle Head, 2010.

FILMS

Man and Boy, Jemmin Inc., 1971.

Hickey & Boggs, United Artists, 1972.

Uptown Saturday Night, First Artists, 1974.

Let's Do It Again, First Artists, 1975.

Mother, Jugs & Speed, 20th Century-Fox, 1976.

A Piece of the Action, First Artists, 1977.

California Suite, Columbia Pictures, 1978.

The Devil and Max Devlin, Walt Disney Productions, 1981.

Bill Cosby: Himself, Jemmin Inc., 1983.

Leonard Part 6, Columbia Pictures, 1986.

Bill Cosby: 49 (VHS), COC Productions, 1987.

Ghost Dad, Universal Pictures, 1990.

The Meteor Man, Metro-Goldwyn-Mayer, 1993.

Jack, Buena Vista Pictures, 1996.

To Mr. Sapolsky, with Love (VHS), COC, 1996.

Fat Albert, 20th Century-Fox, 2004.

Far from Finished (DVD), Comedy Central, 2013.

Books

Fatherhood, Doubleday, 1986.*

Time Flies, Doubleday, 1987.*

Love and Marriage, Doubleday, 1989.

Childhood, Putnam, 1991.

Kids Say the Darndest Things, Bantam Books, 1998.

Congratulations! Now What? A Book for Graduates, Hyperion, 1999.

American Schools: The $100 Billion Challenge (with Dwight Allen), IPublish, 2000.

Cosbyology: Essays and Observations from the Doctor of Comedy, Hyperion, 2001.

I Am What I Ate . . . and I'm Frightened!!!, HarperEntertainment, 2003.

Friends of a Feather: One of Life's Little Fables (with Erika Cosby), HarperEntertainment, 2003.

Come On, People: On the Path from Victims to Victors (with Alvin Poussaint), Thomas Nelson, 2007.

* Reached #1 on *New York Times* Nonfiction Bestseller List.

I Didn't Ask to Be Born (But I'm Glad I Was), Center Street, 2011.

NOTES

Prologue

"Thank you for my childhood": Author travel and interviews with Bill Cosby and fans in New York City, Richmond, Virginia, and Greenville, South Carolina, Apr. 19–20, 2013.

Then Wilder shares a story: Author interview with L. Douglas Wilder.

An interviewer once asked him if he had fifty dollars in his pocket: "Bill Cosby on Jonathan Winters," YouTube, Jan. 3, 2011.

1 Granddad Samuel's Bible

The basketball game took place: Foreword by Bill Cosby in *Lombardi's Left Side,* by Herb Adderley, Dave Robinson, and Royce Boyles, Ascend Books, 2012; Cosby appearance on *The David Letterman Show,* Mar. 19, 2013.

One hundred and twenty-five years before that basketball game: "From Maria to Bill

Cosby: A Case Study in Tracing Black Slave Ancestry," *National Genealogical Society Quarterly,* Mar. 1987.

What the Cosby family found in Philadelphia: Philadelphia Divided: Race and Politics in the City of Brotherly Love, by James Wolfinger, University of North Carolina Press, 2007, Introduction and chapter 1.

one of the southern migrants who found a manufacturing job: Author interview with Tony Williams, Cosby's friend who worked with Samuel Cosby at the Tube Works; *Munitions Manufacture in the Philadelphia Ordnance District,* by William Bradford Williams, A. Pomerantz & Co., 1921, Ch. XLVI.

The family moved into a row house on West Godfrey Avenue: Author interview with Cosby.

The young family moved into a row house at 6058 Beechwood Street: Author interview with Johnny Baines.

Bill Sr. headed to a local tavern: Cosby interview with Lawrence Linderman, *Playboy,* May 1969.

". . . I thought the world had ended": Author interview with Baines.

The house on Stewart Street was a dilapidated hovel: Author interview with Cosby.

Granddad Samuel read stories aloud to him: Cosby interview with Paul Farhi, "Bill

Cosby's Gift for Gag: It's in His Genes via a Sock," *Washington Post,* Oct. 26, 2009.

Bill would tag after him — like "an open basket": Cosby interview with Gloria Campisi, "A Native Son, His Pain in City's Project Led Him to Success," *Philadelphia Daily News,* Jan. 17, 1997.

Gertrude had her own ways of making her grandson feel special: Cosby interview with Amy Calder, "Goodness: Bill Cosby Coming to Maine to Share His Talents with Us," *Kennebec Journal,* May 16, 2011.

Aboard the USS West Virginia: "Cook Third Class Doris Miller, USN," Naval History & Heritage website.

The second development was the arrival of public housing: "Philadelphia Divided," Chapter 3; "Richard Allen Homes," Historical Society of Pennsylvania website.

Apartment A at 919 Parrish Place: Author interview with Cosby; *Childhood,* by Bill Cosby, G. P. Putnam & Sons, 1991.

2. A Place in the Projects

Anna Pearl Hite emerged from a small row house in Germantown: Author interview with Cosby.

One year, the Colored girls banded together: Biography of Margaret Roselle Hawkins on The Links, Incorporated website.

His first-grade teacher was so impressed:

Cosby address to master's degree graduates of Columbia University's Teachers College, May 1998.

From the beginning, they had nicknames for each other: Author interview with Bootsie Barnes and Skeet Matthews.

The ultimate punishment: Childhood, Cosby, p. 126.

he found that he had a special gift for mimicry: Author interview with Cosby; *Childhood,* Cosby, p. 123.

Bill heard a commercial for a popular brand of cereal: Cosby performance in Richmond, Virginia, Apr. 19, 2013.

"Hey, Shorty, you're really *poor, man!":* Cosby interview with Linderman, *Playboy,* 1969.

When Bill joined the Boy Scouts: Author interview with Cosby.

Although Bill loved bikes: Cosby interview with Lawrence Linderman, *Playboy,* Dec. 1985.

"If your father sold all that wine he drank . . .": Cosby remarks at Graterford Prison, *Hard-headed Boys,* Nicetown Records, 1985.

Sometimes Anna's instructions would take the form of funny warnings: Cosby interview with Dan Goodgame, "I Do Believe in Control," *Time,* June 24, 2011.

leftovers of lobster thermidor and Chateaubriand: Cosby interview with Bill Boggs, BillBoggsTV, YouTube.

"Shorty, your brother sure looks sickly!": Author interview with Cosby.

Mrs. McKinney revealed the results to her class: Cosbyology, by Bill Cosby, Hyperion, 2001, pp. 49–51.

At eleven years old, they started to have summer jobs: Author interview with Barnes and Matthews.

Miss Forchic started by giving Bill a new place in her classroom: Cosby interview with Diana Nollen, "Bill Cosby Helps Reopen Paramount with Family Friendly Show," Hooplanow.com, Nov. 15, 2012.

"Shorty's the teacher's pet!": Author interview with Barnes and Matthews.

As a fifth grader, he had been made a crossing guard: Childhood, Cosby, pp. 93–96.

"I'm just afraid," she wrote: Cosby interview with Veronic Dudo, "Stars at the Shore: Bill Cosby," CBSPhilly, July 25, 2012.

3. Lost in Germantown

put an end to the happy-go-lucky existence: Author interview with Barnes and Matthews.

For Cos, the icebreaker was jazz: Cosby interview with Don Heckman, *International Review of Music,* June 2010.

he used jazz as a pretext to meet pretty girls: Childhood, Cosby, pp. 181–183.

he couldn't afford to rent a tuxedo: Cosby with

Linderman, *Playboy,* 1969.

In eighth grade, his allergy to homework caught up with him: Cosbyology, pp. 55–70.

another black student was trying to enroll in a new school: Linda Brown interview for *Black/White & Brown,* PBS documentary produced by KTWU, 2004.

They were more interested in developments in the jazz world: Cosby interview with Jake Feinberg, *The Jake Feinberg Show,* KWFM 1330, Sept. 22, 2012.

"Don't play football until you're twenty-one years old!": Cosby interview with Linderman, *Playboy,* 1985; *Cosbyology,* pp. 125–136.

It was a narrow little house: Author interviews with Cosby and Williams.

but also trying to play the drums: Author interview with Cosby; Cosby interview with Feinberg, *The Jake Feinberg Show;* Cosby appearance on *The Dick Cavett Show,* Feb. 21, 1973.

as soon as he experienced the new marvel, he was hooked: Author interview with Cosby; *Seriously Funny: The Rebel Comedians of the 1950s and 1960s,* by Gerald Nachman, Pantheon, 2003, pp. 562–590.

greatest obsession in high school was the "Down Cats": Author interview with Joe Johnson Jr.; Cosby interview with Linderman, *Playboy,* 1969.

Miles Davis was playing a matinee with his

band: "Miles and Style," by Bill Cosby in *Miles Davis: The Complete Illustrated History,* Voyageur Press, 2012.

His grades had gone from bad to worse: Author interview with Cosby.

Rookie had a next-door neighbor named Raymond Travis: Author interview with Raymond Travis.

"As a kid in Philadelphia," he said, "I gravitated to athletics": "The Case of the Scholarly 'Spy,' " by Joanne Stang, *New York Times,* Sept. 10, 1965.

"I had no backup plan": Author interview with Cosby.

he decided on which branch of the military to join: Cosby speeches at the Lone Sailor Awards, 2010, and Honorary Chief Petty Officer ceremony, Feb. 17, 2011.

4. The Navy Way

The RDC was hovering over Cosby: Cosby speeches at the Lone Sailor Awards and Honorary Chief Petty Officer ceremony; Cosby appearance on *Late Night with Jimmy Fallon,* Jan. 18, 2012.

It was called Argentia: Uprooted! The Argentia Story, by Eileen Houlihan, Creative Book Publishers, 1992.

a young black pilot named Ronald Crockett: Author interview with Ronald Crockett.

Cosby seized any opportunity to play sports in

the military: Stars in Blue: Movie Actors in America's Sea Services, by James E. Wise Jr. and Anne Collier Rehill, Naval Institute Press, 1997, pp. 255–258.

the football coach at Quantico: Author interview with Ben Moore's daughter, Diane Fearon.

Her name was Lieutenant Jean Lamb: Author interview with Jean Lamb Heath.

Another patient was a Marine Corps officer from Mississippi: Author interview with Lamb Heath; Cosby interview with Michael Sragow, "Cosby's Take on Twain Humor," Baltimore Sun, Nov. 1, 2009.

a mulatto serviceman named Tony Reynolds: Author interview with Lamb Heath.

Cosby experienced another epiphany: Author interview with Cosby.

"a mental sin": "Stars in Blue," p. 255.

Cosby went over to the Owls squad: Author interview with Gavin White.

he felt as if his entire wasted school career were passing before his eyes: Author interview with Cosby.

5. The Bar at Temple

Cosby wanted to run the 220-yard hurdles: Author interview with White.

Cosby could also take a hit: Cosby interview with George Vecsey, "Cosby Can Laugh Now, But Football Was Serious Business,"

New York Times, Dec. 4, 2010.

he befriended a nineteen-year-old black sopho-more: Author interview with Don Council.

Coach White also came to rely on Cosby as a morale officer: Author interview with White.

White was what he called an abolitionist: Author interview with Cosby.

White was surprised and touched to receive a letter from Cosby: Cosby letter to White, summer 1961.

he was riding the bench when he heard a fan of the other team shouting insults: Author interviews with White and Council.

Council had seen evidence of Cosby's hot side: Author interview with Council; Miles *Davis and American Culture,* edited by Gerald Lyn Early, Missouri Historical Society Press, 2001, pp. 90–91.

He applied for membership in Local 274 of the American Federation of Musicians: Cosby union application in the Charles L. Blockson Afro-American Collection, Temple University.

a saxophonist named Tony Williams: Author interview with Williams.

Cosby decided to write about the first time he lost a tooth: Author interview with Cosby; Cosby interview with John Liberty, "Comedian Talks About the Navy, His Early Writing and His Favorite Period of a Long, Decorated Career," MLive, Jan. 9, 2013.

He began to fantasize about a future as a comedy writer: Cosby interview with Liberty, MLive; *"I Started Out as a Child,"* Bill Cosby, Warner Bros. Records, 1964.

Cosby took a job as a bartender: Author interview with Williams.

he came across a new album: 2000 Years with Carl Reiner and Mel Brooks, Capitol Records, 1960.

Cosby fell in love with the album: Author interview with Johnson.

a black comic named Pop Foster: Author interviews with Cosby and Johnson.

One of the performers was another Temple University student named Alix Dobkin: Herb Gart interview with David Wilson, BerkshireFineArts.com, Apr. 9, 2012.

As Dobkin remembered it: "My Village Life," by Alix Dobkin, excerpted from *My Red Blood: A Memoir of Growing Up Communist, Coming Onto the Greenwich Village Folk Scene and Coming Out in the Feminist Movement,* Alyson Books, 2009.

Cosby and Council had been sitting at the Showboat for several hours: Author interview with Council.

he thought about the ways comedy could resemble jazz: Author interviews with Cosby, Williams, and Sonny Rollins.

Cosby would have another epiphany: Author interview with Cosby.

6. "Noah" in the Village

The Gaslight Café had a tiny storeroom: Author interview with Cosby; Tom Paxton interview with Ken Paulson, "Speaking Freely" series, The Newseum, Washington, DC, Nov. 29, 2000.

he had to deal with an unexpected setback: Author interview with Cosby; *My Village Life,* Dobkin.

The Gaslight Café had started its life: "How Do You Bury a Cellar?," by Al Aronowitz, The Blacklisted Journalist, Column Six, Feb. 1, 1996.

Hood told Cosby that his job description was to keep the crowd amused: Author interview with Cosby.

One night he wandered into a new place and found Cedar Walton: Cosby interview with Heckman, *International Review of Music.*

Tom Paxton was impressed with how quickly Cosby's act was evolving: Author interview with Paxton.

word of Cosby's presence in the Village reached the New York Times: "Comic Turns Quips into Tuition," by Paul Gardner, *New York Times,* June 25, 1964; author interview with Gardner.

When Herb Gart opened a copy of the New York Times: Gart radio interview on therainbow.com.

Cosby couldn't help but identify with Gregory:

847

Author interview with Cosby.

Gart gave him recordings of performers he thought Cosby should study: Cosby: The Life of a Comedy Legend, by Ronald L. Smith, Prometheus Books, 1997, pp. 39–41.

he was going to work clean: Author interview with Cosby.

For Roy Silver, there was also a Bob Dylan story: "Roy Silver — The Lost Interview" on *Bob Dylan: Together Through Life* DVD/CD collection, Columbia, 2009; *The Witmark Demos: 1962–1964; The Bootleg Series: Volume 9,* liner notes by Colin Escott, July 2010.

"He was kind of like a hustler type": Dylan interview on "Roy Silver — The Lost Interview."

In a memoir, Weintraub would write: Bruce Lee, Woodstock and Me, by Fred Weintraub, with David Fields, Brooktree Canyon Press, 2011, pp. 182–185.

Silver told a Life *magazine reporter that Cosby "threatened to punch me . . .":* "I Am Two People, Man," by Thomas B. Morgan, *Life,* Apr. 11, 1969, p. 78.

Cosby had a different recollection: Author interview with Cosby.

Cosby noticed a ripple of audience reaction: Author interview with Cosby; "A Nut in Every Car," on *Bill Cosby Is a Very Funny*

848

Fellow — Right!, Warner Bros. Records, 1963.

So Cosby started working on a routine: Author interview with Cosby: "Noah: Right!," on *Bill Cosby Is a Very Funny Fellow — Right!.*

His friend Don Council talked him out of it: Author interview with Council.

Cosby was offered a Friday night date at Philadelphia's Town Hall that paid $250: *Cosby: The Life of a Comedy Legend,* Smith, pp. 49–50.

he confided in his friend Don Council: Author interviews with Council and Cosby.

he outdid them all in likeability: *The Bitter End: Hanging Out at America's Nightclub,* by Paul Colby, Cooper Square Press, 2002, pp. 69–84.

7. Two Blind Dates

The scene was a familiar one: History and Founders items on www.oblatesisters.com.

From the nuns, Camille learned the rules: "Oblate Nuns Get Deserved Praise from Cosby's Wife," by Gregory Kane, *Baltimore Sun,* July 10, 2004; "Baltimore School Honors the Cosbys," by Mary Gail Hare, *Baltimore Sun,* Apr. 20, 2012.

Cosby lived at the home of Ron Crockett on Bryant Street: Author interview with Crockett.

"six half smokes and a good woman!": "Bill

Cosby Recalls Ben's Chili Bowl," by Joseph Weber, *Washington Post,* Oct. 9, 2009.

This is someone Cos should meet!: Author interview with Crockett.

Cosby asked Camille to marry him: Author interview with Cosby; "Life with Bill Cosby," *Ebony,* Sept. 1966, p. 34.

When Cosby's family found out what was happening: Author interview with Crockett.

Cosby was encouraged to see the first mention of his name in Billboard: "Bud & Travis: As Themselves," *Billboard,* June 1, 1963, p. 10.

Silver knew the talent coordinator for the late-night program: Author interview with Sheldon Schultz.

Cosby was scheduled next to last in the order of guests: Schultz's booking notes for *The Tonight Show,* Aug. 6, 1963.

He came out from behind the stage curtain: Author interview with Cosby.

Shelly Schultz had never heard anything like it: Author interview with Schultz.

When The Tonight Show *aired later that night:* Author interview with Cosby.

Cosby needed the help of a talent agency: Author interview with Schultz; "Industry Profile: Jay Jacobs," by Jane Cohen and Bob Grossweiner, celebrityaccess.com.

Billboard *confirmed how it had happened:* "WB Signs New Comic Cosby," *Billboard,* Aug. 24, 1963, p. 14.

liner notes written by the older comic: Bill Cosby *Is a Very Funny Fellow — Right!,* liner notes by Allan Sherman.

more clubs started calling: Author interview with Cosby.

8. "Riggie" in Chicago

"Everything okay, Mr. Cosby?": Cosby has told this story with slight variations in a commencement address to the Juilliard School in 2002 (excerpted in *Take This Advice: The Best Graduation Speeches Ever Given,* edited by Sandra Bark, Simon Spotlight Entertainment, 2005), a commencement address at Carnegie Mellon University in 2007, and in *Cosbyology,* pp. 155–157.

a kind of negative ego: Author interview with Cosby.

His name was Ed Weinberger: "I Am Two People, Man," Morgan, *Life,* p. 77.

He called it "loading the boat": Author interview with Cosby.

one of the best three minutes of comedy he had ever written: Author interview with Cosby; "The Playground," on *Wonderfulness,* Warner Bros. Records, 1965.

King looked up from his written text and started to improvise: "Mahalia Jackson, and King's Improvisation," by Drew Hansen, *New York Times,* Aug. 27, 2013.

Paar liked to boast that he had run a film clip of

the Beatles: "Jack Paar Reminisces," by Nan Robertson, *New York Times,* Feb. 20, 1984.

He later remembered Paar: Cosby interviewed for "Jack Paar: As I Was Saying," PBS *American Masters* documentary, 1997.

Come on, Jack: Author interview with Cosby.

Cosby came out from behind the curtain looking shy and awkward: Cosby appearance on *The Jack Paar Show,* Sept. 27, 1963.

The next Monday, Marty Litke: Author interview with Cosby.

Billboard *included it in the magazine's "Pop Special Merit" picks: Billboard,* Oct. 26, 1963, p. 43.

Cosby was on a plane to Los Angeles: Hootenanny, Season 2, Episode 13.

in the middle of the rehearsal: Author interview with Cosby.

He told Shelly Schultz to get him back on The Tonight Show: Author interview with Schultz.

he called the Hanks home, and Camille answered: Author interview with Cosby.

a lighthearted item about the wedding: "Comedian Bill Cosby Marries Md. U. Co-Ed," *Jet,* Feb. 13, 1964, p. 59.

Stymie Crockett was the only guest on the groom's side: Author interview with Crockett.

Camille had never flown before: Author interview with Cosby.

Cosby was obsessed with John Coltrane: Cosby interview with Feinberg, *The Jake Feinberg Show.*

During the honeymoon road trip: Author interview with Crockett.

9. "Sheldon's Folly"

It was a Thursday night: The Official Dick Van Dyke Show Book, by Vince Waldron, Chicago Review Press, 2011, p. 127; Schultz's booking notes for *The Tonight Show,* Dec. 5, 1963.

Cosby was thrilled to meet Carl Reiner: Cosby interview with Linderman, *Playboy,* 1969.

Van Dyke recalled that the cast barely got any work done: The Official Dick Van Dyke Book, Waldron, p. 127.

Leonard invited him to his office: Cosby interview with Linderman, *Playboy,* 1969.

In Sheldon Leonard's mind, he had spent a lifetime: Leonard interview with Sam Denoff for the Archive of American Television, July 11, 1996.

Felton had offered the starring role: I Spy: A History and Episode Guide to the Groundbreaking Television Series, by Marc Cushman and Linda J. LaRosa, McFarland & Company, 2007, p. 15.

"I like your idea, kid, but I like mine better": Culp commentary on DVD of *I Spy, Season 1,* Image Entertainment, 2008; Culp inter-

view with Stephen J. Abramson for the Archive of American Television, Nov. 6, 2007.

he felt as if a depth charge had gone off in his head: I Spy, Cushman and LaRosa, p. 19.

Leonard was closing in on a unique financial arrangement: I Spy, Cushman and LaRosa, pp. 3, 20.

Leonard was ready to make his final pitch: Leonard interview with Denoff, AAT.

he invited the three men to spend the afternoon with him and Camille: And the Show Goes On, by Sheldon Leonard, Limelight, 1995, p. 146; author interview with Leonard's son, Steve Bershad.

David Friedkin had a son named Gregory: I Spy, Cushman and LaRosa, p. 25.

After the show, Leonard asked to meet with Cosby: Cosby interview with Linderman, *Playboy,* 1969; *I Spy,* Cushman and LaRosa, pp. 25, 26.

The manager met with Leonard: And the Show Goes On, Leonard, p. 146.

he had even performed for the president of the United States: Author interview with Cosby; "Big Names at Show Include One Lyndon B. Johnson," by Richard F. Shepard, *New York Times,* May 23, 1964.

he had been profiled for the first time in Ebony: " 'Raceless' Bill Cosby," *Ebony,* May 1964, pp. 131–140.

a national closed-circuit TV concert: "NAACP

Hails TV Spectacular," *Jet,* May 28, 1964, pp. 58–61.

He agreed to an interview for Jet: " 'Not Trying to Hide Fact I'm a Negro': Comic Bill Cosby," by Chester Higgins, *Jet,* Aug. 16, 1964, pp. 62, 63.

It was a hot August day: I Spy, Cushman and LaRosa, pp. 27, 28; Culp commentary on DVD of *I Spy, Season 1;* Culp interview with Abramson, AAT.

10. "Television's Jackie Robinson"

Cosby peered through the cracks: And the Show Goes On, Leonard, pp. 149, 150; *I Spy,* Cushman and LaRosa, p. 33.

Cosby had another idea: Author interview with Cosby.

a "one-third, two-third" guarantee: Culp interview with Abramson, AAT.

Leonard had scouted some stunning locales: I Spy, Cushman and LaRosa, pp. 32–34; "Affair in T'Sien Cha," on DVD of *I Spy: Season 1.*

Leonard had bought a vicuna coat: And the Show Goes On, Leonard, pp. 151, 152.

He arranged to bump into Leonard: Culp commentary on DVD of *I Spy, Season 1;* Culp interview with Abramson, AAT; *I Spy,* Cushman and LaRosa, p. 34.

Cosby was back on the road performing: "People and Places," by Mike Gross, *Bill-*

board, Nov. 14, 1964, p. 10.

Cosby did find Culp's daily phone calls odd at first: I Spy, Cushman and LaRosa, pp. 37, 38.

he was humble about his new career: "Cosby to Appear in TV Spy Series," *New York Times,* Nov. 16, 1964.

I Started Out as a Child, *was getting rave reviews: Billboard,* Oct. 31, 1964, p. 20; Nov. 28, 1964, p. 37; Dec. 12, 1964, p. 6.

Cosby had accepted an engagement at the Shoreham Hotel: Billboard, Dec. 12, p. 28.

Variety *made that impossible:* "Television's Jackie Robinson," by George Rosen, *Variety,* Dec. 23, 1964, p. 19.

Where are the heroes for black kids?: "Bill Cosby Tells Need for Black Heroes," *Jet,* Oct. 19, 1967, pp. 54–58.

Bob Culp was having a less merry Christmas: Culp commentary on DVD of *I Spy: Season 1.*

Earle Hagen, the veteran TV composer: I Spy, Cushman and LaRosa, p. 38.

The next day, Culp went to see Fine: Culp commentary on DVD of *I Spy: Season 1.*

In a seven-page ad in Variety: *Variety,* Feb. 17, 1965, pp. 25–31.

They also granted access to Charles L. Mee Jr.: "That's the Truth — and Other Cosby Stories," Charles L. Mee Jr., *New York Times,* Mar. 14, 1965.

a network publicist handed him a press release: *Brief Encounters: From Einstein to Elvis,* by Tom Mackin, Author House, 2008, p. 283.

11. Mr. Crosley and Mr. Cups

Cosby and Culp went to check out the dressing rooms: Culp commentary on DVD of *I Spy, Season 1.*

They had discovered other things in common: Culp interview with Abramson, AAT.

they were back in Asia in the middle of a heat wave: Culp commentary on DVD of *I Spy, Season 1.*

"divine bullshit": I Spy, Cushman and LaRosa, p. 53.

they were filming a scene on a ferryboat: Culp commentary on DVD of *I Spy, Season 1.*

"My father drank . . .": I Spy, Cushman and LaRosa, p. 66.

how to film men of such different complexions: I Spy, Cushman and LaRosa, p. 46.

just in time to attend the Grammy Awards: "Roger Miller the Smash (Sic!) Winner in Grammy Awards," *Daily Variety,* Apr. 14, 1965, p. 2.

On the album cover, Cosby held a volleyball: Why Is There Air?, by Bill Cosby, Warner Bros. Records, 1965, liner notes by Stan Cornyn.

Cosby was wearing a new sweater: Culp commentary on DVD of *I Spy, Season 1.*

the two men did have one heart-to-heart: Culp commentary on DVD of *I Spy, Season 1;* Culp interview with Abramson, AAT; *I Spy,* Cushman and LaRosa, p. 59.

there had been speculation in the press: "Cosby in 'Spy' Puts NBC Dixie Affils on Spot," *Variety,* Apr. 7, 1965, p. 1; " 'I Spy' with Negro Is Widely Booked," by Val Adams, *New York Times,* Sept. 10, 1965.

Tinker hated the corny plot: Culp commentary and "So Long, Patrick Henry" on DVD of *I Spy, Season 1.*

the mischievous actors couldn't resist ad-libbing a jab: I Spy, Cushman and LaRosa, p. 56.

The Saturday Evening Post *gave the job:* "Bill Cosby: Variety Is the Life of Spies," by Stanley Karnow, *Saturday Evening Post,* Sept. 25, 1965, pp. 86–88.

most singled out Cosby's performance: I Spy, Cushman and LaRosa, pp. 56, 57.

By the third episode of the season: "Carry Me Back to Old Tsing-Tao" on DVD of *I Spy, Season 1; I Spy,* Cushman and LaRosa, p. 51.

An episode entitled "Dragon's Teeth": I Spy, Cushman and LaRosa, p. 66.

Culp's Valentine's gift to Cosby: "The Loser" on DVD of *I Spy, Season 1; I Spy* Cushman and LaRosa, p. 70.

12. A World of "Wonderfulness"

As Cosby was checking in: Culp commentary on DVD of *I Spy, Season 1.*

Baby Erika came, too: I Spy, Cushman and LaRosa, p. 75.

Cosby would remember the trip fondly: "The Case of the Scholarly 'Spy,' " Stang, *New York Times,* Sept. 10, 1965.

Leonard had agreed to let Culp direct the episode: Culp commentary on DVD of *I Spy, Season 1;* Cosby performance at the Ruth Eckerd Hall, Clearwater, Florida, Mar. 27, 2010.

it didn't take long for the same thing to happen to Bob Culp and France Nuyen: Culp commentary on DVD of *I Spy, Season 1; I Spy,* Cushman and LaRosa, pp. 101, 110–220.

four months on prime-time television had propelled his earning power: " 'Spy' Skyrockets Cosby's Nitery Pay," *Daily Variety,* Jan. 20, 1966, p. 1; "Cosby, Getz Hot 32G in Port., Seattle Gigs," *Daily Variety,* Feb. 16, 1966, p. 51.

Sold Bill Cosby short at a few bucks: Cosby interview with Linderman, *Playboy,* 1969.

When he returned to Harrah's: "Nevada Nitery Reviews," *Daily Variety,* Mar. 14, 1966, p. 9; "Just for Variety," by Army Archerd, *Daily Variety,* Apr. 28, 1966, p. 2; *Revenge,* by Bill Cosby, Warner Bros. Records, 1966; *Horror Stars on Radio,* by Ronald L. Smith,

McFarland & Company, 2010, pp. 242–244.

I Spy *finished its first season in strong shape: I Spy,* Cushman and LaRosa, p. 143.

Then came the Emmy nominations: Culp commentary on DVD of *I Spy, Season 1;* "NBC Wins TV Acad Awards Race," *Daily Variety,* May 23, 1966, p. 1; *I Spy,* Cushman and LaRosa, pp. 148–150.

Cosby was switching planes at O'Hare Airport: Miles: The Autobiography, by Miles Davis with Quincy Troupe, Touchstone, 1989, p. 303.

an attorney for the NAACP visited the show's head writer: "Fine, Friedkin Plot 'Spy' Spinoff; 2 SG Series Iffy," by Dave Kaufman, *Daily Variety,* Feb. 22, 1966, p. 12.

Because Leonard had gone almost a half million dollars over his budget: "Just for Variety," by Army Archerd, *Daily Variety,* Jan. 14, 1966, p. 2; "Lori," on DVD of *I Spy, Season 2; I Spy* Cushman and LaRosa, p. 162.

NBC aired another Scotty love story two weeks later: "Trial by Treehouse" on DVD of *I Spy, Season 2; I Spy,* Cushman and LaRosa, p. 169; "Just for Variety," by Army Archerd, *Daily Variety,* Apr. 28, 1966.

Bob Culp, meanwhile, seized the opportunity: Culp commentary on *I Spy, Season 2; I Spy,* Cushman and LaRosa, p. 190.

Leonard hadn't minded their improvising at first: Leonard interview with Denoff, AAT; *I Spy,* Cushman and LaRosa, pp. 186, 187.

he was pleased with the Italian love story: "Tonia" on DVD of *I Spy, Season 2;* "Just for Variety," by Army Archerd, *Daily Variety,* Aug. 26, 1966.

his on-screen love life would not cross the color line: "Color Him Funny," *Newsweek,* Jan. 31, 1966, p. 76.

After watching "Tonia": I Spy, Cushman and LaRosa, p. 218.

13. Bigger Than *I Spy*

When Ebony *magazine asked Bill and Camille Cosby:* "Life with Bill Cosby," *Ebony,* Sept. 1966, pp. 34–42.

the real news in the Cosby family: "Bill Cosby Fast Facts," by CNN Library, cnn.com; "Two Daughters," on *Revenge,* by Bill Cosby, Warner Bros. Records, 1967.

Sheldon Leonard had given him equal billing: I Spy, Cushman and LaRosa, p. 189.

Cosby had received a raise: Author interview with Cosby.

For Anna, the realization that the wayward boy: I Spy, Cushman and LaRosa, p. 256.

he hung out with the head writers for The Dick Van Dyke Show: *Silver Throat: Bill Cosby Sings,* liner notes by Bill Persky and Sam Denoff.

When Cannonball and Nat Adderley: Jet, Sept. 22, 1966, p. 44; Cosby remarks at a reception for the Anthony Quinn Foundation, Aug. 2011.

Cosby also made time for the inner-city school kids: "Just for Variety," by Army Archerd, *Daily Variety,* Jan. 10, 1967, p. 2; author interview with Crockett.

Kelly and Scotty are locked up together in a jail cell: "Sophia" on DVD of *I Spy, Season 2.*

Culp was too wrapped up in his affair with France Nuyen: Culp commentary on DVD of *I Spy, Season 2.*

the women took over all the closet space: I Spy, Cushman and LaRosa, p. 227.

Leonard took Cosby to film an episode of I Spy *in Philadelphia:* "Cops and Robbers" on DVD of *I Spy, Season 2; I Spy,* Cushman and LaRosa, p. 147.

Roy Silver booked Cosby into Harrah's: "Just for Variety," by Army Archerd, *Daily Variety,* Feb. 16, 1967, p. 2; *Daily Variety,* Mar. 15, 1967, p. 63; "Two Daughters" and "Buck, Buck," on *Revenge,* 1967; *Daily Variety,* June 15, 1967, p. 5.

trying to figure out who Fat Albert was: Author interviews with Cosby, Barnes, Matthews, and Baines.

Leonard's original plan: "New Greek Regime Green-lights 'I Spy,' " *Daily Variety,* May 4, 1967, p. 1; *And the Show Goes On,* Leonard, pp. 182–186.

Culp carried a clipboard: Culp commentary
on DVD of *I Spy, Season 3.*

*This time, Cosby found it hard to be happy: I
Spy,* Cushman and LaRosa, p. 267.

Belafonte made a crude joke: "Just for Variety," by Army Archerd, *Daily Variety,* Aug.
17, 1967, p. 2.

*Cosby and Culp went out of their way to cel-
ebrate each other's birthdays:* "Just for Variety," by Army Archerd, *Daily Variety,* July
13, p. 2, and Aug. 17, p. 2.

Leonard was trying to figure out where to take
I Spy *next: And the Show Goes On,* Leon-
ard, pp.193–195; *I Spy,* Cushman and La-
Rosa, pp. 310–313.

*they would phone each other with withering
critiques:* Culp commentary on DVD of *I
Spy, Season 3.*

Leonard was also distracted by a new venture:
I Spy, Cushman and LaRosa, pp. 368–372.

*Cosby and Culp knew none of this in January
1968:* Culp commentary and "Home to
Judgment" on DVD of *I Spy, Season 3.*

Bob Culp would take a break from acting: I Spy,
Cushman and LaRosa, pp. 379–383.

*Sheldon Leonard's career, too, would never be
the same: I Spy,* Cushman and LaRosa, pp.
375–377.

*Cosby and Culp had also revived and rein-
vented the "buddy genre": I Spy,* Cushman
and LaRosa, pp. 188, 189; "Colorblind

Buddies in Black and White," by Jamie Ma-
lanowski, *New York Times,* Nov. 10, 2002.

*But Bill Cosby wasn't looking back: Daily Vari-
ety,* Jan. 9, 1968, p. 2; Jan. 17, 1968, p. 50;
Variety, Feb. 28, 1968, p. 49.

*an electric performance of his longest and most
memorable comic monologue yet:* Liner
notes and "To Russell, My Brother, Whom
I Slept With," on *To Russell, My Brother,
Whom I Slept With,* by Bill Cosby, Warner
Bros. Records, 1968.

yet another idea was germinating: "Life with
Bill Cosby," *Ebony,* p. 40.

14. Black Is Beautiful

Cosby was at the University of Kansas: Liner
notes by Bill Cosby, *Bill Cosby Presents
Badfoot Brown and the Bunions Bradford
Funeral and Marching Band,* UNI Records,
1971; "Cosby Was in Lawrence When King
Was Slain," ljworld.com, Oct. 2, 2004.

*Cosby called his agents and told them to cancel
the five concerts:* "King's Death Affects
Showbiz," *Daily Variety,* Apr. 8, 1968, p. 1.

The next call he got was from Bob Culp: I Spy,
Cushman and LaRosa, p. 380.

*The service was held at the Ebenezer Baptist
Church:* Special issue of *Jet,* "King's
Widow: Bereavement to Battlefield," Apr.
25, 1968.

Cosby and Culp were part of a group that was

driven by bus: Cosby liner notes, *Badfoot Brown; I Spy,* Cushman and LaRosa, p. 381.

When Cosby showed up for the Emmy awards: "CBS, NBC in Emmy Tie: 20 Each," *Daily Variety,* May 20, 1968, p. 1.

By this time, Cosby had made up the concerts: "3 Bill Cosby Gigs Gross $96,100," *Daily Variety,* Apr. 29, 1968, p. 2.

he knew where he wanted to go next: Author interviews with Cosby and his 1968 road manager, Joe Gannon; "Apollo Audience, a Tough Jury, Acquits Cosby," by Vincent Canby, *New York Times,* June 17, 1968; "House Review," *Variety,* June 19, 1968, p. 65.

Cosby traveled to Washington, DC, for June 19: Coverage of June 'Teenth Solidarity Day," *Jet,* July 4, 1968, pp. 6–14.

Cosby would spend much of his time helping Belafonte organize a benefit: Author interviews with Cosby and Gannon; "Benefit Bash for SCLC Grosses $138,900, H'w'd Bowl Record," *Daily Variety,* July 19, 1968, p. 6.

Cosby had hosted an hour-long TV special on black history: Black History: Lost, Stolen or Strayed, CBS, July 2, 1968; "Cosby Promised His Teacher He'd Never Sing 'Old Black Joe' Again," by Joanne Stang, *New York Times,* June 30, 1968.

Roy Silver was driving a hard bargain: "Stay

Tuned: Bill Cosby," by Stan Cornyn, rhino.com.

Taking $2 million of Cosby's money: "I Am Two People, Man," Morgan, *Life,* p. 80; "Bill Cosby's Firm in 5-Pix W7 Deal," *Daily Variety,* Jan. 10, 1968, p. 1.

He had little taste for political activism: "Hollywood Cross-Cuts," by Army Archerd, *Variety,* Jan. 1, 1969, p. 22.

Interviewed about the presidential contest: Cosby interview with Stewart Thompson, WGBH, 1969 on openvault.wgbh.org.

Cosby had given a Newsweek *reporter hours of his time:* "Color-Blind Comic," *Newsweek,* May 20, 1968, p. 92.

He chose Playboy *magazine to do it:* Cosby interview with Linderman, *Playboy,* 1969.

The Second Bill Cosby Special *aired on NBC: The Second Bill Cosby Show,* NBC, Apr. 3, 1969; *Lift Every Voice and Sing: A Celebration of the Negro National Anthem,* edited by Julian Bond and Sondra Kathryn Wilson, Random House, 2001.

15. Bust in Beverly Hills

"Call Roy," Cosby said: Author interview with Jeff Wald.

he was bragging to the press that the company would soon be making $50 million a year: "Code Name for 'Spy' Cosby — $15. Mil," *Variety,* Sept. 25, 1968, p. 50.

Wald's first big assignment: Author interview with Wald; "Stay Tuned: Bill Cosby," Cornyn; Roy Silver obituary on variety .com, Nov. 4, 2003.

They signed the Turtles: Excerpt from *Shell Shocked: My Life with the Turtles,* by Howard Kaylan with Jeff Tamarkin, on rolling stone.com, Feb. 25, 2013.

rumors swirled about the troubles in the film division: Author interview with Wald; "A Tale of Two Films: The Picasso Summer (1969)," by Kimberly Lindbergs, on TCM's "Movie Morlocks" blog, Apr. 12, 2012.

The only time that Jeff Wald caught more than a fleeting glimpse of Cosby: Author interview with Wald.

they learned that twenty-nine staffers had been fired: "Campbell-Silver-Cosby Overstaffed: 29 Fired," *Variety,* Feb. 19, 1969, p. 42.

when Bruce Campbell screened a rough cut of The Picasso Summer: "A Tale of Two Films," Linbergs, 2012.

"Bill and I are building something big here!": Author interview with Ron DeBlasio.

He was also part of William Morris royalty: The Agency: William Morris and the Hidden History of Show Business, by Frank Rose, HarperBusiness, 1995, p. 211.

"Bill, there's been some pilfering going on": Author interview with Cosby.

he had always known that he wasn't as rich as

everyone assumed: "The Pleasures and Problems of Being Bill Cosby," *Ebony,* July 1969, pp. 144–154.

Now he faced the prospect that he could end up broke: Author interviews with Cosby and DeBlasio.

Brokaw phoned the two young managers: Author interview with Wald.

The event was to raise money: "Stars Pay $100 per Plate," by Peter Bailey, *Jet,* May 29, 1969, pp. 24–32.

Two days later, le tout *Hollywood:* "Cosby, Silver, Campbell Split," *Daily Variety,* May 13, 1969, p. 1.

Silver's grandiose bid to become a Hollywood mogul imploded: "Filmways May Take Over Debt-Ridden Campbell-Silver," *Daily Variety,* Dec. 5, 1969, p. 25.

Cosby walked away from the crash of Roy Silver's production company: Author interviews with Cosby, Wald, and Council; "Cosby Makes Millions Teaching Manners and Moral Lessons on TV," by Ronald E. Kisner, *Jet,* May 11, 1978, p. 61.

he was granted the wish he had been making for six years: "The Pleasures and Problems of Being Bill Cosby," *Ebony,* July 1969.

16. More Situation Than Comedy

Quincy Jones was in the booth: Jones interview with John Burlingame for the Archive of

American Television, Nov. 13, 2002.

NBC executives were counting on Bill Cosby's debut: "Spurning Debbie, P&G Eyes Cosby for Its Sun. Slot," *Variety,* Feb. 5, 1969, p. 39; "Light and Airy," by Jack Hellman, *Daily Variety,* May 12, 1969, p. 10.

For the June "press tour": Author interview with Herb Schlosser.

Cosby had agreed to a fairly conventional premise: "Just for Variety," by Army Archerd, *Daily Variety,* July 16, 1968, p. 2; "Hollywood Cross-Cuts," Archerd, *Variety,* Jan. 1, 1969.

Cosby concluded that the detective angle was "a bunch of crap": Brief Encounters, Mackin, pp. 284–286.

Cosby had tightened his inner circle: Cosby interview on *The Bill Cosby Show, Season One,* DVD, Shout Factory, 2006.

all the people their show would confound: Brief Encounters, Mackin, p. 286; "Light and Airy," Hellman, *Daily Variety,* May 12, 1969, p. 10.

Cosby's goal was to show that a black man doesn't always have to be angry: Herb Schlosser interview with Bill Cosby at the Museum of the Moving Image, Feb. 15, 2011.

For the pilot episode: "The Fatal Phone Call," "The Gumball Incident," and "Rules Is

Rules," on *The Bill Cosby Show, Season One.*

When it came to casting: Brief Encounters, Mackin, pp. 284, 285.

Cosby took special pleasure in showcasing black guest stars: Cosby interview, "Lover's Quarrel" and "A Christmas Ballad," on *The Bill Cosby Show, Season One.*

some memorable white guest stars as well: Cosby interview and "The Elevator Doesn't Stop Here," on *The Bill Cosby Show, Season One.*

a training ground for blacks in Hollywood: Brief Encounters, Mackin, p. 284.

he ran afoul of the Hollywood trade unions: Schlosser interview with Cosby, MOTMI.

An even bigger fight was over the laugh track: "Charles Douglass, 93; Gave TV Its Laugh Track," by Adam Bernstein, *Washington Post,* Apr. 24, 2003; Cosby interview on *The Bill Cosby Show, Season One.*

Critics didn't quite know what to make of the show: "Another Year in the Life of a Juvenile Delinquent," by Jack Gould, Sept. 28, 1969; "Television Reviews," *Daily Variety,* Sept. 15, 1969, p. 11; "Television Reviews," *Variety,* Sept. 17, 1969, p. 34.

Black Power advocates criticized Cosby: "Can 'Just for Laughs' Be Real for Blacks?," by Faith Berry, *New York Times,* Dec. 7, 1969; "Bill Cosby Is Not Malcolm X, He's Bill

Cosby," by A. S. "Doc" Young, *New York Times,* Dec. 21, 1969.

Come Emmy season: "NBC's 80.Contenders Top Emmy Field," *Variety,* May 6, 1970, p. 64.

A sign of the feuding came in June: "Light and Airy," by Jack Hellman, *Daily Variety,* June 22, 1970, p. 10.

Looking back, Cosby would maintain: Cosby interview on *The Bill Cosby Show, Season One.*

Whatever qualms NBC might have had: Cosby interview with Schlosser, MOTMI.

Yet when NBC executives looked back: Author interview with Schlosser.

17. Fat Albert's New Home

Ever since the Roaring Twenties: "Driving the Mohawk Trail in Massachusetts," by Mark Vanhoenacker, *New York Times,* Oct. 4, 2012.

Bill and Camille Cosby found their dream house: "Comedian-Actor Bill Cosby Buys $65,000 Home, Land," *Jet,* Sept. 16, 1971, p. 15.

The story of how Bill Cosby made that improbable move: Author interview with Dwight Allen.

Like Temple University, he could sense that it was a "step school": Cosby interview with Doug Most, "Bill Cosby, in His Own Words," *Boston Globe,* Apr. 20, 2013.

Camille was instantly supportive of the idea: Bill Cosby: In Words and Pictures, by Robert E. Johnson, Johnson Publishing Company, 1986, pp. 898–104; "Oprah Talks to Camille Cosby" in *O: The Oprah Magazine,* May/June 2000.

Cosby had always thought of himself as "East Coast": Cosby interview with Feinberg, *The Jack Feinberg Show.*

he told friends and reporters that he planned to move to Massachusetts: "Just for Variety," by Army Archerd, *Daily Variety,* Sept. 22, 1970, p. 2.

"All I want is a parking space": Author interview with Allen.

"a remake of Here Comes Mr. Jordan: "Not Just Passing, WB Bets," *Variety,* Nov. 5, 1969, p. 7.

another longtime dream: to make a family Western with a black hero: "Man and Boy: New Cosby Film Depicts Black Family's Struggle in West After Civil War," by Louie Robinson, *Ebony,* Apr. 1971, pp. 42–54.

In a lukewarm review: Review of *Man and Boy,* by Roger Ebert, rogerebert.com, Dec. 23, 1971.

Van Peebles was determined to shoot an underground movie: Sweet Sweetback's Baadasssss Song: A Guerrilla Filmmaking Manifesto, by Melvin Van Peebles, Thunder's Mouth Press, 2004.

CBS was after him: "1972. CBS Series for Bill Cosby," *Daily Variety,* May 20, 1971, p. 1.

Sesame Street had just launched: Author interview with Joan Ganz Cooney; Cooney essay and "Then and Now" interviews included in *The Best of The Electric Company,* DVD, Shout Factory, 2006.

charmed by Cosby but astonished at his relaxed attitude: Author interview with Cooney; "Rita Moreno Remembers Outtakes," on *The Best of The Electric Company.*

the most successful program for school-aged children: Walter J. Podrazik essay included on *The Best of the Electric Company.*

He was starting to talk with Dwight Allen: Author interview with Allen.

It wasn't the first time the idea of a Fat Albert show had come up: Author interview with Ken Mundie; "Television Reviews," *Variety,* Nov. 19, 1969, p. 38.

When Cosby met with Lou Scheimer: Scheimer interview with David McLees included in *Fat Albert's Greatest Hits* DVD, Urban-Works, 2004; *Fat Albert and the Cosby Kids,* by L. Wayne Hicks, tvparty.com.

First were the characters: Cosby interview with Dave Itzkoff, "Hey, Hey, Hey, Bill Cosby on 'Fat Albert,' Yesterday and Today," *New York Times,* June 12, 2013.

Cosby based Mushmouth on a boy: Scheimer

interview with McLees.

Hoping for a big hit: "Schlatter Producing 'Cosby,'" *Variety,* Mar. 8, 1972, p. 32.

Groucho Marx made what would be his last appearance on TV: The New Bill Cosby Show, 1973, available on YouTube.

cemented a new friendship: "Just for Variety," by Army Archerd, *Daily Variety,* May 2, 1974, p. 2; *Hello, I Must Be Going: Groucho and His Friends,* Introduction by Bill Cosby, Doubleday & Company, 1992.

When Russell Cosby heard about the time slot: Author interview with Bill Cosby.

Meanwhile, Fat Albert and the Cosby Kids: *TV Guide,* Apr. 17–23, 1993, p. 75; Scheimer interview with McLees, UrbanWorks.

Cosby would also visit Filmation headquarters: Cosby interview with Itzkoff, *New York Times.*

18. Playboy of the West

In the 1970s, the largest hotel in Las Vegas: "The Las Vegas Hilton: Looking Back," on Two Way Hard Three: A Las Vegas Casino & Design Blog, ratevegas.com.

As he was playing tennis on the Hilton deck: Author interview with Lamb Heath; "The Story of Black Watch, or Bill Cosby Goes to the Dogs," by Jean Heath, *The Great Dane Reporter,* 1976.

One was his East Coast existence: Variety,

Aug. 15, 1973, p. 30, and June 25, 1975, p. 77.

a new inspiration, the poet Carl Sandburg: Author interview with Cosby: "Laughing Corn," by Carl Sandburg; "Carl Sandburg's Biography" on carl-sandburg.com.

he could feed his voracious appetite for tennis: Bill Cosby: In Words and Pictures, Johnson, pp. 92–97; *Daily Variety,* Feb. 25, 1975, p. 2; May 19, 1975, p. 2; *Variety,* Sept. 15, 1976, p. 93.

a second playground in Las Vegas: " 'Gimme' People at Vegas Hotel Peeve Bill Cosby, Blasts Album Moochers," *Variety,* Oct. 1, 1969, p. 1; "International, Las Vegas Hilton," on lvstriphistory.com; reviews of Cosby shows at the Las Vegas Hilton in *Daily Variety,* Dec. 28, 1973, p. 12; May 28, 1975, p. 22; July 23, 1976, p. 12; Nov. 4, 1976, p. 13; Feb. 25, 1977, p. 20; and in *Variety,* Aug. 15, 1974, p. 14; Sept. 11, 1974, p. 73; Apr. 28, 1976, p. 69.

On one of those nights, Shelly Schultz: Author interview with Schultz.

tame attempts to capture the licentious zeitgeist: "Mile-High Notes from Reno-Tahoe," by Forest Church, *Daily Variety,* Jan. 21, 1974; *Bill Cosby Is Not Himself These Days,* Capitol/EMI Records, 1976.

an unexpected professional opportunity: "Presley Pullout Puts Hilton, L.V., in Booking Bind," *Variety,* Aug. 27, 1975, p. 49.

Two years earlier, Cosby had spotted a tall, striking, twenty-year-old brunette: Cosby interview with Dan Rather, *CBS News*, Jan. 26, 1997 (unaired); " '70s Affair Haunts Star at Tragic Time," by K. C. Baker and Linda Yglesias, *New York Daily News,* Feb. 2, 1977; "Cosby Says He Bought Silence After Affair," CNN.com, July 15, 1997.

It was only ten minutes into the screening: This Life, by Sidney Poitier, Coronet Books, 1980, pp. 394–404.

a revolutionary new financial arrangement: "Looking at First Artists," on the Barbra-timeless blog, May 2008.

he wanted to involve more black talent: Sidney Poitier: Man, Actor, Icon, by Aram Goudsouzian, University of North Carolina Press, 2004, pp. 345–347.

Cosby liked Wesley's script: "Uptown Saturday Night: Hilarious New Black Movie," by Clarence Brown, *Jet,* July 25, 1974, pp. 58–61; *Jet,* Jan. 31, 1974; *Uptown Saturday Night,* Warner Home Video, 2004.

an important reunion for him and Cosby: Author interview with Ron DeBlasio; "The Official Biography of Richard Pryor," richard pryor.com.

he told the inmates that the comedian he would most like to see: Cosby remarks at Graterford Prison on *Hardheaded Boys,* Nicetown Records.

After he reemerged on the national scene: Author interview with Ron DeBlasio.

Cosby and Pryor would appear together in another movie: California Suite DVD, Image Entertainment, 2010; "The Current Cinema," by Pauline Kael, Jan. 8, 1979, pp. 49–51; Cosby letter in *Daily Variety,* Jan. 10, 1979, p. 56.

Cosby had also seen yet another TV show fail: Cos entry on TV.com; "On All Channels," by Dave Kaufman, *Daily Variety,* Dec. 7, 1976, p. 8, and Dec. 1, 1977, p. 12.

So instead he went to the Playboy Mansion: "Just for Variety," by Army Archerd, Sept. 30, 1976, p. 2; "The Case of Bill Cosby vs. Tommy Smothers," WFMU's Beware of the Blog, wfmu.org, 2006.

Cosby did have something to feel proud of that fall: "An Integration of the Visual Media Via 'Fat Albert and the Cosby Kids' into the Elementary School Curriculum as a Teaching Aid and Vehicle to Achieve Increased Learning," by William Henry Cosby Jr., University of Massachusetts, 1976; *Jet,* Feb. 24, 1977, p. 14.

19. The Art of Jell-O

On a sunny May morning: "That Doctorate After Bill Cosby's Name Is No Honorary Freebie," by Gail Jennes, *People,* June 6, 1977; Cosby interview with Most, *Boston*

Globe; author interview with Dwight Allen.

he appeared on another Ebony *cover:* Cover photo and "Dr. Bill Cosby: He's a Comedian, Actor, Philosopher, Author, Educator and Family Man," by Louie Robinson, *Ebony,* June 1977, pp. 130–136.

"Madison Avenue is afraid of the dark": "The Nat "King" Cole Show: From the Small Screen to Your Computer Screen, Finally," by Karen Grisby Bates, The Record, npr.org, Feb. 15, 2011.

As a cigar lover, he had noticed the White Owl ads: "Bill Cosby Looks Back on His Life in Commercials," by Rance Crain, *Advertising Age,* Mar. 28, 2011; Bill Cosby White Owl commercial on YouTube.

the product that Cosby had always dreamed of selling: Author interview with Grace Leong; Cosby interview with Doug Miles and Don Henderson, WSLR Radio, Jan. 9, 2011; "Bill Cosby Looks Back on His Life in Commercials," Crain, *Advertising Age.*

his reputation for clashing with the people who made advertising: Author interviews with Grace Leong and Phylicia Rashad; Cosby interview with Miles and Henderson, WSLR; "Bill Cosby Looks Back on His Life in Commercials," Crain, *Advertising Age.*

no one could argue with Cosby's results: "A Poet in the Supermarket," by Dana Gioia, *New York Times,* Oct. 28, 2007; *For God,*

Country & Coca-Cola, by Mark Pendergrast, Basic Books, 2013, p. 321; author interview with Clare Bisceglia.

Cosby was also playing a behind-the-scenes role: "Commercial Success: Celebrities Such as Bill Cosby and Gladys Knight Are Selling Their Image to Pitch National Brands," by Stephen Gayle, *Black Enterprise,* Dec. 1981, pp. 51–56.

Cosby's career as a pitchman had changed the manner in which he lived: Author interview with David Brokaw.

"David Driskell? This is Bill Cosby": Author interview with David Driskell.

The Cosbys had begun acquiring art in the late sixties: Introduction, by Camille O. Cosby in *The Other Side of Color: African American Art in the Collection of Camille O. and William H. Cosby Jr.,* by David C. Driskell, Pomegranate Communications, 2001.

For three days: Author interview with Driskell; Introduction by William H. Cosby Jr., in *The Other Side of Color,* Driskell.

Cosby was now focused on what his own five children were learning: Author interview with Cosby; "Bill Cosby Tells Why He Is Tough on His Children," *Jet,* May 30, 1983, pp. 60–63; *Bill Cosby: In Words and Pictures,* Johnson, pp. 116–131; Cosby interview with Rather, CBS News.

Cosby was coming to grips with the frustrations

of being a middle-aged man: "Bill Cosby Talks About: Middle Age and Other Aggravations," by Bill Cosby, *Ebony,* Dec. 1980, pp. 116–124.

Cosby didn't tell Ebony *readers:* Cosby interview with Rather, CBS News.

new opportunities to indulge his love of jazz: Author interviews with George Wein and Sonny Rollins; Davis with Troupe, *Miles: The Autobiography,* p. 348; *Miles Davis: The Complete Illustrated History,* p. 61.

he decided to make a concert film: Bill Cosby: Himself DVD, Fox Home, 2004; *Variety,* Apr. 15, 1983, p. 19; *Daily Variety,* May 25, 1983, p. 2.

a new generation of aspiring stand-up comedians rediscovered Cosby: "The 30th Anniversary of *Bill Cosby: Himself* — an All-Star Salute," by Nathaniel Penn, GQ.com, May 2013.

trying to help Sammy Davis Jr. make a comeback: Author interview with David Brokaw; Cosby remarks at Graterford Prison on *Hardheaded Boys; Sammy: An Autobiography,* by Sammy Davis Jr. and Jane and Burt Boyar, Farrar, Straus and Giroux, 2000, pp. 499, 500; " '2.Friends' 214G So Far," *Variety,* Nov. 9, 1983, p. 76.

20. "Meet Your New Family"

Marcy Carsey and Tom Werner were desperate: Author interviews with Marcy Carsey and Tom Werner: Carsey and Werner interview with Karen Herman for the Archive of American Television, Mar. 10, 2003; Larry Auerbach interview with Dan Pasternack for the Archive of American Television, May 21, 2003.

"You will not be a chauffeur!": Cosby interview with Linderman, *Playboy,* 1985.

Now Carsey and Werner had to figure out how to make the numbers work: Auerbach interview with Pasternack, AAT; *The Cosby Show: Audience, Impact, and Implications,* by Linda K. Fuller, Greenwood Press, 1992, pp. 46–55.

a network prepared to add a new situation comedy to its roster: Author interviews with Carsey and Werner; Carsey and Werner interviews with Herman, AAT.

"Please God, help me be quiet": Author interview with Phylicia Rashad; Rashad interview with John Colucci for the Archive of American Television, Oct. 22, 2007.

the month leading up to that moment had been a mad scramble: Author interviews with Carsey, Werner, and Jay Sandrich; Cosby interview for *The Cosby Show: 25th Anniversary Commemorative Edition* DVD set, First Look Studios, 2008; Cosby interview with Linderman, *Playboy,* 1985.

As Tom Werner was reviewing casting tapes: Author interviews with Werner and Sandrich; "A Look Back" on *The Cosby Show* DVD set; "Keshia Knight Pulliam: Coping with Success at 7," by Marilyn Marshall, *Ebony,* Dec. 1986, pp. 27–34.

For the Huxtable boy: Cosby interview on *The Cosby Show* DVD set; Malcolm-Jamal Warner remarks at the Mark Twain Prize for American Humor ceremony broadcast on PBS, Nov. 4, 2009.

"May the Lord watch over thee and me": Rashad interview with Colucci, AAT.

one day of rehearsal before taping the presentation: Author interviews with Carsey, Werner, and Sandrich; Cosby interview and "Pilot," on *The Cosby Show* DVD set.

21. The Serfs of Flatbush

It was Earl Pomerantz's first call to Bill Cosby: "Story of a Writer — Part Fifteen B," by Earl Pomerantz, Just Thinking . . . blog, June 19, 2008.

The Vitagraph studio was almost a century old: Author interviews with Sandrich and Werner; "Story of a Writer — Part Fifteen D, by Earl Pomerantz, Just Thinking . . . blog, June 23, 2008; "MOMA Celebrates Vitagraph Studios," by Francis Morrone, *New York Sun,* Nov. 10, 2006.

the arcane rules of New York City's craft unions: Garvin Eddy interview with Stephen Abramson for the Archive for American Television, May 21, 2010.

another step to ensure the realism of the show: Author interview with Alvin Poussaint.

Cosby resumed his hazing of Earl Pomerantz: "Story of a Writer — Part Fifteen C," by Earl Pomerantz, Just Thinking . . . blog, June 20, 2008; author interview with Tom Werner.

"Either we peel them off": Author interview with Marcy Carsey.

They set their sights on Elliot Schoenman: "Paying It Forward: The Cosby Show Changed the Way We Saw and Wrote Television," by Neely Swanson, Written By (journal of the Writers Guild of America), Summer 2012, pp. 20–27.

"NBC never stopped being nervous": Author interviews with Carsey, Werner, and Sandrich.

"I'm not lonely!": Author interview with Rashad.

virtually everyone in the TV world considered that a stretch: "Being First Is Often Fatal for New Series," by David Bianculli, *Philadelphia Inquirer,* Aug. 30, 1984; "It's Humor vs. The Hunk as Cosby, Selleck Clash," by Mike Boone, *The Gazette,* Sept. 26, 1984; " 'The Cosby Show' Off to a Good Start on NBC," by Fred Rothenberg, AP, Sept.

24, 1984; "Cosby Triumphs in TV Ratings," *Tri-City Herald,* Sept. 26, 1984.

they never expected it to do so well so quickly: Author interviews with Carsey and Werner.

22. The Master at Work

Jay Sandrich didn't know what else to do: Author interview with Sandrich; "The Slumber Party," on *The Cosby Show* DVD set.

indisputably the hottest new program of the 1984–1985 TV season: "Year of the Sitcom for the TV Nets," by Bob Knight, *Variety,* Dec. 4, 1985 p. 1; " 'Cagney & Lacey,' Cosby Show Capture Top Emmys," by Lee Margulies, *Los Angeles Times,* Sept. 23, 1985; "The Cosby Show," Fuller, pp. 36–44.

Cosby wanted to see the same characteristic in Clair: Phylicia Rashad remarks on the Mark Twain Prize broadcast, PBS, Nov. 4, 2009.

it didn't feel right to him with just four children: Cosby interview on *The Cosby Show* DVD set; Cosby interview with Linderman, *Playboy,* 1985; author interview with Sandrich.

Cosby was treating his TV children almost as if they were his own: Author interview with Rashad; *The Cosby Show Scrapbook,* Sharon Publications, 1986.

he would sometimes slip: Author interview with Carsey.

"Apples aren't funny": Author interview with Jack Gelbart.

a DustBuster on the living room set: "Looking Back," on *The Cosby Show* DVD.

a crazy-quilt wool and leather sweater: Koos Van Den Akker interview with Vice.com, "Koos and the Cosby Sweaters," Mar. 25, 2009.

a show about kids keeping secrets from their parents: Author interview with Sandrich; "Denise's Friend," on *The Cosby Show* DVD set.

the core message that Cosby wanted to drive home about healthy families: "TV's Top Mom & Dad," by Robert E. Johnson, *Ebony,* Feb. 1986, p. 30.

ideas for what could be funny: Author interviews with Carsey, Sandrich, and Gelbart; Cosby interview and "The Juicer," "Jitterbug Break," "Mr. Sandman," "Full House," "Cliff's Wet Adventure," and "Happy Anniversary," on *The Cosby Show* DVD set.

one of the hundred greatest TV shows of all time: TV Guide, June 28–July 4, 1997; *Saturday Night Live,* NBC, Feb. 18, 2012.

23. "It's Not an Invention"

Phylicia Rashad was doing a round of press interviews: Author interviews with Rashad; Rashad interview with Colucci, AAT; *Black*

Bourgeoisie, E. Franklin Frazier, Free Press, 1965; "The Negro Family: The Case for National Action," US Department of Labor, Mar. 1965.

the criticism that "the Huxtables aren't real": Author interviews with Cosby, Poussaint, and Susan Fales-Hill; *Darkest America: Black Minstrelsy from Slavery to Hip-Hop,* by Yuval Taylor and Jake Austen, W. W. Norton and Company, 2012; "TV's Black World Turns — But Stays Unreal," by Henry Louis Gates Jr., *New York Times,* Nov. 12, 1989; *Bill Cosby: In Words and Pictures,* Johnson Publishing Co., Inc., p. 164.

First was his beloved jazz music: Author interviews with Sandrich, Gelbart, and Rashad; "Play It Again, Vanessa," "Cliff's Birthday," "Play It Again, Russell," "The Younger Woman," "A Touch of Wonder," "Grampy and Nu-Nu Visit the Huxtables," and opening credit sequences, seasons 1–8, on the *The Cosby Show* DVD set.

Cosby also showcased other forms of black music: "Not Everybody Loves the Blues" and "A Touch of Wonder," on *The Cosby Show* DVD set; Questlove interview with John Oliver, *The Daily Show,* Comedy Central, June 25, 2013.

Cosby used the show to celebrate African American painters: Author interview with Driskell; "The Auction," on *The Cosby*

Show DVD; "Cos and Affection for a Black Artist," by Jacqueline Trescott, *Washington Post,* Nov. 30, 1997.

Cosby injected politics into The Cosby Show *as well:* Author interviews with Poussaint and Fales-Hill; "Cosby's Fast Track," by Harry F. Waters, *Newsweek,* Sept. 2, 1985, pp. 50–56; "Vanessa's Bad Grade," "The March," "The Birth (Part 2)," "Olivia Comes Out of the Closet," and "The Storyteller," on *The Cosby Show* DVD set.

Cosby pushed to hire blacks behind the camera: Author interviews with Fales-Hill and Holly Robinson Peete; "Paying It Forward," Swanson, Written By (journal of the Writers Guild of America), p. 26; "Mother, May I?," on *The Cosby Show* DVD set.

Cosby loved Temple University: Author interviews with Cosby and Fales-Hill; "Historically Black Colleges and Universities, 1976–2001," by Stephen Provasnik and Linda F. Shafer, National Center for Education Statistics, 2004; "Breaking with Tradition," "The Card Game," and "Shakespeare," on *The Cosby Show* DVD set.

a spin-off show based on life at Hillman College: Author interviews with Fales-Hill, Rashad, and Joanne Curley Kerner; "Hillman," on *The Cosby Show* DVD set.

the abrupt departure of Lisa Bonet: Author interviews with Fales-Hill and Curley Kerner; "Lisa Bonet: The Growing Pains of a Rising Star," by Lynn Norment, *Ebony,* Dec. 1987, pp. 150–156; "Different Touch to 'A Different World,' " by Diane Haithman, *Los Angeles Times,* Oct. 6, 1988; "Nielsen to Scope Blacks," *Black Enterprise,* Oct. 1990, p. 18.

24. "A Vein of Gold"

Johnetta Cole was about to meet with the senior staff: Johnetta Cole interview with Camille Cosby at the Benjamin Franklin Creativity Laureate Award ceremony at the Smithsonian Institution, Washington, DC, Apr. 8, 2011.

Twenty million dollars was almost half the size: "A Black College Gets a Gift of $20 Million," by Lee A. Daniels, *New York Times,* Nov. 8, 1988; Author interview with Poussaint.

that vein had turned into a gold mine: "Of the Show Biz Rich, Bill Cosby is Top Star," by Al Delugach, *Los Angeles Times,* Sept. 7, 1987.

the most lucrative syndication deal in television history: The Cosby Show, Fuller, pp. 46–55, " 'Cosby Show' Syndication: 'Arrogant' Hardball," by James Warren, *Chicago Tribune,* May 4, 1988; " 'Cosby' Gives New Meaning to a Deal," by Kenneth R. Clark, *Chicago Tribune,* May 9, 1988; "The Owners of 'The Cosby Show' sued Viacom," *Los*

*Angeles Time*s, Mar. 13, 1987; Auerbach interview with Pasternack, AAT.

In addition to the donation to Spelman: "Bill Cosby Makes College Donations," *Rome News-Tribune,* Dec. 19, 1988, p. 14.

giving away his money in spontaneous and anonymous ways: Author interviews with Cosby, Rashad, Gelbart, and Bershad; "Cosby's Fast Track," by Waters, *Newsweek;* "Mom and Dad Huxtable Do Vegas," by Dennis McDougal, *Los Angeles Time*s, Mar. 4, 1990.

Cosby's most extravagant gestures: "Bill Cosby's 'I Love My Wife' Party," *Jet,* Sept. 1, 1986, pp. 52–55; Rashad interview with Colucci, AAT; "Competency Trial Set for Former Cosby Aide," by Dennis McDougal, *Los Angeles Time*s, Mar. 14, 1990.

coworkers would catch him in a melancholy mood: Author interview with Sandrich; "The World According to THE COS," by Lawrence Christon, *Los Angeles Time*s, Dec. 10, 1989.

a bitter dispute with one of his oldest friends: Author interviews with sources close to Cosby.

the declining health of his mother: Author interview with Lamb Heath: "Bill Cosby Tells How Wife Saved His Mother's Life," *Jet,* Oct. 19, 1987, pp. 14–16.

another drama all the more vexing: "Illegitimate Claim?," by Tom Gliatto, *People,* July 28, 1997.

An even bigger drama was unfolding around Cosby's daughter Erinn: Author interview with Allison Samuels; Cosby interview with Linderman, *Playboy,* 1985; "Cosby Daughter: Tyson Assaulted Her," Associated Press, May 8, 1992; "The World According to THE COS," Christon, *Los Angeles Times*; "Bill Cosby's Tough Love," by William Raspberry, *Washington Post,* Dec. 13, 1989: "Cosby's Comments," *Los Angeles Times,* Dec. 24, 1989.

25. Ennis and Theo

Ennis Cosby was attending a low-key Quaker boarding school: Author interview with Bill Cosby and travel to George School; review and video of May 1984 musical revue, *Among Friends,* georgeschool.org; Cosby interview with Linderman, *Playboy,* 1985; "Good-bye, Friend," by Peter Castro, *People,* Feb. 3, 1997.

When it came time for Ennis to apply to college: Author interview with Cosby; "Young Cosby Wanted to Give Back," by Ennis William Cosby, *Philadelphia Inquirer,* Jan. 29, 1997; "Good-bye, Friend," Castro, *People.*

Cosby was thrilled about Ennis's breakthrough: "Theo's Gift," "Theo's Final Final," "Theo and the Kids (Part 1)," "Theo and the Kids

(Part 2)," "Theo's Future," "And So, We Commence (Part 1)," and "And So, We Commence (Part 2)," on *The Cosby Show* DVD set.

The premise had run its course: Author interviews with Cosby, Carsey and Jeff Jarvis; "KNBC Interrupts LA Riot Coverage for Finale of the Cosby Show," on "LA Riots Anniversary: 8 Infamous Videos," by Brittany Jones-Cooper, *The Daily Beast,* Apr. 26, 2012; "Critic's Notebook; Waging a Ratings War, 'Cosby' vs. 'Simpsons,' " by John J. O'Connor, *New York Times,* Nov. 27, 1990; "It's Cosby's Brood vs. the Radical Dude," by Tim Appelo, *Entertainment Weekly,* Aug. 31, 1990; "Seinfeld Ten Years Later," by Stephen Winzenburg, *Television Quarterly,* Spring/Summer 2008, pp. 57–61.

By the 1990s, a more obvious impact was already evident: Author interviews with Carsey and Werner; "Paying It Forward," Swanson, Written By (journal of the Writers Guild of America); "New Direction Charted for NBC," by Bill Carter, *New York Times,* July 19, 1989; Author interview with Schlosser.

scholars were examining that social impact: Author interviews with Cosby and Rashad; *Enlightened Racism: The Cosby Show, Audiences, and the Myth of the American Dream,* by Sut Jhally and Justin M. Lewis, Westview Press, 1992; " 'The Biggest Show in The World': Race and the Global Popularity of *The Cosby Show,*" by Timothy Havens, *Media, Culture & Society,* SAGE Publications, vol. 22: 371–391.

it led US network executives to rethink their assumptions: "The Demise of the Black Sitcom," starpulse.com, Aug. 13, 2008.

one was determined not to show any gratitude: Eddy Murphy Raw, Paramount Pictures, 1987; Cosby interview with Ryan Cormier, "Still a Stand-up Guy," *Wilmington Delaware News Journal,* July 20, 2007; author interview with DeBlasio.

reminders that not everything he did turned to gold: Author interview with Bisceglia; "Through Slick and Thin Paul Weiland, Ad-man Turned Hollywood Film-Maker, Talks About Stars, Egos and His Latest Movie, *City Slickers II,*" Simon Hattenstone, *The Guardian,* Sept. 22, 1994; "He Rode into Hollywood on a Chariot of Fire, but David Puttnam's Job at Columbia Went Up in Smoke," by Margo Dougherty, *People,* Nov. 16, 1987; "The Best-Seller Blues: Hard Lessons from a Cosby Book," by Gayle Feldman, *New York Times,* June 10, 1990.

A Different World was left to fend for itself: Author interview with Fales-Hill; "A 'Different' Take on the LA Riots," by Greg

Braxton, *Los Angeles Times*, Aug. 13, 1992.

26. A Gift Marked Tiffany

On the day that Cosby's mother died: Author interview with Rashad; Cosby interview with Rather, CBS News.

Alvin Poussaint had seen clues: Author interview with Poussaint; "Kennedy Center Honors Bill Cosby," by Ann Oldenburg, *USA Today,* Dec. 1998.

he didn't like what he saw: "Life After the Cosby Show," by Laura B. Randolph, *Ebony,* May 1994, pp. 100–104; "Newest TV Hall of Famers Take Bow at Disney," by Catherine Hinton, *Orlando Sentinel,* Oct. 4, 1992; "Cosby Condemns 'Massacre' of Black Images Depicted by 'Drive-By' White Writers," *Jet,* Oct. 26, 1992, pp. 58–60.

Cosby wanted to buy the entire network: "The Media Business: Bill Cosby Trying to Buy NBC from G.E.," by Bill Carter, *New York Times,* Oct. 29, 1992; "Does Cosby Have Ingredients for NBC Purchase?," by Alan Citron and John Lippman, *Los Angeles Times,* June 15, 1993; "Bill Cosby: The Man Who Would be King?," by Lisa Bernhard, *Total TV,* Jan. 1994.

a remake of the old Groucho Marx game show: Author interview with Johnathan Rodgers; "Star Power Powers Syndies," by Ray Bennett, *Daily Variety,* Sept. 11, 1992; "All

Bets Are Off: Cosby's Syndie 'Life' Looks Weak," by Jim Benson, *Daily Variety,* Oct. 1, 1992; "The Doctor Is Out," by Greg Braxton, *Los Angeles Time*s, Sept. 15, 1996.

Cosby's next attempt at a TV comeback was an hour-long drama: Author interview with Cosby; "Life After the Cosby Show," Randolph, *Ebony,* 1994; "Camouflage," episode 10 of *The Cosby Mysteries,* on YouTube; "Guess Who's Coming to Criticize Dinner," episode of *The Simpsons; Saturday Night Live,* Feb. 5, 1994.

On the surface, Les Moonves and Sam Haskell: Promises I Made My Mother, by Sam Haskell, Ballantine Books, 2009, pp. 89–93; Leslie Moonves interview with Dan Pasternack for the Archive of American Television, Dec. 19–20, 2006.

Moonves wanted Cosby so badly: "CBS Has Cos to Celebrate," by Brian Lowry, *Daily Variety,* Dec. 4, 1985, p. 4.

he had decided that it had two major problems: Author interviews with Curley Kerner and Rashad: "Just Cos: CBS Dumps Producer," by Brian Lowry, *Daily Variety,* Apr. 8, 1996, p. 1; "Crotchety Cosby?," *The Gazette,* Apr. 11, 1996, p. D1; "Cosby Show: Rashad in, Hopkins Out," by Joe Flint, *Daily Variety,* Apr. 22, 1986, p. 5; "Cast Changes on 'Cosby' Render Pilot Obsolete," by Marilyn Beck and Stacy Jenel Smith, *Los Angeles*

Daily News, Aug. 27, 1996.

America was eager to sample Bill Cosby in a new comedy: "Cosby: Bull's Eye," by Joe Flint, *Daily Variety,* Sept. 18, 1996, p. 1; "Dad's So Grumpy Now: The Cosby Persona Goes into a New Phase of Life," by John J. O'Connor, *New York Times,* Sept. 16, 1996; "Old Cos, New Cos: Both Good," by David Zurawick, *Baltimore Sun,* Sept. 16, 1996.

Cosby was genuinely surprised — and wary: "Just for Variety," by Army Archerd, *Daily Variety,* Sept. 19, 1996, p. 2; "Networks' Attention Turns to Redemption," by Stuart Miller, *Variety,* Nov. 4–10, 1996, p. 30.

Camille had emerged as a public figure: "Oprah Talks to Camille Cosby," *O,* 2000; "Just for Variety," Archerd, *Daily Variety,* Sept. 19, 1996.

The future looked particularly bright for Ennis Cosby: Cosby interview with Rather, CBS News; "Young Cosby Wanted to Give Back," Ennis Cosby, *Philadelphia Inquirer;* "Ennis Cosby Is Recalled as Devoted to Teaching," by John T. McQuiston, *New York Times,* Jan. 17, 1997; "Cosby Son Remembered for His Modest Style," by Charisse Jones, *New York Times,* Jan. 18, 1997.

he had already helped turn around the life of one grateful student: "A Well-Known Name Overcomes a Label," by Lena Williams, *New*

York Times, Aug. 4, 1996; "Dad Learns to Read: How Russell Cosby Overcame Dyslexia," by Susan Friedman, Family Education Network, 1998; "Russell Cosby Earns College Degree as Promise to Slain Nephew Ennis," *Jet,* Nov. 10, 1997, p. 23.

now everyone in the family could laugh about it: Cosby interview with Rather, CBS News; "1997," peopleschoice.com; Author interview with Curley Kerner.

27. Nightmare Off the 405

this was the hardest thing she had ever had to do: Author interview with Curley Kerner.

McBride walked him through everything the police knew so far: "Bill Cosby's Son Is Slain Along Freeway," by B. Drummond Ayres Jr., *New York Times,* Jan. 17, 1997; "Cosby's Son Killed," by Adam Sandler, *Daily Variety,* Jan. 17, p. 8; "Bill Cosby's Son Is Shot to Death in Los Angeles," by Carol Morello, *Philadelphia Inquirer,* Jan. 17, 1997; "Key Witness in Cosby Killing 'Traumatized,'" CNN.com, Jan. 17, 1997; "Mystery Witness Enters Spotlight," by James Rainey, *Los Angeles Times,* June 24, 1998; author interview with David Brokaw; Cosby interview with Rather, CBS News; "Oprah Talks with Camille Cosby," *O.*

he had a difficult time with death: Author interview with Poussaint.

Ed Lewis arrived at the family town house: Author interviews with Lewis and Curley Kerner; "Good-bye, Friend," Castro, *People;* "CNN Apology on Pictures," *New York Times,* Jan. 17, 1997; "Police Hold Off on Sketch of Killer Because Witness Is Traumatized," by Deborah Hastings, Associated Press, Jan. 18, 1997.

Throughout the day, thousands of people had phoned: "Good-bye, Friend," Castro, *People;* "A Much-Watched Brokaw Send-off," *Los Angeles Times,* Dec. 3, 2004; "Pal to Continue Ennis' Ed Work," by Patrice O'Shaughnessy, *New York Daily News,* Jan. 19, 1997.

Once two days had passed: Cosby interview with Rather, CBS News; "Police Release Sketches of Suspect and Potential Witness in Cosby Killing," by B. Drummond Ayres Jr., *New York Times,* Jan. 18, 1997; "Ennis Laid to Rest at Home," by Rafael A. Olmeda, Corky Siemaszko, and Denene Millner, *New York Daily News,* Jan. 20, 1997.

The burial took place later that day: Author interviews with Cosby and Howard Bingham; Cosby interview with Rather, CBS News.

28. The Trials of "Job"

Cosby couldn't stay away any longer: Cosby interview with Rather, CBS News; "Cosby Embraces Dignity, Then Laughter," by Lawrie Mifflin, *New York Times,* Jan. 28, 1997; "Just for Variety," by Army Archerd, *Daily Variety,* Jan. 29, 1997, p. 2; author interview with Curley Kerner.

the private drama that Cosby had worked to keep hidden: "Bill Cosby Was Target of Extortion Plot," by David W. Chen, *New York Times,* Jan. 21, 1997; "Cosby Extortion Scheme: Did Good Deed Go Awry?," by Charisse Jones, *New York Times,* Jan. 22, 1997; "Bail Is Set at $250,000 Each for 2 in Cosby Extortion Case," by Jan Hoffman, *New York Times,* Jan. 25, 1997; *People* cover, Feb. 3, 1997.

another dramatic turn in the Jackson story: "Dad Claim in Cos Case: Truck Driver Says He'll Take Paternity Test," by K. C. Baker, Michelle Caruso, Corky Siemaszko, and Greg B. Smith, *New York Daily News,* Jan. 25, 1997; Cosby interview with Rather, CBS News.

Cosby had legitimized the story: "Bill Cosby Unplugged," by Frank Rich, *New York Times,* Jan. 29, 1997.

Rather walked into an audio booth: Rather track for unaired *60 Minutes* piece on Bill Cosby, Jan. 29, 1997; "CBS Says It Would

Be Unseemly to Broadcast Cosby Interview," by Lawrie Mifflin, *New York Times,* Jan. 31, 1997; " '60 Min.' Axes Cosby Seg," by Gary Levin, *Daily Variety,* Jan. 31, 1997, p. 1; author interview with Andrew Heyward.

had enraged a central figure in the drama: "Camille Cosby 'Emotionally Abused' by Tabloids," by W. Speers, *Philadelphia Inquirer,* Feb. 7, 1997; "Cosbys to *National Enquirer:* No, We're Not Grateful," by Stacy Finz, *Los Angeles Daily News,* Mar. 25, 1997.

The suspect's name was Mikail Markhasev: "Young Russian Immigrant Charged with Cosby Killing" and "Suspect in Cosby Killing 'a Kid Really Hard Beyond His Years,' " by B. Drummond Ayres Jr., *New York Times,* Mar. 13 and Mar. 15, 1997.

the extortion case against Autumn Jackson moved forward: "Man Pleads Guilty to Charges Tied to Cosby Extortion," by Lynette Holloway, *New York Times,* Jan. 29, 1997; "Illegitimate Claim?," Gliatto, *People;* "Bill Takes Paternity Test, Wants to End Riddle of Autumn Kinship," by Greg B. Smith and Larry Sutton, *New York Daily News,* July 29, 1997.

When Mikail Markhasev went on trial: "A Messy Murder Trial: The Ennis Cosby Case Draws to a Close as Both Sides Falter," by

Sharon Waxman, *Washington Post,* July 3, 1998; "Man Convicted in Cosby Death; Faces Life Term," by James Sterngold, *New York Times,* July 8, 1998.

Camille Cosby had come to see larger forces behind her son's murder: "America Taught My Son's Killer to Hate Blacks," by Camille Cosby, *USA Today,* July 8, 1998; "Cosby's Wife Ups the Dialogue on Racism," by Linda Wright Moore, *Philadelphia Inquirer,* July 16, 1998; "Mrs. Cosby's Racial Paranoia," by David Horowitz, Salon.com, July 13, 1998; "Camille Cosby Comments on Response to Her USA Today Article About Racism in the USA," *USA Today,* July 29, 1998.

a specific explanation for the killing: Author interview with DeBlasio; "A Messy Murder Trial" and "Guilty Verdict in Cosby Case," by Sharon Waxman, *Washington Post,* July 3 and July 8, 1998.

Of all the explanations for his son's death: "Camille Cosby Calls for Boycott on Violence in Music, Shows Son's Killer 'Was Riding with Satan,' Her Husband Said in Ceremony," by Roy H. Campbell, *Philadelphia Inquirer,* Apr. 6, 1997.

29. A Death in the TV Family

the first day that the full cast and crew of his CBS show went back to work: Author inter-

900

views with Curley Kerner and Gelbart; Cosby interview with Rather, CBS News.

Cosby flew to West Palm Beach to perform stand-up: Author interview with Poussaint; "Always a Master of Timing, Cosby Decides the Time to Return Is Now," by Will Lester, Associated Press, Feb. 2, 1997; "With Show, Cosby Acts on His Vow to Move On," by Mireya Navarro, *New York Times,* Feb. 2, 1997.

He was giving the memory of Ennis a physical presence: Author interviews with Allison Samuels and George Wein; "Cosby's Darkest Hours," by Allison Samuels, *Newsweek,* Jan. 21, 2007.

Ennis could still be a raw topic: Author interview with Grace Leong and Gavin White.

a bizarre story he was writing about Cosby: "Cosby Has Family, Friends Worried," by William Bunch, Knight Ridder Tribune, July 5, 2002; "Cos Mystic Mystery" and "Cosby's Musical Mystic in New 'Jam,' " *New York Post,* July 2, 2002, and July 7, 2002.

The first time Ray Romano was introduced to stand-up comedy: Romano on *The Green Room with Paul Provenza,* Showtime, 2011; "Ray Romano's Road to Fame: Everybody Loves Raymond," by Carl Kolchak, Yahoo! Voices, Apr. 14, 2006; Moonves interview with Pasternak, AAT; Phil Rosenthal interview with Karen Herman for the Archive of American Television, Apr. 13, 2005; *Promises I Made My Mother,* Haskell, p. 93.

Cosby *was a respectable success, but it wasn't a hit:* Author interview with Curley Kerner; Moonves interview with Pasternack, AAT; "Madeline Kahn, a Retrospective," by Tony Sokol, DenOfGeek.com, Feb. 28, 2013, "Dating Games," *Cosby* on YouTube.

Curley Kerner was encouraged to hear about the new head writer: Author interviews with Curley Kerner and Tom Straw; "The Episode Episode," and "Judgment Day," *Cosby* on YouTube.

Madeline Kahn had been diagnosed with ovarian cancer: "Actress Madeline Kahn Dead of Ovarian Cancer at 57," Associated Press, Dec. 4, 1999; "This Old Friend" and "Loving Madeline," *Cosby* on YouTube.

Cosby was too proud and competitive: Author interview with Straw; "CBS and Bill Cosby Announce Finale for 'Cosby,' " PRNewswire, Mar. 24, 2000; Moonves interview with Pasternack, AAT; "Nickelodeon's Newest Cartoon: Cosby's Little Bill and His Charm," by Ed Bark, *Dallas Morning News,* Nov. 28, 1999.

a quest to put education reform on the national agenda: Author interview with Allen; *American Education: The 100 Billion Dollar Challenge,* by Dwight Allen and William H.

Cosby Jr., iPublish.com, 2000.

an important moment of personal closure: "Killer of Bill Cosby's Son Confesses," by Twila Decker, *Los Angeles Time*s, Feb. 10, 2001; "Ennis Cosby's Convicted Killer Confesses, Drops Appeal," Associated Press, Feb. 10, 2001.

a phone message that revived his spirits: "Bush Honors 12 with Presidential Medal of Freedom," *New York Times,* July 9, 2002; "2008 Presidential Medal of Freedom Ceremony," YouTube; Cosby appearance on *The Late Show with David Letterman,* CBS, July 26, 2002.

30. Prophet of Pound Cake

The event was billed as a celebration: Invitation to "*Brown v. Board of Education* 50th Anniversary Commemoration," howard .edu.

Cosby was in no mood to cheer: Author interview with Cosby and Wilder; "Some Blacks Find Nuggets of Truth in Cosby's Speech," by Hamil R. Harris, *Washington Post,* May 26, 2004.

The other man was Kenneth Clark: Author interview with Poussaint; "Kenneth Clark, Who Fought Segregation, Dies," by Richard Severo, *New York Times,* May 2, 2005; "Kenneth Clark Dies; Helped Desegregate Schools," by Joe Holley, *Washington Post,*

May 3, 2005.

Cosby came up to receive his award: Author interview with Wilder; "Dr. Bill Cosby Speaks at the 50th Anniversary Commemoration of the *Brown v. Topeka Board of Education* Supreme Court Decision" full transcript, rci.rutgers.edu.

the evening's hosts were not amused: Author interview with Wilder; "Bill Cosby: Poor Blacks Can't Speak English," WorldNet Daily.com, May 20, 2004; "Beyond What Bill Cosby Said," by Theodore M. Shaw, *Washington Post,* May 27, 2004.

Suddenly Cosby's speech was news: "Reliable Source," by Richard Leiby, *Washington Post,* May 19, 2004; "Some Blacks Find Nuggets of Truth in Cosby's Speech," Harris, *Washington Post; The O'Reilly Factor,* Fox News, June 1, 2004.

Among African Americans, reaction broke down: " 'Fix It, Brother,' " by Colbert I. King, *Washington Post,* May 22, 2004; "Ebonics! Weird Names! $500 Shoes!" and "Mushmouth Revisited," by Ta-Nehisi Coates, *Village Voice,* May 18, 2004, and July 6, 2004.

Another black critic was even more sweeping: Is Bill Cosby Right? (Or Has the Black Middle Class Lost Its Mind?), by Michael Eric Dyson, Basic Books, 2005; "Insult Comic," by Reihan Salam, New Republic Online, May 4, 2005.

he went back on the offensive: "Debate Continues as Cosby Again Criticizes Black Youths," by Hamil R. Harris and Paul Farhi, *Washington Post,* July 3, 2004; "Tough Talk: Bill Cosby," *PBS NewsHour,* July 15, 2004.

Once Michael Eric Dyson's book came out: Author interview with Cosby; "Dr. Huxtable and Mr. Hyde," by Robert Huber, *Philadelphia,* June 9, 2006.

a three-front crusade: Author interview with Stanley Battle; "Cosby Calls to Absent Fathers," by Brent Jones, *Baltimore Sun,* Aug. 23, 2006; "Dr. Bill Cosby's Fireside Chats," *Educator,* Fall 2009; *Come On, People: On the Path from Victims to Victors* by Bill Cosby and Alvin F. Poussaint, MD, Thomas Nelson, 2007; Cosby appearance on *Meet the Press,* Oct. 14, 2007; Cosby appearance on *Oprah,* Oct. 17, 2007.

at least one critic had come to see Cosby in a different light: "This Is How We Lost to the White Man," by Ta-Nehisi Coates, *The Atlantic,* May 2008; "Fear of a Black Pundit: Ta-Nehisi Coates Raises His Voice in American Media," by Jordan Michael Smith, *New York Observer,* Mar. 5, 2013; "The Cosby Crusade," Coates interview on theatlantic.com, May 1, 2008.

31. "The Cosby Effect"

the tingle of history in the air: Cosby appearance on *Meet the Press,* Jan. 11, 2009; " 'Cosby' Equals Obama Election? Cosby Mulls It Over," by Lynn Elber, Associated Press, Nov. 12, 2008; Chris Wallace and Karl Rove on the Fox News Channel, Nov. 4, 2008; "Before Obama, There Was Bill Cosby," by Tim Arango, *New York Times,* Nov. 8, 2008.

a memorable milestone on the road to Obama's victory: "Ossie Davis and Bill Cosby Address the Congressional Black Caucus," Motown Records, 1972.

It's what had eventually won Cosby over to Obama: Author interview with Cosby and Wilder; " 'Cosby' Equals Obama Election?," Elber, AP; "Barack Obama's Speech on Father's Day," June 15, 2008, YouTube.

he was appalled by the state of the country: Author interviews with Cosby and Stanley Battle; "The Art of Survival in the Richard Allen Homes," by Roger Cohn, the Alicia Patterson Foundation, 1984; Cosby and Battle appearance on *Today,* NBC, Apr. 7, 2011; " 'R2' Gang Leaves Trail of Violence," "Cosby Challenges the Ville," and "Cosby Helps Launch 'Southern Academy,' " *New Haven Independent,* Mar. 26, 2010, Nov. 24, 2010, and June 10, 2011; "Bill Cosby in Newhallville, New Haven, CT, 11/23/

10," Parts 1–5, YouTube.

Cosby saw something other than racism at play: "Bill Cosby Weighs in on Trayvon Martin Case," by Deborah Simmons, *Washington Times*, Apr. 7, 2012; "Trayvon Martin's Death Is Like Ennis Cosby's," by Allison Samuels, July 14, 2013; Cosby interview with Richard Harris for "After Newtown: Guns in America," PBS.

The news of Robert Culp's death came as a shock: "Actor Robert Culp Dies After Falling at His Hollywood Home," *Los Angeles Times,* Mar. 24, 2010; "Bill Cosby Remembers Robert Culp" (Cosby performance at Ruth Eckerd Hall, Clearwater, Florida, Mar. 27, 2010), YouTube.

So many of Cosby's professional abolitionists were gone now: "Obituaries: Sheldon Leonard," *Variety,* Jan. 20–26, 1997, p. 50; "Alan Ribback, Gate of Horn Nightclub Owner in '50s, '60s," *Chicago Sun-Times,* Sept. 1, 1993; "Roy Silver," Variety.com, Nov. 4, 2003; author interviews with DeBlasio and Schultz.

he accepted the lifetime achievement award named after his very first influence: "Twelfth Knight: It's Cosby's Time to Claim the Twain Prize," by Paul Farhi, *Washington Post,* Oct. 27, 2009; "The Kennedy Center Mark Twain Prize for American Humor," PBS, Nov. 4, 2009; *The Dick Cavett Show:*

Comic Legends — Bill Cosby, YouTube.

Epilogue

Even when Cosby isn't on the road now: Author interviews with Cosby and David Brokaw; *Far from Finished,* Comedy Central, Nov. 26, 2013; Cosby interview with Andrew Boris and Robyn Taylor, *The Boris and Robyn Show,* WPDH, May 12, 2014; Guest Programmer (Bill Cosby), Turner Classic Movies, Jan. 23, 2005, *The Loneliness of the Long Distance Runner* (1962), DVD, Warner Home Video, 2007.

PHOTO CREDITS

21. NBC
22. Courtesy of Carsey-Werner Productions
23. Courtesy of Spelman College
24. Courtesy of Bill Cosby
25. Courtesy of Bill Cosby
26. Courtesy of Carsey-Werner Productions
27. AP Photo/George School, Mark Oster-man
28. AP Photo/David Karp
29. AP Photo/Sasa Kralj
30. Susan Tusa/Detroit Free Press/ZUMA PRESS.com
31. AP Photo/Jacquelyn Martin
32. AP Photo/Alex Menendez

ABOUT THE AUTHOR

Mark Whitaker is the author of the critically acclaimed memoir *My Long Trip Home*. The former managing editor of CNN, he was previously Washington bureau chief for NBC News and a reporter and editor at *Newsweek,* where he rose to become the first African American leader of a national newsweekly.

The employees of Thorndike Press hope you have enjoyed this Large Print book. All our Thorndike, Wheeler, and Kennebec Large Print titles are designed for easy reading, and all our books are made to last. Other Thorndike Press Large Print books are available at your library, through selected bookstores, or directly from us.

For information about titles, please call:
(800) 223-1244

or visit our Web site at:
http://gale.cengage.com/thorndike

To share your comments, please write:
Publisher
Thorndike Press
10 Water St., Suite 310
Waterville, ME 04901